D1255976

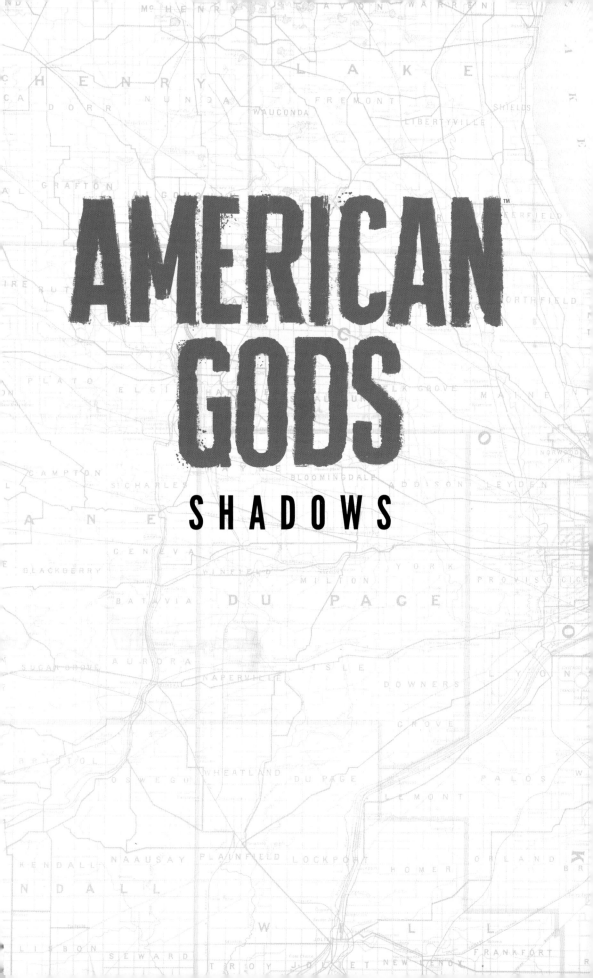

AMERICAN GODS

SHADOWS

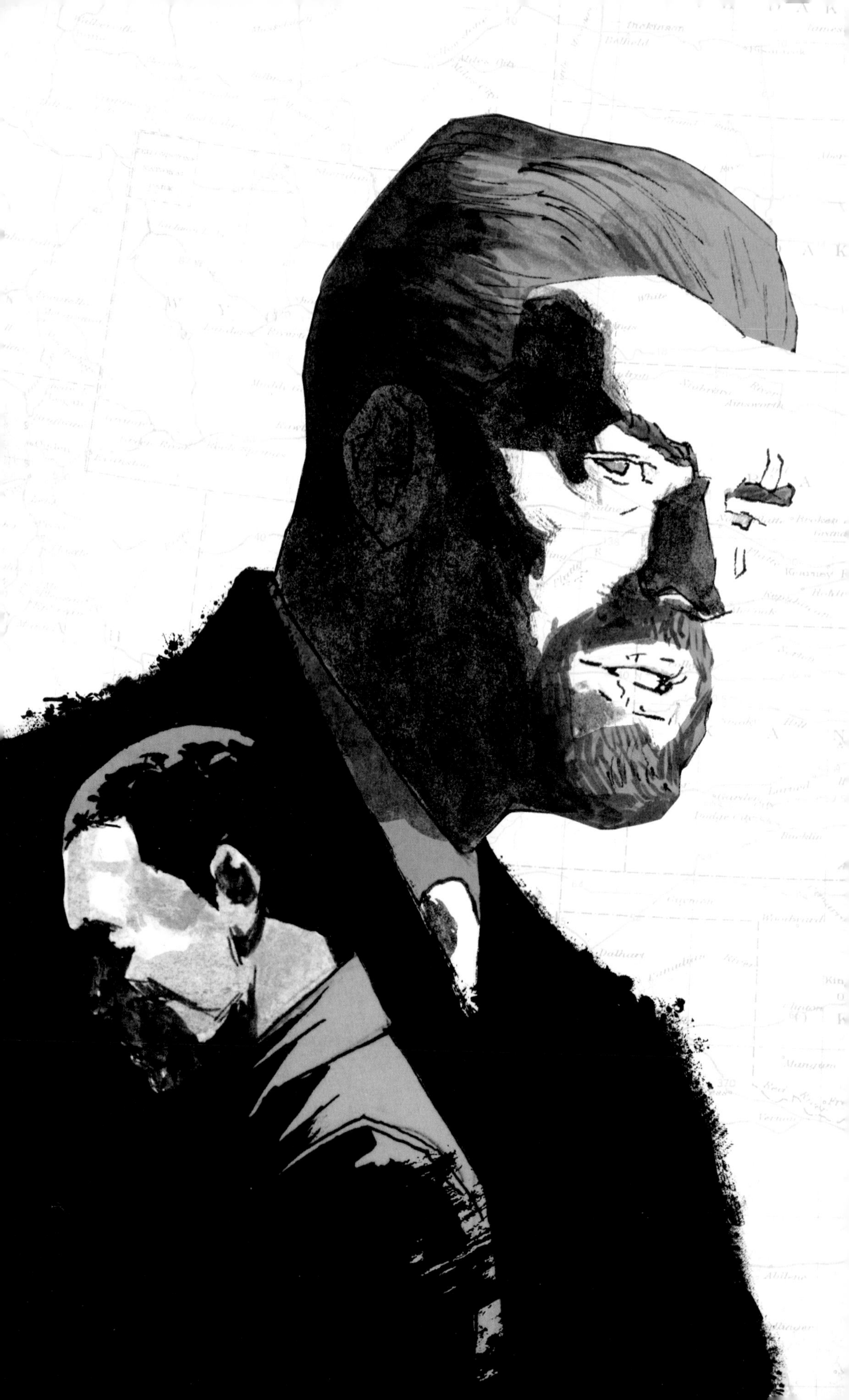

AMERICAN GODS™

SHADOWS

Story and words by
NEIL GAIMAN

Script and layouts by
P. CRAIG RUSSELL

Art by
SCOTT HAMPTON

Letters by
RICK PARKER

Chapter title pages by **GLENN FABRY** with **ADAM BROWN**

Chapter design pages by **DAVID MACK**

"Somewhere in America" from Chapter One by **P. CRAIG RUSSELL** and **LOVERN KINDZIERSKI**

"Coming to America" from Chapter Three by **WALTER SIMONSON** and **LAURA MARTIN**

"Coming to America" from Chapter Four by **COLLEEN DORAN**

"Coming to America" from Chapter Eight by **GLENN FABRY** and **ADAM BROWN**

Cover by **DAVID MACK**

DARK HORSE BOOKS

PUBLISHER MIKE RICHARDSON   EDITOR **DANIEL CHABON**   ASSISTANT EDITOR **RACHEL ROBERTS**

DESIGNER **ETHAN KIMBERLING**   DIGITAL ART TECHNICIAN **CHRISTIANNE GOUDREAU**

I want to thank my "co-director" *Jaime Hodge* for her help in making *American Gods* one of the most rewarding books of my career. I couldn't ask for a better artistic collaborator. —**Scott Hampton**

 Facebook.com/DarkHorseComics   Twitter.com/DarkHorseComics

Advertising Sales: (503) 905-2537
International Licensing: (503) 905-2377

To find a comics shop in your area, visit comicshoplocator.com.

NEIL GAIMAN'S AMERICAN GODS™

This volume collects issues #1 through #9 of the Dark Horse comic-book series *American Gods: Shadows*.

Published by Dark Horse Books
A division of Dark Horse Comics, Inc.
10956 SE Main Street
Milwaukie, OR 97222

DarkHorse.com

First hardcover edition: February 2018
ISBN 978-1-50670-386-2

10 9 8 7 6 5 4 3 2 1
Printed in Hong Kong

Library of Congress Cataloging-in-Publication Data

Names: Gaiman, Neil, author. | Russell, P. Craig, author, illustrator. | Hampton, Scott, artist. | Parker, Rick, 1946- letterer.
Title: American Gods : shadows / story and words by Neil Gaiman ; script and layouts by P. Craig Russell ; art by Scott Hampton ; letters by Rick Parker.
Description: First hardcover edition. | Milwaukie, OR : Dark Horse Books, 2018- | v. 1. "This volume collects issues #1 through #9 of the Dark Horse comic-book series American Gods: Shadows"
Identifiers: LCCN 2017048023| ISBN 9781506703862 (volume 1) | ISBN 9781506707303 (volume 2) | ISBN 9781506707310 (volume 3)
Subjects: LCSH: Comic books, strips, etc. | BISAC: COMICS & GRAPHIC NOVELS / Media Tie-In. | COMICS & GRAPHIC NOVELS / Fantasy. | COMICS & GRAPHIC NOVELS / General.
Classification: LCC PN6728.A485 G35 2018 | DDC 741.5/973--dc23
LC record available at https://lccn.loc.gov/2017048023

Neil Hankerson Executive Vice President
Tom Weddle Chief Financial Officer
Randy Stradley Vice President of Publishing
Nick McWhorter Chief Business Development Officer
Matt Parkinson Vice President of Marketing
David Scroggy Vice President of Product Development
Dale LaFountain Vice President of Information Technology
Cara Niece Vice President of Production and Scheduling
Mark Bernardi Vice President of Book Trade and Digital Sales
Ken Lizzi General Counsel
Dave Marshall Editor in Chief
Davey Estrada Editorial Director
Scott Allie Executive Senior Editor
Chris Warner Senior Books Editor
Cary Grazzini Director of Specialty Projects
Lia Ribacchi Art Director
Vanessa Todd Director of Print Purchasing
Matt Dryer Director of Digital Art and Prepress
Michael Gombos Director of International Publishing and Licensing

CHAPTER ONE

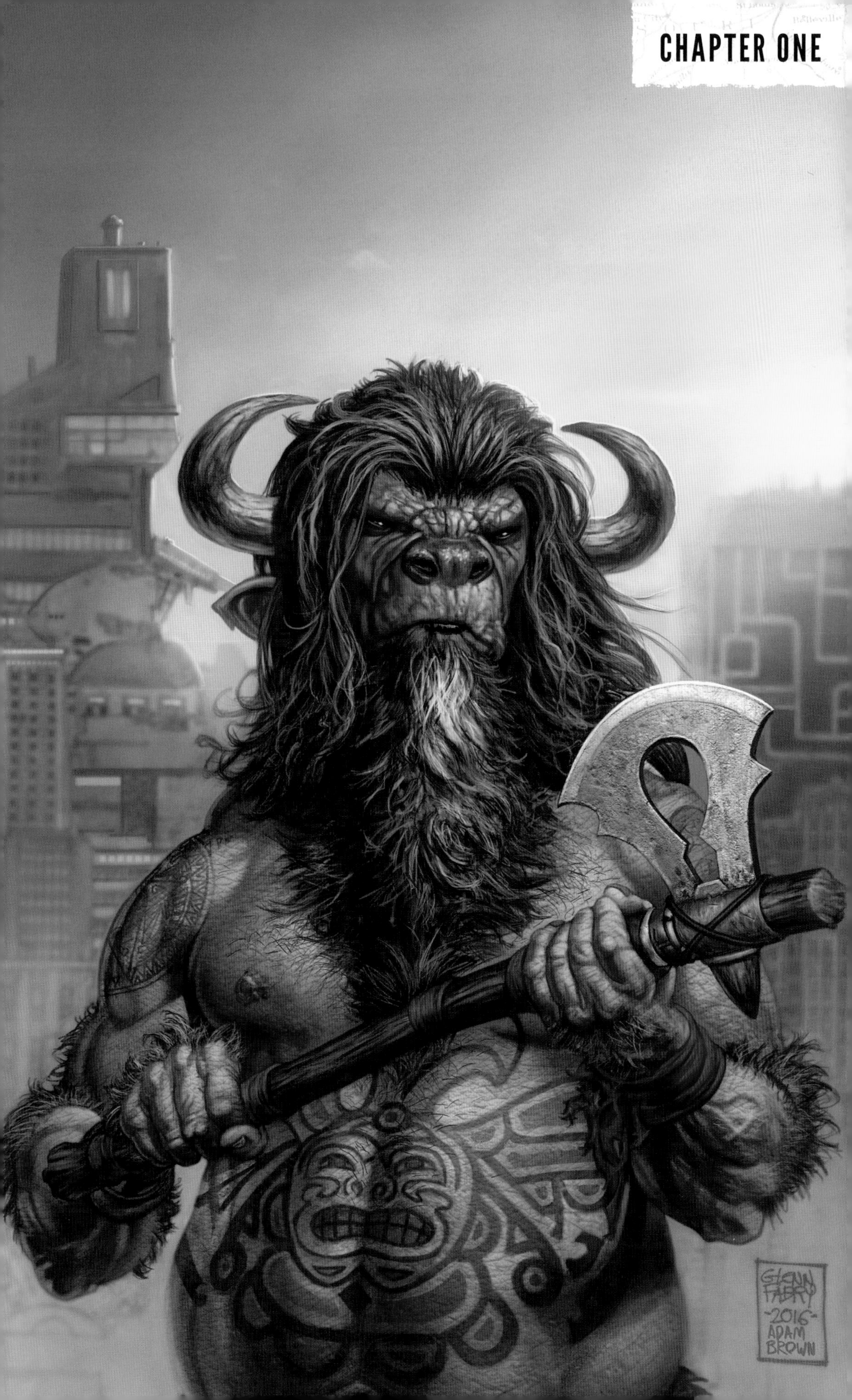
GLENN FABRY
-2016-
ADAM BROWN

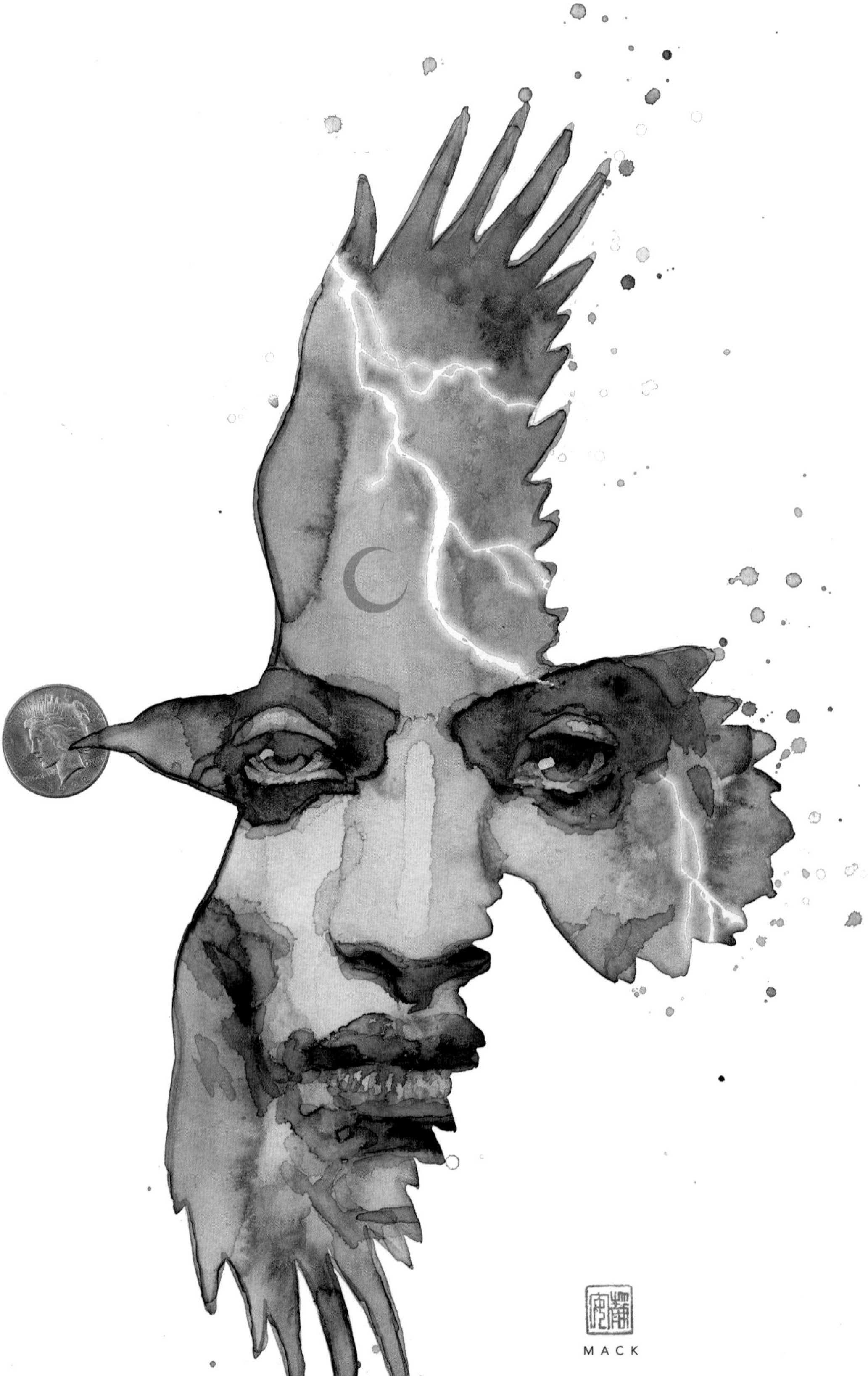
MACK

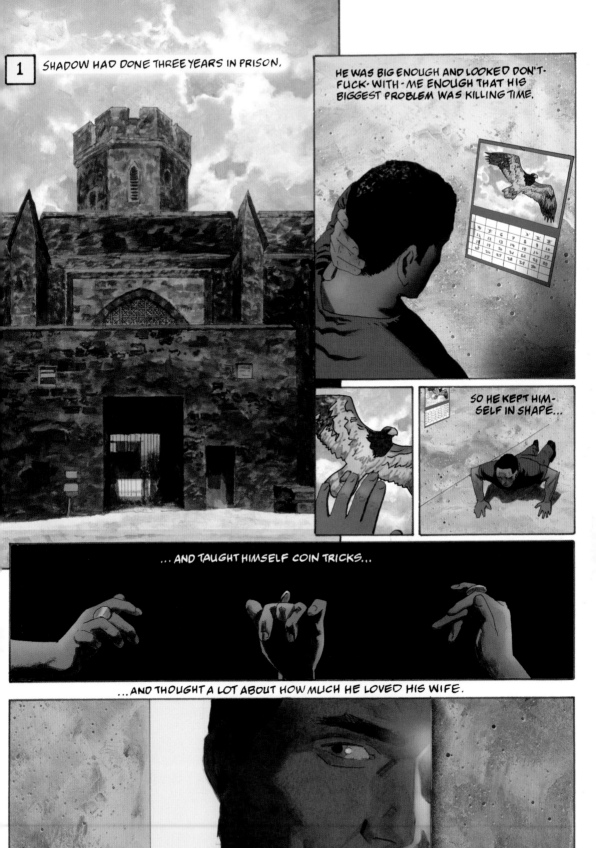

1 SHADOW HAD DONE THREE YEARS IN PRISON,

HE WAS BIG ENOUGH AND LOOKED DON'T-FUCK-WITH-ME ENOUGH THAT HIS BIGGEST PROBLEM WAS KILLING TIME.

SO HE KEPT HIM-SELF IN SHAPE...

... AND TAUGHT HIMSELF COIN TRICKS...

...AND THOUGHT A LOT ABOUT HOW MUCH HE LOVED HIS WIFE.

THE BEST THING--IN SHADOW'S OPINION, PERHAPS THE ONLY GOOD THING--ABOUT BEING IN PRISON WAS A FEELING OF RELIEF. THE FEELING THAT HE HAD PLUNGED AS LOW AS HE COULD PLUNGE AND HE'D HIT BOTTOM. HE DIDN'T WORRY THAT THE MAN WAS GOING TO GET HIM, BECAUSE THE MAN HAD GOT HIM.

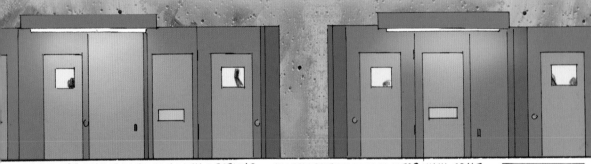

HE DID NOT AWAKE IN PRISON WITH A FEELING OF DREAD; HE WAS NO LONGER SCARED OF WHAT TOMORROW MIGHT BRING BECAUSE YESTERDAY HAD BROUGHT IT.

SHADOW TRIED NOT TO TALK TOO MUCH. SOMEWHERE AROUND THE MIDDLE OF YEAR TWO HE MENTIONED HIS THEORY TO LOW KEY LYESMITH, HIS CELLMATE.

IT DOESN'T MATTER WHAT YOU'VE DONE, WHAT YOU'VE BEEN CONVICTED OF.

THAT'S TRUE. IT'S EVEN BETTER WHEN YOU'VE BEEN SENTENCED TO DEATH.

WHAT'S IMPORTANT IS THAT THEY'VE *GOT* YOU.

THAT'S WHEN YOU REMEMBER THE JOKES ABOUT THE GUYS WHO KICKED THEIR BOOTS OFF AS THE NOOSE FLIPPED AROUND THEIR NECKS BECAUSE THEIR FRIENDS ALWAYS TOLD THEM THEY'D DIE WITH THEIR BOOTS ON.

IS THAT A JOKE?

DAMN RIGHT. GALLOWS HUMOR. BEST KIND THERE IS--*BANG*, THE WORST HAS HAPPENED, YOU GET A FEW DAYS FOR IT TO SINK IN, THEN YOU'RE RIDING THE CART ON YOUR WAY TO DO THE DANCE ON *NOTHING*.

WHEN DID THEY LAST HANG A MAN IN THIS STATE?

HOW THE HELL SHOULD *I* KNOW?

TELL YOU WHAT, THOUGH.

THIS COUNTRY STARTED GOING TO HELL WHEN THEY STOPPED HANGING FOLKS. NO GALLOWS DIRT. NO GALLOWS DEALS.

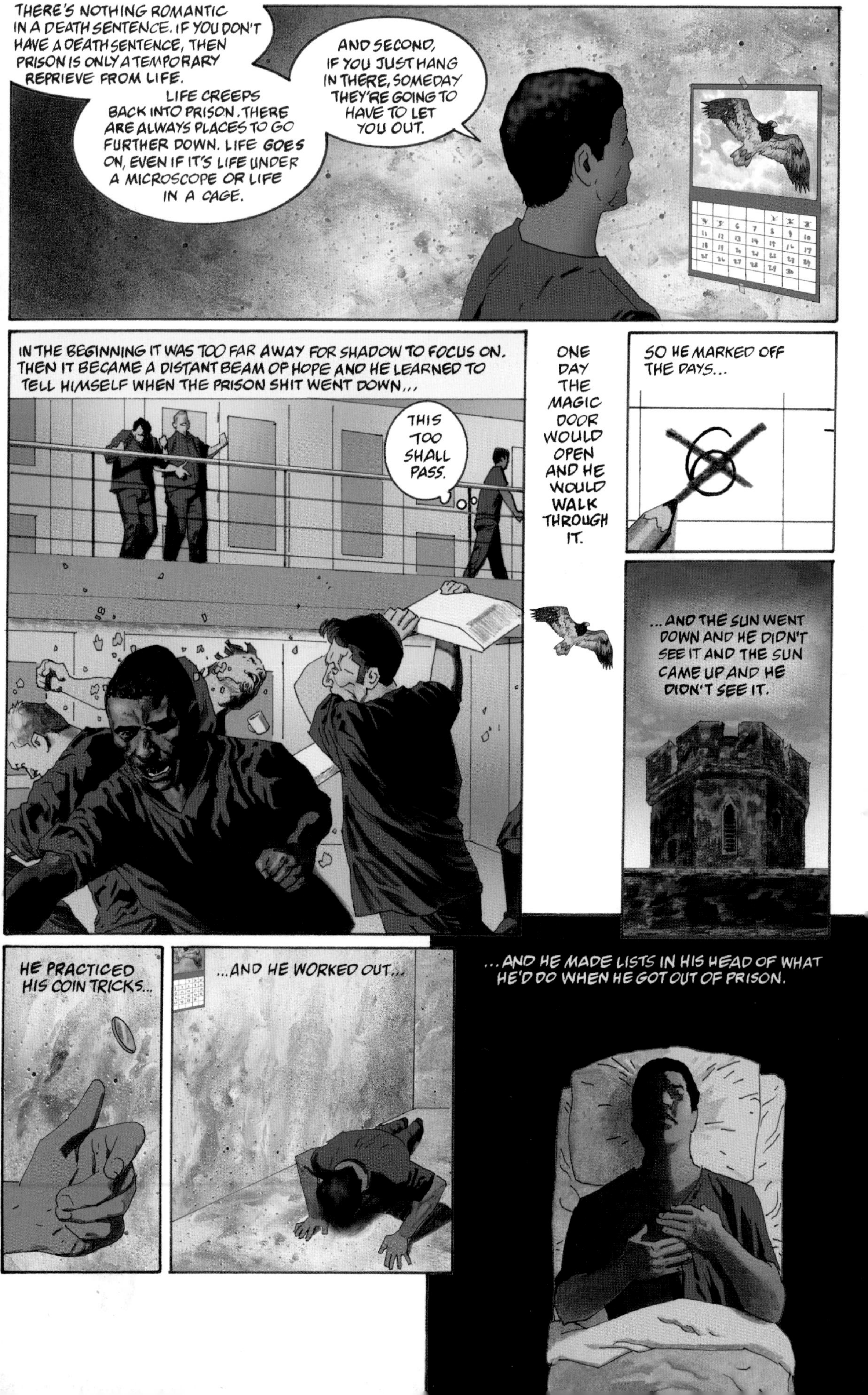
THERE'S NOTHING ROMANTIC IN A DEATH SENTENCE. IF YOU DON'T HAVE A DEATH SENTENCE, THEN PRISON IS ONLY A TEMPORARY REPRIEVE FROM LIFE.
LIFE CREEPS BACK INTO PRISON. THERE ARE ALWAYS PLACES TO GO FURTHER DOWN. LIFE GOES ON, EVEN IF IT'S LIFE UNDER A MICROSCOPE OR LIFE IN A CAGE.
AND SECOND, IF YOU JUST HANG IN THERE, SOMEDAY THEY'RE GOING TO HAVE TO LET YOU OUT.
IN THE BEGINNING IT WAS TOO FAR AWAY FOR SHADOW TO FOCUS ON. THEN IT BECAME A DISTANT BEAM OF HOPE AND HE LEARNED TO TELL HIMSELF WHEN THE PRISON SHIT WENT DOWN...
THIS TOO SHALL PASS.
ONE DAY THE MAGIC DOOR WOULD OPEN AND HE WOULD WALK THROUGH IT.
SO HE MARKED OFF THE DAYS...
...AND THE SUN WENT DOWN AND HE DIDN'T SEE IT AND THE SUN CAME UP AND HE DIDN'T SEE IT.
HE PRACTICED HIS COIN TRICKS...
...AND HE WORKED OUT...
...AND HE MADE LISTS IN HIS HEAD OF WHAT HE'D DO WHEN HE GOT OUT OF PRISON.

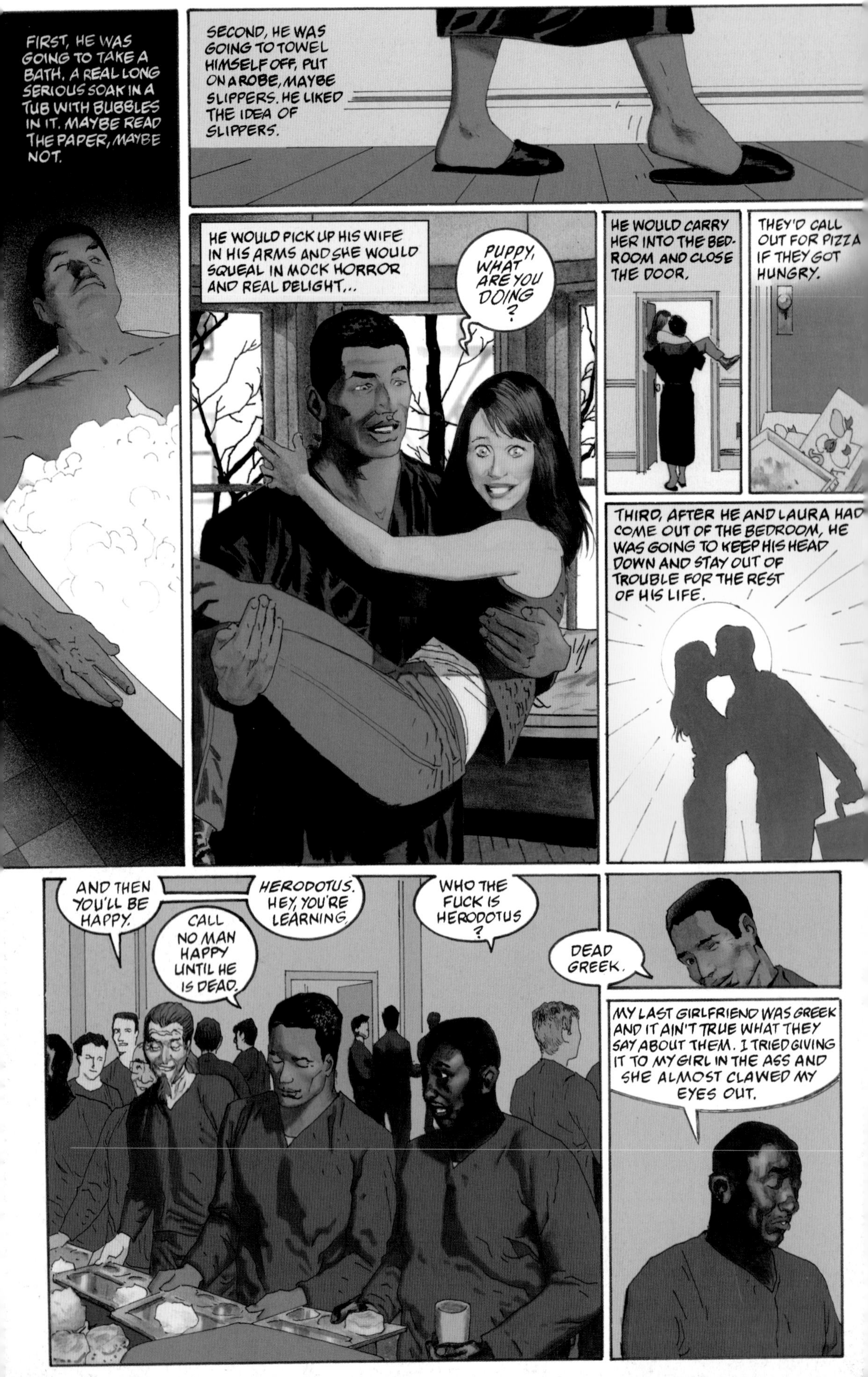
FIRST, HE WAS GOING TO TAKE A BATH. A REAL LONG SERIOUS SOAK IN A TUB WITH BUBBLES IN IT. MAYBE READ THE PAPER, MAYBE NOT.
SECOND, HE WAS GOING TO TOWEL HIMSELF OFF, PUT ON A ROBE, MAYBE SLIPPERS. HE LIKED THE IDEA OF SLIPPERS.
HE WOULD PICK UP HIS WIFE IN HIS ARMS AND SHE WOULD SQUEAL IN MOCK HORROR AND REAL DELIGHT...
PUPPY, WHAT ARE YOU DOING?
HE WOULD CARRY HER INTO THE BED-ROOM AND CLOSE THE DOOR.
THEY'D CALL OUT FOR PIZZA IF THEY GOT HUNGRY.
THIRD, AFTER HE AND LAURA HAD COME OUT OF THE BEDROOM, HE WAS GOING TO KEEP HIS HEAD DOWN AND STAY OUT OF TROUBLE FOR THE REST OF HIS LIFE.
AND THEN YOU'LL BE HAPPY.
CALL NO MAN HAPPY UNTIL HE IS DEAD.
HERODOTUS. HEY, YOU'RE LEARNING.
WHO THE FUCK IS HERODOTUS?
DEAD GREEK.
MY LAST GIRLFRIEND WAS GREEK AND IT AIN'T TRUE WHAT THEY SAY ABOUT THEM. I TRIED GIVING IT TO MY GIRL IN THE ASS AND SHE ALMOST CLAWED MY EYES OUT.

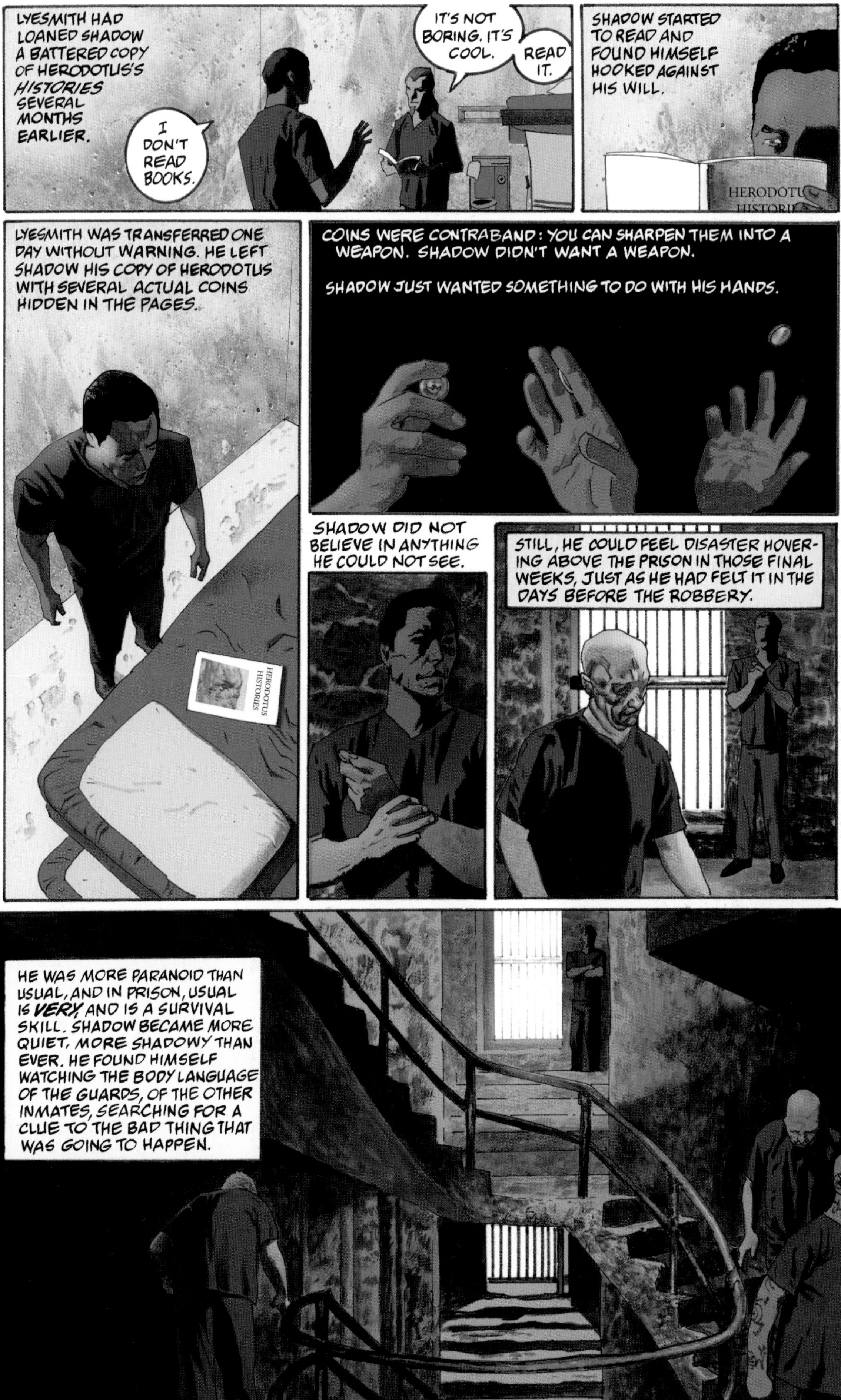
LYESMITH HAD LOANED SHADOW A BATTERED COPY OF HERODOTUS'S *HISTORIES* SEVERAL MONTHS EARLIER.
I DON'T READ BOOKS.
IT'S NOT BORING. IT'S COOL.
READ IT.
SHADOW STARTED TO READ AND FOUND HIMSELF HOOKED AGAINST HIS WILL.
LYESMITH WAS TRANSFERRED ONE DAY WITHOUT WARNING. HE LEFT SHADOW HIS COPY OF HERODOTUS WITH SEVERAL ACTUAL COINS HIDDEN IN THE PAGES.
HERODOTUS HISTORIES
COINS WERE CONTRABAND: YOU CAN SHARPEN THEM INTO A WEAPON. SHADOW DIDN'T WANT A WEAPON.
SHADOW JUST WANTED SOMETHING TO DO WITH HIS HANDS.
SHADOW DID NOT BELIEVE IN ANYTHING HE COULD NOT SEE.
STILL, HE COULD FEEL DISASTER HOVERING ABOVE THE PRISON IN THOSE FINAL WEEKS, JUST AS HE HAD FELT IT IN THE DAYS BEFORE THE ROBBERY.
HE WAS MORE PARANOID THAN USUAL, AND IN PRISON, USUAL IS ***VERY***, AND IS A SURVIVAL SKILL. SHADOW BECAME MORE QUIET, MORE SHADOWY THAN EVER. HE FOUND HIMSELF WATCHING THE BODY LANGUAGE OF THE GUARDS, OF THE OTHER INMATES, SEARCHING FOR A CLUE TO THE BAD THING THAT WAS GOING TO HAPPEN.

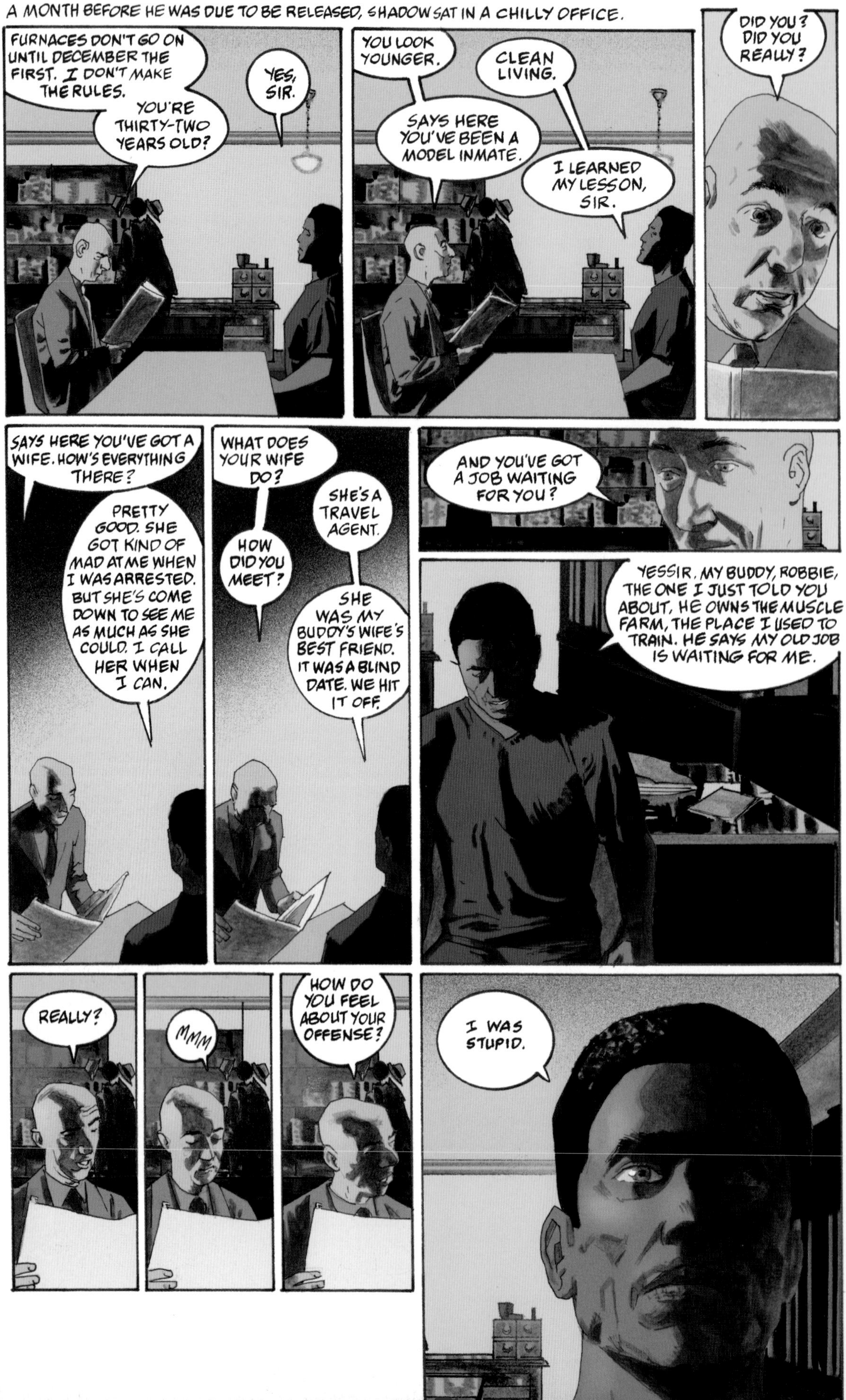
A MONTH BEFORE HE WAS DUE TO BE RELEASED, SHADOW SAT IN A CHILLY OFFICE.
FURNACES DON'T GO ON UNTIL DECEMBER THE FIRST. I DON'T MAKE THE RULES.
YOU'RE THIRTY-TWO YEARS OLD?
YES, SIR.
YOU LOOK YOUNGER.
CLEAN LIVING.
SAYS HERE YOU'VE BEEN A MODEL INMATE.
I LEARNED MY LESSON, SIR.
DID YOU? DID YOU REALLY?
SAYS HERE YOU'VE GOT A WIFE. HOW'S EVERYTHING THERE?
PRETTY GOOD. SHE GOT KIND OF MAD AT ME WHEN I WAS ARRESTED. BUT SHE'S COME DOWN TO SEE ME AS MUCH AS SHE COULD. I CALL HER WHEN I CAN.
WHAT DOES YOUR WIFE DO?
SHE'S A TRAVEL AGENT.
HOW DID YOU MEET?
SHE WAS MY BUDDY'S WIFE'S BEST FRIEND. IT WAS A BLIND DATE. WE HIT IT OFF.
AND YOU'VE GOT A JOB WAITING FOR YOU?
YESSIR. MY BUDDY, ROBBIE, THE ONE I JUST TOLD YOU ABOUT, HE OWNS THE MUSCLE FARM, THE PLACE I USED TO TRAIN. HE SAYS MY OLD JOB IS WAITING FOR ME.
REALLY?
MMM
HOW DO YOU FEEL ABOUT YOUR OFFENSE?
I WAS STUPID.

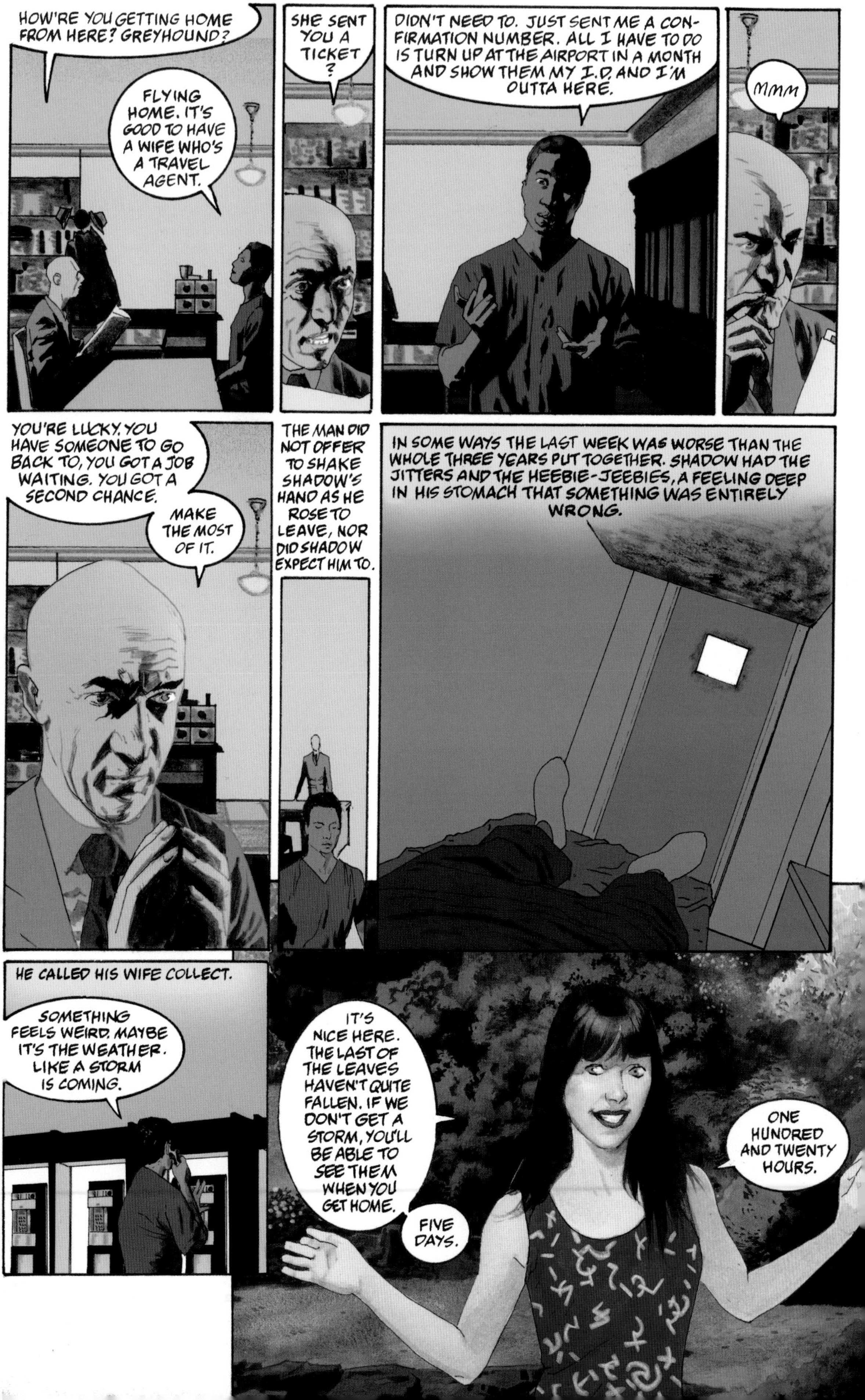
HOW'RE YOU GETTING HOME FROM HERE? GREYHOUND?
FLYING HOME. IT'S GOOD TO HAVE A WIFE WHO'S A TRAVEL AGENT.
SHE SENT YOU A TICKET?
DIDN'T NEED TO. JUST SENT ME A CONFIRMATION NUMBER. ALL I HAVE TO DO IS TURN UP AT THE AIRPORT IN A MONTH AND SHOW THEM MY I.D. AND I'M OUTTA HERE.
MMM
YOU'RE LUCKY. YOU HAVE SOMEONE TO GO BACK TO, YOU GOT A JOB WAITING. YOU GOT A SECOND CHANCE.
MAKE THE MOST OF IT.
THE MAN DID NOT OFFER TO SHAKE SHADOW'S HAND AS HE ROSE TO LEAVE, NOR DID SHADOW EXPECT HIM TO.
IN SOME WAYS THE LAST WEEK WAS WORSE THAN THE WHOLE THREE YEARS PUT TOGETHER. SHADOW HAD THE JITTERS AND THE HEEBIE-JEEBIES, A FEELING DEEP IN HIS STOMACH THAT SOMETHING WAS ENTIRELY WRONG.
HE CALLED HIS WIFE COLLECT.
SOMETHING FEELS WEIRD. MAYBE IT'S THE WEATHER. LIKE A STORM IS COMING.
IT'S NICE HERE. THE LAST OF THE LEAVES HAVEN'T QUITE FALLEN. IF WE DON'T GET A STORM, YOU'LL BE ABLE TO SEE THEM WHEN YOU GET HOME.
FIVE DAYS.
ONE HUNDRED AND TWENTY HOURS.

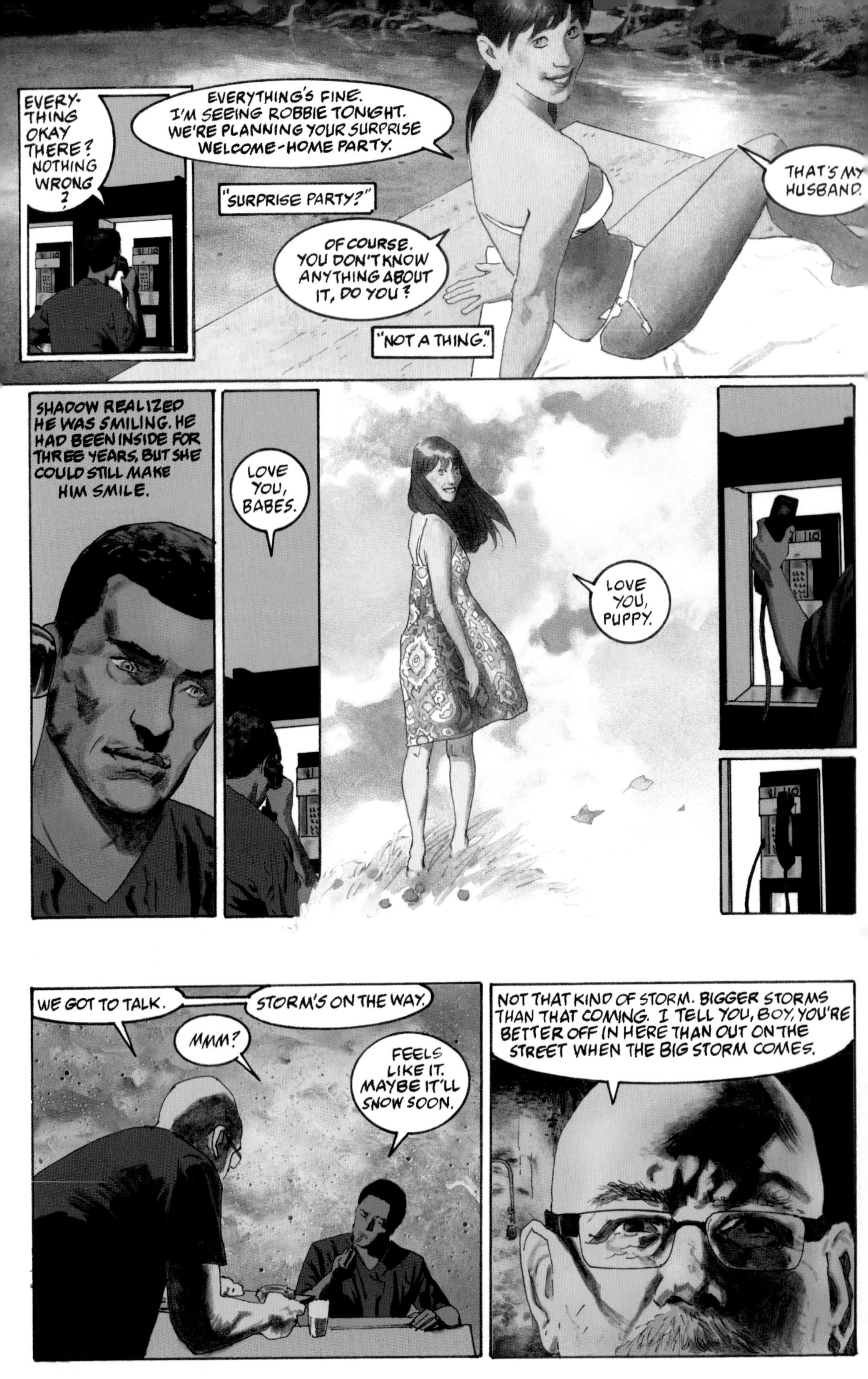
EVERY-THING OKAY THERE? NOTHING WRONG?
EVERYTHING'S FINE. I'M SEEING ROBBIE TONIGHT. WE'RE PLANNING YOUR SURPRISE WELCOME-HOME PARTY.
THAT'S MY HUSBAND.
"SURPRISE PARTY?"
OF COURSE. YOU DON'T KNOW ANYTHING ABOUT IT, DO YOU?
"NOT A THING."
SHADOW REALIZED HE WAS SMILING. HE HAD BEEN INSIDE FOR THREE YEARS, BUT SHE COULD STILL MAKE HIM SMILE.
LOVE YOU, BABES.
LOVE YOU, PUPPY.
WE GOT TO TALK.
STORM'S ON THE WAY.
MMM?
FEELS LIKE IT. MAYBE IT'LL SNOW SOON.
NOT THAT KIND OF STORM. BIGGER STORMS THAN THAT COMING. I TELL YOU, BOY, YOU'RE BETTER OFF IN HERE THAN OUT ON THE STREET WHEN THE BIG STORM COMES.

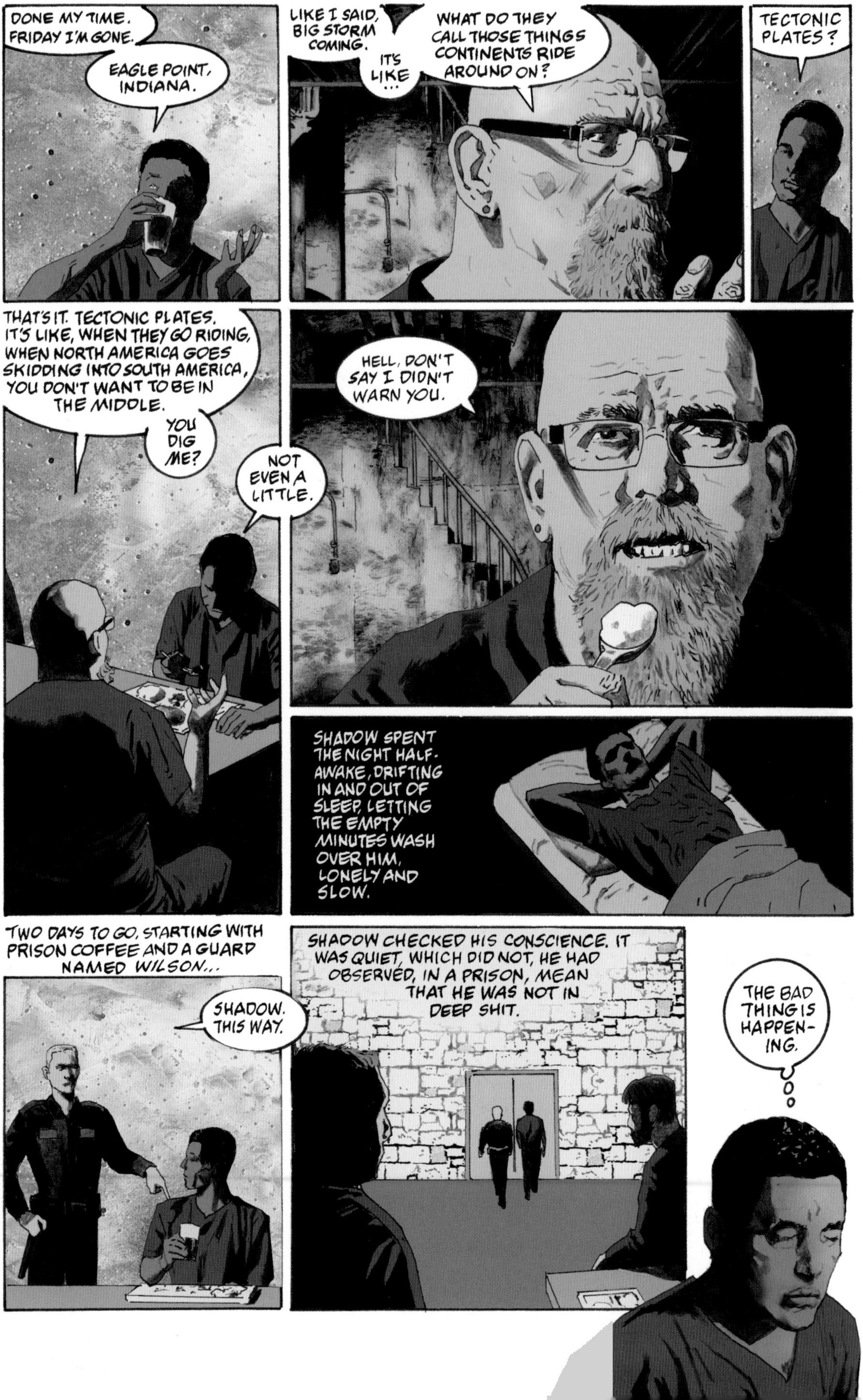
DONE MY TIME. FRIDAY I'M GONE.
EAGLE POINT, INDIANA.
LIKE I SAID, BIG STORM COMING.
IT'S LIKE ...
WHAT DO THEY CALL THOSE THINGS CONTINENTS RIDE AROUND ON?
TECTONIC PLATES?
THAT'S IT. TECTONIC PLATES. IT'S LIKE, WHEN THEY GO RIDING, WHEN NORTH AMERICA GOES SKIDDING INTO SOUTH AMERICA, YOU DON'T WANT TO BE IN THE MIDDLE.
YOU DIG ME?
NOT EVEN A LITTLE.
HELL, DON'T SAY I DIDN'T WARN YOU.
SHADOW SPENT THE NIGHT HALF-AWAKE, DRIFTING IN AND OUT OF SLEEP, LETTING THE EMPTY MINUTES WASH OVER HIM, LONELY AND SLOW.
TWO DAYS TO GO, STARTING WITH PRISON COFFEE AND A GUARD NAMED WILSON...
SHADOW. THIS WAY.
SHADOW CHECKED HIS CONSCIENCE. IT WAS QUIET, WHICH DID NOT, HE HAD OBSERVED, IN A PRISON, MEAN THAT HE WAS NOT IN DEEP SHIT.
THE BAD THING IS HAPPENING.

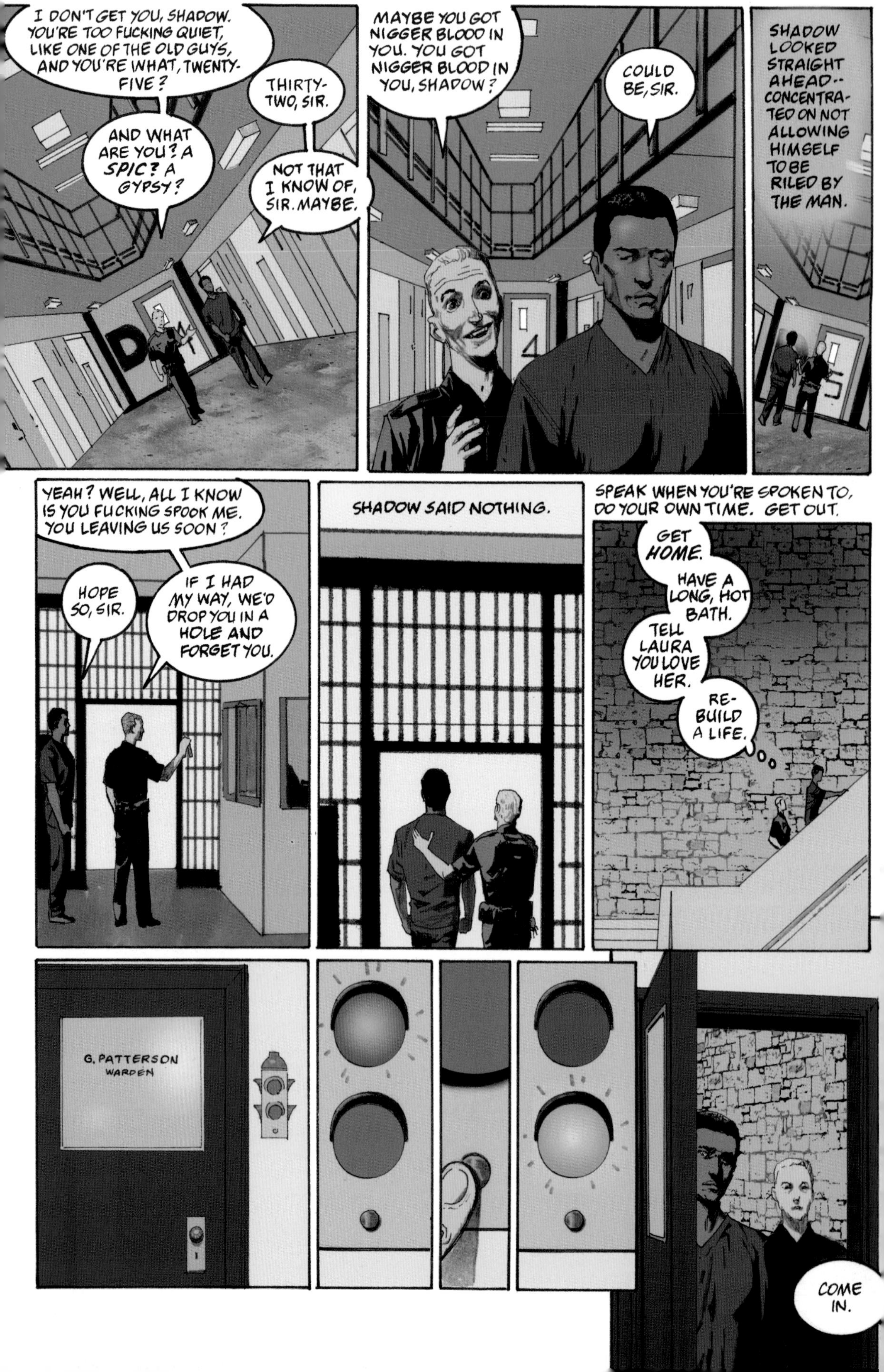
I DON'T GET YOU, SHADOW. YOU'RE TOO FUCKING QUIET, LIKE ONE OF THE OLD GUYS, AND YOU'RE WHAT, TWENTY-FIVE?
THIRTY-TWO, SIR.
AND WHAT ARE YOU? A SPIC? A GYPSY?
NOT THAT I KNOW OF, SIR. MAYBE.
MAYBE YOU GOT NIGGER BLOOD IN YOU. YOU GOT NIGGER BLOOD IN YOU, SHADOW?
COULD BE, SIR.
SHADOW LOOKED STRAIGHT AHEAD-- CONCENTRATED ON NOT ALLOWING HIMSELF TO BE RILED BY THE MAN.
YEAH? WELL, ALL I KNOW IS YOU FUCKING SPOOK ME. YOU LEAVING US SOON?
HOPE SO, SIR.
IF I HAD MY WAY, WE'D DROP YOU IN A HOLE AND FORGET YOU.
SHADOW SAID NOTHING.
SPEAK WHEN YOU'RE SPOKEN TO, DO YOUR OWN TIME. GET OUT.
GET HOME.
HAVE A LONG, HOT BATH.
TELL LAURA YOU LOVE HER.
RE-BUILD A LIFE.
G. PATTERSON
WARDEN
COME IN.

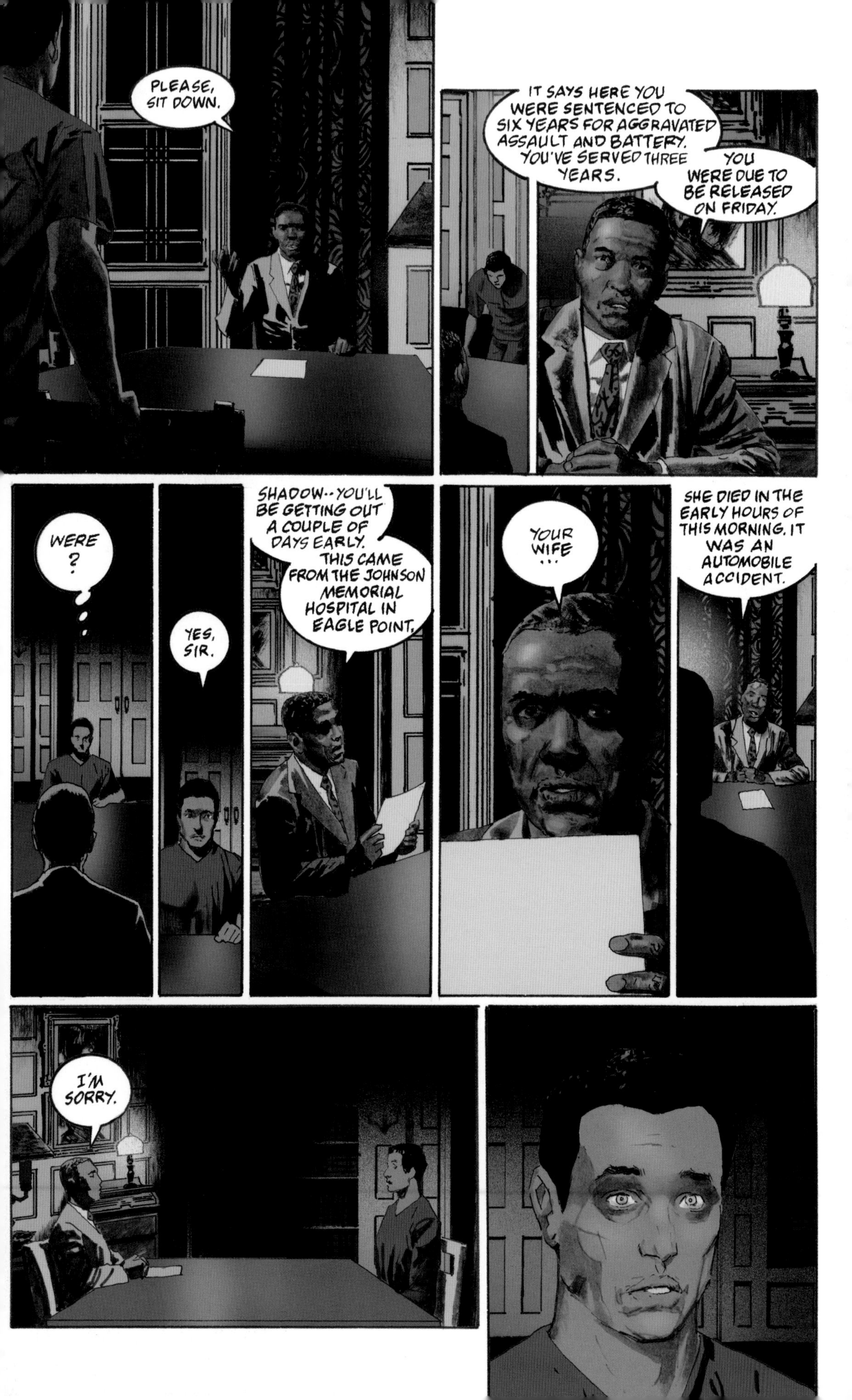
PLEASE, SIT DOWN.
IT SAYS HERE YOU WERE SENTENCED TO SIX YEARS FOR AGGRAVATED ASSAULT AND BATTERY. YOU'VE SERVED THREE YEARS.
YOU WERE DUE TO BE RELEASED ON FRIDAY.
WERE ?
YES, SIR.
SHADOW.. YOU'LL BE GETTING OUT A COUPLE OF DAYS EARLY.
THIS CAME FROM THE JOHNSON MEMORIAL HOSPITAL IN EAGLE POINT.
YOUR WIFE ...
SHE DIED IN THE EARLY HOURS OF THIS MORNING. IT WAS AN AUTOMOBILE ACCIDENT.
I'M SORRY.

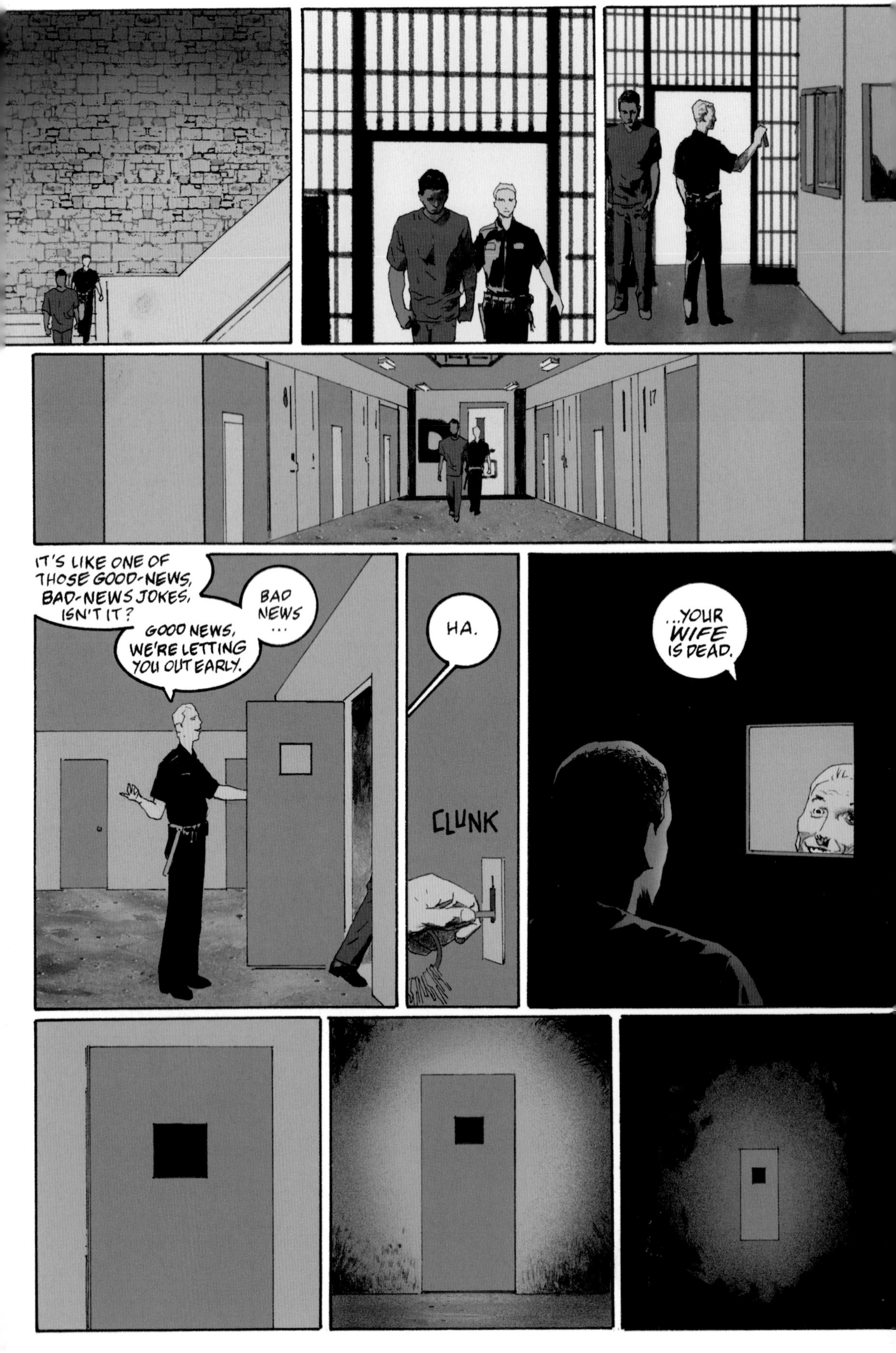
IT'S LIKE ONE OF THOSE GOOD-NEWS, BAD-NEWS JOKES, ISN'T IT?
GOOD NEWS, WE'RE LETTING YOU OUT EARLY.
BAD NEWS ...
HA.
CLUNK
...YOUR WIFE IS DEAD.

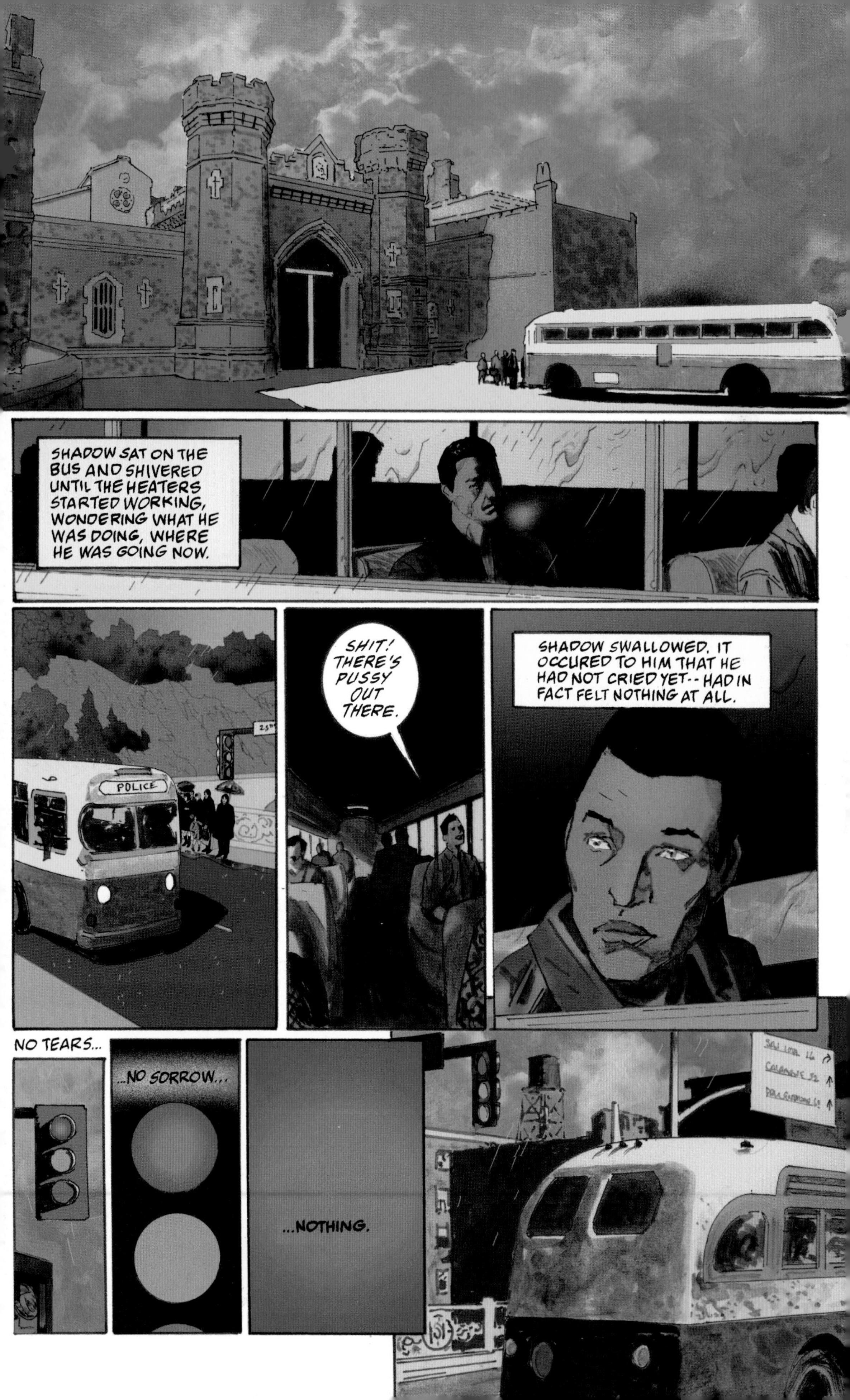
SHADOW SAT ON THE BUS AND SHIVERED UNTIL THE HEATERS STARTED WORKING, WONDERING WHAT HE WAS DOING, WHERE HE WAS GOING NOW.
POLICE
SHIT! THERE'S PUSSY OUT THERE.
SHADOW SWALLOWED. IT OCCURED TO HIM THAT HE HAD NOT CRIED YET-- HAD IN FACT FELT NOTHING AT ALL.
NO TEARS...
...NO SORROW...
...NOTHING.

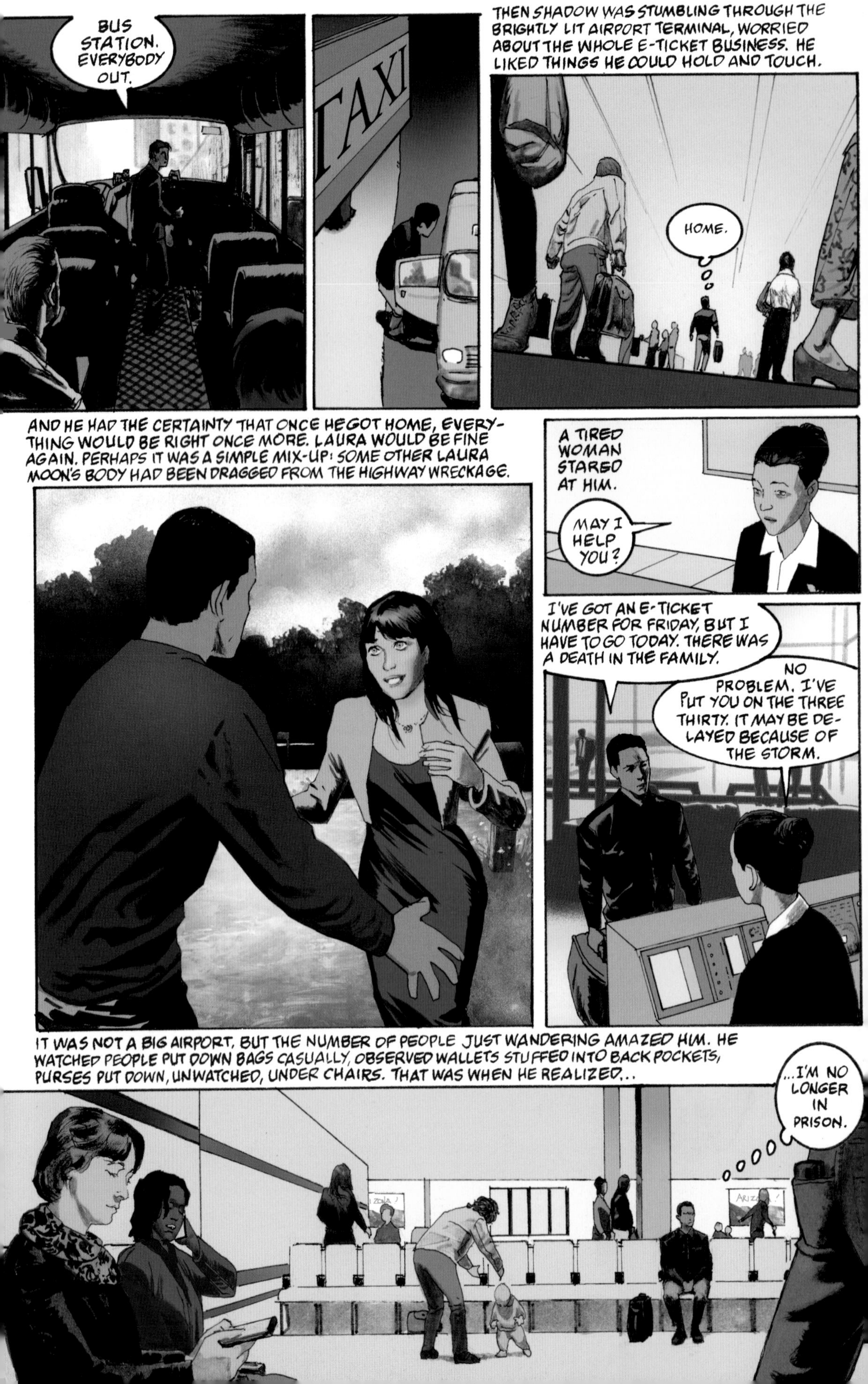
BUS STATION. EVERYBODY OUT.
TAXI
THEN SHADOW WAS STUMBLING THROUGH THE BRIGHTLY LIT AIRPORT TERMINAL, WORRIED ABOUT THE WHOLE E-TICKET BUSINESS. HE LIKED THINGS HE COULD HOLD AND TOUCH.
HOME.
AND HE HAD THE CERTAINTY THAT ONCE HE GOT HOME, EVERYTHING WOULD BE RIGHT ONCE MORE. LAURA WOULD BE FINE AGAIN. PERHAPS IT WAS A SIMPLE MIX-UP: SOME OTHER LAURA MOON'S BODY HAD BEEN DRAGGED FROM THE HIGHWAY WRECKAGE.
A TIRED WOMAN STARED AT HIM.
MAY I HELP YOU?
I'VE GOT AN E-TICKET NUMBER FOR FRIDAY, BUT I HAVE TO GO TODAY. THERE WAS A DEATH IN THE FAMILY.
NO PROBLEM. I'VE PUT YOU ON THE THREE THIRTY. IT MAY BE DELAYED BECAUSE OF THE STORM.
IT WAS NOT A BIG AIRPORT, BUT THE NUMBER OF PEOPLE JUST WANDERING AMAZED HIM. HE WATCHED PEOPLE PUT DOWN BAGS CASUALLY, OBSERVED WALLETS STUFFED INTO BACK POCKETS, PURSES PUT DOWN, UNWATCHED, UNDER CHAIRS. THAT WAS WHEN HE REALIZED...
...I'M NO LONGER IN PRISON.

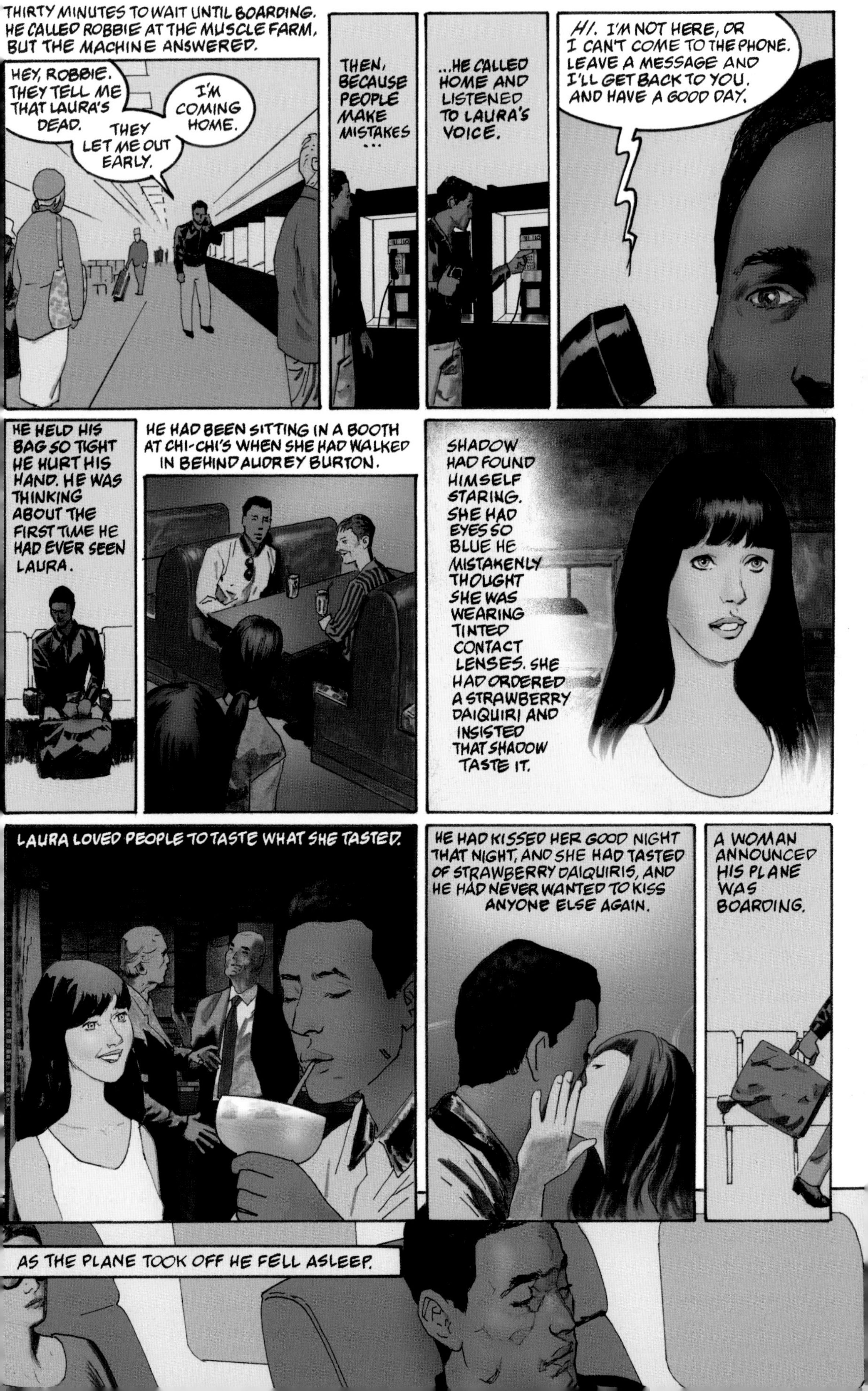
THIRTY MINUTES TO WAIT UNTIL BOARDING. HE CALLED ROBBIE AT THE MUSCLE FARM, BUT THE MACHINE ANSWERED.
HEY, ROBBIE. THEY TELL ME THAT LAURA'S DEAD.
THEY LET ME OUT EARLY.
I'M COMING HOME.
THEN, BECAUSE PEOPLE MAKE MISTAKES...
...HE CALLED HOME AND LISTENED TO LAURA'S VOICE.
HI. I'M NOT HERE, OR I CAN'T COME TO THE PHONE. LEAVE A MESSAGE AND I'LL GET BACK TO YOU. AND HAVE A GOOD DAY.
HE HELD HIS BAG SO TIGHT HE HURT HIS HAND. HE WAS THINKING ABOUT THE FIRST TIME HE HAD EVER SEEN LAURA.
HE HAD BEEN SITTING IN A BOOTH AT CHI-CHI'S WHEN SHE HAD WALKED IN BEHIND AUDREY BURTON.
SHADOW HAD FOUND HIMSELF STARING. SHE HAD EYES SO BLUE HE MISTAKENLY THOUGHT SHE WAS WEARING TINTED CONTACT LENSES. SHE HAD ORDERED A STRAWBERRY DAIQUIRI AND INSISTED THAT SHADOW TASTE IT.
LAURA LOVED PEOPLE TO TASTE WHAT SHE TASTED.
HE HAD KISSED HER GOOD NIGHT THAT NIGHT, AND SHE HAD TASTED OF STRAWBERRY DAIQUIRIS, AND HE HAD NEVER WANTED TO KISS ANYONE ELSE AGAIN.
A WOMAN ANNOUNCED HIS PLANE WAS BOARDING.
AS THE PLANE TOOK OFF HE FELL ASLEEP.

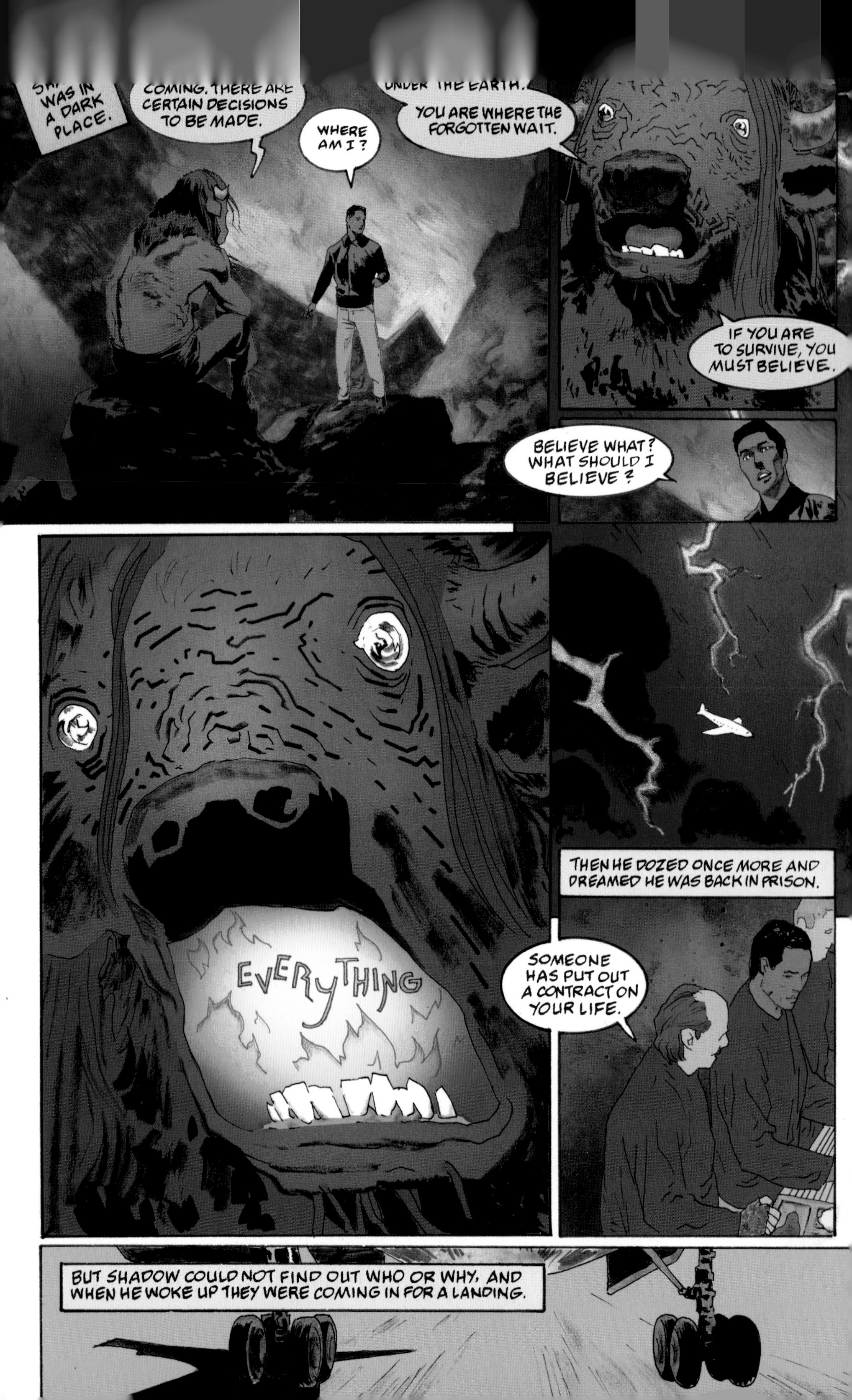
WAS IN A DARK PLACE.
COMING. THERE ARE CERTAIN DECISIONS TO BE MADE.
WHERE AM I?
UNDER THE EARTH.
YOU ARE WHERE THE FORGOTTEN WAIT.
IF YOU ARE TO SURVIVE, YOU MUST BELIEVE.
BELIEVE WHAT? WHAT SHOULD I BELIEVE?
EVERYTHING
THEN HE DOZED ONCE MORE AND DREAMED HE WAS BACK IN PRISON.
SOMEONE HAS PUT OUT A CONTRACT ON YOUR LIFE.
BUT SHADOW COULD NOT FIND OUT WHO OR WHY, AND WHEN HE WOKE UP THEY WERE COMING IN FOR A LANDING.

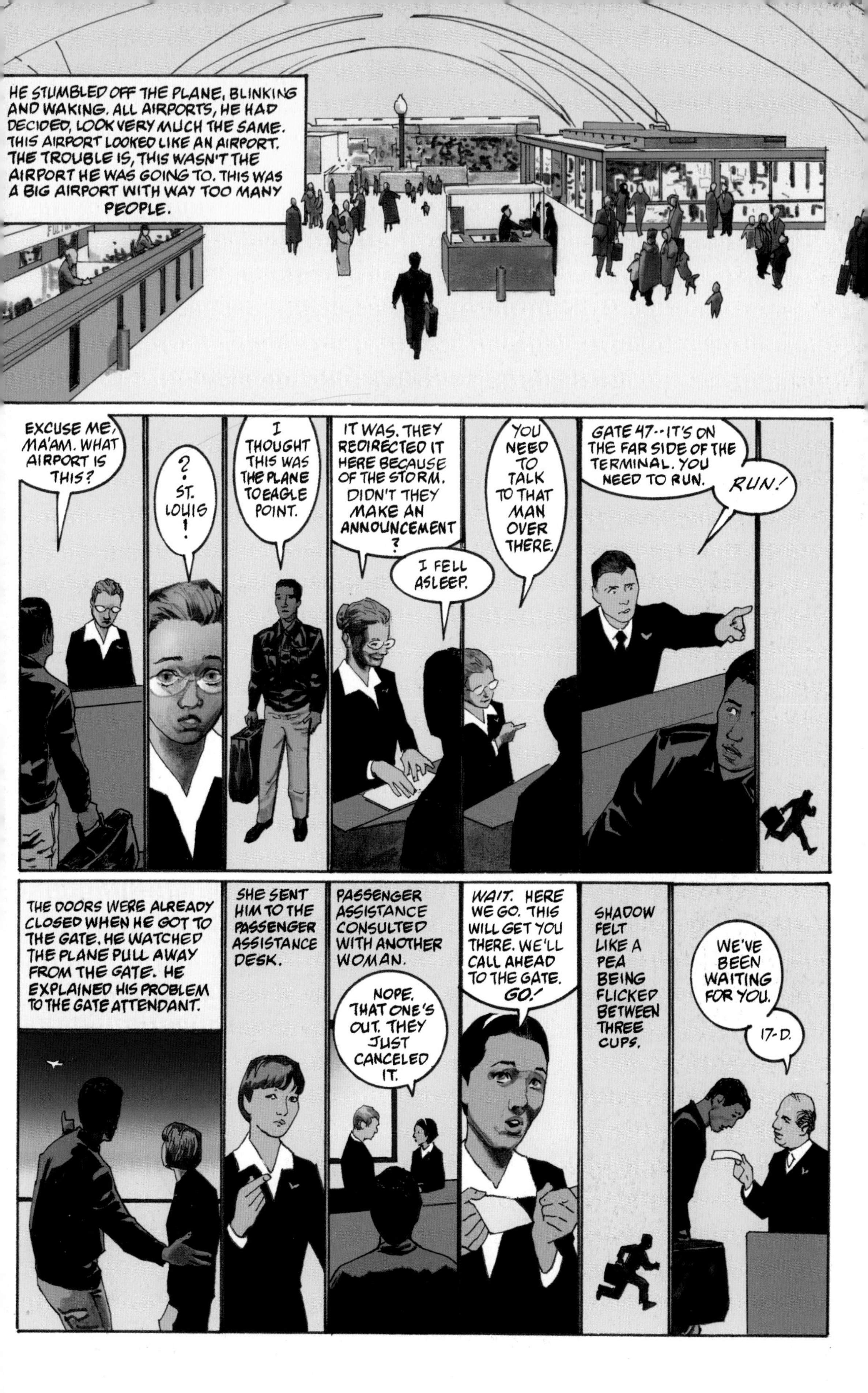
HE STUMBLED OFF THE PLANE, BLINKING AND WAKING. ALL AIRPORTS, HE HAD DECIDED, LOOK VERY MUCH THE SAME. THIS AIRPORT LOOKED LIKE AN AIRPORT. THE TROUBLE IS, THIS WASN'T THE AIRPORT HE WAS GOING TO. THIS WAS A BIG AIRPORT WITH WAY TOO MANY PEOPLE.
EXCUSE ME, MA'AM. WHAT AIRPORT IS THIS?
? ST. LOUIS !
I THOUGHT THIS WAS THE PLANE TO EAGLE POINT.
IT WAS. THEY REDIRECTED IT HERE BECAUSE OF THE STORM. DIDN'T THEY MAKE AN ANNOUNCEMENT ?
I FELL ASLEEP.
YOU NEED TO TALK TO THAT MAN OVER THERE.
GATE 47--IT'S ON THE FAR SIDE OF THE TERMINAL. YOU NEED TO RUN.
RUN!
THE DOORS WERE ALREADY CLOSED WHEN HE GOT TO THE GATE. HE WATCHED THE PLANE PULL AWAY FROM THE GATE. HE EXPLAINED HIS PROBLEM TO THE GATE ATTENDANT.
SHE SENT HIM TO THE PASSENGER ASSISTANCE DESK.
PASSENGER ASSISTANCE CONSULTED WITH ANOTHER WOMAN.
NOPE. THAT ONE'S OUT. THEY JUST CANCELED IT.
WAIT. HERE WE GO. THIS WILL GET YOU THERE. WE'LL CALL AHEAD TO THE GATE. GO!
SHADOW FELT LIKE A PEA BEING FLICKED BETWEEN THREE CUPS.
WE'VE BEEN WAITING FOR YOU.
17-D.

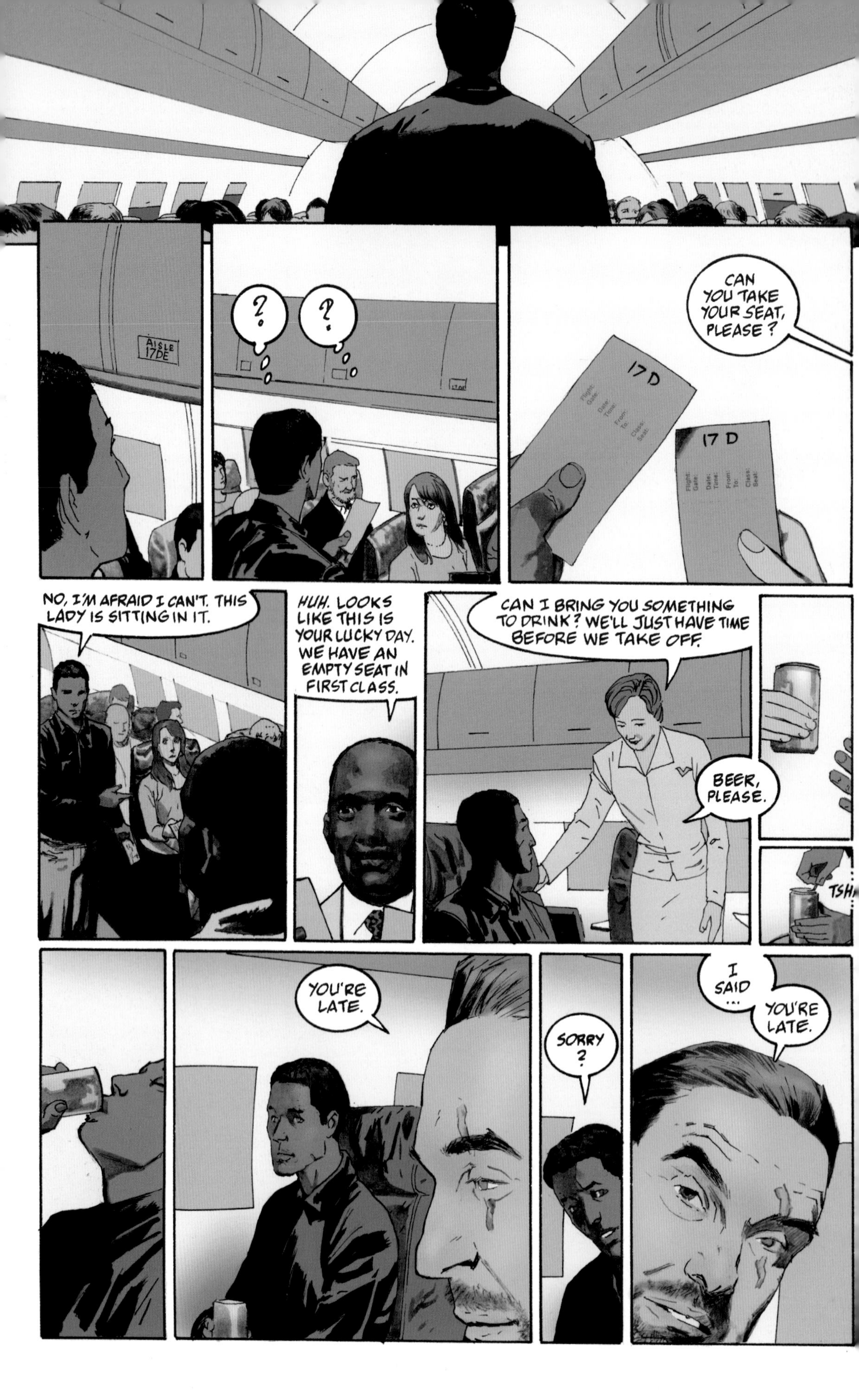
AISLE 17DE
?
?
CAN YOU TAKE YOUR SEAT, PLEASE?
17 D
17 D
NO, I'M AFRAID I CAN'T. THIS LADY IS SITTING IN IT.
HUH. LOOKS LIKE THIS IS YOUR LUCKY DAY. WE HAVE AN EMPTY SEAT IN FIRST CLASS.
CAN I BRING YOU SOMETHING TO DRINK? WE'LL JUST HAVE TIME BEFORE WE TAKE OFF.
BEER, PLEASE.
TSH
YOU'RE LATE.
SORRY?
I SAID...
YOU'RE LATE.

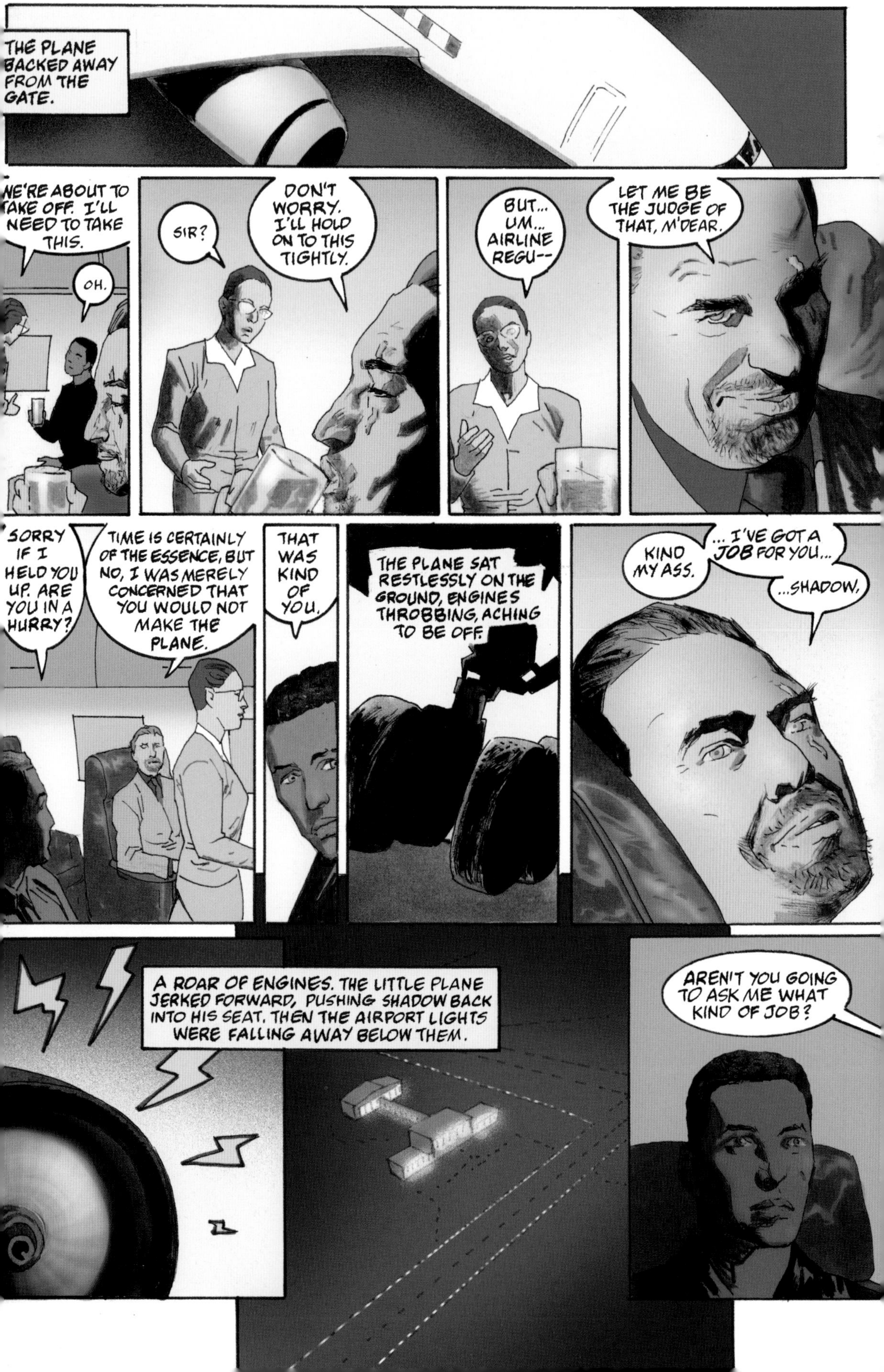
THE PLANE BACKED AWAY FROM THE GATE.
WE'RE ABOUT TO TAKE OFF. I'LL NEED TO TAKE THIS.
OH.
SIR?
DON'T WORRY. I'LL HOLD ON TO THIS TIGHTLY.
BUT... UM... AIRLINE REGU--
LET ME BE THE JUDGE OF THAT, M'DEAR.
SORRY IF I HELD YOU UP. ARE YOU IN A HURRY?
TIME IS CERTAINLY OF THE ESSENCE, BUT NO, I WAS MERELY CONCERNED THAT YOU WOULD NOT MAKE THE PLANE.
THAT WAS KIND OF YOU.
THE PLANE SAT RESTLESSLY ON THE GROUND, ENGINES THROBBING, ACHING TO BE OFF.
KIND MY ASS.
... I'VE GOT A JOB FOR YOU...
...SHADOW.
A ROAR OF ENGINES. THE LITTLE PLANE JERKED FORWARD, PUSHING SHADOW BACK INTO HIS SEAT. THEN THE AIRPORT LIGHTS WERE FALLING AWAY BELOW THEM.
AREN'T YOU GOING TO ASK ME WHAT KIND OF JOB?

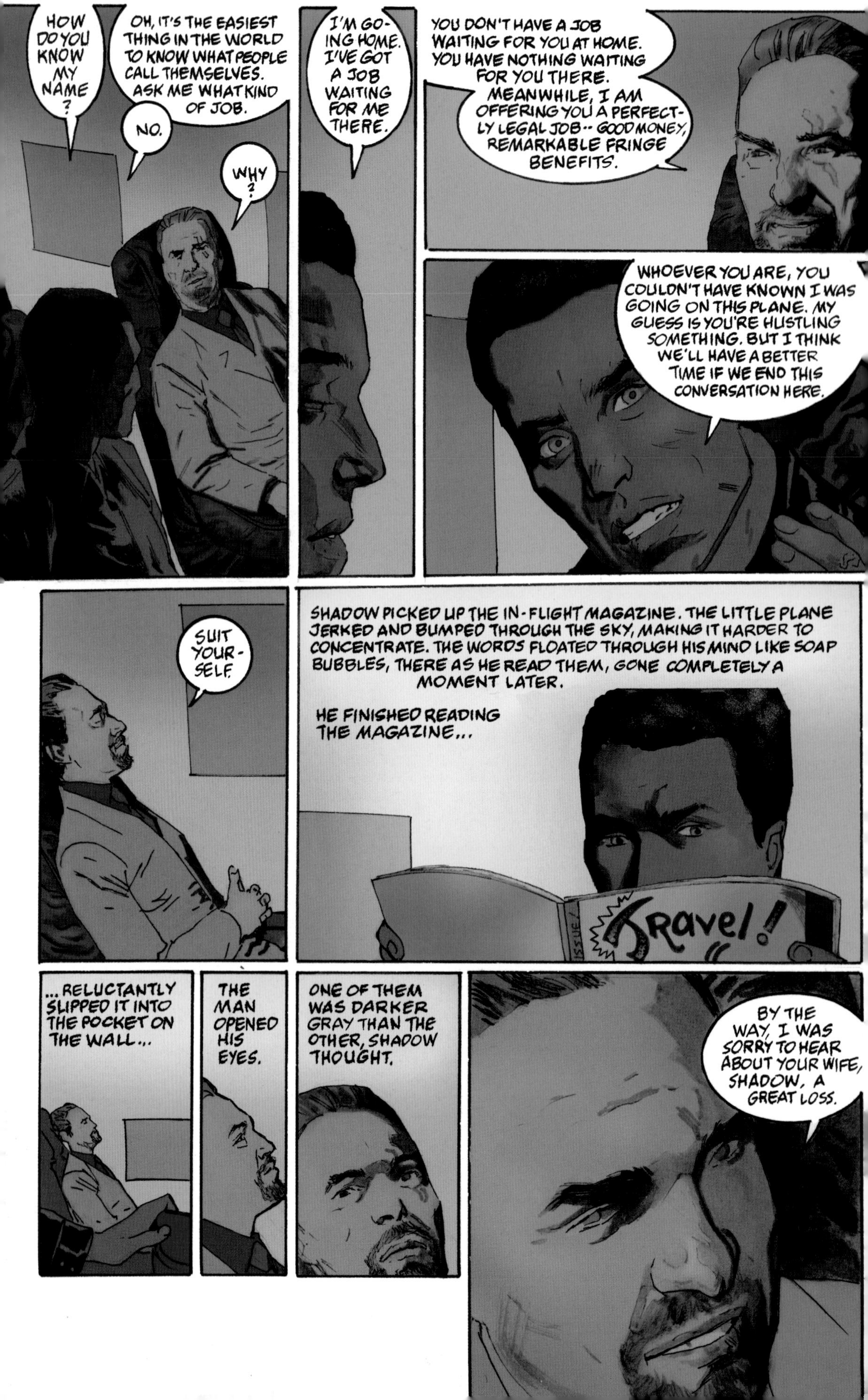

HOW DO YOU KNOW MY NAME?
OH, IT'S THE EASIEST THING IN THE WORLD TO KNOW WHAT PEOPLE CALL THEMSELVES. ASK ME WHAT KIND OF JOB.
NO.
WHY?
I'M GOING HOME. I'VE GOT A JOB WAITING FOR ME THERE.
YOU DON'T HAVE A JOB WAITING FOR YOU AT HOME. YOU HAVE NOTHING WAITING FOR YOU THERE.
MEANWHILE, I AM OFFERING YOU A PERFECTLY LEGAL JOB -- GOOD MONEY, REMARKABLE FRINGE BENEFITS.
WHOEVER YOU ARE, YOU COULDN'T HAVE KNOWN I WAS GOING ON THIS PLANE. MY GUESS IS YOU'RE HUSTLING SOMETHING. BUT I THINK WE'LL HAVE A BETTER TIME IF WE END THIS CONVERSATION HERE.
SUIT YOURSELF.
SHADOW PICKED UP THE IN-FLIGHT MAGAZINE. THE LITTLE PLANE JERKED AND BUMPED THROUGH THE SKY, MAKING IT HARDER TO CONCENTRATE. THE WORDS FLOATED THROUGH HIS MIND LIKE SOAP BUBBLES, THERE AS HE READ THEM, GONE COMPLETELY A MOMENT LATER.
HE FINISHED READING THE MAGAZINE...
Travel!
...RELUCTANTLY SLIPPED IT INTO THE POCKET ON THE WALL...
THE MAN OPENED HIS EYES.
ONE OF THEM WAS DARKER GRAY THAN THE OTHER, SHADOW THOUGHT.
BY THE WAY, I WAS SORRY TO HEAR ABOUT YOUR WIFE, SHADOW. A GREAT LOSS.

SHADOW TOOK A DEEP BREATH. COUNTED TO FIVE.

SO WAS I.

IF IT COULD BUT HAVE BEEN ANY OTHER WAY.

SHE DIED IN A CAR CRASH. IT'S A FAST WAY TO GO. IT COULD HAVE BEEN WORSE.

SHADOW, IT'S NOT A JOKE. IT'S NOT A TRICK. I CAN PAY YOU BETTER THAN ANY OTHER JOB YOU WILL FIND WILL PAY YOU. YOU'RE AN EX-CON. THERE IS NOT A LONG LINE OF PEOPLE ELBOWING EACH OTHER OUT OF THE WAY TO HIRE YOU.

MISTER WHOEVER-THE-FUCK YOU ARE, THERE ISN'T ENOUGH MONEY IN THE WORLD.

THE MAN GRINNED. SHADOW FOUND HIMSELF REMEMBERING A P.B.S. SHOW ABOUT CHIMPANZEES. WHEN A CHIMP SMILES, IT'S ONLY TO BARE ITS TEETH IN A GRIMACE OF HATE OR AGGRESSION. IT'S A THREAT.

THIS GRIN WAS ONE OF THOSE.

SURE, THERE'S MONEY ENOUGH. THERE MAY BE A LITTLE RISK, OF COURSE, BUT IF YOU SURVIVE, YOU CAN HAVE WHATEVER YOUR HEART DESIRES.

YOU COULD BE THE NEXT KING OF AMERICA.

WHO ARE YOU?

AH, YES. THE AGE OF INFORMATION. WHY DON'T YOU CALL ME WEDNESDAY? MISTER WEDNESDAY. ALTHOUGH GIVEN THE WEATHER, IT MIGHT AS WELL BE THURSDAY, EH?

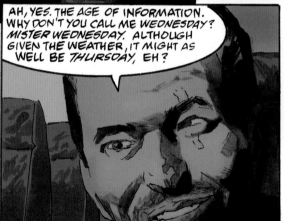

WHAT'S YOUR REAL NAME?

WORK FOR ME LONG ENOUGH AND I MAY EVEN TELL YOU THAT. *THERE.* JOB OFFER. NO ONE EXPECTS YOU TO SAY YES IMMEDIATELY.

TAKE YOUR TIME.

I DON'T THINK SO. I DON'T LIKE YOU. I DON'T WANT TO WORK WITH YOU.

LIKE I SAY, DON'T RUSH INTO IT.

TAKE YOUR TIME.

Z Z Z

THE PLANE LANDED WITH A BUMP AND A FEW PASSENGERS GOT OFF. IT WAS A LITTLE AIRPORT IN THE MIDDLE OF NOWHERE AND THERE WERE STILL TWO LITTLE AIRPORTS TO GO BEFORE EAGLE POINT.

MISTER WEDNESDAY.

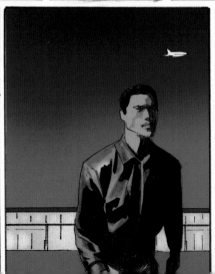

BUDGET RENT-A-CAR

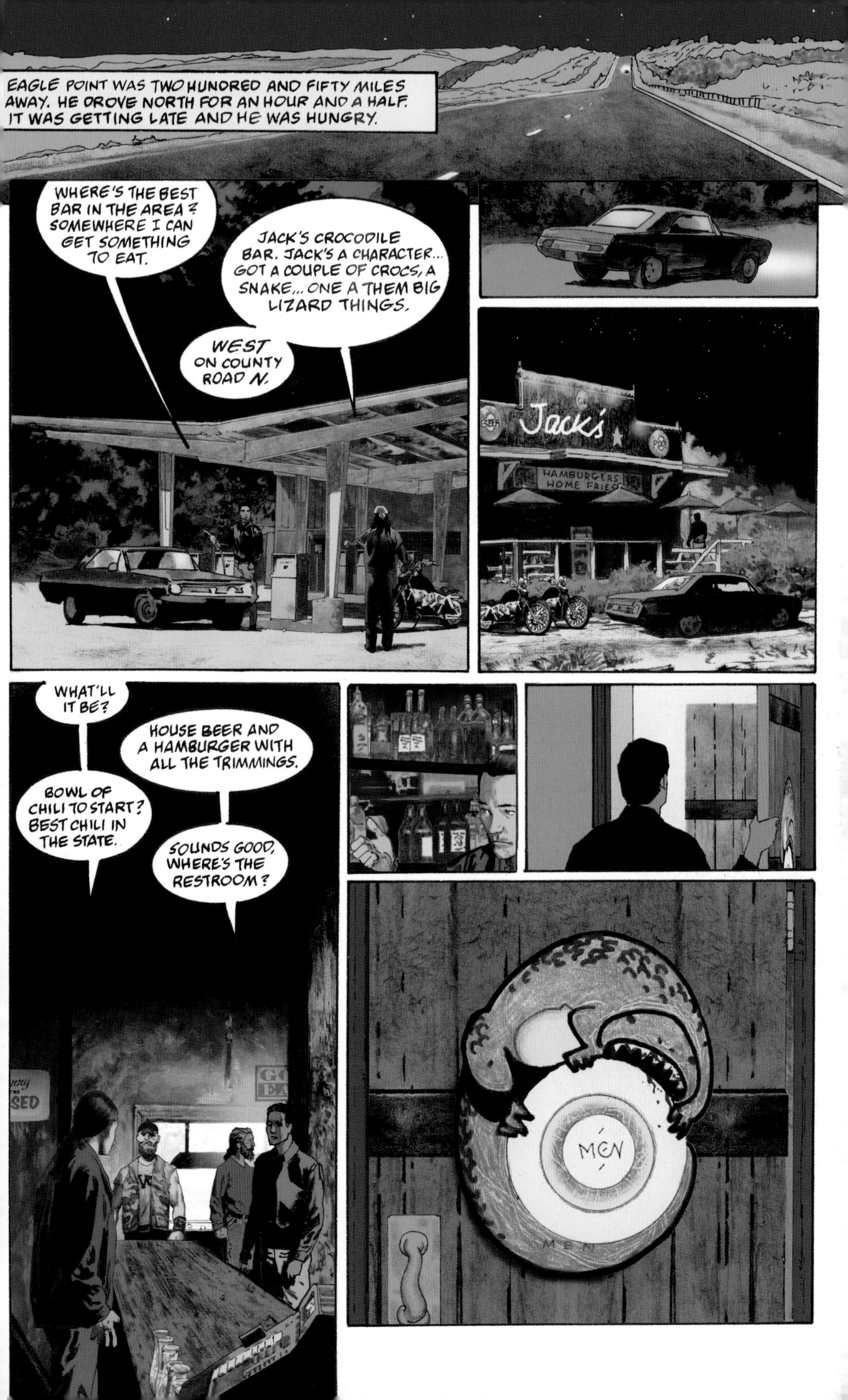
EAGLE POINT WAS TWO HUNDRED AND FIFTY MILES AWAY. HE DROVE NORTH FOR AN HOUR AND A HALF. IT WAS GETTING LATE AND HE WAS HUNGRY.
WHERE'S THE BEST BAR IN THE AREA? SOMEWHERE I CAN GET SOMETHING TO EAT.
JACK'S CROCODILE BAR. JACK'S A CHARACTER... GOT A COUPLE OF CROCS, A SNAKE... ONE A THEM BIG LIZARD THINGS.
WEST ON COUNTY ROAD N.
Jack's
BEER
POOL
HAMBURGERS HOME FRIES
WHAT'LL IT BE?
HOUSE BEER AND A HAMBURGER WITH ALL THE TRIMMINGS.
BOWL OF CHILI TO START? BEST CHILI IN THE STATE.
SOUNDS GOOD, WHERE'S THE RESTROOM?
MEN

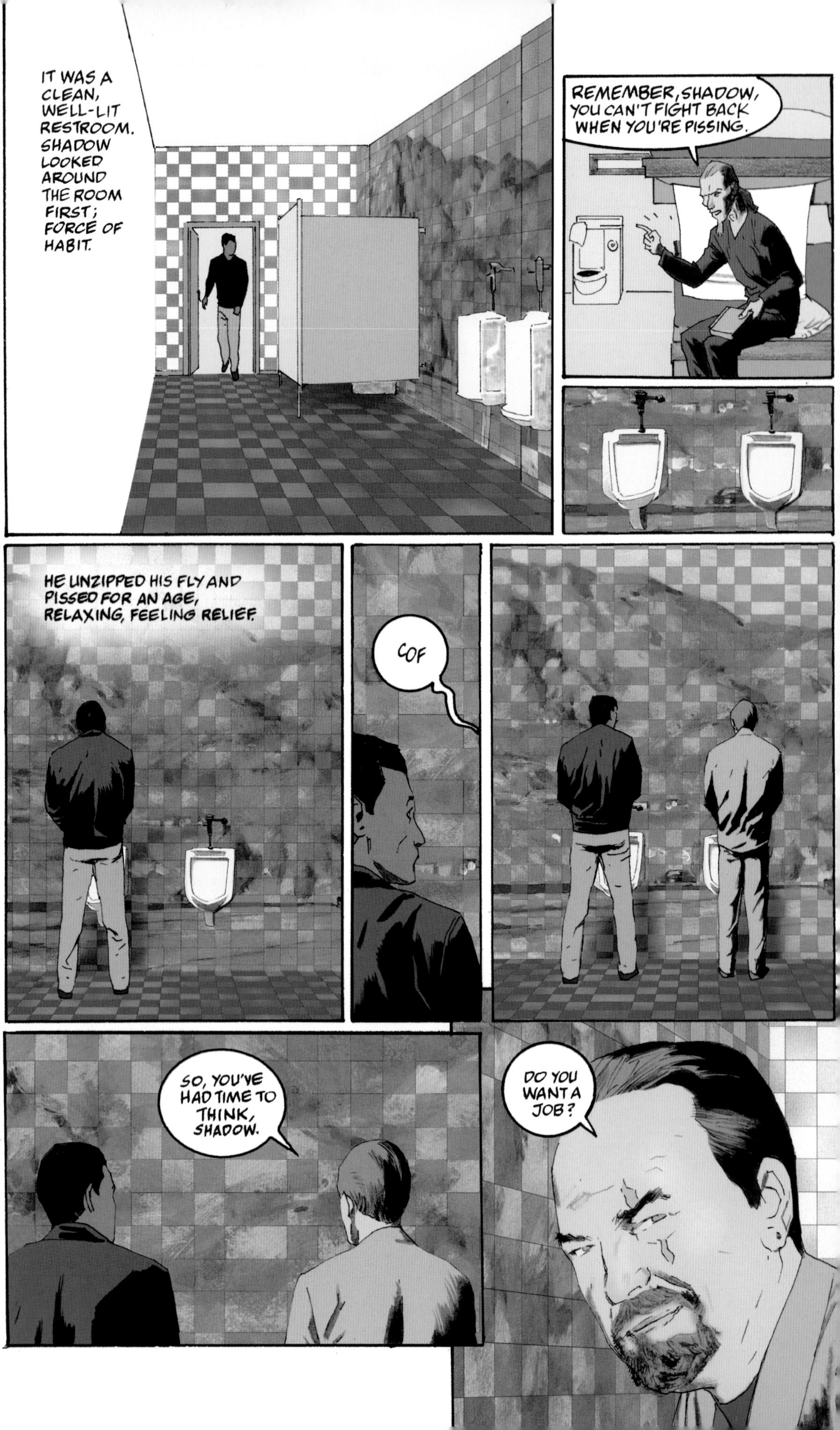
IT WAS A CLEAN, WELL-LIT RESTROOM. SHADOW LOOKED AROUND THE ROOM FIRST; FORCE OF HABIT.
REMEMBER, SHADOW, YOU CAN'T FIGHT BACK WHEN YOU'RE PISSING.
HE UNZIPPED HIS FLY AND PISSED FOR AN AGE, RELAXING, FEELING RELIEF.
COF
SO, YOU'VE HAD TIME TO THINK, SHADOW.
DO YOU WANT A JOB?

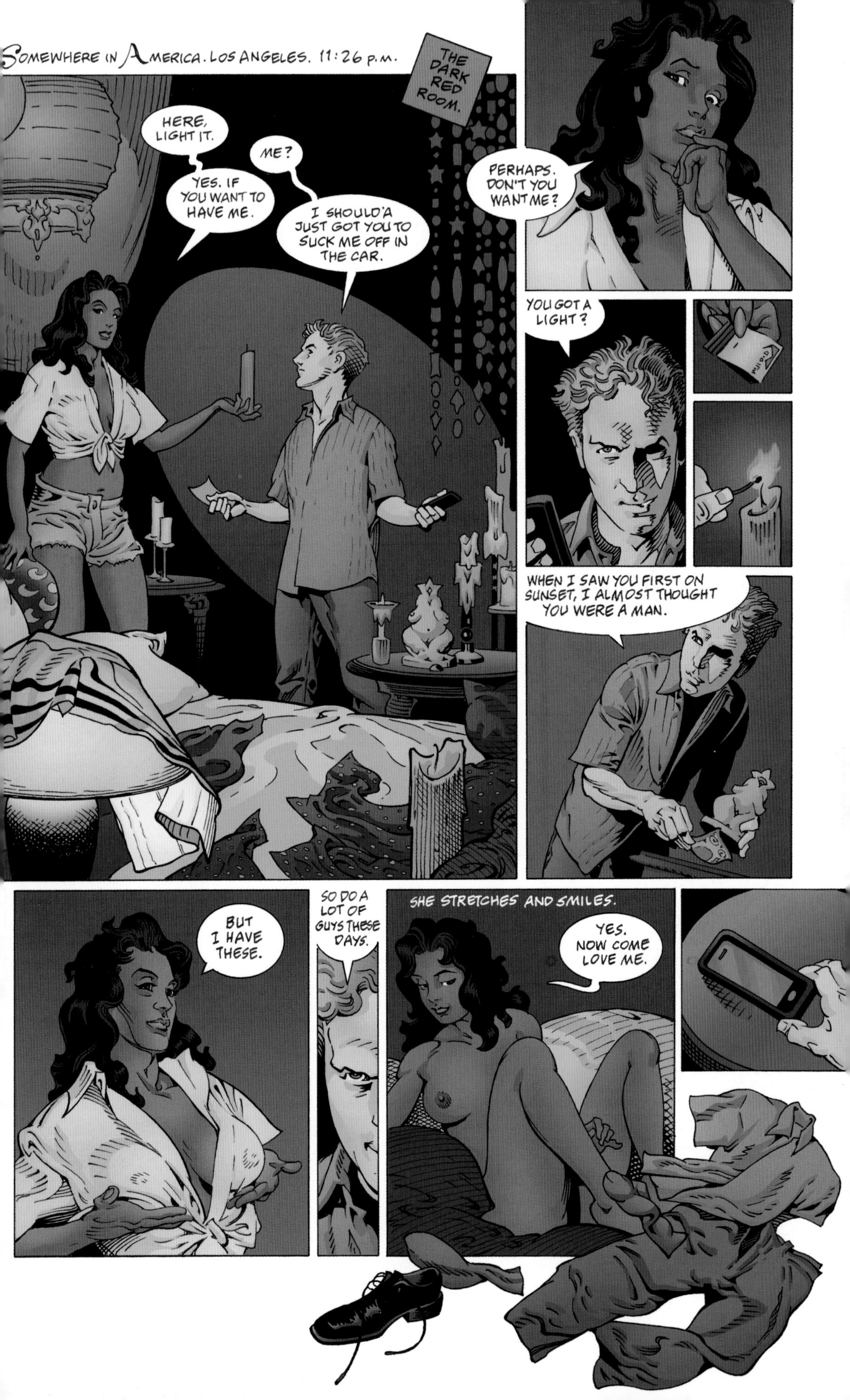
Somewhere in America. Los Angeles. 11:26 p.m.
THE DARK RED ROOM.
HERE, LIGHT IT.
ME?
YES. IF YOU WANT TO HAVE ME.
I SHOULD'A JUST GOT YOU TO SUCK ME OFF IN THE CAR.
PERHAPS. DON'T YOU WANT ME?
YOU GOT A LIGHT?
WHEN I SAW YOU FIRST ON SUNSET, I ALMOST THOUGHT YOU WERE A MAN.
BUT I HAVE THESE.
SO DO A LOT OF GUYS THESE DAYS.
SHE STRETCHES AND SMILES.
YES. NOW COME LOVE ME.

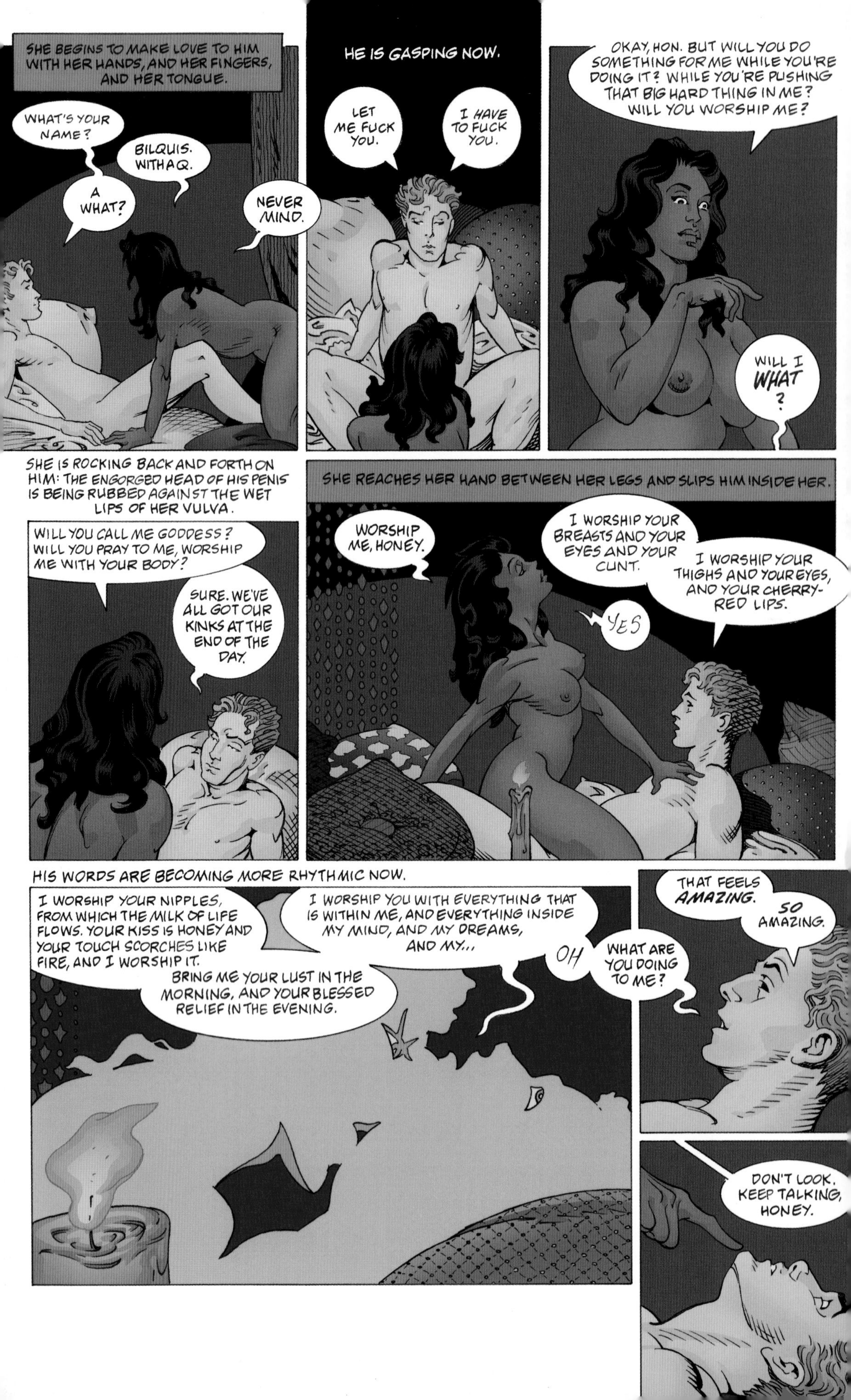
SHE BEGINS TO MAKE LOVE TO HIM WITH HER HANDS, AND HER FINGERS, AND HER TONGUE.
WHAT'S YOUR NAME?
BILQUIS. WITH A Q.
A WHAT?
NEVER MIND.
HE IS GASPING NOW.
LET ME FUCK YOU.
I HAVE TO FUCK YOU.
OKAY, HON. BUT WILL YOU DO SOMETHING FOR ME WHILE YOU'RE DOING IT? WHILE YOU'RE PUSHING THAT BIG HARD THING IN ME? WILL YOU WORSHIP ME?
WILL I WHAT?
SHE IS ROCKING BACK AND FORTH ON HIM: THE ENGORGED HEAD OF HIS PENIS IS BEING RUBBED AGAINST THE WET LIPS OF HER VULVA.
WILL YOU CALL ME GODDESS? WILL YOU PRAY TO ME, WORSHIP ME WITH YOUR BODY?
SURE. WE'VE ALL GOT OUR KINKS AT THE END OF THE DAY.
SHE REACHES HER HAND BETWEEN HER LEGS AND SLIPS HIM INSIDE HER.
WORSHIP ME, HONEY.
I WORSHIP YOUR BREASTS AND YOUR EYES AND YOUR CUNT.
I WORSHIP YOUR THIGHS AND YOUR EYES, AND YOUR CHERRY-RED LIPS.
YES
HIS WORDS ARE BECOMING MORE RHYTHMIC NOW.
I WORSHIP YOUR NIPPLES, FROM WHICH THE MILK OF LIFE FLOWS. YOUR KISS IS HONEY AND YOUR TOUCH SCORCHES LIKE FIRE, AND I WORSHIP IT.
BRING ME YOUR LUST IN THE MORNING, AND YOUR BLESSED RELIEF IN THE EVENING.
I WORSHIP YOU WITH EVERYTHING THAT IS WITHIN ME, AND EVERYTHING INSIDE MY MIND, AND MY DREAMS, AND MY...
OH
WHAT ARE YOU DOING TO ME?
THAT FEELS AMAZING.
SO AMAZING.
DON'T LOOK. KEEP TALKING, HONEY.

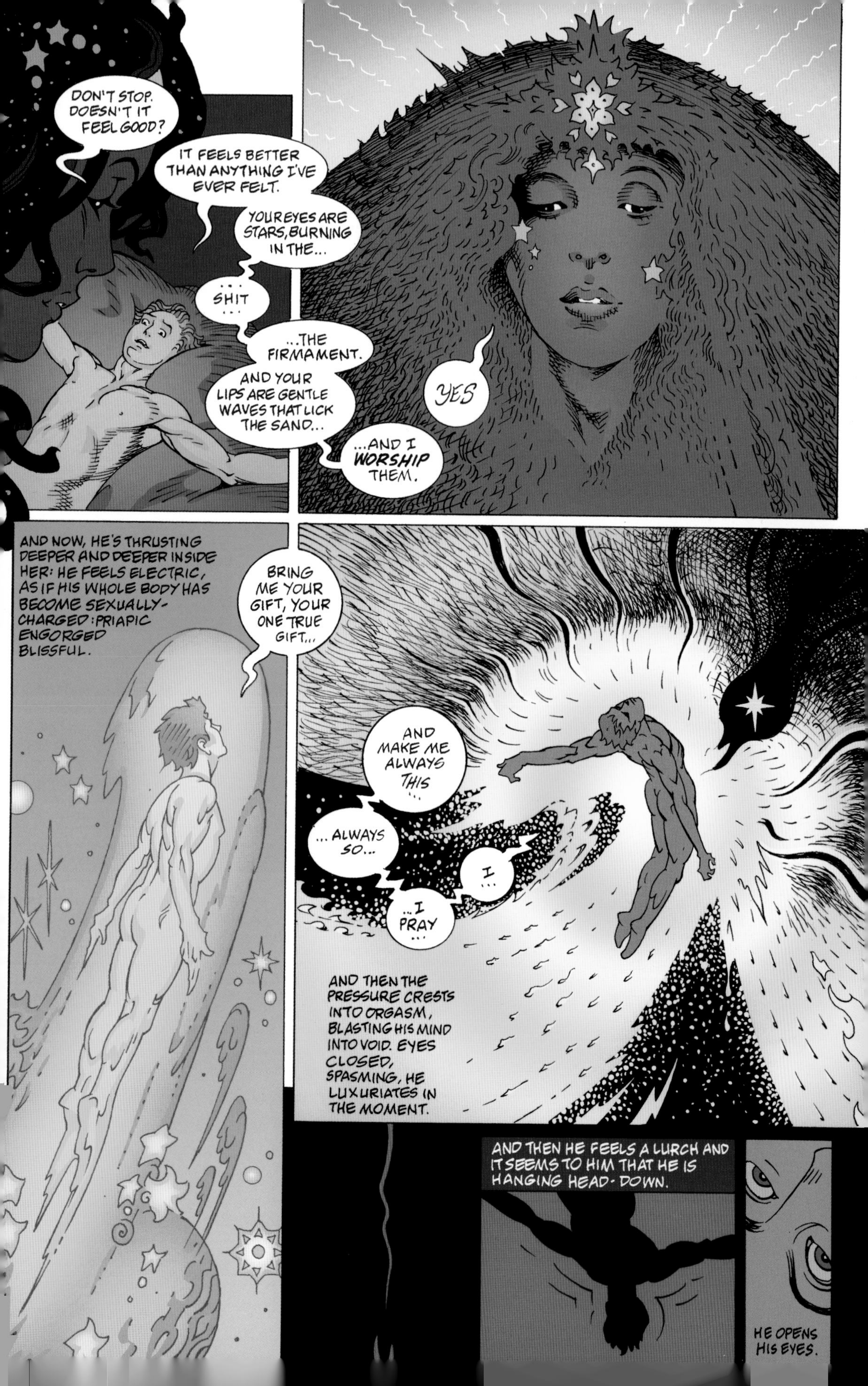
DON'T STOP. DOESN'T IT FEEL GOOD?
IT FEELS BETTER THAN ANYTHING I'VE EVER FELT.
YOUR EYES ARE STARS, BURNING IN THE...
...SHIT...
...THE FIRMAMENT.
AND YOUR LIPS ARE GENTLE WAVES THAT LICK THE SAND...
YES
...AND I **WORSHIP** THEM.
AND NOW, HE'S THRUSTING DEEPER AND DEEPER INSIDE HER: HE FEELS ELECTRIC, AS IF HIS WHOLE BODY HAS BECOME SEXUALLY-CHARGED: PRIAPIC ENGORGED BLISSFUL.
BRING ME YOUR GIFT, YOUR ONE TRUE GIFT...
AND MAKE ME ALWAYS THIS...
...ALWAYS SO...
I...
...I PRAY...
AND THEN THE PRESSURE CRESTS INTO ORGASM, BLASTING HIS MIND INTO VOID. EYES CLOSED, SPASMING, HE LUXURIATES IN THE MOMENT.
AND THEN HE FEELS A LURCH AND IT SEEMS TO HIM THAT HE IS HANGING HEAD-DOWN.
HE OPENS HIS EYES.

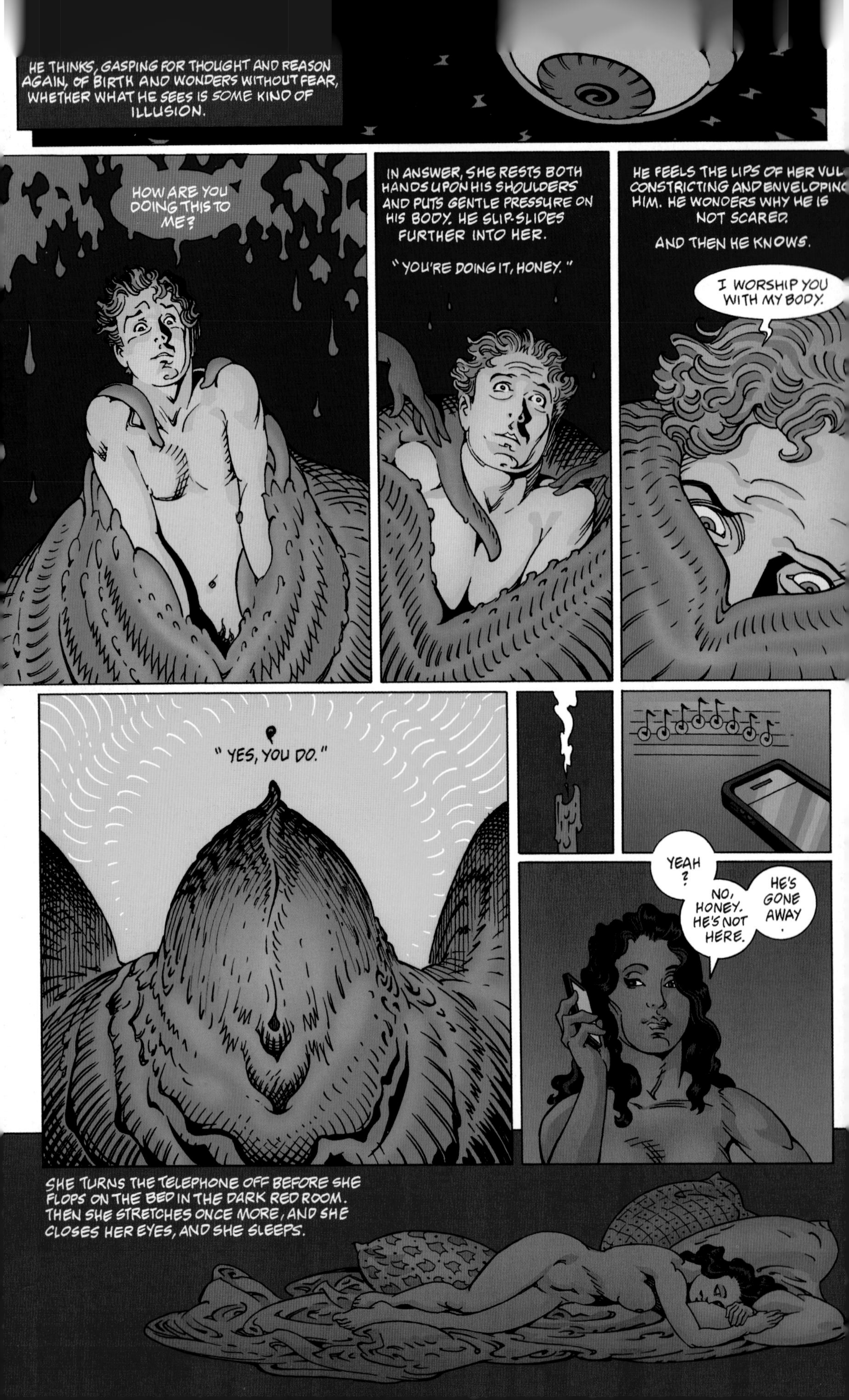
HE THINKS, GASPING FOR THOUGHT AND REASON AGAIN, OF BIRTH AND WONDERS WITHOUT FEAR, WHETHER WHAT HE SEES IS SOME KIND OF ILLUSION.
HOW ARE YOU DOING THIS TO ME?
IN ANSWER, SHE RESTS BOTH HANDS UPON HIS SHOULDERS AND PUTS GENTLE PRESSURE ON HIS BODY. HE SLIP-SLIDES FURTHER INTO HER.
"YOU'RE DOING IT, HONEY."
HE FEELS THE LIPS OF HER VUL
CONSTRICTING AND ENVELOPING HIM. HE WONDERS WHY HE IS NOT SCARED.
AND THEN HE KNOWS.
I WORSHIP YOU WITH MY BODY.
"YES, YOU DO."
YEAH?
NO, HONEY. HE'S NOT HERE.
HE'S GONE AWAY.
SHE TURNS THE TELEPHONE OFF BEFORE SHE FLOPS ON THE BED IN THE DARK RED ROOM. THEN SHE STRETCHES ONCE MORE, AND SHE CLOSES HER EYES, AND SHE SLEEPS.

CHAPTER TWO

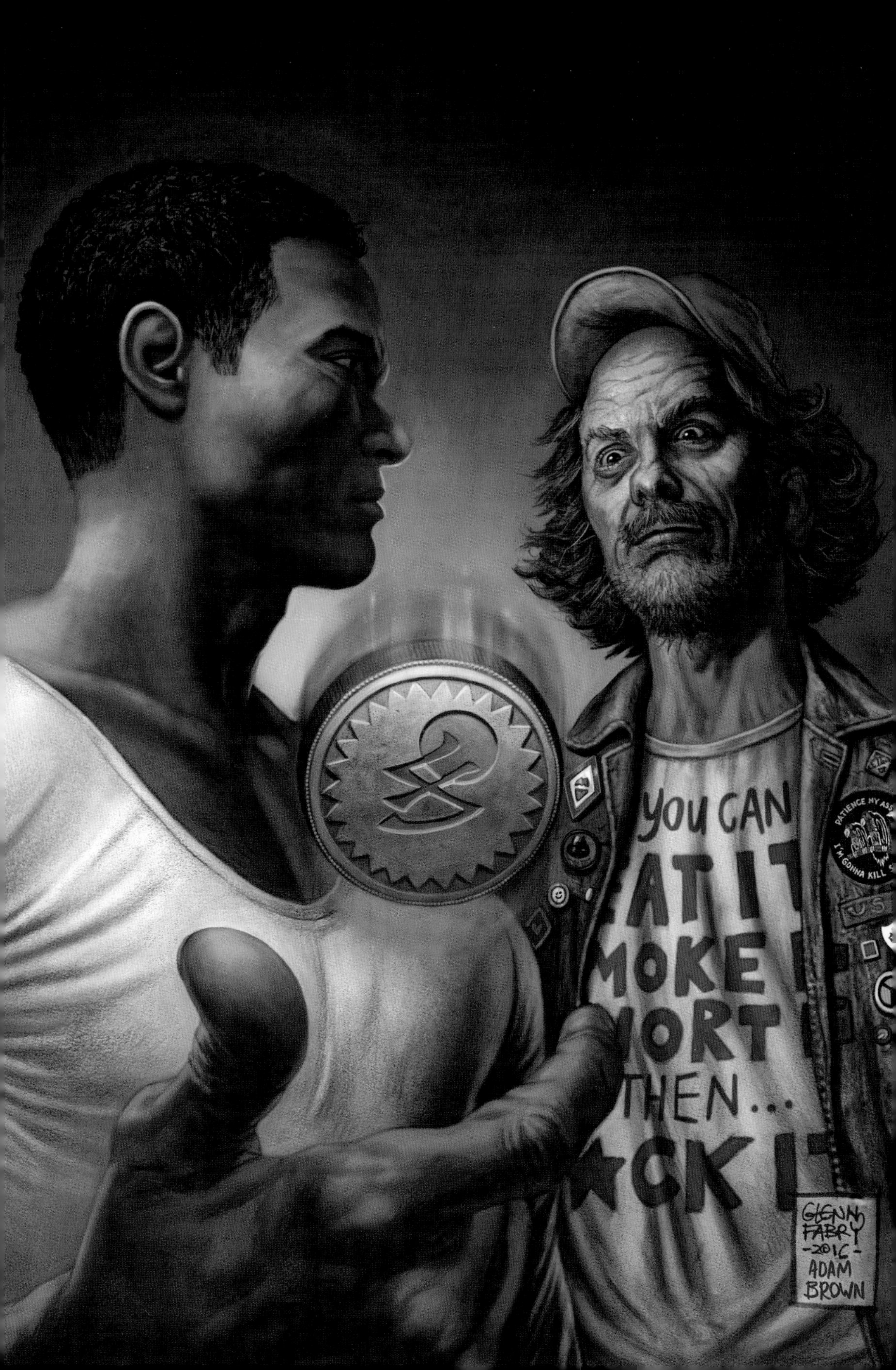

YOU CAN
THEN...
PATIENCE MY ASS
GLENN FABRY -2016- ADAM BROWN

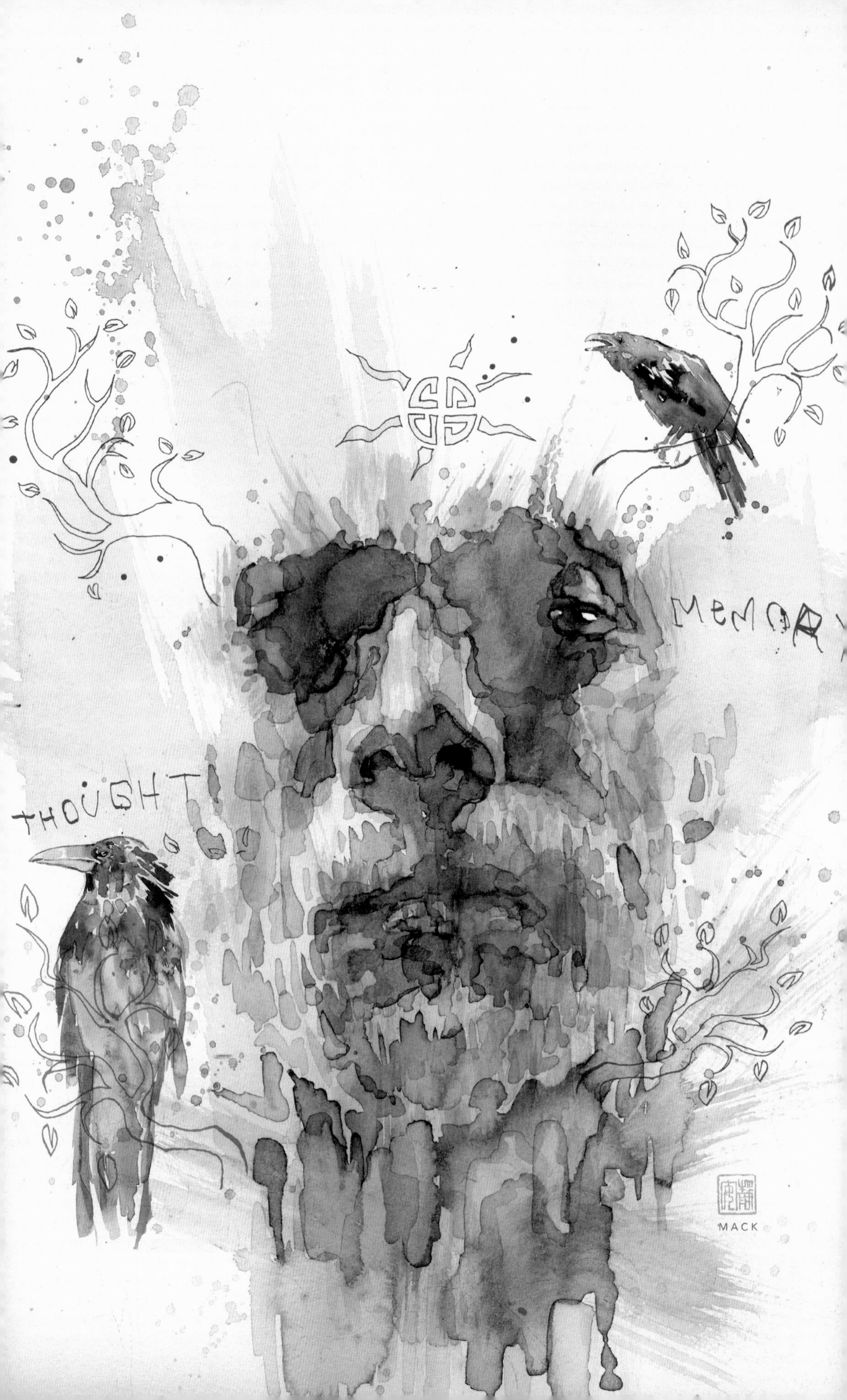
THOUGHT
MEMORY
MACK

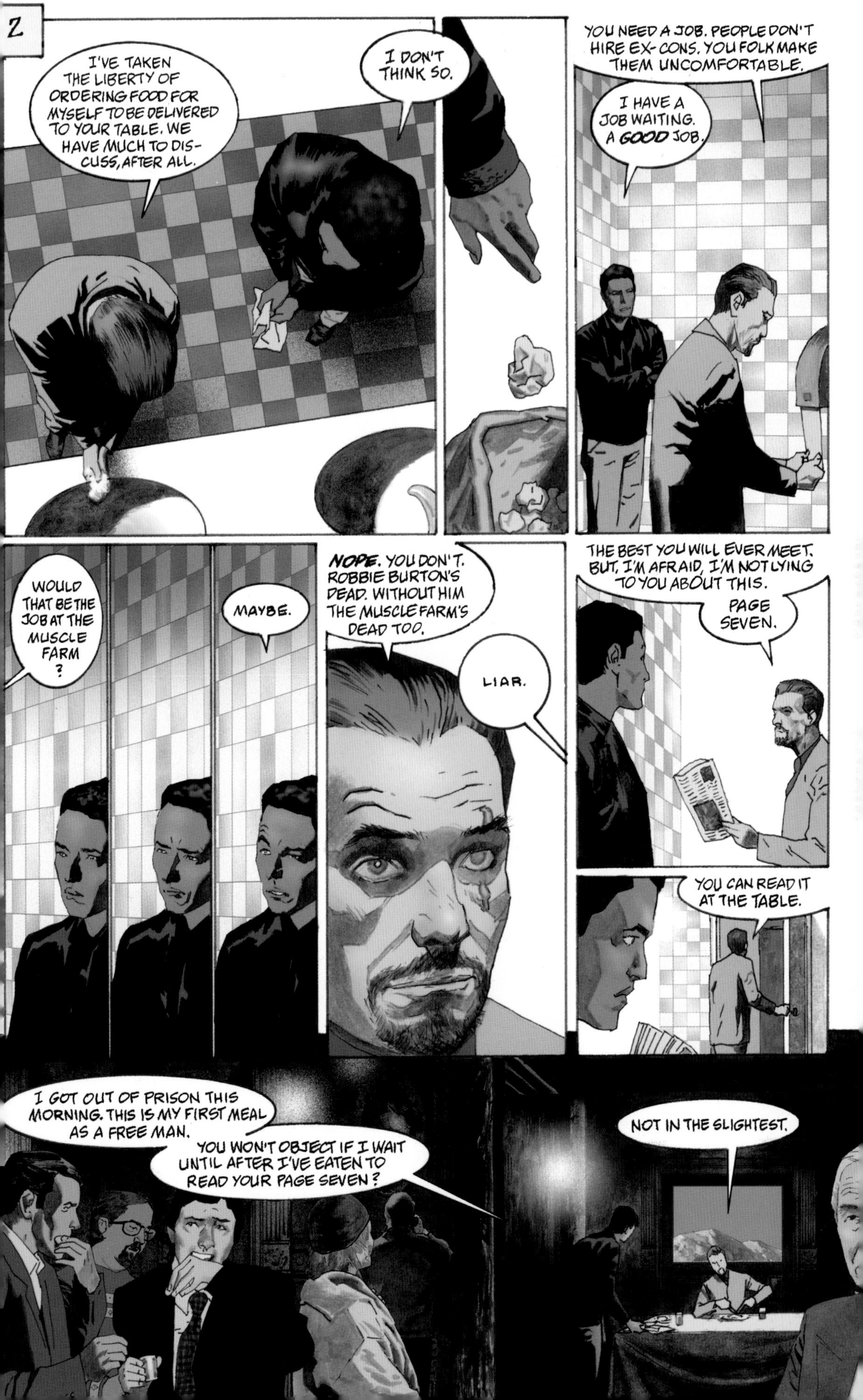
2
I'VE TAKEN THE LIBERTY OF ORDERING FOOD FOR MYSELF TO BE DELIVERED TO YOUR TABLE. WE HAVE MUCH TO DISCUSS, AFTER ALL.
I DON'T THINK SO.
YOU NEED A JOB. PEOPLE DON'T HIRE EX-CONS. YOU FOLK MAKE THEM UNCOMFORTABLE.
I HAVE A JOB WAITING. A GOOD JOB.
WOULD THAT BE THE JOB AT THE MUSCLE FARM?
MAYBE.
NOPE. YOU DON'T. ROBBIE BURTON'S DEAD. WITHOUT HIM THE MUSCLE FARM'S DEAD TOO.
LIAR.
THE BEST YOU WILL EVER MEET. BUT, I'M AFRAID, I'M NOT LYING TO YOU ABOUT THIS.
PAGE SEVEN.
YOU CAN READ IT AT THE TABLE.
I GOT OUT OF PRISON THIS MORNING. THIS IS MY FIRST MEAL AS A FREE MAN.
YOU WON'T OBJECT IF I WAIT UNTIL AFTER I'VE EATEN TO READ YOUR PAGE SEVEN?
NOT IN THE SLIGHTEST.

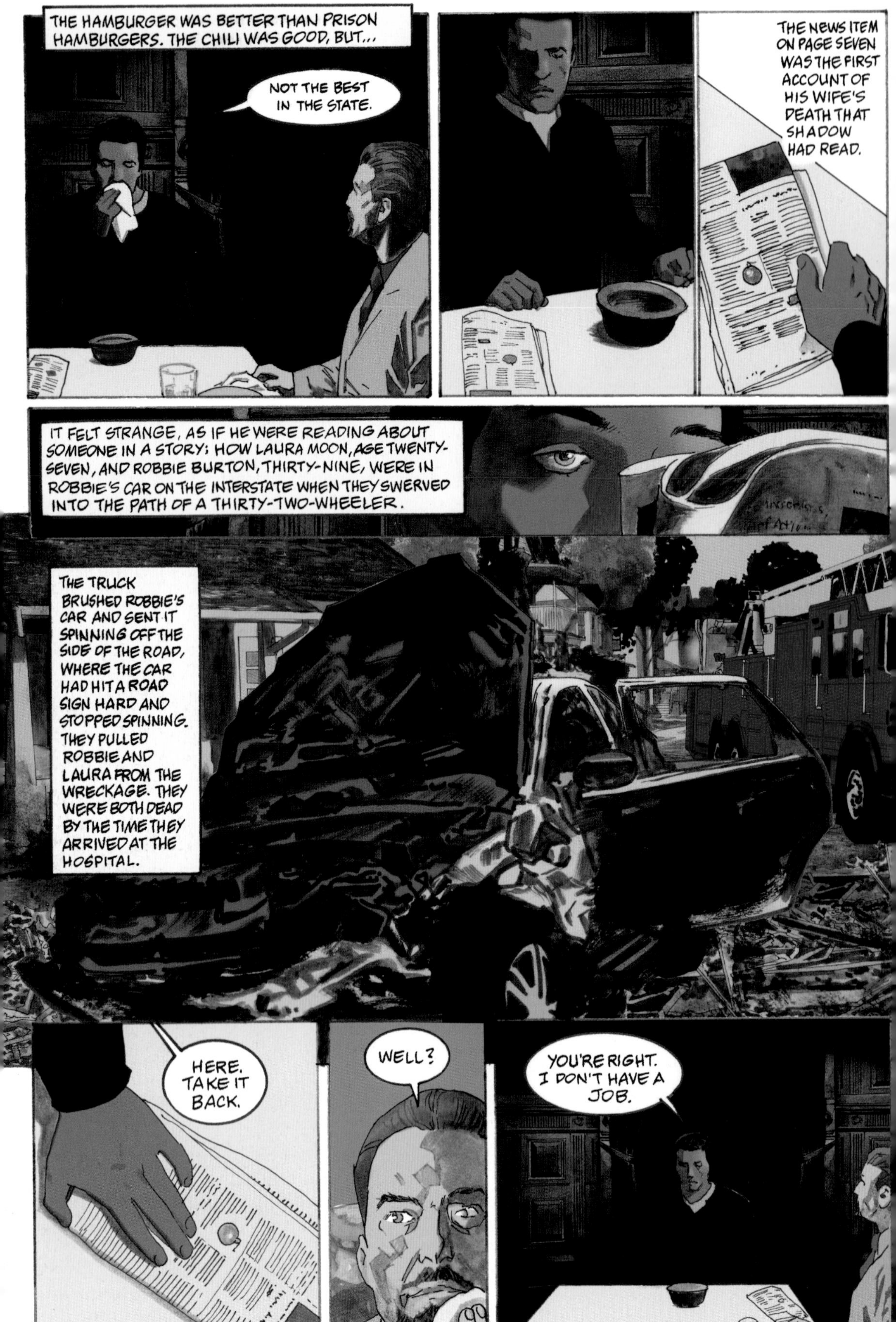
THE HAMBURGER WAS BETTER THAN PRISON HAMBURGERS. THE CHILI WAS GOOD, BUT...
NOT THE BEST IN THE STATE.
THE NEWS ITEM ON PAGE SEVEN WAS THE FIRST ACCOUNT OF HIS WIFE'S DEATH THAT SHADOW HAD READ.
IT FELT STRANGE, AS IF HE WERE READING ABOUT SOMEONE IN A STORY; HOW LAURA MOON, AGE TWENTY-SEVEN, AND ROBBIE BURTON, THIRTY-NINE, WERE IN ROBBIE'S CAR ON THE INTERSTATE WHEN THEY SWERVED INTO THE PATH OF A THIRTY-TWO-WHEELER.
THE TRUCK BRUSHED ROBBIE'S CAR AND SENT IT SPINNING OFF THE SIDE OF THE ROAD, WHERE THE CAR HAD HIT A ROAD SIGN HARD AND STOPPED SPINNING. THEY PULLED ROBBIE AND LAURA FROM THE WRECKAGE. THEY WERE BOTH DEAD BY THE TIME THEY ARRIVED AT THE HOSPITAL.
HERE. TAKE IT BACK.
WELL?
YOU'RE RIGHT. I DON'T HAVE A JOB.

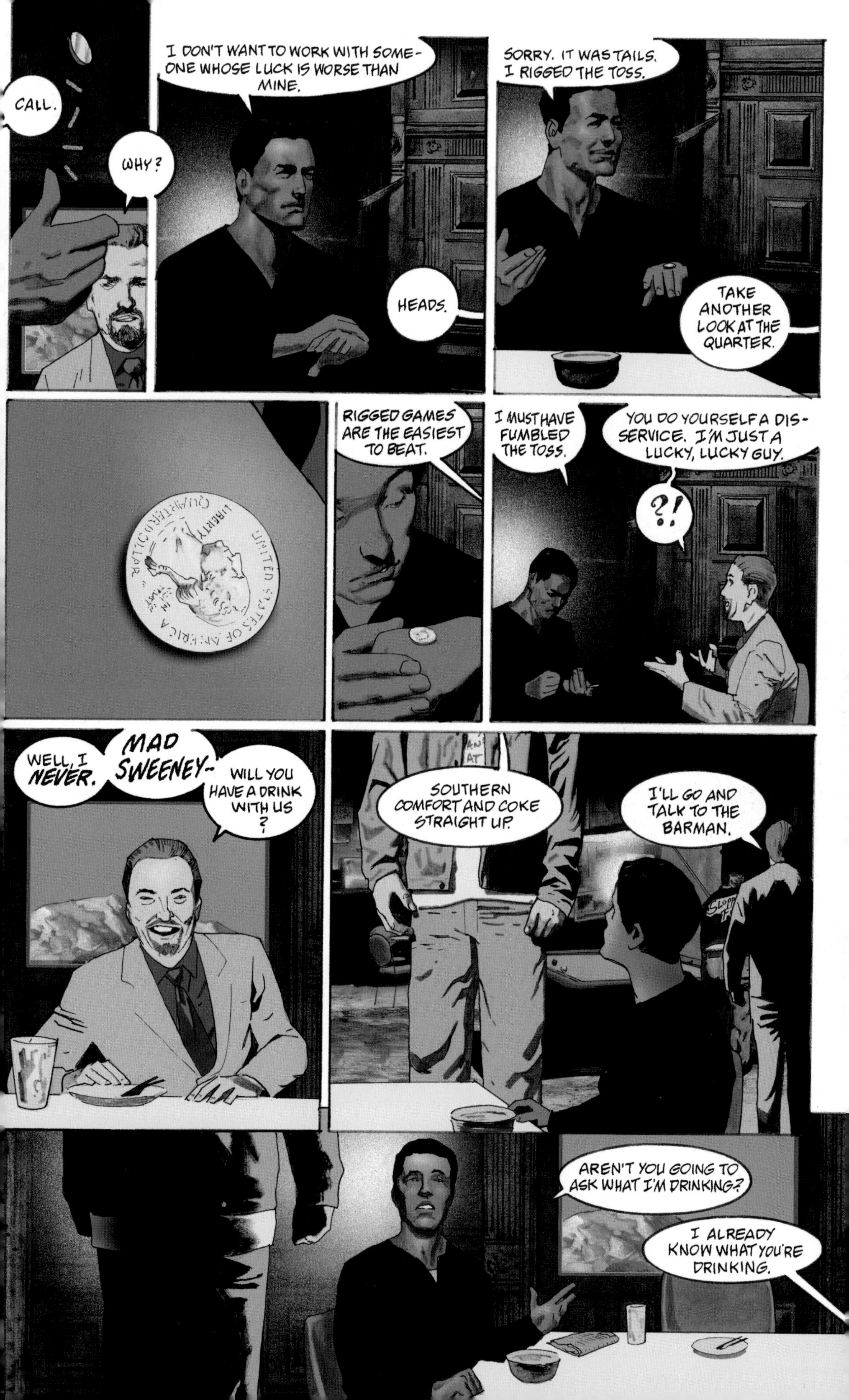
CALL.
WHY?
I DON'T WANT TO WORK WITH SOME-ONE WHOSE LUCK IS WORSE THAN MINE.
HEADS.
SORRY. IT WAS TAILS. I RIGGED THE TOSS.
TAKE ANOTHER LOOK AT THE QUARTER.
RIGGED GAMES ARE THE EASIEST TO BEAT.
I MUST HAVE FUMBLED THE TOSS.
YOU DO YOURSELF A DIS-SERVICE. I'M JUST A LUCKY, LUCKY GUY.
?!
WELL, I NEVER.
MAD SWEENEY-
WILL YOU HAVE A DRINK WITH US?
SOUTHERN COMFORT AND COKE STRAIGHT UP.
I'LL GO AND TALK TO THE BARMAN.
AREN'T YOU GOING TO ASK WHAT I'M DRINKING?
I ALREADY KNOW WHAT YOU'RE DRINKING.

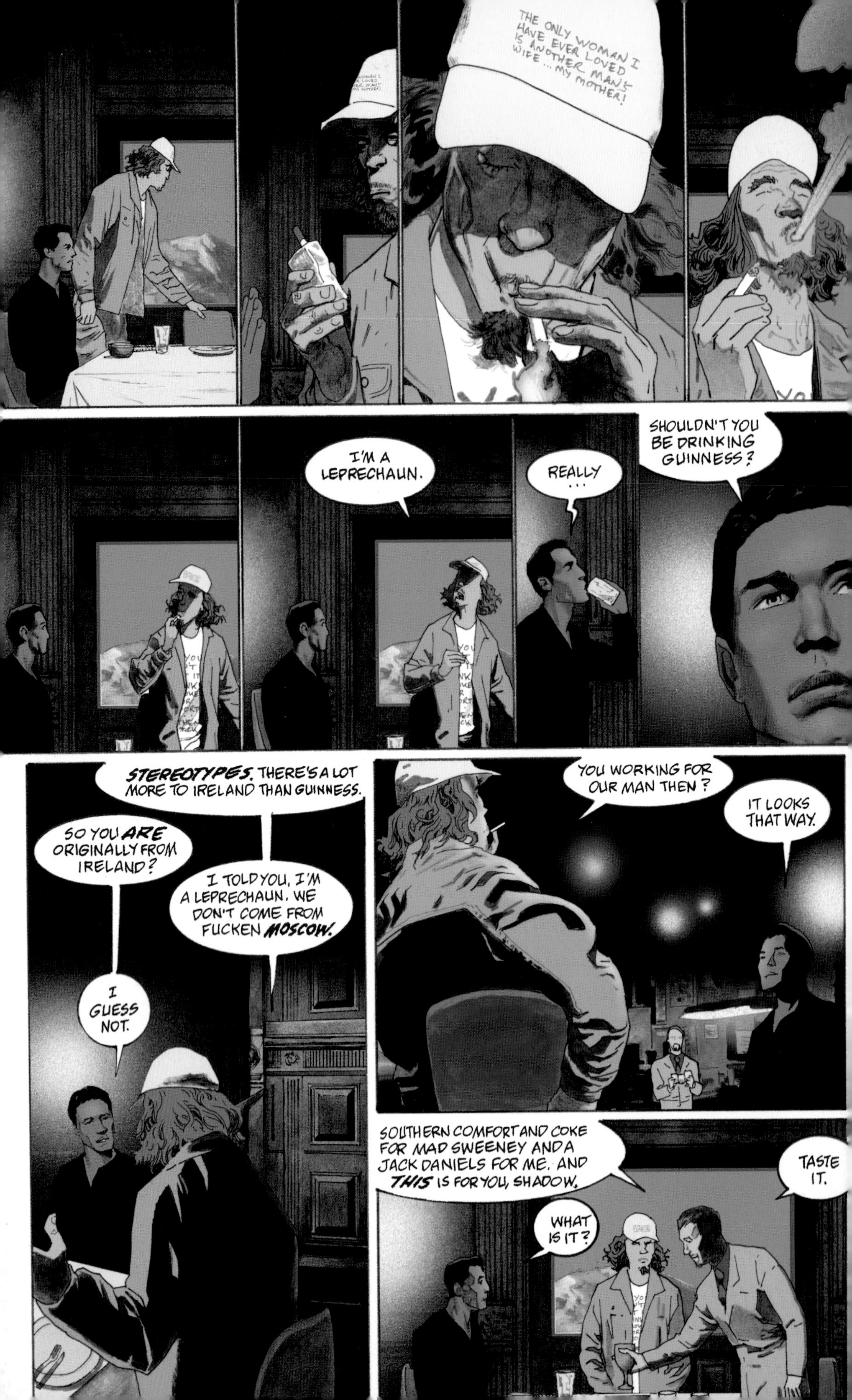
THE ONLY WOMAN I HAVE EVER LOVED IS ANOTHER MAN'S WIFE ... MY MOTHER!
I'M A LEPRECHAUN.
REALLY ...
SHOULDN'T YOU BE DRINKING GUINNESS?
STEREOTYPES. THERE'S A LOT MORE TO IRELAND THAN GUINNESS.
SO YOU ARE ORIGINALLY FROM IRELAND?
I TOLD YOU, I'M A LEPRECHAUN. WE DON'T COME FROM FUCKEN MOSCOW.
I GUESS NOT.
YOU WORKING FOR OUR MAN THEN?
IT LOOKS THAT WAY.
SOUTHERN COMFORT AND COKE FOR MAD SWEENEY AND A JACK DANIELS FOR ME. AND THIS IS FOR YOU, SHADOW.
TASTE IT.
WHAT IS IT?

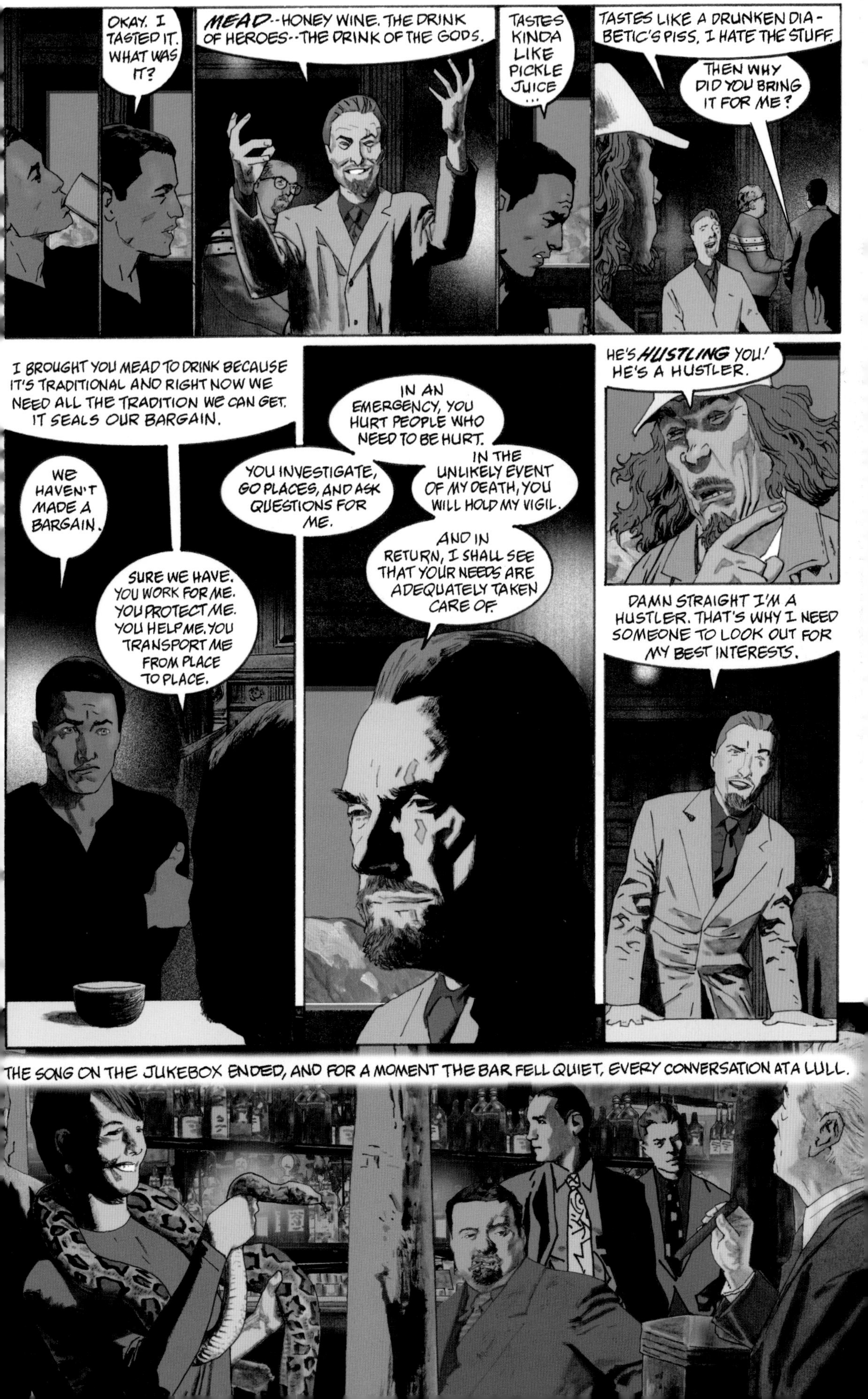
OKAY. I TASTED IT. WHAT WAS IT?
MEAD--HONEY WINE. THE DRINK OF HEROES--THE DRINK OF THE GODS.
TASTES KINDA LIKE PICKLE JUICE...
TASTES LIKE A DRUNKEN DIABETIC'S PISS. I HATE THE STUFF.
THEN WHY DID YOU BRING IT FOR ME?
I BROUGHT YOU MEAD TO DRINK BECAUSE IT'S TRADITIONAL AND RIGHT NOW WE NEED ALL THE TRADITION WE CAN GET. IT SEALS OUR BARGAIN.
WE HAVEN'T MADE A BARGAIN.
SURE WE HAVE. YOU WORK FOR ME. YOU PROTECT ME. YOU HELP ME. YOU TRANSPORT ME FROM PLACE TO PLACE.
YOU INVESTIGATE, GO PLACES, AND ASK QUESTIONS FOR ME.
IN AN EMERGENCY, YOU HURT PEOPLE WHO NEED TO BE HURT.
IN THE UNLIKELY EVENT OF MY DEATH, YOU WILL HOLD MY VIGIL.
AND IN RETURN, I SHALL SEE THAT YOUR NEEDS ARE ADEQUATELY TAKEN CARE OF.
HE'S HUSTLING YOU! HE'S A HUSTLER.
DAMN STRAIGHT I'M A HUSTLER. THAT'S WHY I NEED SOMEONE TO LOOK OUT FOR MY BEST INTERESTS.
THE SONG ON THE JUKEBOX ENDED, AND FOR A MOMENT THE BAR FELL QUIET, EVERY CONVERSATION AT A LULL.

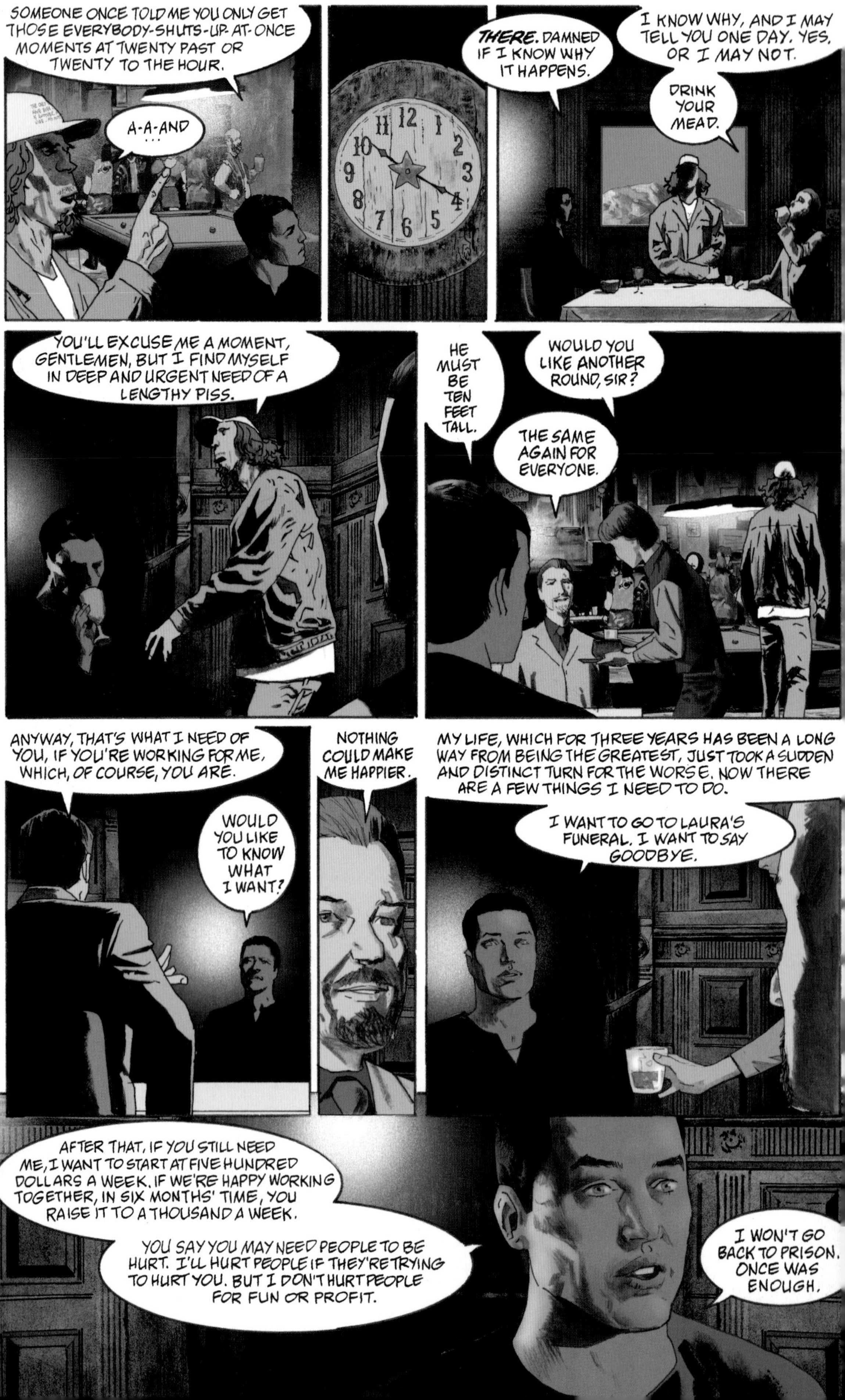
SOMEONE ONCE TOLD ME YOU ONLY GET THOSE EVERYBODY-SHUTS-UP-AT-ONCE MOMENTS AT TWENTY PAST OR TWENTY TO THE HOUR.
A-A-AND . . .
THERE. DAMNED IF I KNOW WHY IT HAPPENS.
I KNOW WHY, AND I MAY TELL YOU ONE DAY. YES, OR I MAY NOT.
DRINK YOUR MEAD.
YOU'LL EXCUSE ME A MOMENT, GENTLEMEN, BUT I FIND MYSELF IN DEEP AND URGENT NEED OF A LENGTHY PISS.
HE MUST BE TEN FEET TALL.
WOULD YOU LIKE ANOTHER ROUND, SIR?
THE SAME AGAIN FOR EVERYONE.
ANYWAY, THAT'S WHAT I NEED OF YOU, IF YOU'RE WORKING FOR ME, WHICH, OF COURSE, YOU ARE.
WOULD YOU LIKE TO KNOW WHAT I WANT?
NOTHING COULD MAKE ME HAPPIER.
MY LIFE, WHICH FOR THREE YEARS HAS BEEN A LONG WAY FROM BEING THE GREATEST, JUST TOOK A SUDDEN AND DISTINCT TURN FOR THE WORSE. NOW THERE ARE A FEW THINGS I NEED TO DO.
I WANT TO GO TO LAURA'S FUNERAL. I WANT TO SAY GOODBYE.
AFTER THAT, IF YOU STILL NEED ME, I WANT TO START AT FIVE HUNDRED DOLLARS A WEEK. IF WE'RE HAPPY WORKING TOGETHER, IN SIX MONTHS' TIME, YOU RAISE IT TO A THOUSAND A WEEK.
YOU SAY YOU MAY NEED PEOPLE TO BE HURT. I'LL HURT PEOPLE IF THEY'RE TRYING TO HURT YOU. BUT I DON'T HURT PEOPLE FOR FUN OR PROFIT.
I WON'T GO BACK TO PRISON. ONCE WAS ENOUGH.

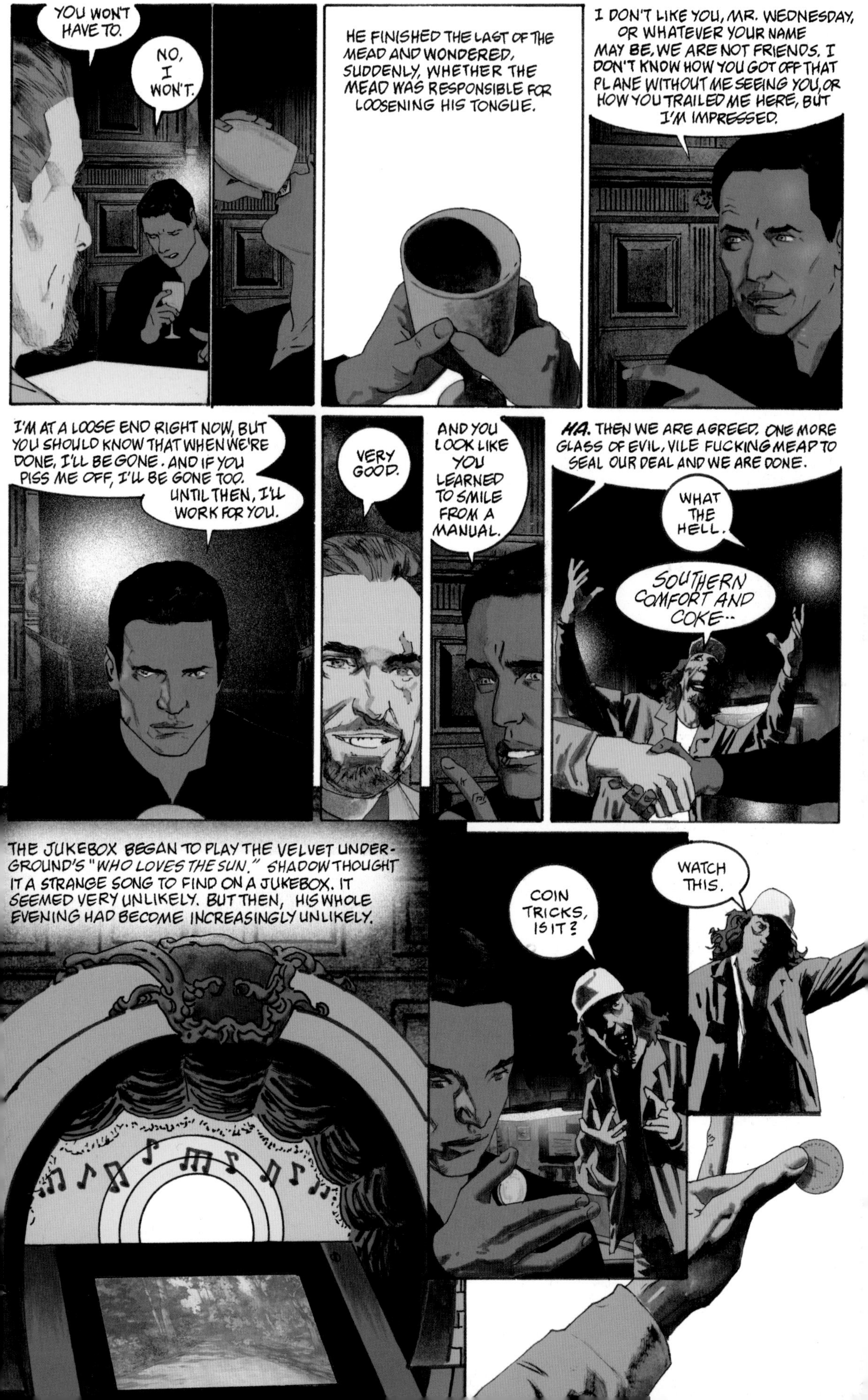
YOU WON'T HAVE TO.
NO, I WON'T.
HE FINISHED THE LAST OF THE MEAD AND WONDERED, SUDDENLY, WHETHER THE MEAD WAS RESPONSIBLE FOR LOOSENING HIS TONGUE.
I DON'T LIKE YOU, MR. WEDNESDAY, OR WHATEVER YOUR NAME MAY BE. WE ARE NOT FRIENDS. I DON'T KNOW HOW YOU GOT OFF THAT PLANE WITHOUT ME SEEING YOU, OR HOW YOU TRAILED ME HERE, BUT I'M IMPRESSED.
I'M AT A LOOSE END RIGHT NOW, BUT YOU SHOULD KNOW THAT WHEN WE'RE DONE, I'LL BE GONE. AND IF YOU PISS ME OFF, I'LL BE GONE TOO.
UNTIL THEN, I'LL WORK FOR YOU.
VERY GOOD.
AND YOU LOOK LIKE YOU LEARNED TO SMILE FROM A MANUAL.
HA. THEN WE ARE AGREED. ONE MORE GLASS OF EVIL, VILE FUCKING MEAD TO SEAL OUR DEAL AND WE ARE DONE.
WHAT THE HELL.
SOUTHERN COMFORT AND COKE..
THE JUKEBOX BEGAN TO PLAY THE VELVET UNDERGROUND'S "WHO LOVES THE SUN." SHADOW THOUGHT IT A STRANGE SONG TO FIND ON A JUKEBOX. IT SEEMED VERY UNLIKELY. BUT THEN, HIS WHOLE EVENING HAD BECOME INCREASINGLY UNLIKELY.
COIN TRICKS, IS IT?
WATCH THIS.

SWEENEY DROPPED THE LARGE COIN, GOLDEN AND SHINING INTO THE GLASS.

THEN HE TOOK A COIN FROM A CANDLE FLAME, ANOTHER FROM HIS BEARD, A THIRD FROM SHADOW'S EMPTY LEFT HAND.

THEN HE CURLED HIS FINGERS OVER THE GLASS, AND BLEW HARD, AND SEVERAL MORE GOLDEN COINS DROPPED INTO THE GLASS.

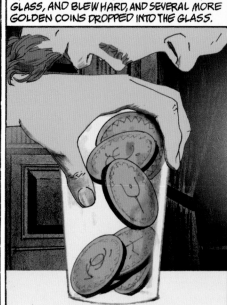

HE TIPPED THE COINS INTO HIS POCKET...

...TAPPED THE POCKET TO SHOW IT WAS EMPTY.

THERE-- THAT'S A COIN TRICK FOR YOU.

I NEED TO KNOW HOW YOU DID IT.

I DID IT. THAT'S HOW I DID IT.

ALL THE WAYS OF DOING *THE MISER'S DREAM* I'VE READ ABOUT, YOU'D BE HIDING THE COINS IN THE HAND THAT HOLDS THE GLASS, AND DROPPING THEM IN WHILE YOU PRODUCE AND VANISH THE COIN IN YOUR RIGHT HAND.

SOUNDS LIKE A HELL OF A LOT OF WORK TO ME. IT'S EASIER JUST TO PICK THEM OUT OF THE AIR.

MEAD FOR YOU, SHADOW. I'LL STICK WITH MR. JACK DANIELS AND FOR THE FREELOADING IRISHMAN, A BOTTLED BEER, SOMETHING DARK FOR PREFERENCE.

FREE-LOADER, IS IT?

MAY THE STORM PASS OVER US AND LEAVE US HALE AND UNHARMED.

A FINE TOAST BUT IT WON'T..

DO I HAVE TO DRINK THIS?

YES, I'M AFRAID YOU DO, IT SEALS OU DEAL. THIRD TIME'S THE CHARM, EH?

SHIT.

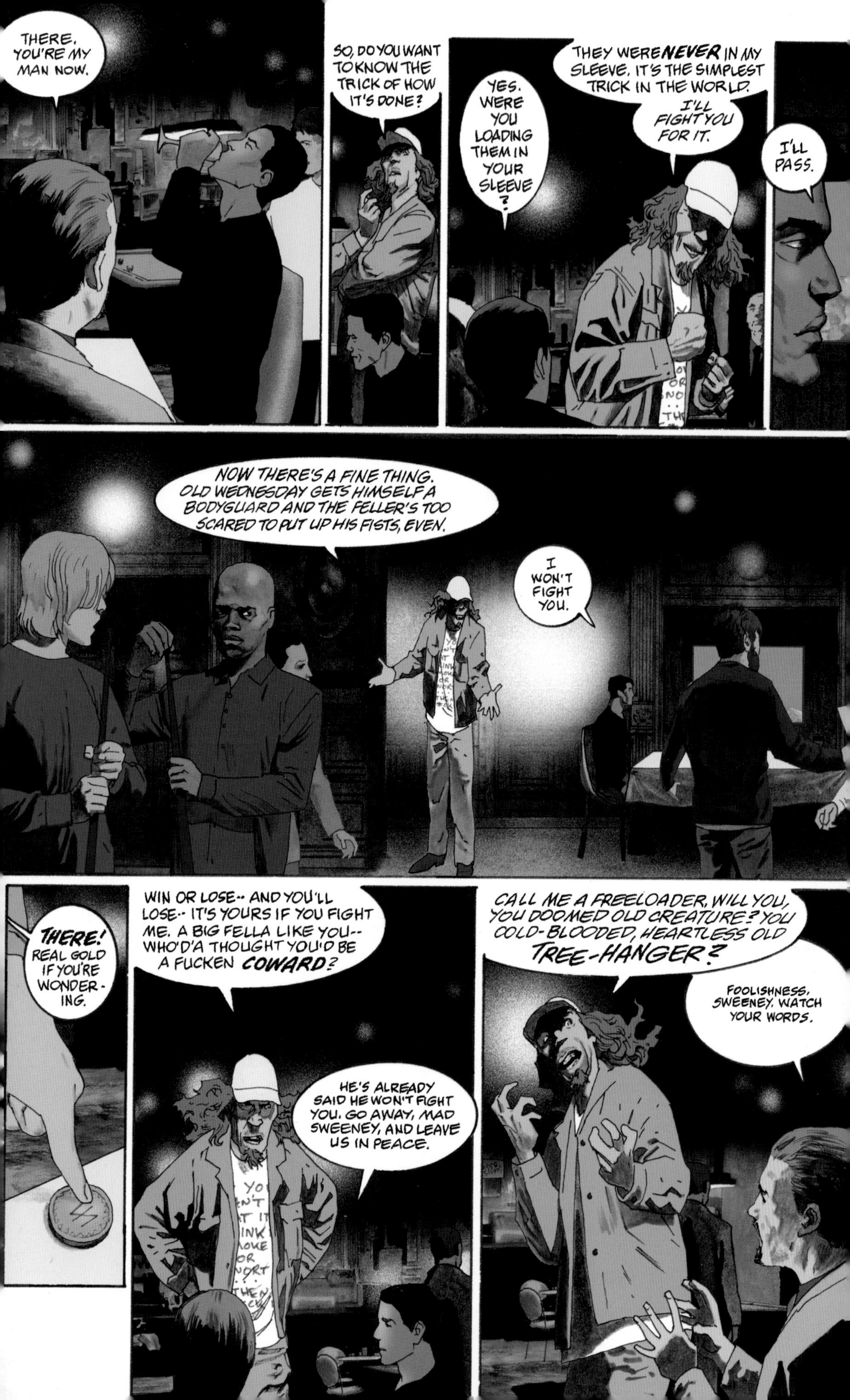
THERE. YOU'RE MY MAN NOW.
SO, DO YOU WANT TO KNOW THE TRICK OF HOW IT'S DONE?
YES. WERE YOU LOADING THEM IN YOUR SLEEVE?
THEY WERE NEVER IN MY SLEEVE. IT'S THE SIMPLEST TRICK IN THE WORLD.
I'LL FIGHT YOU FOR IT.
I'LL PASS.
NOW THERE'S A FINE THING. OLD WEDNESDAY GETS HIMSELF A BODYGUARD AND THE FELLER'S TOO SCARED TO PUT UP HIS FISTS, EVEN.
I WON'T FIGHT YOU.
THERE! REAL GOLD IF YOU'RE WONDERING.
WIN OR LOSE-- AND YOU'LL LOSE-- IT'S YOURS IF YOU FIGHT ME. A BIG FELLA LIKE YOU-- WHO'D'A THOUGHT YOU'D BE A FUCKEN COWARD?
HE'S ALREADY SAID HE WON'T FIGHT YOU. GO AWAY, MAD SWEENEY, AND LEAVE US IN PEACE.
CALL ME A FREELOADER, WILL YOU, YOU DOOMED OLD CREATURE? YOU COLD-BLOODED, HEARTLESS OLD TREE-HANGER?
FOOLISHNESS, SWEENEY. WATCH YOUR WORDS.

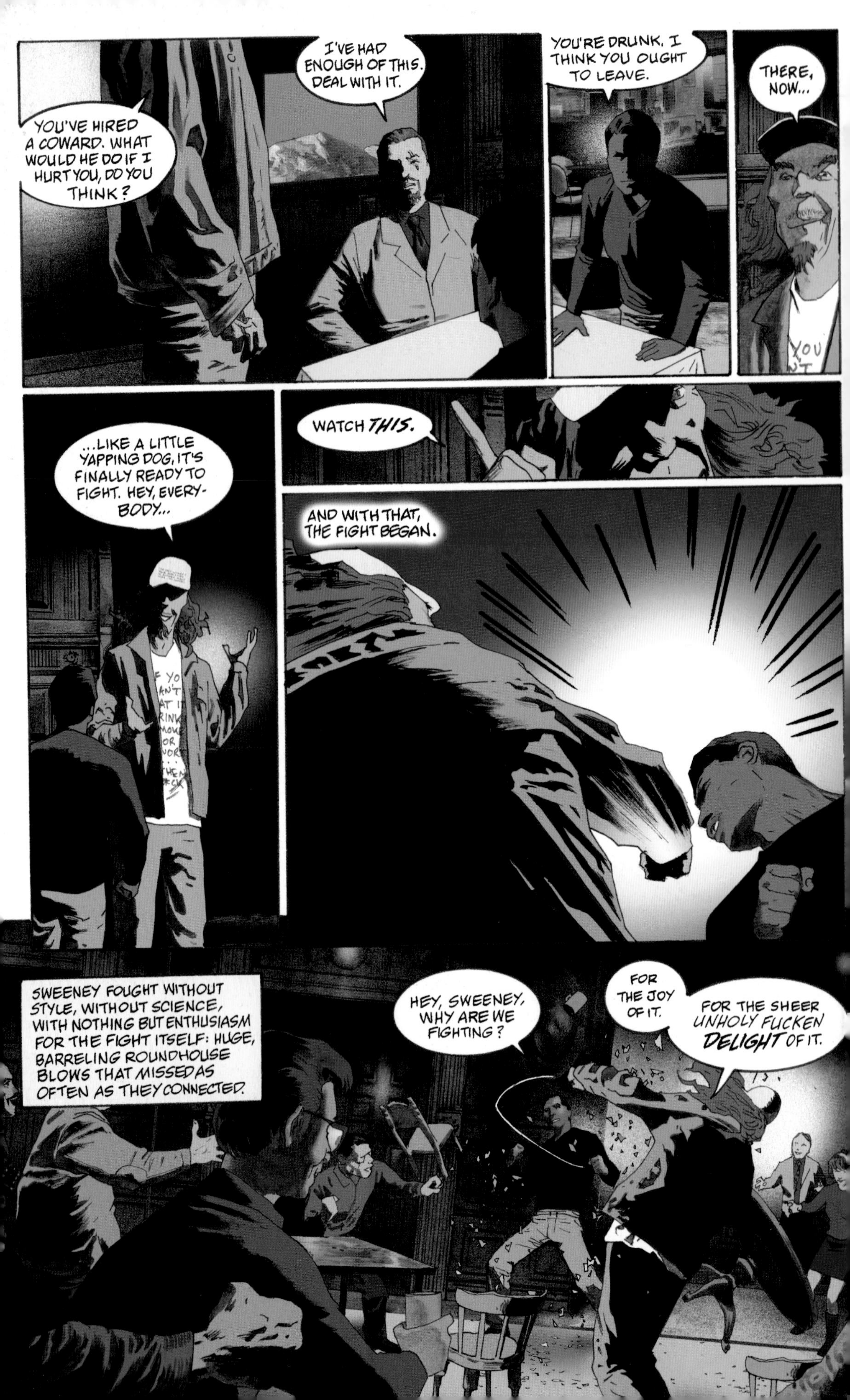
YOU'VE HIRED A COWARD. WHAT WOULD HE DO IF I HURT YOU, DO YOU THINK?
I'VE HAD ENOUGH OF THIS. DEAL WITH IT.
YOU'RE DRUNK. I THINK YOU OUGHT TO LEAVE.
THERE, NOW...
...LIKE A LITTLE YAPPING DOG, IT'S FINALLY READY TO FIGHT. HEY, EVERY-BODY...
WATCH THIS.
AND WITH THAT, THE FIGHT BEGAN.
SWEENEY FOUGHT WITHOUT STYLE, WITHOUT SCIENCE, WITH NOTHING BUT ENTHUSIASM FOR THE FIGHT ITSELF: HUGE, BARRELING ROUNDHOUSE BLOWS THAT MISSED AS OFTEN AS THEY CONNECTED.
HEY, SWEENEY, WHY ARE WE FIGHTING?
FOR THE JOY OF IT.
FOR THE SHEER UNHOLY FUCKEN DELIGHT OF IT.

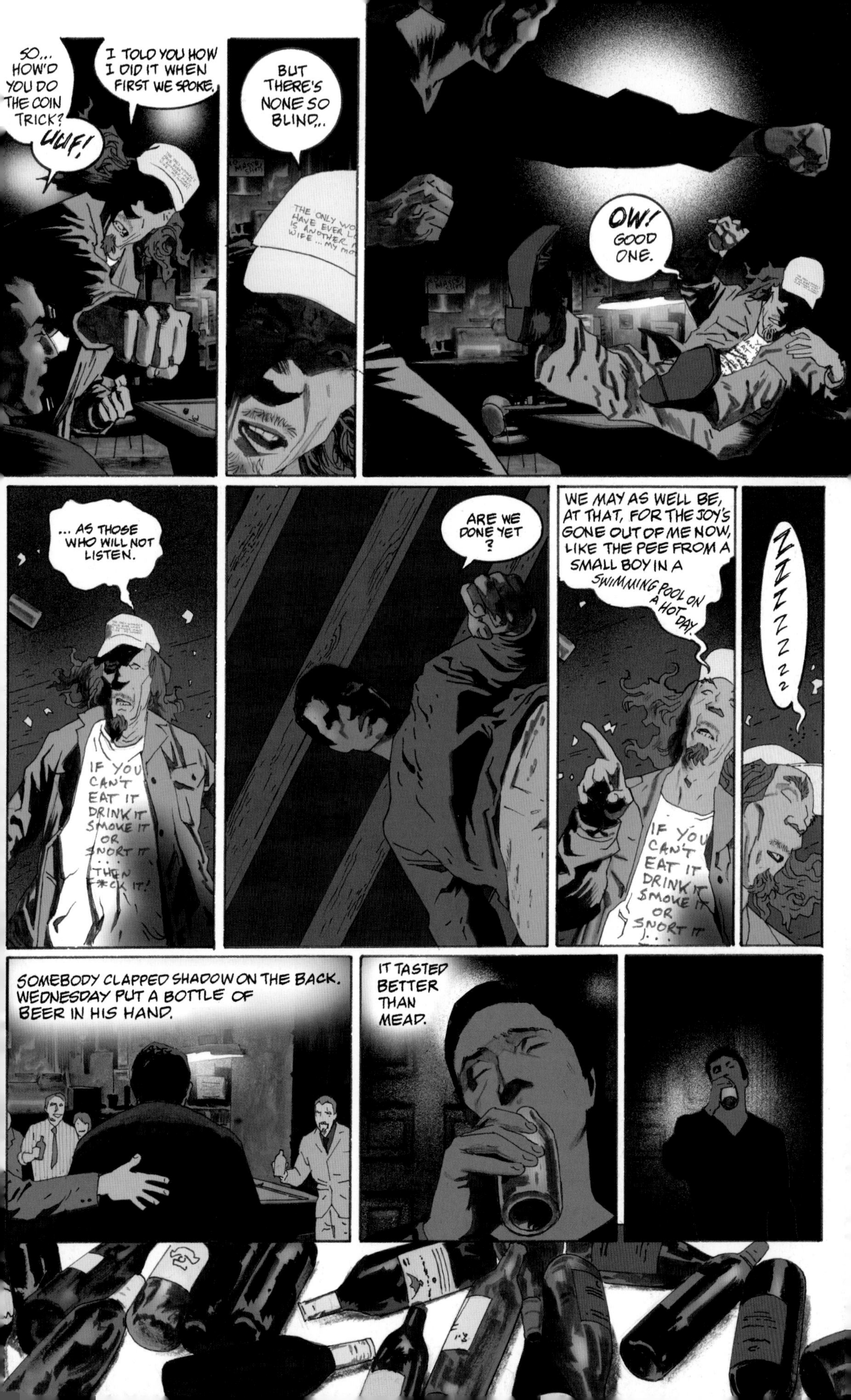
SO... HOW'D YOU DO THE COIN TRICK?
UUF!
I TOLD YOU HOW I DID IT WHEN FIRST WE SPOKE.
BUT THERE'S NONE SO BLIND...
OW! GOOD ONE.
... AS THOSE WHO WILL NOT LISTEN.
IF YOU CAN'T EAT IT DRINK IT SMOKE IT OR SNORT IT . . . THEN F*CK IT!
ARE WE DONE YET?
WE MAY AS WELL BE, AT THAT, FOR THE JOY'S GONE OUT OF ME NOW, LIKE THE PEE FROM A SMALL BOY IN A SWIMMING POOL ON A HOT DAY.
IF YOU CAN'T EAT IT DRINK IT SMOKE IT OR SNORT IT . . .
ZZZZZZzz
SOMEBODY CLAPPED SHADOW ON THE BACK. WEDNESDAY PUT A BOTTLE OF BEER IN HIS HAND.
IT TASTED BETTER THAN MEAD.

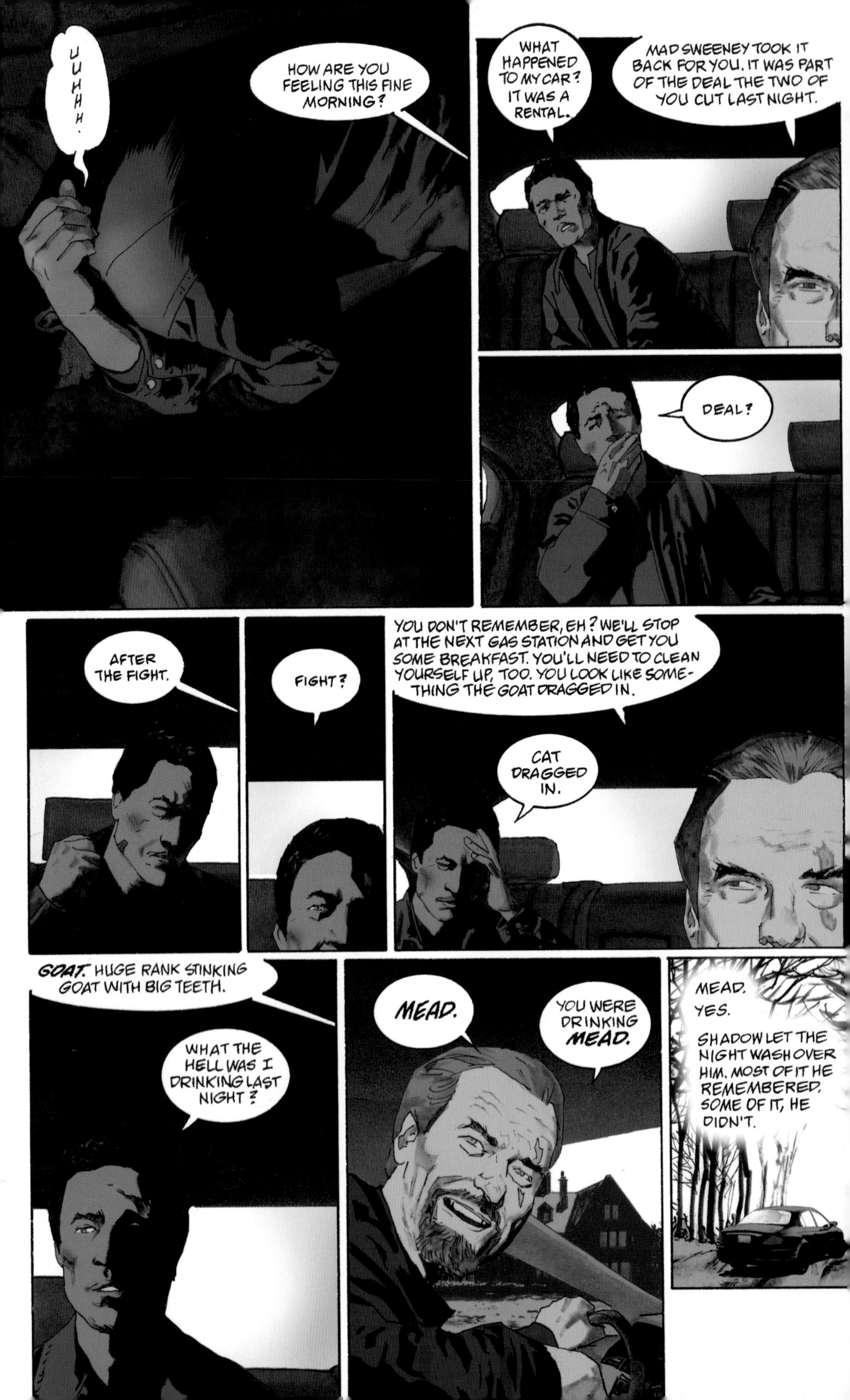

UHHH.
HOW ARE YOU FEELING THIS FINE MORNING?
WHAT HAPPENED TO MY CAR? IT WAS A RENTAL.
MAD SWEENEY TOOK IT BACK FOR YOU. IT WAS PART OF THE DEAL THE TWO OF YOU CUT LAST NIGHT.
DEAL?
AFTER THE FIGHT.
FIGHT?
YOU DON'T REMEMBER, EH? WE'LL STOP AT THE NEXT GAS STATION AND GET YOU SOME BREAKFAST. YOU'LL NEED TO CLEAN YOURSELF UP, TOO. YOU LOOK LIKE SOME-THING THE GOAT DRAGGED IN.
CAT DRAGGED IN.
GOAT. HUGE RANK STINKING GOAT WITH BIG TEETH.
WHAT THE HELL WAS I DRINKING LAST NIGHT?
MEAD.
YOU WERE DRINKING MEAD.
MEAD.
YES.
SHADOW LET THE NIGHT WASH OVER HIM. MOST OF IT HE REMEMBERED, SOME OF IT, HE DIDN'T.

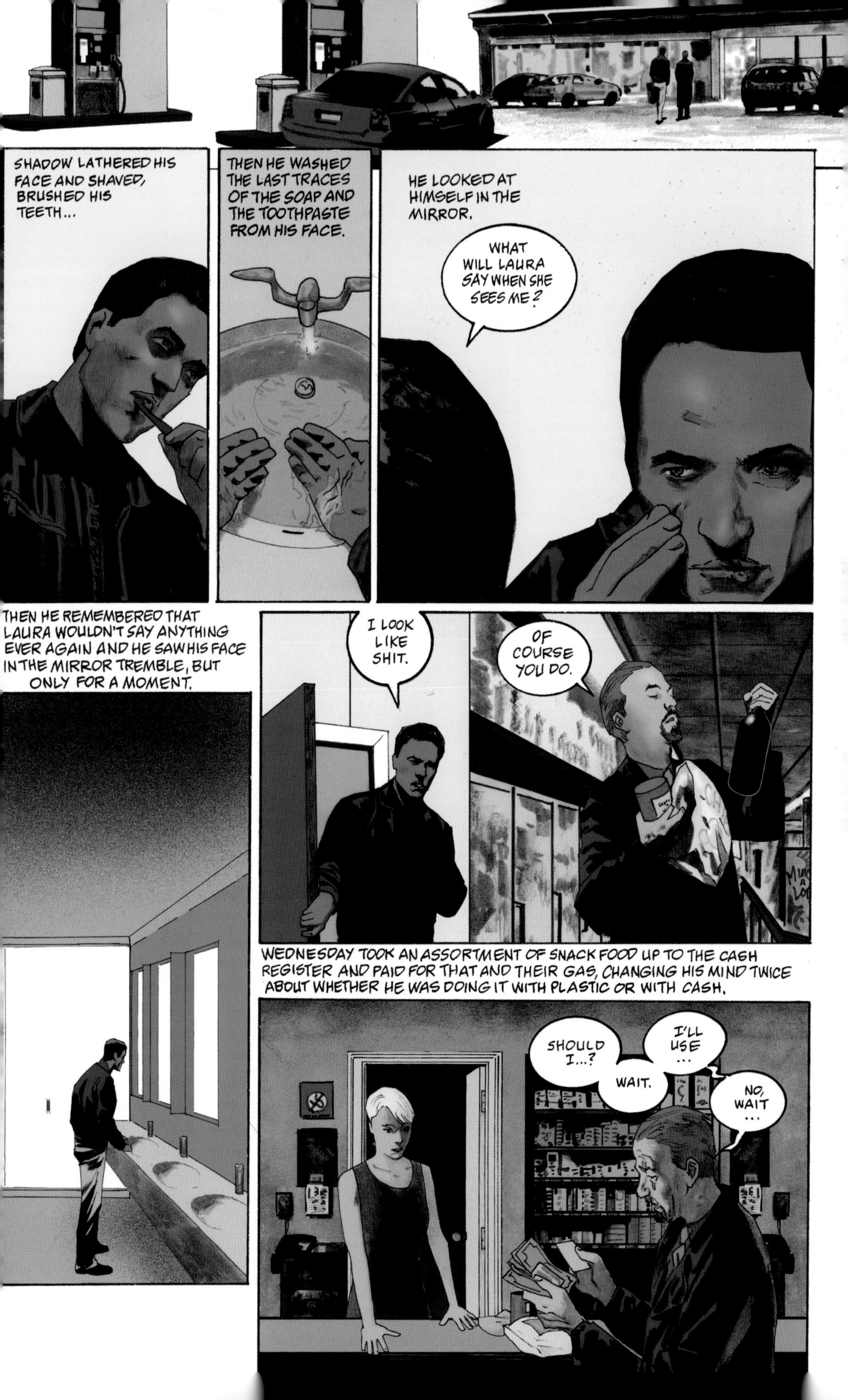
SHADOW LATHERED HIS FACE AND SHAVED, BRUSHED HIS TEETH...
THEN HE WASHED THE LAST TRACES OF THE SOAP AND THE TOOTHPASTE FROM HIS FACE.
HE LOOKED AT HIMSELF IN THE MIRROR.
WHAT WILL LAURA SAY WHEN SHE SEES ME?
THEN HE REMEMBERED THAT LAURA WOULDN'T SAY ANYTHING EVER AGAIN AND HE SAW HIS FACE IN THE MIRROR TREMBLE, BUT ONLY FOR A MOMENT.
I LOOK LIKE SHIT.
OF COURSE YOU DO.
WEDNESDAY TOOK AN ASSORTMENT OF SNACK FOOD UP TO THE CASH REGISTER AND PAID FOR THAT AND THEIR GAS, CHANGING HIS MIND TWICE ABOUT WHETHER HE WAS DOING IT WITH PLASTIC OR WITH CASH.
SHOULD I...?
WAIT.
I'LL USE ...
NO, WAIT ...

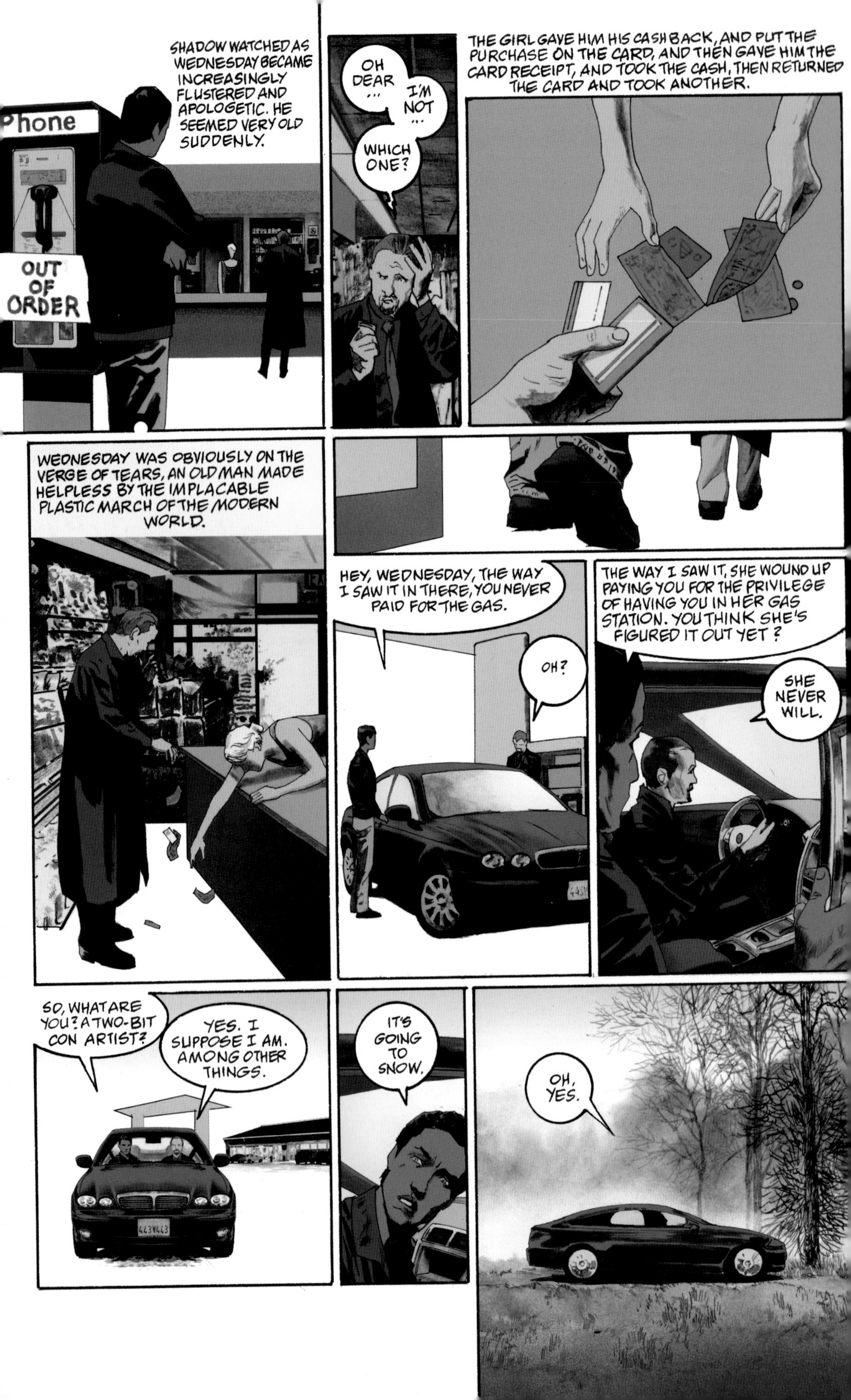
SHADOW WATCHED AS WEDNESDAY BECAME INCREASINGLY FLUSTERED AND APOLOGETIC. HE SEEMED VERY OLD SUDDENLY.
Phone
OUT OF ORDER
OH DEAR ...
I'M NOT ...
WHICH ONE?
THE GIRL GAVE HIM HIS CASH BACK, AND PUT THE PURCHASE ON THE CARD, AND THEN GAVE HIM THE CARD RECEIPT, AND TOOK THE CASH, THEN RETURNED THE CARD AND TOOK ANOTHER.
WEDNESDAY WAS OBVIOUSLY ON THE VERGE OF TEARS, AN OLD MAN MADE HELPLESS BY THE IMPLACABLE PLASTIC MARCH OF THE MODERN WORLD.
HEY, WEDNESDAY, THE WAY I SAW IT IN THERE, YOU NEVER PAID FOR THE GAS.
OH?
THE WAY I SAW IT, SHE WOUND UP PAYING YOU FOR THE PRIVILEGE OF HAVING YOU IN HER GAS STATION. YOU THINK SHE'S FIGURED IT OUT YET?
SHE NEVER WILL.
SO, WHAT ARE YOU? A TWO-BIT CON ARTIST?
YES. I SUPPOSE I AM. AMONG OTHER THINGS.
IT'S GOING TO SNOW.
OH, YES.

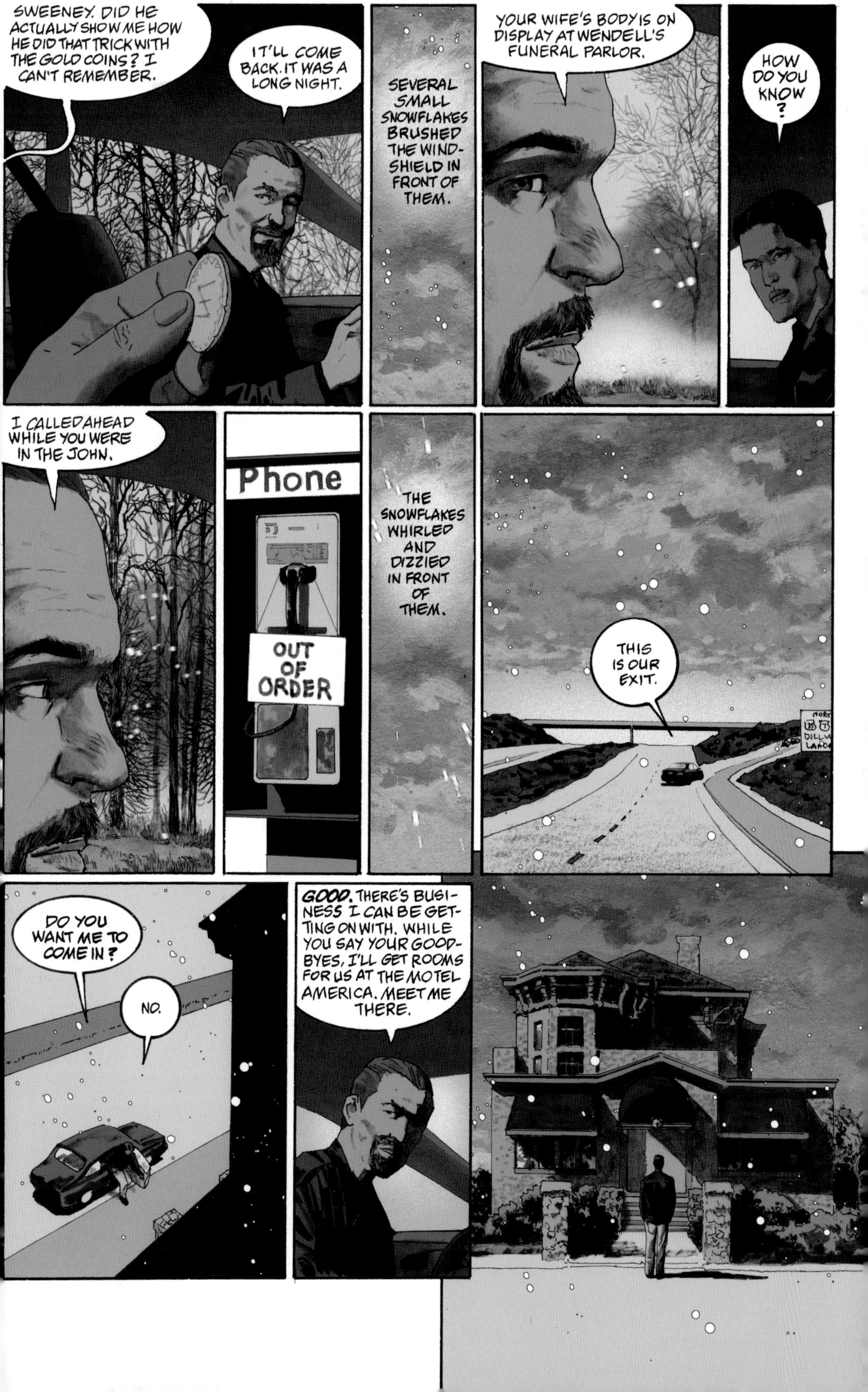
SWEENEY. DID HE ACTUALLY SHOW ME HOW HE DID THAT TRICK WITH THE GOLD COINS? I CAN'T REMEMBER.
IT'LL COME BACK. IT WAS A LONG NIGHT.
SEVERAL SMALL SNOWFLAKES BRUSHED THE WIND-SHIELD IN FRONT OF THEM.
YOUR WIFE'S BODY IS ON DISPLAY AT WENDELL'S FUNERAL PARLOR.
HOW DO YOU KNOW?
I CALLED AHEAD WHILE YOU WERE IN THE JOHN.
Phone
OUT OF ORDER
THE SNOWFLAKES WHIRLED AND DIZZIED IN FRONT OF THEM.
THIS IS OUR EXIT.
DO YOU WANT ME TO COME IN?
NO.
GOOD. THERE'S BUSI-NESS I CAN BE GET-TING ON WITH. WHILE YOU SAY YOUR GOOD-BYES, I'LL GET ROOMS FOR US AT THE MOTEL AMERICA. MEET ME THERE.

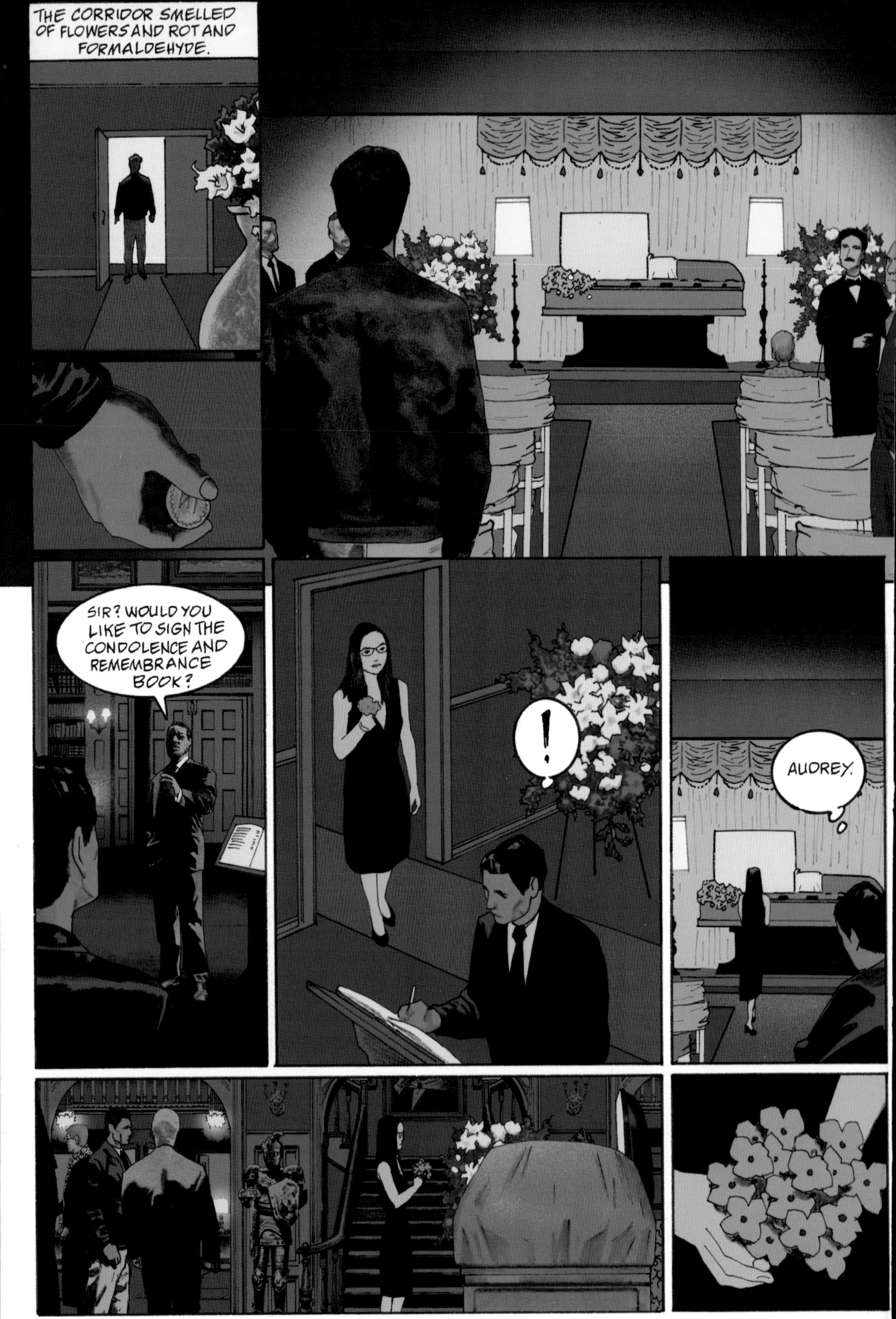
THE CORRIDOR SMELLED OF FLOWERS AND ROT AND FORMALDEHYDE.
SIR? WOULD YOU LIKE TO SIGN THE CONDOLENCE AND REMEMBRANCE BOOK?
!
AUDREY.

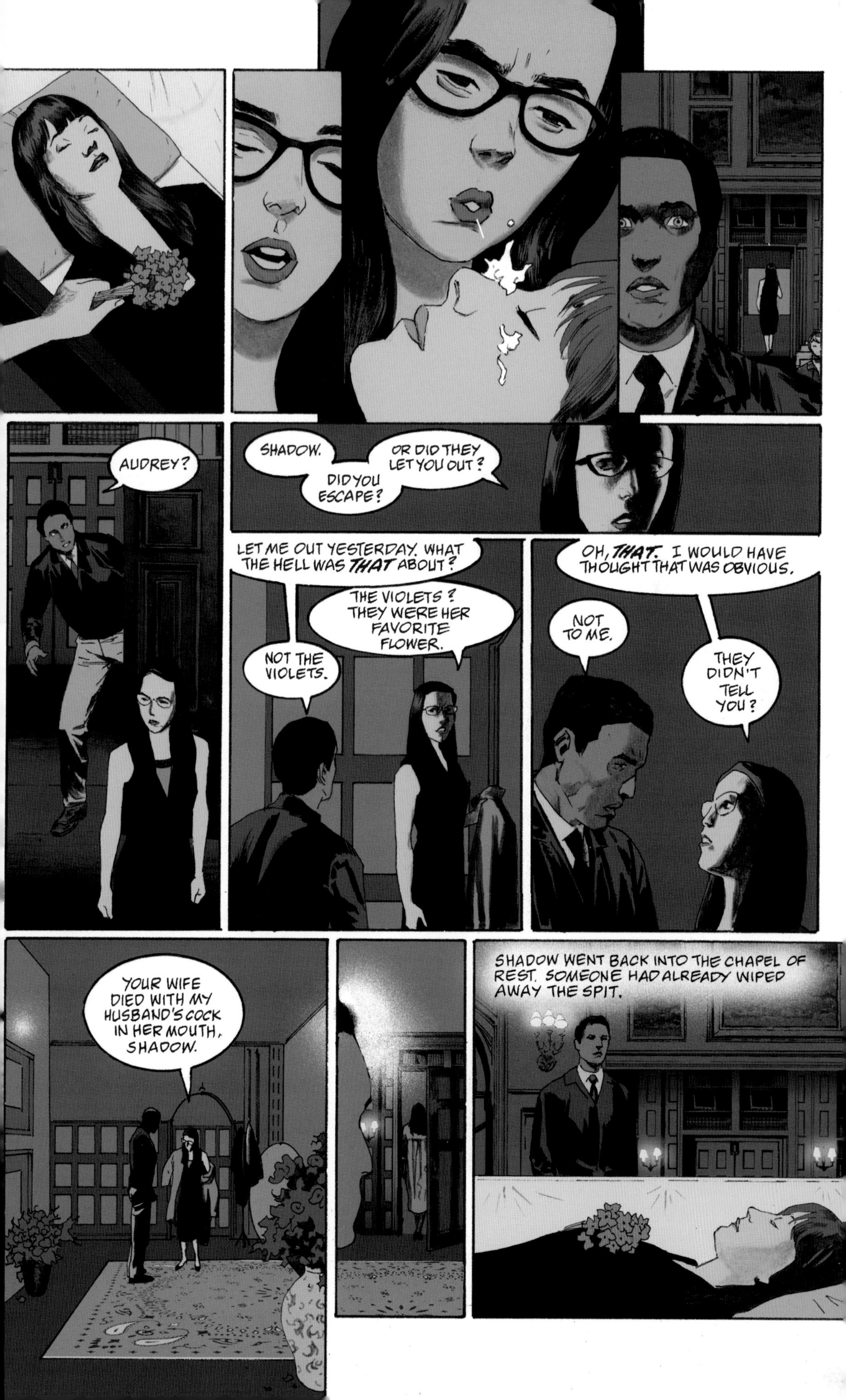
AUDREY?
SHADOW.
DID YOU ESCAPE?
OR DID THEY LET YOU OUT?
LET ME OUT YESTERDAY. WHAT THE HELL WAS THAT ABOUT?
NOT THE VIOLETS.
THE VIOLETS? THEY WERE HER FAVORITE FLOWER.
OH, THAT. I WOULD HAVE THOUGHT THAT WAS OBVIOUS.
NOT TO ME.
THEY DIDN'T TELL YOU?
YOUR WIFE DIED WITH MY HUSBAND'S COCK IN HER MOUTH, SHADOW.
SHADOW WENT BACK INTO THE CHAPEL OF REST. SOMEONE HAD ALREADY WIPED AWAY THE SPIT.

LAURA WAS INTERRED IN A SMALL NONDENOMINATIONAL CEMETERY ON THE EDGE OF TOWN.

THE SHORT SERVICE ENDED. THE PEOPLE WENT AWAY. SHADOW DID NOT LEAVE. THERE WAS SOMETHING HE WANTED TO SAY TO LAURA, AND HE WAS PREPARED TO WAIT UNTIL HE KNEW WHAT IT WAS.

THE WORLD SLOWLY BEGAN TO LOSE LIGHT AND COLOR. SHADOW BURROWED HIS HANDS INTO HIS POCKETS FOR WARMTH, AND HIS FINGERS CLOSED ABOUT THE GOLD COIN.

HE WALKED OVER TO THE GRAVE.

THIS IS FOR YOU.

GOOD NIGHT, LAURA.

I'M SORRY.

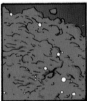

YOU WANT A LIFT, SHADOW?

NO, AUDREY. NOT FROM YOU.

I THOUGHT SHE WAS MY BEST FRIEND AND ALL THE TIME SHE WAS FUCKING HIM BEHIND MY BACK.

PLEASE GO AWAY, AUDREY.

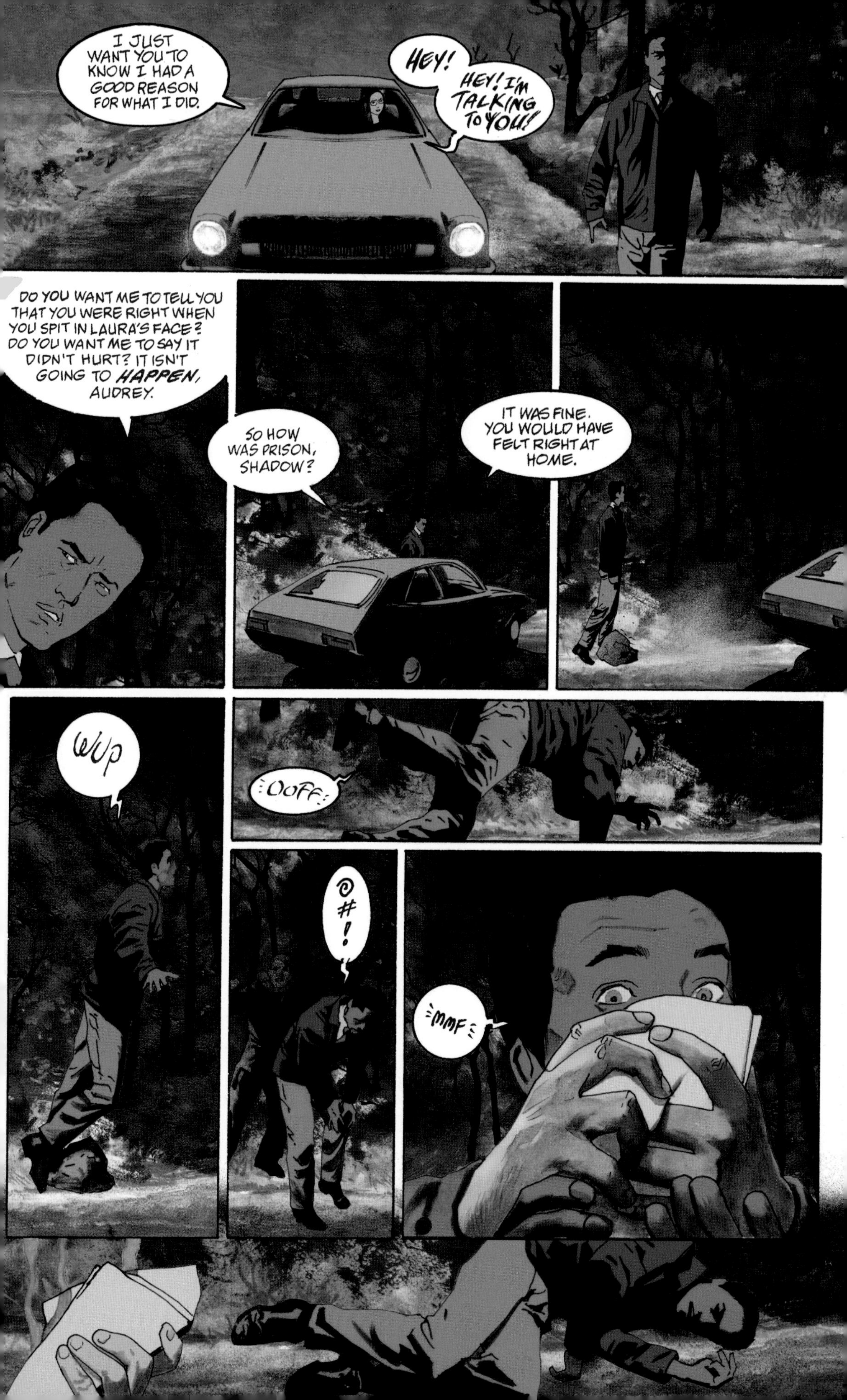
I JUST WANT YOU TO KNOW I HAD A GOOD REASON FOR WHAT I DID.
HEY!
HEY! I'M TALKING TO YOU!
DO YOU WANT ME TO TELL YOU THAT YOU WERE RIGHT WHEN YOU SPIT IN LAURA'S FACE? DO YOU WANT ME TO SAY IT DIDN'T HURT? IT ISN'T GOING TO HAPPEN, AUDREY.
SO HOW WAS PRISON, SHADOW?
IT WAS FINE. YOU WOULD HAVE FELT RIGHT AT HOME.
WUP
OOFF
@#!
MMF

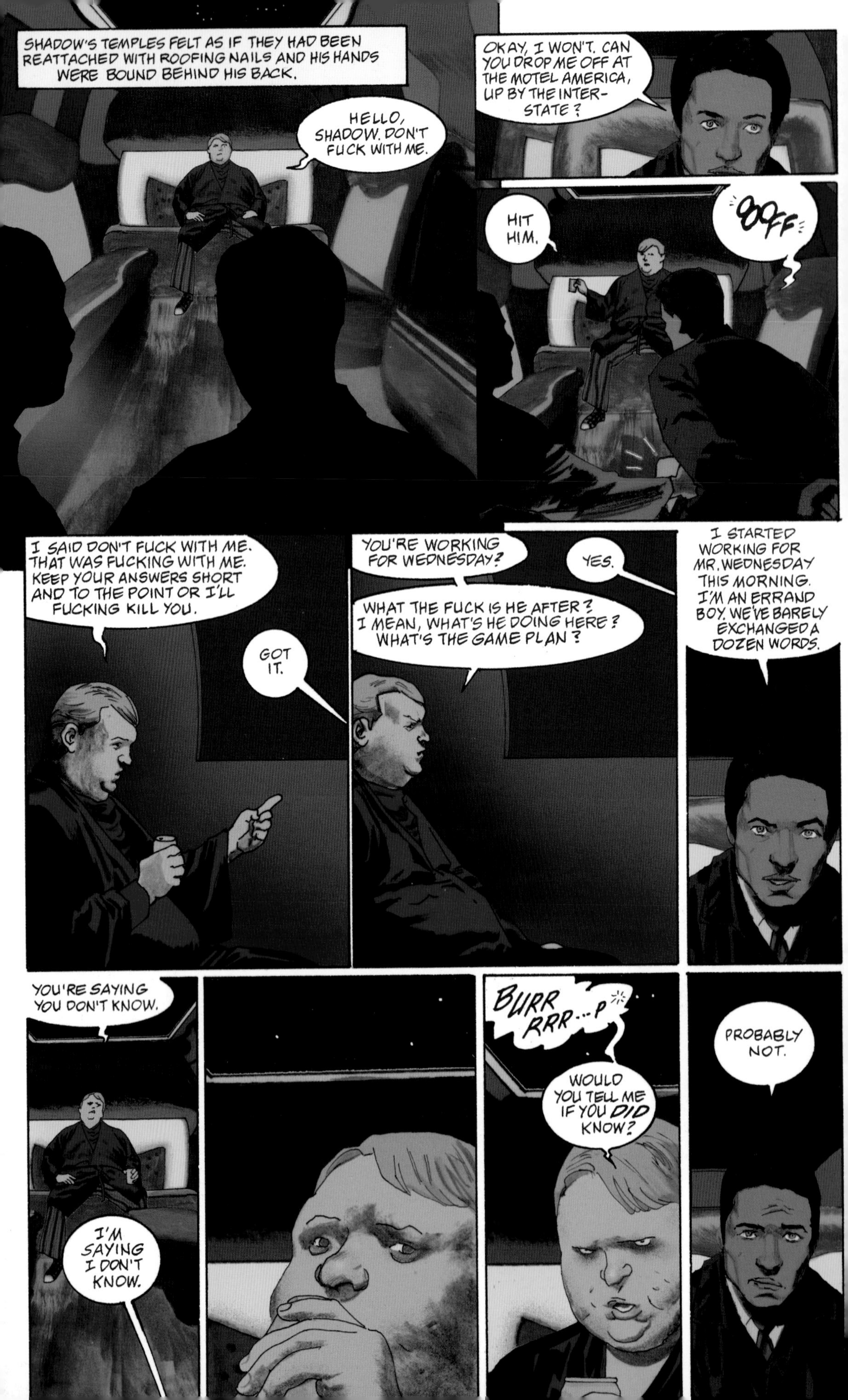
SHADOW'S TEMPLES FELT AS IF THEY HAD BEEN REATTACHED WITH ROOFING NAILS AND HIS HANDS WERE BOUND BEHIND HIS BACK.
HELLO, SHADOW. DON'T FUCK WITH ME.
OKAY, I WON'T. CAN YOU DROP ME OFF AT THE MOTEL AMERICA, UP BY THE INTER-STATE?
HIT HIM.
OOFF
I SAID DON'T FUCK WITH ME. THAT WAS FUCKING WITH ME. KEEP YOUR ANSWERS SHORT AND TO THE POINT OR I'LL FUCKING KILL YOU.
GOT IT.
YOU'RE WORKING FOR WEDNESDAY?
YES.
WHAT THE FUCK IS HE AFTER? I MEAN, WHAT'S HE DOING HERE? WHAT'S THE GAME PLAN?
I STARTED WORKING FOR MR. WEDNESDAY THIS MORNING. I'M AN ERRAND BOY. WE'VE BARELY EXCHANGED A DOZEN WORDS.
YOU'RE SAYING YOU DON'T KNOW.
I'M SAYING I DON'T KNOW.
BURR RRR...P
WOULD YOU TELL ME IF YOU DID KNOW?
PROBABLY NOT.

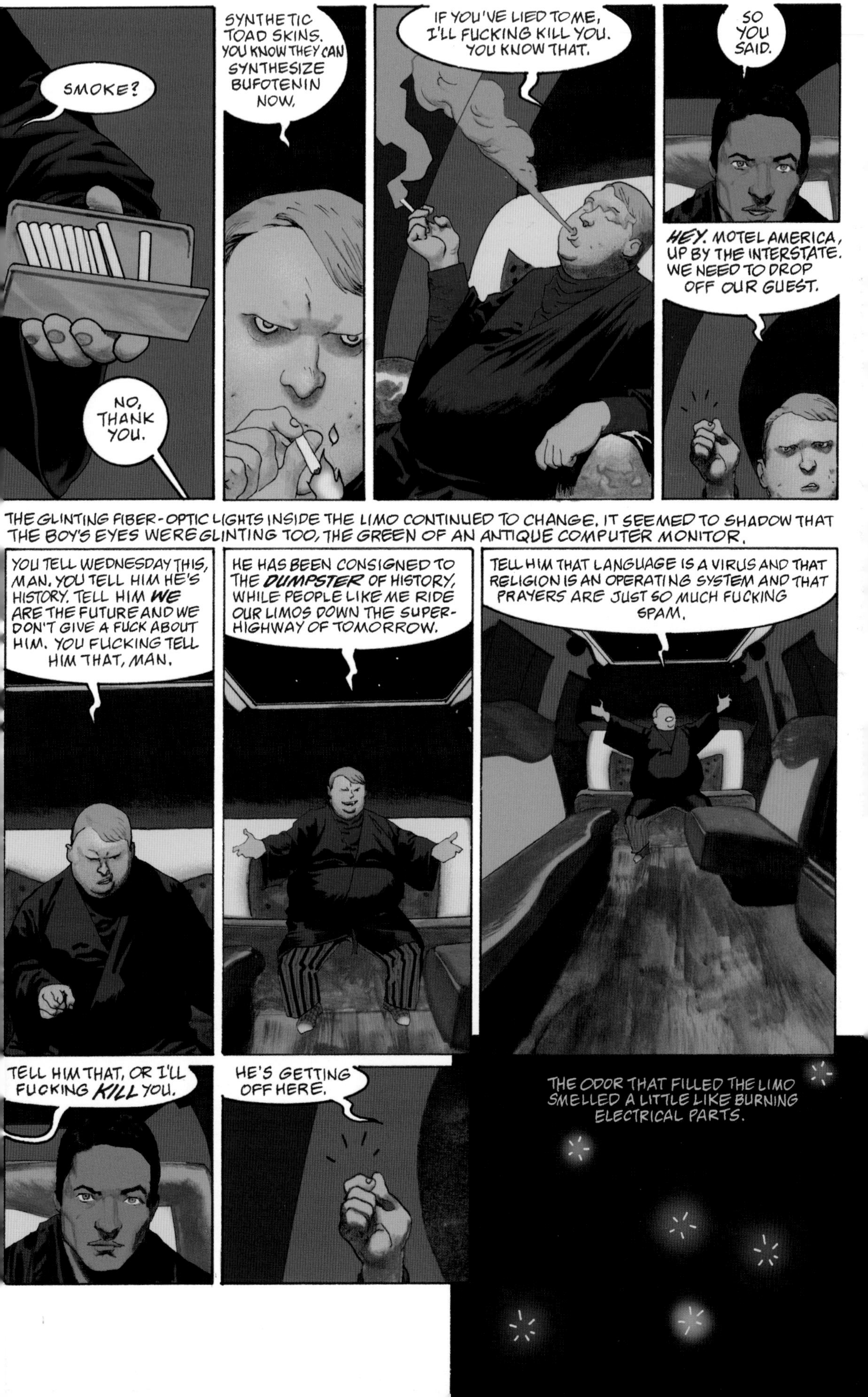
SMOKE?
NO, THANK YOU.
SYNTHETIC TOAD SKINS. YOU KNOW THEY CAN SYNTHESIZE BUFOTENIN NOW.
IF YOU'VE LIED TO ME, I'LL FUCKING KILL YOU. YOU KNOW THAT.
SO YOU SAID.
HEY. MOTEL AMERICA, UP BY THE INTERSTATE. WE NEED TO DROP OFF OUR GUEST.
THE GLINTING FIBER-OPTIC LIGHTS INSIDE THE LIMO CONTINUED TO CHANGE. IT SEEMED TO SHADOW THAT THE BOY'S EYES WERE GLINTING TOO, THE GREEN OF AN ANTIQUE COMPUTER MONITOR.
YOU TELL WEDNESDAY THIS, MAN. YOU TELL HIM HE'S HISTORY. TELL HIM WE ARE THE FUTURE AND WE DON'T GIVE A FUCK ABOUT HIM. YOU FUCKING TELL HIM THAT, MAN.
HE HAS BEEN CONSIGNED TO THE DUMPSTER OF HISTORY, WHILE PEOPLE LIKE ME RIDE OUR LIMOS DOWN THE SUPER-HIGHWAY OF TOMORROW.
TELL HIM THAT LANGUAGE IS A VIRUS AND THAT RELIGION IS AN OPERATING SYSTEM AND THAT PRAYERS ARE JUST SO MUCH FUCKING SPAM.
TELL HIM THAT, OR I'LL FUCKING KILL YOU.
HE'S GETTING OFF HERE.
THE ODOR THAT FILLED THE LIMO SMELLED A LITTLE LIKE BURNING ELECTRICAL PARTS.

SHADOW REALIZED THAT HE HAD NOT YET GOT A CLEAR LOOK AT EITHER OF THE PEOPLE WHO HAD BEEN IN THE BACK SEAT WITH HIM. HE DID NOT KNOW IF THEY WERE MEN OR WOMEN, OLD OR YOUNG.

THE INSIDE OF THE CAR WAS NOW ONE WRITHING CLOUD OF SMOKE IN WHICH TWO LIGHTS GLINTED, COPPER-COLORED LIKE THE BEAUTIFUL EYES OF A TOAD.

GOOD TALKING TO YOU.

YOU SHOULD KNOW THAT *IF* WE DO FUCKING KILL YOU, THEN WE'LL JUST DELETE YOU. YOU GOT THAT? ONE CLICK AND YOU'RE OVERWRITTEN WITH RANDOM ONES AND ZEROS. UNDELETE IS NOT AN OPTION.

IT'S ALL ABOUT THE DOMINANT FUCKING PARADIGM, SHADOW. NOTHING ELSE IS IMPORTANT.

AND HEY...

≥FFFT≤

VRRRRRR

SORRY TO HEAR ABOUT YOUR OLD LADY.

Perry's RESTAURANT

TACO BEEF DRIVE THRU

BURGER LAND

COW-ART

Hom Tow n

MOTEL

POOL

SHADOW WAS A COUPLE OF HUNDRED YARDS AWAY FROM HIS MOTEL AND HE WALKED THERE BREATHING THE COLD AIR, PAST RED AND YELLOW AND BLUE LIGHTS ADVERTISING EVERY KIND OF FAST FOOD A MAN COULD IMAGINE, AS LONG AS IT WAS A HAMBURGER, AND HE REACHED THE MOTEL AMERICA WITHOUT INCIDENT.

CHAPTER THREE

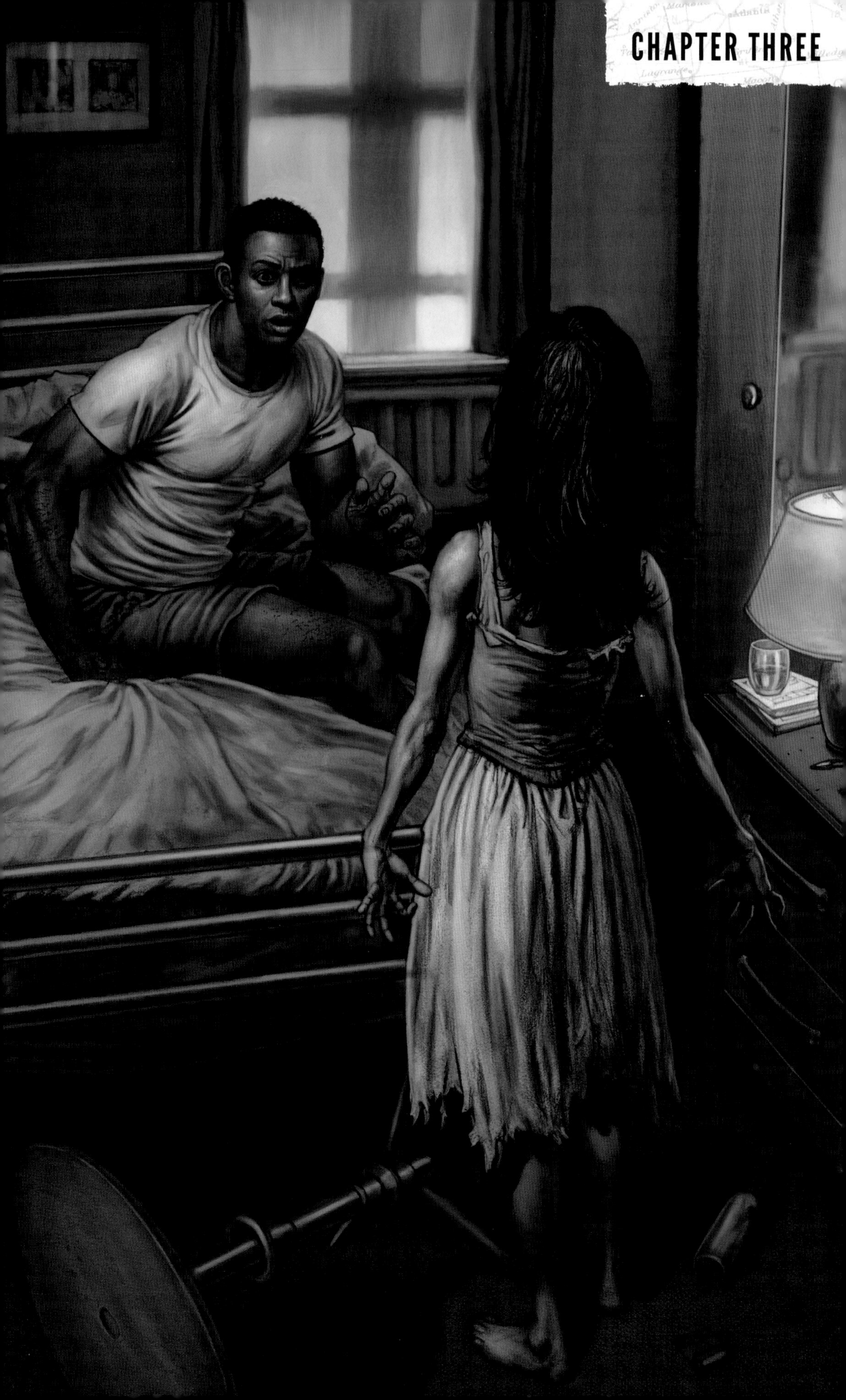

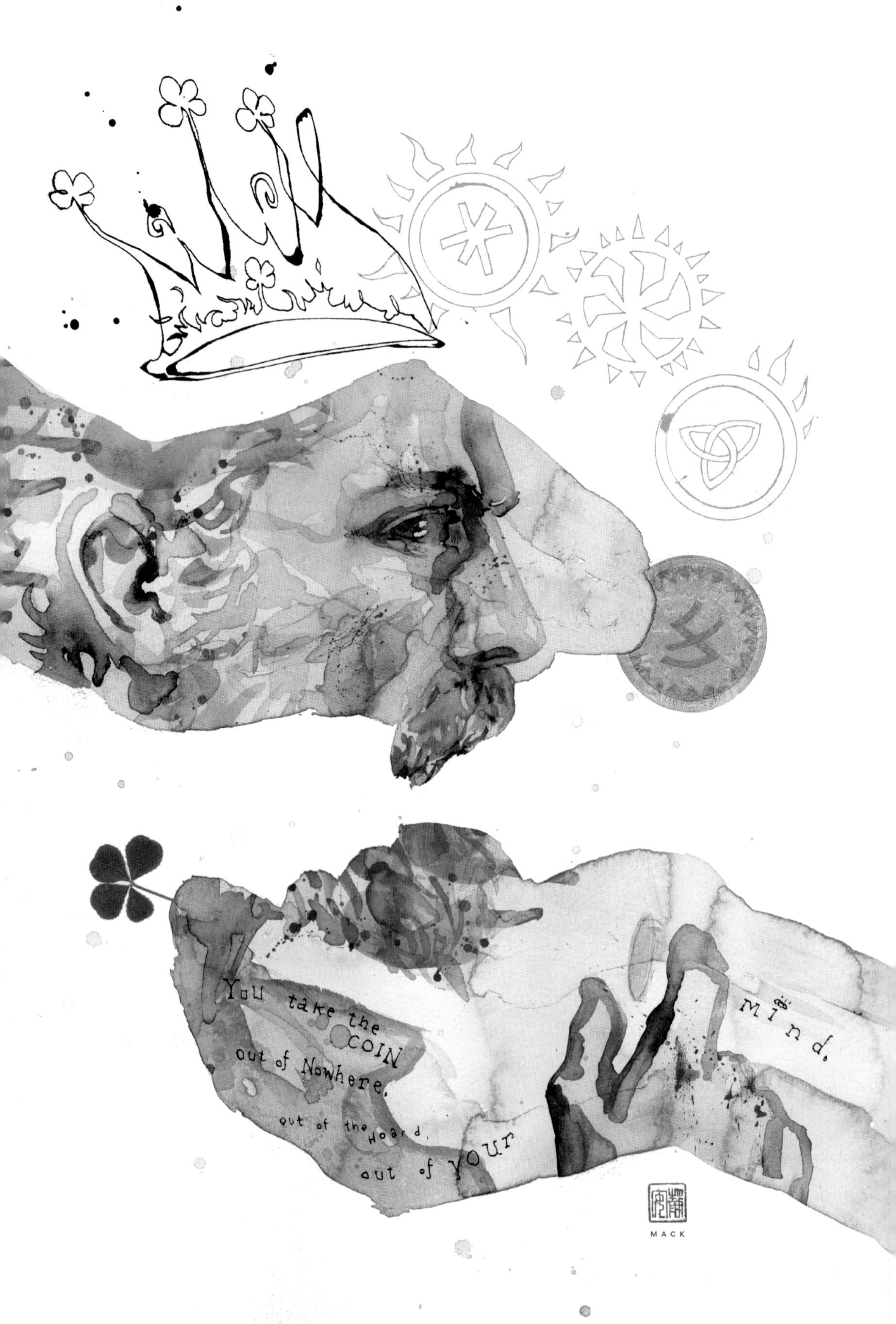
You take the COIN
out of Nowhere,
out of the Hoard,
out of your
mind.
MACK

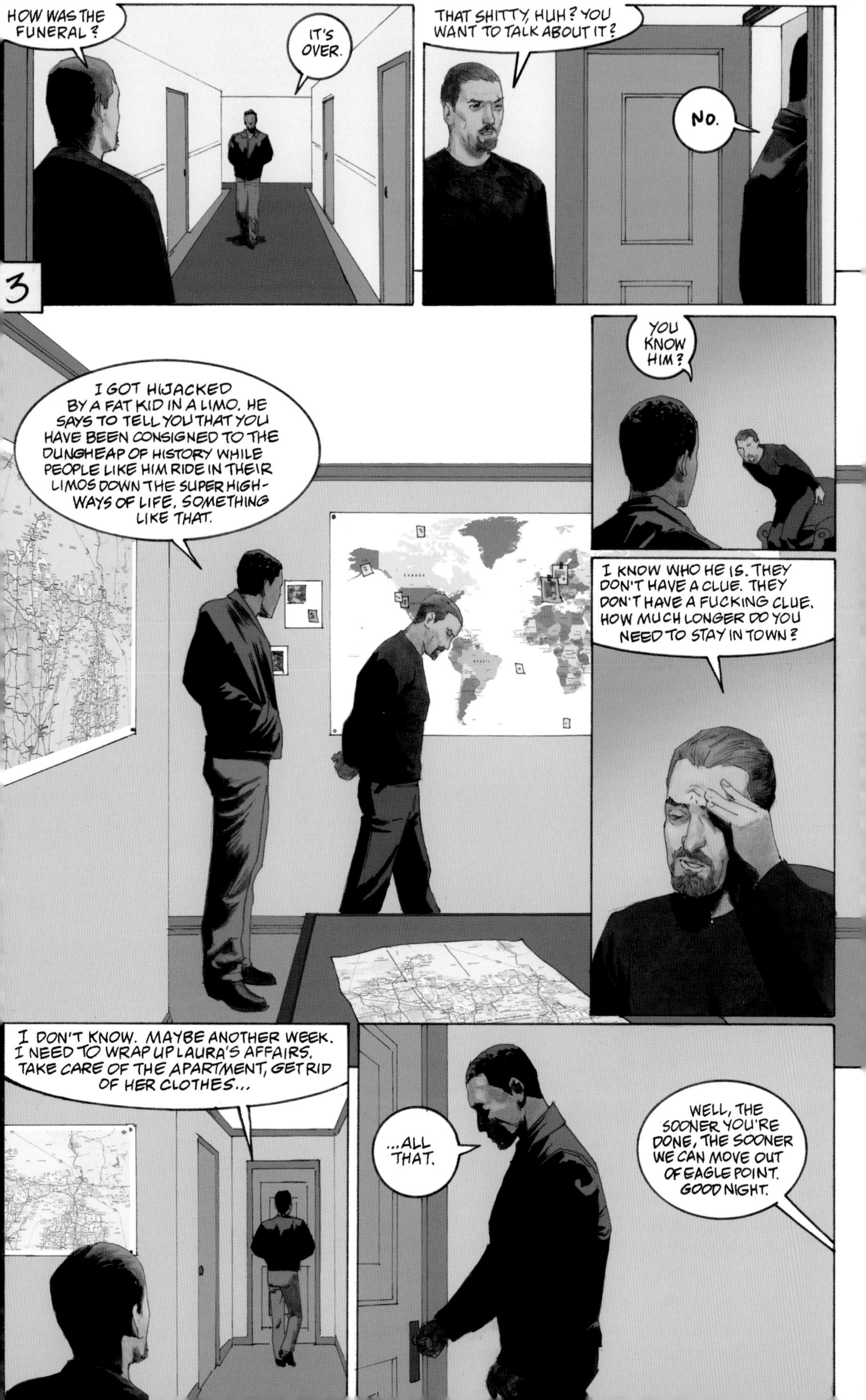

HOW WAS THE FUNERAL?
IT'S OVER.
THAT SHITTY, HUH? YOU WANT TO TALK ABOUT IT?
NO.
3
I GOT HIJACKED BY A FAT KID IN A LIMO. HE SAYS TO TELL YOU THAT YOU HAVE BEEN CONSIGNED TO THE DUNGHEAP OF HISTORY WHILE PEOPLE LIKE HIM RIDE IN THEIR LIMOS DOWN THE SUPER HIGH-WAYS OF LIFE. SOMETHING LIKE THAT.
YOU KNOW HIM?
I KNOW WHO HE IS. THEY DON'T HAVE A CLUE. THEY DON'T HAVE A FUCKING CLUE. HOW MUCH LONGER DO YOU NEED TO STAY IN TOWN?
I DON'T KNOW. MAYBE ANOTHER WEEK. I NEED TO WRAP UP LAURA'S AFFAIRS. TAKE CARE OF THE APARTMENT, GET RID OF HER CLOTHES...
...ALL THAT.
WELL, THE SOONER YOU'RE DONE, THE SOONER WE CAN MOVE OUT OF EAGLE POINT. GOOD NIGHT.

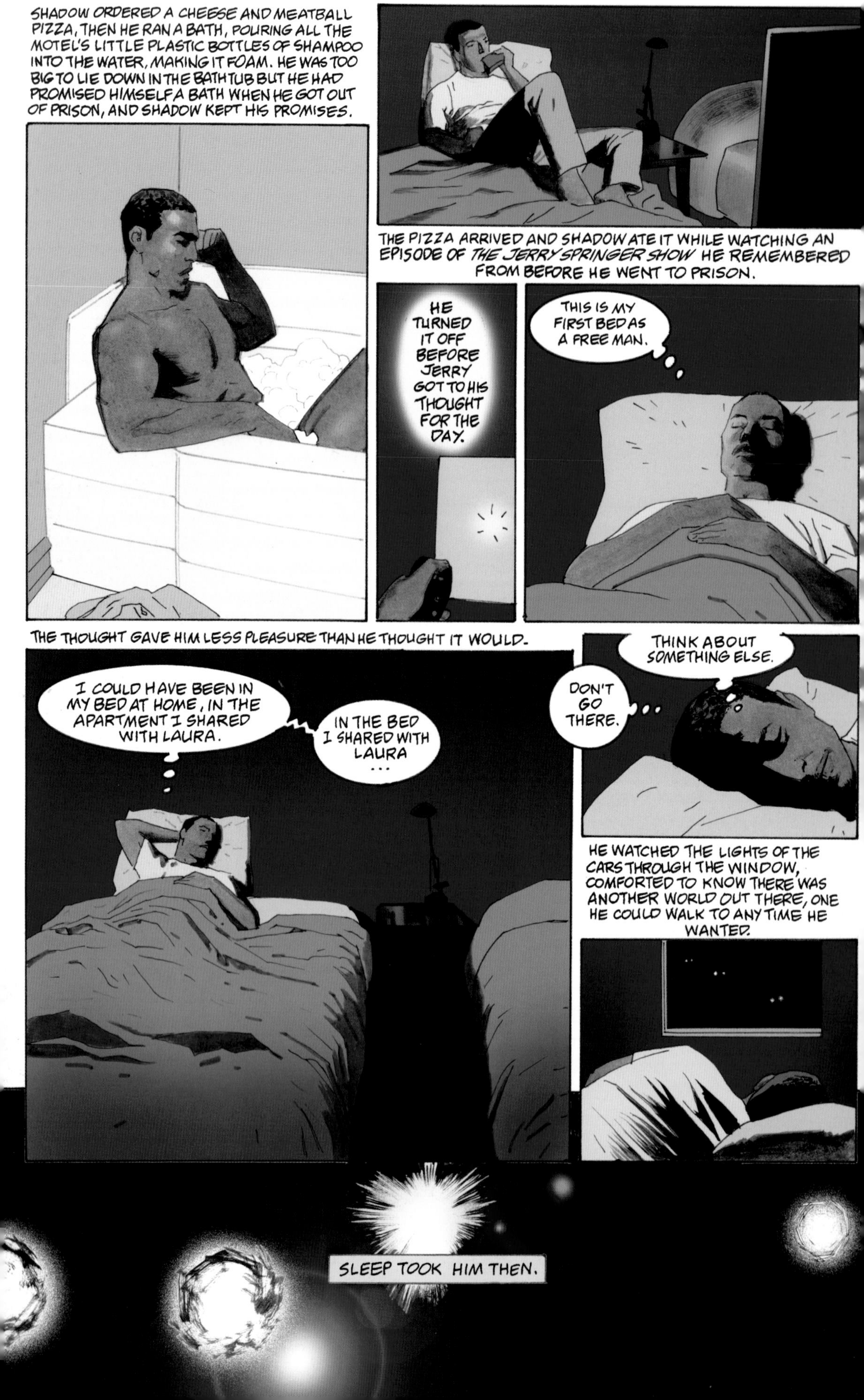
SHADOW ORDERED A CHEESE AND MEATBALL PIZZA, THEN HE RAN A BATH, POURING ALL THE MOTEL'S LITTLE PLASTIC BOTTLES OF SHAMPOO INTO THE WATER, MAKING IT FOAM. HE WAS TOO BIG TO LIE DOWN IN THE BATHTUB BUT HE HAD PROMISED HIMSELF A BATH WHEN HE GOT OUT OF PRISON, AND SHADOW KEPT HIS PROMISES.
THE PIZZA ARRIVED AND SHADOW ATE IT WHILE WATCHING AN EPISODE OF *THE JERRY SPRINGER SHOW* HE REMEMBERED FROM BEFORE HE WENT TO PRISON.
HE TURNED IT OFF BEFORE JERRY GOT TO HIS THOUGHT FOR THE DAY.
THIS IS MY FIRST BED AS A FREE MAN.
THE THOUGHT GAVE HIM LESS PLEASURE THAN HE THOUGHT IT WOULD.
I COULD HAVE BEEN IN MY BED AT HOME, IN THE APARTMENT I SHARED WITH LAURA.
IN THE BED I SHARED WITH LAURA ...
THINK ABOUT SOMETHING ELSE.
DON'T GO THERE.
HE WATCHED THE LIGHTS OF THE CARS THROUGH THE WINDOW, COMFORTED TO KNOW THERE WAS ANOTHER WORLD OUT THERE, ONE HE COULD WALK TO ANY TIME HE WANTED.
SLEEP TOOK HIM THEN.

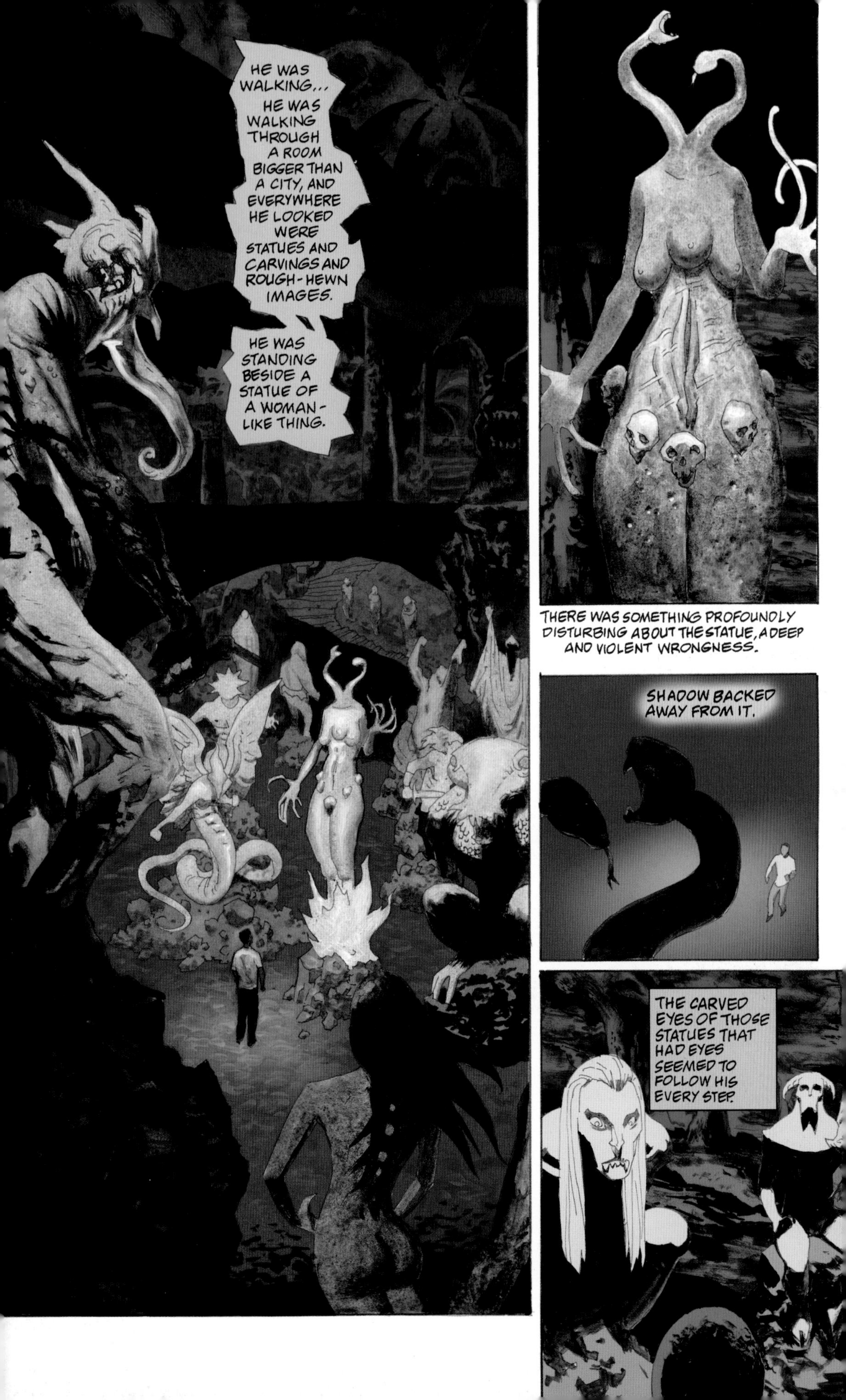
HE WAS WALKING... HE WAS WALKING THROUGH A ROOM BIGGER THAN A CITY, AND EVERYWHERE HE LOOKED WERE STATUES AND CARVINGS AND ROUGH-HEWN IMAGES.
HE WAS STANDING BESIDE A STATUE OF A WOMAN-LIKE THING.
THERE WAS SOMETHING PROFOUNDLY DISTURBING ABOUT THE STATUE, A DEEP AND VIOLENT WRONGNESS.
SHADOW BACKED AWAY FROM IT.
THE CARVED EYES OF THOSE STATUES THAT HAD EYES SEEMED TO FOLLOW HIS EVERY STEP.

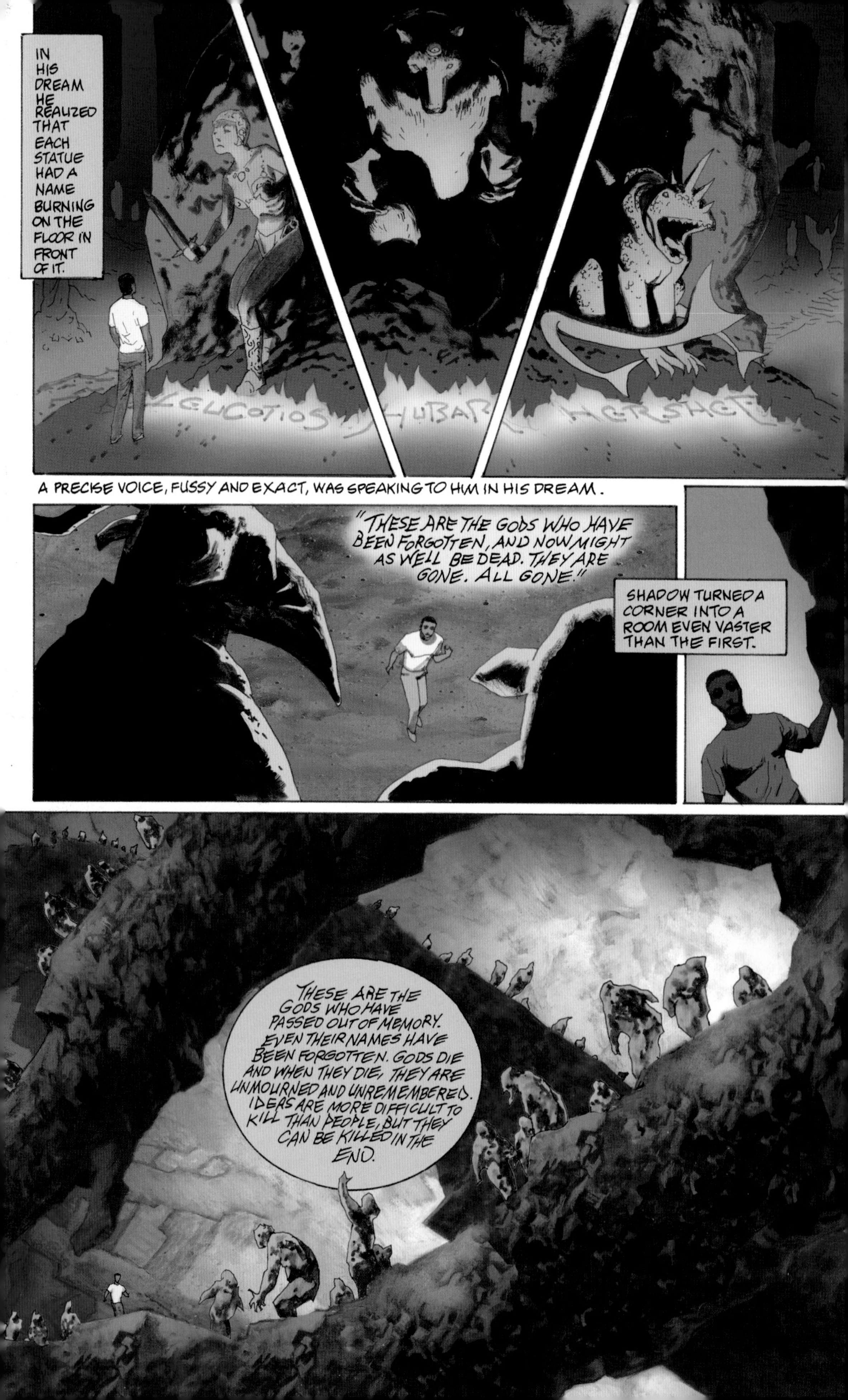
IN HIS DREAM HE REALIZED THAT EACH STATUE HAD A NAME BURNING ON THE FLOOR IN FRONT OF IT.
LEUCOTIOS
HUBAR
HERSHEF
A PRECISE VOICE, FUSSY AND EXACT, WAS SPEAKING TO HIM IN HIS DREAM.
"THESE ARE THE GODS WHO HAVE BEEN FORGOTTEN, AND NOW MIGHT AS WELL BE DEAD. THEY ARE GONE. ALL GONE."
SHADOW TURNED A CORNER INTO A ROOM EVEN VASTER THAN THE FIRST.
THESE ARE THE GODS WHO HAVE PASSED OUT OF MEMORY. EVEN THEIR NAMES HAVE BEEN FORGOTTEN. GODS DIE AND WHEN THEY DIE, THEY ARE UNMOURNED AND UNREMEMBERED. IDEAS ARE MORE DIFFICULT TO KILL THAN PEOPLE, BUT THEY CAN BE KILLED IN THE END.

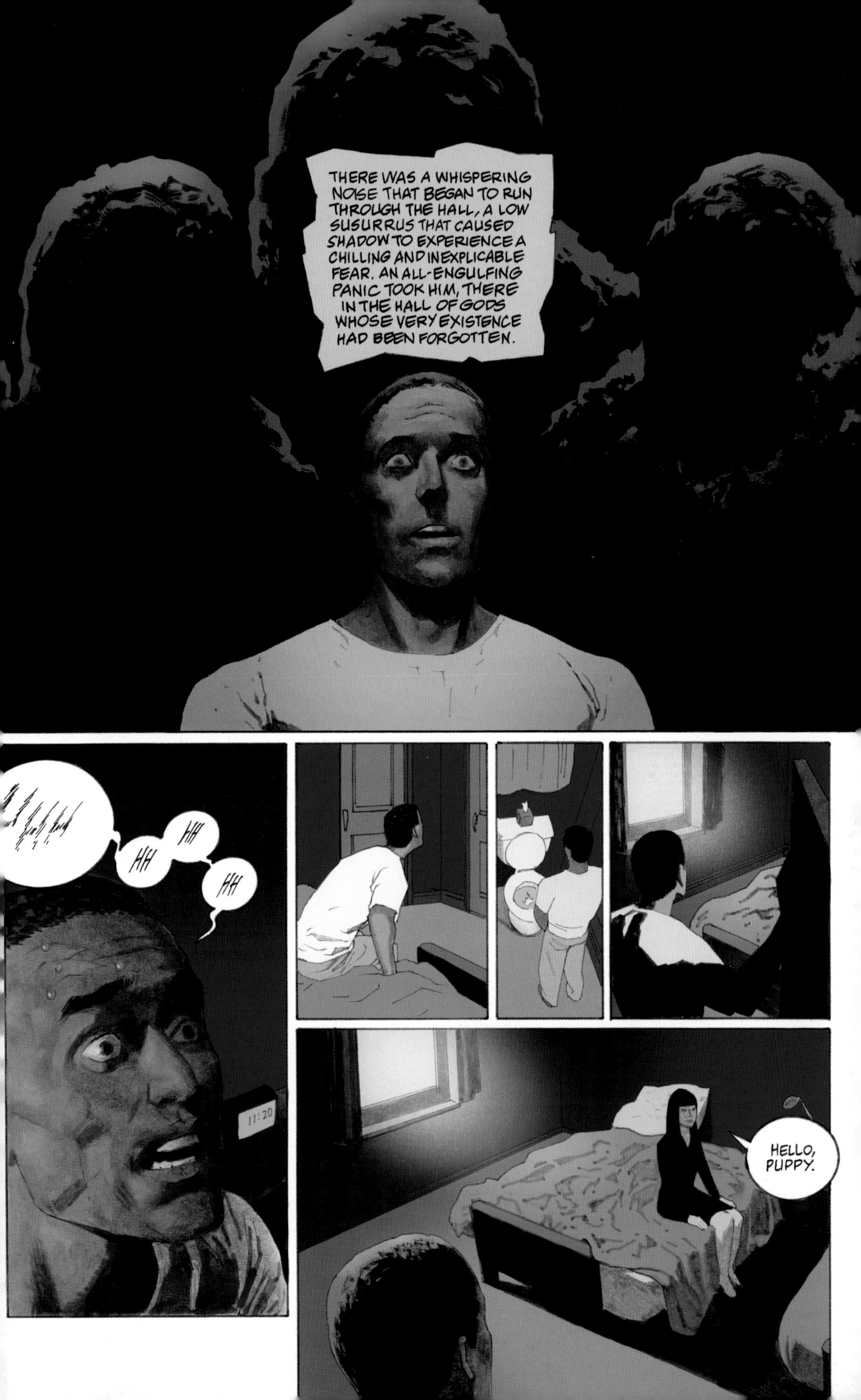
THERE WAS A WHISPERING NOISE THAT BEGAN TO RUN THROUGH THE HALL, A LOW SUSURRUS THAT CAUSED SHADOW TO EXPERIENCE A CHILLING AND INEXPLICABLE FEAR. AN ALL-ENGULFING PANIC TOOK HIM, THERE IN THE HALL OF GODS WHOSE VERY EXISTENCE HAD BEEN FORGOTTEN.
HH
HH
HH
11:20
HELLO, PUPPY.

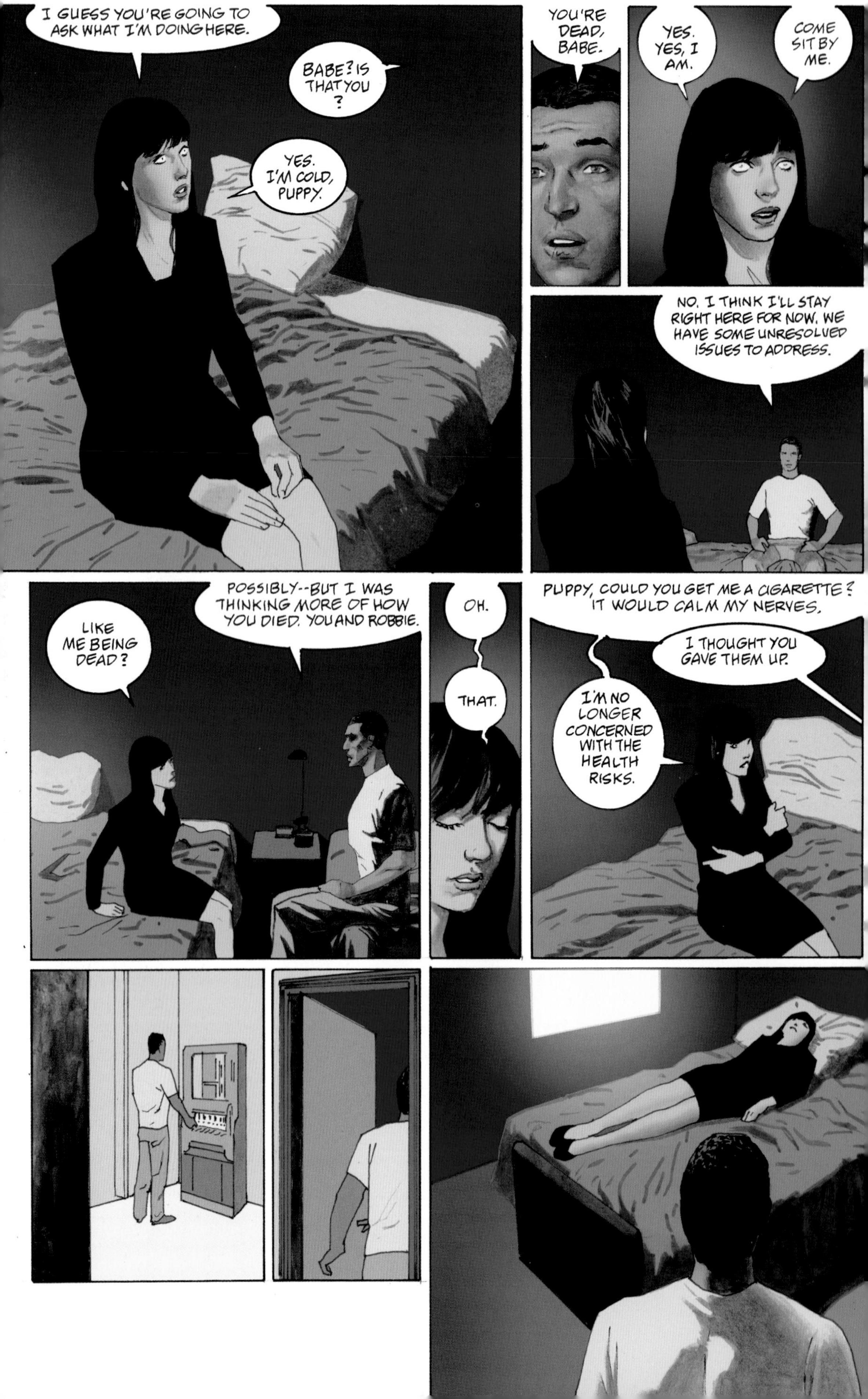
I GUESS YOU'RE GOING TO ASK WHAT I'M DOING HERE.
BABE? IS THAT YOU ?
YES. I'M COLD, PUPPY.
YOU'RE DEAD, BABE.
YES. YES, I AM.
COME SIT BY ME.
NO. I THINK I'LL STAY RIGHT HERE FOR NOW. WE HAVE SOME UNRESOLVED ISSUES TO ADDRESS.
LIKE ME BEING DEAD?
POSSIBLY--BUT I WAS THINKING MORE OF HOW YOU DIED. YOU AND ROBBIE.
OH.
THAT.
PUPPY, COULD YOU GET ME A CIGARETTE? IT WOULD CALM MY NERVES.
I THOUGHT YOU GAVE THEM UP.
I'M NO LONGER CONCERNED WITH THE HEALTH RISKS.

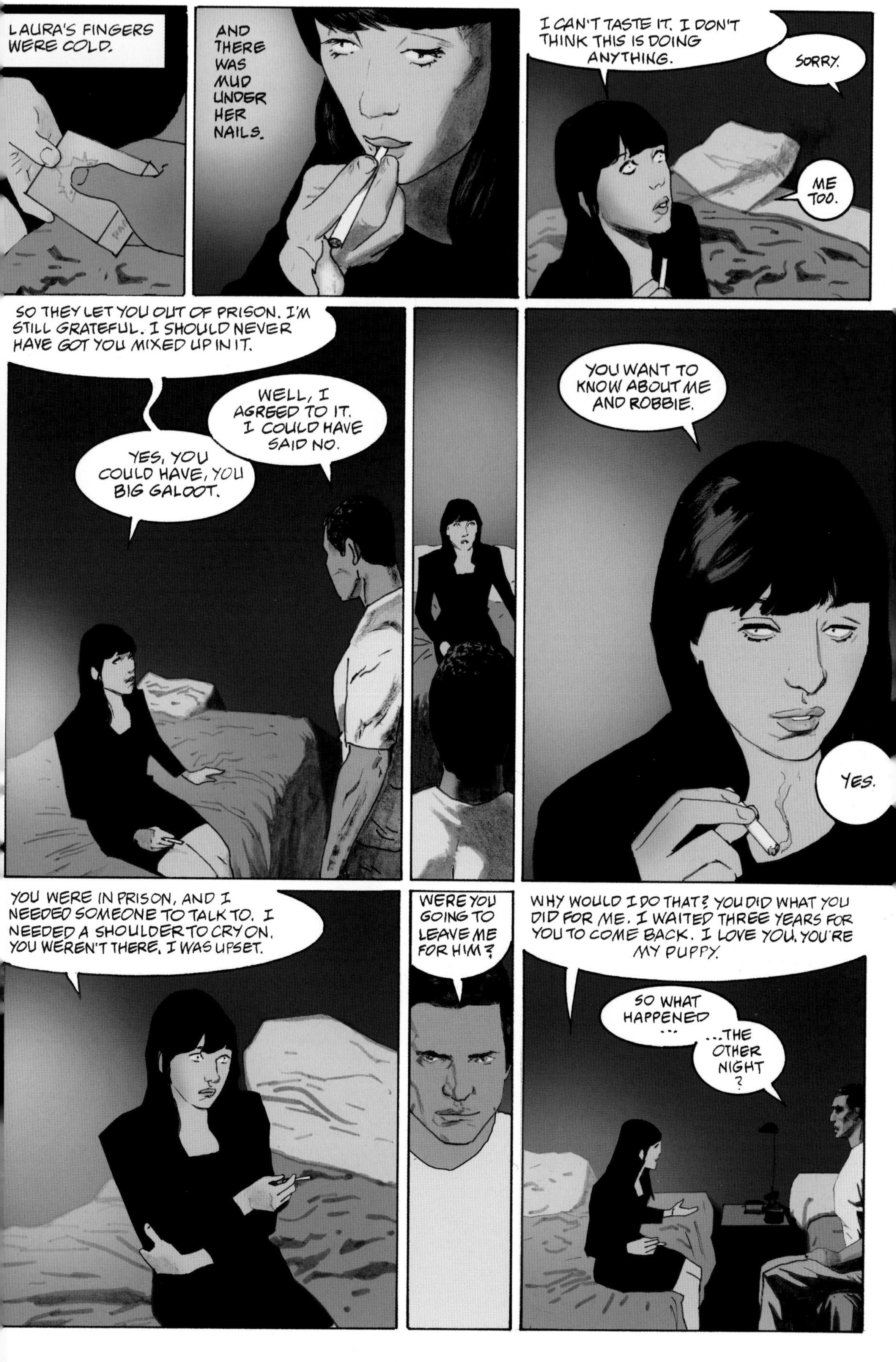
LAURA'S FINGERS WERE COLD.
AND THERE WAS MUD UNDER HER NAILS.
I CAN'T TASTE IT. I DON'T THINK THIS IS DOING ANYTHING.
SORRY.
ME TOO.
SO THEY LET YOU OUT OF PRISON. I'M STILL GRATEFUL. I SHOULD NEVER HAVE GOT YOU MIXED UP IN IT.
WELL, I AGREED TO IT. I COULD HAVE SAID NO.
YES, YOU COULD HAVE, YOU BIG GALOOT.
YOU WANT TO KNOW ABOUT ME AND ROBBIE.
YES.
YOU WERE IN PRISON, AND I NEEDED SOMEONE TO TALK TO. I NEEDED A SHOULDER TO CRY ON. YOU WEREN'T THERE. I WAS UPSET.
WERE YOU GOING TO LEAVE ME FOR HIM?
WHY WOULD I DO THAT? YOU DID WHAT YOU DID FOR ME. I WAITED THREE YEARS FOR YOU TO COME BACK. I LOVE YOU. YOU'RE MY PUPPY.
SO WHAT HAPPENED ...
...THE OTHER NIGHT ?

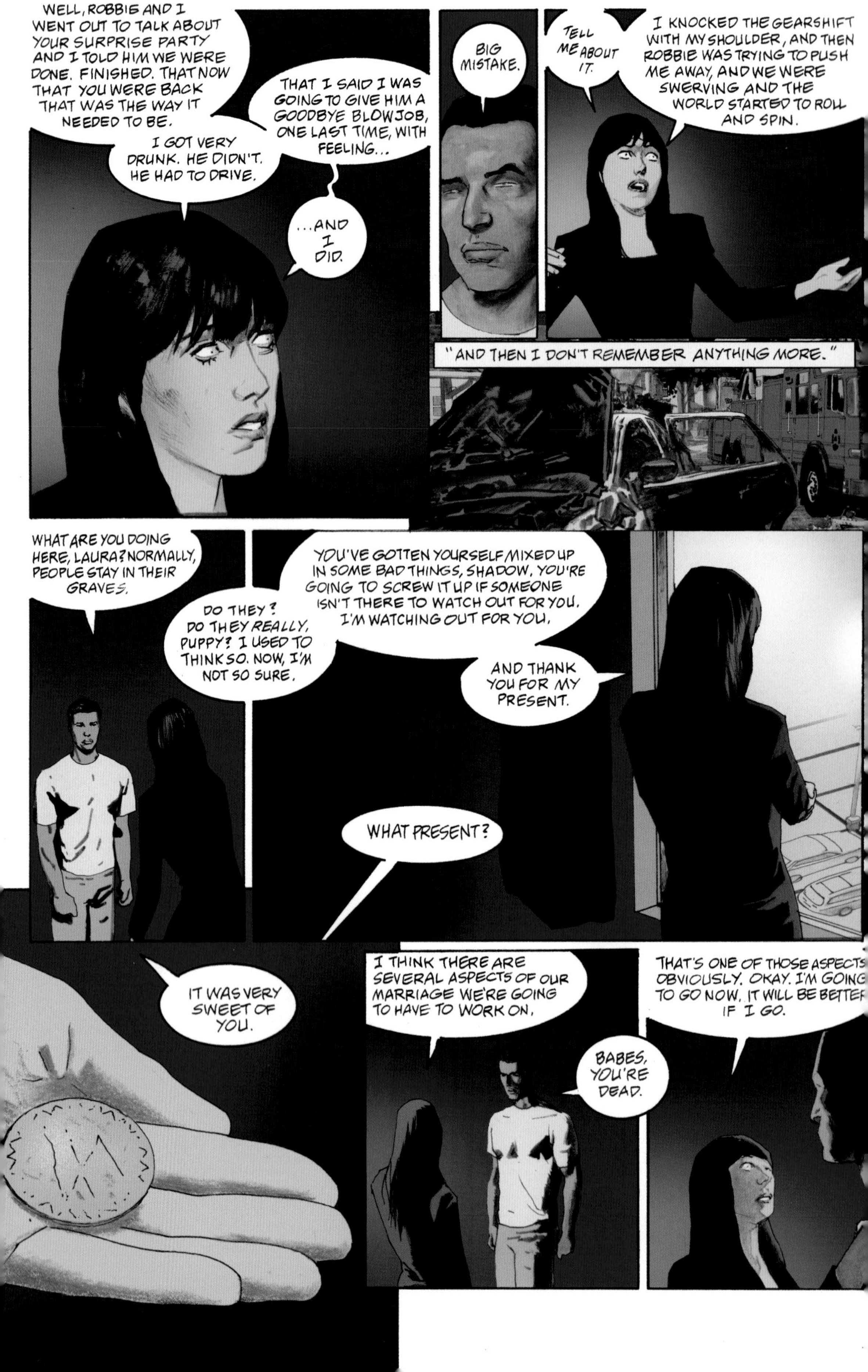
WELL, ROBBIE AND I WENT OUT TO TALK ABOUT YOUR SURPRISE PARTY AND I TOLD HIM WE WERE DONE. FINISHED. THAT NOW THAT YOU WERE BACK THAT WAS THE WAY IT NEEDED TO BE.
I GOT VERY DRUNK. HE DIDN'T. HE HAD TO DRIVE.
THAT I SAID I WAS GOING TO GIVE HIM A GOODBYE BLOWJOB, ONE LAST TIME, WITH FEELING...
...AND I DID.
BIG MISTAKE.
TELL ME ABOUT IT.
I KNOCKED THE GEARSHIFT WITH MY SHOULDER, AND THEN ROBBIE WAS TRYING TO PUSH ME AWAY, AND WE WERE SWERVING AND THE WORLD STARTED TO ROLL AND SPIN.
"AND THEN I DON'T REMEMBER ANYTHING MORE."
WHAT ARE YOU DOING HERE, LAURA? NORMALLY, PEOPLE STAY IN THEIR GRAVES.
DO THEY? DO THEY REALLY, PUPPY? I USED TO THINK SO. NOW, I'M NOT SO SURE.
YOU'VE GOTTEN YOURSELF MIXED UP IN SOME BAD THINGS, SHADOW. YOU'RE GOING TO SCREW IT UP IF SOMEONE ISN'T THERE TO WATCH OUT FOR YOU. I'M WATCHING OUT FOR YOU.
AND THANK YOU FOR MY PRESENT.
WHAT PRESENT?
IT WAS VERY SWEET OF YOU.
I THINK THERE ARE SEVERAL ASPECTS OF OUR MARRIAGE WE'RE GOING TO HAVE TO WORK ON.
BABES, YOU'RE DEAD.
THAT'S ONE OF THOSE ASPECTS OBVIOUSLY. OKAY. I'M GOING TO GO NOW. IT WILL BE BETTER IF I GO.

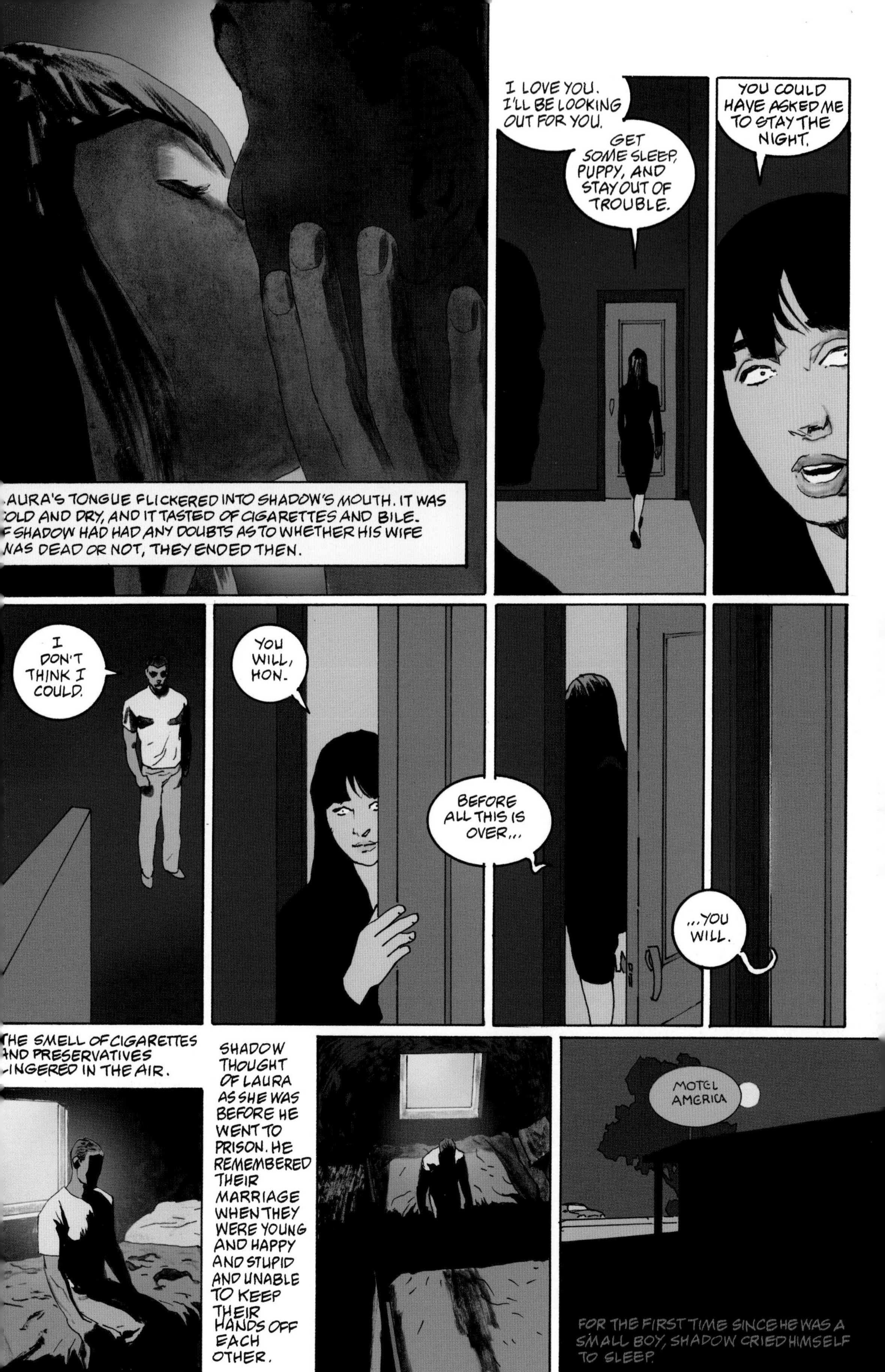

LAURA'S TONGUE FLICKERED INTO SHADOW'S MOUTH. IT WAS
OLD AND DRY, AND IT TASTED OF CIGARETTES AND BILE.
F SHADOW HAD HAD ANY DOUBTS AS TO WHETHER HIS WIFE
NAS DEAD OR NOT, THEY ENDED THEN.
I LOVE YOU. I'LL BE LOOKING OUT FOR YOU.
GET SOME SLEEP, PUPPY, AND STAY OUT OF TROUBLE.
YOU COULD HAVE ASKED ME TO STAY THE NIGHT.
I DON'T THINK I COULD.
YOU WILL, HON.
BEFORE ALL THIS IS OVER...
...YOU WILL.
THE SMELL OF CIGARETTES
AND PRESERVATIVES
INGERED IN THE AIR.
SHADOW THOUGHT OF LAURA AS SHE WAS BEFORE HE WENT TO PRISON. HE REMEMBERED THEIR MARRIAGE WHEN THEY WERE YOUNG AND HAPPY AND STUPID AND UNABLE TO KEEP THEIR HANDS OFF EACH OTHER.
MOTEL AMERICA
FOR THE FIRST TIME SINCE HE WAS A SMALL BOY, SHADOW CRIED HIMSELF TO SLEEP.

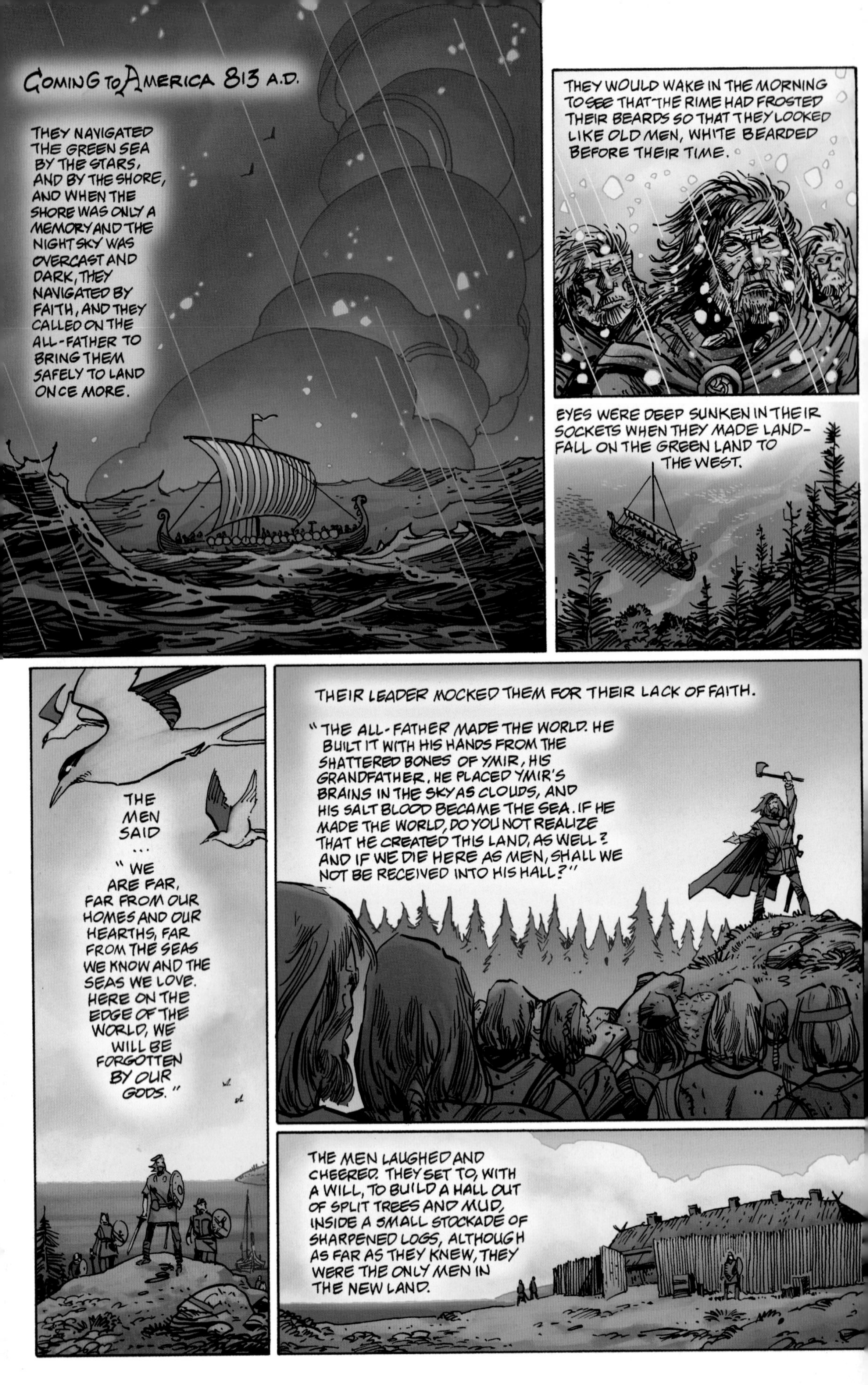
COMING TO AMERICA 813 A.D.
THEY NAVIGATED THE GREEN SEA BY THE STARS, AND BY THE SHORE, AND WHEN THE SHORE WAS ONLY A MEMORY AND THE NIGHT SKY WAS OVERCAST AND DARK, THEY NAVIGATED BY FAITH, AND THEY CALLED ON THE ALL-FATHER TO BRING THEM SAFELY TO LAND ONCE MORE.
THEY WOULD WAKE IN THE MORNING TO SEE THAT THE RIME HAD FROSTED THEIR BEARDS SO THAT THEY LOOKED LIKE OLD MEN, WHITE BEARDED BEFORE THEIR TIME.
EYES WERE DEEP SUNKEN IN THEIR SOCKETS WHEN THEY MADE LANDFALL ON THE GREEN LAND TO THE WEST.
THE MEN SAID ... "WE ARE FAR, FAR FROM OUR HOMES AND OUR HEARTHS, FAR FROM THE SEAS WE KNOW AND THE SEAS WE LOVE. HERE ON THE EDGE OF THE WORLD, WE WILL BE FORGOTTEN BY OUR GODS."
THEIR LEADER MOCKED THEM FOR THEIR LACK OF FAITH.
"THE ALL-FATHER MADE THE WORLD. HE BUILT IT WITH HIS HANDS FROM THE SHATTERED BONES OF YMIR, HIS GRANDFATHER. HE PLACED YMIR'S BRAINS IN THE SKY AS CLOUDS, AND HIS SALT BLOOD BECAME THE SEA. IF HE MADE THE WORLD, DO YOU NOT REALIZE THAT HE CREATED THIS LAND, AS WELL? AND IF WE DIE HERE AS MEN, SHALL WE NOT BE RECEIVED INTO HIS HALL?"
THE MEN LAUGHED AND CHEERED. THEY SET TO, WITH A WILL, TO BUILD A HALL OUT OF SPLIT TREES AND MUD, INSIDE A SMALL STOCKADE OF SHARPENED LOGS, ALTHOUGH AS FAR AS THEY KNEW, THEY WERE THE ONLY MEN IN THE NEW LAND.

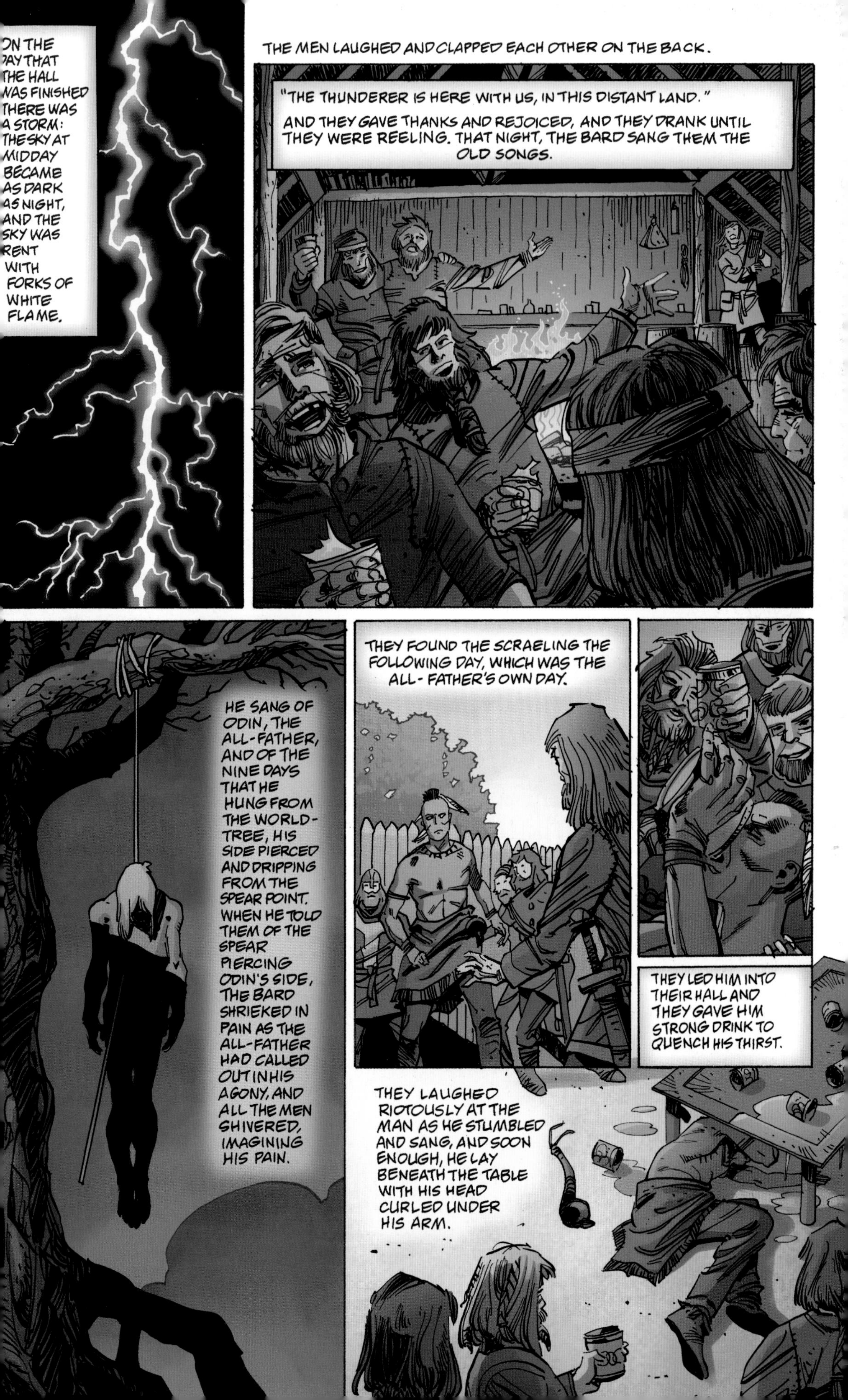
ON THE DAY THAT THE HALL WAS FINISHED THERE WAS A STORM: THE SKY AT MIDDAY BECAME AS DARK AS NIGHT, AND THE SKY WAS RENT WITH FORKS OF WHITE FLAME.
THE MEN LAUGHED AND CLAPPED EACH OTHER ON THE BACK.
"THE THUNDERER IS HERE WITH US, IN THIS DISTANT LAND."
AND THEY GAVE THANKS AND REJOICED, AND THEY DRANK UNTIL THEY WERE REELING. THAT NIGHT, THE BARD SANG THEM THE OLD SONGS.
HE SANG OF ODIN, THE ALL-FATHER, AND OF THE NINE DAYS THAT HE HUNG FROM THE WORLD-TREE, HIS SIDE PIERCED AND DRIPPING FROM THE SPEAR POINT. WHEN HE TOLD THEM OF THE SPEAR PIERCING ODIN'S SIDE, THE BARD SHRIEKED IN PAIN AS THE ALL-FATHER HAD CALLED OUT IN HIS AGONY, AND ALL THE MEN SHIVERED, IMAGINING HIS PAIN.
THEY FOUND THE SCRAELING THE FOLLOWING DAY, WHICH WAS THE ALL-FATHER'S OWN DAY.
THEY LED HIM INTO THEIR HALL AND THEY GAVE HIM STRONG DRINK TO QUENCH HIS THIRST.
THEY LAUGHED RIOTOUSLY AT THE MAN AS HE STUMBLED AND SANG, AND SOON ENOUGH, HE LAY BENEATH THE TABLE WITH HIS HEAD CURLED UNDER HIS ARM.

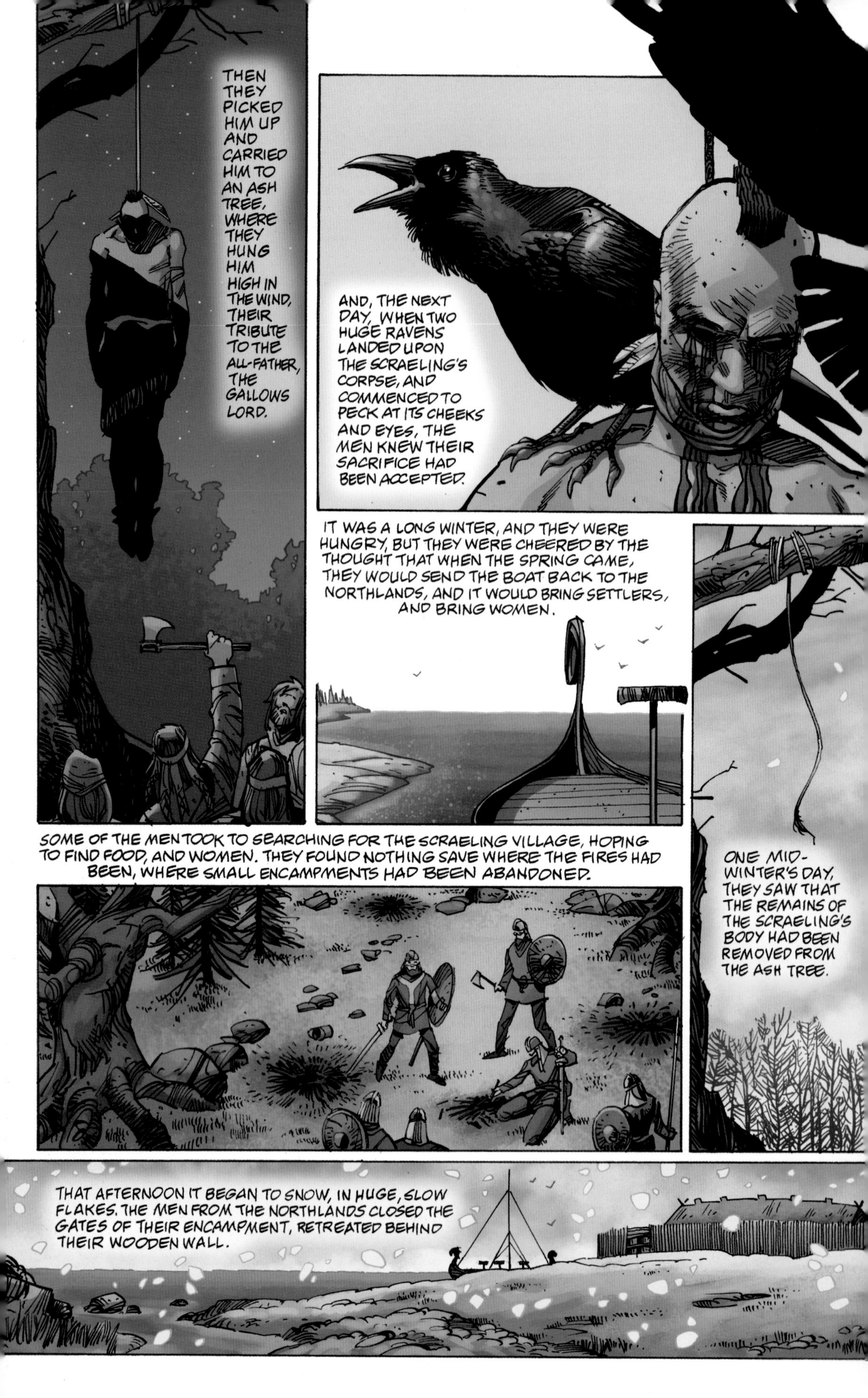
THEN THEY PICKED HIM UP AND CARRIED HIM TO AN ASH TREE, WHERE THEY HUNG HIM HIGH IN THE WIND, THEIR TRIBUTE TO THE ALL-FATHER, THE GALLOWS LORD.
AND, THE NEXT DAY, WHEN TWO HUGE RAVENS LANDED UPON THE SCRAELING'S CORPSE, AND COMMENCED TO PECK AT ITS CHEEKS AND EYES, THE MEN KNEW THEIR SACRIFICE HAD BEEN ACCEPTED.
IT WAS A LONG WINTER, AND THEY WERE HUNGRY, BUT THEY WERE CHEERED BY THE THOUGHT THAT WHEN THE SPRING CAME, THEY WOULD SEND THE BOAT BACK TO THE NORTHLANDS, AND IT WOULD BRING SETTLERS, AND BRING WOMEN.
SOME OF THE MEN TOOK TO SEARCHING FOR THE SCRAELING VILLAGE, HOPING TO FIND FOOD, AND WOMEN. THEY FOUND NOTHING SAVE WHERE THE FIRES HAD BEEN, WHERE SMALL ENCAMPMENTS HAD BEEN ABANDONED.
ONE MID-WINTER'S DAY, THEY SAW THAT THE REMAINS OF THE SCRAELING'S BODY HAD BEEN REMOVED FROM THE ASH TREE.
THAT AFTERNOON IT BEGAN TO SNOW, IN HUGE, SLOW FLAKES. THE MEN FROM THE NORTHLANDS CLOSED THE GATES OF THEIR ENCAMPMENT, RETREATED BEHIND THEIR WOODEN WALL.

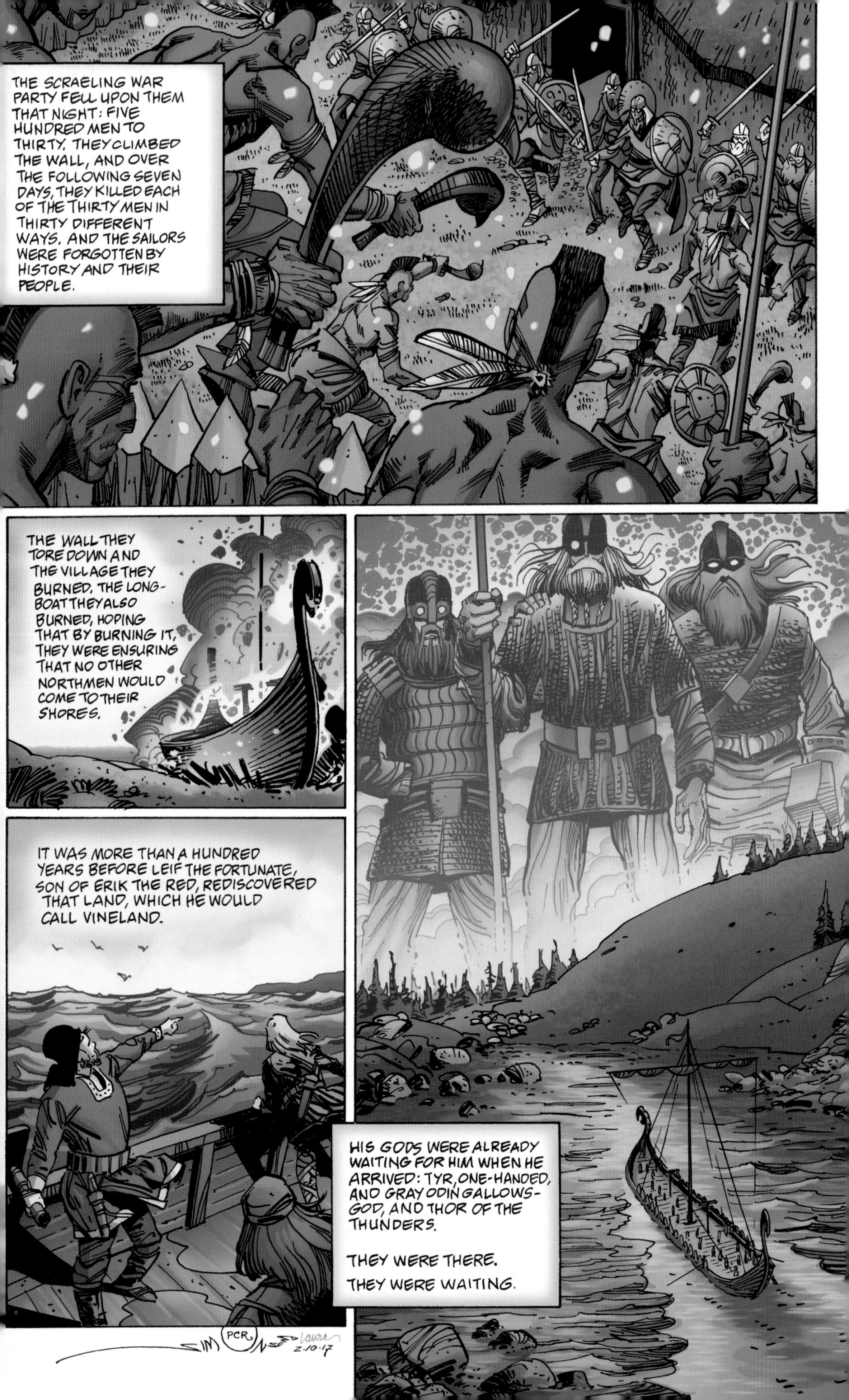
THE SCRAELING WAR PARTY FELL UPON THEM THAT NIGHT: FIVE HUNDRED MEN TO THIRTY. THEY CLIMBED THE WALL, AND OVER THE FOLLOWING SEVEN DAYS, THEY KILLED EACH OF THE THIRTY MEN IN THIRTY DIFFERENT WAYS. AND THE SAILORS WERE FORGOTTEN BY HISTORY AND THEIR PEOPLE.
THE WALL THEY TORE DOWN AND THE VILLAGE THEY BURNED. THE LONG-BOAT THEY ALSO BURNED, HOPING THAT BY BURNING IT, THEY WERE ENSURING THAT NO OTHER NORTHMEN WOULD COME TO THEIR SHORES.
IT WAS MORE THAN A HUNDRED YEARS BEFORE LEIF THE FORTUNATE, SON OF ERIK THE RED, REDISCOVERED THAT LAND, WHICH HE WOULD CALL VINELAND.
HIS GODS WERE ALREADY WAITING FOR HIM WHEN HE ARRIVED: TYR, ONE-HANDED, AND GRAY ODIN GALLOWS-GOD, AND THOR OF THE THUNDERS.
THEY WERE THERE.
THEY WERE WAITING.
SIM PCR NSOD Laura 2.10.17

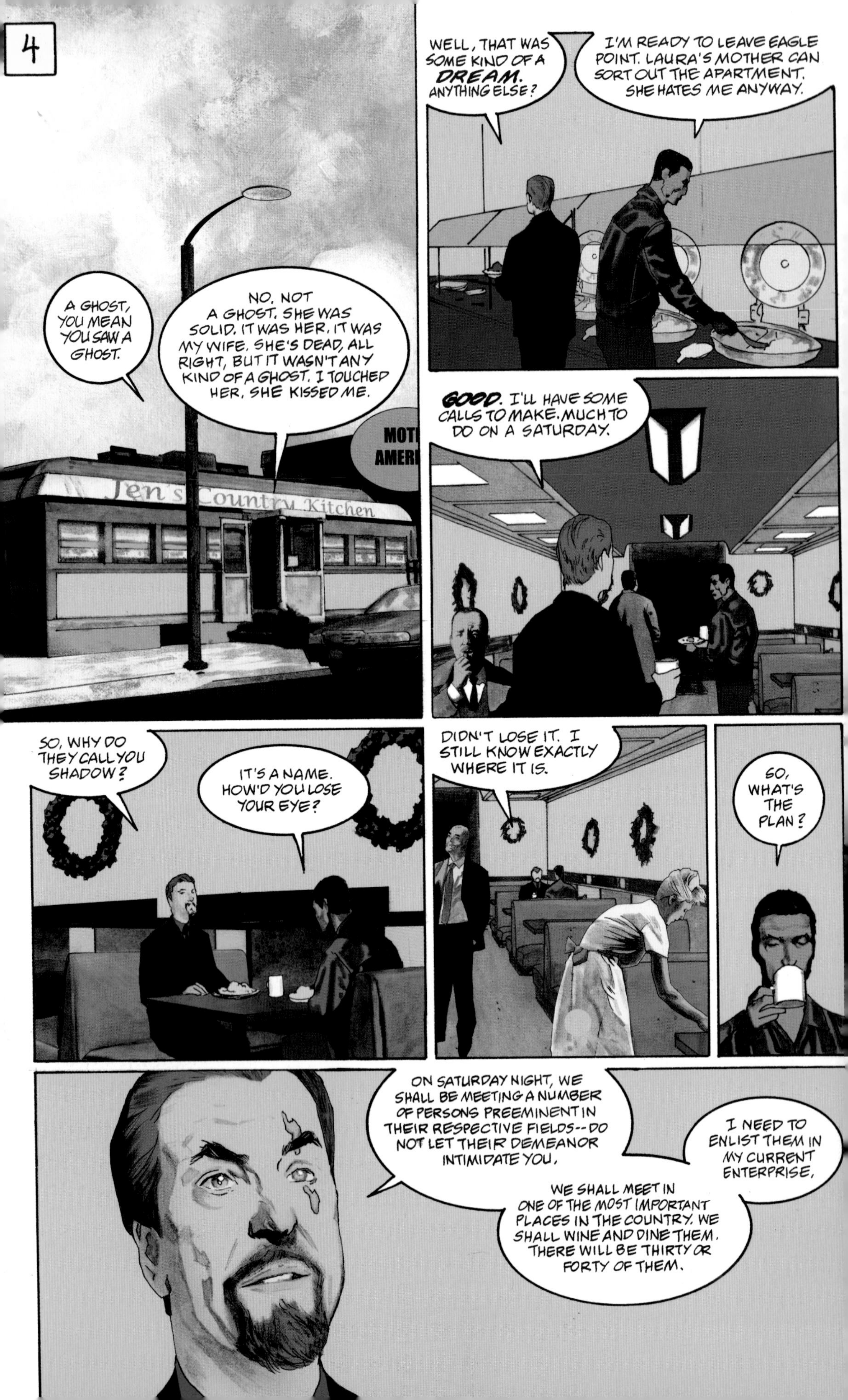
4
A GHOST, YOU MEAN YOU SAW A GHOST.
NO. NOT A GHOST. SHE WAS SOLID. IT WAS HER. IT WAS MY WIFE. SHE'S DEAD, ALL RIGHT, BUT IT WASN'T ANY KIND OF A GHOST. I TOUCHED HER. SHE KISSED ME.
Jen's Country Kitchen
WELL, THAT WAS SOME KIND OF A DREAM. ANYTHING ELSE?
I'M READY TO LEAVE EAGLE POINT. LAURA'S MOTHER CAN SORT OUT THE APARTMENT. SHE HATES ME ANYWAY.
GOOD. I'LL HAVE SOME CALLS TO MAKE. MUCH TO DO ON A SATURDAY.
SO, WHY DO THEY CALL YOU SHADOW?
IT'S A NAME. HOW'D YOU LOSE YOUR EYE?
DIDN'T LOSE IT. I STILL KNOW EXACTLY WHERE IT IS.
SO, WHAT'S THE PLAN?
ON SATURDAY NIGHT, WE SHALL BE MEETING A NUMBER OF PERSONS PREEMINENT IN THEIR RESPECTIVE FIELDS--DO NOT LET THEIR DEMEANOR INTIMIDATE YOU.
I NEED TO ENLIST THEM IN MY CURRENT ENTERPRISE.
WE SHALL MEET IN ONE OF THE MOST IMPORTANT PLACES IN THE COUNTRY. WE SHALL WINE AND DINE THEM. THERE WILL BE THIRTY OR FORTY OF THEM.

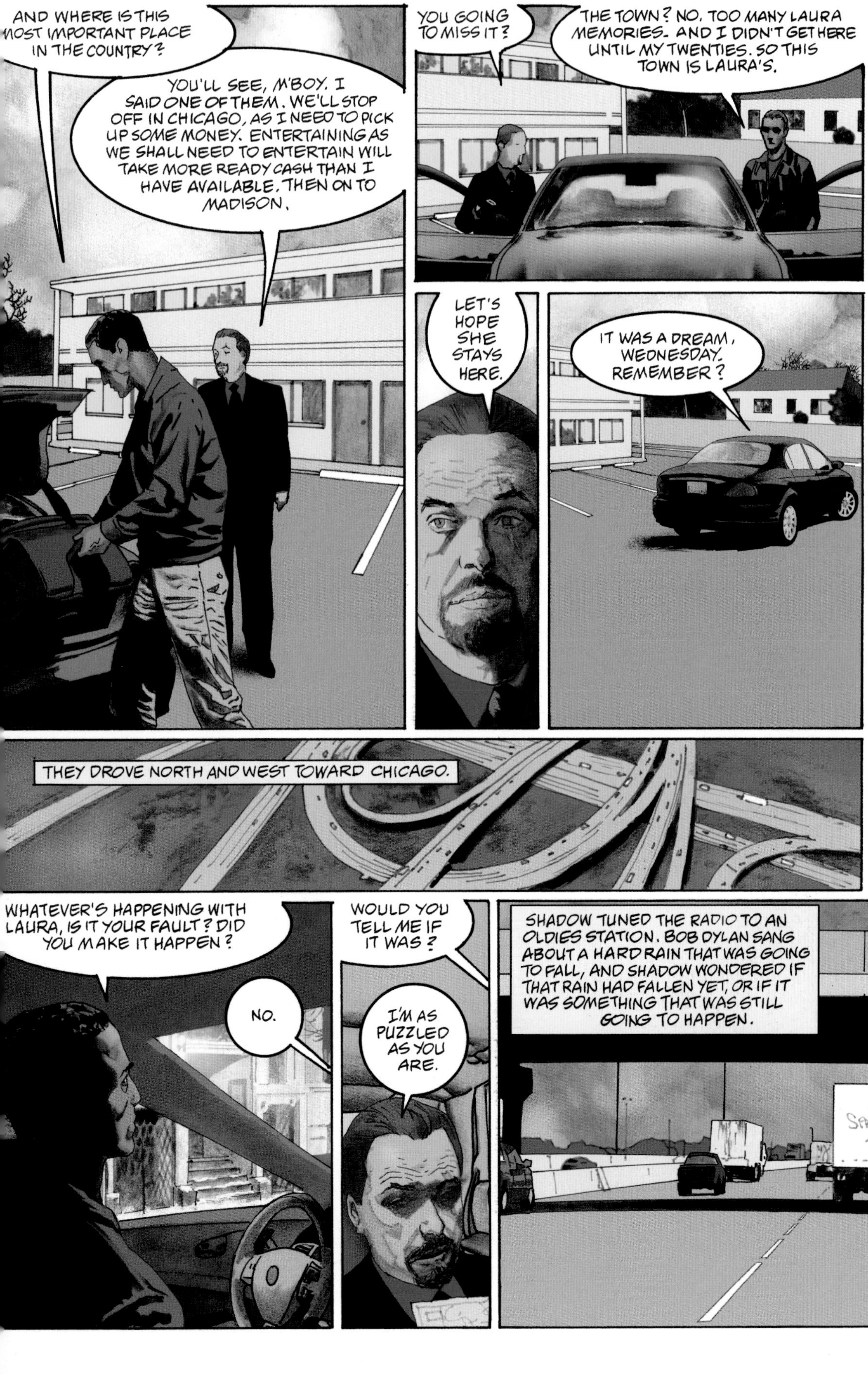
AND WHERE IS THIS MOST IMPORTANT PLACE IN THE COUNTRY?
YOU'LL SEE, M'BOY. I SAID ONE OF THEM. WE'LL STOP OFF IN CHICAGO, AS I NEED TO PICK UP SOME MONEY. ENTERTAINING AS WE SHALL NEED TO ENTERTAIN WILL TAKE MORE READY CASH THAN I HAVE AVAILABLE. THEN ON TO MADISON.
YOU GOING TO MISS IT?
THE TOWN? NO. TOO MANY LAURA MEMORIES. AND I DIDN'T GET HERE UNTIL MY TWENTIES. SO THIS TOWN IS LAURA'S.
LET'S HOPE SHE STAYS HERE.
IT WAS A DREAM, WEDNESDAY. REMEMBER?
THEY DROVE NORTH AND WEST TOWARD CHICAGO.
WHATEVER'S HAPPENING WITH LAURA, IS IT YOUR FAULT? DID YOU MAKE IT HAPPEN?
NO.
WOULD YOU TELL ME IF IT WAS?
I'M AS PUZZLED AS YOU ARE.
SHADOW TUNED THE RADIO TO AN OLDIES STATION. BOB DYLAN SANG ABOUT A HARD RAIN THAT WAS GOING TO FALL, AND SHADOW WONDERED IF THAT RAIN HAD FALLEN YET, OR IF IT WAS SOMETHING THAT WAS STILL GOING TO HAPPEN.

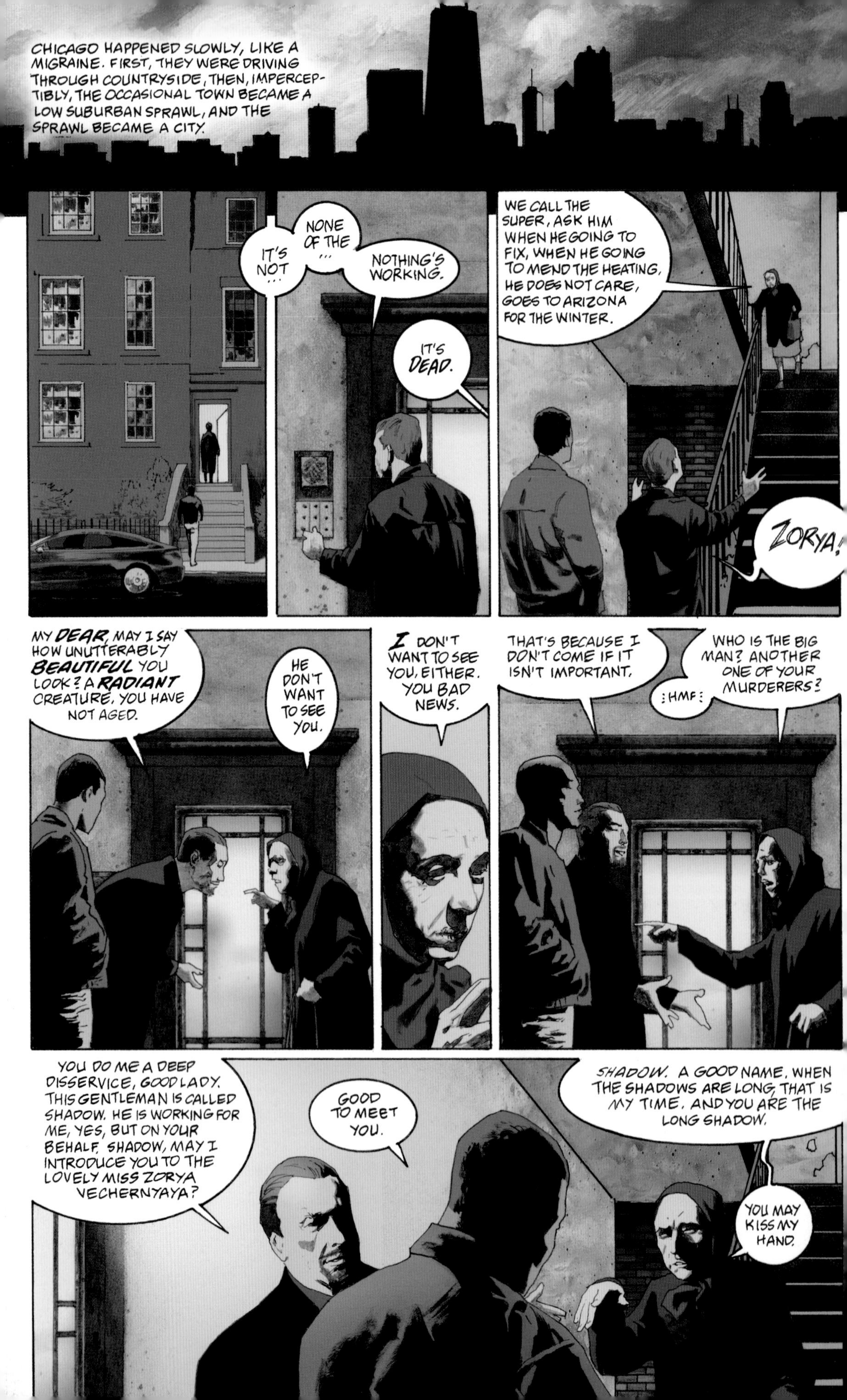
CHICAGO HAPPENED SLOWLY, LIKE A MIGRAINE. FIRST, THEY WERE DRIVING THROUGH COUNTRYSIDE, THEN, IMPERCEPTIBLY, THE OCCASIONAL TOWN BECAME A LOW SUBURBAN SPRAWL, AND THE SPRAWL BECAME A CITY.
IT'S NOT ...
NONE OF THE ...
NOTHING'S WORKING.
IT'S DEAD.
WE CALL THE SUPER, ASK HIM WHEN HE GOING TO FIX, WHEN HE GOING TO MEND THE HEATING, HE DOES NOT CARE, GOES TO ARIZONA FOR THE WINTER.
ZORYA!
MY DEAR, MAY I SAY HOW UNUTTERABLY BEAUTIFUL YOU LOOK? A RADIANT CREATURE. YOU HAVE NOT AGED.
HE DON'T WANT TO SEE YOU.
I DON'T WANT TO SEE YOU, EITHER. YOU BAD NEWS.
THAT'S BECAUSE I DON'T COME IF IT ISN'T IMPORTANT.
:HMF:
WHO IS THE BIG MAN? ANOTHER ONE OF YOUR MURDERERS?
YOU DO ME A DEEP DISSERVICE, GOOD LADY. THIS GENTLEMAN IS CALLED SHADOW. HE IS WORKING FOR ME, YES, BUT ON YOUR BEHALF. SHADOW, MAY I INTRODUCE YOU TO THE LOVELY MISS ZORYA VECHERNYAYA?
GOOD TO MEET YOU.
SHADOW. A GOOD NAME. WHEN THE SHADOWS ARE LONG, THAT IS MY TIME. AND YOU ARE THE LONG SHADOW.
YOU MAY KISS MY HAND.

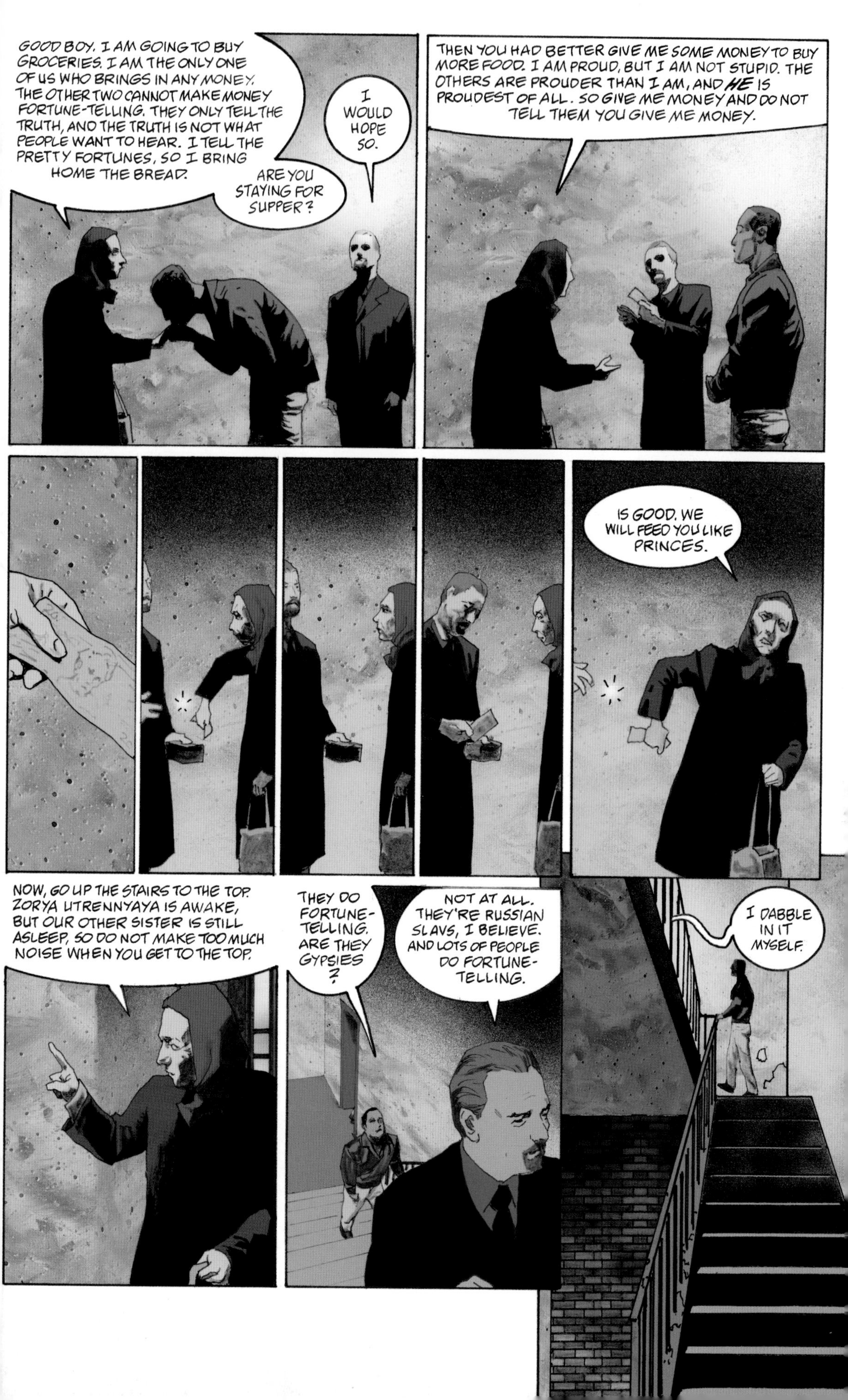
GOOD BOY. I AM GOING TO BUY GROCERIES. I AM THE ONLY ONE OF US WHO BRINGS IN ANY MONEY. THE OTHER TWO CANNOT MAKE MONEY FORTUNE-TELLING. THEY ONLY TELL THE TRUTH, AND THE TRUTH IS NOT WHAT PEOPLE WANT TO HEAR. I TELL THE PRETTY FORTUNES, SO I BRING HOME THE BREAD.
ARE YOU STAYING FOR SUPPER?
I WOULD HOPE SO.
THEN YOU HAD BETTER GIVE ME SOME MONEY TO BUY MORE FOOD. I AM PROUD, BUT I AM NOT STUPID. THE OTHERS ARE PROUDER THAN I AM, AND HE IS PROUDEST OF ALL. SO GIVE ME MONEY AND DO NOT TELL THEM YOU GIVE ME MONEY.
IS GOOD. WE WILL FEED YOU LIKE PRINCES.
NOW, GO UP THE STAIRS TO THE TOP. ZORYA UTRENNYAYA IS AWAKE, BUT OUR OTHER SISTER IS STILL ASLEEP, SO DO NOT MAKE TOO MUCH NOISE WHEN YOU GET TO THE TOP.
THEY DO FORTUNE-TELLING. ARE THEY GYPSIES?
NOT AT ALL. THEY'RE RUSSIAN SLAVS, I BELIEVE. AND LOTS OF PEOPLE DO FORTUNE-TELLING.
I DABBLE IN IT MYSELF.

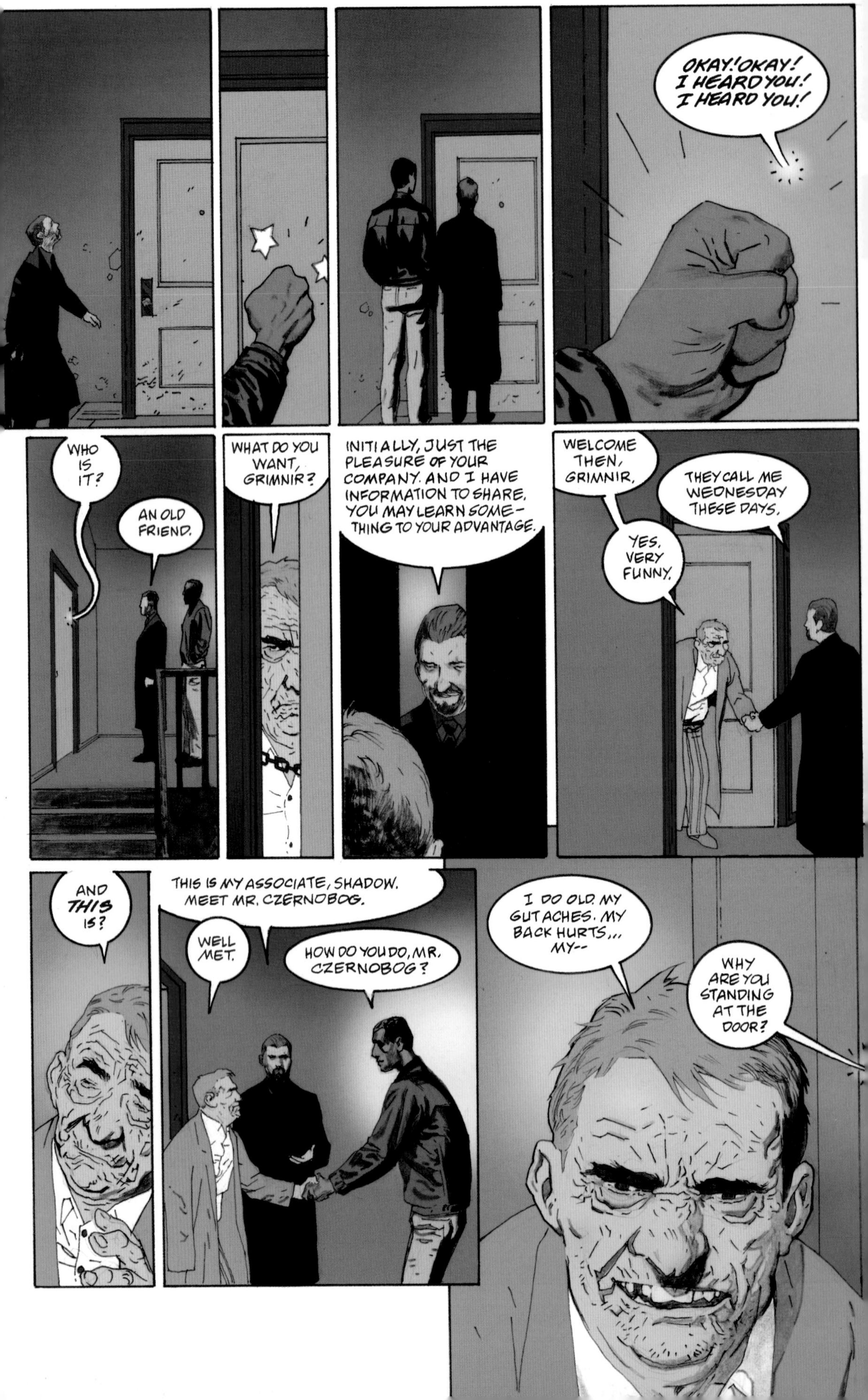
OKAY! OKAY! I HEARD YOU! I HEARD YOU!
WHO IS IT?
AN OLD FRIEND.
WHAT DO YOU WANT, GRIMNIR?
INITIALLY, JUST THE PLEASURE OF YOUR COMPANY. AND I HAVE INFORMATION TO SHARE. YOU MAY LEARN SOME-THING TO YOUR ADVANTAGE.
WELCOME THEN, GRIMNIR,
THEY CALL ME WEDNESDAY THESE DAYS.
YES. VERY FUNNY.
AND THIS IS?
THIS IS MY ASSOCIATE, SHADOW. MEET MR. CZERNOBOG.
WELL MET.
HOW DO YOU DO, MR. CZERNOBOG?
I DO OLD. MY GUT ACHES. MY BACK HURTS,,, MY--
WHY ARE YOU STANDING AT THE DOOR?

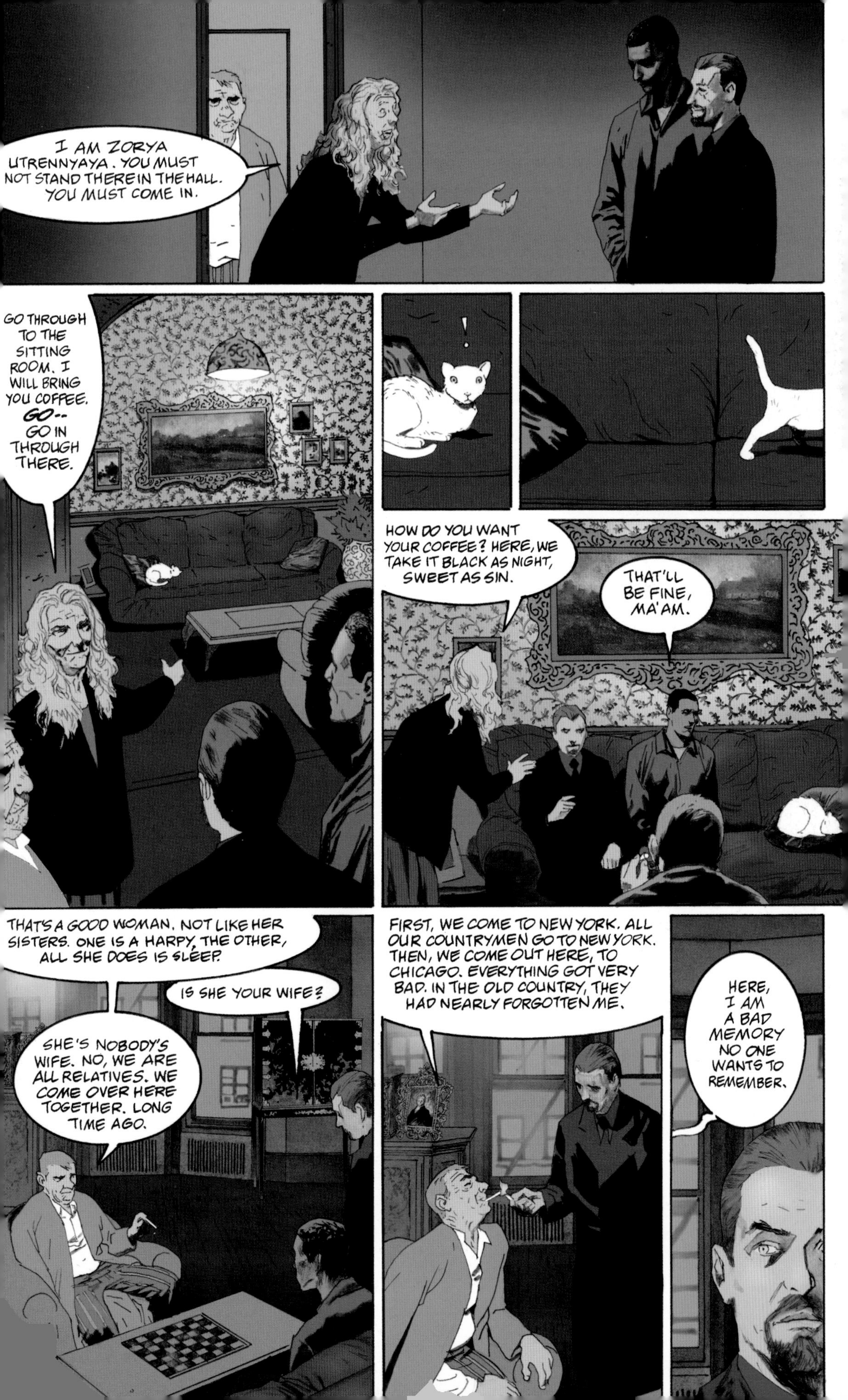
I AM ZORYA UTRENNYAYA. YOU MUST NOT STAND THERE IN THE HALL. YOU MUST COME IN.
GO THROUGH TO THE SITTING ROOM. I WILL BRING YOU COFFEE. GO-- GO IN THROUGH THERE.
!
HOW DO YOU WANT YOUR COFFEE? HERE, WE TAKE IT BLACK AS NIGHT, SWEET AS SIN.
THAT'LL BE FINE, MA'AM.
THAT'S A GOOD WOMAN. NOT LIKE HER SISTERS. ONE IS A HARPY, THE OTHER, ALL SHE DOES IS SLEEP.
IS SHE YOUR WIFE?
SHE'S NOBODY'S WIFE. NO, WE ARE ALL RELATIVES. WE COME OVER HERE TOGETHER. LONG TIME AGO.
FIRST, WE COME TO NEW YORK. ALL OUR COUNTRYMEN GO TO NEW YORK. THEN, WE COME OUT HERE, TO CHICAGO. EVERYTHING GOT VERY BAD. IN THE OLD COUNTRY, THEY HAD NEARLY FORGOTTEN ME.
HERE, I AM A BAD MEMORY NO ONE WANTS TO REMEMBER.

YOU KNOW WHAT I DID WHEN I GOT TO CHICAGO?

NO.

I GET JOB IN THE *MEAT* BUSINESS, ON THE KILL FLOOR. I WAS A *KNOCKER.* WE TAKE THE SLEDGEHAMMER AND WE *KNOCK* THE COW DOWN...

BAM!

IT TAKES STRENGTH IN THE ARMS, YES?

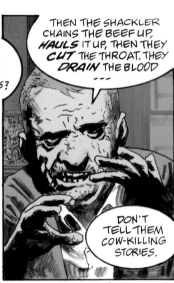

THEN THE SHACKLER CHAINS THE BEEF UP, *HAULS* IT UP, THEN THEY *CUT* THE THROAT. THEY *DRAIN* THE BLOOD ---

DON'T TELL THEM COW-KILLING STORIES.

ZORYA VECHERNYAYA IS DOING SHOPPING. SHE WILL BE SOON BACK.

WE MET HER DOWNSTAIRS. SHE SAYS SHE TELLS FORTUNES.

YES, IN THE TWILIGHT, THAT IS THE TIME FOR LIES. I DO NOT TELL GOOD LIES. AND OUR SISTER, ZORYA POLUNOCHNAYA, SHE CAN TELL NO LIES AT ALL.

THE COFFEE WAS EVEN SWEETER AND STRONGER THAN SHADOW HAD EXPECTED.

UH... WHERE'S...

DOOR ON LEFT. END OF HALL.

VOICES RAISED DOWN THE HALL.

YOU BRING TROUBLE! NOTHING BUT TROUBLE! I WILL NOT LISTEN. YOU WILL GET OUT OF MY HOUSE!

IS THERE A PROBLEM?

HE IS THE PROBLEM! *HE* IS! YOU TELL HIM THAT THERE IS NOTHING WILL MAKE ME HELP HIM! I WANT HIM TO GO! I WANT HIM OUT OF HERE! BOTH OF YOU *GO!*

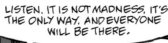

PLEASE, PLEASE BE QUIET, YOU WAKE UP ZORYA POLUNOCHNAYA.

YOU ARE LIKE HIM, YOU WANT ME TO JOIN HIS MADNESS!

LISTEN, IT IS NOT MADNESS, IT'S THE ONLY WAY. AND EVERYONE WILL BE THERE.

YOU KNOW WHO I AM. YOU KNOW WHAT THESE HANDS HAVE DONE. YOU WANT MY BROTHER, NOT ME. AND HE'S GONE.

IS SOMETHING WRONG?

NOTHING IS WRONG, MY SISTER, GO BACK TO SLEEP.

SEE? SEE WHAT YOU DO WITH ALL YOUR SHOUTING? YOU GO BACK IN THERE AND SIT DOWN. SIT!

IT DOESN'T HAVE TO BE FOR YOU. IF IT IS FOR YOUR BROTHER, IT IS FOR YOU AS WELL. THAT'S ONE PLACE YOU DUALISTIC TYPES HAVE IT OVER THE REST OF US, EH? TALKING OF BIELEBOG, HAVE YOU HEARD ANYTHING FROM HIM?

NONE OF US HAVE.

I AM ALMOST FORGOTTEN, BUT STILL, THEY REMEMBER ME A LITTLE, HERE AND IN THE OLD COUNTRY.

DO YOU HAVE A BROTHER?

NO, NOT THAT I KNOW OF.

I HAVE A BROTHER. THEY SAY YOU PUT US TOGETHER, WE ARE LIKE ONE PERSON. WHEN WE WERE YOUNG, HIS HAIR, IT IS VERY BLOND. AND PEOPLE SAY, HE IS THE GOOD ONE. MY HAIR IS VERY DARK, AND PEOPLE SAY I AM THE ROGUE, YOU KNOW? I AM THE BAD ONE.

AND NOW, TIME PASSES, OUR HAIR IS GRAY AND YOU WOULD NOT KNOW WHO WAS LIGHT, WHO WAS DARK.

WERE YOU CLOSE?

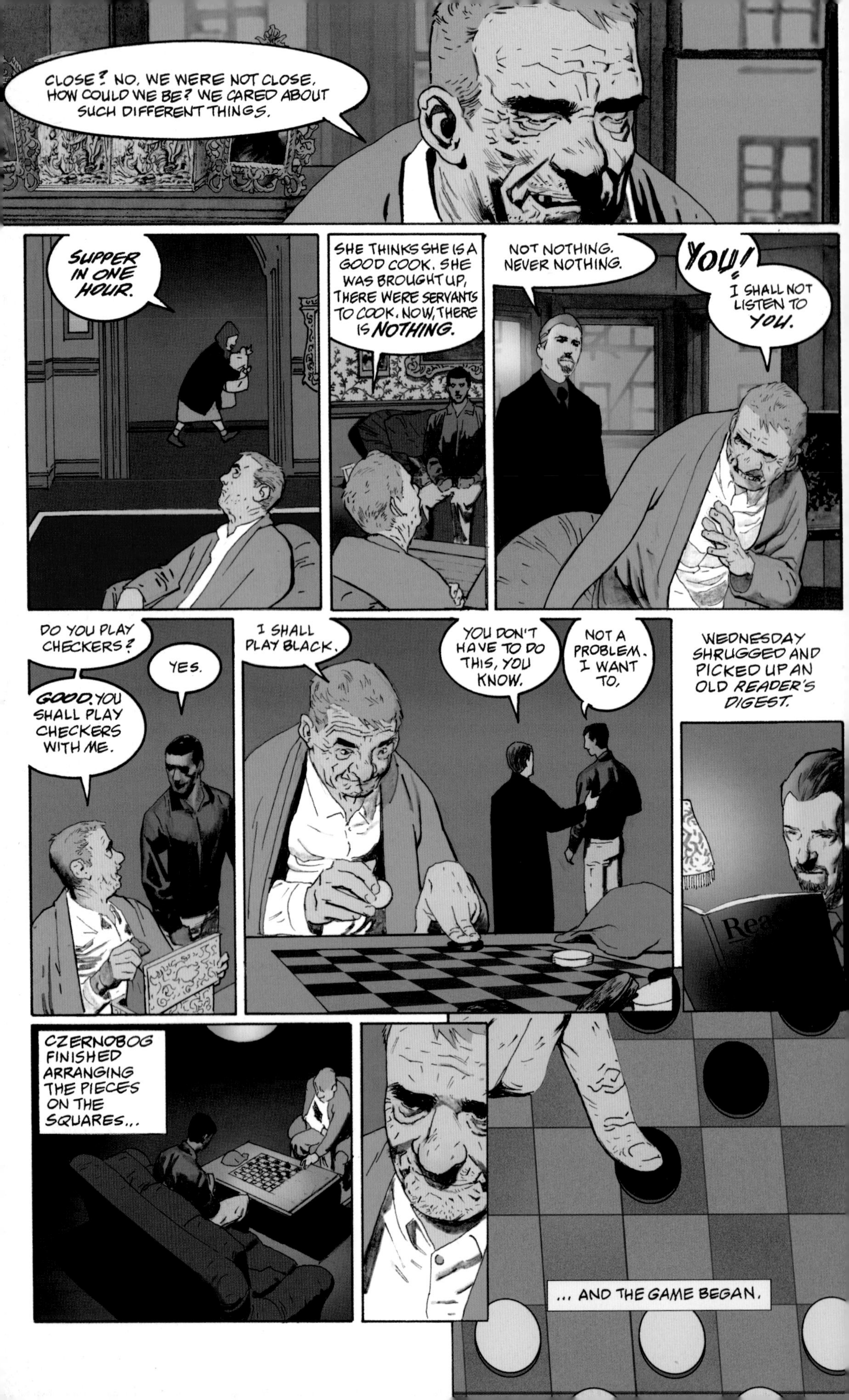
CLOSE? NO, WE WERE NOT CLOSE. HOW COULD WE BE? WE CARED ABOUT SUCH DIFFERENT THINGS.
SUPPER IN ONE HOUR.
SHE THINKS SHE IS A GOOD COOK. SHE WAS BROUGHT UP, THERE WERE SERVANTS TO COOK. NOW, THERE IS NOTHING.
NOT NOTHING. NEVER NOTHING.
YOU!
I SHALL NOT LISTEN TO YOU.
DO YOU PLAY CHECKERS?
YES.
GOOD. YOU SHALL PLAY CHECKERS WITH ME.
I SHALL PLAY BLACK.
YOU DON'T HAVE TO DO THIS, YOU KNOW.
NOT A PROBLEM. I WANT TO.
WEDNESDAY SHRUGGED AND PICKED UP AN OLD READER'S DIGEST.
CZERNOBOG FINISHED ARRANGING THE PIECES ON THE SQUARES...
... AND THE GAME BEGAN.

CHAPTER FOUR

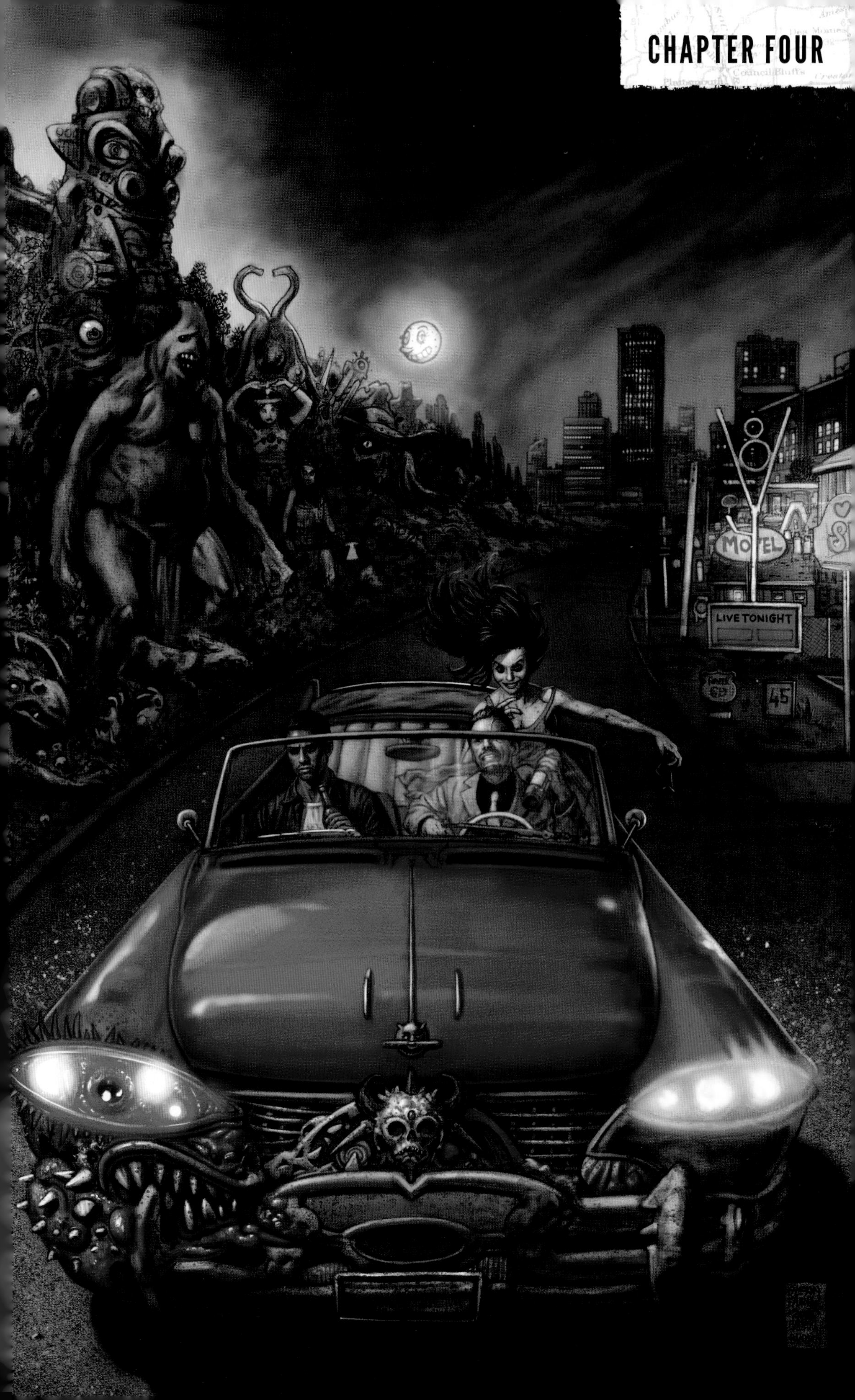
MOTEL
LIVE TONIGHT
45

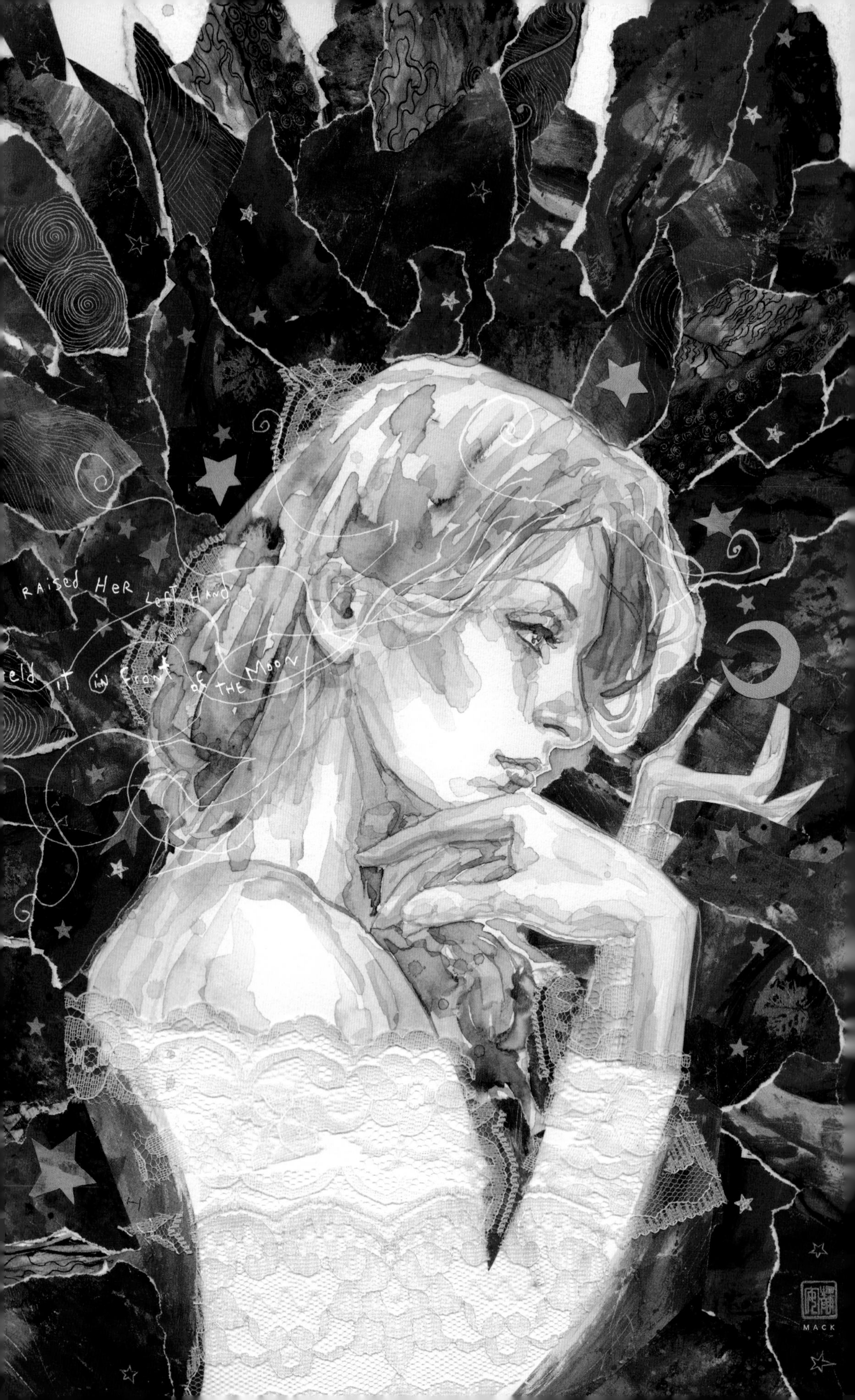
RAISED HER LEFT HAND
eld IT IN front OF THE MOON
MACK

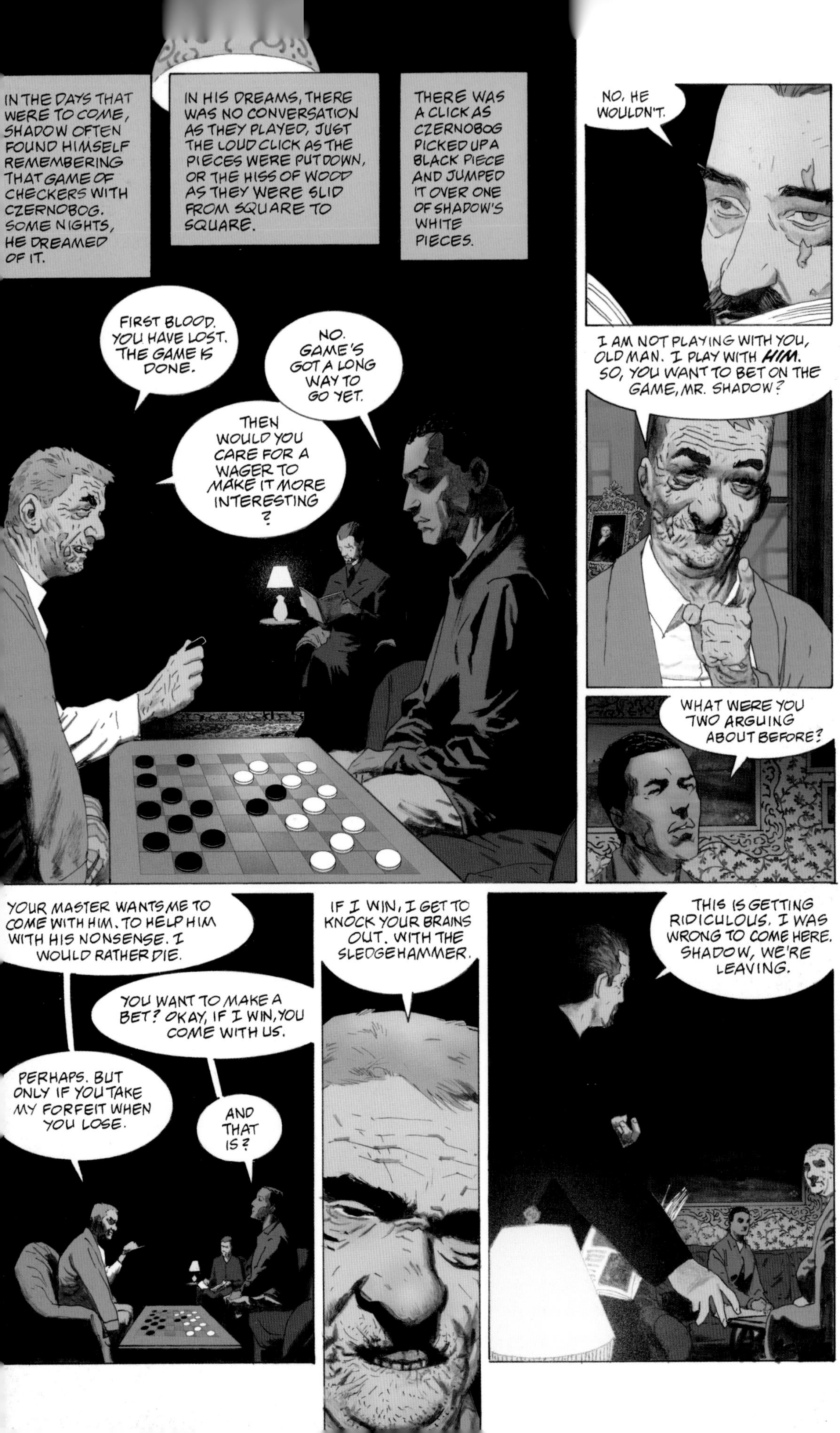
IN THE DAYS THAT WERE TO COME, SHADOW OFTEN FOUND HIMSELF REMEMBERING THAT GAME OF CHECKERS WITH CZERNOBOG. SOME NIGHTS, HE DREAMED OF IT.
IN HIS DREAMS, THERE WAS NO CONVERSATION AS THEY PLAYED, JUST THE LOUD CLICK AS THE PIECES WERE PUT DOWN, OR THE HISS OF WOOD AS THEY WERE SLID FROM SQUARE TO SQUARE.
THERE WAS A CLICK AS CZERNOBOG PICKED UP A BLACK PIECE AND JUMPED IT OVER ONE OF SHADOW'S WHITE PIECES.
FIRST BLOOD. YOU HAVE LOST. THE GAME IS DONE.
NO. GAME'S GOT A LONG WAY TO GO YET.
THEN WOULD YOU CARE FOR A WAGER TO MAKE IT MORE INTERESTING ?
NO, HE WOULDN'T.
I AM NOT PLAYING WITH YOU, OLD MAN. I PLAY WITH ***HIM***. SO, YOU WANT TO BET ON THE GAME, MR. SHADOW?
WHAT WERE YOU TWO ARGUING ABOUT BEFORE?
YOUR MASTER WANTS ME TO COME WITH HIM. TO HELP HIM WITH HIS NONSENSE. I WOULD RATHER DIE.
YOU WANT TO MAKE A BET? OKAY, IF I WIN, YOU COME WITH US.
PERHAPS. BUT ONLY IF YOU TAKE MY FORFEIT WHEN YOU LOSE.
AND THAT IS?
IF I WIN, I GET TO KNOCK YOUR BRAINS OUT. WITH THE SLEDGEHAMMER.
THIS IS GETTING RIDICULOUS. I WAS WRONG TO COME HERE. SHADOW, WE'RE LEAVING.

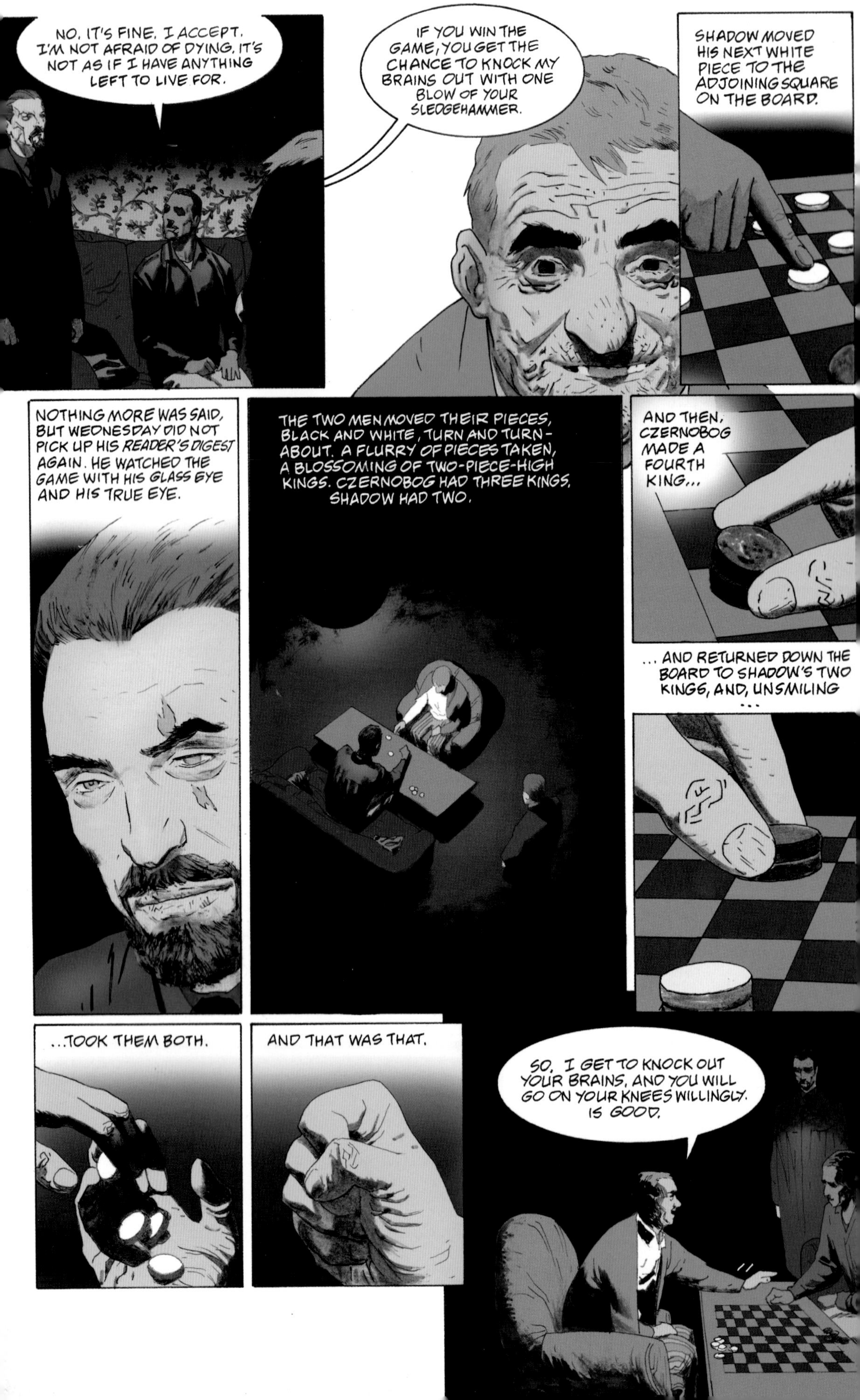
NO. IT'S FINE. I ACCEPT. I'M NOT AFRAID OF DYING. IT'S NOT AS IF I HAVE ANYTHING LEFT TO LIVE FOR.
IF YOU WIN THE GAME, YOU GET THE CHANCE TO KNOCK MY BRAINS OUT WITH ONE BLOW OF YOUR SLEDGEHAMMER.
SHADOW MOVED HIS NEXT WHITE PIECE TO THE ADJOINING SQUARE ON THE BOARD.
NOTHING MORE WAS SAID, BUT WEDNESDAY DID NOT PICK UP HIS *READER'S DIGEST* AGAIN. HE WATCHED THE GAME WITH HIS GLASS EYE AND HIS TRUE EYE.
THE TWO MEN MOVED THEIR PIECES, BLACK AND WHITE, TURN AND TURN-ABOUT. A FLURRY OF PIECES TAKEN, A BLOSSOMING OF TWO-PIECE-HIGH KINGS. CZERNOBOG HAD THREE KINGS, SHADOW HAD TWO.
AND THEN, CZERNOBOG MADE A FOURTH KING...
... AND RETURNED DOWN THE BOARD TO SHADOW'S TWO KINGS, AND, UNSMILING ...
...TOOK THEM BOTH.
AND THAT WAS THAT.
SO, I GET TO KNOCK OUT YOUR BRAINS, AND YOU WILL GO ON YOUR KNEES WILLINGLY. IS *GOOD*.

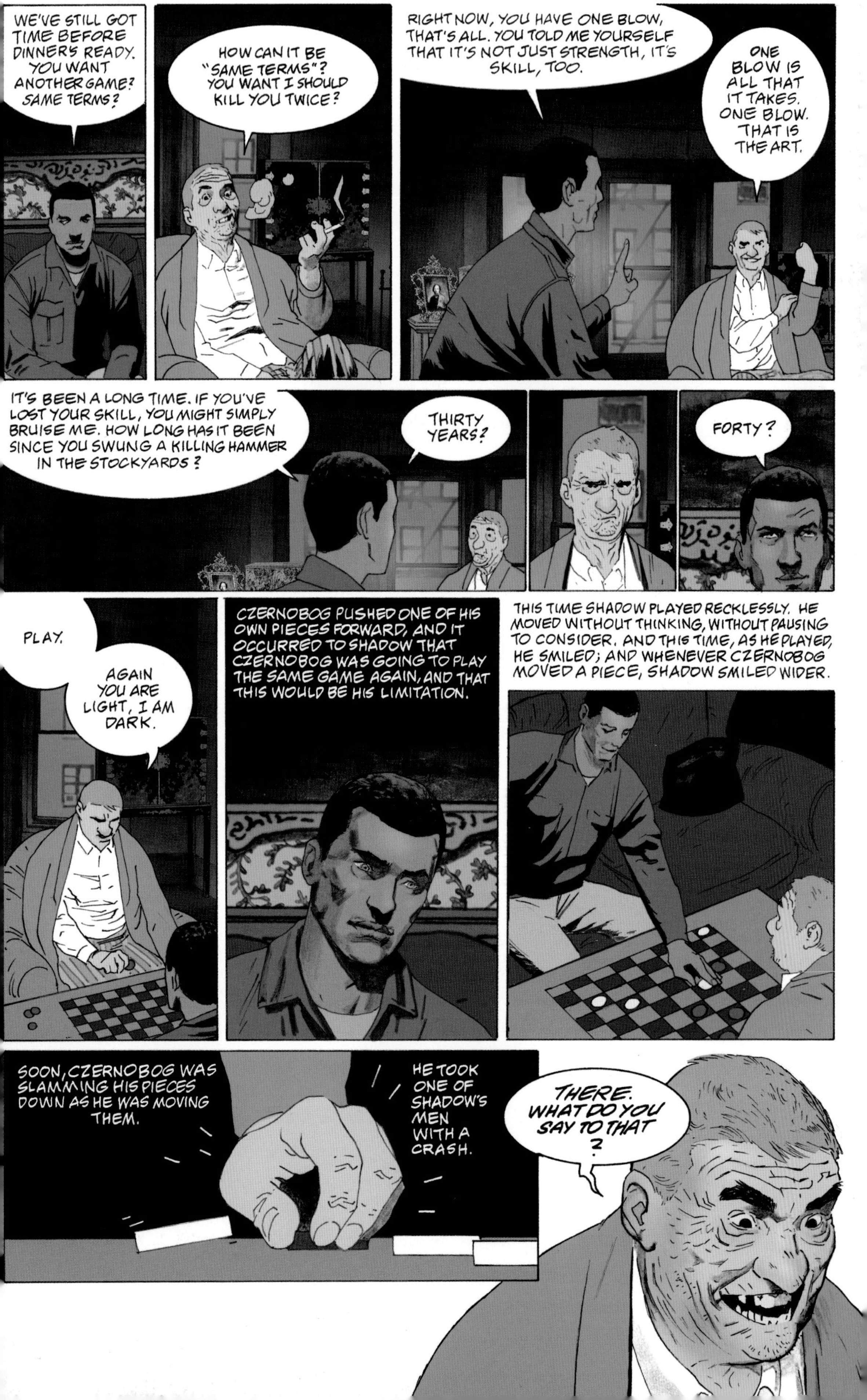
WE'VE STILL GOT TIME BEFORE DINNER'S READY. YOU WANT ANOTHER GAME? SAME TERMS?
HOW CAN IT BE "SAME TERMS"? YOU WANT I SHOULD KILL YOU TWICE?
RIGHT NOW, YOU HAVE ONE BLOW, THAT'S ALL. YOU TOLD ME YOURSELF THAT IT'S NOT JUST STRENGTH, IT'S SKILL, TOO.
ONE BLOW IS ALL THAT IT TAKES. ONE BLOW. THAT IS THE ART.
IT'S BEEN A LONG TIME. IF YOU'VE LOST YOUR SKILL, YOU MIGHT SIMPLY BRUISE ME. HOW LONG HAS IT BEEN SINCE YOU SWUNG A KILLING HAMMER IN THE STOCKYARDS?
THIRTY YEARS?
FORTY?
PLAY.
AGAIN YOU ARE LIGHT, I AM DARK.
CZERNOBOG PUSHED ONE OF HIS OWN PIECES FORWARD, AND IT OCCURRED TO SHADOW THAT CZERNOBOG WAS GOING TO PLAY THE SAME GAME AGAIN, AND THAT THIS WOULD BE HIS LIMITATION.
THIS TIME SHADOW PLAYED RECKLESSLY. HE MOVED WITHOUT THINKING, WITHOUT PAUSING TO CONSIDER. AND THIS TIME, AS HE PLAYED, HE SMILED; AND WHENEVER CZERNOBOG MOVED A PIECE, SHADOW SMILED WIDER.
SOON, CZERNOBOG WAS SLAMMING HIS PIECES DOWN AS HE WAS MOVING THEM.
HE TOOK ONE OF SHADOW'S MEN WITH A CRASH.
THERE. WHAT DO YOU SAY TO THAT?

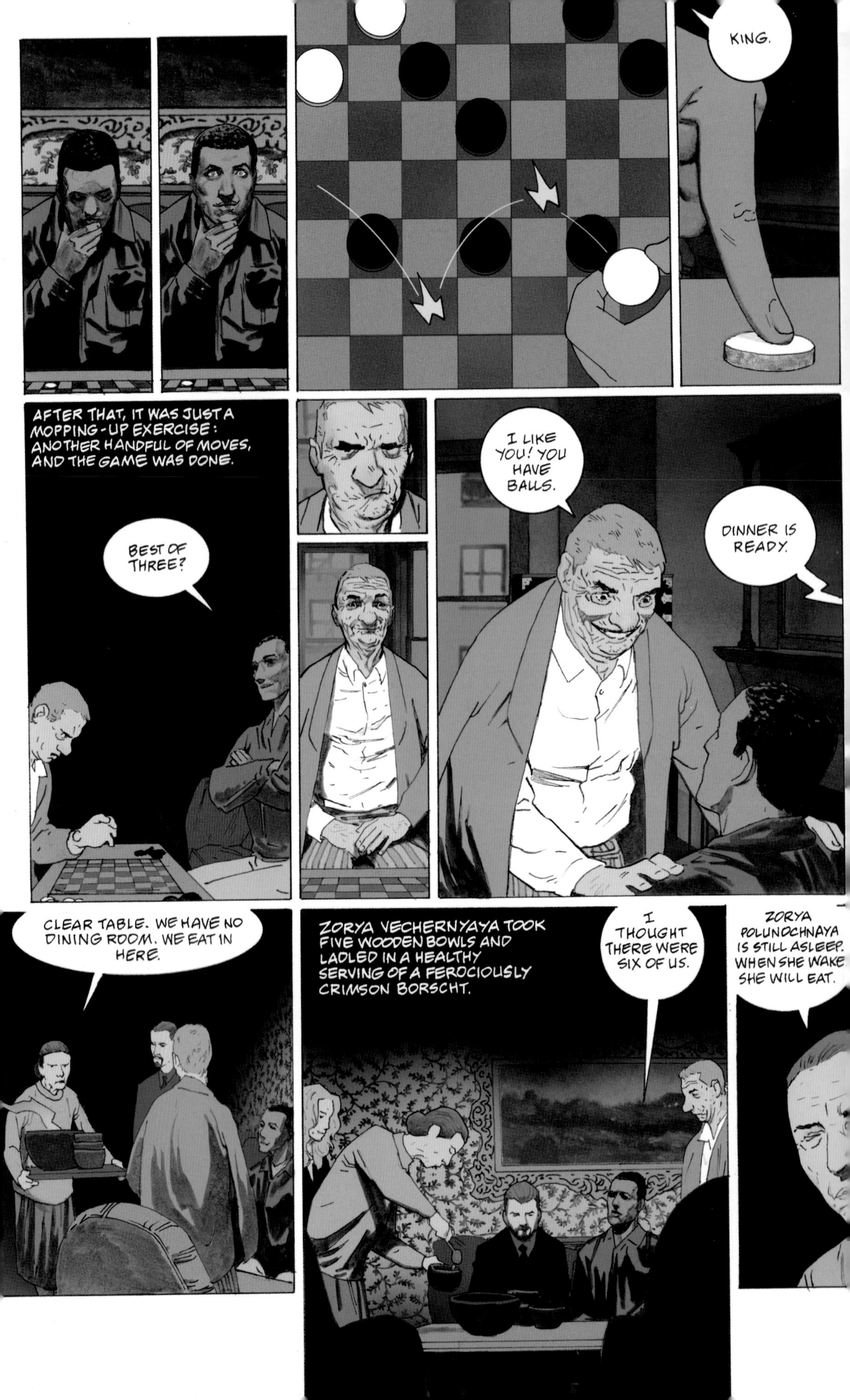
KING.
AFTER THAT, IT WAS JUST A MOPPING-UP EXERCISE: ANOTHER HANDFUL OF MOVES, AND THE GAME WAS DONE.
BEST OF THREE?
I LIKE YOU! YOU HAVE BALLS.
DINNER IS READY.
CLEAR TABLE. WE HAVE NO DINING ROOM. WE EAT IN HERE.
ZORYA VECHERNYAYA TOOK FIVE WOODEN BOWLS AND LADLED IN A HEALTHY SERVING OF A FEROCIOUSLY CRIMSON BORSCHT.
I THOUGHT THERE WERE SIX OF US.
ZORYA POLUNOCHNAYA IS STILL ASLEEP. WHEN SHE WAKE SHE WILL EAT.

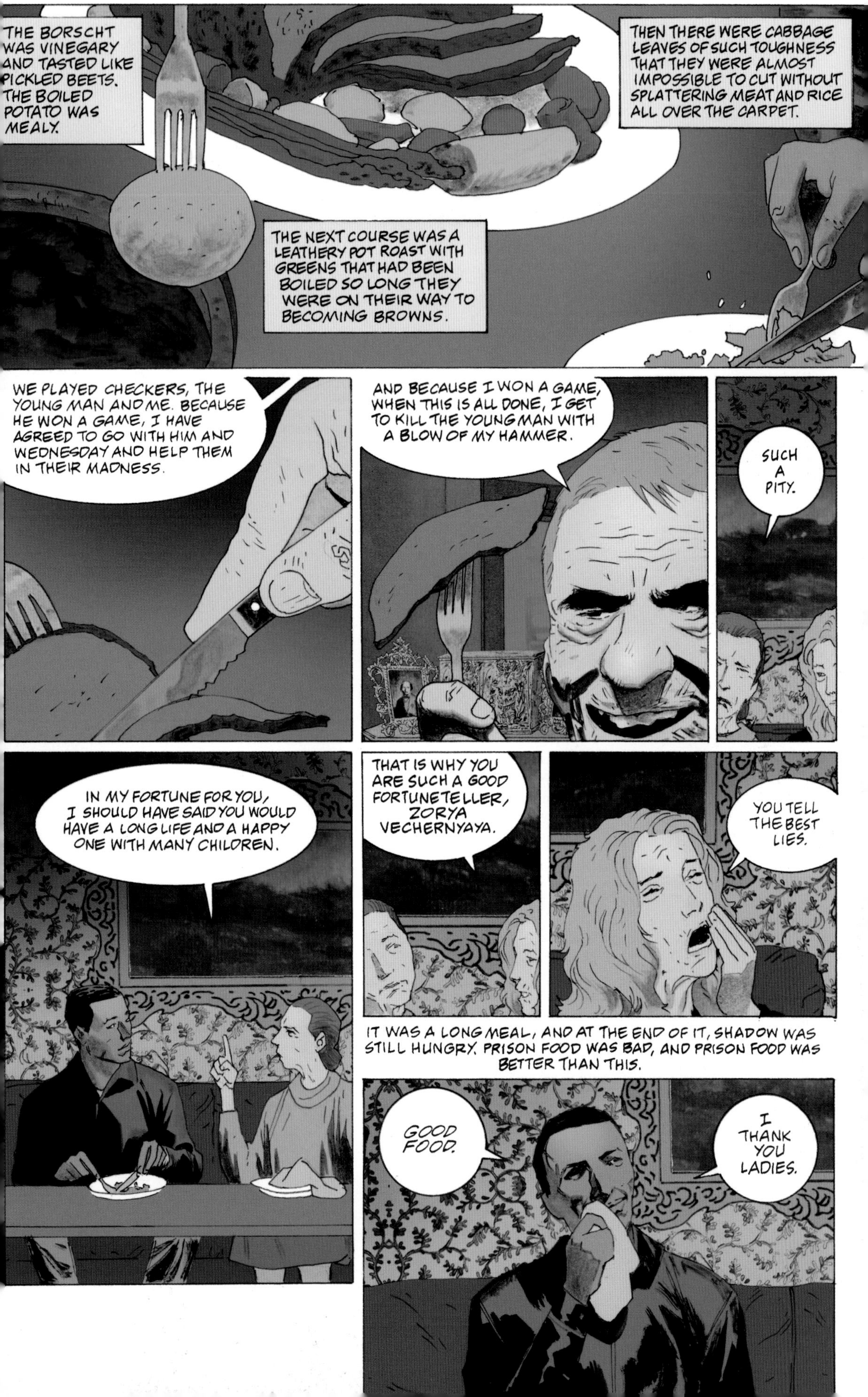
THE BORSCHT WAS VINEGARY AND TASTED LIKE PICKLED BEETS. THE BOILED POTATO WAS MEALY.
THEN THERE WERE CABBAGE LEAVES OF SUCH TOUGHNESS THAT THEY WERE ALMOST IMPOSSIBLE TO CUT WITHOUT SPLATTERING MEAT AND RICE ALL OVER THE CARPET.
THE NEXT COURSE WAS A LEATHERY POT ROAST WITH GREENS THAT HAD BEEN BOILED SO LONG THEY WERE ON THEIR WAY TO BECOMING BROWNS.
WE PLAYED CHECKERS, THE YOUNG MAN AND ME. BECAUSE HE WON A GAME, I HAVE AGREED TO GO WITH HIM AND WEDNESDAY AND HELP THEM IN THEIR MADNESS.
AND BECAUSE I WON A GAME, WHEN THIS IS ALL DONE, I GET TO KILL THE YOUNG MAN WITH A BLOW OF MY HAMMER.
SUCH A PITY.
IN MY FORTUNE FOR YOU, I SHOULD HAVE SAID YOU WOULD HAVE A LONG LIFE AND A HAPPY ONE WITH MANY CHILDREN.
THAT IS WHY YOU ARE SUCH A GOOD FORTUNETELLER, ZORYA VECHERNYAYA.
YOU TELL THE BEST LIES.
IT WAS A LONG MEAL, AND AT THE END OF IT, SHADOW WAS STILL HUNGRY. PRISON FOOD WAS BAD, AND PRISON FOOD WAS BETTER THAN THIS.
GOOD FOOD.
I THANK YOU LADIES.

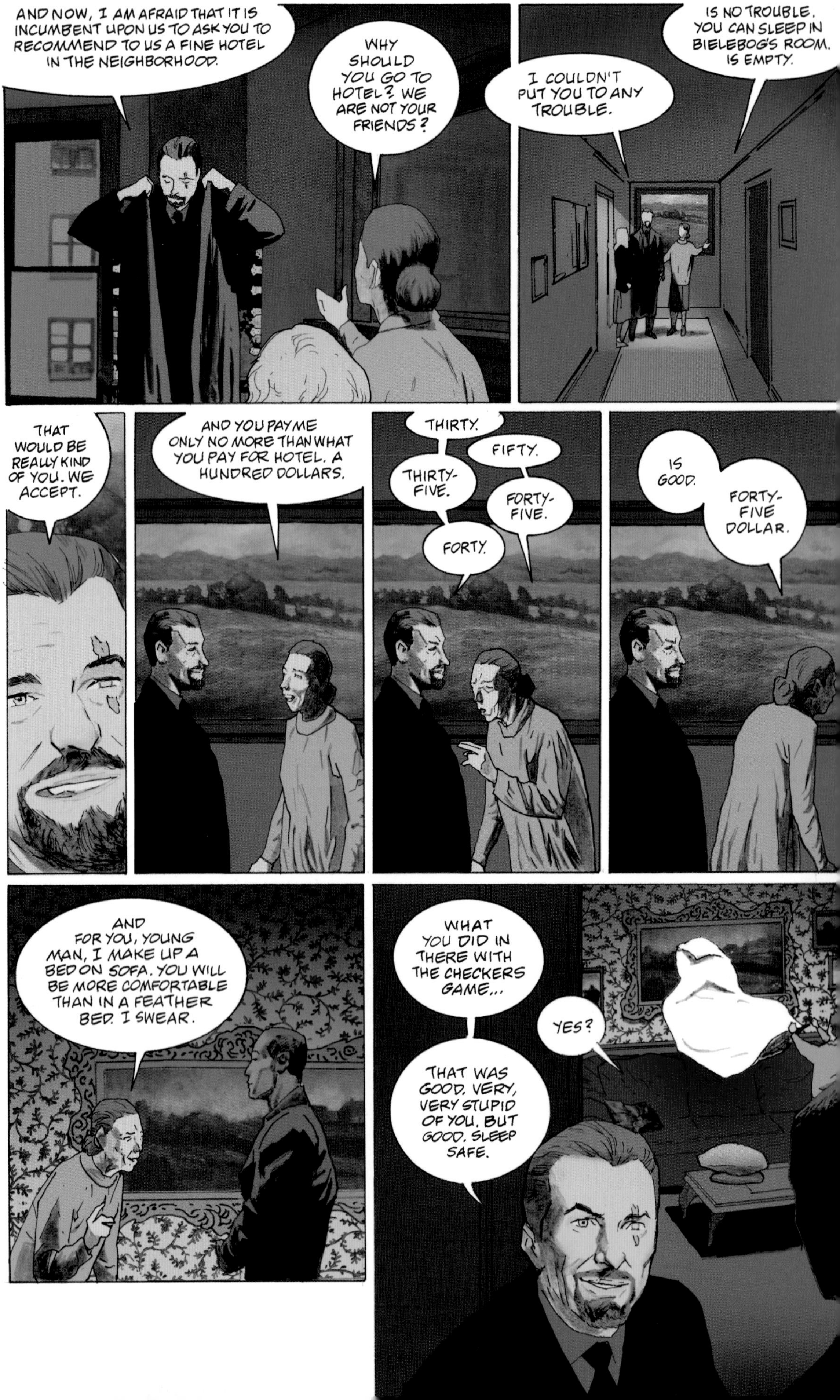
AND NOW, I AM AFRAID THAT IT IS INCUMBENT UPON US TO ASK YOU TO RECOMMEND TO US A FINE HOTEL IN THE NEIGHBORHOOD.
WHY SHOULD YOU GO TO HOTEL? WE ARE NOT YOUR FRIENDS?
I COULDN'T PUT YOU TO ANY TROUBLE.
IS NO TROUBLE. YOU CAN SLEEP IN BIELEBOG'S ROOM. IS EMPTY.
THAT WOULD BE REALLY KIND OF YOU. WE ACCEPT.
AND YOU PAY ME ONLY NO MORE THAN WHAT YOU PAY FOR HOTEL. A HUNDRED DOLLARS.
THIRTY.
FIFTY.
THIRTY-FIVE.
FORTY-FIVE.
FORTY.
IS GOOD.
FORTY-FIVE DOLLAR.
AND FOR YOU, YOUNG MAN, I MAKE UP A BED ON SOFA. YOU WILL BE MORE COMFORTABLE THAN IN A FEATHER BED. I SWEAR.
WHAT YOU DID IN THERE WITH THE CHECKERS GAME...
YES?
THAT WAS GOOD. VERY, VERY STUPID OF YOU. BUT GOOD. SLEEP SAFE.

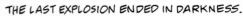THE LAST EXPLOSION ENDED IN DARKNESS.

THERE WERE EXPLOSIONS IN SHADOW'S DREAM: HE WAS RUNNING THROUGH A MINEFIELD. HE FELT WARM BLOOD RUNNING DOWN HIS FACE. SOMEONE WAS SHOOTING AT HIM.

I MUST BE DREAMING. I THINK I JUST DIED.

LAURA?

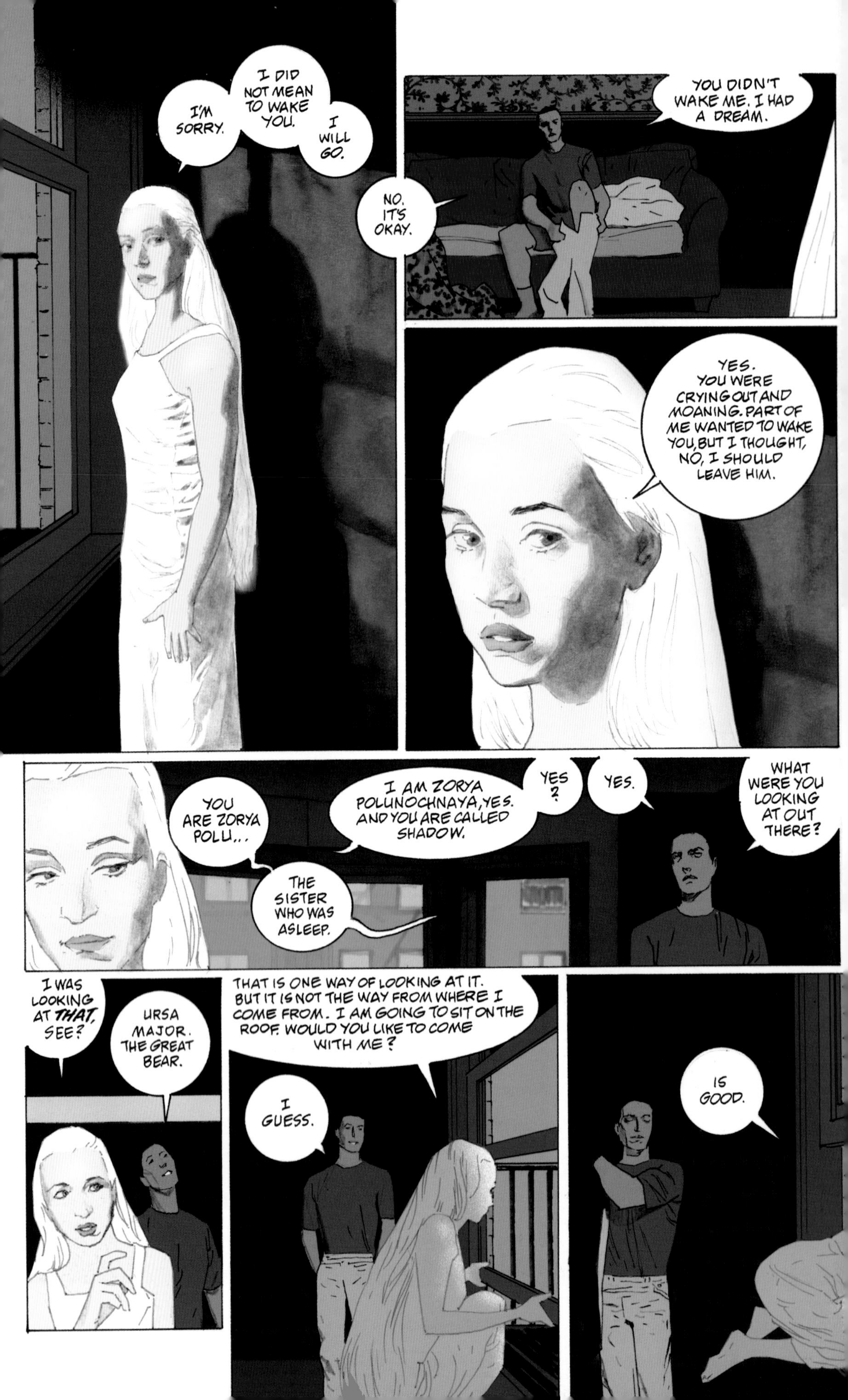
I'M SORRY.
I DID NOT MEAN TO WAKE YOU.
I WILL GO.
NO. IT'S OKAY.
YOU DIDN'T WAKE ME. I HAD A DREAM.
YES. YOU WERE CRYING OUT AND MOANING. PART OF ME WANTED TO WAKE YOU, BUT I THOUGHT, NO, I SHOULD LEAVE HIM.
YOU ARE ZORYA POLU...
THE SISTER WHO WAS ASLEEP.
I AM ZORYA POLUNOCHNAYA, YES. AND YOU ARE CALLED SHADOW.
YES?
YES.
WHAT WERE YOU LOOKING AT OUT THERE?
I WAS LOOKING AT THAT, SEE?
URSA MAJOR. THE GREAT BEAR.
THAT IS ONE WAY OF LOOKING AT IT. BUT IT IS NOT THE WAY FROM WHERE I COME FROM. I AM GOING TO SIT ON THE ROOF. WOULD YOU LIKE TO COME WITH ME?
I GUESS.
IS GOOD.

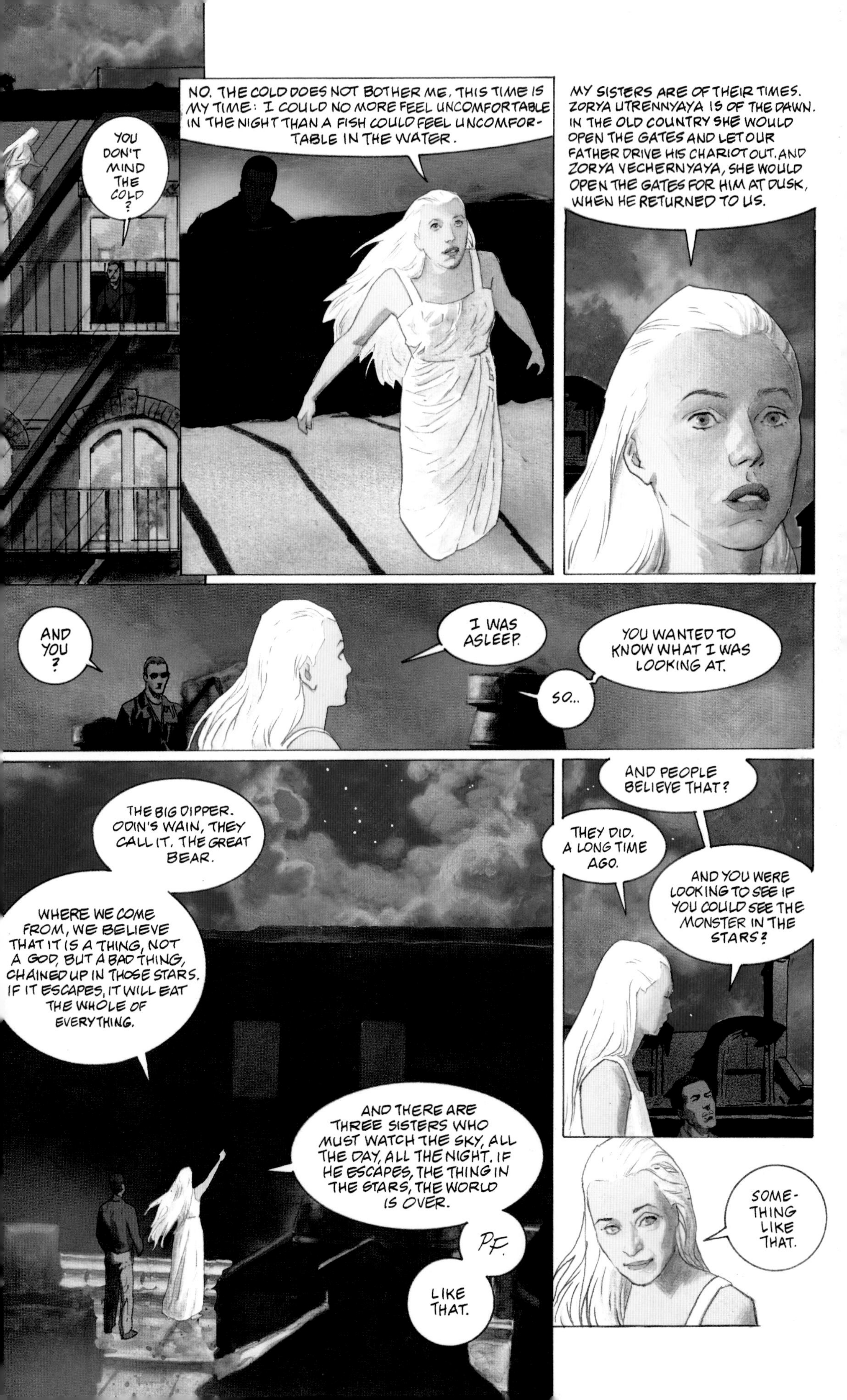

YOU DON'T MIND THE COLD?
NO. THE COLD DOES NOT BOTHER ME. THIS TIME IS MY TIME: I COULD NO MORE FEEL UNCOMFORTABLE IN THE NIGHT THAN A FISH COULD FEEL UNCOMFORTABLE IN THE WATER.
MY SISTERS ARE OF THEIR TIMES. ZORYA UTRENNYAYA IS OF THE DAWN. IN THE OLD COUNTRY SHE WOULD OPEN THE GATES AND LET OUR FATHER DRIVE HIS CHARIOT OUT. AND ZORYA VECHERNYAYA, SHE WOULD OPEN THE GATES FOR HIM AT DUSK, WHEN HE RETURNED TO US.
AND YOU?
I WAS ASLEEP.
SO...
YOU WANTED TO KNOW WHAT I WAS LOOKING AT.
THE BIG DIPPER. ODIN'S WAIN, THEY CALL IT. THE GREAT BEAR.
WHERE WE COME FROM, WE BELIEVE THAT IT IS A THING, NOT A GOD, BUT A BAD THING, CHAINED UP IN THOSE STARS. IF IT ESCAPES, IT WILL EAT THE WHOLE OF EVERYTHING.
AND THERE ARE THREE SISTERS WHO MUST WATCH THE SKY, ALL THE DAY, ALL THE NIGHT. IF HE ESCAPES, THE THING IN THE STARS, THE WORLD IS OVER.
LIKE THAT.
AND PEOPLE BELIEVE THAT?
THEY DID. A LONG TIME AGO.
AND YOU WERE LOOKING TO SEE IF YOU COULD SEE THE MONSTER IN THE STARS?
SOME-THING LIKE THAT.

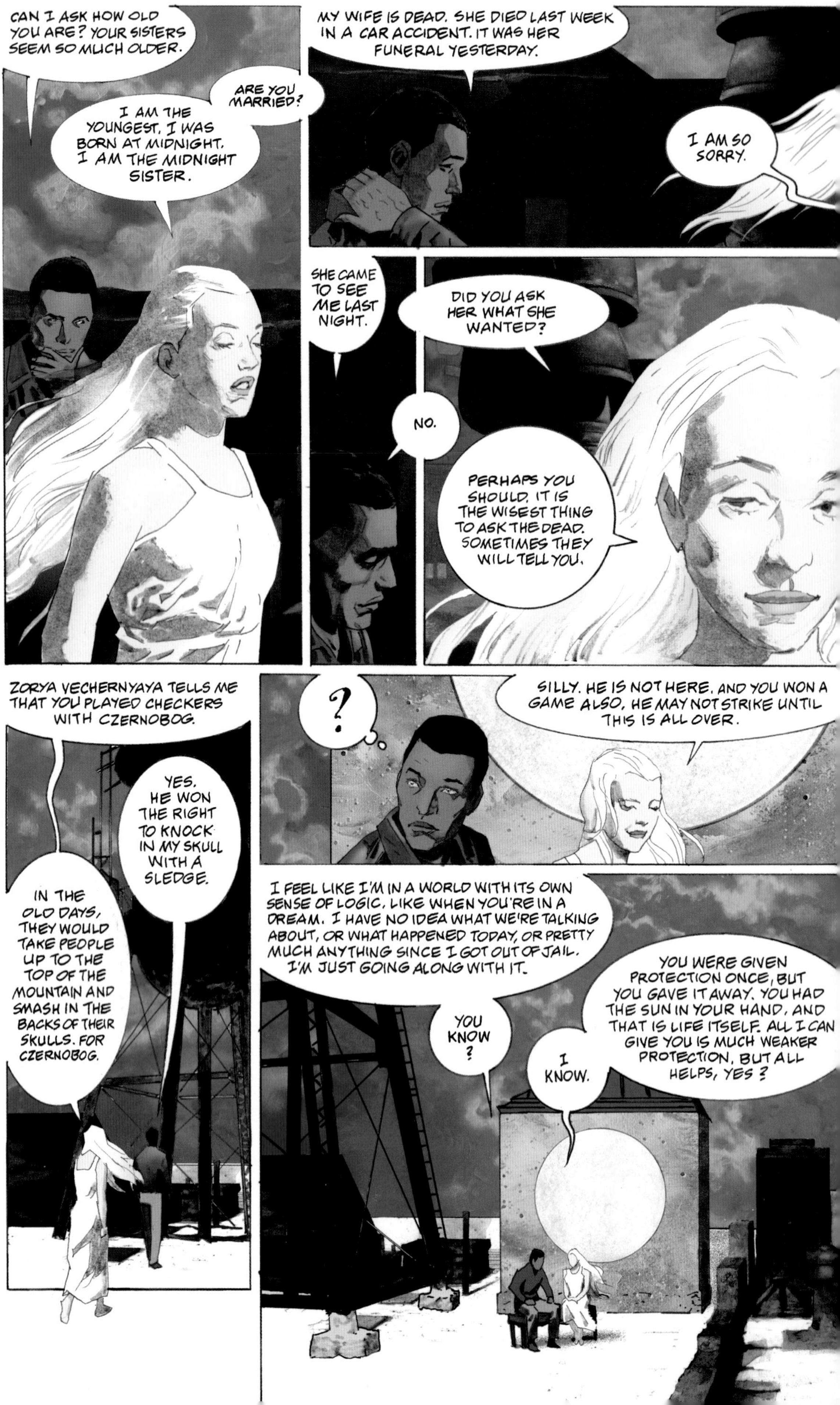
CAN I ASK HOW OLD YOU ARE? YOUR SISTERS SEEM SO MUCH OLDER.
I AM THE YOUNGEST. I WAS BORN AT MIDNIGHT. I AM THE MIDNIGHT SISTER.
ARE YOU MARRIED?
MY WIFE IS DEAD. SHE DIED LAST WEEK IN A CAR ACCIDENT. IT WAS HER FUNERAL YESTERDAY.
I AM SO SORRY.
SHE CAME TO SEE ME LAST NIGHT.
DID YOU ASK HER WHAT SHE WANTED?
NO.
PERHAPS YOU SHOULD. IT IS THE WISEST THING TO ASK THE DEAD. SOMETIMES THEY WILL TELL YOU.
ZORYA VECHERNYAYA TELLS ME THAT YOU PLAYED CHECKERS WITH CZERNOBOG.
YES. HE WON THE RIGHT TO KNOCK IN MY SKULL WITH A SLEDGE.
IN THE OLD DAYS, THEY WOULD TAKE PEOPLE UP TO THE TOP OF THE MOUNTAIN AND SMASH IN THE BACKS OF THEIR SKULLS. FOR CZERNOBOG.
?
SILLY. HE IS NOT HERE. AND YOU WON A GAME ALSO. HE MAY NOT STRIKE UNTIL THIS IS ALL OVER.
I FEEL LIKE I'M IN A WORLD WITH ITS OWN SENSE OF LOGIC. LIKE WHEN YOU'RE IN A DREAM. I HAVE NO IDEA WHAT WE'RE TALKING ABOUT, OR WHAT HAPPENED TODAY, OR PRETTY MUCH ANYTHING SINCE I GOT OUT OF JAIL. I'M JUST GOING ALONG WITH IT.
I KNOW.
YOU KNOW?
YOU WERE GIVEN PROTECTION ONCE, BUT YOU GAVE IT AWAY. YOU HAD THE SUN IN YOUR HAND. AND THAT IS LIFE ITSELF. ALL I CAN GIVE YOU IS MUCH WEAKER PROTECTION, BUT ALL HELPS, YES?

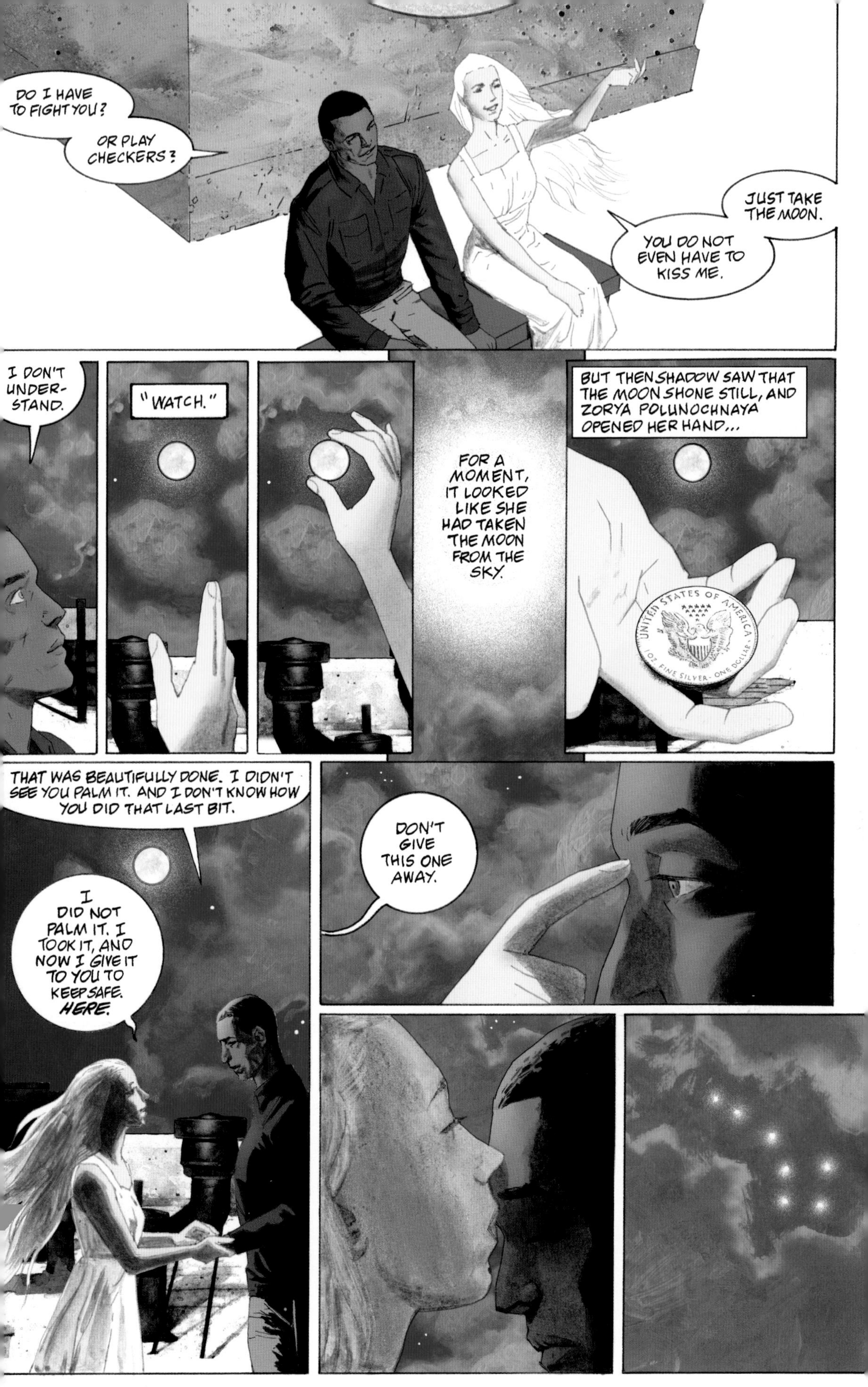
DO I HAVE TO FIGHT YOU?
OR PLAY CHECKERS?
JUST TAKE THE MOON.
YOU DO NOT EVEN HAVE TO KISS ME.
I DON'T UNDER-STAND.
"WATCH."
FOR A MOMENT, IT LOOKED LIKE SHE HAD TAKEN THE MOON FROM THE SKY.
BUT THEN SHADOW SAW THAT THE MOON SHONE STILL, AND ZORYA POLUNOCHNAYA OPENED HER HAND...
UNITED STATES OF AMERICA
1 OZ. FINE SILVER - ONE DOLLAR
THAT WAS BEAUTIFULLY DONE. I DIDN'T SEE YOU PALM IT. AND I DON'T KNOW HOW YOU DID THAT LAST BIT.
I DID NOT PALM IT. I TOOK IT, AND NOW I GIVE IT TO YOU TO KEEP SAFE. *HERE.*
DON'T GIVE THIS ONE AWAY.

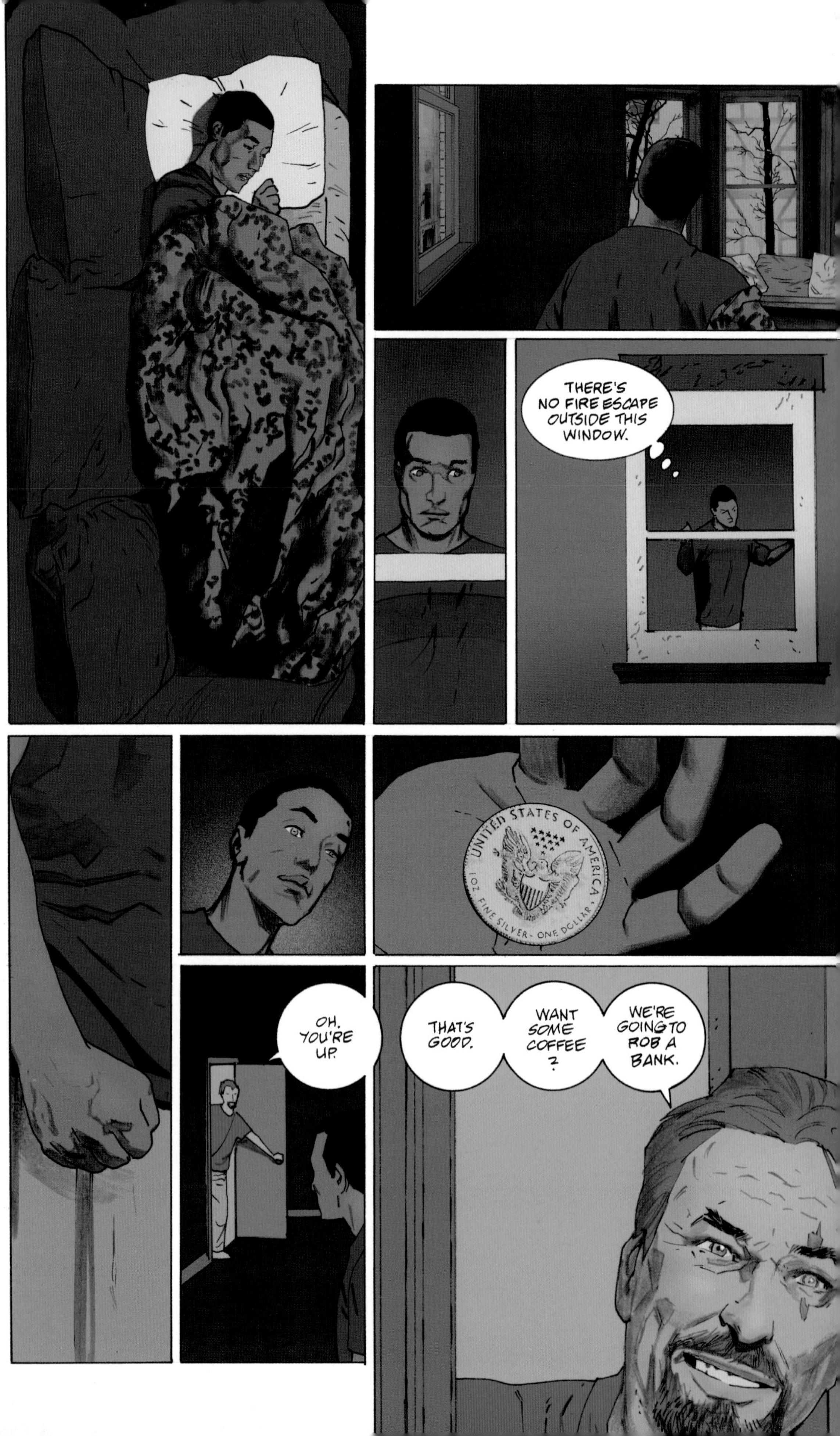
THERE'S NO FIRE ESCAPE OUTSIDE THIS WINDOW.
UNITED STATES OF AMERICA
1 OZ. FINE SILVER - ONE DOLLAR
OH. YOU'RE UP.
THAT'S GOOD.
WANT SOME COFFEE ?
WE'RE GOING TO ROB A BANK.

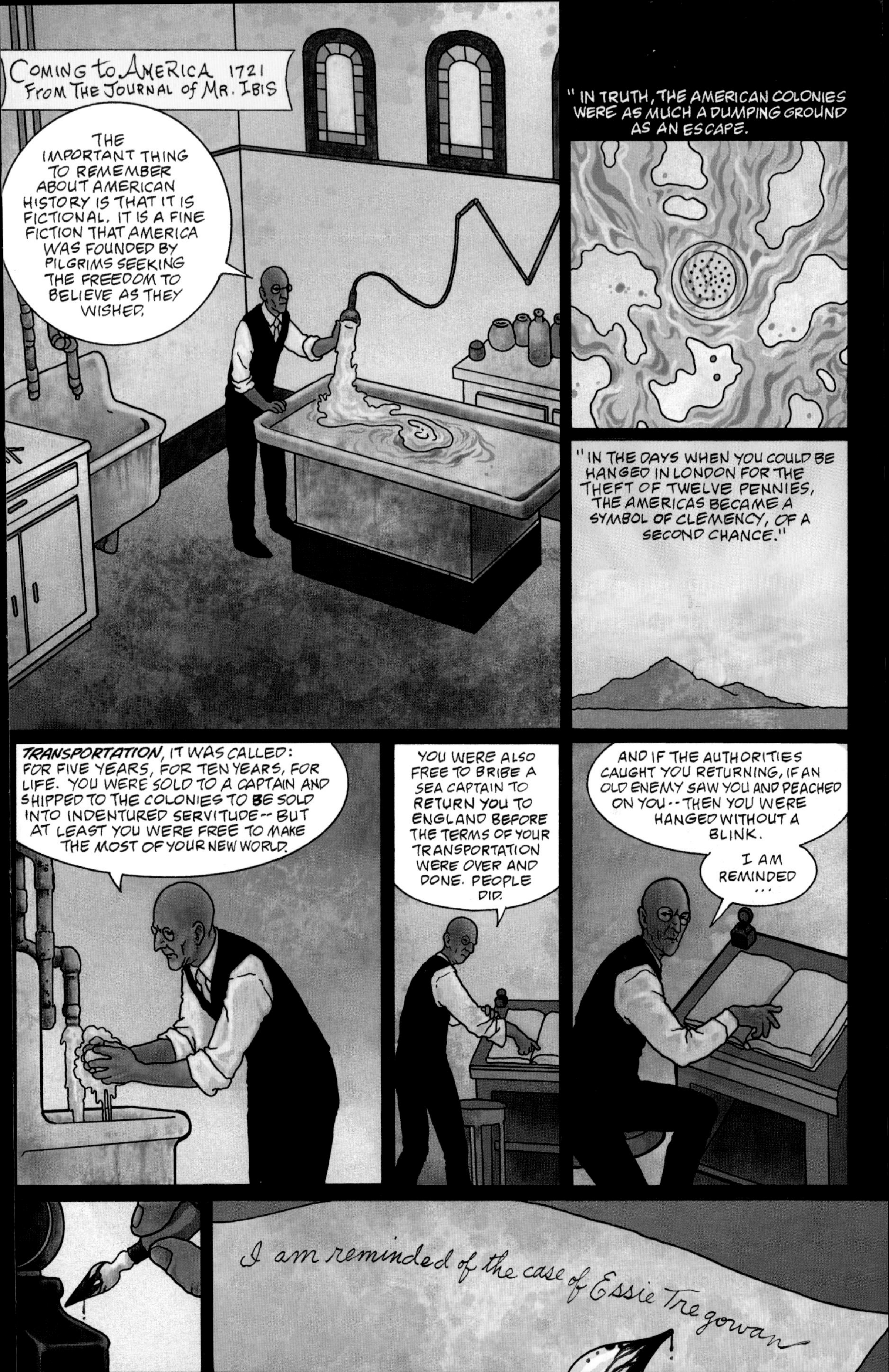
Coming to America 1721 From The Journal of Mr. Ibis
THE IMPORTANT THING TO REMEMBER ABOUT AMERICAN HISTORY IS THAT IT IS FICTIONAL. IT IS A FINE FICTION THAT AMERICA WAS FOUNDED BY PILGRIMS SEEKING THE FREEDOM TO BELIEVE AS THEY WISHED.
"IN TRUTH, THE AMERICAN COLONIES WERE AS MUCH A DUMPING GROUND AS AN ESCAPE.
"IN THE DAYS WHEN YOU COULD BE HANGED IN LONDON FOR THE THEFT OF TWELVE PENNIES, THE AMERICAS BECAME A SYMBOL OF CLEMENCY, OF A SECOND CHANCE."
TRANSPORTATION, IT WAS CALLED: FOR FIVE YEARS, FOR TEN YEARS, FOR LIFE. YOU WERE SOLD TO A CAPTAIN AND SHIPPED TO THE COLONIES TO BE SOLD INTO INDENTURED SERVITUDE-- BUT AT LEAST YOU WERE FREE TO MAKE THE MOST OF YOUR NEW WORLD.
YOU WERE ALSO FREE TO BRIBE A SEA CAPTAIN TO RETURN YOU TO ENGLAND BEFORE THE TERMS OF YOUR TRANSPORTATION WERE OVER AND DONE. PEOPLE DID.
AND IF THE AUTHORITIES CAUGHT YOU RETURNING, IF AN OLD ENEMY SAW YOU AND PEACHED ON YOU -- THEN YOU WERE HANGED WITHOUT A BLINK.
I AM REMINDED ...
I am reminded of the case of Essie Tregowan

ESSIE CAME FROM A LITTLE CLIFFTOP VILLAGE IN CORNWALL, IN THE SOUTHWEST OF ENGLAND, WHERE HER FAMILY HAD LIVED FROM TIME OUT OF MIND. HER FATHER WAS A FISHERMAN AND HER MOTHER A COOK AT THE SQUIRE'S HOUSE.

AT THE AGE OF TWELVE, ESSIE BEGAN TO WORK THERE ALSO, IN THE SCULLERY.

SHE WAS A THIN LITTLE THING WHO WAS FOREVER SLIPPING OFF TO LISTEN TO STORIES AND TALES IF ANYONE WAS TELLING THEM.

TALES OF THE PISKIES AND THE SPRIGGANS AND THE BLACK DOGS OF THE MOORS. AND, THOUGH THE SQUIRE LAUGHED AT SUCH THINGS, THE KITCHEN FOLK ALWAYS PUT OUT A SAUCER OF THE CREAMIEST MILK AT NIGHT, PUT IT OUTSIDE THE KITCHEN DOOR...

...FOR THE PISKIES.

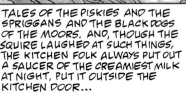

YEARS PASSED AND ESSIE WAS NO LONGER A THIN LITTLE THING WHEN HER EYES LIGHTED ON BARTHOLOMEW, THE SQUIRE'S EIGHTEEN-YEAR-OLD SON, HOME FROM RUGBY.

AND THAT NIGHT, SHE WENT TO THE STANDING STONE AT THE EDGE OF THE WOODLAND, AND SHE PUT SOME BREAD THAT BARTHOLOMEW HAD LEFT UNEATEN ON THE STONE, WRAPPED IN A CUT STRAND OF HER OWN HAIR.

AND ON THE VERY NEXT DAY, BARTHOLOMEW LOOKED ON HER APPROVINGLY WITH HIS OWN EYES. THE DANGEROUS BLUE OF A SKY WHEN A STORM IS COMING.

HE HAD SUCH DANGEROUS EYES, SAID ESSIE TREGOWAN.

SOON ENOUGH, BARTHOLOMEW WENT UP TO OXFORD, AND WHEN ESSIE'S CONDITION BECAME APPARENT, SHE WAS DISMISSED.

AS A FAVOR TO ESSIE'S MOTHER, WHO WAS A VERY FINE COOK, THE SQUIRE'S WIFE PREVAILED UPON HER HUSBAND TO RETURN THE FORMER MAIDEN TO THE SCULLERY.

WITHIN THE YEAR, SHE TOOK FOR HER NEW BEAU A MAN FROM A NEIGHBORING VILLAGE, WITH A BAD REPUTATION, WHO WENT BY THE NAME OF JOSIAH HORNER.

BUT THE BABE WAS STILL-BORN.

AND ONE NIGHT, WHEN THE FAMILY SLEPT, ESSIE UNBOLTED THE SIDE DOOR, TO LET HER LOVER IN. HE RIFLED THE HOUSE WHILE THE FAMILY SLEPT ON. SUSPICION IMMEDIATELY FELL ON SOMEONE IN THE HOUSE.

ESSIE, BY DENYING EVERYTHING, WAS CONVICTED OF NOTHING UNTIL JOSIAH HORNER WAS CAUGHT PASSING ONE OF THE SQUIRE'S NOTES, AND HE AND ESSIE WENT TO TRIAL.

HORNER WAS CONVICTED AND *TURNED OFF.*

BUT THE JUDGE TOOK PITY ON ESSIE AND HE SENTENCED HER TO SEVEN YEARS' TRANSPORTATION. SHE WAS TO BE TRANSPORTED ON A SHIP UNDER THE COMMAND OF ONE CAPTAIN CLARKE.

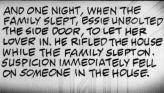

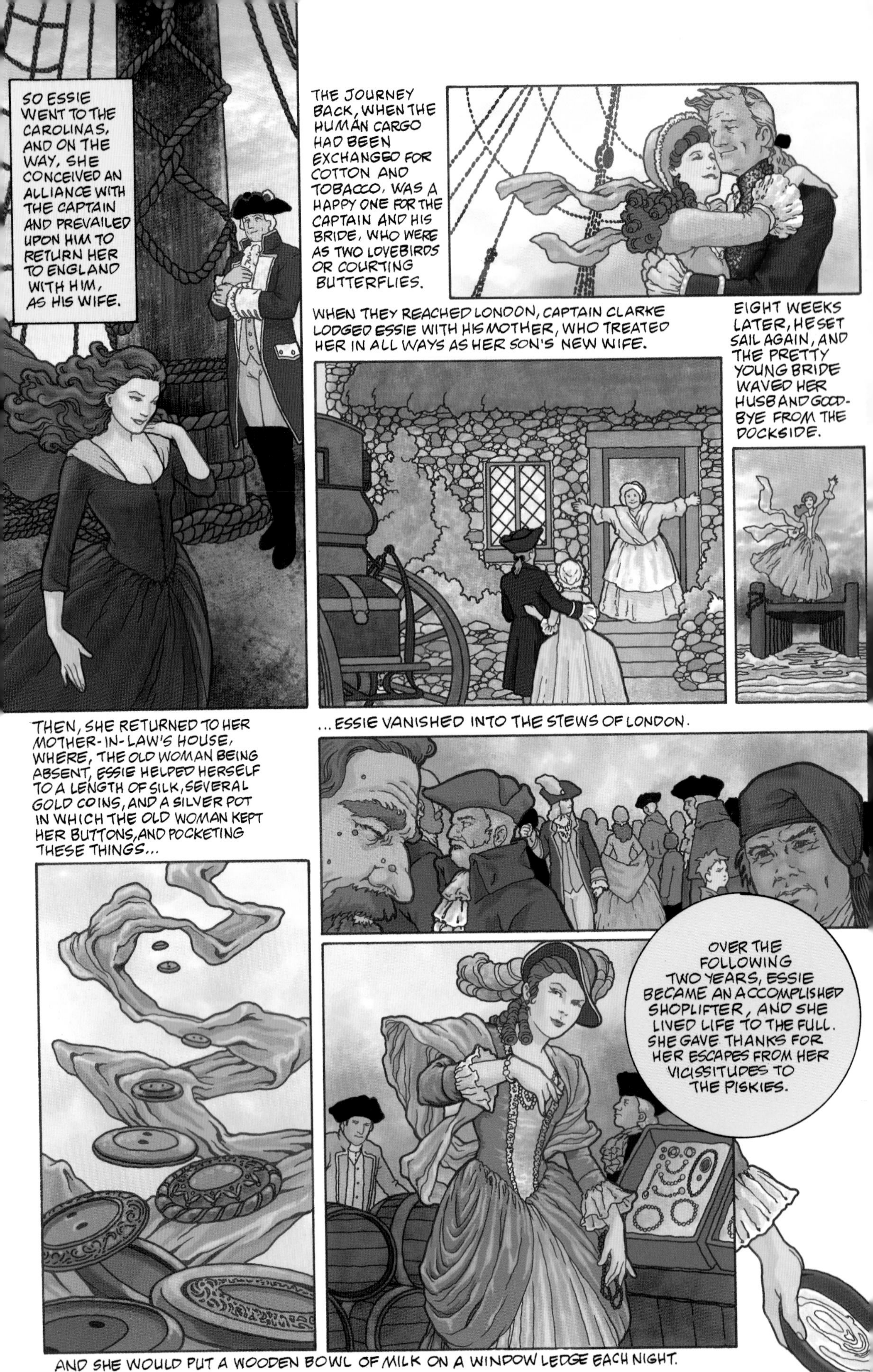
SO ESSIE WENT TO THE CAROLINAS, AND ON THE WAY, SHE CONCEIVED AN ALLIANCE WITH THE CAPTAIN AND PREVAILED UPON HIM TO RETURN HER TO ENGLAND WITH HIM, AS HIS WIFE.
THE JOURNEY BACK, WHEN THE HUMAN CARGO HAD BEEN EXCHANGED FOR COTTON AND TOBACCO, WAS A HAPPY ONE FOR THE CAPTAIN AND HIS BRIDE, WHO WERE AS TWO LOVEBIRDS OR COURTING BUTTERFLIES.
WHEN THEY REACHED LONDON, CAPTAIN CLARKE LODGED ESSIE WITH HIS MOTHER, WHO TREATED HER IN ALL WAYS AS HER SON'S NEW WIFE.
EIGHT WEEKS LATER, HE SET SAIL AGAIN, AND THE PRETTY YOUNG BRIDE WAVED HER HUSBAND GOOD-BYE FROM THE DOCKSIDE.
THEN, SHE RETURNED TO HER MOTHER-IN-LAW'S HOUSE, WHERE, THE OLD WOMAN BEING ABSENT, ESSIE HELPED HERSELF TO A LENGTH OF SILK, SEVERAL GOLD COINS, AND A SILVER POT IN WHICH THE OLD WOMAN KEPT HER BUTTONS, AND POCKETING THESE THINGS...
...ESSIE VANISHED INTO THE STEWS OF LONDON.
OVER THE FOLLOWING TWO YEARS, ESSIE BECAME AN ACCOMPLISHED SHOPLIFTER, AND SHE LIVED LIFE TO THE FULL. SHE GAVE THANKS FOR HER ESCAPES FROM HER VICISSITUDES TO THE PISKIES.
AND SHE WOULD PUT A WOODEN BOWL OF MILK ON A WINDOW LEDGE EACH NIGHT.

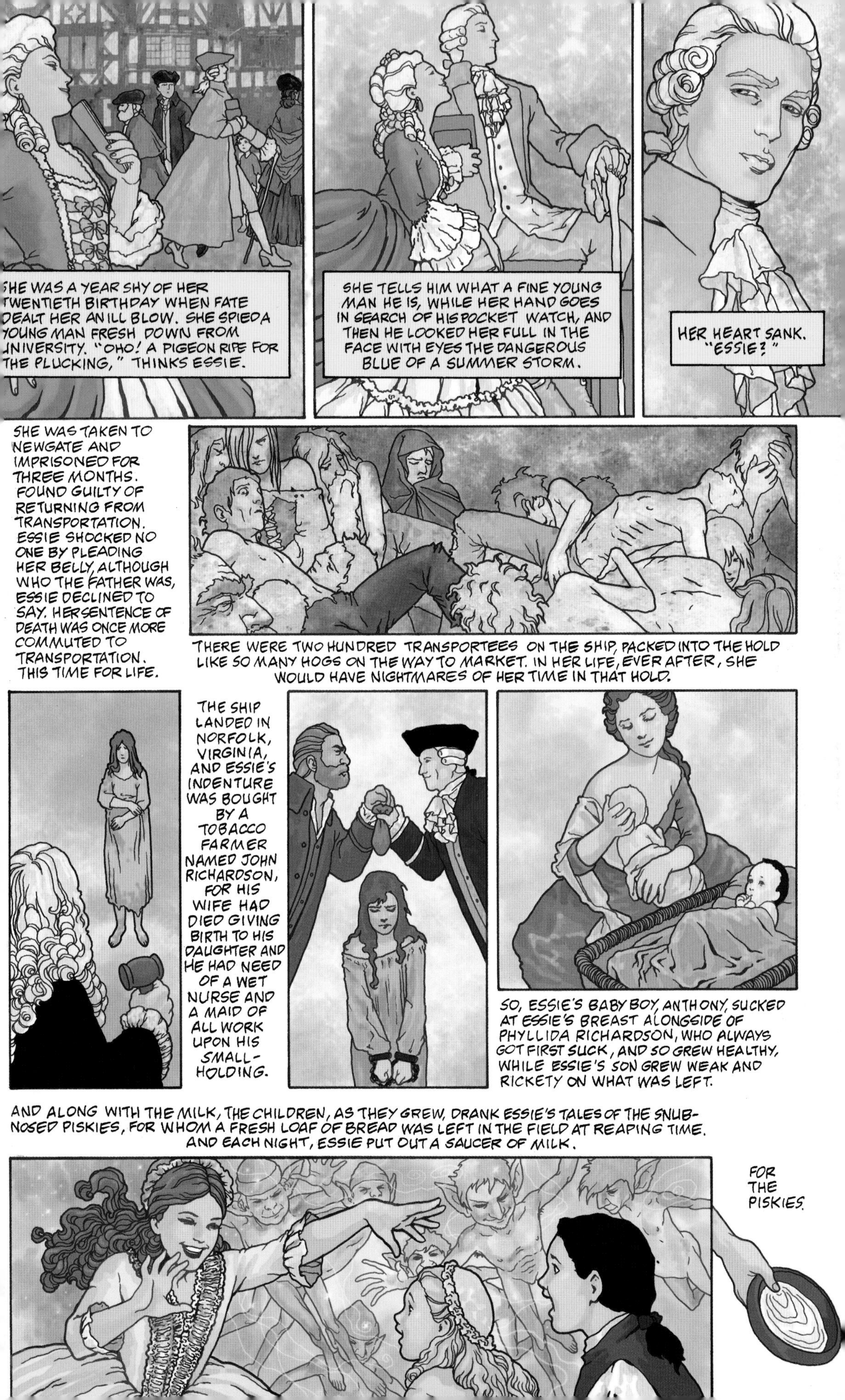
SHE WAS A YEAR SHY OF HER TWENTIETH BIRTHDAY WHEN FATE DEALT HER AN ILL BLOW. SHE SPIED A YOUNG MAN FRESH DOWN FROM UNIVERSITY. "OHO! A PIGEON RIPE FOR THE PLUCKING," THINKS ESSIE.
SHE TELLS HIM WHAT A FINE YOUNG MAN HE IS, WHILE HER HAND GOES IN SEARCH OF HIS POCKET WATCH, AND THEN HE LOOKED HER FULL IN THE FACE WITH EYES THE DANGEROUS BLUE OF A SUMMER STORM.
HER HEART SANK.
"ESSIE?"
SHE WAS TAKEN TO NEWGATE AND IMPRISONED FOR THREE MONTHS. FOUND GUILTY OF RETURNING FROM TRANSPORTATION. ESSIE SHOCKED NO ONE BY PLEADING HER BELLY, ALTHOUGH WHO THE FATHER WAS, ESSIE DECLINED TO SAY. HER SENTENCE OF DEATH WAS ONCE MORE COMMUTED TO TRANSPORTATION. THIS TIME FOR LIFE.
THERE WERE TWO HUNDRED TRANSPORTEES ON THE SHIP, PACKED INTO THE HOLD LIKE SO MANY HOGS ON THE WAY TO MARKET. IN HER LIFE, EVER AFTER, SHE WOULD HAVE NIGHTMARES OF HER TIME IN THAT HOLD.
THE SHIP LANDED IN NORFOLK, VIRGINIA, AND ESSIE'S INDENTURE WAS BOUGHT BY A TOBACCO FARMER NAMED JOHN RICHARDSON, FOR HIS WIFE HAD DIED GIVING BIRTH TO HIS DAUGHTER AND HE HAD NEED OF A WET NURSE AND A MAID OF ALL WORK UPON HIS SMALL-HOLDING.
SO, ESSIE'S BABY BOY, ANTHONY, SUCKED AT ESSIE'S BREAST ALONGSIDE OF PHYLLIDA RICHARDSON, WHO ALWAYS GOT FIRST SUCK, AND SO GREW HEALTHY, WHILE ESSIE'S SON GREW WEAK AND RICKETY ON WHAT WAS LEFT.
AND ALONG WITH THE MILK, THE CHILDREN, AS THEY GREW, DRANK ESSIE'S TALES OF THE SNUB-NOSED PISKIES, FOR WHOM A FRESH LOAF OF BREAD WAS LEFT IN THE FIELD AT REAPING TIME. AND EACH NIGHT, ESSIE PUT OUT A SAUCER OF MILK.
FOR THE PISKIES.

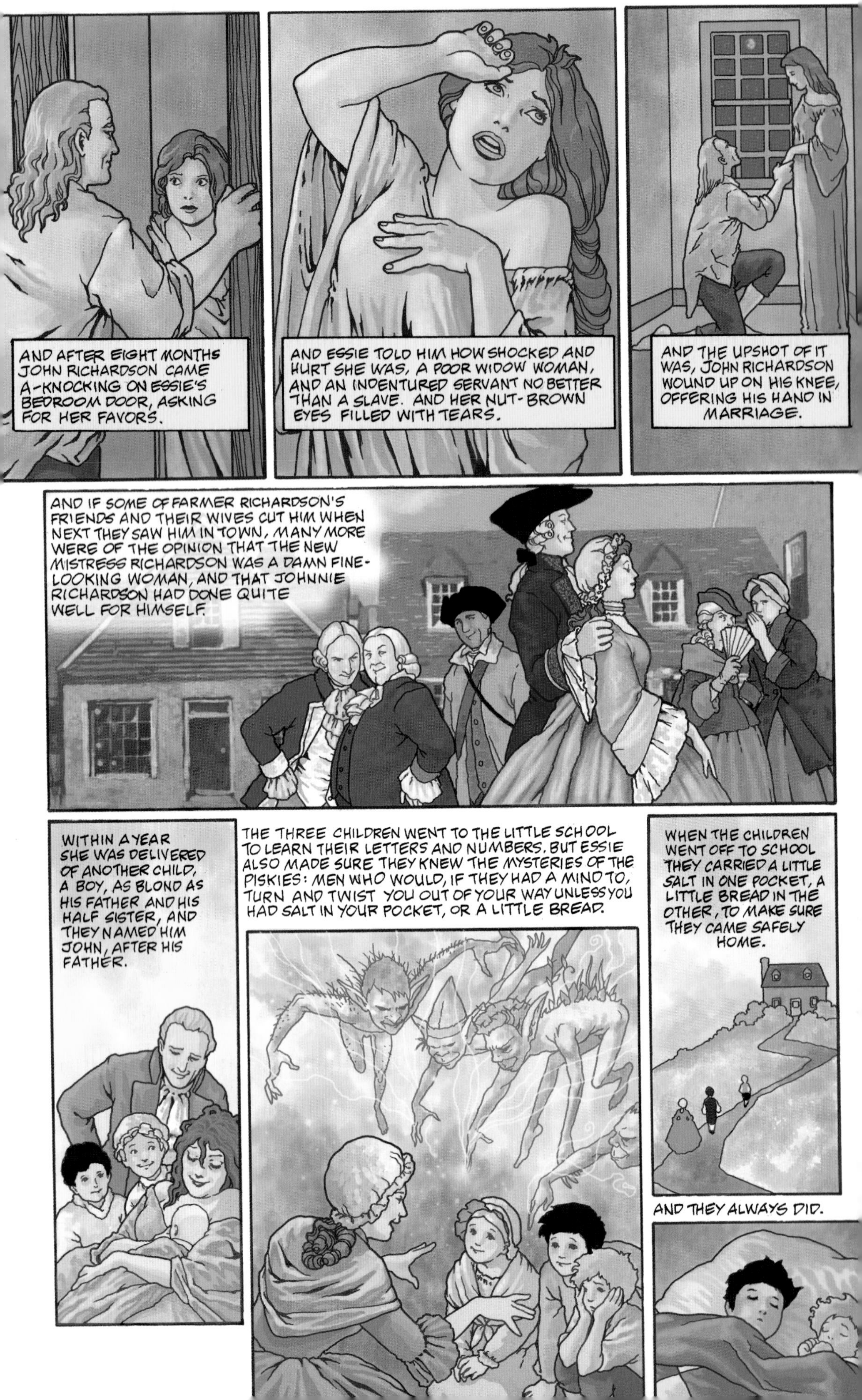
AND AFTER EIGHT MONTHS JOHN RICHARDSON CAME A-KNOCKING ON ESSIE'S BEDROOM DOOR, ASKING FOR HER FAVORS.
AND ESSIE TOLD HIM HOW SHOCKED AND HURT SHE WAS, A POOR WIDOW WOMAN, AND AN INDENTURED SERVANT NO BETTER THAN A SLAVE. AND HER NUT-BROWN EYES FILLED WITH TEARS.
AND THE UPSHOT OF IT WAS, JOHN RICHARDSON WOUND UP ON HIS KNEE, OFFERING HIS HAND IN MARRIAGE.
AND IF SOME OF FARMER RICHARDSON'S FRIENDS AND THEIR WIVES CUT HIM WHEN NEXT THEY SAW HIM IN TOWN, MANY MORE WERE OF THE OPINION THAT THE NEW MISTRESS RICHARDSON WAS A DAMN FINE-LOOKING WOMAN, AND THAT JOHNNIE RICHARDSON HAD DONE QUITE WELL FOR HIMSELF.
WITHIN A YEAR SHE WAS DELIVERED OF ANOTHER CHILD, A BOY, AS BLOND AS HIS FATHER AND HIS HALF SISTER, AND THEY NAMED HIM JOHN, AFTER HIS FATHER.
THE THREE CHILDREN WENT TO THE LITTLE SCHOOL TO LEARN THEIR LETTERS AND NUMBERS. BUT ESSIE ALSO MADE SURE THEY KNEW THE MYSTERIES OF THE PISKIES: MEN WHO WOULD, IF THEY HAD A MIND TO, TURN AND TWIST YOU OUT OF YOUR WAY UNLESS YOU HAD SALT IN YOUR POCKET, OR A LITTLE BREAD.
WHEN THE CHILDREN WENT OFF TO SCHOOL THEY CARRIED A LITTLE SALT IN ONE POCKET, A LITTLE BREAD IN THE OTHER, TO MAKE SURE THEY CAME SAFELY HOME.
AND THEY ALWAYS DID.

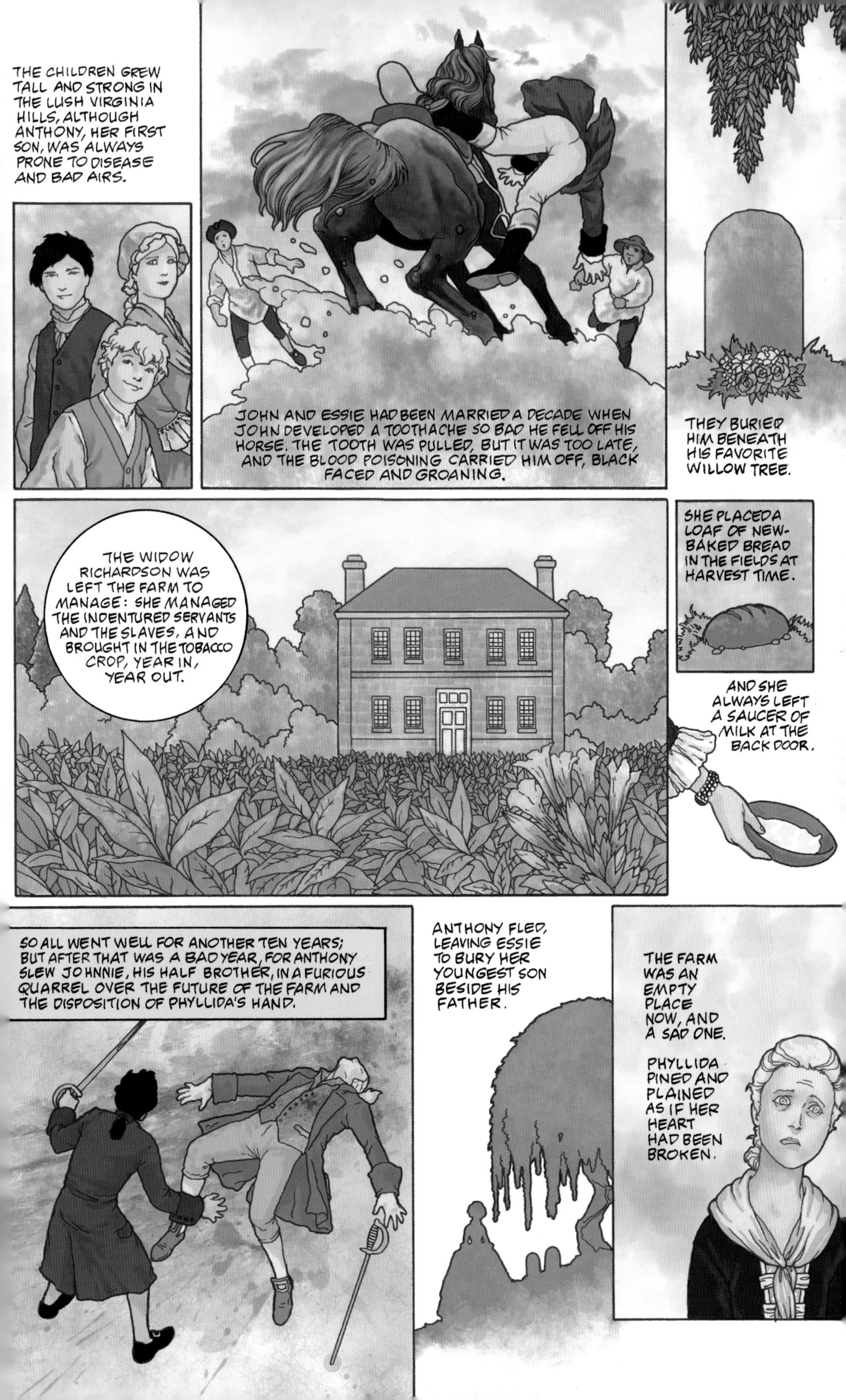
THE CHILDREN GREW TALL AND STRONG IN THE LUSH VIRGINIA HILLS, ALTHOUGH ANTHONY, HER FIRST SON, WAS ALWAYS PRONE TO DISEASE AND BAD AIRS.
JOHN AND ESSIE HAD BEEN MARRIED A DECADE WHEN JOHN DEVELOPED A TOOTHACHE SO BAD HE FELL OFF HIS HORSE. THE TOOTH WAS PULLED, BUT IT WAS TOO LATE, AND THE BLOOD POISONING CARRIED HIM OFF, BLACK FACED AND GROANING.
THEY BURIED HIM BENEATH HIS FAVORITE WILLOW TREE.
THE WIDOW RICHARDSON WAS LEFT THE FARM TO MANAGE: SHE MANAGED THE INDENTURED SERVANTS AND THE SLAVES, AND BROUGHT IN THE TOBACCO CROP, YEAR IN, YEAR OUT.
SHE PLACED A LOAF OF NEW-BAKED BREAD IN THE FIELDS AT HARVEST TIME.
AND SHE ALWAYS LEFT A SAUCER OF MILK AT THE BACK DOOR.
SO ALL WENT WELL FOR ANOTHER TEN YEARS; BUT AFTER THAT WAS A BAD YEAR, FOR ANTHONY SLEW JOHNNIE, HIS HALF BROTHER, IN A FURIOUS QUARREL OVER THE FUTURE OF THE FARM AND THE DISPOSITION OF PHYLLIDA'S HAND.
ANTHONY FLED, LEAVING ESSIE TO BURY HER YOUNGEST SON BESIDE HIS FATHER.
THE FARM WAS AN EMPTY PLACE NOW, AND A SAD ONE.
PHYLLIDA PINED AND PLAINED AS IF HER HEART HAD BEEN BROKEN.

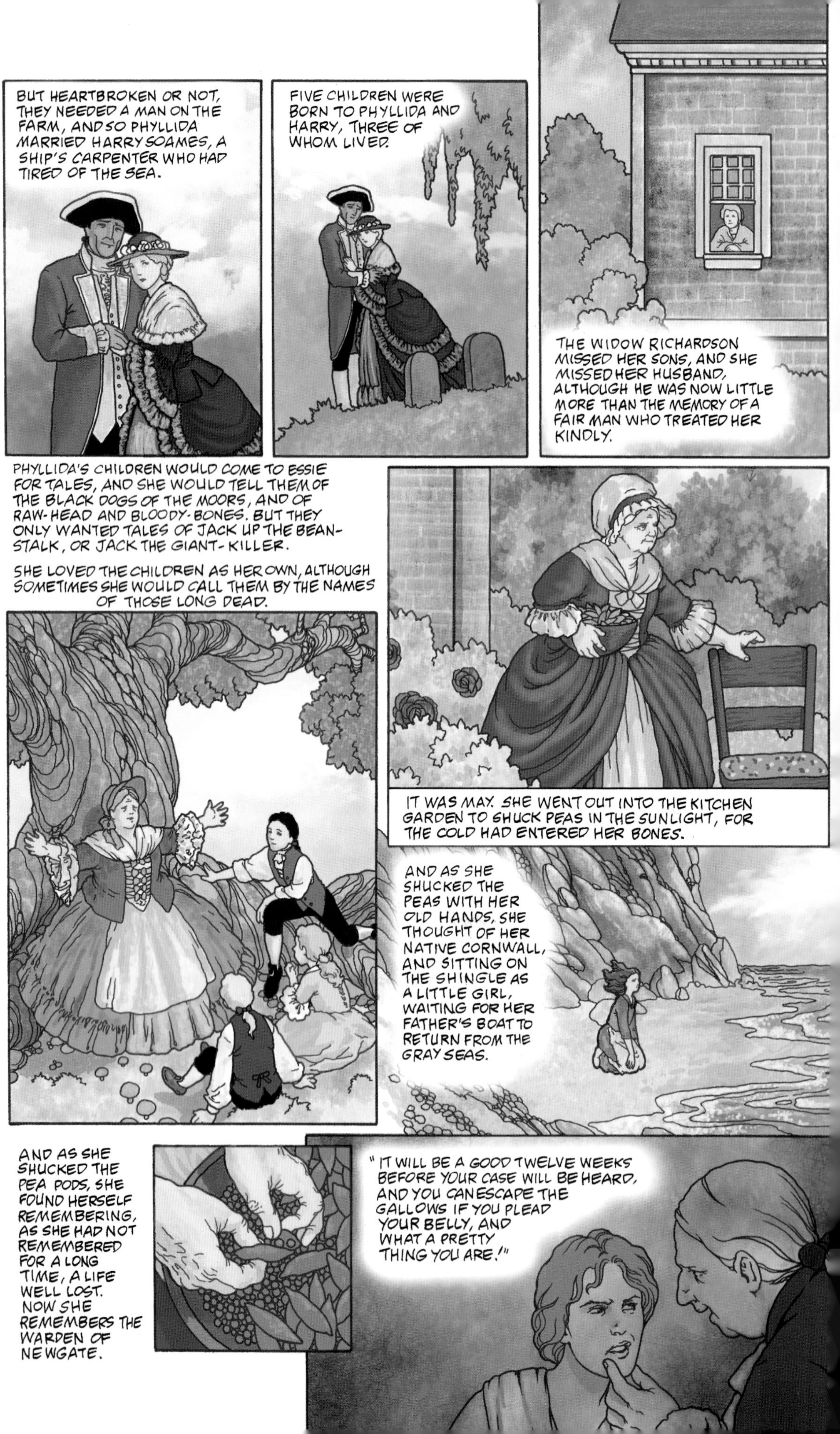
BUT HEARTBROKEN OR NOT, THEY NEEDED A MAN ON THE FARM, AND SO PHYLLIDA MARRIED HARRY SOAMES, A SHIP'S CARPENTER WHO HAD TIRED OF THE SEA.
FIVE CHILDREN WERE BORN TO PHYLLIDA AND HARRY, THREE OF WHOM LIVED.
THE WIDOW RICHARDSON MISSED HER SONS, AND SHE MISSED HER HUSBAND, ALTHOUGH HE WAS NOW LITTLE MORE THAN THE MEMORY OF A FAIR MAN WHO TREATED HER KINDLY.
PHYLLIDA'S CHILDREN WOULD COME TO ESSIE FOR TALES, AND SHE WOULD TELL THEM OF THE BLACK DOGS OF THE MOORS, AND OF RAW-HEAD AND BLOODY-BONES. BUT THEY ONLY WANTED TALES OF JACK UP THE BEAN-STALK, OR JACK THE GIANT-KILLER.
SHE LOVED THE CHILDREN AS HER OWN, ALTHOUGH SOMETIMES SHE WOULD CALL THEM BY THE NAMES OF THOSE LONG DEAD.
IT WAS MAY. SHE WENT OUT INTO THE KITCHEN GARDEN TO SHUCK PEAS IN THE SUNLIGHT, FOR THE COLD HAD ENTERED HER BONES.
AND AS SHE SHUCKED THE PEAS WITH HER OLD HANDS, SHE THOUGHT OF HER NATIVE CORNWALL, AND SITTING ON THE SHINGLE AS A LITTLE GIRL, WAITING FOR HER FATHER'S BOAT TO RETURN FROM THE GRAY SEAS.
AND AS SHE SHUCKED THE PEA PODS, SHE FOUND HERSELF REMEMBERING, AS SHE HAD NOT REMEMBERED FOR A LONG TIME, A LIFE WELL LOST. NOW SHE REMEMBERS THE WARDEN OF NEWGATE.
"IT WILL BE A GOOD TWELVE WEEKS BEFORE YOUR CASE WILL BE HEARD, AND YOU CAN ESCAPE THE GALLOWS IF YOU PLEAD YOUR BELLY, AND WHAT A PRETTY THING YOU ARE!"

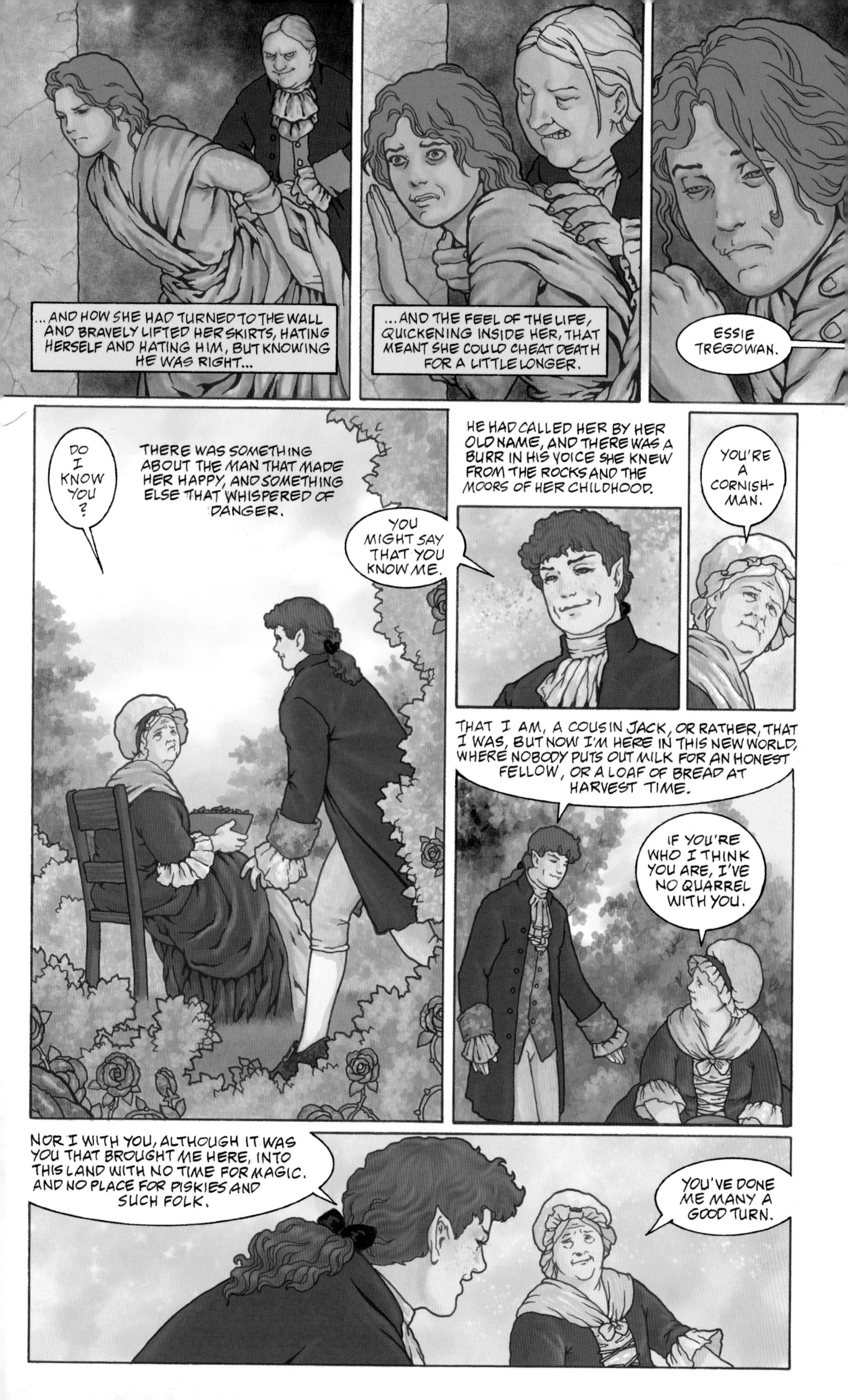
...AND HOW SHE HAD TURNED TO THE WALL AND BRAVELY LIFTED HER SKIRTS, HATING HERSELF AND HATING HIM, BUT KNOWING HE WAS RIGHT...
...AND THE FEEL OF THE LIFE, QUICKENING INSIDE HER, THAT MEANT SHE COULD CHEAT DEATH FOR A LITTLE LONGER.
ESSIE TREGOWAN.
DO I KNOW YOU?
THERE WAS SOMETHING ABOUT THE MAN THAT MADE HER HAPPY, AND SOMETHING ELSE THAT WHISPERED OF DANGER.
YOU MIGHT SAY THAT YOU KNOW ME.
HE HAD CALLED HER BY HER OLD NAME, AND THERE WAS A BURR IN HIS VOICE SHE KNEW FROM THE ROCKS AND THE MOORS OF HER CHILDHOOD.
YOU'RE A CORNISH-MAN.
THAT I AM, A COUSIN JACK, OR RATHER, THAT I WAS, BUT NOW I'M HERE IN THIS NEW WORLD, WHERE NOBODY PUTS OUT MILK FOR AN HONEST FELLOW, OR A LOAF OF BREAD AT HARVEST TIME.
IF YOU'RE WHO I THINK YOU ARE, I'VE NO QUARREL WITH YOU.
NOR I WITH YOU, ALTHOUGH IT WAS YOU THAT BROUGHT ME HERE, INTO THIS LAND WITH NO TIME FOR MAGIC. AND NO PLACE FOR PISKIES AND SUCH FOLK.
YOU'VE DONE ME MANY A GOOD TURN.

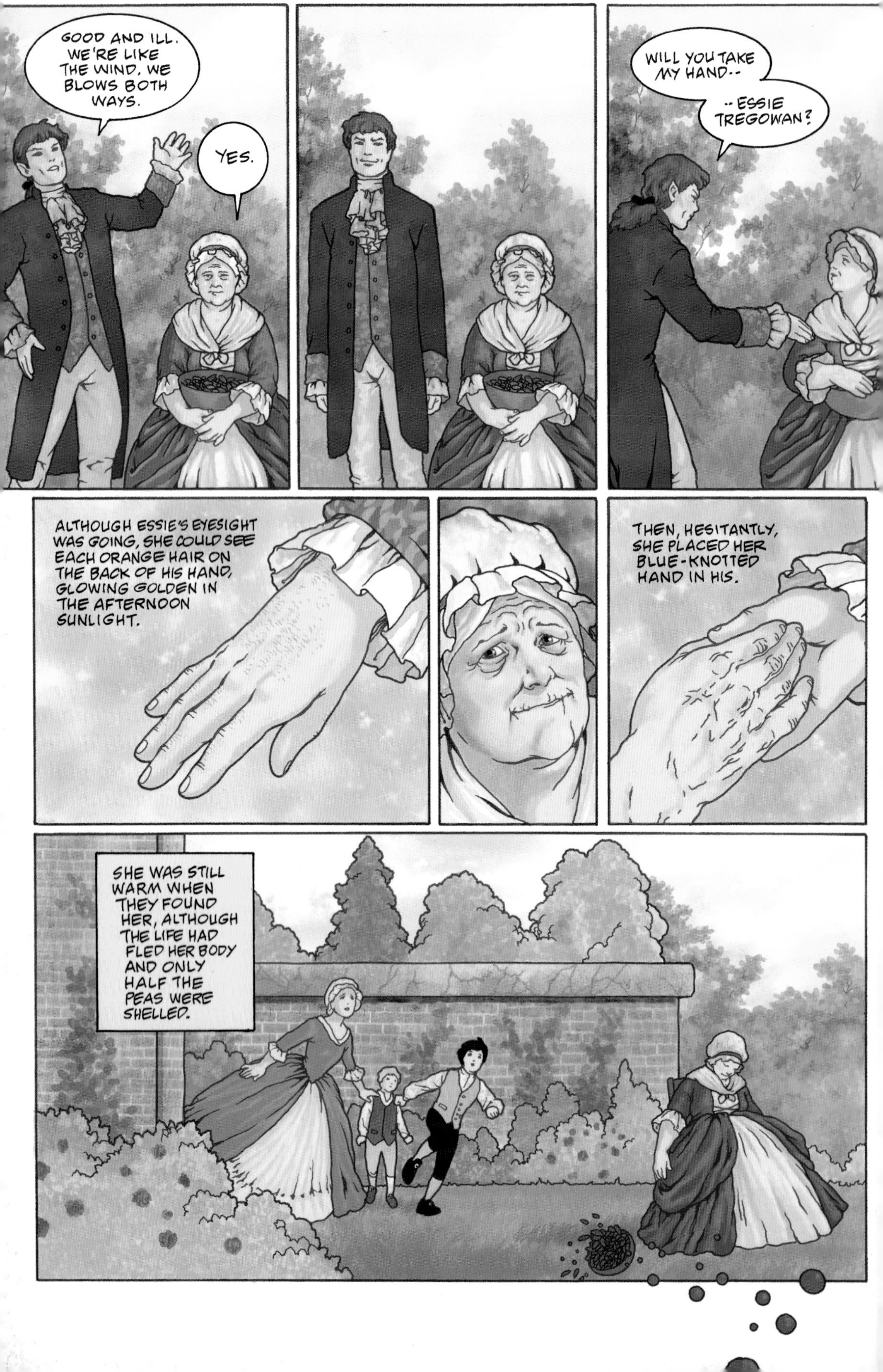
GOOD AND ILL. WE'RE LIKE THE WIND. WE BLOWS BOTH WAYS.
YES.
WILL YOU TAKE MY HAND--
--ESSIE TREGOWAN?
ALTHOUGH ESSIE'S EYESIGHT WAS GOING, SHE COULD SEE EACH ORANGE HAIR ON THE BACK OF HIS HAND, GLOWING GOLDEN IN THE AFTERNOON SUNLIGHT.
THEN, HESITANTLY, SHE PLACED HER BLUE-KNOTTED HAND IN HIS.
SHE WAS STILL WARM WHEN THEY FOUND HER, ALTHOUGH THE LIFE HAD FLED HER BODY AND ONLY HALF THE PEAS WERE SHELLED.

CHAPTER FIVE

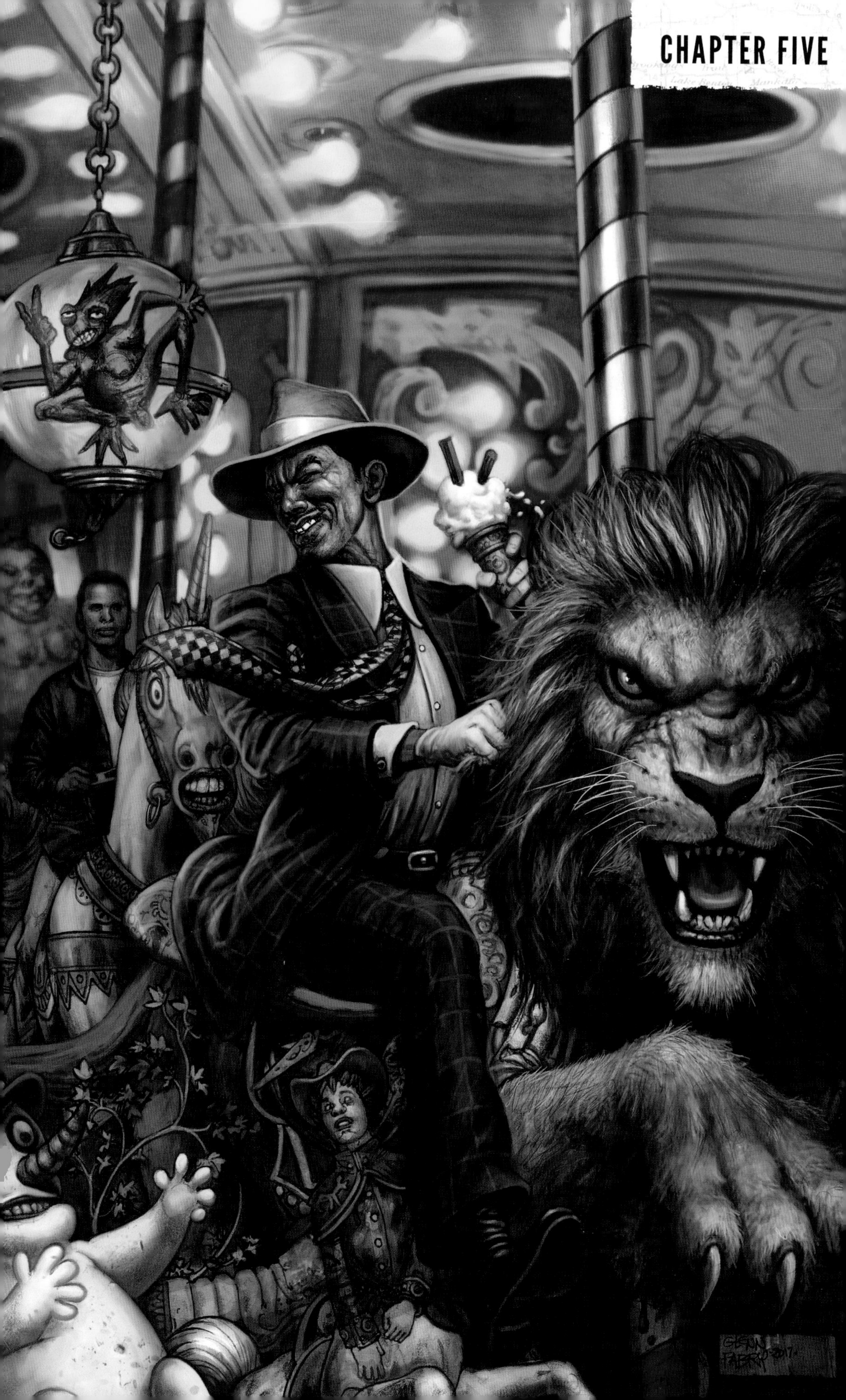

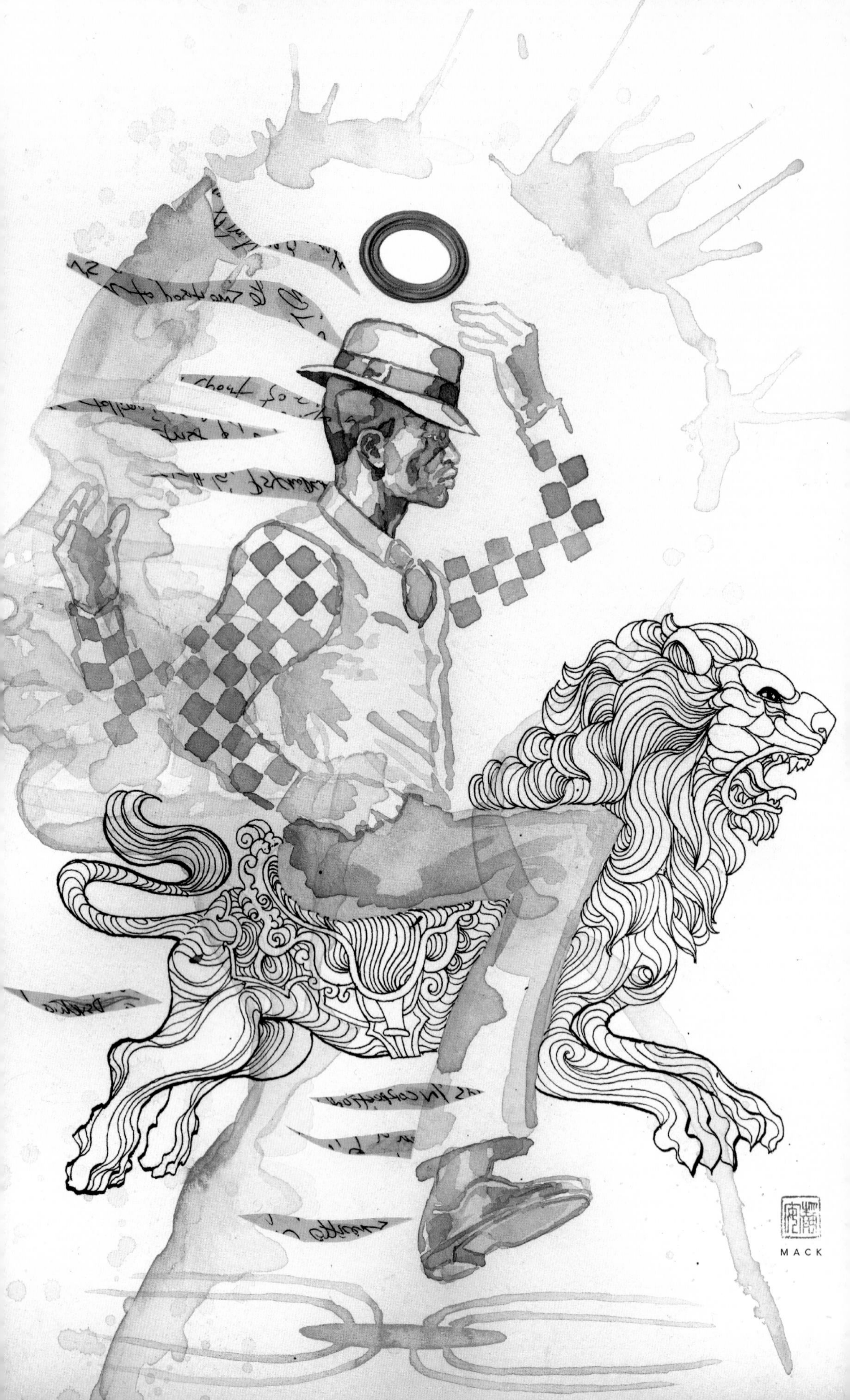
MACK

5 ONLY ZORYA UTRENNYAYA WAS AWAKE TO SAY GOODBYE TO THEM THAT SATURDAY MORNING.

THANK YOU FOR YOUR HOSPITALITY, DEAR LADY. YOU AND YOUR LOVELY SISTERS REMAIN AS RADIANT AS THE SKY ITSELF.

YOU ARE A BAD OLD MAN. KEEP SAFE. I WOULD NOT LIKE TO HEAR THAT YOU WERE GONE FOR GOOD.

IT WOULD DISTRESS ME EQUALLY, MY DEAR.

ZORYA POLUNOCHNAYA THINKS VERY HIGHLY OF YOU. I ALSO.

THANK YOU. THANKS FOR DINNER.

YOU LIKED?

"YOU MUST COME AGAIN."

THE SILVER DOLLAR WAS COLD IN SHADOW'S HAND, BIGGER AND HEAVIER THAN ANY COINS HE HAD USED SO FAR. HE CLASSIC-PALMED IT. THEN STRAIGHTENED HIS HAND TO A FRONT PALM POSITION AND FUMBLED IT...

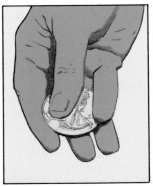

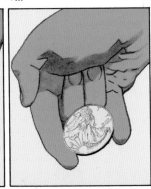

...EVER SO SLIGHTLY.

YOU CANNOT AFFORD TO BE CARELESS WITH PEOPLE'S GIFTS, SHADOW. SOMETHING LIKE THIS, YOU NEED TO HANG ON TO IT.

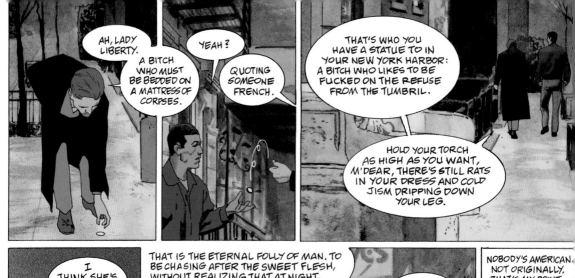

AH, LADY LIBERTY. A BITCH WHO MUST BE BEDDED ON A MATTRESS OF CORPSES.

YEAH?

QUOTING SOMEONE FRENCH.

THAT'S WHO YOU HAVE A STATUE TO IN YOUR NEW YORK HARBOR: A BITCH WHO LIKES TO BE FUCKED ON THE REFUSE FROM THE TUMBRIL.

HOLD YOUR TORCH AS HIGH AS YOU WANT, M'DEAR, THERE'S STILL RATS IN YOUR DRESS AND COLD JISM DRIPPING DOWN YOUR LEG.

I THINK SHE'S BEAUTIFUL.

THAT IS THE ETERNAL FOLLY OF MAN. TO BE CHASING AFTER THE SWEET FLESH, WITHOUT REALIZING THAT AT NIGHT, YOU'RE RUBBING YOURSELF AGAINST WORM FOOD.

NO OFFENSE MEANT.

SO YOU AREN'T AMERICAN?

NOBODY'S AMERICAN. NOT ORIGINALLY. THAT'S MY POINT.

GOOD JOB LAST NIGHT WITH CZERNOBOG, BY THE WAY. YOU ENLISTED HIM MORE WHOLE-HEARTEDLY THAN EVER I COULD.

ONLY BECAUSE HE GETS TO KILL ME AFTERWARD.

NOT NECESSARILY. HE'S OLD AND THE KILLING STROKE MIGHT MERELY LEAVE YOU PARALYZED FOR LIFE. SO YOU SHOULD HAVE MUCH TO LOOK FORWARD TO, SHOULD MISTER CZERNOBOG SURVIVE THE COMING DIFFICULTIES.

AND THERE'S SOME QUESTION OF THIS?

FUCK YES.

THIS IS THE BANK I SHALL BE ROBBING. THEY DON'T CLOSE FOR ANOTHER FEW HOURS. LET'S GO IN AND SAY HELLO.

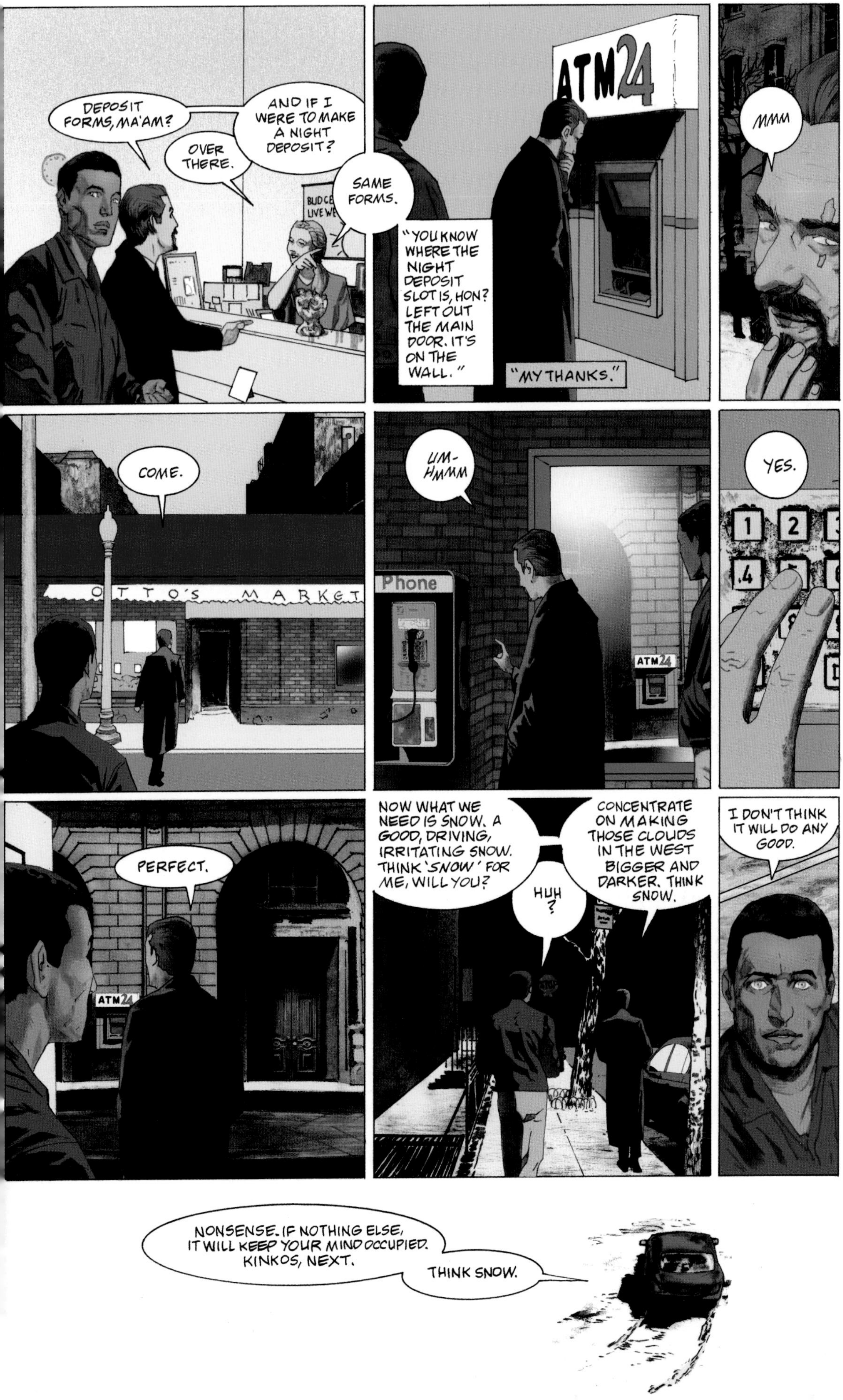
DEPOSIT FORMS, MA'AM?
OVER THERE.
AND IF I WERE TO MAKE A NIGHT DEPOSIT?
SAME FORMS.
ATM24
"YOU KNOW WHERE THE NIGHT DEPOSIT SLOT IS, HON? LEFT OUT THE MAIN DOOR. IT'S ON THE WALL."
"MY THANKS."
MMM
COME.
OTTO'S MARKET
UM-HMMM
Phone
ATM24
YES.
PERFECT.
ATM24
NOW WHAT WE NEED IS SNOW. A GOOD, DRIVING, IRRITATING SNOW. THINK 'SNOW' FOR ME, WILL YOU?
HUH?
CONCENTRATE ON MAKING THOSE CLOUDS IN THE WEST BIGGER AND DARKER. THINK SNOW.
I DON'T THINK IT WILL DO ANY GOOD.
NONSENSE. IF NOTHING ELSE, IT WILL KEEP YOUR MIND OCCUPIED. KINKOS, NEXT.
THINK SNOW.

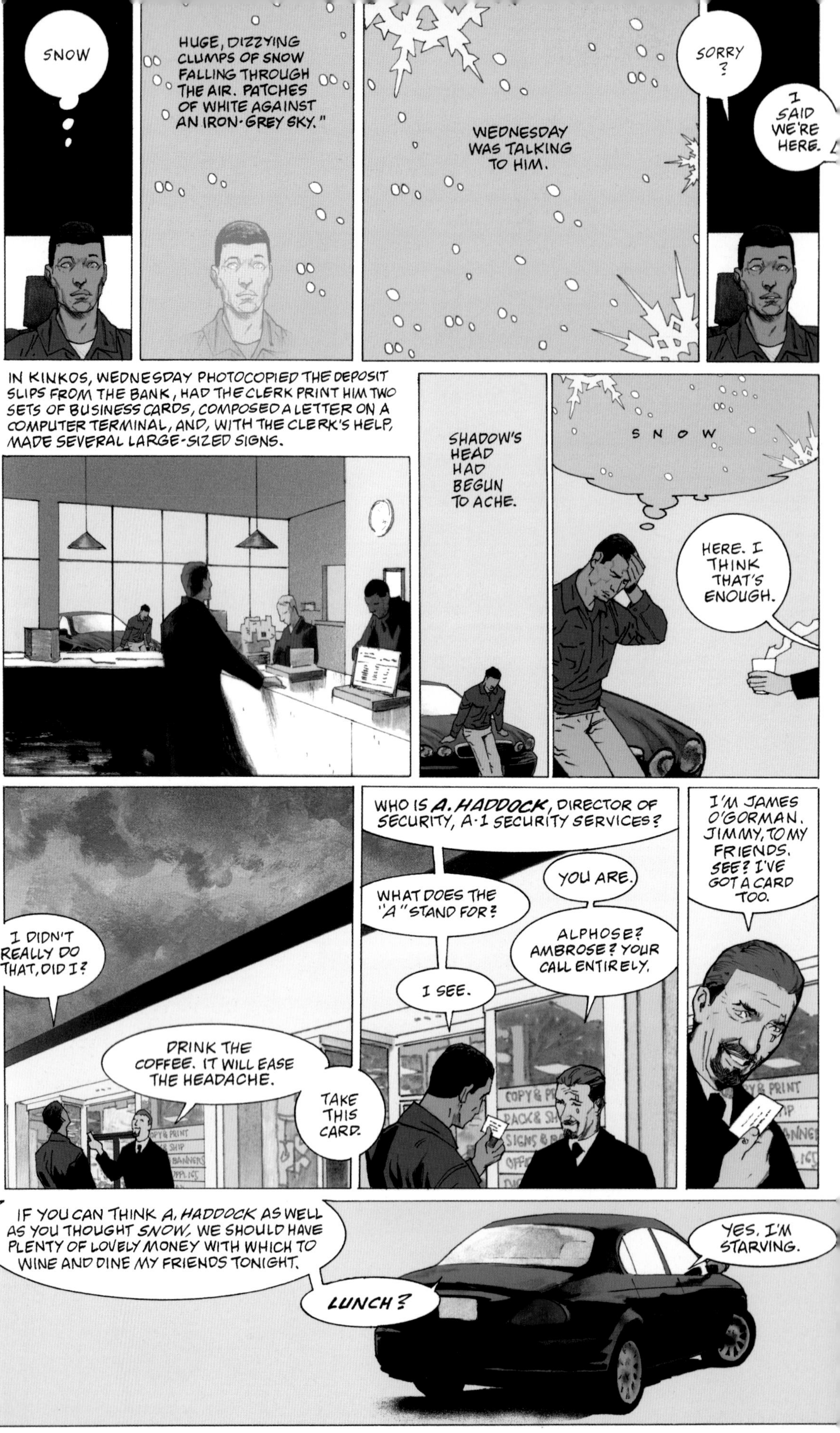
SNOW
HUGE, DIZZYING CLUMPS OF SNOW FALLING THROUGH THE AIR. PATCHES OF WHITE AGAINST AN IRON-GREY SKY."
WEDNESDAY WAS TALKING TO HIM.
SORRY ?
I SAID WE'RE HERE.
IN KINKOS, WEDNESDAY PHOTOCOPIED THE DEPOSIT SLIPS FROM THE BANK, HAD THE CLERK PRINT HIM TWO SETS OF BUSINESS CARDS, COMPOSED A LETTER ON A COMPUTER TERMINAL, AND, WITH THE CLERK'S HELP, MADE SEVERAL LARGE-SIZED SIGNS.
SHADOW'S HEAD HAD BEGUN TO ACHE.
S N O W
HERE. I THINK THAT'S ENOUGH.
I DIDN'T REALLY DO THAT, DID I?
DRINK THE COFFEE. IT WILL EASE THE HEADACHE.
TAKE THIS CARD.
WHO IS A. HADDOCK, DIRECTOR OF SECURITY, A-1 SECURITY SERVICES?
YOU ARE.
WHAT DOES THE "A" STAND FOR?
ALPHOSE? AMBROSE? YOUR CALL ENTIRELY.
I SEE.
I'M JAMES O'GORMAN. JIMMY, TO MY FRIENDS. SEE? I'VE GOT A CARD TOO.
IF YOU CAN THINK A. HADDOCK AS WELL AS YOU THOUGHT SNOW, WE SHOULD HAVE PLENTY OF LOVELY MONEY WITH WHICH TO WINE AND DINE MY FRIENDS TONIGHT.
LUNCH?
YES. I'M STARVING.

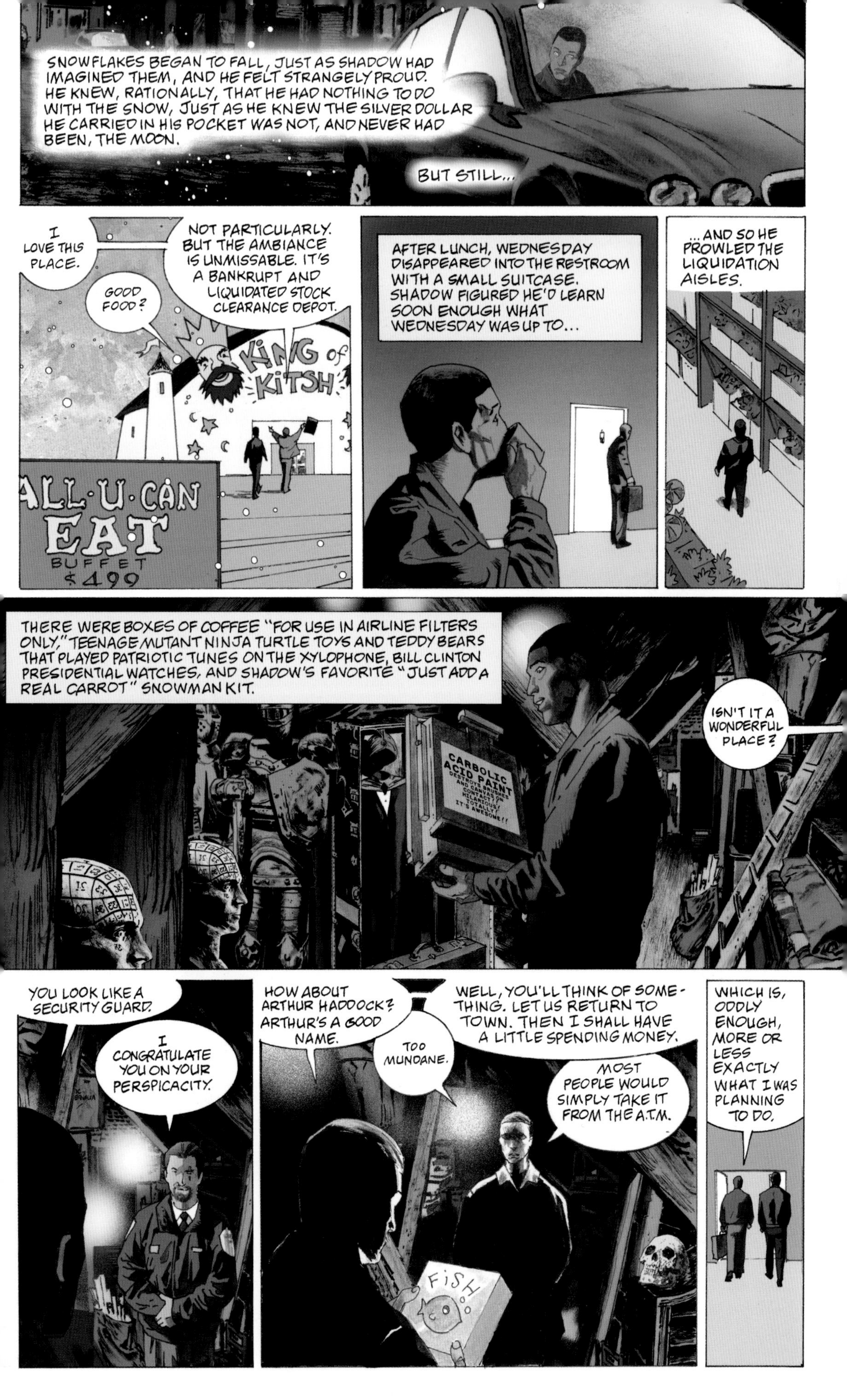
SNOWFLAKES BEGAN TO FALL, JUST AS SHADOW HAD IMAGINED THEM, AND HE FELT STRANGELY PROUD. HE KNEW, RATIONALLY, THAT HE HAD NOTHING TO DO WITH THE SNOW, JUST AS HE KNEW THE SILVER DOLLAR HE CARRIED IN HIS POCKET WAS NOT, AND NEVER HAD BEEN, THE MOON.
BUT STILL...
I LOVE THIS PLACE.
GOOD FOOD?
NOT PARTICULARLY. BUT THE AMBIANCE IS UNMISSABLE. IT'S A BANKRUPT AND LIQUIDATED STOCK CLEARANCE DEPOT.
KiNG of KiTSH
ALL-U-CAN EAT
BUFFET
$499
AFTER LUNCH, WEDNESDAY DISAPPEARED INTO THE RESTROOM WITH A SMALL SUITCASE. SHADOW FIGURED HE'D LEARN SOON ENOUGH WHAT WEDNESDAY WAS UP TO...
...AND SO HE PROWLED THE LIQUIDATION AISLES.
THERE WERE BOXES OF COFFEE "FOR USE IN AIRLINE FILTERS ONLY," TEENAGE MUTANT NINJA TURTLE TOYS AND TEDDY BEARS THAT PLAYED PATRIOTIC TUNES ON THE XYLOPHONE, BILL CLINTON PRESIDENTIAL WATCHES, AND SHADOW'S FAVORITE "JUST ADD A REAL CARROT" SNOWMAN KIT.
CARBOLIC ACID PAINT
ISN'T IT A WONDERFUL PLACE?
YOU LOOK LIKE A SECURITY GUARD.
I CONGRATULATE YOU ON YOUR PERSPICACITY.
HOW ABOUT ARTHUR HADDOCK? ARTHUR'S A GOOD NAME.
TOO MUNDANE.
WELL, YOU'LL THINK OF SOMETHING. LET US RETURN TO TOWN. THEN I SHALL HAVE A LITTLE SPENDING MONEY.
MOST PEOPLE WOULD SIMPLY TAKE IT FROM THE A.T.M.
FiSH
WHICH IS, ODDLY ENOUGH, MORE OR LESS EXACTLY WHAT I WAS PLANNING TO DO.

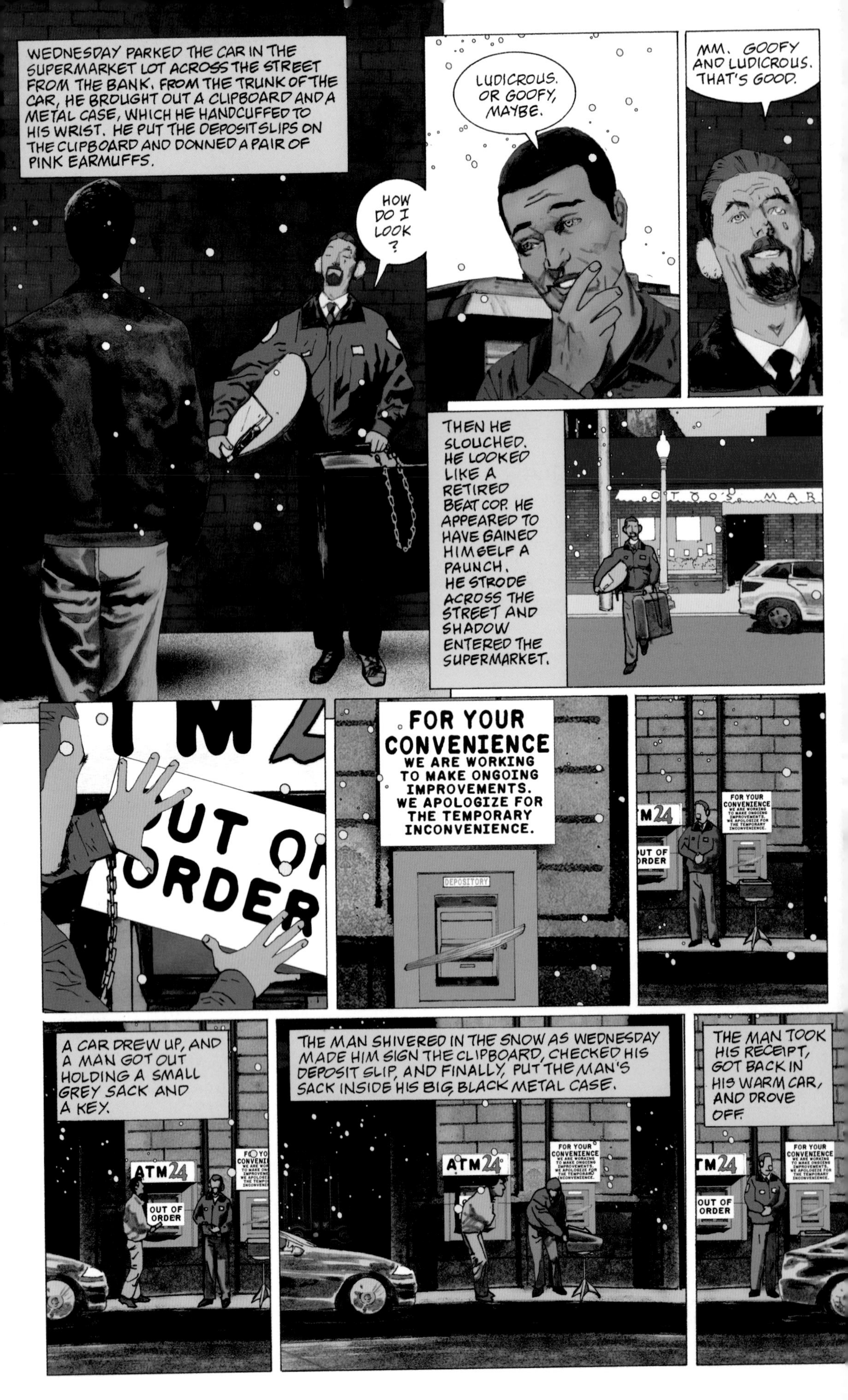
WEDNESDAY PARKED THE CAR IN THE SUPERMARKET LOT ACROSS THE STREET FROM THE BANK. FROM THE TRUNK OF THE CAR, HE BROUGHT OUT A CLIPBOARD AND A METAL CASE, WHICH HE HANDCUFFED TO HIS WRIST. HE PUT THE DEPOSIT SLIPS ON THE CLIPBOARD AND DONNED A PAIR OF PINK EARMUFFS.
HOW DO I LOOK ?
LUDICROUS. OR GOOFY, MAYBE.
MM. GOOFY AND LUDICROUS. THAT'S GOOD.
THEN HE SLOUCHED. HE LOOKED LIKE A RETIRED BEAT COP. HE APPEARED TO HAVE GAINED HIMSELF A PAUNCH. HE STRODE ACROSS THE STREET AND SHADOW ENTERED THE SUPERMARKET.
OTTO'S MAR
OUT OF ORDER
FOR YOUR CONVENIENCE WE ARE WORKING TO MAKE ONGOING IMPROVEMENTS. WE APOLOGIZE FOR THE TEMPORARY INCONVENIENCE.
DEPOSITORY
A CAR DREW UP, AND A MAN GOT OUT HOLDING A SMALL GREY SACK AND A KEY.
THE MAN SHIVERED IN THE SNOW AS WEDNESDAY MADE HIM SIGN THE CLIPBOARD, CHECKED HIS DEPOSIT SLIP, AND FINALLY, PUT THE MAN'S SACK INSIDE HIS BIG, BLACK METAL CASE.
THE MAN TOOK HIS RECEIPT, GOT BACK IN HIS WARM CAR, AND DROVE OFF.

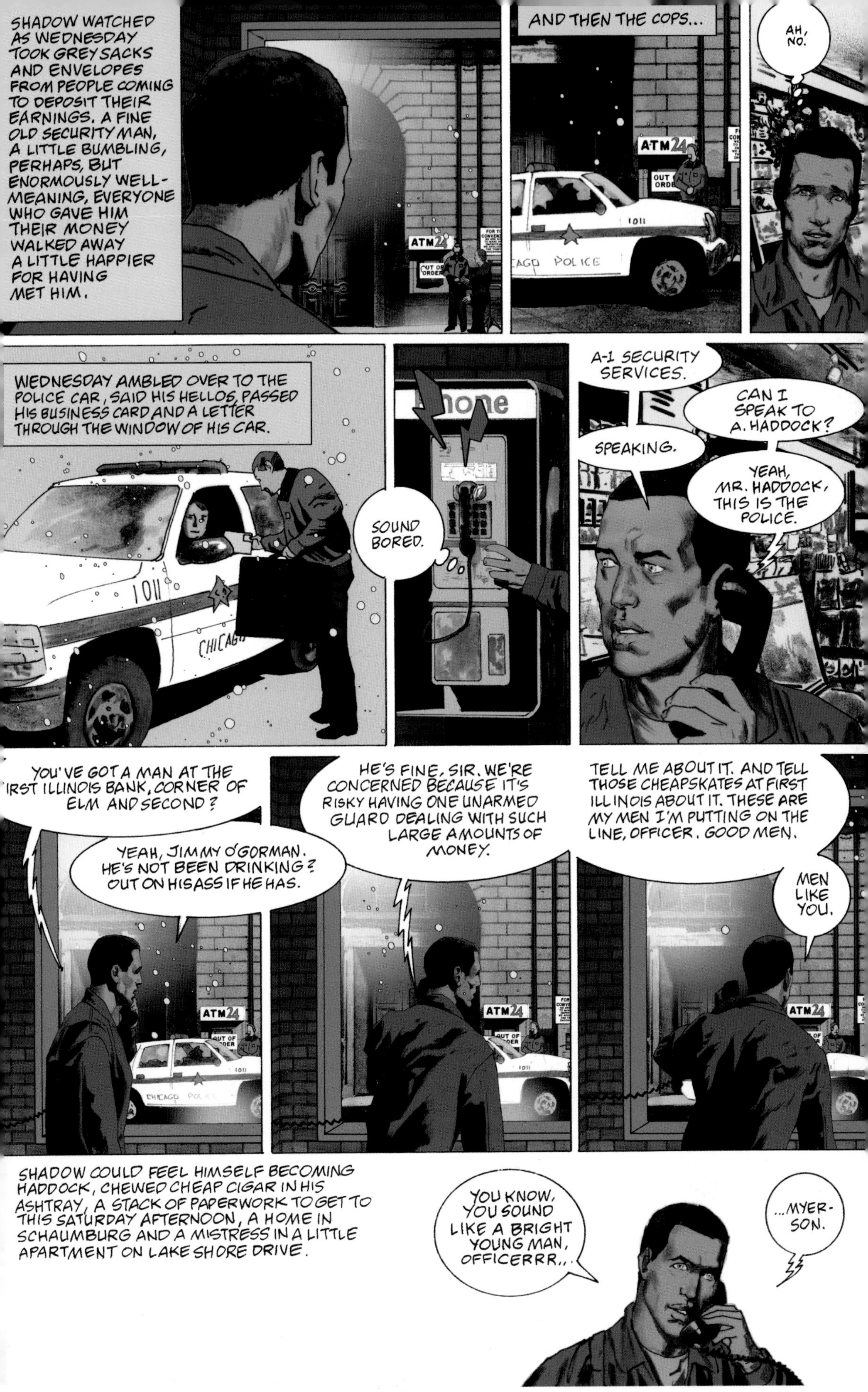

SHADOW WATCHED AS WEDNESDAY TOOK GREY SACKS AND ENVELOPES FROM PEOPLE COMING TO DEPOSIT THEIR EARNINGS. A FINE OLD SECURITY MAN, A LITTLE BUMBLING, PERHAPS, BUT ENORMOUSLY WELL-MEANING, EVERYONE WHO GAVE HIM THEIR MONEY WALKED AWAY A LITTLE HAPPIER FOR HAVING MET HIM.
ATM24
OUT OF ORDER
AND THEN THE COPS...
ATM24
CHICAGO POLICE
AH, NO.
WEDNESDAY AMBLED OVER TO THE POLICE CAR, SAID HIS HELLOS, PASSED HIS BUSINESS CARD AND A LETTER THROUGH THE WINDOW OF HIS CAR.
1011
CHICAGO
Phone
SOUND BORED.
A-1 SECURITY SERVICES.
CAN I SPEAK TO A. HADDOCK?
SPEAKING.
YEAH, MR. HADDOCK, THIS IS THE POLICE.
YOU'VE GOT A MAN AT THE FIRST ILLINOIS BANK, CORNER OF ELM AND SECOND?
YEAH, JIMMY O'GORMAN. HE'S NOT BEEN DRINKING? OUT ON HIS ASS IF HE HAS.
HE'S FINE, SIR. WE'RE CONCERNED BECAUSE IT'S RISKY HAVING ONE UNARMED GUARD DEALING WITH SUCH LARGE AMOUNTS OF MONEY.
TELL ME ABOUT IT. AND TELL THOSE CHEAPSKATES AT FIRST ILLINOIS ABOUT IT. THESE ARE MY MEN I'M PUTTING ON THE LINE, OFFICER. GOOD MEN.
MEN LIKE YOU.
SHADOW COULD FEEL HIMSELF BECOMING HADDOCK, CHEWED CHEAP CIGAR IN HIS ASHTRAY, A STACK OF PAPERWORK TO GET TO THIS SATURDAY AFTERNOON, A HOME IN SCHAUMBURG AND A MISTRESS IN A LITTLE APARTMENT ON LAKE SHORE DRIVE.
YOU KNOW, YOU SOUND LIKE A BRIGHT YOUNG MAN, OFFICERRR...
...MYER-SON.

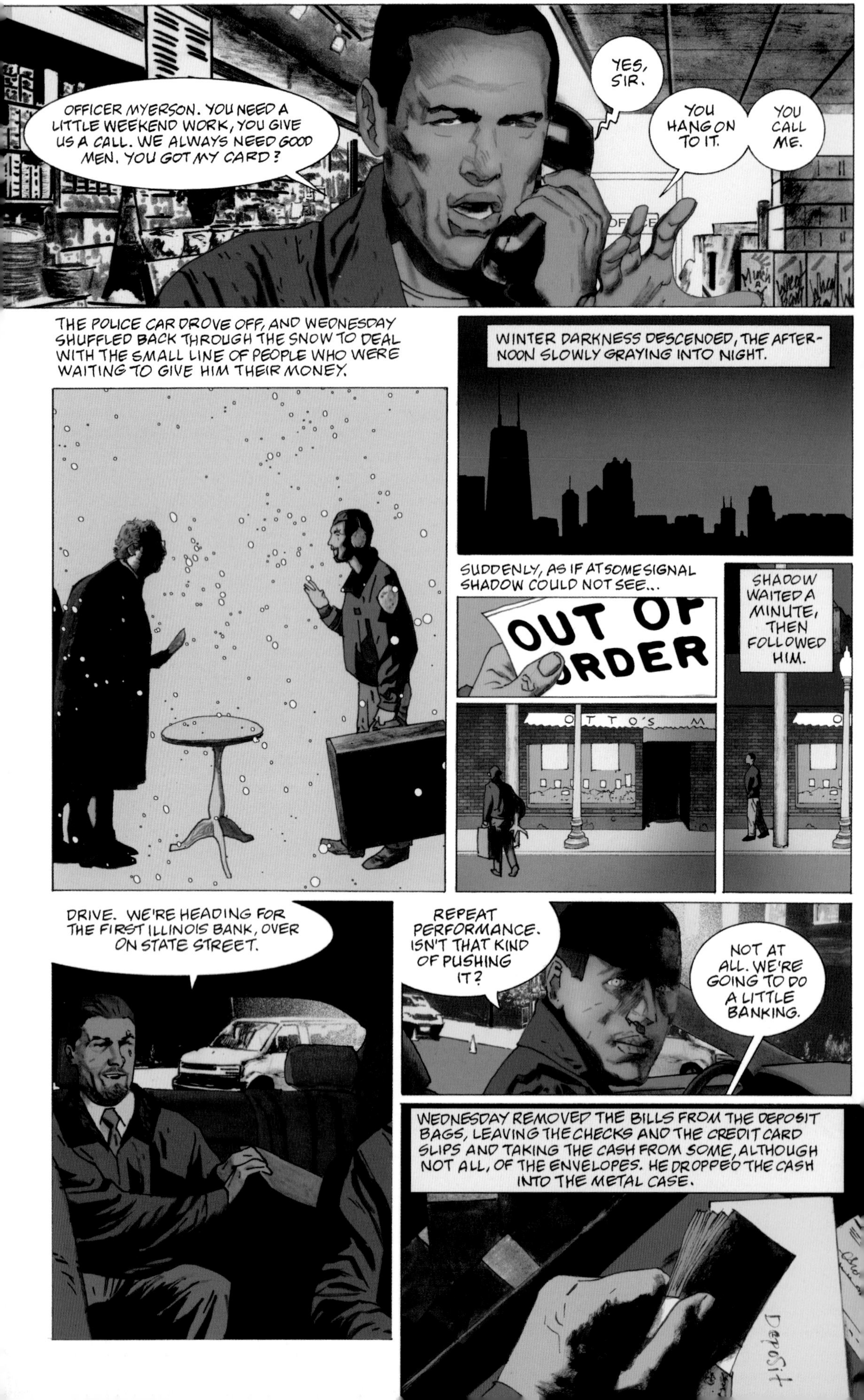
OFFICER MYERSON. YOU NEED A LITTLE WEEKEND WORK, YOU GIVE US A CALL. WE ALWAYS NEED GOOD MEN. YOU GOT MY CARD?
YES, SIR.
YOU HANG ON TO IT.
YOU CALL ME.
THE POLICE CAR DROVE OFF, AND WEDNESDAY SHUFFLED BACK THROUGH THE SNOW TO DEAL WITH THE SMALL LINE OF PEOPLE WHO WERE WAITING TO GIVE HIM THEIR MONEY.
WINTER DARKNESS DESCENDED, THE AFTERNOON SLOWLY GRAYING INTO NIGHT.
SUDDENLY, AS IF AT SOME SIGNAL SHADOW COULD NOT SEE...
OUT OF ORDER
SHADOW WAITED A MINUTE, THEN FOLLOWED HIM.
OTTO'S M
DRIVE. WE'RE HEADING FOR THE FIRST ILLINOIS BANK, OVER ON STATE STREET.
REPEAT PERFORMANCE. ISN'T THAT KIND OF PUSHING IT?
NOT AT ALL. WE'RE GOING TO DO A LITTLE BANKING.
WEDNESDAY REMOVED THE BILLS FROM THE DEPOSIT BAGS, LEAVING THE CHECKS AND THE CREDIT CARD SLIPS AND TAKING THE CASH FROM SOME, ALTHOUGH NOT ALL, OF THE ENVELOPES. HE DROPPED THE CASH INTO THE METAL CASE.
DEPOSIT

SHADOW PULLED UP OUTSIDE THE BANK, STOPPING THE CAR WELL OUT OF CAMERA RANGE.

WAIT HERE.

WEDNESDAY PUSHED THE ENVELOPES THROUGH THE NIGHT DEPOSIT SLOT. THEN HE OPENED THE NIGHT SAFE AND DROPPED IN THE GREY BAGS.

THERE, MY BOY. THAT WILL CONFUSE EVERYTHING.

HERE. YOUR FIRST WEEK'S WAGES.

SO THAT'S WHAT YOU DO TO MAKE MONEY?

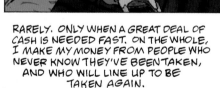

RARELY. ONLY WHEN A GREAT DEAL OF CASH IS NEEDED FAST. ON THE WHOLE, I MAKE MY MONEY FROM PEOPLE WHO NEVER KNOW THEY'VE BEEN TAKEN, AND WHO WILL LINE UP TO BE TAKEN AGAIN.

THAT SWEENEY GUY *SAID* THAT YOU WERE A HUSTLER.

HE WAS RIGHT. BUT THAT IS THE LEAST OF WHAT I AM, AND THE LEAST OF WHAT I NEED FOR YOU, SHADOW.

NOW, YOU'RE HEADING FOR I-90.

FOLLOW THE SIGNS WEST FOR MADISON.

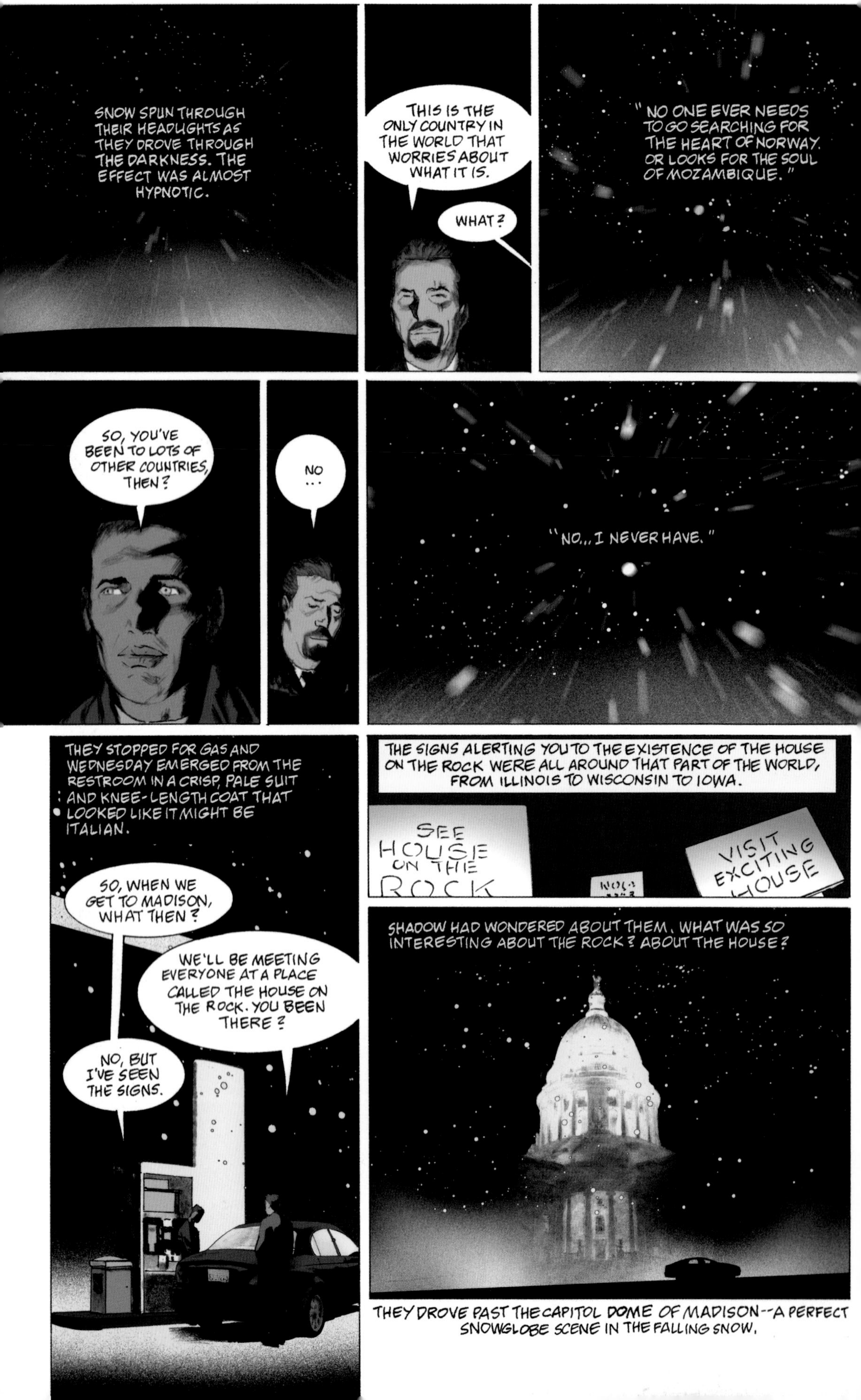

SNOW SPUN THROUGH THEIR HEADLIGHTS AS THEY DROVE THROUGH THE DARKNESS. THE EFFECT WAS ALMOST HYPNOTIC.
THIS IS THE ONLY COUNTRY IN THE WORLD THAT WORRIES ABOUT WHAT IT IS.
WHAT?
"NO ONE EVER NEEDS TO GO SEARCHING FOR THE HEART OF NORWAY. OR LOOKS FOR THE SOUL OF MOZAMBIQUE."
SO, YOU'VE BEEN TO LOTS OF OTHER COUNTRIES, THEN?
NO...
"NO... I NEVER HAVE."
THEY STOPPED FOR GAS AND WEDNESDAY EMERGED FROM THE RESTROOM IN A CRISP, PALE SUIT AND KNEE-LENGTH COAT THAT LOOKED LIKE IT MIGHT BE ITALIAN.
SO, WHEN WE GET TO MADISON, WHAT THEN?
WE'LL BE MEETING EVERYONE AT A PLACE CALLED THE HOUSE ON THE ROCK. YOU BEEN THERE?
NO, BUT I'VE SEEN THE SIGNS.
THE SIGNS ALERTING YOU TO THE EXISTENCE OF THE HOUSE ON THE ROCK WERE ALL AROUND THAT PART OF THE WORLD, FROM ILLINOIS TO WISCONSIN TO IOWA.
SEE HOUSE ON THE ROCK
VISIT EXCITING HOUSE
SHADOW HAD WONDERED ABOUT THEM. WHAT WAS SO INTERESTING ABOUT THE ROCK? ABOUT THE HOUSE?
THEY DROVE PAST THE CAPITOL DOME OF MADISON--A PERFECT SNOWGLOBE SCENE IN THE FALLING SNOW.

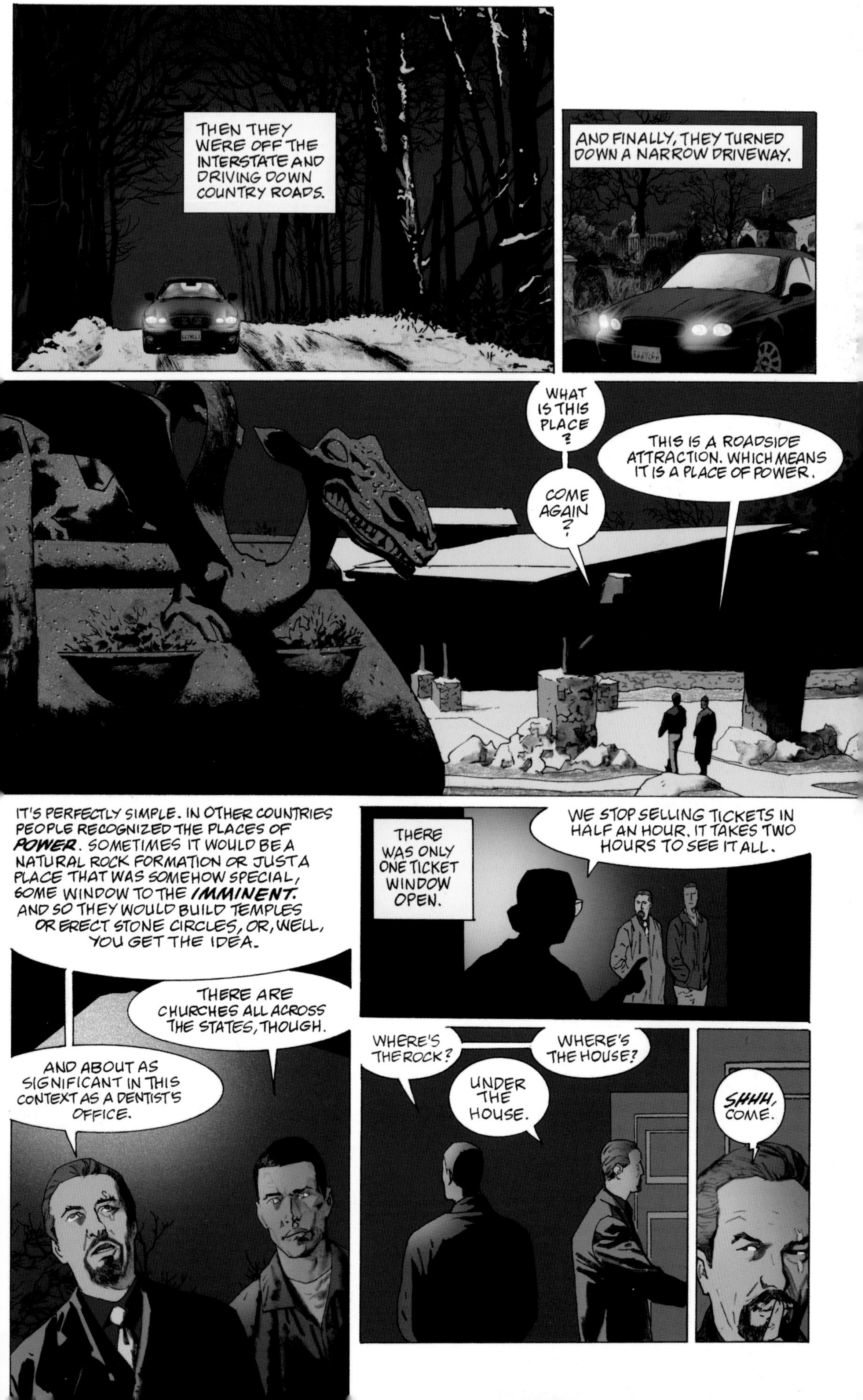
THEN THEY WERE OFF THE INTERSTATE AND DRIVING DOWN COUNTRY ROADS.
AND FINALLY, THEY TURNED DOWN A NARROW DRIVEWAY.
WHAT IS THIS PLACE?
COME AGAIN?
THIS IS A ROADSIDE ATTRACTION. WHICH MEANS IT IS A PLACE OF POWER.
IT'S PERFECTLY SIMPLE. IN OTHER COUNTRIES PEOPLE RECOGNIZED THE PLACES OF POWER. SOMETIMES IT WOULD BE A NATURAL ROCK FORMATION OR JUST A PLACE THAT WAS SOMEHOW SPECIAL, SOME WINDOW TO THE IMMINENT. AND SO THEY WOULD BUILD TEMPLES OR ERECT STONE CIRCLES, OR, WELL, YOU GET THE IDEA.
THERE ARE CHURCHES ALL ACROSS THE STATES, THOUGH.
AND ABOUT AS SIGNIFICANT IN THIS CONTEXT AS A DENTIST'S OFFICE.
THERE WAS ONLY ONE TICKET WINDOW OPEN.
WE STOP SELLING TICKETS IN HALF AN HOUR. IT TAKES TWO HOURS TO SEE IT ALL.
WHERE'S THE ROCK?
WHERE'S THE HOUSE?
UNDER THE HOUSE.
SHHH, COME.

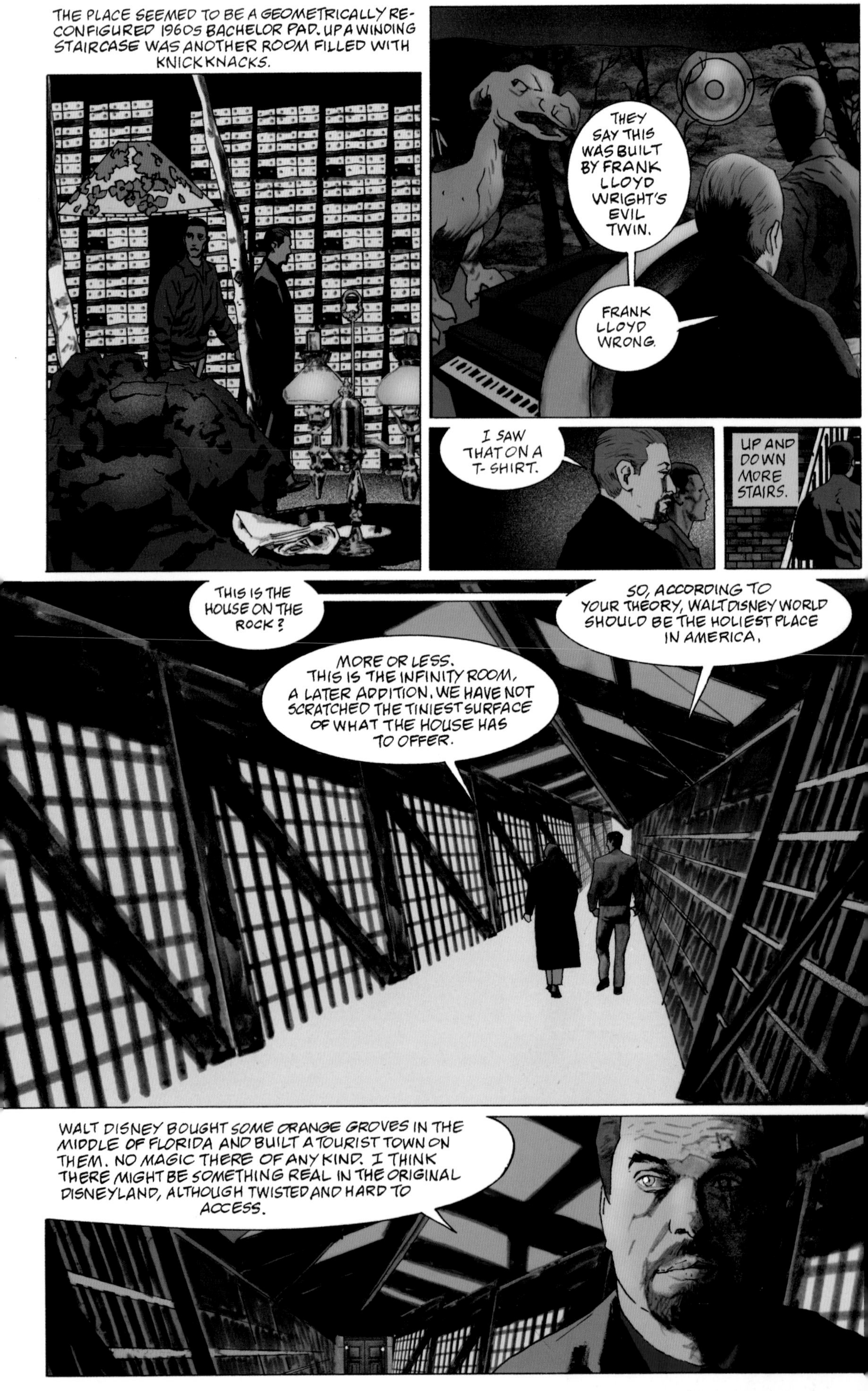
THE PLACE SEEMED TO BE A GEOMETRICALLY RE-CONFIGURED 1960s BACHELOR PAD. UP A WINDING STAIRCASE WAS ANOTHER ROOM FILLED WITH KNICKKNACKS.
THEY SAY THIS WAS BUILT BY FRANK LLOYD WRIGHT'S EVIL TWIN.
FRANK LLOYD WRONG.
I SAW THAT ON A T-SHIRT.
UP AND DOWN MORE STAIRS.
THIS IS THE HOUSE ON THE ROCK?
MORE OR LESS. THIS IS THE INFINITY ROOM, A LATER ADDITION. WE HAVE NOT SCRATCHED THE TINIEST SURFACE OF WHAT THE HOUSE HAS TO OFFER.
SO, ACCORDING TO YOUR THEORY, WALT DISNEY WORLD SHOULD BE THE HOLIEST PLACE IN AMERICA.
WALT DISNEY BOUGHT SOME ORANGE GROVES IN THE MIDDLE OF FLORIDA AND BUILT A TOURIST TOWN ON THEM. NO MAGIC THERE OF ANY KIND. I THINK THERE MIGHT BE SOMETHING REAL IN THE ORIGINAL DISNEYLAND, ALTHOUGH TWISTED AND HARD TO ACCESS.

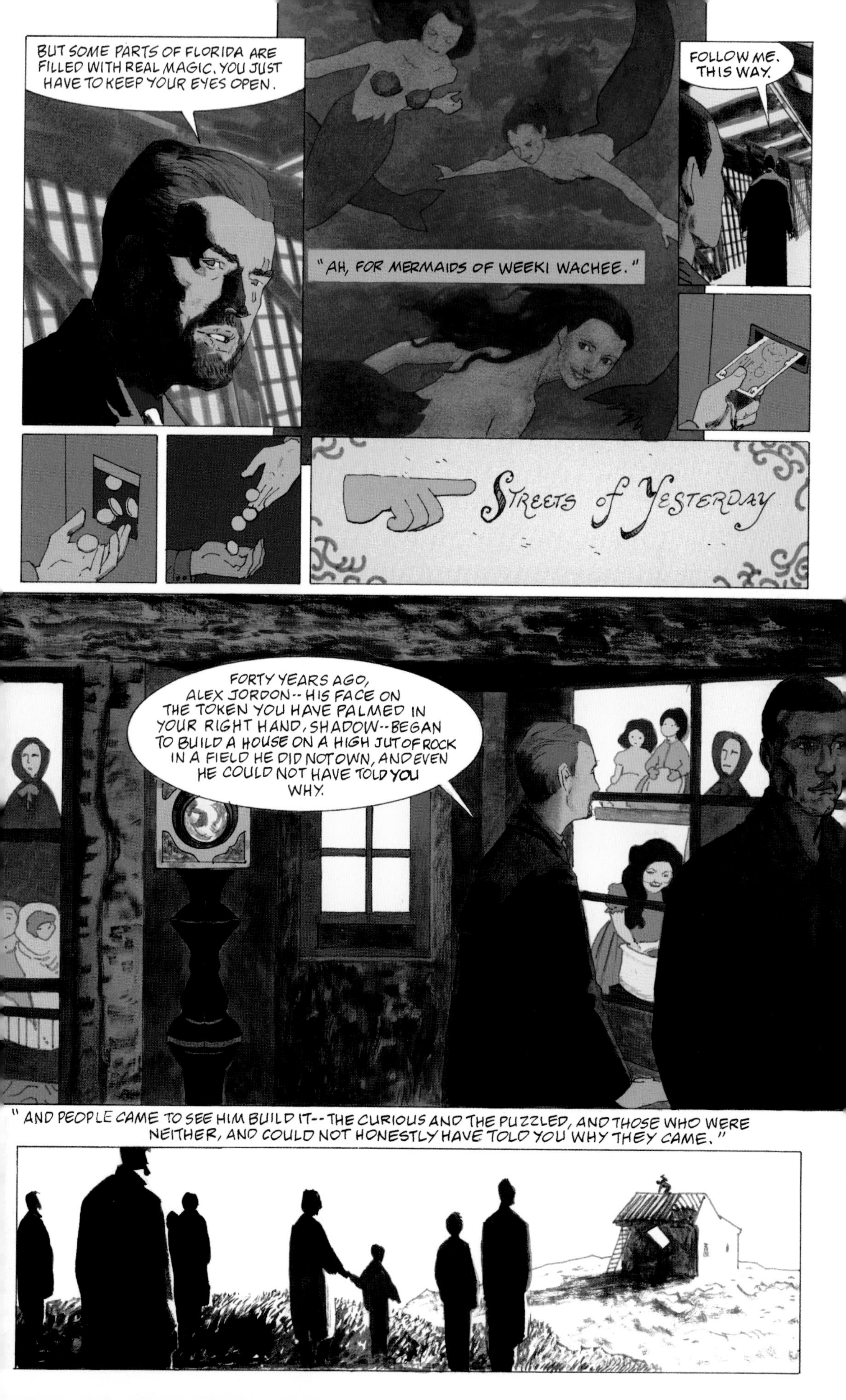
BUT SOME PARTS OF FLORIDA ARE FILLED WITH REAL MAGIC. YOU JUST HAVE TO KEEP YOUR EYES OPEN.
"AH, FOR MERMAIDS OF WEEKI WACHEE."
FOLLOW ME. THIS WAY.
STREETS OF YESTERDAY
FORTY YEARS AGO, ALEX JORDON--HIS FACE ON THE TOKEN YOU HAVE PALMED IN YOUR RIGHT HAND, SHADOW--BEGAN TO BUILD A HOUSE ON A HIGH JUT OF ROCK IN A FIELD HE DID NOT OWN, AND EVEN HE COULD NOT HAVE TOLD YOU WHY.
"AND PEOPLE CAME TO SEE HIM BUILD IT--THE CURIOUS AND THE PUZZLED, AND THOSE WHO WERE NEITHER, AND COULD NOT HONESTLY HAVE TOLD YOU WHY THEY CAME."

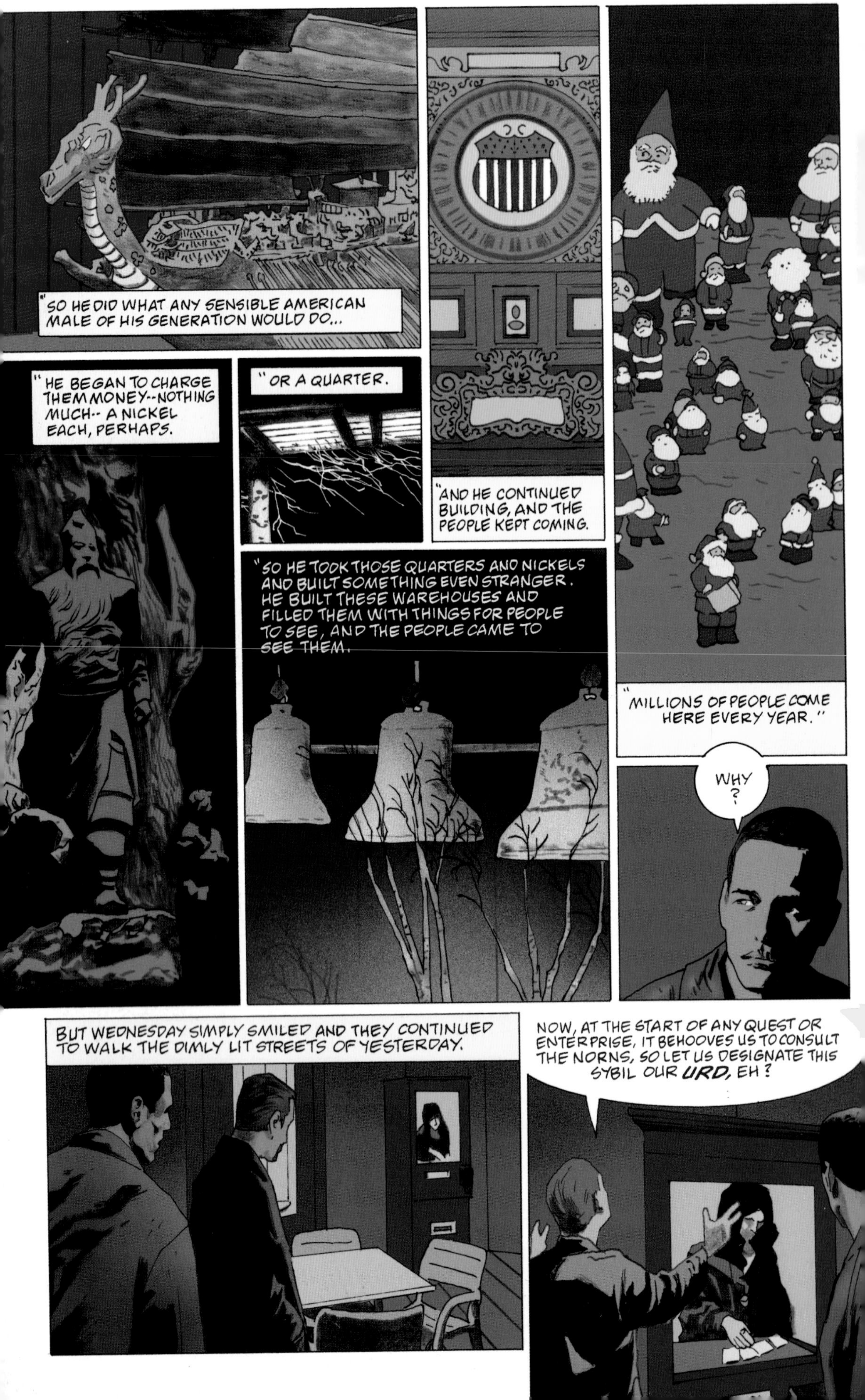
"SO HE DID WHAT ANY SENSIBLE AMERICAN MALE OF HIS GENERATION WOULD DO...
"HE BEGAN TO CHARGE THEM MONEY--NOTHING MUCH-- A NICKEL EACH, PERHAPS.
"OR A QUARTER.
"AND HE CONTINUED BUILDING, AND THE PEOPLE KEPT COMING.
"SO HE TOOK THOSE QUARTERS AND NICKELS AND BUILT SOMETHING EVEN STRANGER. HE BUILT THESE WAREHOUSES AND FILLED THEM WITH THINGS FOR PEOPLE TO SEE, AND THE PEOPLE CAME TO SEE THEM.
"MILLIONS OF PEOPLE COME HERE EVERY YEAR."
WHY?
BUT WEDNESDAY SIMPLY SMILED AND THEY CONTINUED TO WALK THE DIMLY LIT STREETS OF YESTERDAY.
NOW, AT THE START OF ANY QUEST OR ENTERPRISE, IT BEHOOVES US TO CONSULT THE NORNS, SO LET US DESIGNATE THIS SYBIL OUR URD, EH?

CLUNK

RRRRRRRRRRR

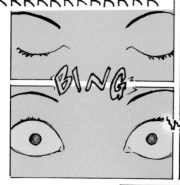

BING

WWWWWRRRRRRRRRRR THHHWWWIPPP

AREN'T YOU GOING TO SHOW IT TO ME? I'LL SHOW YOU MINE.

HMMF

A MAN'S FORTUNE IS HIS OWN AFFAIR. I WOULD NOT ASK TO SEE YOURS.

THHWWWWP

CLUNK

EVERY ENDING IS A NEW BEGINNING YOUR LUCKY NUMBER IS ONE YOUR LUCKY COLOR IS DEAD.

MOTTO: LIKE FATHER, LIKE SON

HUNH!

THEY WENT FURTHER IN, DOWN A RED CORRIDOR.

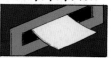

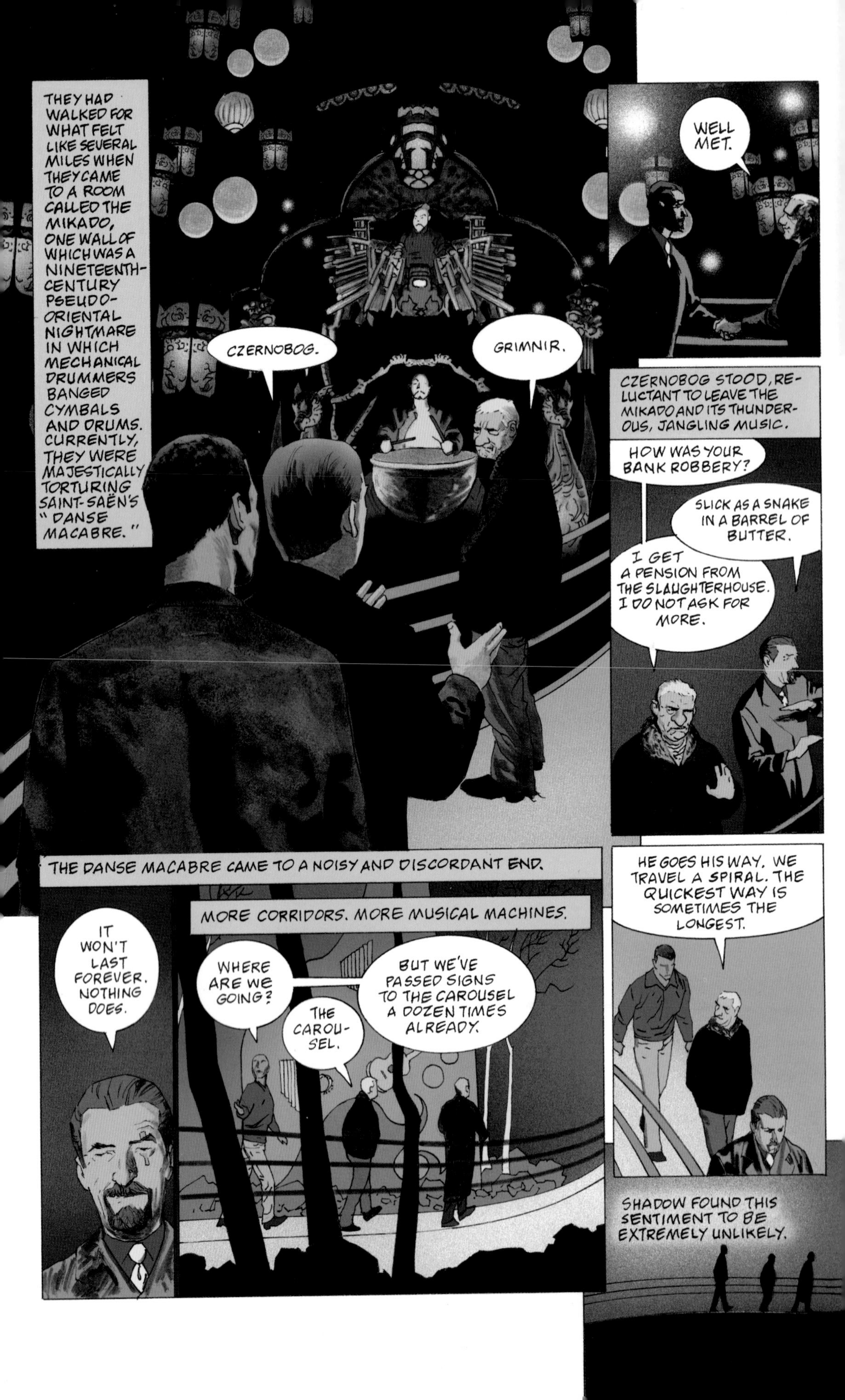
THEY HAD WALKED FOR WHAT FELT LIKE SEVERAL MILES WHEN THEY CAME TO A ROOM CALLED THE MIKADO, ONE WALL OF WHICH WAS A NINETEENTH-CENTURY PSEUDO-ORIENTAL NIGHTMARE IN WHICH MECHANICAL DRUMMERS BANGED CYMBALS AND DRUMS. CURRENTLY, THEY WERE MAJESTICALLY TORTURING SAINT-SAËN'S "DANSE MACABRE."
CZERNOBOG.
GRIMNIR.
WELL MET.
CZERNOBOG STOOD, RELUCTANT TO LEAVE THE MIKADO AND ITS THUNDEROUS, JANGLING MUSIC.
HOW WAS YOUR BANK ROBBERY?
SLICK AS A SNAKE IN A BARREL OF BUTTER.
I GET A PENSION FROM THE SLAUGHTERHOUSE. I DO NOT ASK FOR MORE.
THE DANSE MACABRE CAME TO A NOISY AND DISCORDANT END.
IT WON'T LAST FOREVER. NOTHING DOES.
MORE CORRIDORS. MORE MUSICAL MACHINES.
WHERE ARE WE GOING?
THE CAROUSEL.
BUT WE'VE PASSED SIGNS TO THE CAROUSEL A DOZEN TIMES ALREADY.
HE GOES HIS WAY. WE TRAVEL A SPIRAL. THE QUICKEST WAY IS SOMETIMES THE LONGEST.
SHADOW FOUND THIS SENTIMENT TO BE EXTREMELY UNLIKELY.

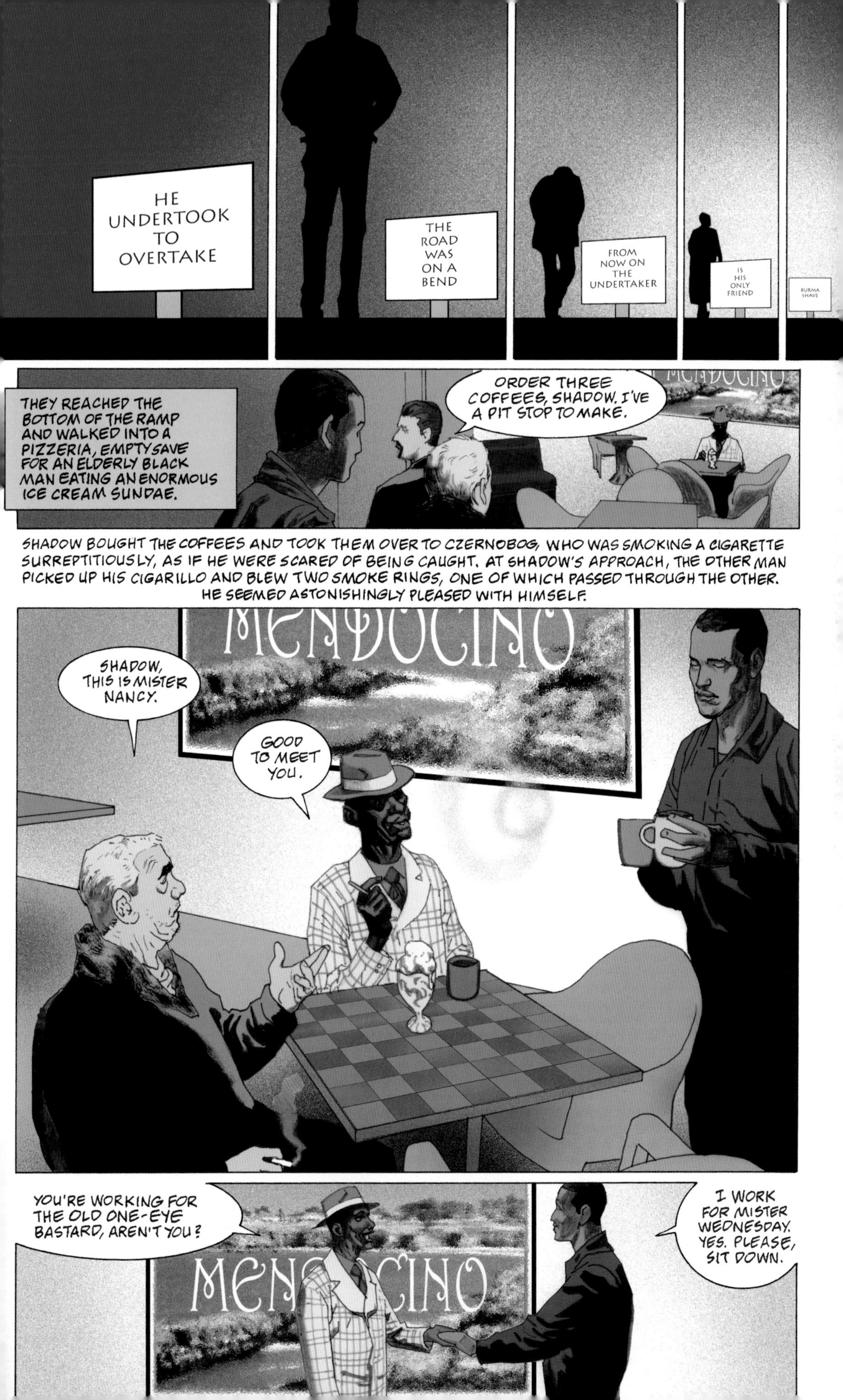
HE UNDERTOOK TO OVERTAKE
THE ROAD WAS ON A BEND
FROM NOW ON THE UNDERTAKER
IS HIS ONLY FRIEND
BURMA SHAVE
THEY REACHED THE BOTTOM OF THE RAMP AND WALKED INTO A PIZZERIA, EMPTY SAVE FOR AN ELDERLY BLACK MAN EATING AN ENORMOUS ICE CREAM SUNDAE.
ORDER THREE COFFEES, SHADOW. I'VE A PIT STOP TO MAKE.
MENDOCINO
SHADOW BOUGHT THE COFFEES AND TOOK THEM OVER TO CZERNOBOG, WHO WAS SMOKING A CIGARETTE SURREPTITIOUSLY, AS IF HE WERE SCARED OF BEING CAUGHT. AT SHADOW'S APPROACH, THE OTHER MAN PICKED UP HIS CIGARILLO AND BLEW TWO SMOKE RINGS, ONE OF WHICH PASSED THROUGH THE OTHER. HE SEEMED ASTONISHINGLY PLEASED WITH HIMSELF.
MENDOCINO
SHADOW, THIS IS MISTER NANCY.
GOOD TO MEET YOU.
YOU'RE WORKING FOR THE OLD ONE-EYE BASTARD, AREN'T YOU?
I WORK FOR MISTER WEDNESDAY. YES. PLEASE, SIT DOWN.

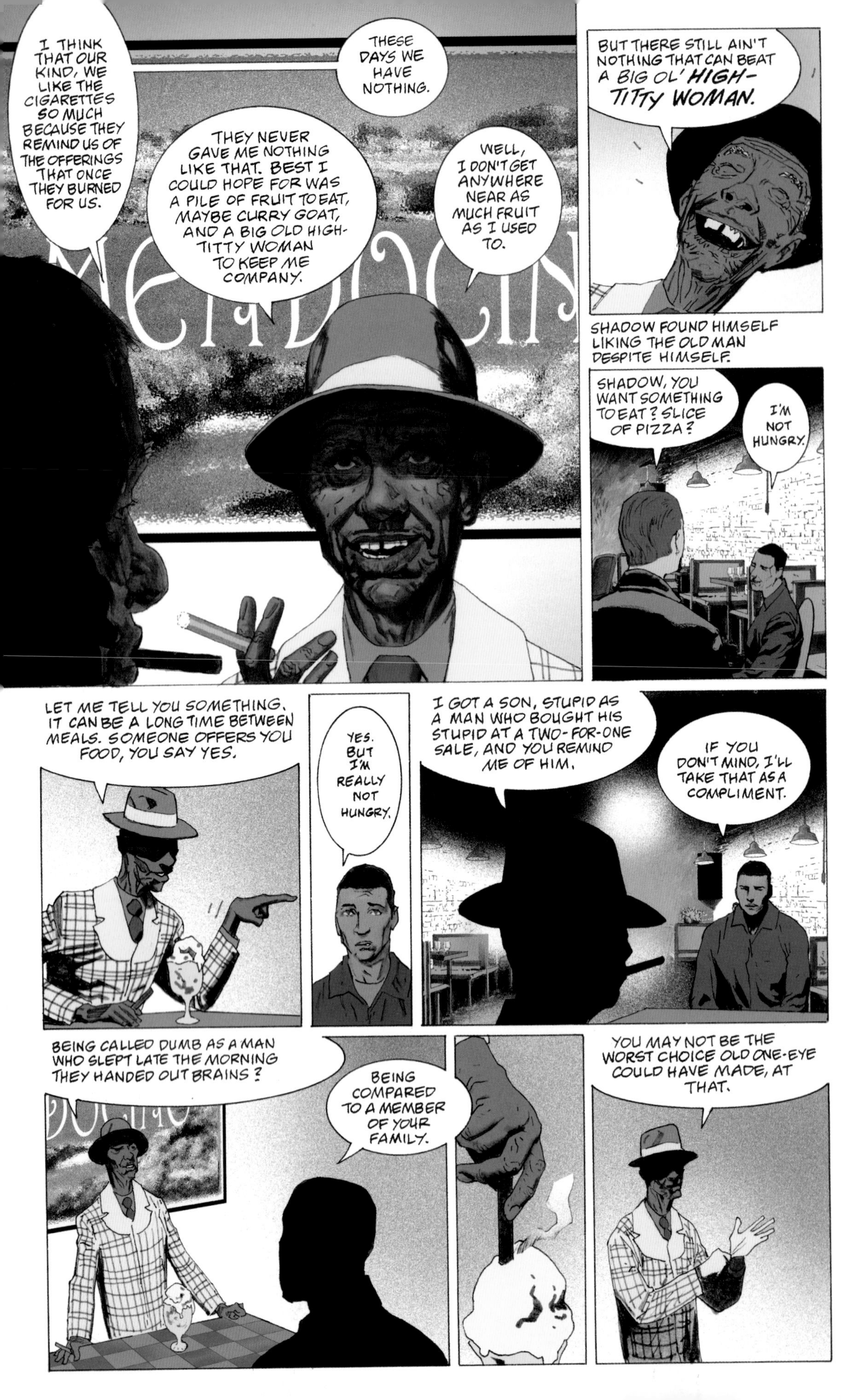

I THINK THAT OUR KIND, WE LIKE THE CIGARETTES SO MUCH BECAUSE THEY REMIND US OF THE OFFERINGS THAT ONCE THEY BURNED FOR US.
THESE DAYS WE HAVE NOTHING.
THEY NEVER GAVE ME NOTHING LIKE THAT. BEST I COULD HOPE FOR WAS A PILE OF FRUIT TO EAT, MAYBE CURRY GOAT, AND A BIG OLD HIGH-TITTY WOMAN TO KEEP ME COMPANY.
WELL, I DON'T GET ANYWHERE NEAR AS MUCH FRUIT AS I USED TO.
MENDOCIN
BUT THERE STILL AIN'T NOTHING THAT CAN BEAT A BIG OL' HIGH-TITTY WOMAN.
SHADOW FOUND HIMSELF LIKING THE OLD MAN DESPITE HIMSELF.
SHADOW, YOU WANT SOMETHING TO EAT? SLICE OF PIZZA?
I'M NOT HUNGRY.
LET ME TELL YOU SOMETHING. IT CAN BE A LONG TIME BETWEEN MEALS. SOMEONE OFFERS YOU FOOD, YOU SAY YES.
YES. BUT I'M REALLY NOT HUNGRY.
I GOT A SON, STUPID AS A MAN WHO BOUGHT HIS STUPID AT A TWO-FOR-ONE SALE, AND YOU REMIND ME OF HIM.
IF YOU DON'T MIND, I'LL TAKE THAT AS A COMPLIMENT.
BEING CALLED DUMB AS A MAN WHO SLEPT LATE THE MORNING THEY HANDED OUT BRAINS?
BEING COMPARED TO A MEMBER OF YOUR FAMILY.
YOU MAY NOT BE THE WORST CHOICE OLD ONE-EYE COULD HAVE MADE, AT THAT.

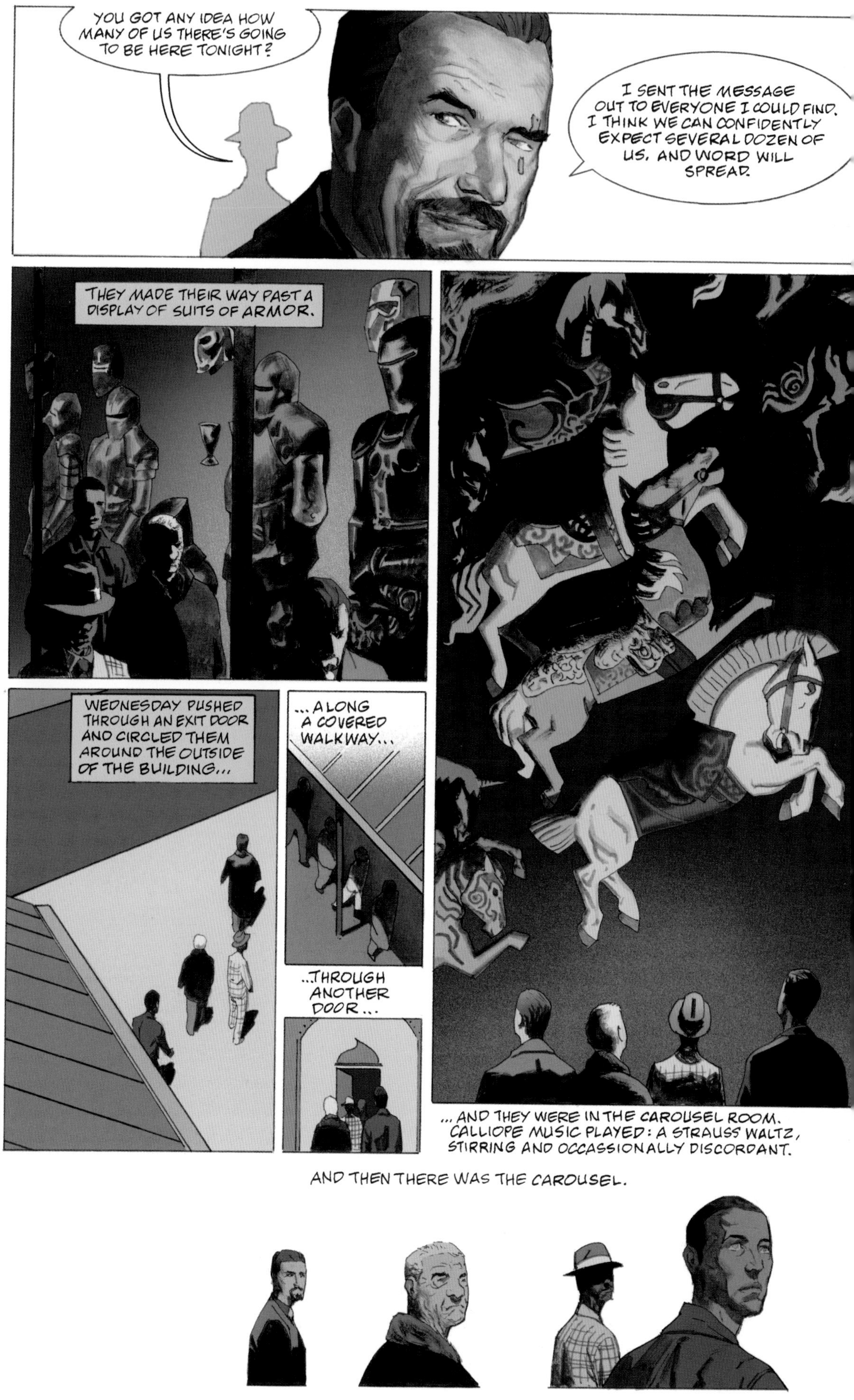
YOU GOT ANY IDEA HOW MANY OF US THERE'S GOING TO BE HERE TONIGHT?
I SENT THE MESSAGE OUT TO EVERYONE I COULD FIND. I THINK WE CAN CONFIDENTLY EXPECT SEVERAL DOZEN OF US. AND WORD WILL SPREAD.
THEY MADE THEIR WAY PAST A DISPLAY OF SUITS OF ARMOR.
WEDNESDAY PUSHED THROUGH AN EXIT DOOR AND CIRCLED THEM AROUND THE OUTSIDE OF THE BUILDING...
...ALONG A COVERED WALKWAY...
...THROUGH ANOTHER DOOR...
...AND THEY WERE IN THE CAROUSEL ROOM. CALLIOPE MUSIC PLAYED: A STRAUSS WALTZ, STIRRING AND OCCASSIONALLY DISCORDANT.
AND THEN THERE WAS THE CAROUSEL.

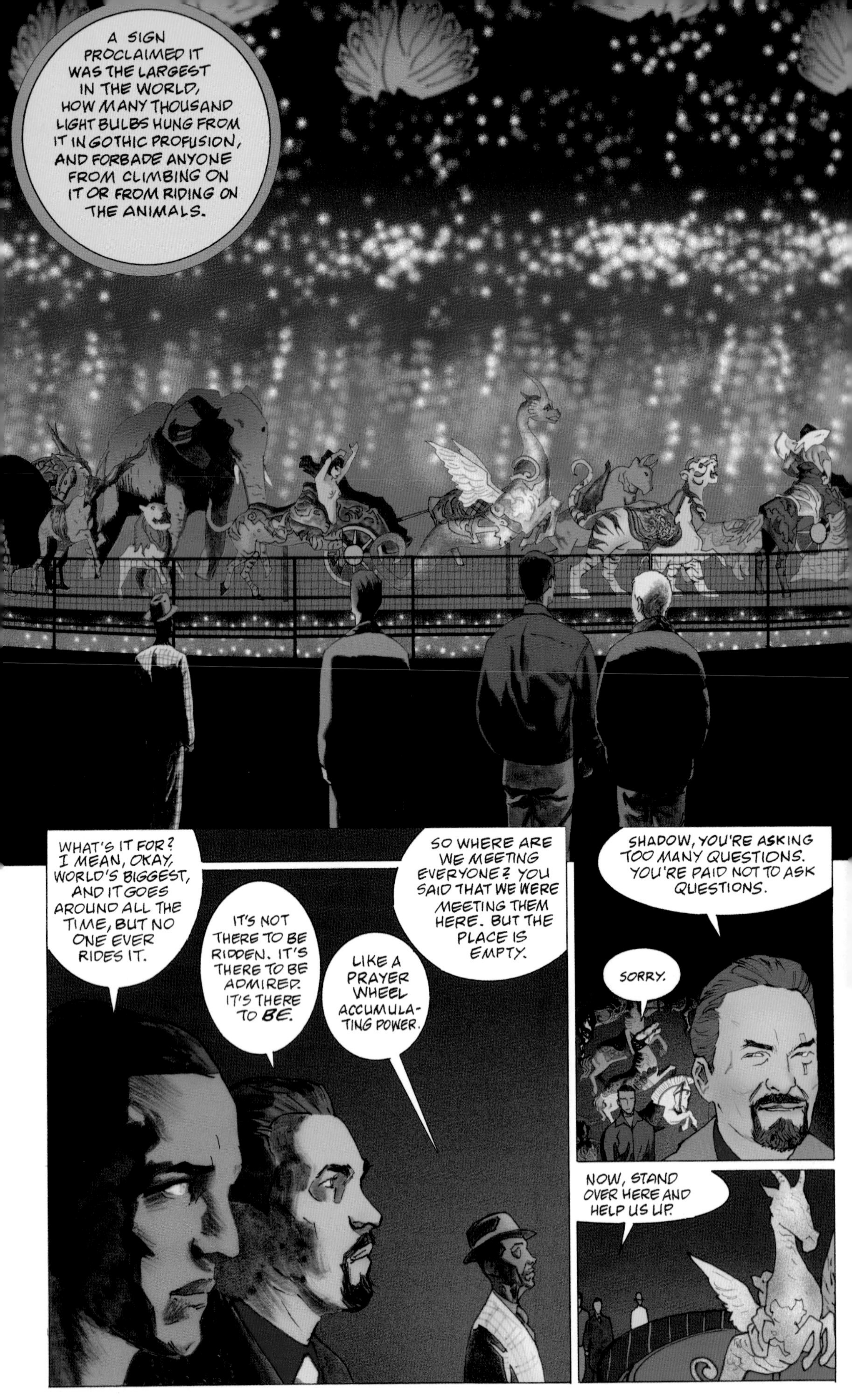
A SIGN PROCLAIMED IT WAS THE LARGEST IN THE WORLD, HOW MANY THOUSAND LIGHT BULBS HUNG FROM IT IN GOTHIC PROFUSION, AND FORBADE ANYONE FROM CLIMBING ON IT OR FROM RIDING ON THE ANIMALS.
WHAT'S IT FOR? I MEAN, OKAY, WORLD'S BIGGEST, AND IT GOES AROUND ALL THE TIME, BUT NO ONE EVER RIDES IT.
IT'S NOT THERE TO BE RIDDEN. IT'S THERE TO BE ADMIRED. IT'S THERE TO BE.
LIKE A PRAYER WHEEL ACCUMULATING POWER.
SO WHERE ARE WE MEETING EVERYONE? YOU SAID THAT WE WERE MEETING THEM HERE. BUT THE PLACE IS EMPTY.
SHADOW, YOU'RE ASKING TOO MANY QUESTIONS. YOU'RE PAID NOT TO ASK QUESTIONS.
SORRY.
NOW, STAND OVER HERE AND HELP US UP.

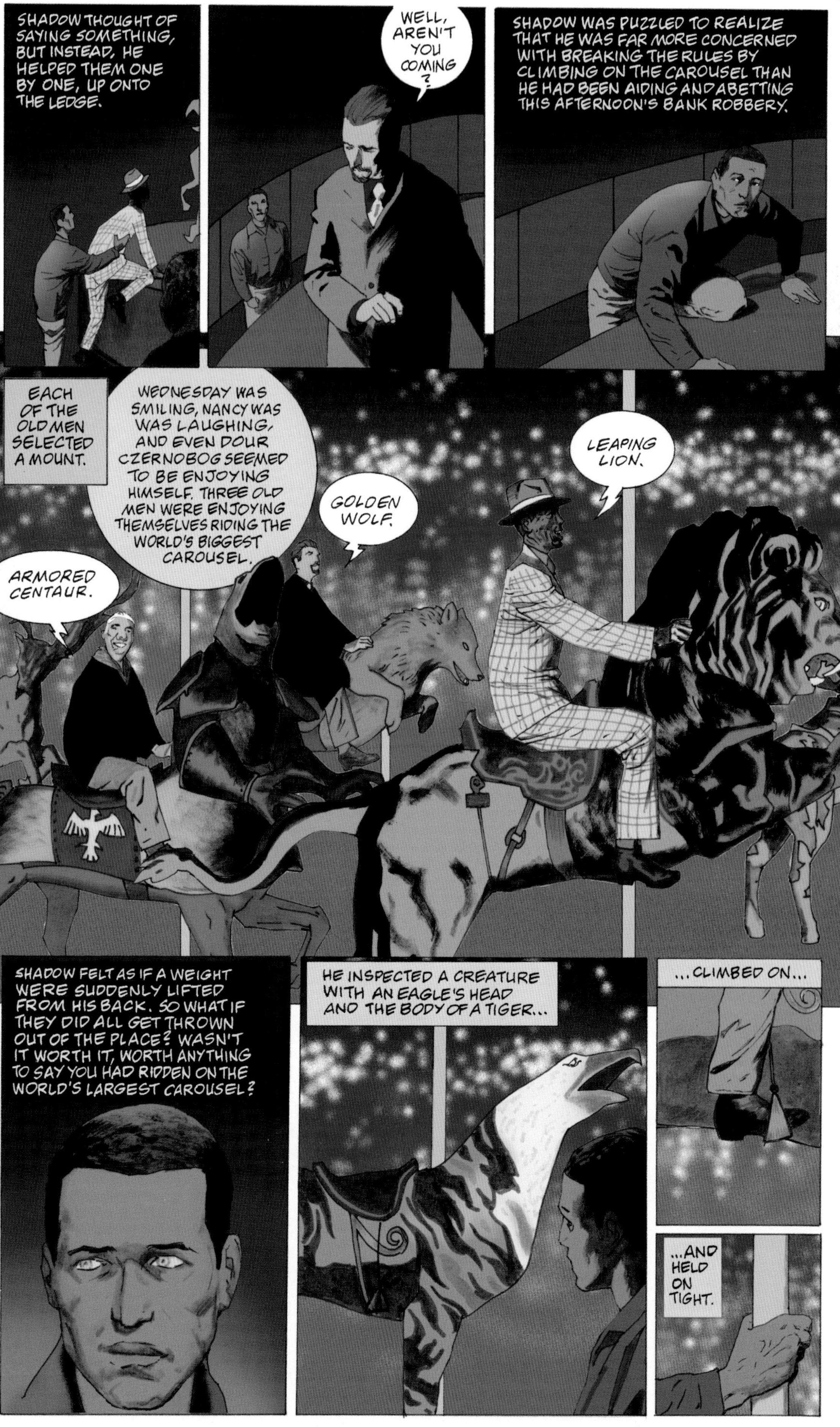

SHADOW THOUGHT OF SAYING SOMETHING, BUT INSTEAD, HE HELPED THEM ONE BY ONE, UP ONTO THE LEDGE.
WELL, AREN'T YOU COMING?
SHADOW WAS PUZZLED TO REALIZE THAT HE WAS FAR MORE CONCERNED WITH BREAKING THE RULES BY CLIMBING ON THE CAROUSEL THAN HE HAD BEEN AIDING AND ABETTING THIS AFTERNOON'S BANK ROBBERY.
EACH OF THE OLD MEN SELECTED A MOUNT.
WEDNESDAY WAS SMILING, NANCY WAS WAS LAUGHING, AND EVEN DOUR CZERNOBOG SEEMED TO BE ENJOYING HIMSELF. THREE OLD MEN WERE ENJOYING THEMSELVES RIDING THE WORLD'S BIGGEST CAROUSEL.
ARMORED CENTAUR.
GOLDEN WOLF.
LEAPING LION.
SHADOW FELT AS IF A WEIGHT WERE SUDDENLY LIFTED FROM HIS BACK. SO WHAT IF THEY DID ALL GET THROWN OUT OF THE PLACE? WASN'T IT WORTH IT, WORTH ANYTHING TO SAY YOU HAD RIDDEN ON THE WORLD'S LARGEST CAROUSEL?
HE INSPECTED A CREATURE WITH AN EAGLE'S HEAD AND THE BODY OF A TIGER...
...CLIMBED ON...
...AND HELD ON TIGHT.

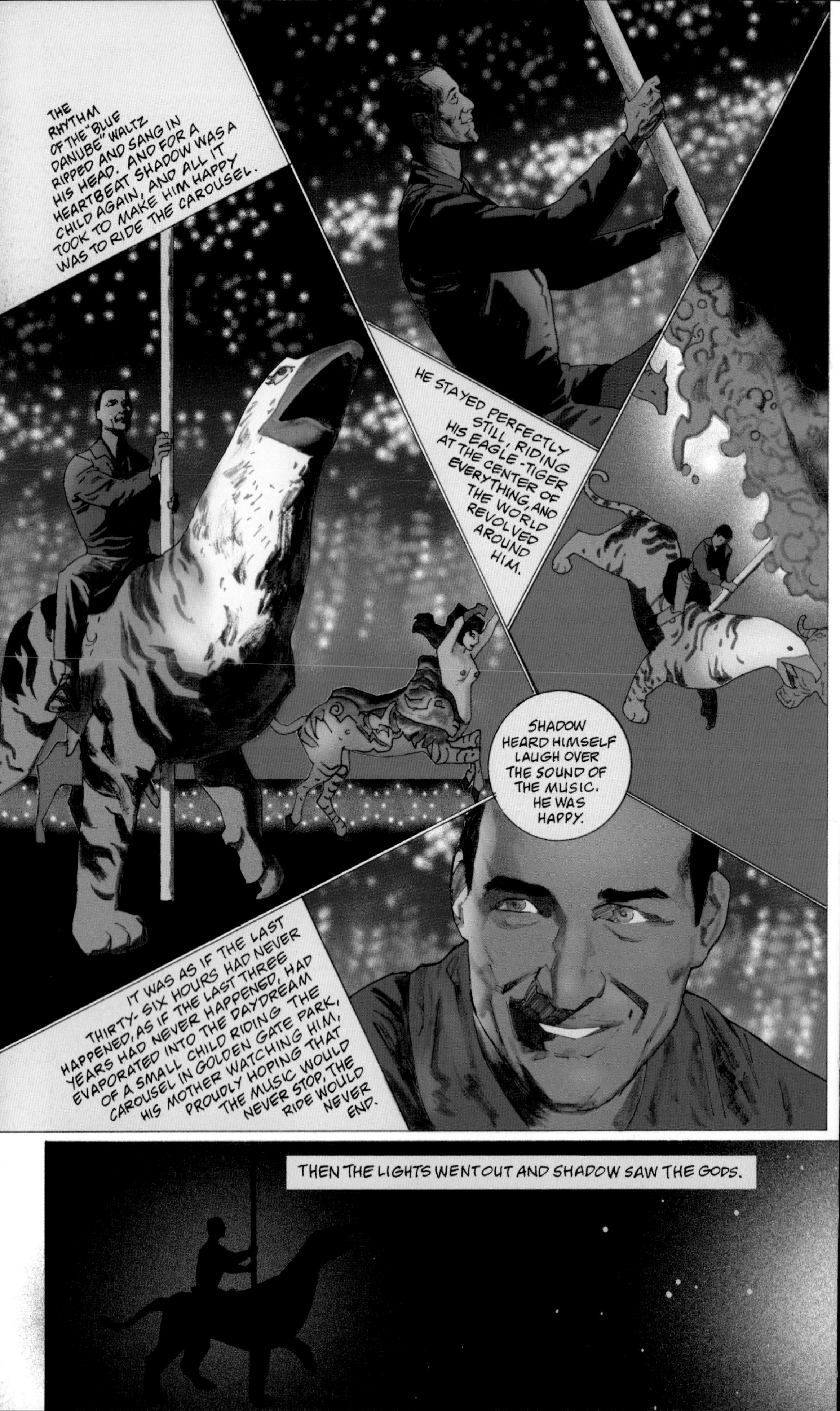
THE RHYTHM OF THE "BLUE DANUBE" WALTZ RIPPED AND SANG IN HIS HEAD. AND FOR A HEARTBEAT SHADOW WAS A CHILD AGAIN, AND ALL IT TOOK TO MAKE HIM HAPPY WAS TO RIDE THE CAROUSEL.
HE STAYED PERFECTLY STILL, RIDING HIS EAGLE-TIGER AT THE CENTER OF EVERYTHING, AND THE WORLD REVOLVED AROUND HIM.
SHADOW HEARD HIMSELF LAUGH OVER THE SOUND OF THE MUSIC. HE WAS HAPPY.
IT WAS AS IF THE LAST THIRTY-SIX HOURS HAD NEVER HAPPENED, AS IF THE LAST THREE YEARS HAD NEVER HAPPENED, HAD EVAPORATED INTO THE DAYDREAM OF A SMALL CHILD RIDING THE CAROUSEL IN GOLDEN GATE PARK, HIS MOTHER WATCHING HIM, PROUDLY HOPING THAT THE MUSIC WOULD NEVER STOP, THE RIDE WOULD NEVER END.
THEN THE LIGHTS WENT OUT AND SHADOW SAW THE GODS.

CHAPTER SIX

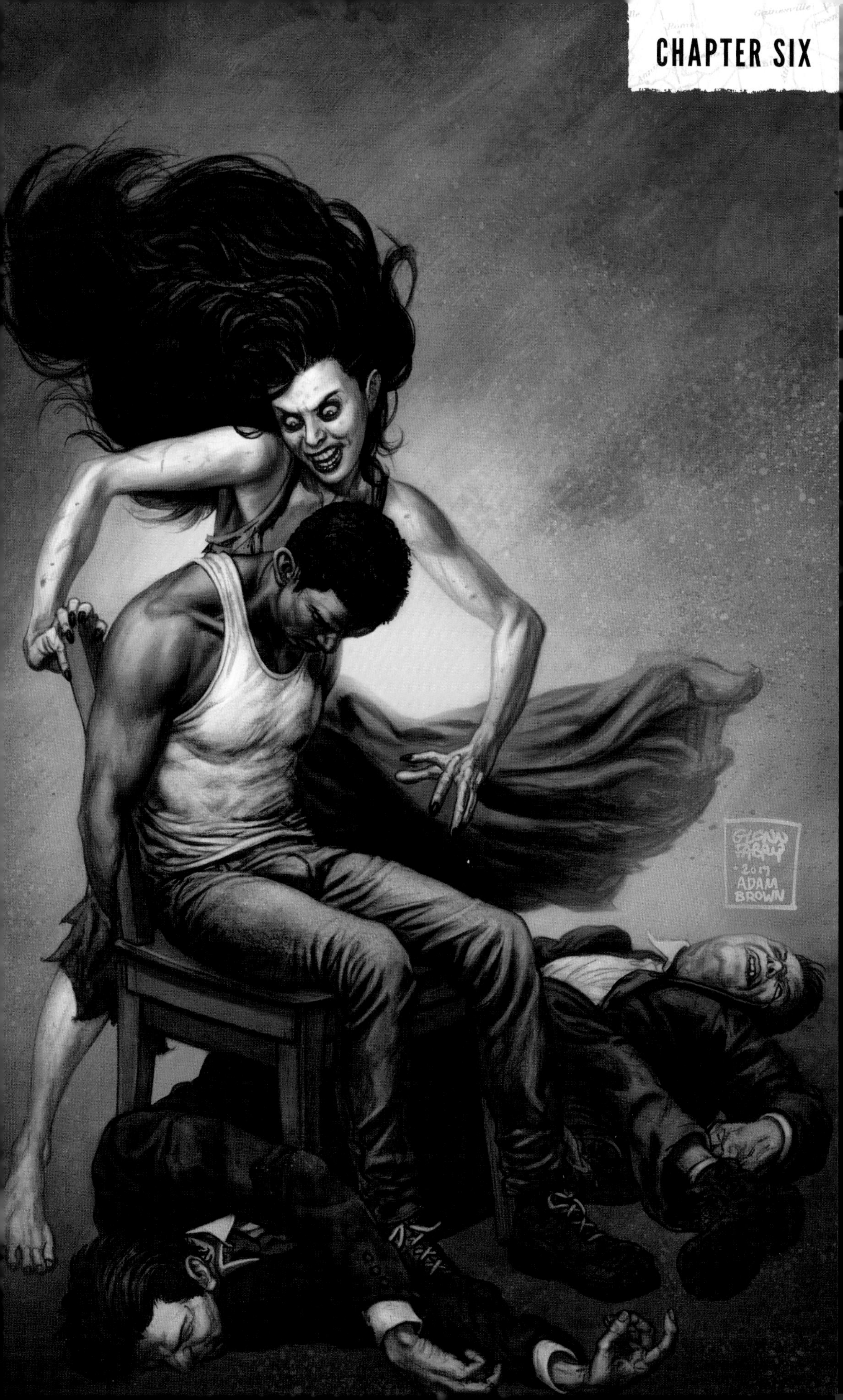

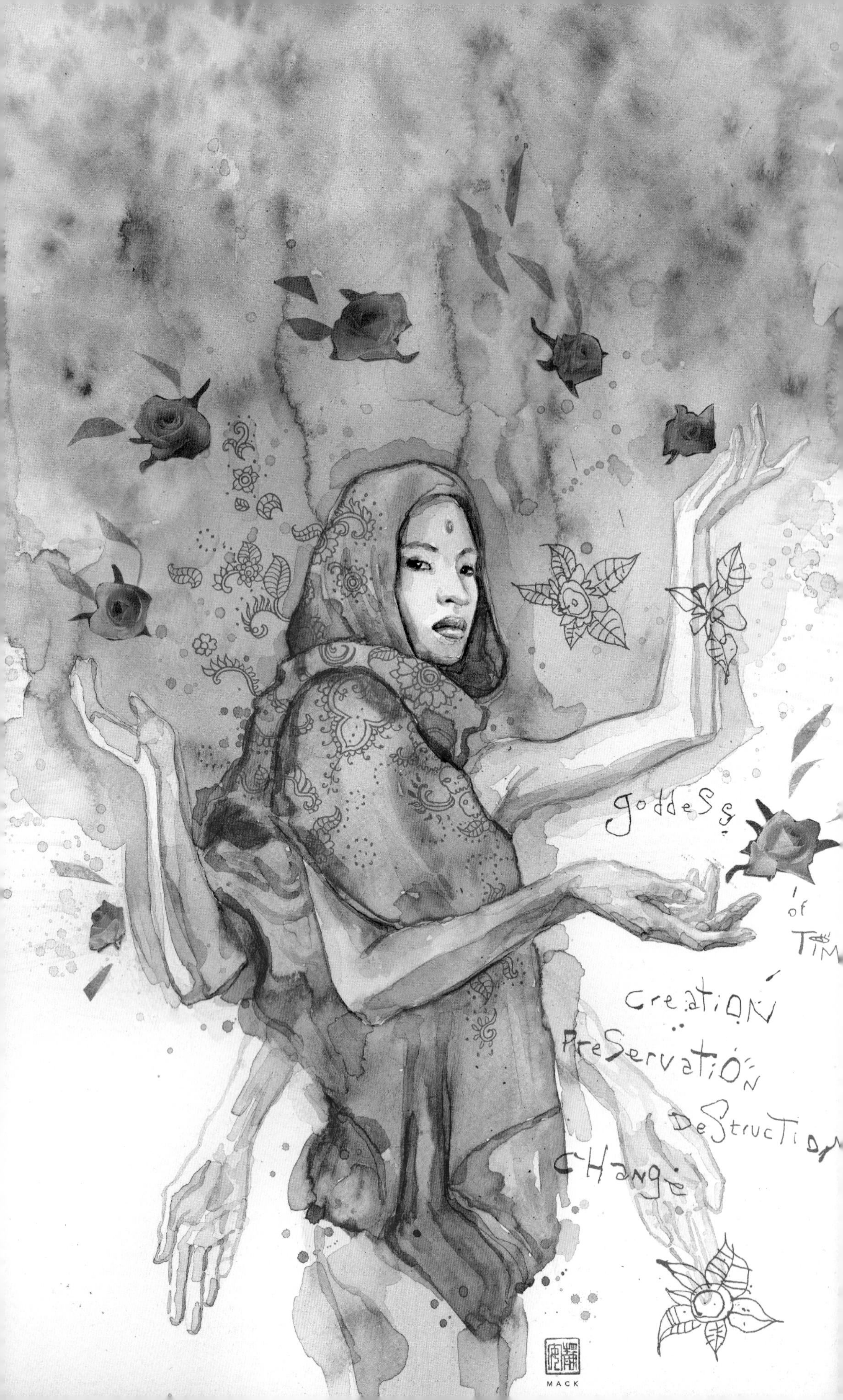
goddess
of
TIM
creation
preservation
destruction
change
MACK

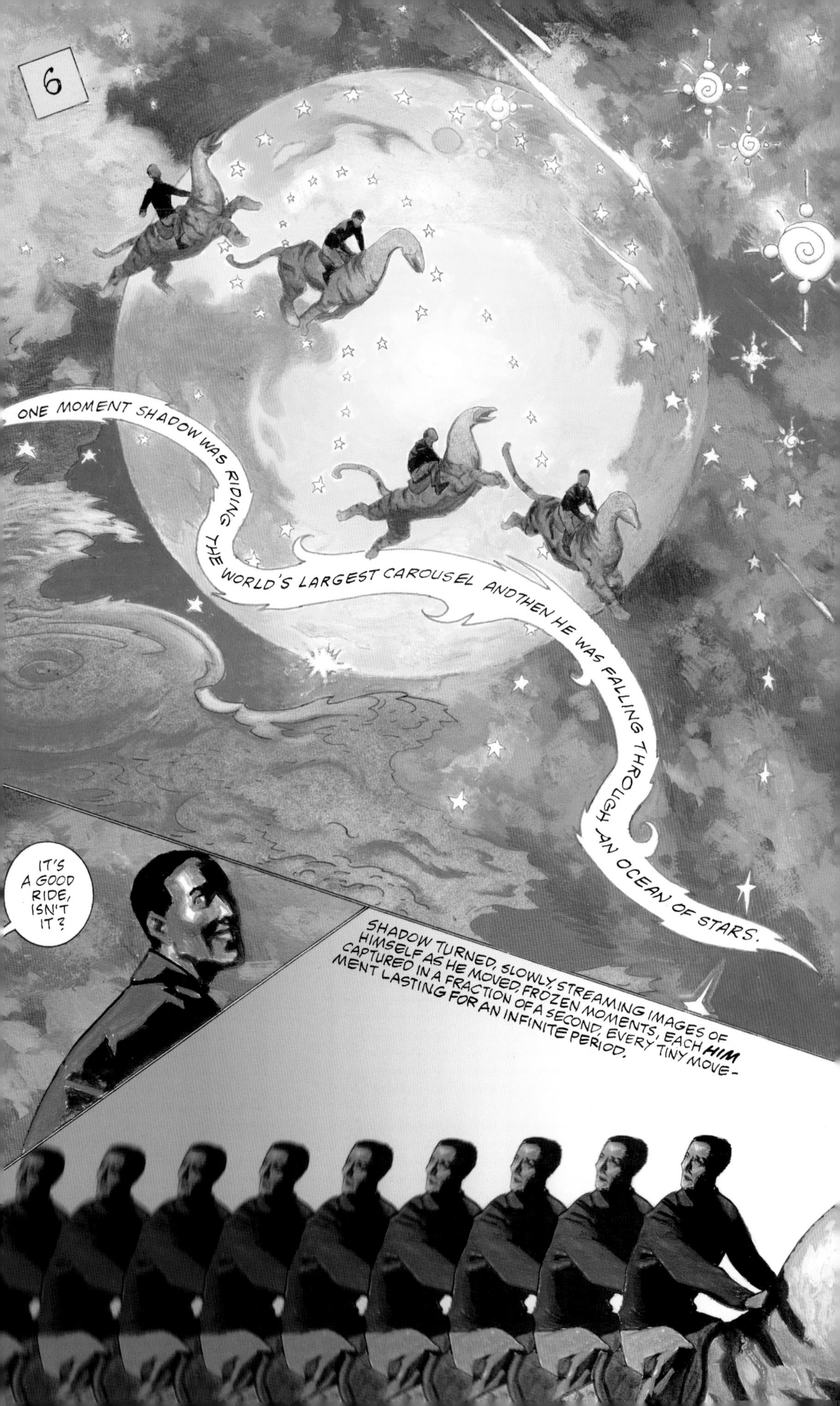
6
ONE MOMENT SHADOW WAS RIDING THE WORLD'S LARGEST CAROUSEL AND THEN HE WAS FALLING THROUGH AN OCEAN OF STARS.
IT'S A GOOD RIDE, ISN'T IT?
SHADOW TURNED, SLOWLY, STREAMING IMAGES OF HIMSELF AS HE MOVED, FROZEN MOMENTS, EACH HIM CAPTURED IN A FRACTION OF A SECOND, EVERY TINY MOVEMENT LASTING FOR AN INFINITE PERIOD.

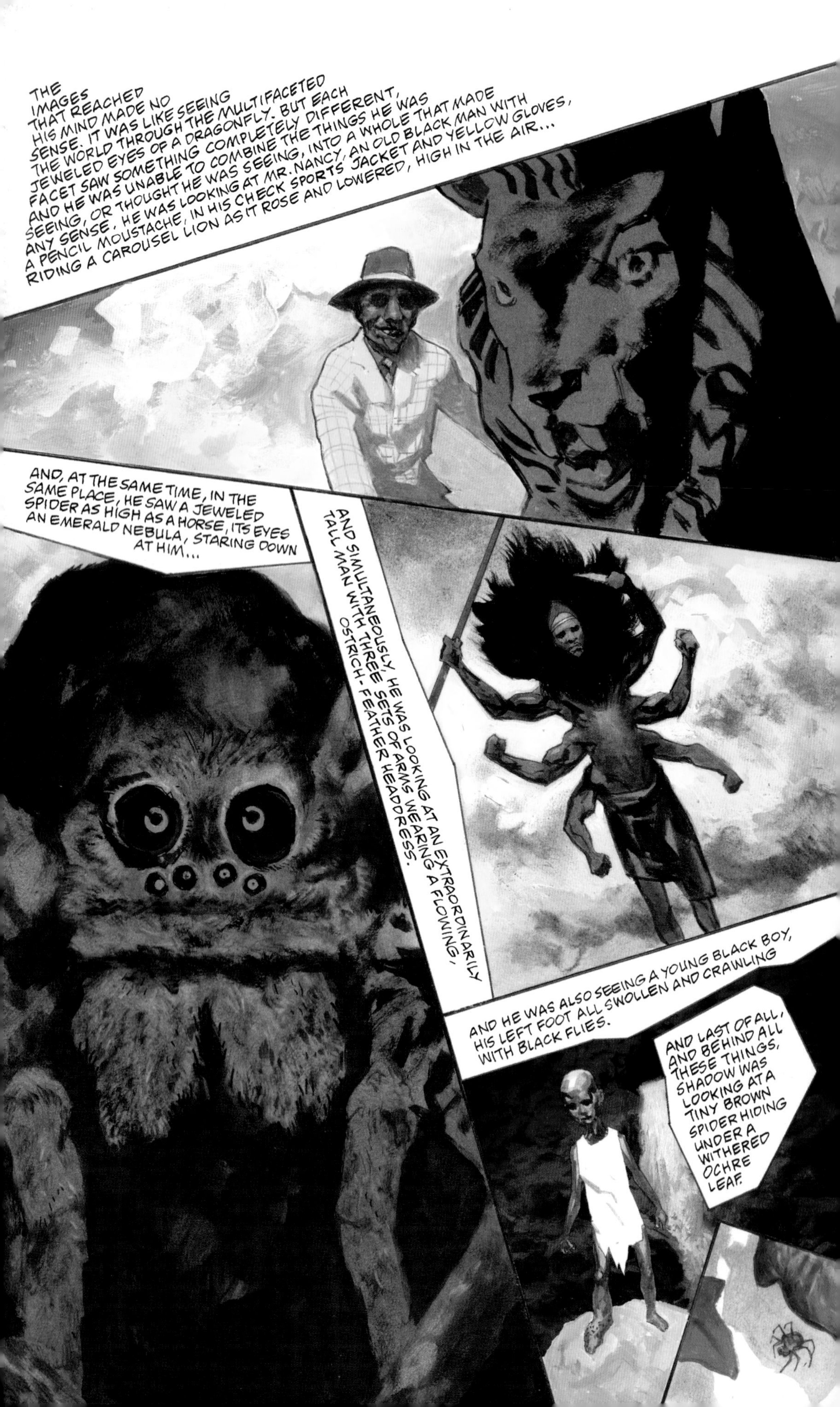
THE IMAGES THAT REACHED HIS MIND MADE NO SENSE. IT WAS LIKE SEEING THE WORLD THROUGH THE MULTIFACETED JEWELED EYES OF A DRAGONFLY. BUT EACH FACET SAW SOMETHING COMPLETELY DIFFERENT, AND HE WAS UNABLE TO COMBINE THE THINGS HE WAS SEEING, OR THOUGHT HE WAS SEEING, INTO A WHOLE THAT MADE ANY SENSE. HE WAS LOOKING AT MR. NANCY, AN OLD BLACK MAN WITH A PENCIL MOUSTACHE, IN HIS CHECK SPORTS JACKET AND YELLOW GLOVES, RIDING A CAROUSEL LION AS IT ROSE AND LOWERED, HIGH IN THE AIR...
AND, AT THE SAME TIME, IN THE SAME PLACE, HE SAW A JEWELED SPIDER AS HIGH AS A HORSE, ITS EYES AN EMERALD NEBULA, STARING DOWN AT HIM...
AND SIMULTANEOUSLY, HE WAS LOOKING AT AN EXTRAORDINARILY TALL MAN WITH THREE SETS OF ARMS WEARING A FLOWING, OSTRICH-FEATHER HEADDRESS.
AND HE WAS ALSO SEEING A YOUNG BLACK BOY, HIS LEFT FOOT ALL SWOLLEN AND CRAWLING WITH BLACK FLIES.
AND LAST OF ALL, AND BEHIND ALL THESE THINGS, SHADOW WAS LOOKING AT A TINY BROWN SPIDER HIDING UNDER A WITHERED OCHRE LEAF.

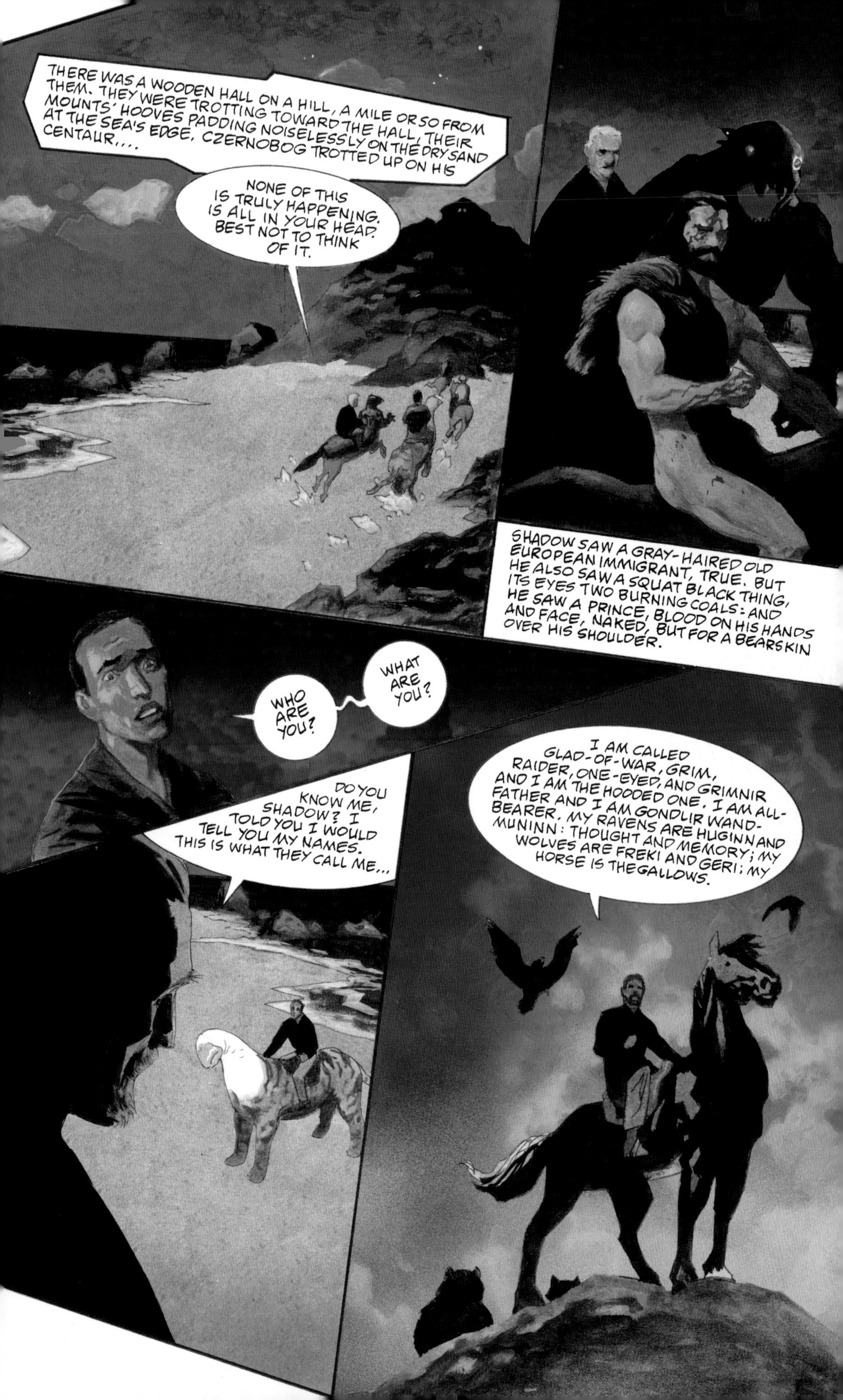
THERE WAS A WOODEN HALL ON A HILL, A MILE OR SO FROM THEM. THEY WERE TROTTING TOWARD THE HALL, THEIR MOUNTS' HOOVES PADDING NOISELESSLY ON THE DRY SAND AT THE SEA'S EDGE. CZERNOBOG TROTTED UP ON HIS CENTAUR....
NONE OF THIS IS TRULY HAPPENING. IS ALL IN YOUR HEAD. BEST NOT TO THINK OF IT.
SHADOW SAW A GRAY-HAIRED OLD EUROPEAN IMMIGRANT, TRUE. BUT HE ALSO SAW A SQUAT BLACK THING, ITS EYES TWO BURNING COALS: AND HE SAW A PRINCE, BLOOD ON HIS HANDS AND FACE, NAKED, BUT FOR A BEARSKIN OVER HIS SHOULDER.
WHO ARE YOU?
WHAT ARE YOU?
DO YOU KNOW ME, SHADOW? I TOLD YOU I WOULD TELL YOU MY NAMES. THIS IS WHAT THEY CALL ME...
I AM CALLED GLAD-OF-WAR, GRIM, RAIDER, ONE-EYED, AND GRIMNIR AND I AM THE HOODED ONE. I AM ALL-FATHER AND I AM GONDLIR WAND-BEARER. MY RAVENS ARE HUGINN AND MUNINN: THOUGHT AND MEMORY; MY WOLVES ARE FREKI AND GERI; MY HORSE IS THE GALLOWS.

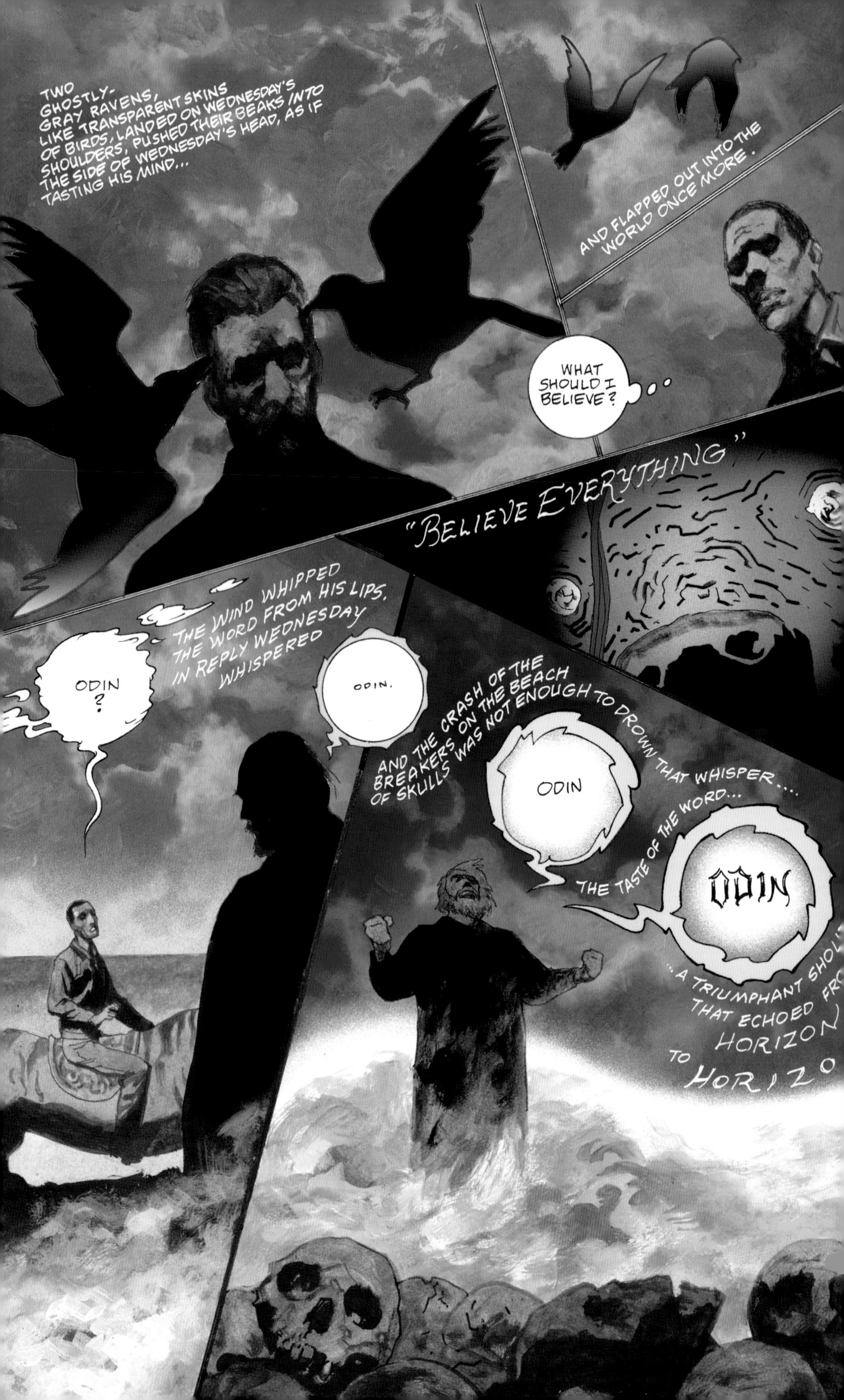
TWO GHOSTLY-GRAY RAVENS, LIKE TRANSPARENT SKINS OF BIRDS, LANDED ON WEDNESDAY'S SHOULDERS, PUSHED THEIR BEAKS INTO THE SIDE OF WEDNESDAY'S HEAD, AS IF TASTING HIS MIND...
AND FLAPPED OUT INTO THE WORLD ONCE MORE.
WHAT SHOULD I BELIEVE?
"BELIEVE EVERYTHING"
THE WIND WHIPPED THE WORD FROM HIS LIPS. IN REPLY WEDNESDAY WHISPERED
ODIN?
ODIN.
AND THE CRASH OF THE BREAKERS ON THE BEACH OF SKULLS WAS NOT ENOUGH TO DROWN THAT WHISPER....
ODIN
THE TASTE OF THE WORD...
ODIN
...A TRIUMPHANT SHOU
THAT ECHOED FRO
HORIZON
TO HORIZO

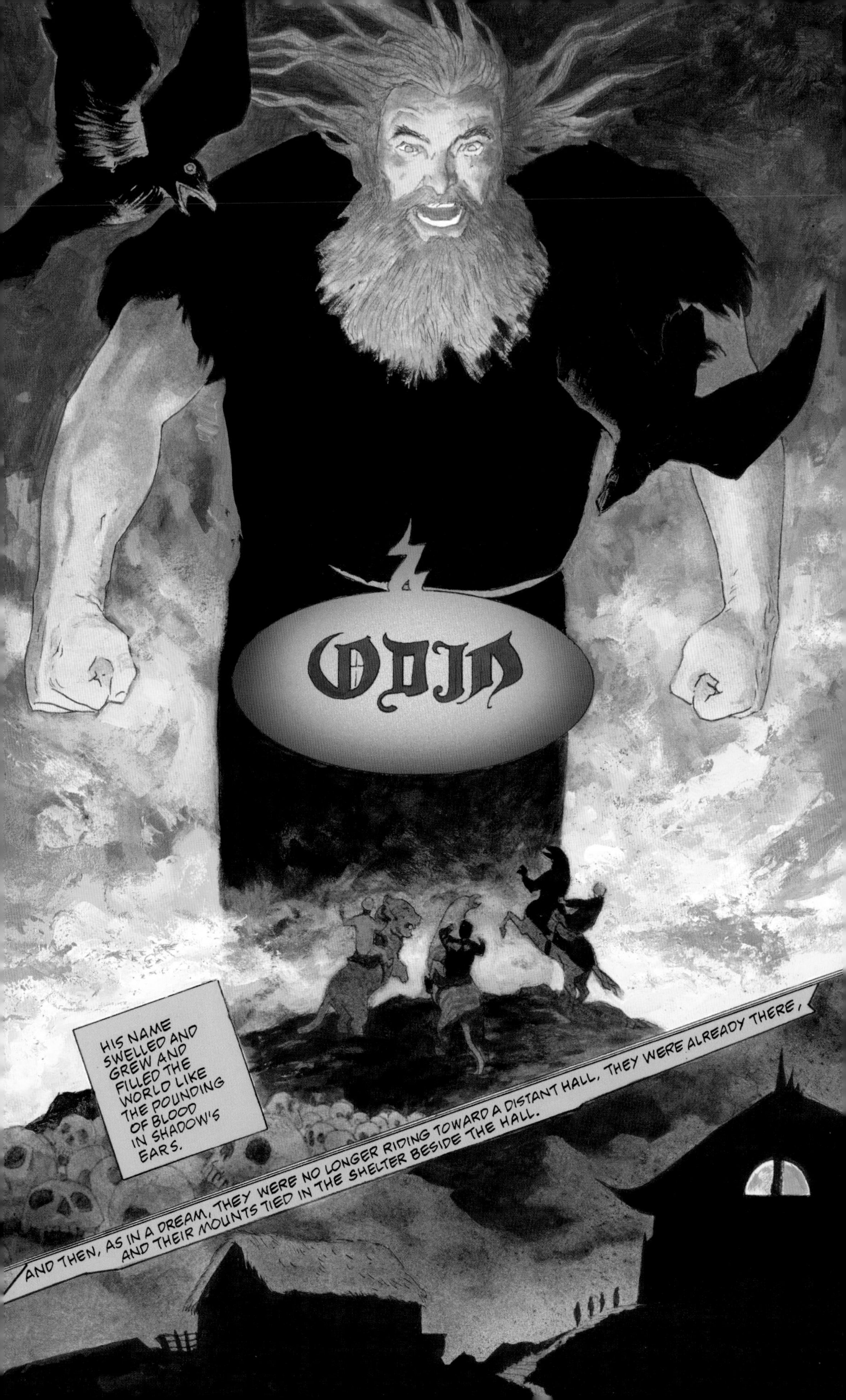
ODIN
HIS NAME SWELLED AND GREW AND FILLED THE WORLD LIKE THE POUNDING OF BLOOD IN SHADOW'S EARS.
AND THEN, AS IN A DREAM, THEY WERE NO LONGER RIDING TOWARD A DISTANT HALL, THEY WERE ALREADY THERE, AND THEIR MOUNTS TIED IN THE SHELTER BESIDE THE HALL.

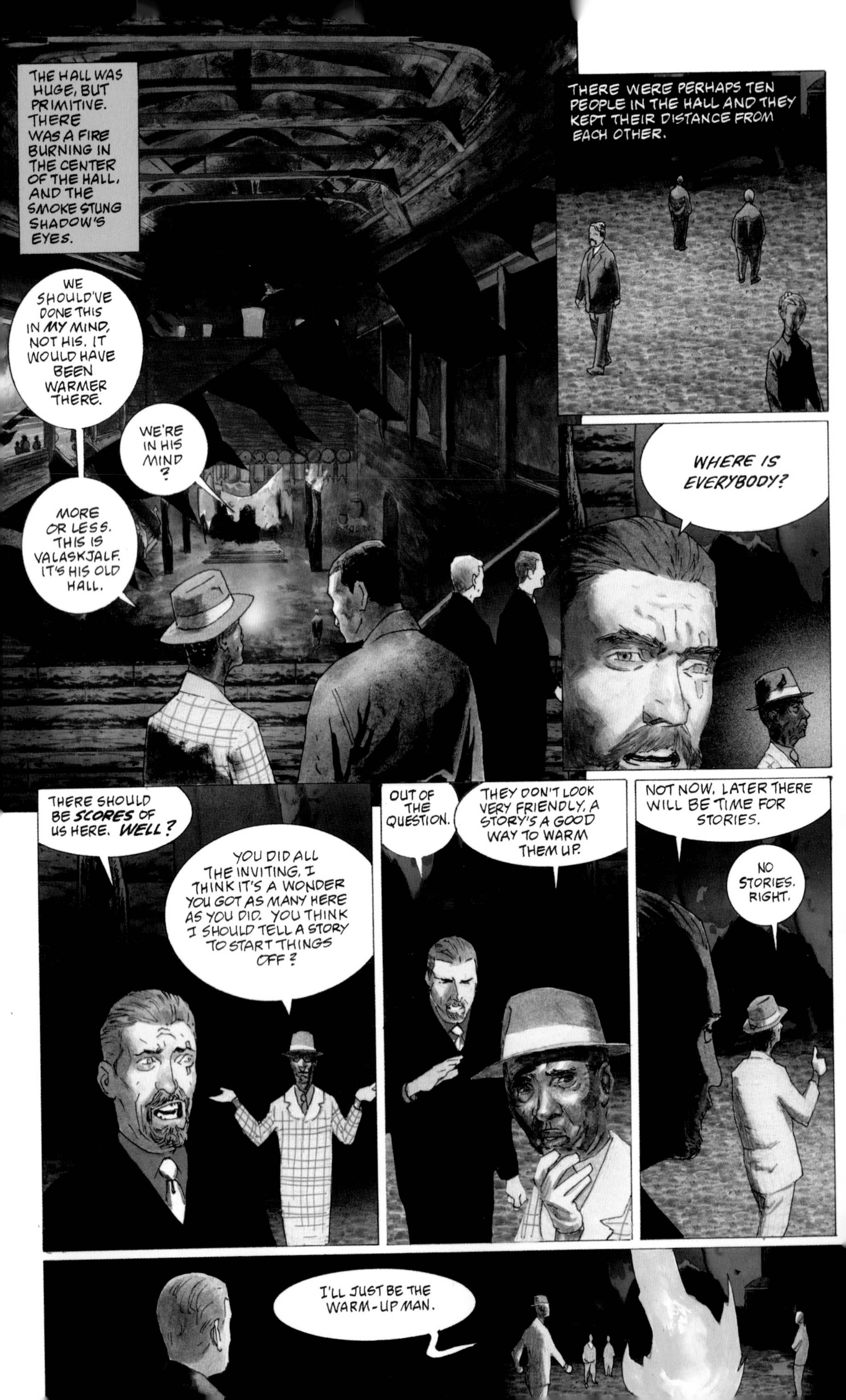
THE HALL WAS HUGE, BUT PRIMITIVE. THERE WAS A FIRE BURNING IN THE CENTER OF THE HALL, AND THE SMOKE STUNG SHADOW'S EYES.
WE SHOULD'VE DONE THIS IN MY MIND, NOT HIS. IT WOULD HAVE BEEN WARMER THERE.
WE'RE IN HIS MIND?
MORE OR LESS. THIS IS VALASKJALF. IT'S HIS OLD HALL.
THERE WERE PERHAPS TEN PEOPLE IN THE HALL AND THEY KEPT THEIR DISTANCE FROM EACH OTHER.
WHERE IS EVERYBODY?
THERE SHOULD BE SCORES OF US HERE. WELL?
YOU DID ALL THE INVITING. I THINK IT'S A WONDER YOU GOT AS MANY HERE AS YOU DID. YOU THINK I SHOULD TELL A STORY TO START THINGS OFF?
OUT OF THE QUESTION.
THEY DON'T LOOK VERY FRIENDLY. A STORY'S A GOOD WAY TO WARM THEM UP.
NOT NOW. LATER THERE WILL BE TIME FOR STORIES.
NO STORIES. RIGHT.
I'LL JUST BE THE WARM-UP MAN.

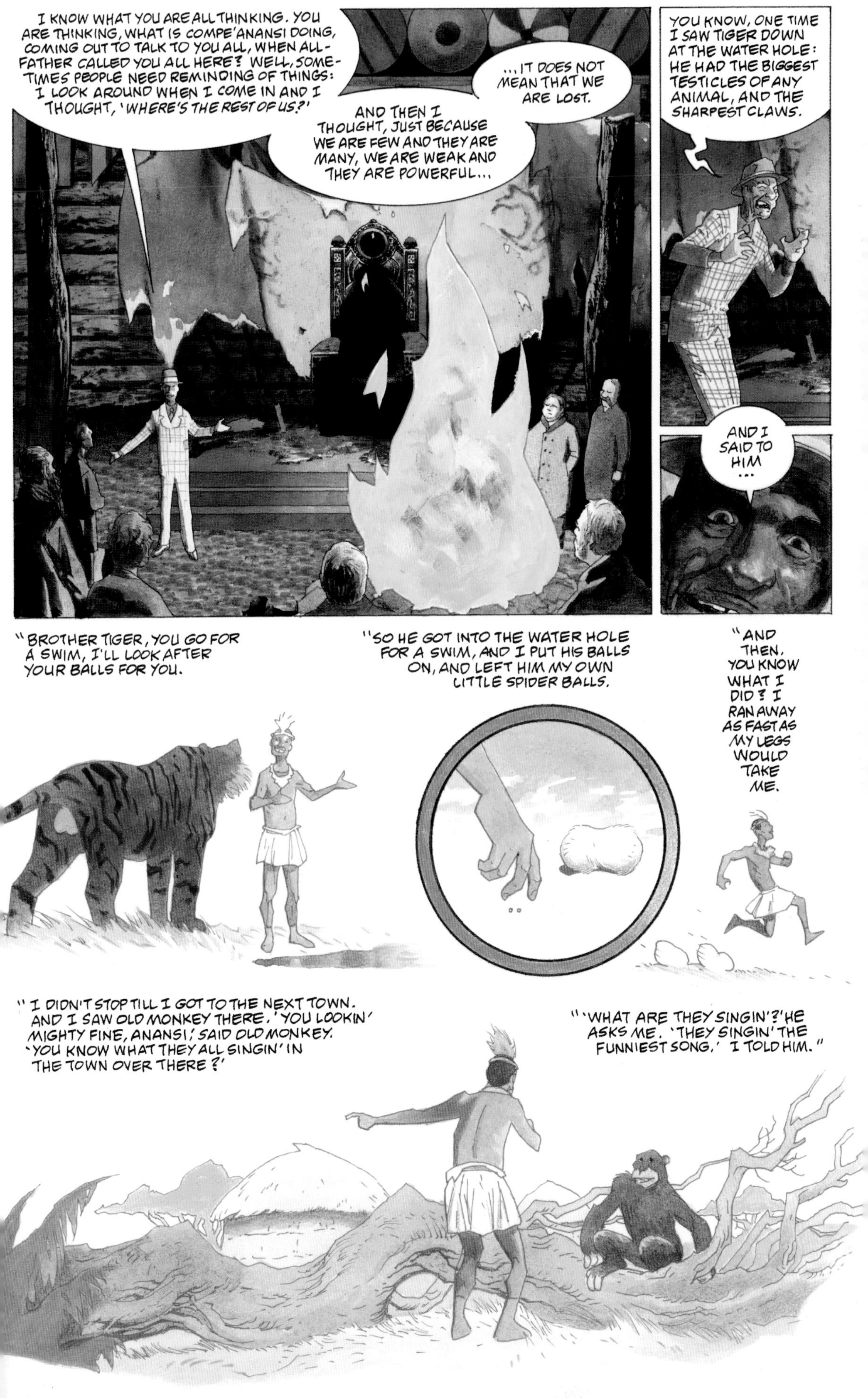

I KNOW WHAT YOU ARE ALL THINKING. YOU ARE THINKING, WHAT IS COMPE'ANANSI DOING, COMING OUT TO TALK TO YOU ALL, WHEN ALL-FATHER CALLED YOU ALL HERE? WELL, SOMETIMES PEOPLE NEED REMINDING OF THINGS: I LOOK AROUND WHEN I COME IN AND I THOUGHT, 'WHERE'S THE REST OF US?'
AND THEN I THOUGHT, JUST BECAUSE WE ARE FEW AND THEY ARE MANY, WE ARE WEAK AND THEY ARE POWERFUL...
...IT DOES NOT MEAN THAT WE ARE LOST.
YOU KNOW, ONE TIME I SAW TIGER DOWN AT THE WATER HOLE: HE HAD THE BIGGEST TESTICLES OF ANY ANIMAL, AND THE SHARPEST CLAWS.
AND I SAID TO HIM ...
"BROTHER TIGER, YOU GO FOR A SWIM, I'LL LOOK AFTER YOUR BALLS FOR YOU.
"SO HE GOT INTO THE WATER HOLE FOR A SWIM, AND I PUT HIS BALLS ON, AND LEFT HIM MY OWN LITTLE SPIDER BALLS.
"AND THEN, YOU KNOW WHAT I DID? I RAN AWAY AS FAST AS MY LEGS WOULD TAKE ME.
"I DIDN'T STOP TILL I GOT TO THE NEXT TOWN. AND I SAW OLD MONKEY THERE. 'YOU LOOKIN' MIGHTY FINE, ANANSI,' SAID OLD MONKEY. 'YOU KNOW WHAT THEY ALL SINGIN' IN THE TOWN OVER THERE?'
"'WHAT ARE THEY SINGIN'?' HE ASKS ME. 'THEY SINGIN' THE FUNNIEST SONG,' I TOLD HIM."

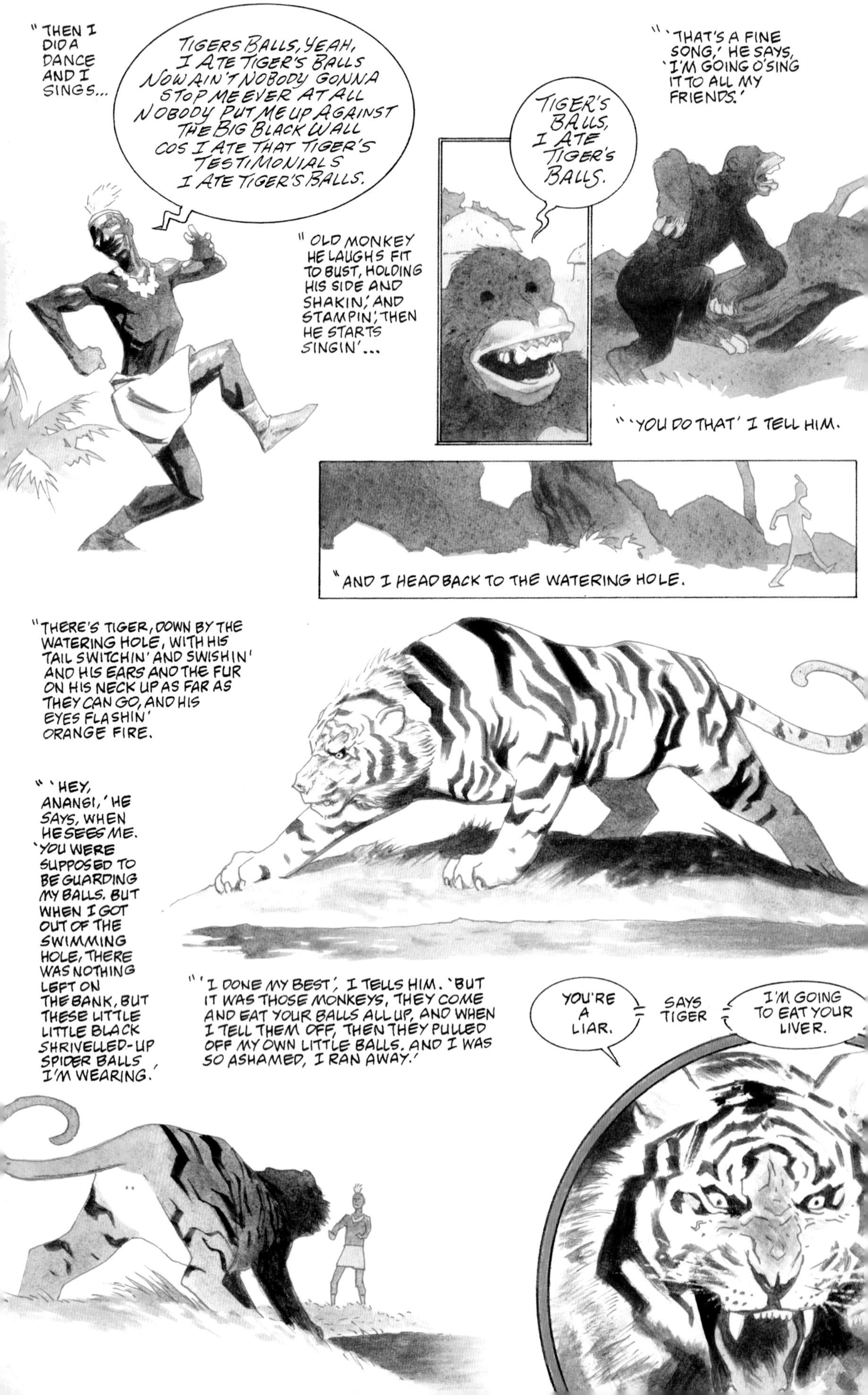

"THEN I DID A DANCE AND I SINGS...
TIGERS BALLS, YEAH, I ATE TIGER'S BALLS NOW AIN'T NOBODY GONNA STOP ME EVER AT ALL NOBODY PUT ME UP AGAINST THE BIG BLACK WALL COS I ATE THAT TIGER'S TESTIMONIALS I ATE TIGER'S BALLS.
"OLD MONKEY HE LAUGHS FIT TO BUST, HOLDING HIS SIDE AND SHAKIN,' AND STAMPIN,' THEN HE STARTS SINGIN'...
TIGER'S BALLS, I ATE TIGER'S BALLS.
"'THAT'S A FINE SONG,' HE SAYS, 'I'M GOING O'SING IT TO ALL MY FRIENDS.'
"'YOU DO THAT' I TELL HIM.
"AND I HEAD BACK TO THE WATERING HOLE.
"THERE'S TIGER, DOWN BY THE WATERING HOLE, WITH HIS TAIL SWITCHIN' AND SWISHIN' AND HIS EARS AND THE FUR ON HIS NECK UP AS FAR AS THEY CAN GO, AND HIS EYES FLASHIN' ORANGE FIRE.
"'HEY, ANANSI,' HE SAYS, WHEN HE SEES ME. 'YOU WERE SUPPOSED TO BE GUARDING MY BALLS. BUT WHEN I GOT OUT OF THE SWIMMING HOLE, THERE WAS NOTHING LEFT ON THE BANK, BUT THESE LITTLE LITTLE BLACK SHRIVELLED-UP SPIDER BALLS I'M WEARING.'
"'I DONE MY BEST,' I TELLS HIM. 'BUT IT WAS THOSE MONKEYS, THEY COME AND EAT YOUR BALLS ALL UP, AND WHEN I TELL THEM OFF, THEN THEY PULLED OFF MY OWN LITTLE BALLS. AND I WAS SO ASHAMED, I RAN AWAY.'
YOU'RE A LIAR.
SAYS TIGER
I'M GOING TO EAT YOUR LIVER.

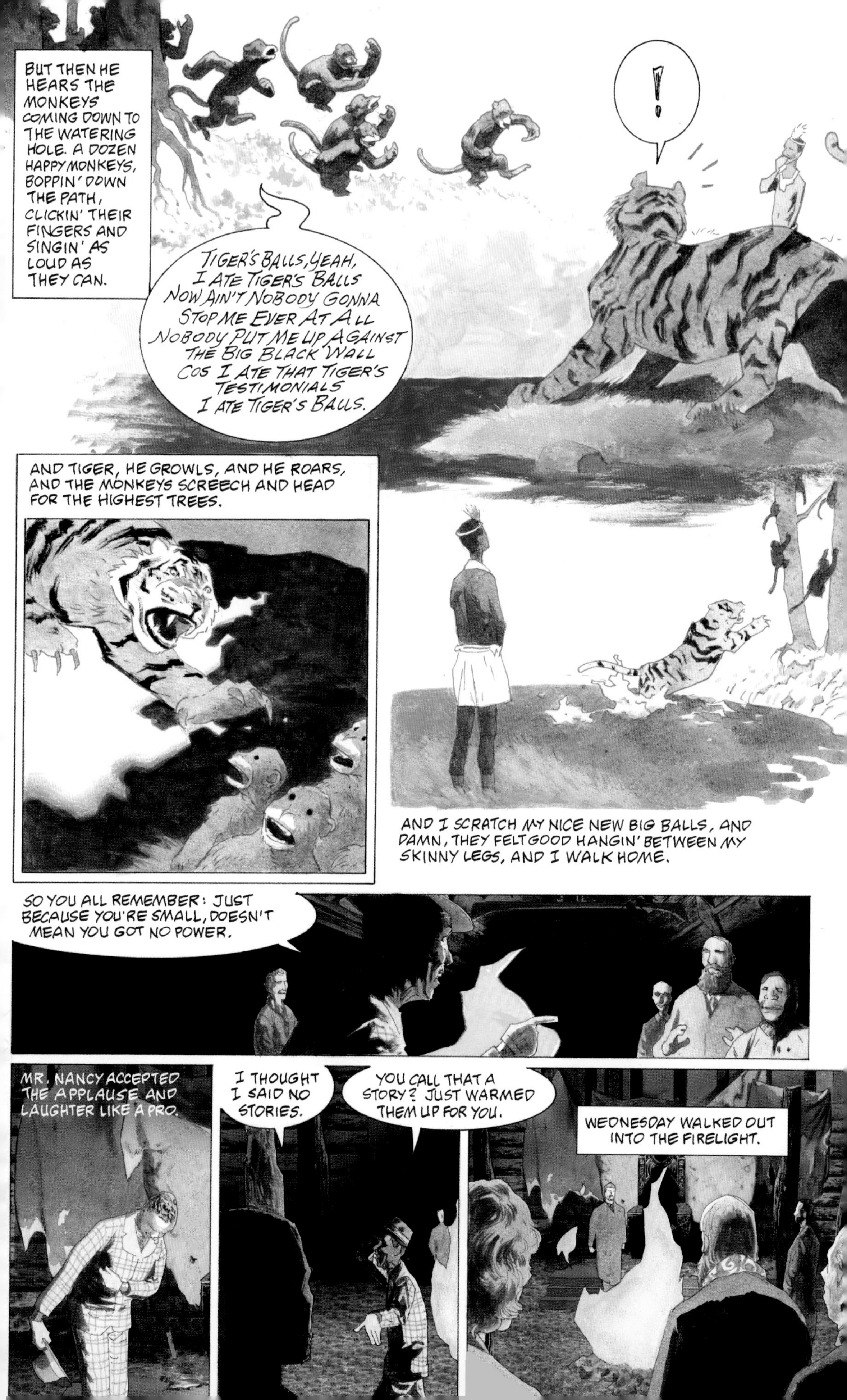

BUT THEN HE HEARS THE MONKEYS COMING DOWN TO THE WATERING HOLE. A DOZEN HAPPY MONKEYS, BOPPIN' DOWN THE PATH, CLICKIN' THEIR FINGERS AND SINGIN' AS LOUD AS THEY CAN.
TIGER'S BALLS, YEAH, I ATE TIGER'S BALLS NOW AIN'T NOBODY GONNA STOP ME EVER AT ALL NOBODY PUT ME UP AGAINST THE BIG BLACK WALL COS I ATE THAT TIGER'S TESTIMONIALS I ATE TIGER'S BALLS.
!
AND TIGER, HE GROWLS, AND HE ROARS, AND THE MONKEYS SCREECH AND HEAD FOR THE HIGHEST TREES.
AND I SCRATCH MY NICE NEW BIG BALLS, AND DAMN, THEY FELT GOOD HANGIN' BETWEEN MY SKINNY LEGS, AND I WALK HOME.
SO YOU ALL REMEMBER: JUST BECAUSE YOU'RE SMALL, DOESN'T MEAN YOU GOT NO POWER.
MR. NANCY ACCEPTED THE APPLAUSE AND LAUGHTER LIKE A PRO.
I THOUGHT I SAID NO STORIES.
YOU CALL THAT A STORY? JUST WARMED THEM UP FOR YOU.
WEDNESDAY WALKED OUT INTO THE FIRELIGHT.

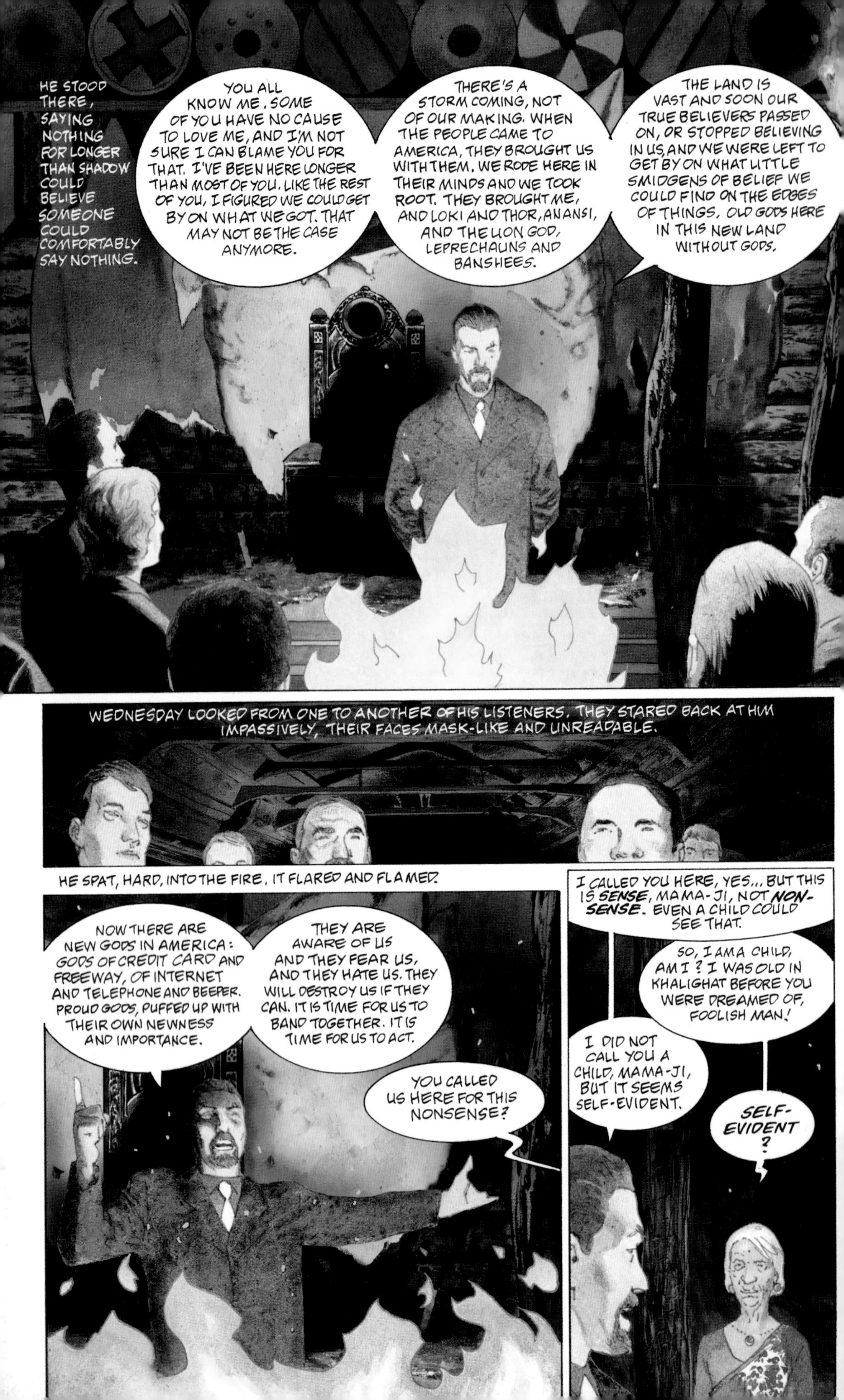
HE STOOD THERE, SAYING NOTHING FOR LONGER THAN SHADOW COULD BELIEVE SOMEONE COULD COMFORTABLY SAY NOTHING.
YOU ALL KNOW ME. SOME OF YOU HAVE NO CAUSE TO LOVE ME, AND I'M NOT SURE I CAN BLAME YOU FOR THAT. I'VE BEEN HERE LONGER THAN MOST OF YOU. LIKE THE REST OF YOU, I FIGURED WE COULD GET BY ON WHAT WE GOT. THAT MAY NOT BE THE CASE ANYMORE.
THERE'S A STORM COMING, NOT OF OUR MAKING. WHEN THE PEOPLE CAME TO AMERICA, THEY BROUGHT US WITH THEM. WE RODE HERE IN THEIR MINDS AND WE TOOK ROOT. THEY BROUGHT ME, AND LOKI AND THOR, ANANSI, AND THE LION GOD, LEPRECHAUNS AND BANSHEES.
THE LAND IS VAST AND SOON OUR TRUE BELIEVERS PASSED ON, OR STOPPED BELIEVING IN US, AND WE WERE LEFT TO GET BY ON WHAT LITTLE SMIDGENS OF BELIEF WE COULD FIND ON THE EDGES OF THINGS. OLD GODS HERE IN THIS NEW LAND WITHOUT GODS.
WEDNESDAY LOOKED FROM ONE TO ANOTHER OF HIS LISTENERS. THEY STARED BACK AT HIM IMPASSIVELY, THEIR FACES MASK-LIKE AND UNREADABLE.
HE SPAT, HARD, INTO THE FIRE. IT FLARED AND FLAMED.
NOW THERE ARE NEW GODS IN AMERICA: GODS OF CREDIT CARD AND FREEWAY, OF INTERNET AND TELEPHONE AND BEEPER. PROUD GODS, PUFFED UP WITH THEIR OWN NEWNESS AND IMPORTANCE.
THEY ARE AWARE OF US AND THEY FEAR US, AND THEY HATE US. THEY WILL DESTROY US IF THEY CAN. IT IS TIME FOR US TO BAND TOGETHER. IT IS TIME FOR US TO ACT.
YOU CALLED US HERE FOR THIS NONSENSE?
I CALLED YOU HERE, YES... BUT THIS IS **SENSE**, MAMA-JI, NOT **NON-SENSE**. EVEN A CHILD COULD SEE THAT.
SO, I AM A CHILD, AM I? I WAS OLD IN KHALIGHAT BEFORE YOU WERE DREAMED OF, FOOLISH MAN!
I DID NOT CALL YOU A CHILD, MAMA-JI, BUT IT SEEMS SELF-EVIDENT.
SELF-EVIDENT?

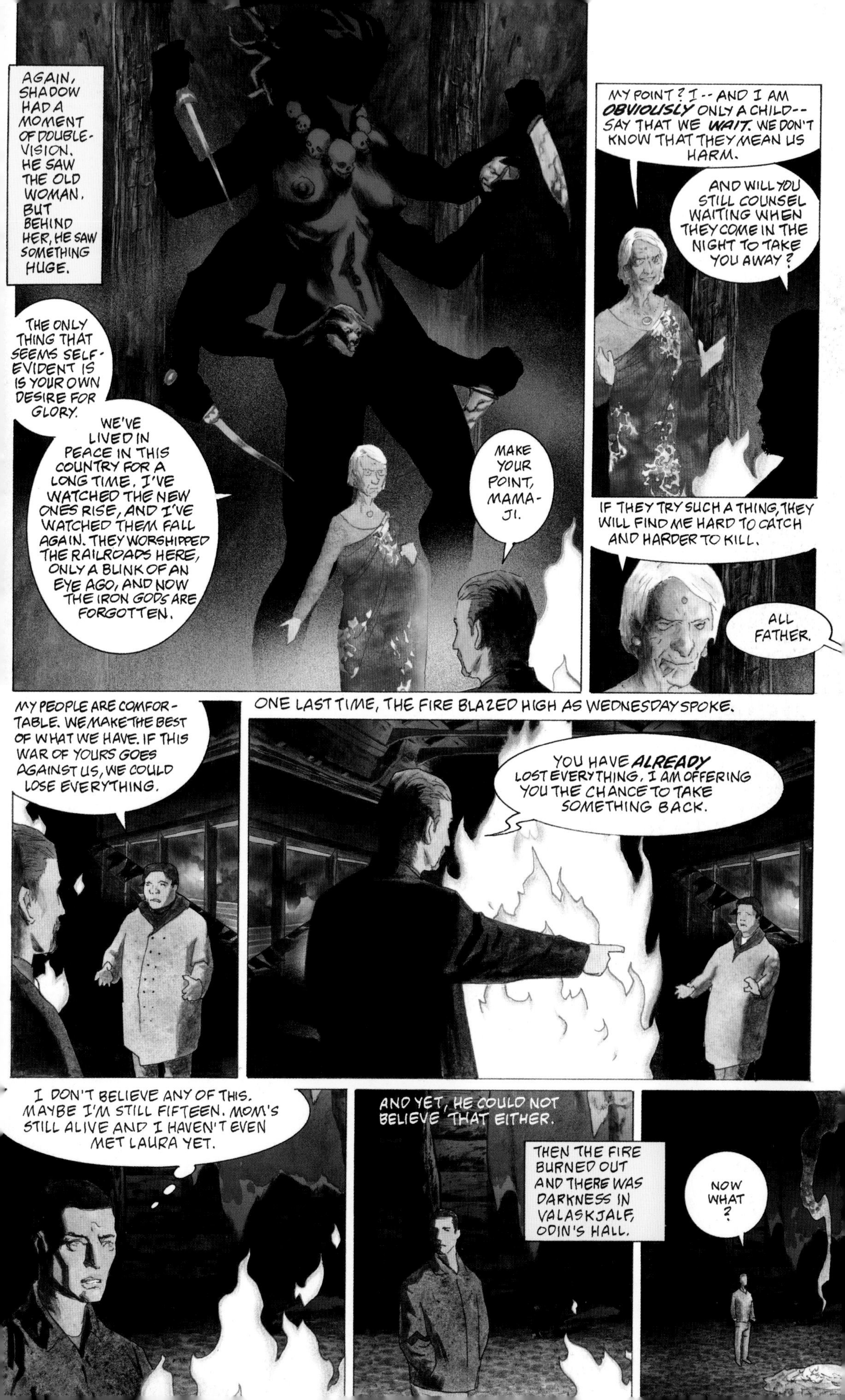
AGAIN, SHADOW HAD A MOMENT OF DOUBLE-VISION. HE SAW THE OLD WOMAN. BUT BEHIND HER, HE SAW SOMETHING HUGE.
THE ONLY THING THAT SEEMS SELF-EVIDENT IS IS YOUR OWN DESIRE FOR GLORY.
WE'VE LIVED IN PEACE IN THIS COUNTRY FOR A LONG TIME. I'VE WATCHED THE NEW ONES RISE, AND I'VE WATCHED THEM FALL AGAIN. THEY WORSHIPPED THE RAILROADS HERE, ONLY A BLINK OF AN EYE AGO, AND NOW THE IRON GODS ARE FORGOTTEN.
MAKE YOUR POINT, MAMA-JI.
MY POINT? I -- AND I AM OBVIOUSLY ONLY A CHILD -- SAY THAT WE WAIT. WE DON'T KNOW THAT THEY MEAN US HARM.
AND WILL YOU STILL COUNSEL WAITING WHEN THEY COME IN THE NIGHT TO TAKE YOU AWAY?
IF THEY TRY SUCH A THING, THEY WILL FIND ME HARD TO CATCH AND HARDER TO KILL.
ALL FATHER.
MY PEOPLE ARE COMFORTABLE. WE MAKE THE BEST OF WHAT WE HAVE. IF THIS WAR OF YOURS GOES AGAINST US, WE COULD LOSE EVERYTHING.
ONE LAST TIME, THE FIRE BLAZED HIGH AS WEDNESDAY SPOKE.
YOU HAVE ALREADY LOST EVERYTHING. I AM OFFERING YOU THE CHANCE TO TAKE SOMETHING BACK.
I DON'T BELIEVE ANY OF THIS. MAYBE I'M STILL FIFTEEN. MOM'S STILL ALIVE AND I HAVEN'T EVEN MET LAURA YET.
AND YET, HE COULD NOT BELIEVE THAT EITHER.
THEN THE FIRE BURNED OUT AND THERE WAS DARKNESS IN VALASKJALF, ODIN'S HALL.
NOW WHAT?

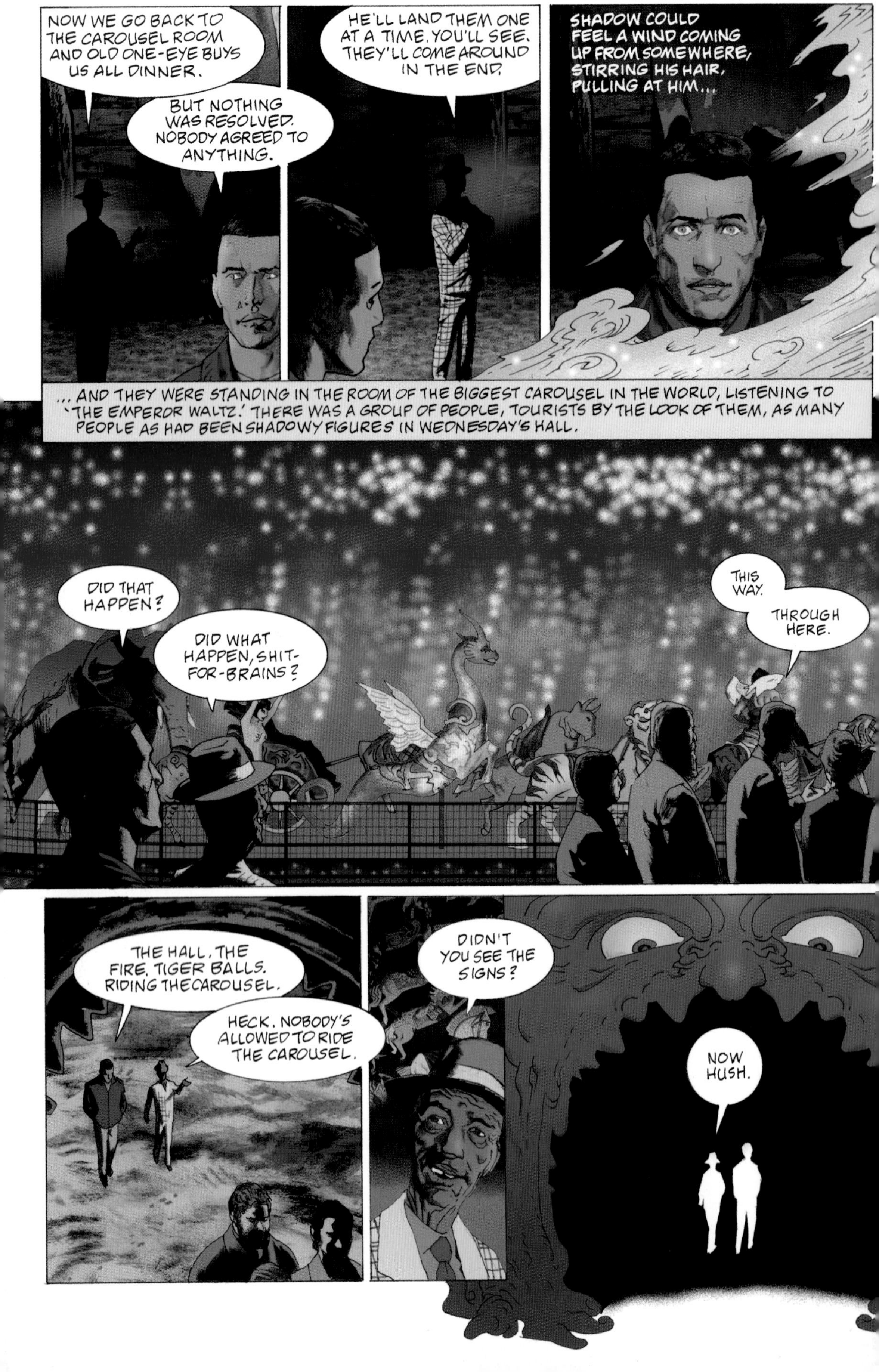
NOW WE GO BACK TO THE CAROUSEL ROOM AND OLD ONE-EYE BUYS US ALL DINNER.
BUT NOTHING WAS RESOLVED. NOBODY AGREED TO ANYTHING.
HE'LL LAND THEM ONE AT A TIME. YOU'LL SEE. THEY'LL COME AROUND IN THE END.
SHADOW COULD FEEL A WIND COMING UP FROM SOMEWHERE, STIRRING HIS HAIR, PULLING AT HIM...
...AND THEY WERE STANDING IN THE ROOM OF THE BIGGEST CAROUSEL IN THE WORLD, LISTENING TO 'THE EMPEROR WALTZ.' THERE WAS A GROUP OF PEOPLE, TOURISTS BY THE LOOK OF THEM, AS MANY PEOPLE AS HAD BEEN SHADOWY FIGURES IN WEDNESDAY'S HALL.
DID THAT HAPPEN?
DID WHAT HAPPEN, SHIT-FOR-BRAINS?
THIS WAY.
THROUGH HERE.
THE HALL. THE FIRE. TIGER BALLS. RIDING THE CAROUSEL.
HECK. NOBODY'S ALLOWED TO RIDE THE CAROUSEL.
DIDN'T YOU SEE THE SIGNS?
NOW HUSH.

SHADOW HAD A CARFUL OF WEDNESDAY'S GUESTS TO FERRY TO THE RESTAURANT: THE WOMAN IN THE RED SARI SAT BESIDE HIM. THERE WERE TWO MEN IN THE BACK SEAT: A PECULIAR-LOOKING YOUNG MAN WHOSE NAME SHADOW HAD NOT CAUGHT, BUT THOUGHT MIGHT BE ELVIS, AND ANOTHER MAN, IN A DARK SUIT, WHO SHADOW COULD NOT REMEMBER.

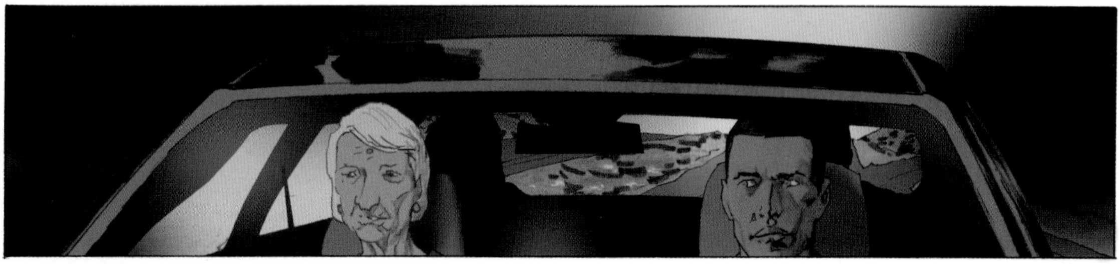

HE HAD STOOD BESIDE THE MAN AS HE GOT INTO THE CAR AND WAS UNABLE TO REMEMBER ANYTHING ABOUT HIM.

HE TURNED AROUND IN THE DRIVER'S SEAT AND LOOKED AT HIM, CAREFULLY NOTING HIS HAIR, CLOTHES, AND FACE.

HE TURNED BACK TO START THE CAR, TO FIND THAT THE MAN HAD SLIPPED FROM HIS MIND.

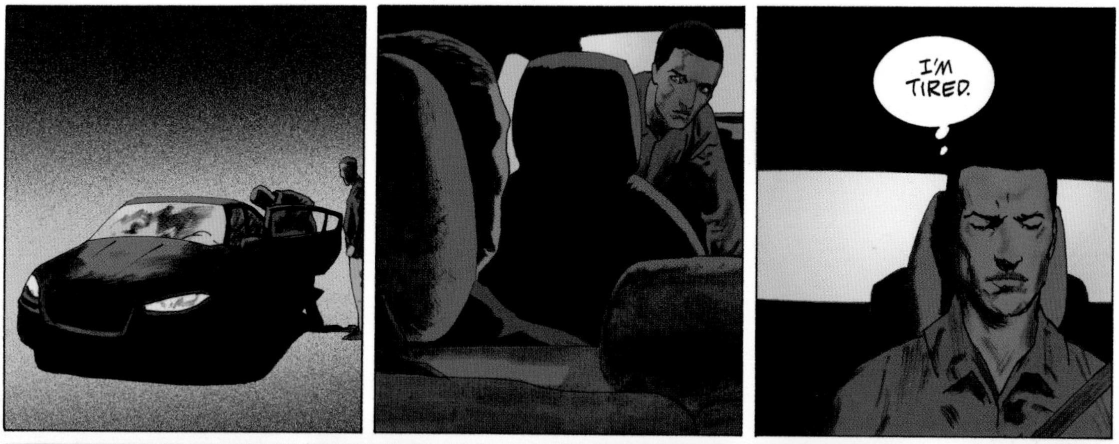
I'M TIRED.

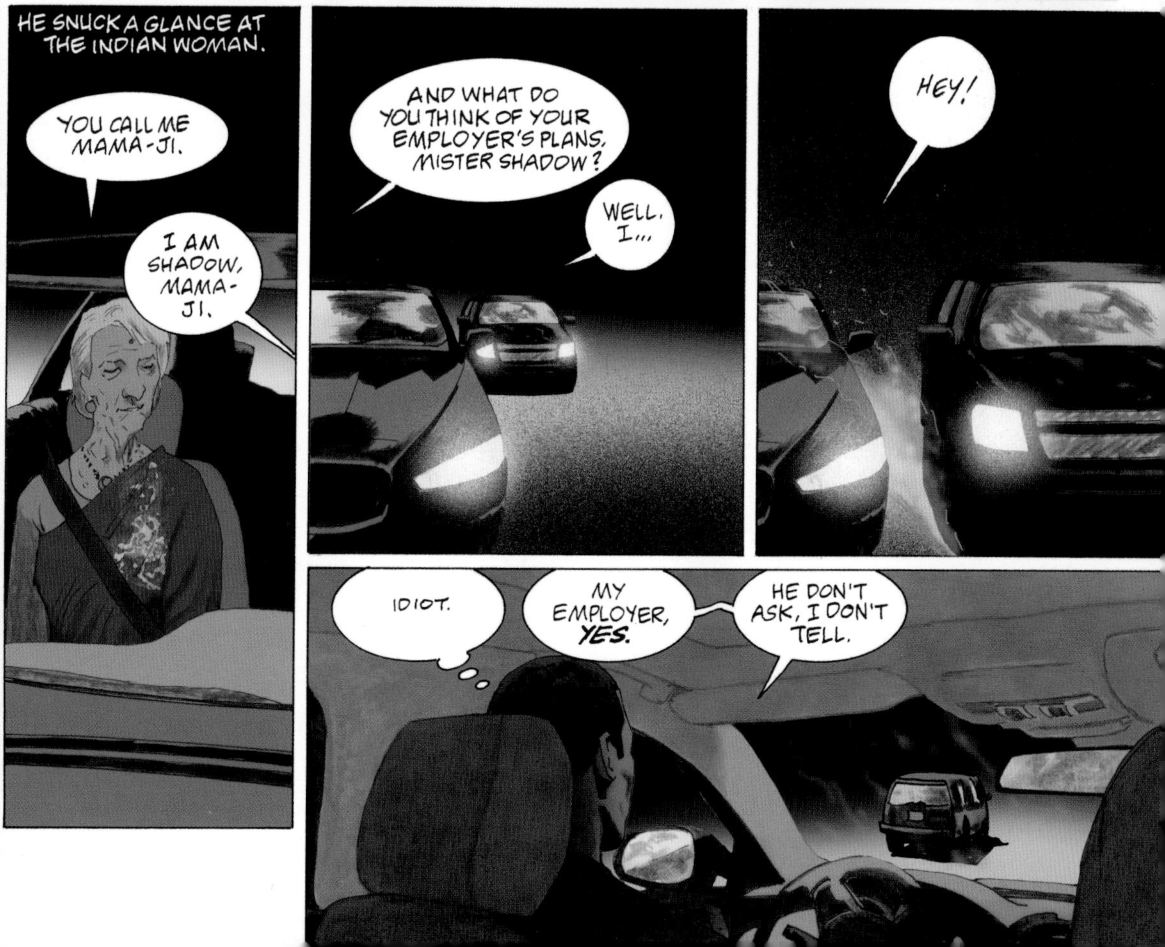
HE SNUCK A GLANCE AT THE INDIAN WOMAN.
YOU CALL ME MAMA-JI.
I AM SHADOW, MAMA-JI.
AND WHAT DO YOU THINK OF YOUR EMPLOYER'S PLANS, MISTER SHADOW?
WELL, I...
HEY!
IDIOT.
MY EMPLOYER, YES.
HE DON'T ASK, I DON'T TELL.

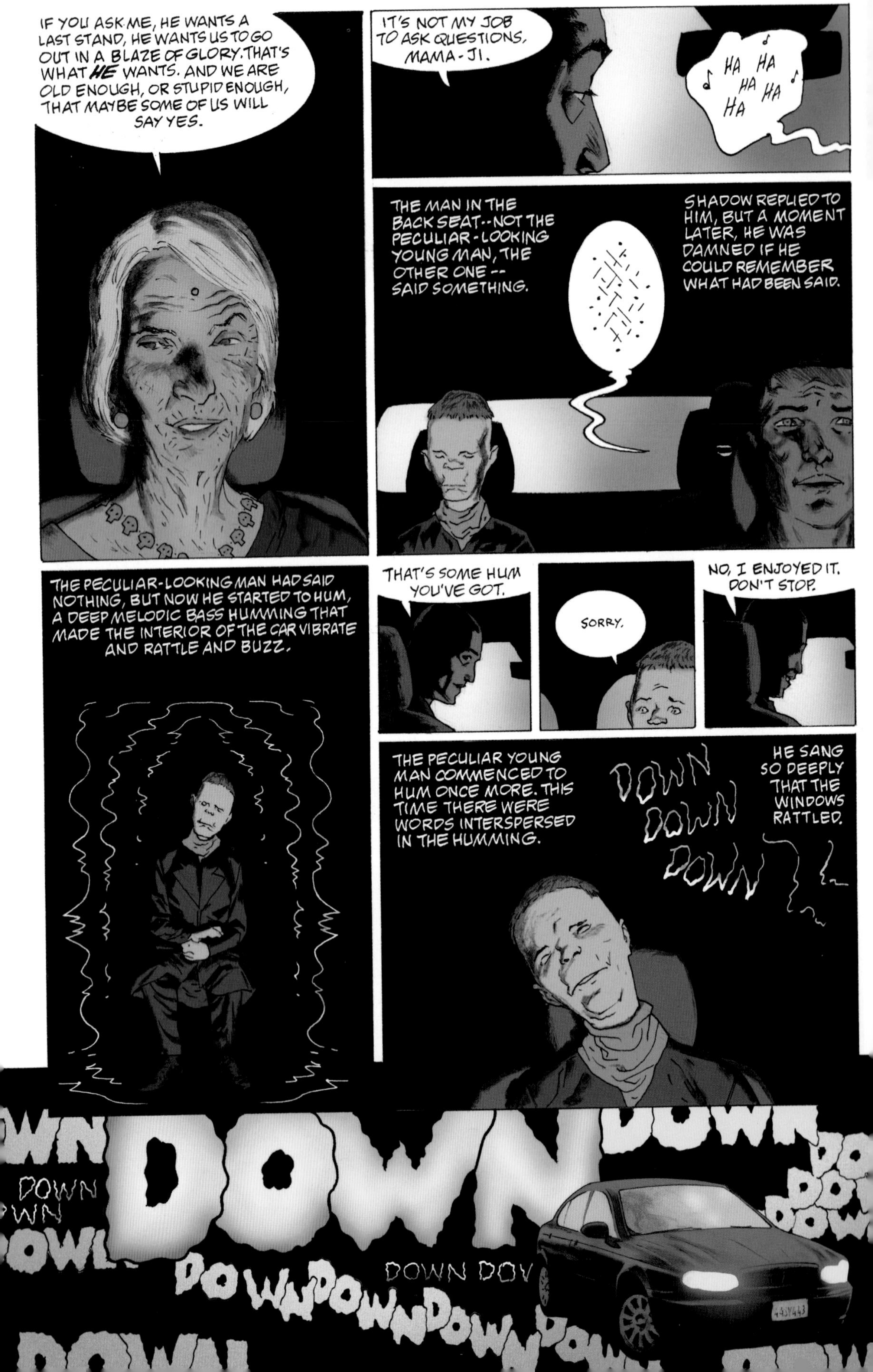
IF YOU ASK ME, HE WANTS A LAST STAND, HE WANTS US TO GO OUT IN A BLAZE OF GLORY. THAT'S WHAT HE WANTS. AND WE ARE OLD ENOUGH, OR STUPID ENOUGH, THAT MAYBE SOME OF US WILL SAY YES.
IT'S NOT MY JOB TO ASK QUESTIONS, MAMA-JI.
HA HA HA HA HA
THE MAN IN THE BACK SEAT--NOT THE PECULIAR-LOOKING YOUNG MAN, THE OTHER ONE--SAID SOMETHING.
SHADOW REPLIED TO HIM, BUT A MOMENT LATER, HE WAS DAMNED IF HE COULD REMEMBER WHAT HAD BEEN SAID.
THE PECULIAR-LOOKING MAN HAD SAID NOTHING, BUT NOW HE STARTED TO HUM, A DEEP MELODIC BASS HUMMING THAT MADE THE INTERIOR OF THE CAR VIBRATE AND RATTLE AND BUZZ.
THAT'S SOME HUM YOU'VE GOT.
SORRY.
NO, I ENJOYED IT. DON'T STOP.
THE PECULIAR YOUNG MAN COMMENCED TO HUM ONCE MORE. THIS TIME THERE WERE WORDS INTERSPERSED IN THE HUMMING.
DOWN DOWN DOWN
HE SANG SO DEEPLY THAT THE WINDOWS RATTLED.
DOWN
DOWN
DOWN

SHADOW PULLED UP AT THE RESTAURANT AND LET HIS PASSENGERS OFF. HE WOULD PARK AT THE BACK OF THE PARKING LOT. HE WANTED TO MAKE THE SHORT WALK BACK, IN THE COLD, TO CLEAR HIS HEAD.

HE PARKED THE CAR BESIDE A BLACK TRUCK.

IS THAT THE TRUCK THAT PASSED US?

I WONDER IF I REALLY HAD *KALI* IN THE FRONT OF MY CAR.

AND THAT GUY IN THE BACK WHOSE FACE I LOOK AT BUT CAN'T READ...

HEY *BUD*, YOU GOT A MATCH?

NO. SORRY, I --

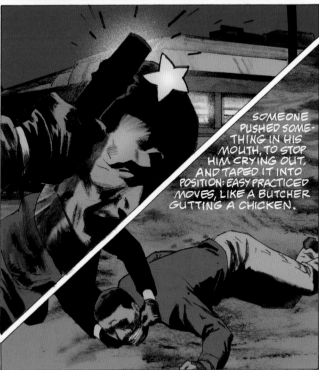

SOMEONE PUSHED SOMETHING IN HIS MOUTH, TO STOP HIM CRYING OUT, AND TAPED IT INTO POSITION: EASY PRACTICED MOVES, LIKE A BUTCHER GUTTING A CHICKEN.

THE QUARRY ARE ALL INSIDE. EVERYONE IN POSITION?

LET'S MOVE IN AND ROUND THEM ALL UP.

WHAT ABOUT THE BIG GUY?

PACKAGE HIM UP. TAKE HIM OUT.

THEY PUT A BAG-LIKE HOOD OVER SHADOW'S HEAD, AND BOUND HIS WRISTS AND ANKLES WITH TAPE, AND PUT HIM IN THE BACK OF THE TRUCK, AND DROVE HIM AWAY.

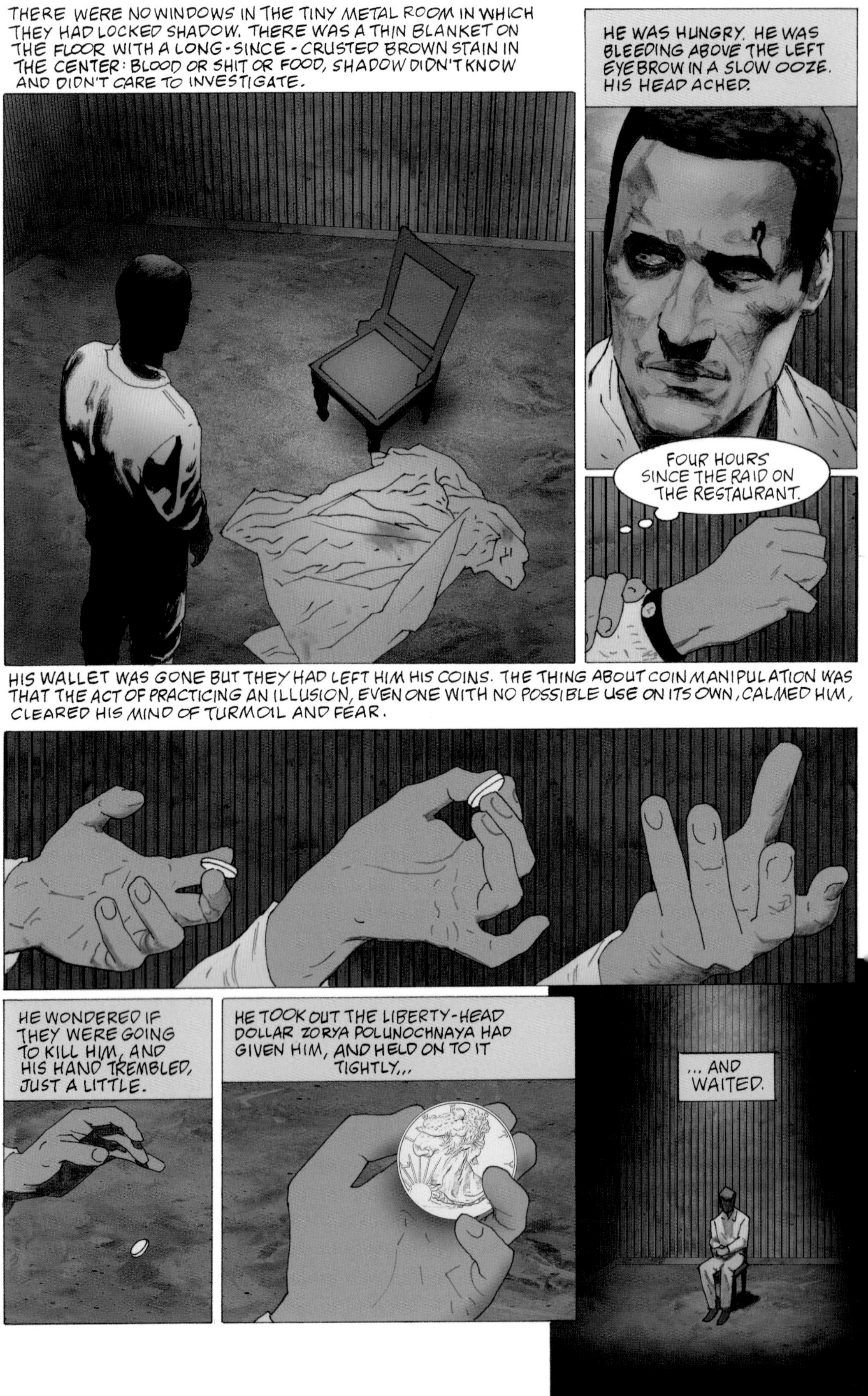
THERE WERE NO WINDOWS IN THE TINY METAL ROOM IN WHICH THEY HAD LOCKED SHADOW. THERE WAS A THIN BLANKET ON THE FLOOR WITH A LONG-SINCE-CRUSTED BROWN STAIN IN THE CENTER: BLOOD OR SHIT OR FOOD, SHADOW DIDN'T KNOW AND DIDN'T CARE TO INVESTIGATE.
HE WAS HUNGRY. HE WAS BLEEDING ABOVE THE LEFT EYEBROW IN A SLOW OOZE. HIS HEAD ACHED.
FOUR HOURS SINCE THE RAID ON THE RESTAURANT.
HIS WALLET WAS GONE BUT THEY HAD LEFT HIM HIS COINS. THE THING ABOUT COIN MANIPULATION WAS THAT THE ACT OF PRACTICING AN ILLUSION, EVEN ONE WITH NO POSSIBLE USE ON ITS OWN, CALMED HIM, CLEARED HIS MIND OF TURMOIL AND FEAR.
HE WONDERED IF THEY WERE GOING TO KILL HIM, AND HIS HAND TREMBLED, JUST A LITTLE.
HE TOOK OUT THE LIBERTY-HEAD DOLLAR ZORYA POLUNOCHNAYA HAD GIVEN HIM, AND HELD ON TO IT TIGHTLY...
... AND WAITED.

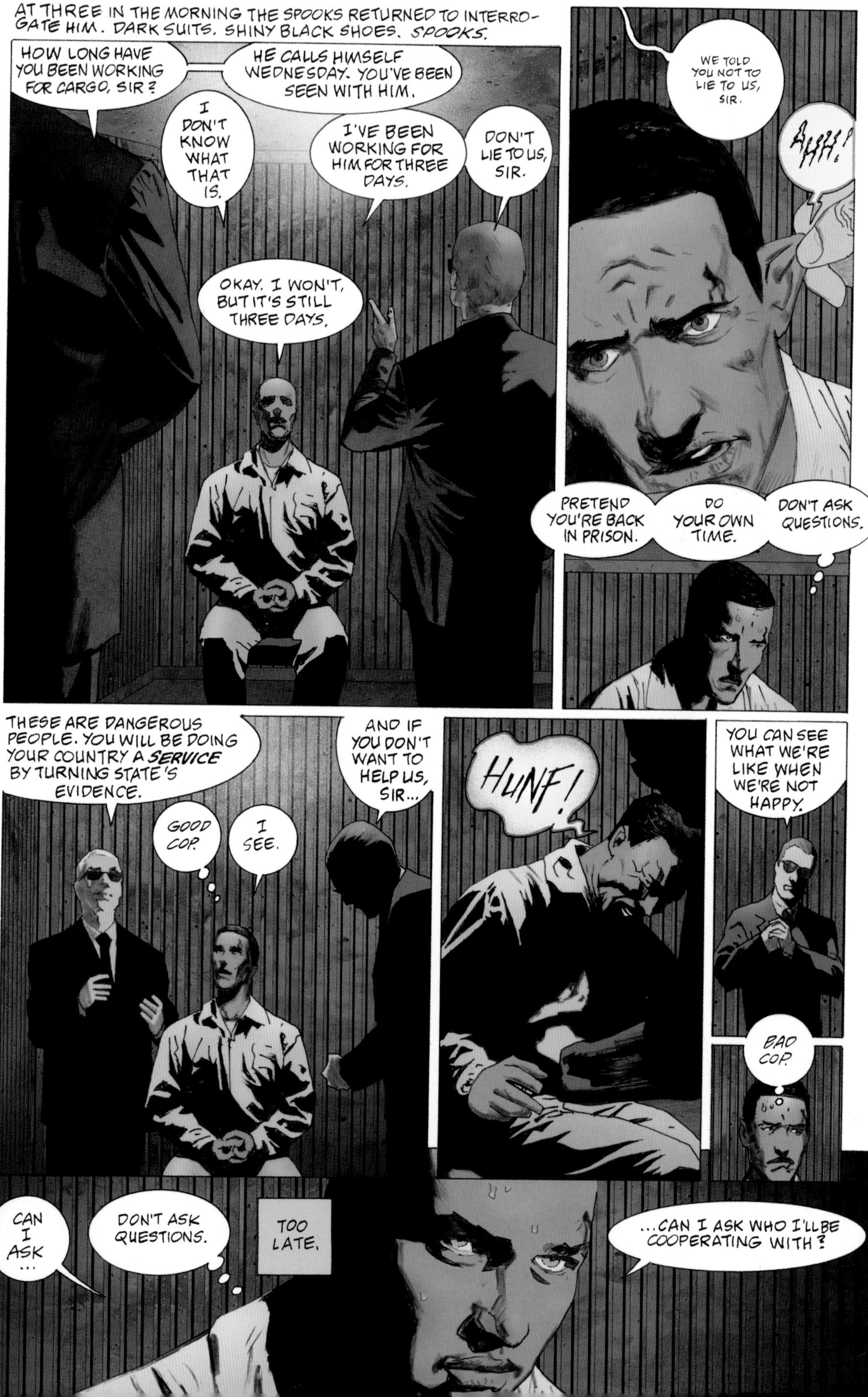
AT THREE IN THE MORNING THE SPOOKS RETURNED TO INTERROGATE HIM. DARK SUITS. SHINY BLACK SHOES. SPOOKS.
HOW LONG HAVE YOU BEEN WORKING FOR CARGO, SIR?
HE CALLS HIMSELF WEDNESDAY. YOU'VE BEEN SEEN WITH HIM.
I DON'T KNOW WHAT THAT IS.
I'VE BEEN WORKING FOR HIM FOR THREE DAYS.
DON'T LIE TO US, SIR.
OKAY. I WON'T, BUT IT'S STILL THREE DAYS.
WE TOLD YOU NOT TO LIE TO US, SIR.
AHH!
PRETEND YOU'RE BACK IN PRISON.
DO YOUR OWN TIME.
DON'T ASK QUESTIONS.
THESE ARE DANGEROUS PEOPLE. YOU WILL BE DOING YOUR COUNTRY A SERVICE BY TURNING STATE'S EVIDENCE.
GOOD COP.
I SEE.
AND IF YOU DON'T WANT TO HELP US, SIR...
HUNF!
YOU CAN SEE WHAT WE'RE LIKE WHEN WE'RE NOT HAPPY.
BAD COP.
CAN I ASK ...
DON'T ASK QUESTIONS.
TOO LATE.
...CAN I ASK WHO I'LL BE COOPERATING WITH?

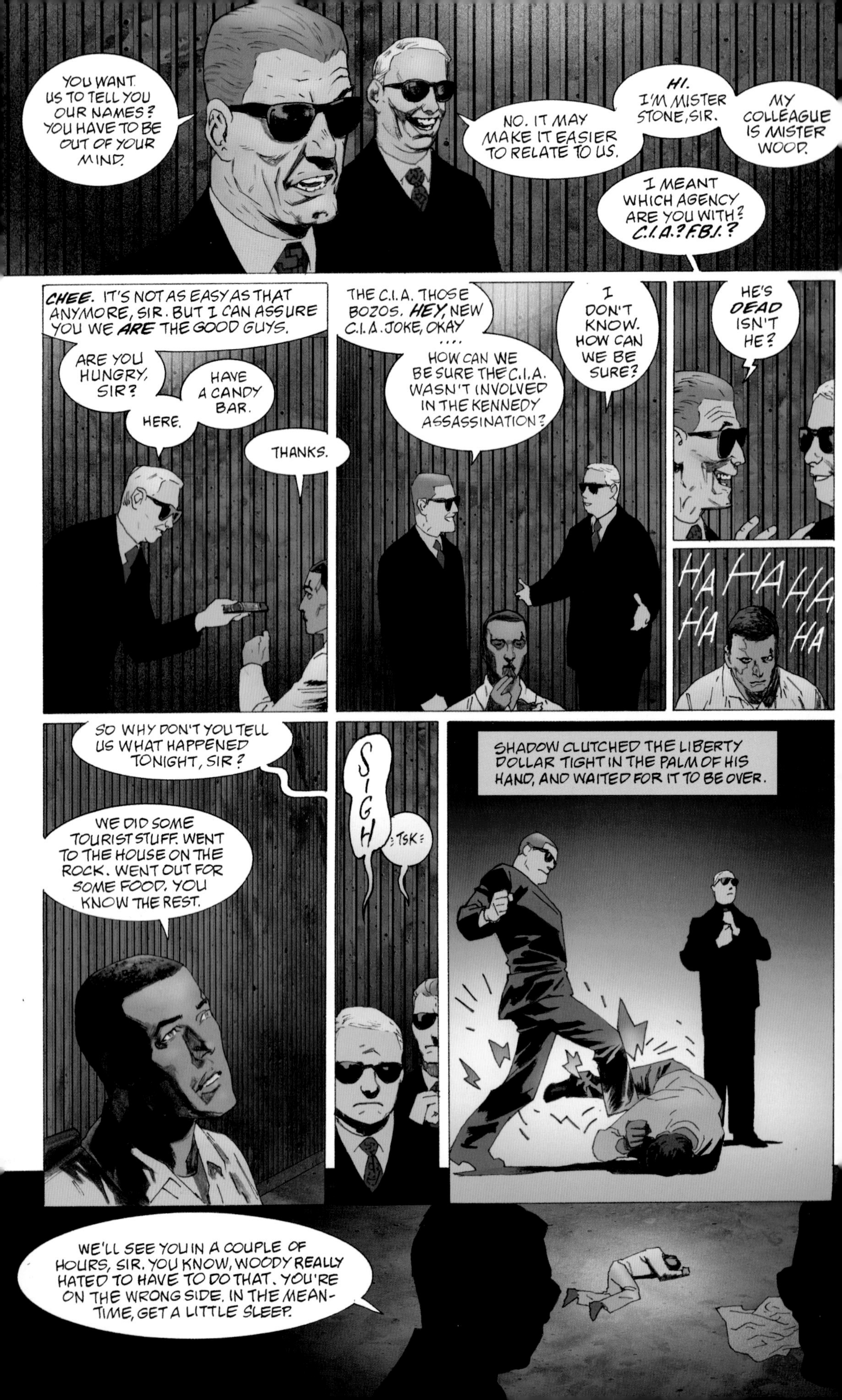
YOU WANT US TO TELL YOU OUR NAMES? YOU HAVE TO BE OUT OF YOUR MIND.
NO. IT MAY MAKE IT EASIER TO RELATE TO US.
HI. I'M MISTER STONE, SIR.
MY COLLEAGUE IS MISTER WOOD.
I MEANT WHICH AGENCY ARE YOU WITH? C.I.A.? F.B.I.?
CHEE. IT'S NOT AS EASY AS THAT ANYMORE, SIR. BUT I CAN ASSURE YOU WE ARE THE GOOD GUYS.
ARE YOU HUNGRY, SIR?
HERE.
HAVE A CANDY BAR.
THANKS.
THE C.I.A. THOSE BOZOS. HEY, NEW C.I.A. JOKE, OKAY ....
HOW CAN WE BE SURE THE C.I.A. WASN'T INVOLVED IN THE KENNEDY ASSASSINATION?
I DON'T KNOW. HOW CAN WE BE SURE?
HE'S DEAD ISN'T HE?
HA HA HA HA HA HA HA HA
SO WHY DON'T YOU TELL US WHAT HAPPENED TONIGHT, SIR?
WE DID SOME TOURIST STUFF. WENT TO THE HOUSE ON THE ROCK. WENT OUT FOR SOME FOOD. YOU KNOW THE REST.
SIGH
TSK
SHADOW CLUTCHED THE LIBERTY DOLLAR TIGHT IN THE PALM OF HIS HAND, AND WAITED FOR IT TO BE OVER.
WE'LL SEE YOU IN A COUPLE OF HOURS, SIR. YOU KNOW, WOODY REALLY HATED TO HAVE TO DO THAT. YOU'RE ON THE WRONG SIDE. IN THE MEAN-TIME, GET A LITTLE SLEEP.

THINK ABOUT IT.

SHADOW PULLED THE THIN BLANKET OVER HIM- SELF, AND HE CLOSED HIS EYES, AND HE HELD ONTO NOTHING, AND HE HELD ONTO DREAMS.

TIME PASSED.

HE WAS FIFTEEN AGAIN, AND HIS MOTHER WAS DYING AND SHE WAS TRYING TO TELL HIM SOMETHING VERY IMPORTANT, AND HE COULDN'T UNDERSTAND HER. A SHAFT OF PAIN MOVED HIM FROM HALF-SLEEP TO HALF-WAKING.

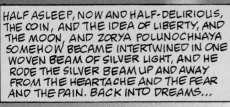

ARE WEDNESDAY AND THE OTHERS STILL AT LIBERTY?

ARE THEY EVEN ALIVE? I HOPE SO.

THE SILVER DOLLAR REMAINED COLD IN HIS RIGHT HAND...

HALF ASLEEP, NOW AND HALF-DELIRIOUS, THE COIN, AND THE IDEA OF LIBERTY, AND THE MOON, AND ZORYA POLUNOCHNAYA SOMEHOW BECAME INTERTWINED IN ONE WOVEN BEAM OF SILVER LIGHT, AND HE RODE THE SILVER BEAM UP AND AWAY FROM THE HEARTACHE AND THE FEAR AND THE PAIN. BACK INTO DREAMS...

FROM FAR AWAY HE COULD HEAR SOME KIND OF NOISE, BUT IT WAS TOO LATE TO THINK ABOUT IT...

... HE BELONGED TO SLEEP NOW.

PUPPY?

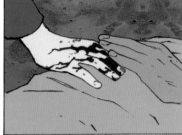

YOU HAVE TO WAKE UP. PLEASE WAKE UP, HON.

AND THERE WAS A MOMENT'S GENTLE RELIEF. HE HAD HAD SUCH A STRANGE DREAM, OF PRISONS AND CON-MEN AND DOWN-AT-THE-HEELS GODS, AND NOW LAURA WAS WAKING HIM TO TELL HIM IT WAS TIME FOR WORK, AND PERHAPS THERE WOULD BE TIME ENOUGH TO STEAL SOME **COFFEE** AND A KISS.

WHERE DID ALL THE BLOOD COME FROM?

OTHER PEOPLE.

WHICH OTHER PEOPLE?

THE GUARDS. IT'S OKAY. I KILLED THEM.

YOU BETTER MOVE. I DON'T THINK I GAVE ANYONE A CHANCE TO RAISE THE ALARM. TAKE A COAT FROM OUT HERE, OR YOU'LL FREEZE YOUR BUTT OFF.

YOU **KILLED** THEM?

IT'S EASIER TO KILL PEOPLE WHEN YOU'RE DEAD YOURSELF. IT'S NOT SUCH A BIG DEAL.

IT'S STILL A BIG DEAL TO ME.

YOU WANT TO STAY HERE UNTIL THE MORNING CREW COMES? I THOUGHT YOU'D LIKE TO GET OUT OF HERE.

THEY'LL THINK I DID IT.

MAYBE.

COME.

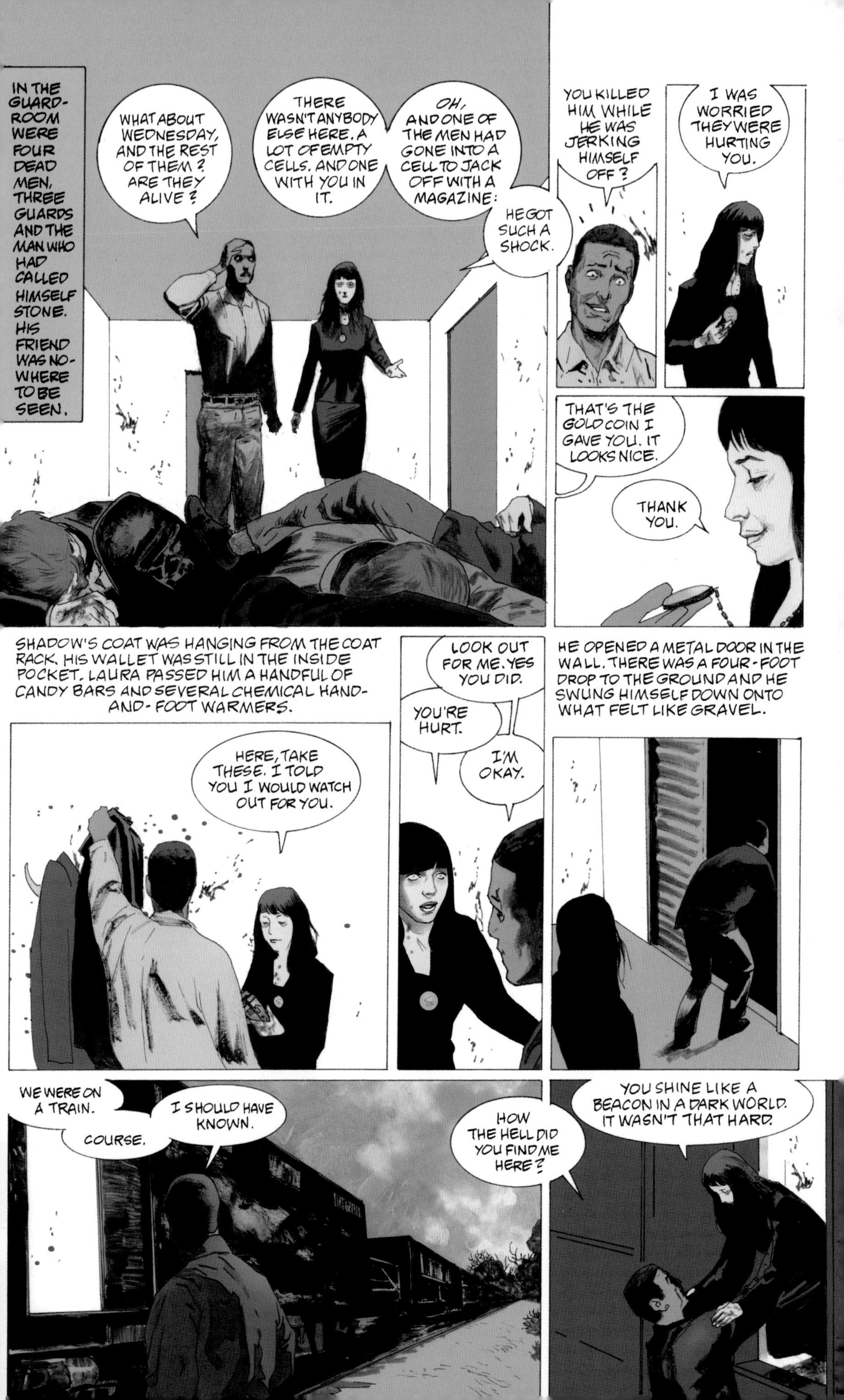

IN THE GUARD-ROOM WERE FOUR DEAD MEN, THREE GUARDS AND THE MAN WHO HAD CALLED HIMSELF STONE. HIS FRIEND WAS NO-WHERE TO BE SEEN.
WHAT ABOUT WEDNESDAY, AND THE REST OF THEM? ARE THEY ALIVE?
THERE WASN'T ANYBODY ELSE HERE. A LOT OF EMPTY CELLS. AND ONE WITH YOU IN IT.
OH, AND ONE OF THE MEN HAD GONE INTO A CELL TO JACK OFF WITH A MAGAZINE.
HE GOT SUCH A SHOCK.
YOU KILLED HIM WHILE HE WAS JERKING HIMSELF OFF?
I WAS WORRIED THEY WERE HURTING YOU.
THAT'S THE GOLD COIN I GAVE YOU. IT LOOKS NICE.
THANK YOU.
SHADOW'S COAT WAS HANGING FROM THE COAT RACK. HIS WALLET WAS STILL IN THE INSIDE POCKET. LAURA PASSED HIM A HANDFUL OF CANDY BARS AND SEVERAL CHEMICAL HAND-AND-FOOT WARMERS.
HERE, TAKE THESE. I TOLD YOU I WOULD WATCH OUT FOR YOU.
LOOK OUT FOR ME. YES YOU DID.
YOU'RE HURT.
I'M OKAY.
HE OPENED A METAL DOOR IN THE WALL. THERE WAS A FOUR-FOOT DROP TO THE GROUND AND HE SWUNG HIMSELF DOWN ONTO WHAT FELT LIKE GRAVEL.
WE WERE ON A TRAIN.
COURSE.
I SHOULD HAVE KNOWN.
HOW THE HELL DID YOU FIND ME HERE?
YOU SHINE LIKE A BEACON IN A DARK WORLD. IT WASN'T THAT HARD.

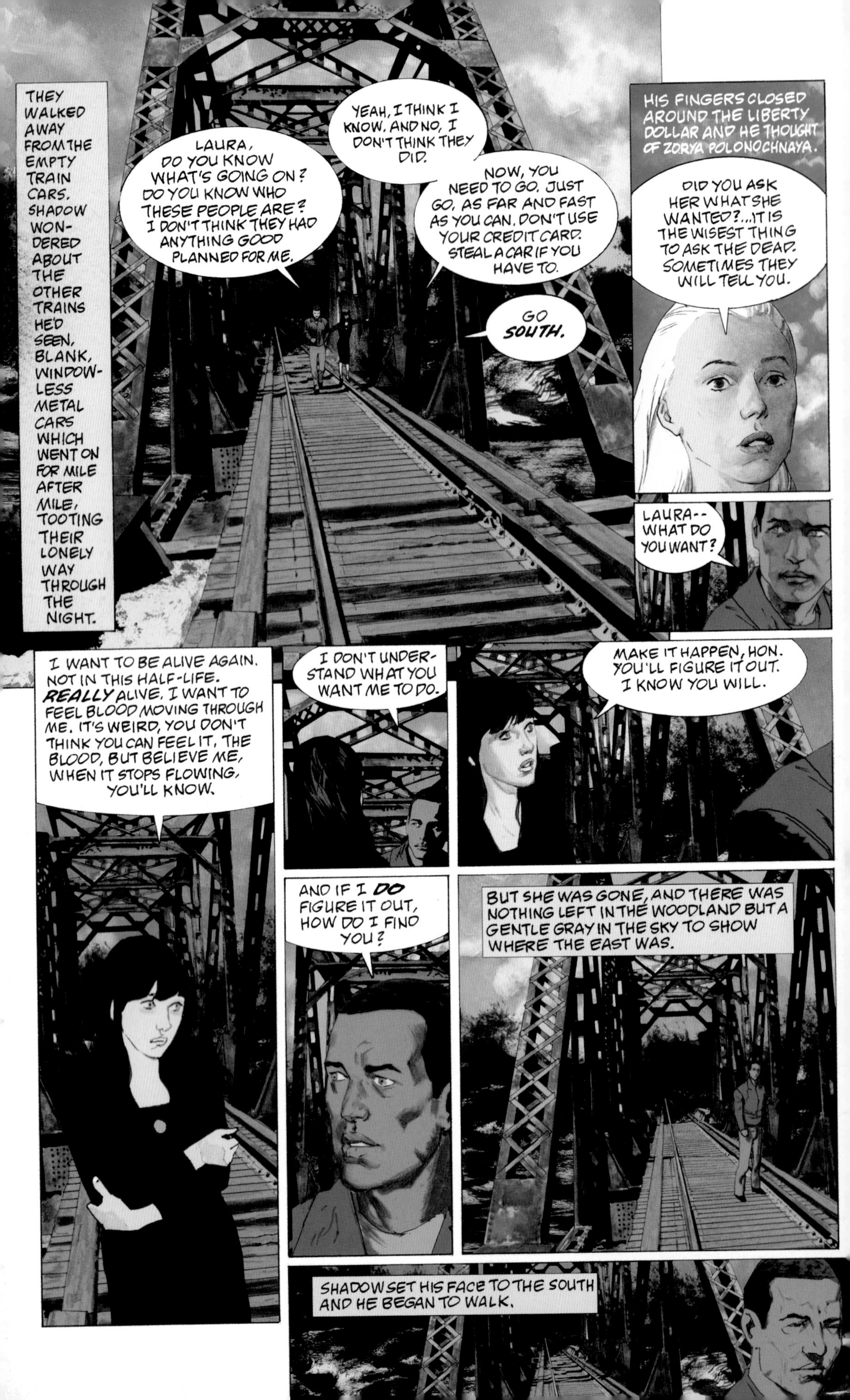
THEY WALKED AWAY FROM THE EMPTY TRAIN CARS. SHADOW WONDERED ABOUT THE OTHER TRAINS HE'D SEEN, BLANK, WINDOWLESS METAL CARS WHICH WENT ON FOR MILE AFTER MILE, TOOTING THEIR LONELY WAY THROUGH THE NIGHT.
LAURA, DO YOU KNOW WHAT'S GOING ON? DO YOU KNOW WHO THESE PEOPLE ARE? I DON'T THINK THEY HAD ANYTHING GOOD PLANNED FOR ME.
YEAH, I THINK I KNOW. AND NO, I DON'T THINK THEY DID.
NOW, YOU NEED TO GO. JUST GO, AS FAR AND FAST AS YOU CAN. DON'T USE YOUR CREDIT CARD. STEAL A CAR IF YOU HAVE TO.
GO SOUTH.
HIS FINGERS CLOSED AROUND THE LIBERTY DOLLAR AND HE THOUGHT OF ZORYA POLONOCHNAYA.
DID YOU ASK HER WHAT SHE WANTED?...IT IS THE WISEST THING TO ASK THE DEAD. SOMETIMES THEY WILL TELL YOU.
LAURA-- WHAT DO YOU WANT?
I WANT TO BE ALIVE AGAIN. NOT IN THIS HALF-LIFE. REALLY ALIVE. I WANT TO FEEL BLOOD MOVING THROUGH ME. IT'S WEIRD, YOU DON'T THINK YOU CAN FEEL IT, THE BLOOD, BUT BELIEVE ME, WHEN IT STOPS FLOWING, YOU'LL KNOW.
I DON'T UNDERSTAND WHAT YOU WANT ME TO DO.
MAKE IT HAPPEN, HON. YOU'LL FIGURE IT OUT. I KNOW YOU WILL.
AND IF I DO FIGURE IT OUT, HOW DO I FIND YOU?
BUT SHE WAS GONE, AND THERE WAS NOTHING LEFT IN THE WOODLAND BUT A GENTLE GRAY IN THE SKY TO SHOW WHERE THE EAST WAS.
SHADOW SET HIS FACE TO THE SOUTH AND HE BEGAN TO WALK.

CHAPTER SEVEN

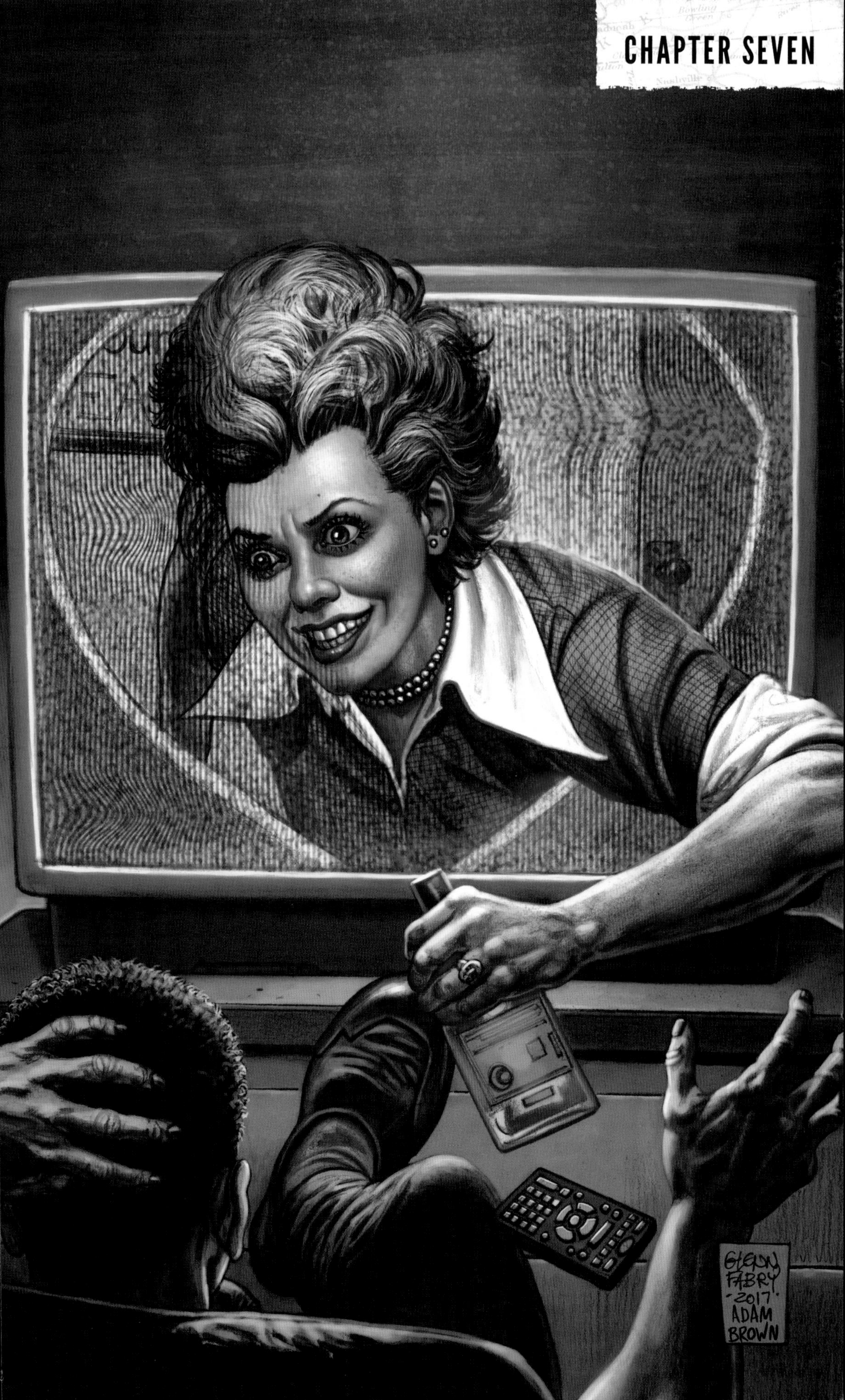
GLENN FABRY
·2017·
ADAM BROWN

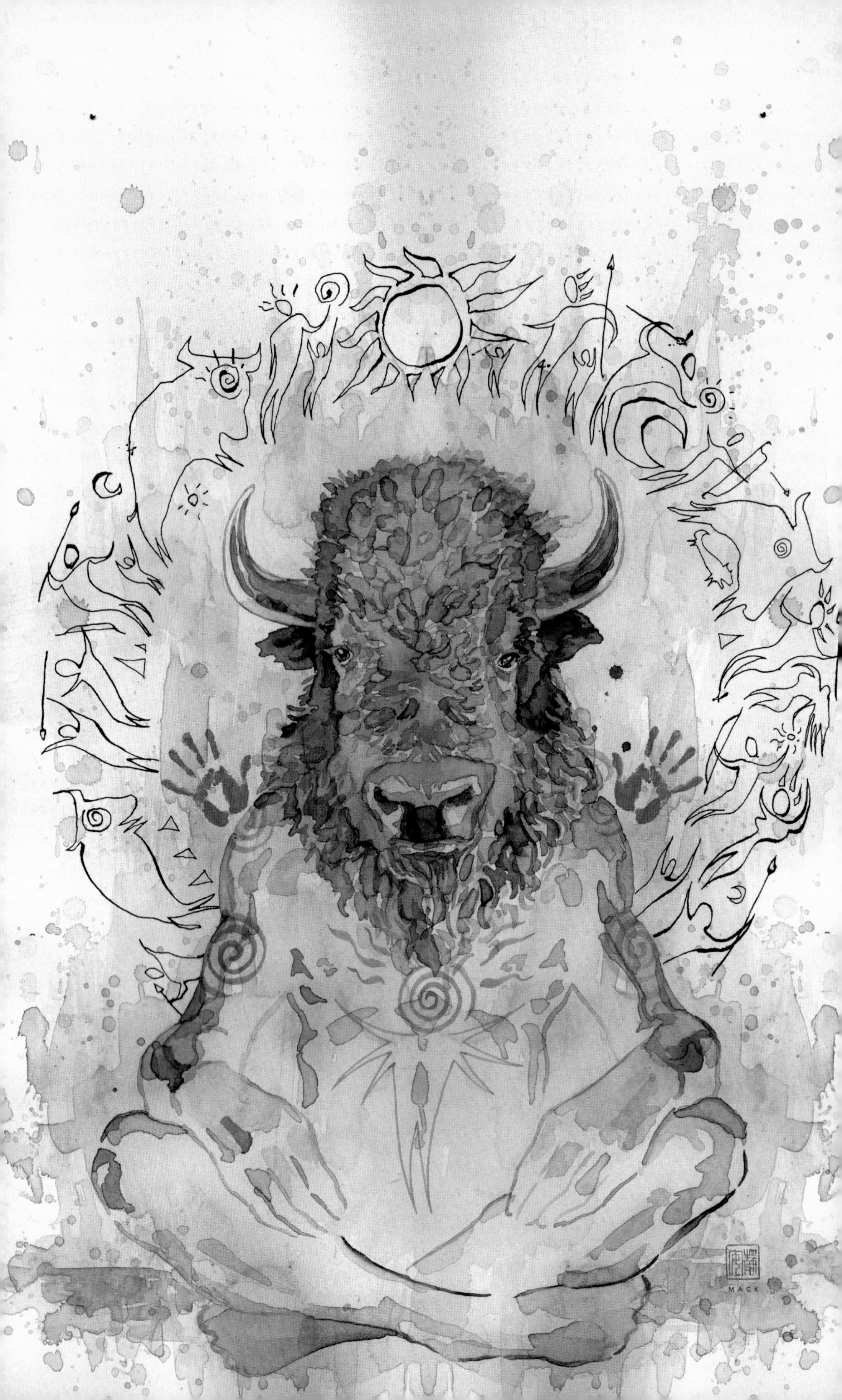
MACK

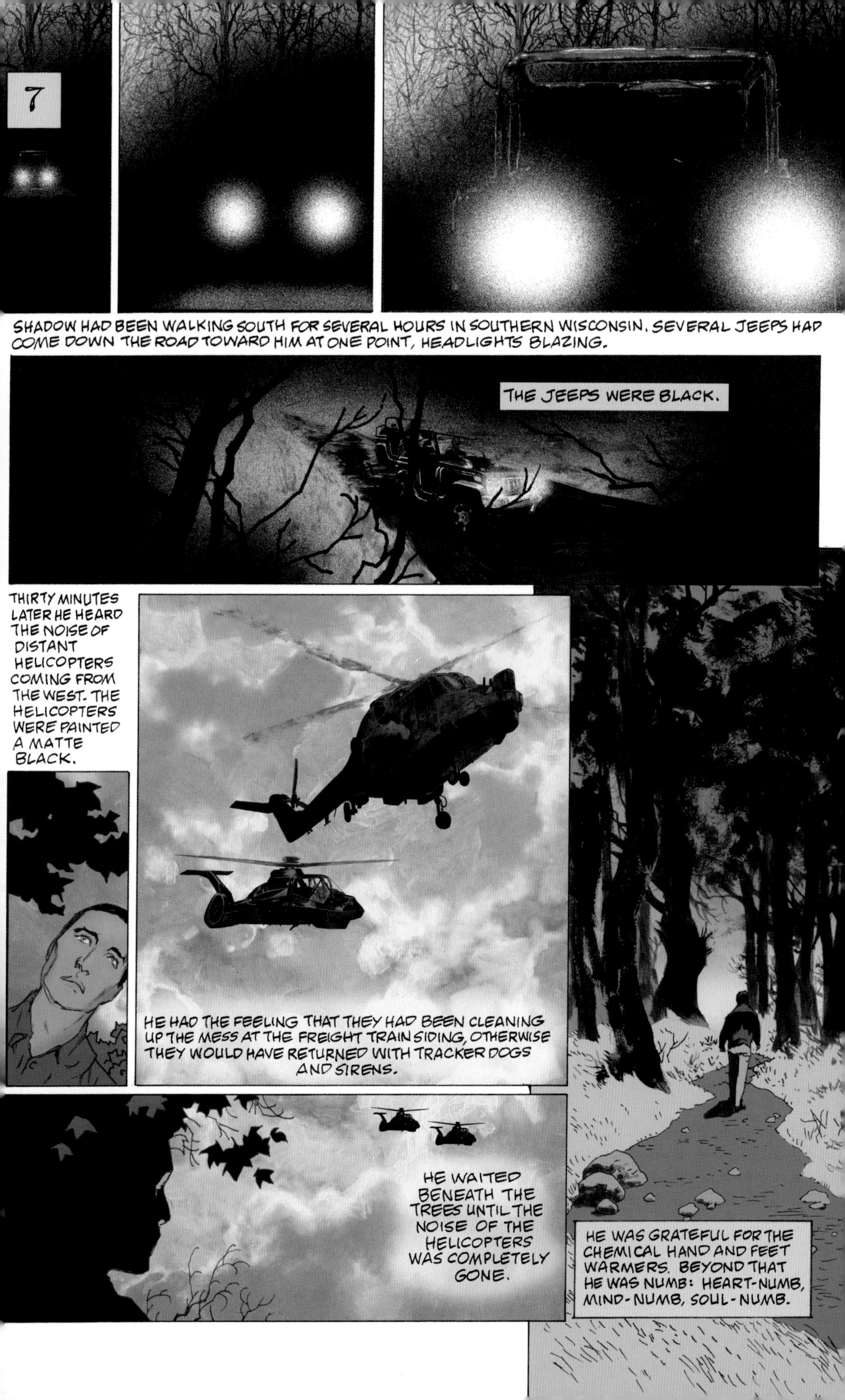
7
SHADOW HAD BEEN WALKING SOUTH FOR SEVERAL HOURS IN SOUTHERN WISCONSIN. SEVERAL JEEPS HAD COME DOWN THE ROAD TOWARD HIM AT ONE POINT, HEADLIGHTS BLAZING.
THE JEEPS WERE BLACK.
THIRTY MINUTES LATER HE HEARD THE NOISE OF DISTANT HELICOPTERS COMING FROM THE WEST. THE HELICOPTERS WERE PAINTED A MATTE BLACK.
HE HAD THE FEELING THAT THEY HAD BEEN CLEANING UP THE MESS AT THE FREIGHT TRAIN SIDING, OTHERWISE THEY WOULD HAVE RETURNED WITH TRACKER DOGS AND SIRENS.
HE WAITED BENEATH THE TREES UNTIL THE NOISE OF THE HELICOPTERS WAS COMPLETELY GONE.
HE WAS GRATEFUL FOR THE CHEMICAL HAND AND FEET WARMERS. BEYOND THAT HE WAS NUMB: HEART-NUMB, MIND-NUMB, SOUL-NUMB.

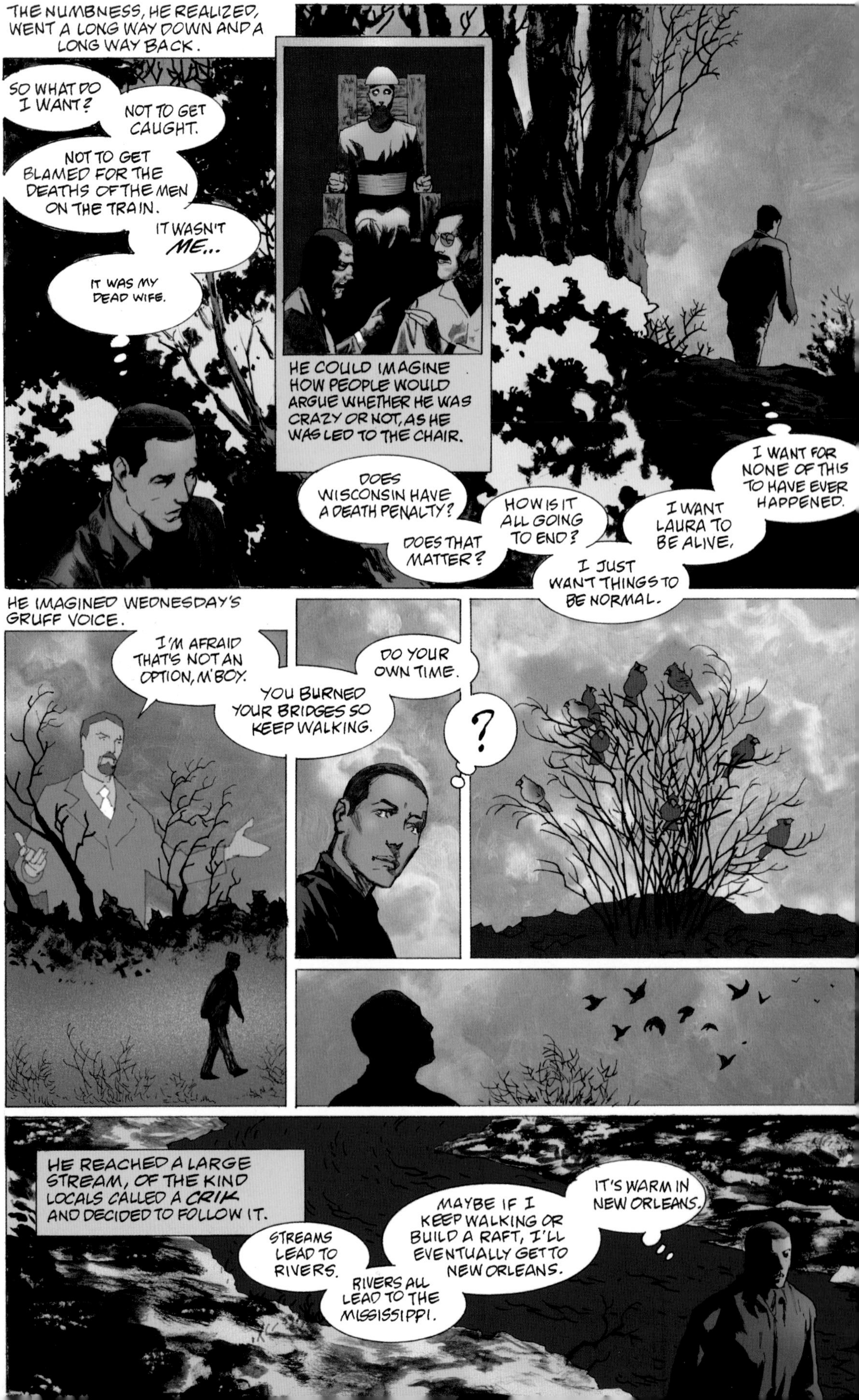
THE NUMBNESS, HE REALIZED, WENT A LONG WAY DOWN AND A LONG WAY BACK.
SO WHAT DO I WANT?
NOT TO GET CAUGHT.
NOT TO GET BLAMED FOR THE DEATHS OF THE MEN ON THE TRAIN.
IT WASN'T ME...
IT WAS MY DEAD WIFE.
HE COULD IMAGINE HOW PEOPLE WOULD ARGUE WHETHER HE WAS CRAZY OR NOT, AS HE WAS LED TO THE CHAIR.
DOES WISCONSIN HAVE A DEATH PENALTY?
DOES THAT MATTER?
HOW IS IT ALL GOING TO END?
I JUST WANT THINGS TO BE NORMAL.
I WANT LAURA TO BE ALIVE.
I WANT FOR NONE OF THIS TO HAVE EVER HAPPENED.
HE IMAGINED WEDNESDAY'S GRUFF VOICE.
I'M AFRAID THAT'S NOT AN OPTION, M'BOY.
YOU BURNED YOUR BRIDGES SO KEEP WALKING.
DO YOUR OWN TIME.
?
HE REACHED A LARGE STREAM, OF THE KIND LOCALS CALLED A CRIK AND DECIDED TO FOLLOW IT.
STREAMS LEAD TO RIVERS.
RIVERS ALL LEAD TO THE MISSISSIPPI.
MAYBE IF I KEEP WALKING OR BUILD A RAFT, I'LL EVENTUALLY GET TO NEW ORLEANS.
IT'S WARM IN NEW ORLEANS.

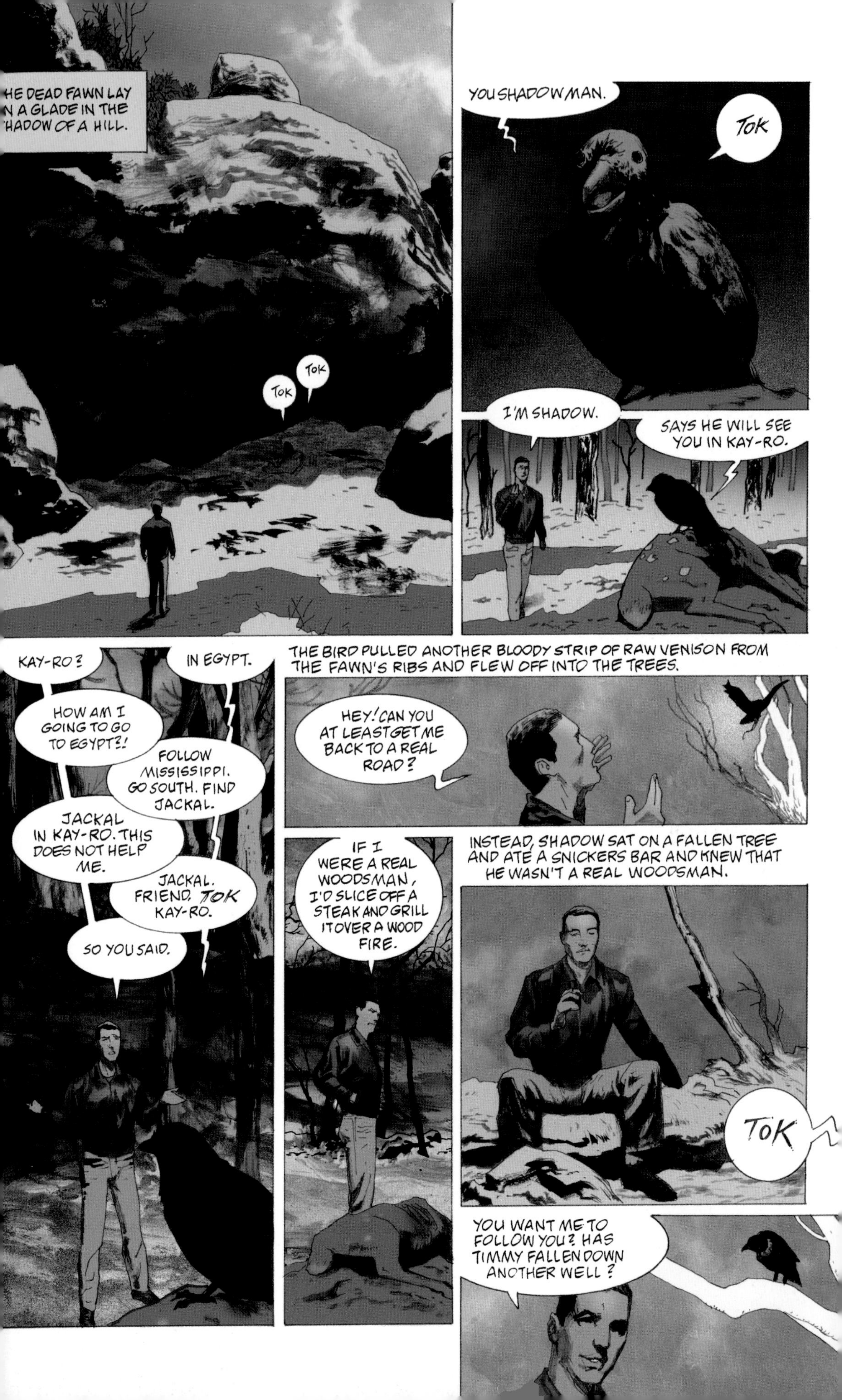
HE DEAD FAWN LAY
N A GLADE IN THE
HADOW OF A HILL.
TOK
TOK
YOU SHADOW MAN.
TOK
I'M SHADOW.
SAYS HE WILL SEE YOU IN KAY-RO.
KAY-RO?
IN EGYPT.
HOW AM I GOING TO GO TO EGYPT?!
FOLLOW MISSISSIPPI. GO SOUTH. FIND JACKAL.
JACKAL IN KAY-RO. THIS DOES NOT HELP ME.
JACKAL. FRIEND. TOK KAY-RO.
SO YOU SAID.
THE BIRD PULLED ANOTHER BLOODY STRIP OF RAW VENISON FROM THE FAWN'S RIBS AND FLEW OFF INTO THE TREES.
HEY! CAN YOU AT LEAST GET ME BACK TO A REAL ROAD?
IF I WERE A REAL WOODSMAN, I'D SLICE OFF A STEAK AND GRILL IT OVER A WOOD FIRE.
INSTEAD, SHADOW SAT ON A FALLEN TREE AND ATE A SNICKERS BAR AND KNEW THAT HE WASN'T A REAL WOODSMAN.
TOK
YOU WANT ME TO FOLLOW YOU? HAS TIMMY FALLEN DOWN ANOTHER WELL?

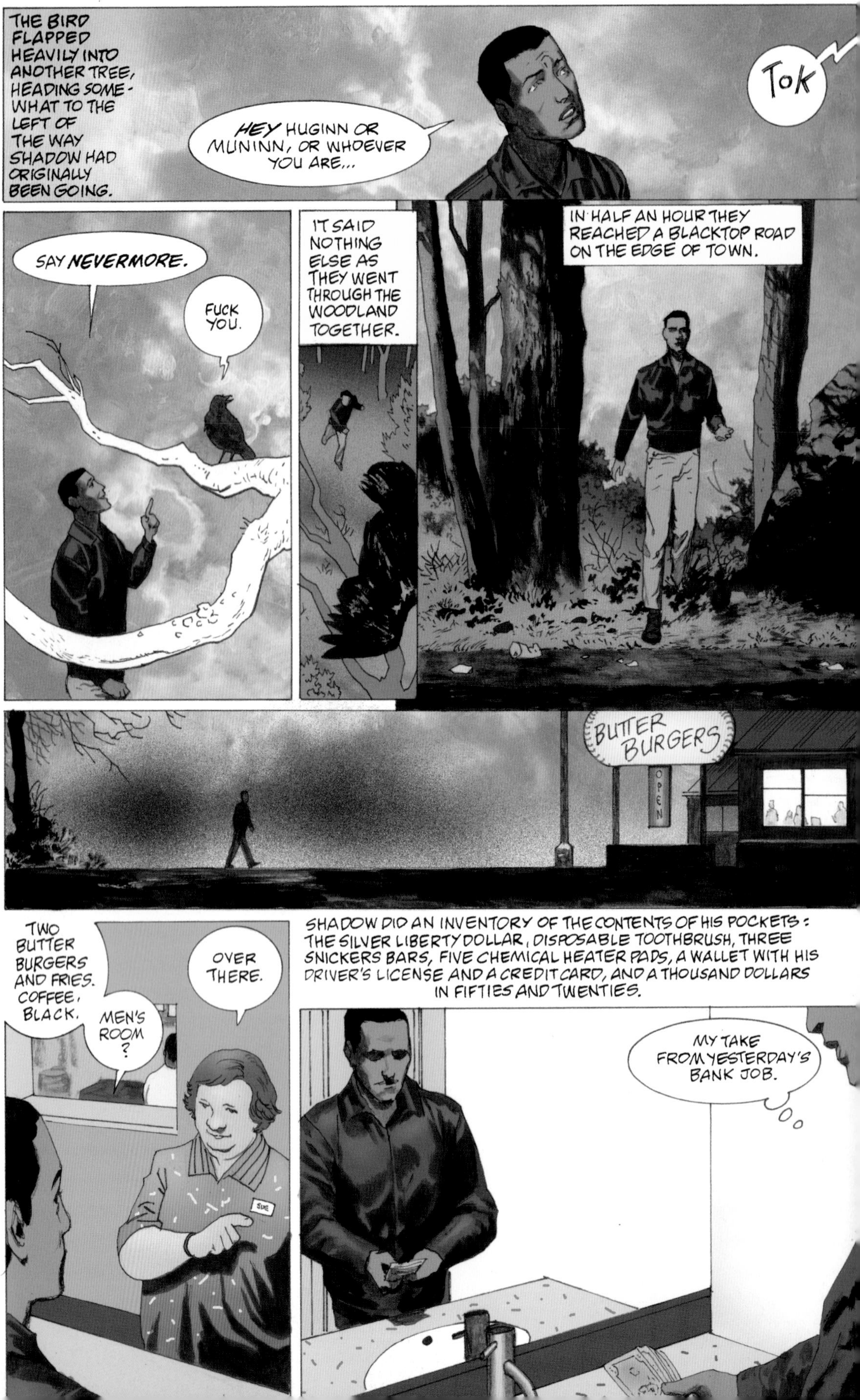
THE BIRD FLAPPED HEAVILY INTO ANOTHER TREE, HEADING SOME-WHAT TO THE LEFT OF THE WAY SHADOW HAD ORIGINALLY BEEN GOING.
HEY HUGINN OR MUNINN, OR WHOEVER YOU ARE...
TOK
SAY NEVERMORE.
FUCK YOU.
IT SAID NOTHING ELSE AS THEY WENT THROUGH THE WOODLAND TOGETHER.
IN HALF AN HOUR THEY REACHED A BLACKTOP ROAD ON THE EDGE OF TOWN.
BUTTER BURGERS
OPEN
TWO BUTTER BURGERS AND FRIES. COFFEE, BLACK.
MEN'S ROOM?
OVER THERE.
SHADOW DID AN INVENTORY OF THE CONTENTS OF HIS POCKETS: THE SILVER LIBERTY DOLLAR, DISPOSABLE TOOTHBRUSH, THREE SNICKERS BARS, FIVE CHEMICAL HEATER PADS, A WALLET WITH HIS DRIVER'S LICENSE AND A CREDIT CARD, AND A THOUSAND DOLLARS IN FIFTIES AND TWENTIES.
MY TAKE FROM YESTERDAY'S BANK JOB.

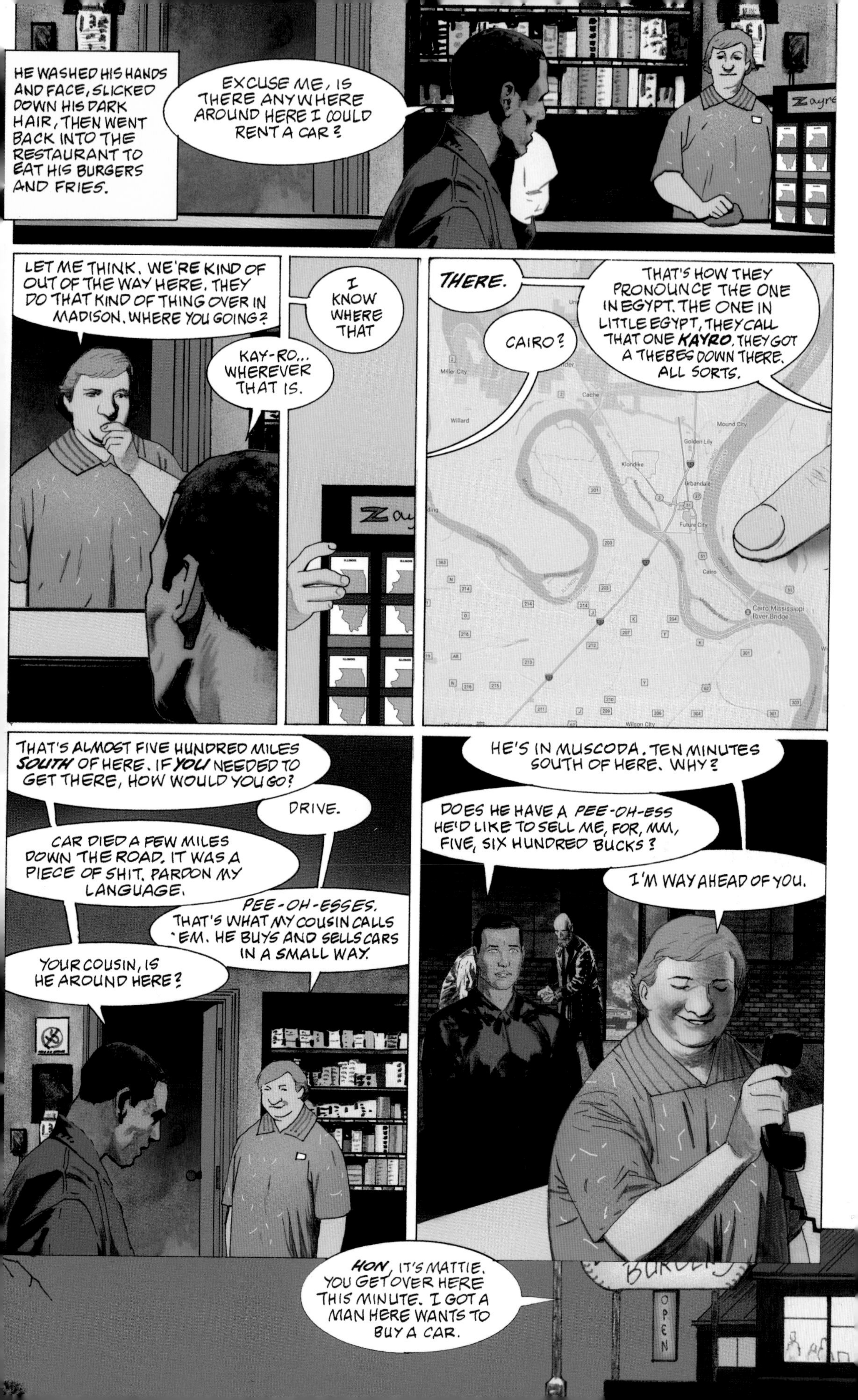

HE WASHED HIS HANDS AND FACE, SLICKED DOWN HIS DARK HAIR, THEN WENT BACK INTO THE RESTAURANT TO EAT HIS BURGERS AND FRIES.
EXCUSE ME, IS THERE ANYWHERE AROUND HERE I COULD RENT A CAR?
Zayre
LET ME THINK. WE'RE KIND OF OUT OF THE WAY HERE. THEY DO THAT KIND OF THING OVER IN MADISON. WHERE YOU GOING?
KAY-RO... WHEREVER THAT IS.
I KNOW WHERE THAT
THERE.
CAIRO?
THAT'S HOW THEY PRONOUNCE THE ONE IN EGYPT. THE ONE IN LITTLE EGYPT, THEY CALL THAT ONE KAYRO. THEY GOT A THEBES DOWN THERE. ALL SORTS.
Miller City
Cache
Willard
Mound City
Golden Lily
Klondike
Urbandale
Future City
Cairo
Cairo Mississippi River Bridge
Wilson City
THAT'S ALMOST FIVE HUNDRED MILES SOUTH OF HERE. IF YOU NEEDED TO GET THERE, HOW WOULD YOU GO?
DRIVE.
CAR DIED A FEW MILES DOWN THE ROAD. IT WAS A PIECE OF SHIT. PARDON MY LANGUAGE.
PEE-OH-ESSES. THAT'S WHAT MY COUSIN CALLS 'EM. HE BUYS AND SELLS CARS IN A SMALL WAY.
YOUR COUSIN, IS HE AROUND HERE?
HE'S IN MUSCODA. TEN MINUTES SOUTH OF HERE. WHY?
DOES HE HAVE A PEE-OH-ESS HE'D LIKE TO SELL ME, FOR, MM, FIVE, SIX HUNDRED BUCKS?
I'M WAY AHEAD OF YOU.
HON, IT'S MATTIE. YOU GET OVER HERE THIS MINUTE. I GOT A MAN HERE WANTS TO BUY A CAR.
OPEN

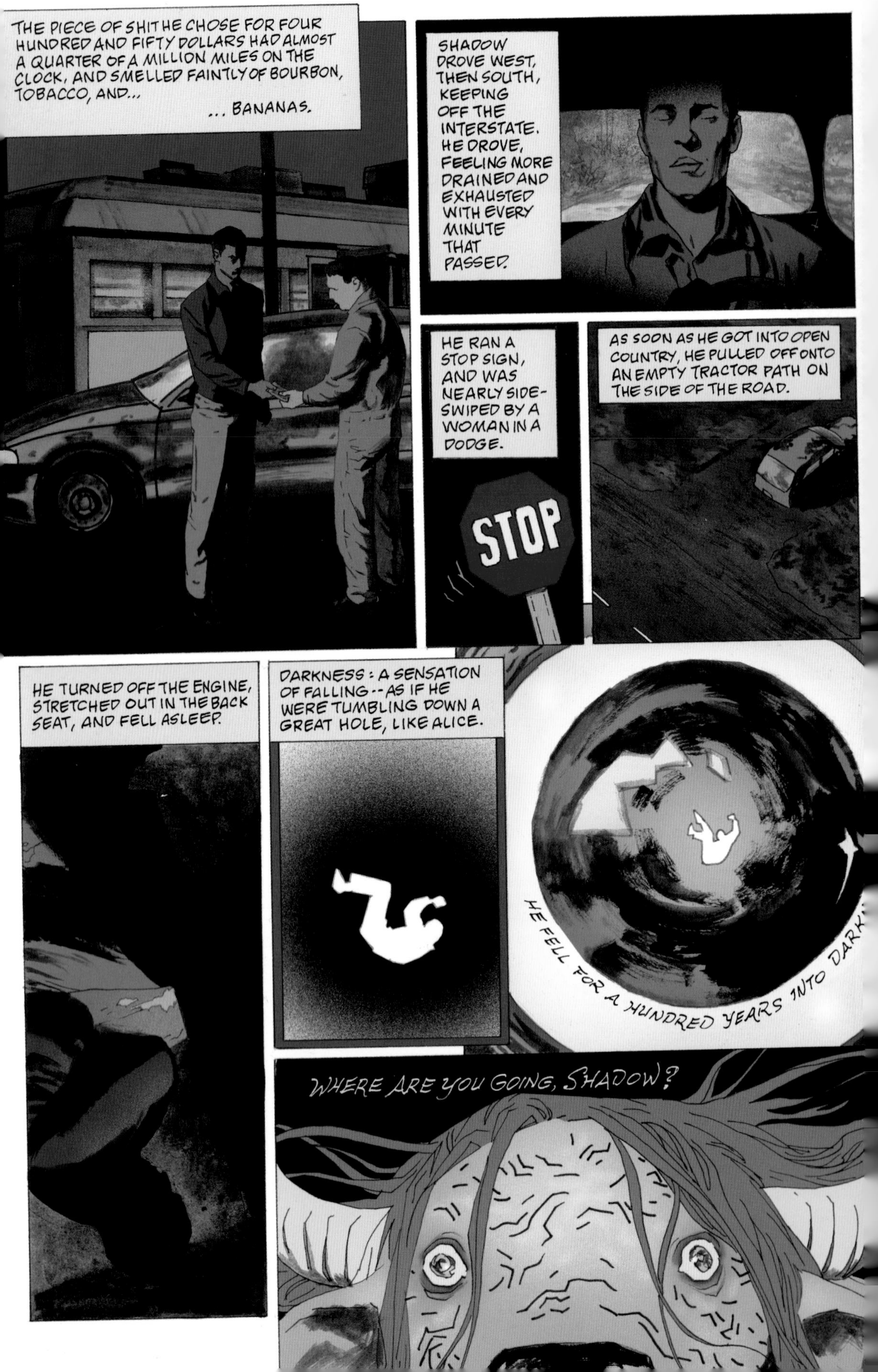
THE PIECE OF SHIT HE CHOSE FOR FOUR HUNDRED AND FIFTY DOLLARS HAD ALMOST A QUARTER OF A MILLION MILES ON THE CLOCK, AND SMELLED FAINTLY OF BOURBON, TOBACCO, AND...
... BANANAS.
SHADOW DROVE WEST, THEN SOUTH, KEEPING OFF THE INTERSTATE. HE DROVE, FEELING MORE DRAINED AND EXHAUSTED WITH EVERY MINUTE THAT PASSED.
HE RAN A STOP SIGN, AND WAS NEARLY SIDE-SWIPED BY A WOMAN IN A DODGE.
STOP
AS SOON AS HE GOT INTO OPEN COUNTRY, HE PULLED OFF ONTO AN EMPTY TRACTOR PATH ON THE SIDE OF THE ROAD.
HE TURNED OFF THE ENGINE, STRETCHED OUT IN THE BACK SEAT, AND FELL ASLEEP.
DARKNESS: A SENSATION OF FALLING--AS IF HE WERE TUMBLING DOWN A GREAT HOLE, LIKE ALICE.
HE FELL FOR A HUNDRED YEARS INTO DARK
WHERE ARE YOU GOING, SHADOW?

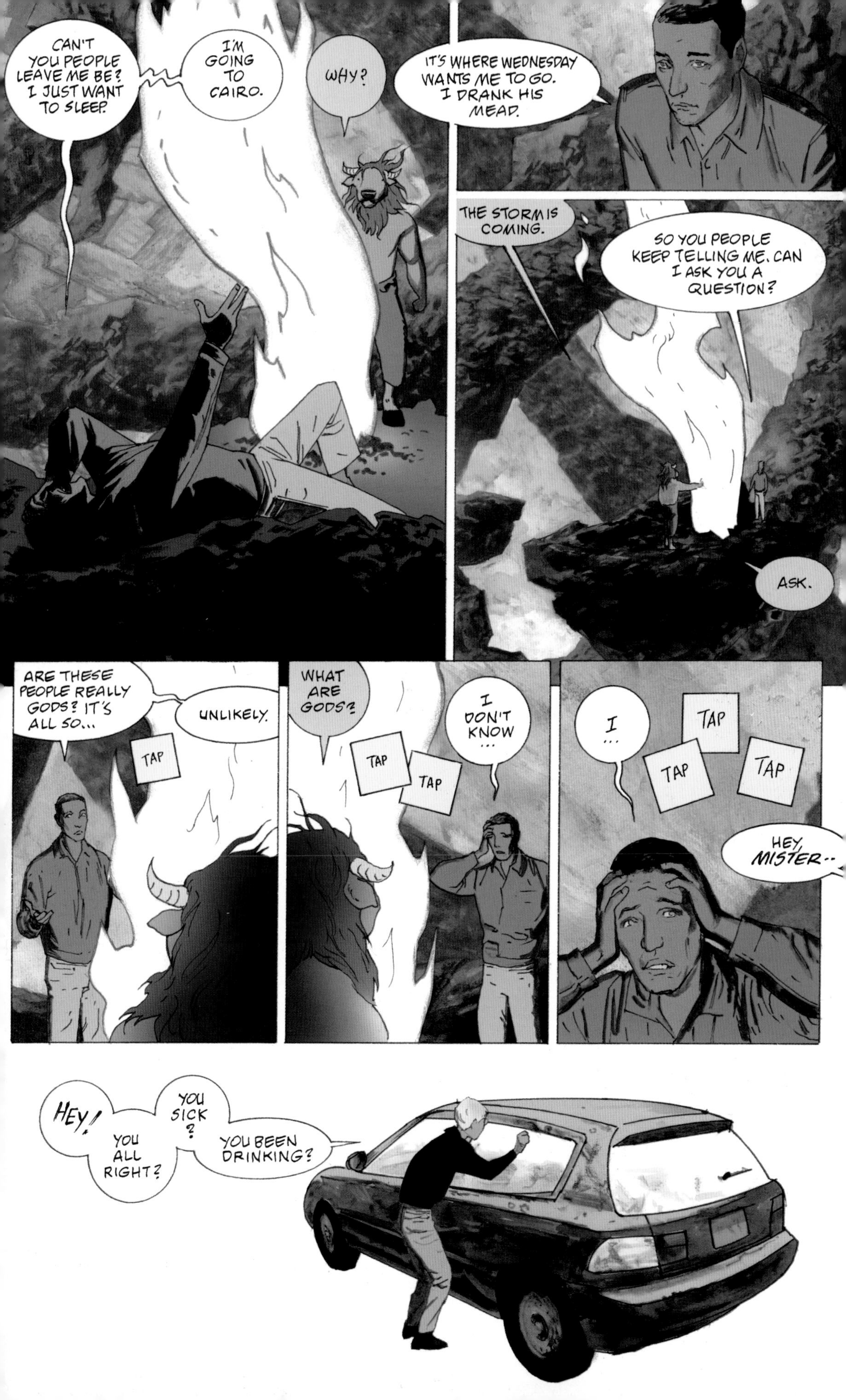
CAN'T YOU PEOPLE LEAVE ME BE? I JUST WANT TO SLEEP.
I'M GOING TO CAIRO.
WHY?
IT'S WHERE WEDNESDAY WANTS ME TO GO. I DRANK HIS MEAD.
THE STORM IS COMING.
SO YOU PEOPLE KEEP TELLING ME. CAN I ASK YOU A QUESTION?
ASK.
ARE THESE PEOPLE REALLY GODS? IT'S ALL SO...
UNLIKELY.
TAP
WHAT ARE GODS?
TAP
TAP
I DON'T KNOW ...
I ...
TAP
TAP
TAP
HEY, MISTER--
HEY!
YOU ALL RIGHT?
YOU SICK?
YOU BEEN DRINKING?

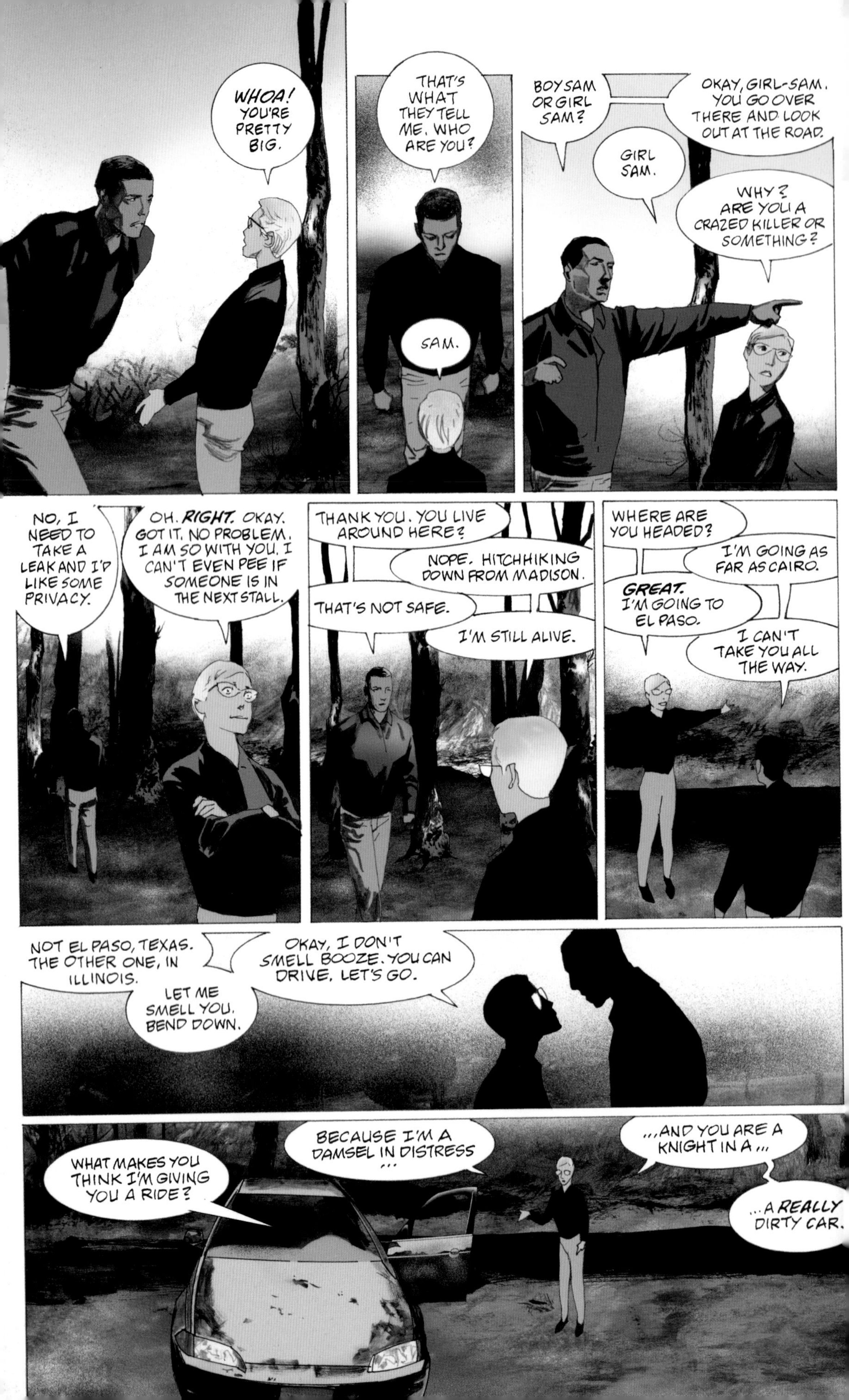
WHOA! YOU'RE PRETTY BIG.
THAT'S WHAT THEY TELL ME. WHO ARE YOU?
SAM.
BOY SAM OR GIRL SAM?
GIRL SAM.
OKAY, GIRL-SAM. YOU GO OVER THERE AND LOOK OUT AT THE ROAD.
WHY? ARE YOU A CRAZED KILLER OR SOMETHING?
NO, I NEED TO TAKE A LEAK AND I'D LIKE SOME PRIVACY.
OH. RIGHT. OKAY. GOT IT. NO PROBLEM. I AM SO WITH YOU. I CAN'T EVEN PEE IF SOMEONE IS IN THE NEXT STALL.
THANK YOU. YOU LIVE AROUND HERE?
NOPE. HITCHHIKING DOWN FROM MADISON.
THAT'S NOT SAFE.
I'M STILL ALIVE.
WHERE ARE YOU HEADED?
I'M GOING AS FAR AS CAIRO.
GREAT. I'M GOING TO EL PASO.
I CAN'T TAKE YOU ALL THE WAY.
NOT EL PASO, TEXAS. THE OTHER ONE, IN ILLINOIS.
LET ME SMELL YOU. BEND DOWN.
OKAY, I DON'T SMELL BOOZE. YOU CAN DRIVE. LET'S GO.
WHAT MAKES YOU THINK I'M GIVING YOU A RIDE?
BECAUSE I'M A DAMSEL IN DISTRESS ...
...AND YOU ARE A KNIGHT IN A ...
...A REALLY DIRTY CAR.

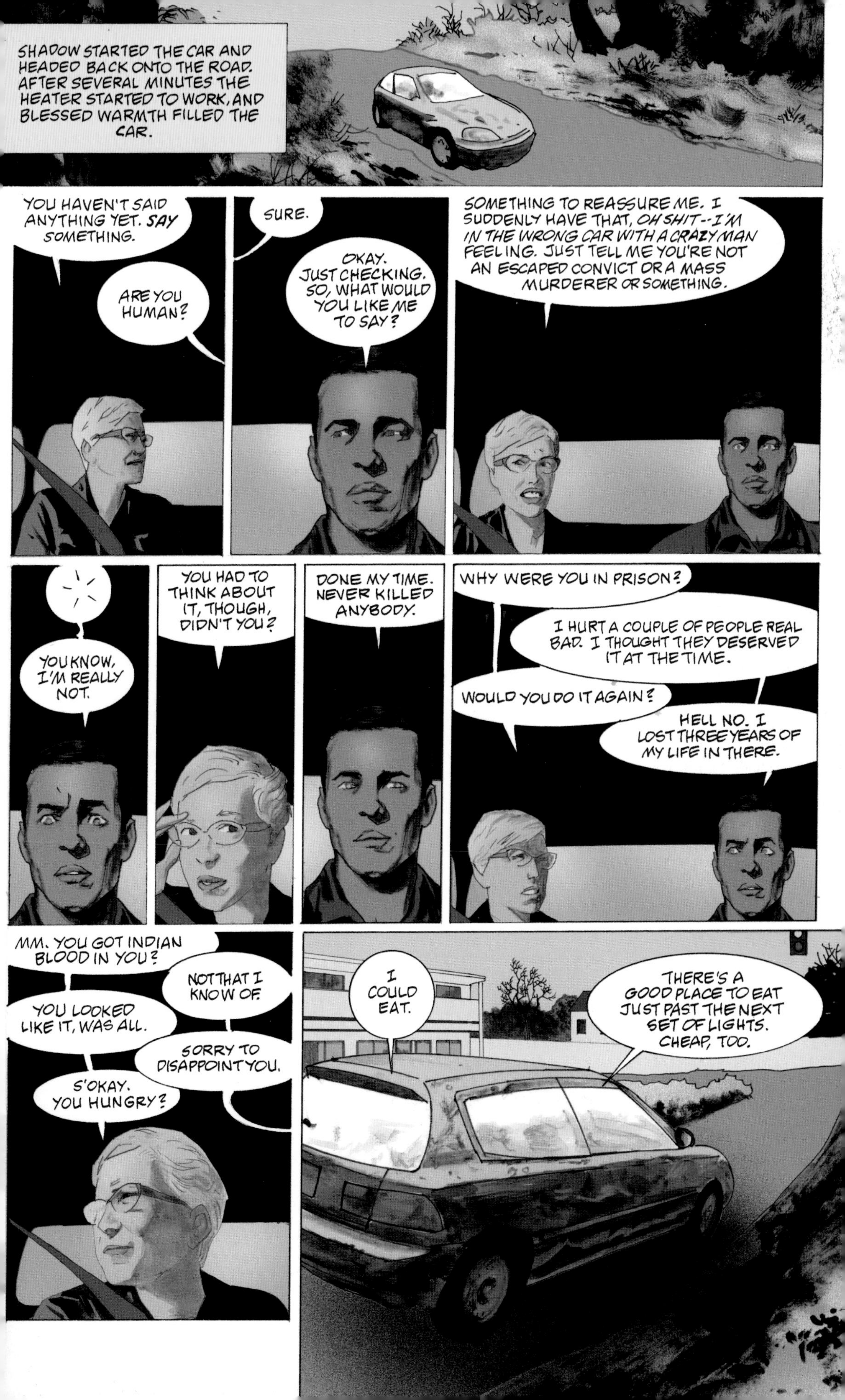
SHADOW STARTED THE CAR AND HEADED BACK ONTO THE ROAD. AFTER SEVERAL MINUTES THE HEATER STARTED TO WORK, AND BLESSED WARMTH FILLED THE CAR.
YOU HAVEN'T SAID ANYTHING YET. SAY SOMETHING.
ARE YOU HUMAN?
SURE.
OKAY. JUST CHECKING. SO, WHAT WOULD YOU LIKE ME TO SAY?
SOMETHING TO REASSURE ME. I SUDDENLY HAVE THAT, OH SHIT--I'M IN THE WRONG CAR WITH A CRAZY MAN FEELING. JUST TELL ME YOU'RE NOT AN ESCAPED CONVICT OR A MASS MURDERER OR SOMETHING.
YOU KNOW, I'M REALLY NOT.
YOU HAD TO THINK ABOUT IT, THOUGH, DIDN'T YOU?
DONE MY TIME. NEVER KILLED ANYBODY.
WHY WERE YOU IN PRISON?
I HURT A COUPLE OF PEOPLE REAL BAD. I THOUGHT THEY DESERVED IT AT THE TIME.
WOULD YOU DO IT AGAIN?
HELL NO. I LOST THREE YEARS OF MY LIFE IN THERE.
MM. YOU GOT INDIAN BLOOD IN YOU?
NOT THAT I KNOW OF.
YOU LOOKED LIKE IT, WAS ALL.
SORRY TO DISAPPOINT YOU.
S'OKAY. YOU HUNGRY?
I COULD EAT.
THERE'S A GOOD PLACE TO EAT JUST PAST THE NEXT SET OF LIGHTS. CHEAP, TOO.

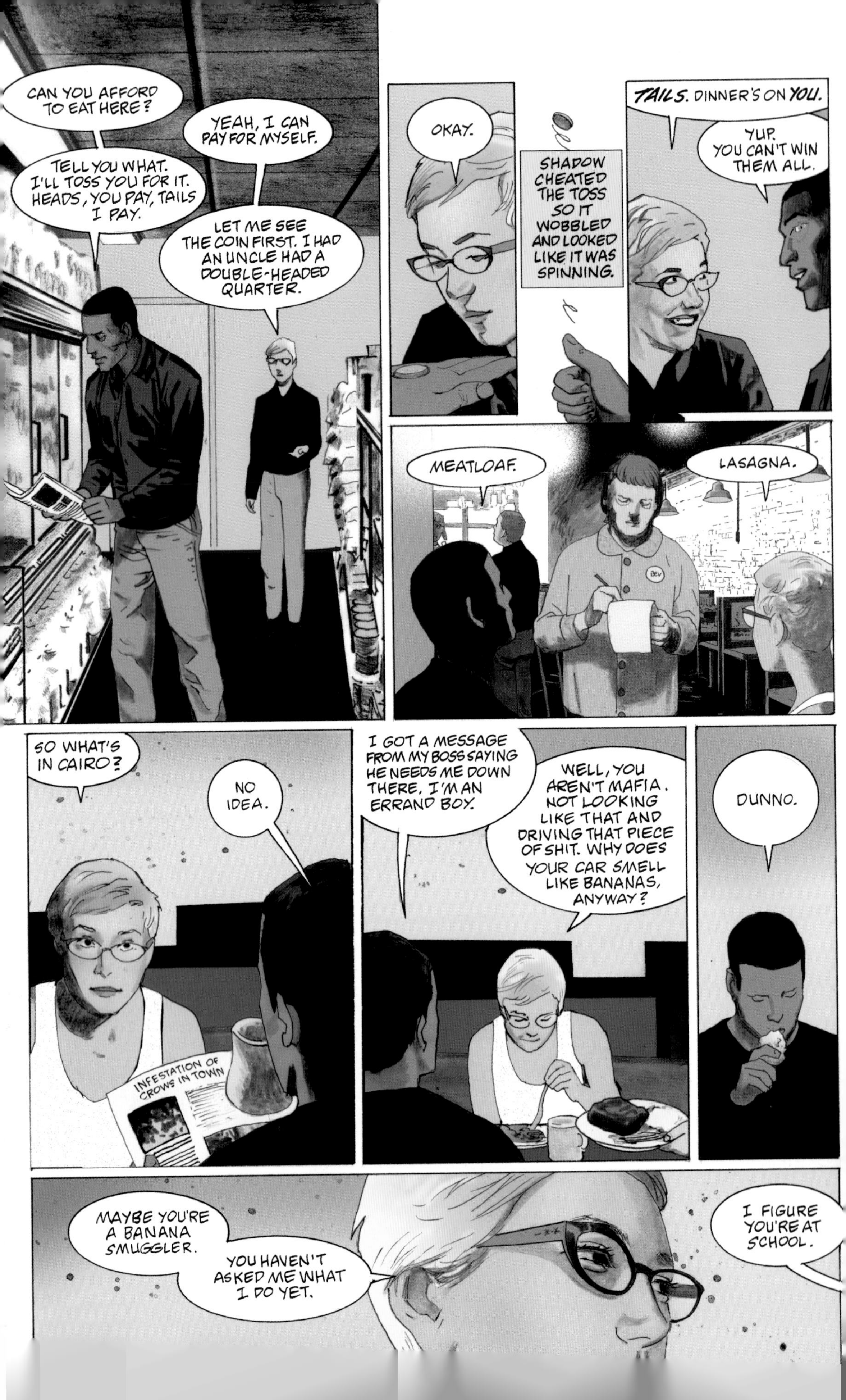
CAN YOU AFFORD TO EAT HERE?
YEAH, I CAN PAY FOR MYSELF.
TELL YOU WHAT. I'LL TOSS YOU FOR IT. HEADS, YOU PAY, TAILS I PAY.
LET ME SEE THE COIN FIRST. I HAD AN UNCLE HAD A DOUBLE-HEADED QUARTER.
OKAY.
SHADOW CHEATED THE TOSS SO IT WOBBLED AND LOOKED LIKE IT WAS SPINNING.
TAILS. DINNER'S ON YOU.
YUP. YOU CAN'T WIN THEM ALL.
MEATLOAF.
LASAGNA.
BEV
SO WHAT'S IN CAIRO?
NO IDEA.
INFESTATION OF CROWS IN TOWN
I GOT A MESSAGE FROM MY BOSS SAYING HE NEEDS ME DOWN THERE. I'M AN ERRAND BOY.
WELL, YOU AREN'T MAFIA. NOT LOOKING LIKE THAT AND DRIVING THAT PIECE OF SHIT. WHY DOES YOUR CAR SMELL LIKE BANANAS, ANYWAY?
DUNNO.
MAYBE YOU'RE A BANANA SMUGGLER.
YOU HAVEN'T ASKED ME WHAT I DO YET.
I FIGURE YOU'RE AT SCHOOL.

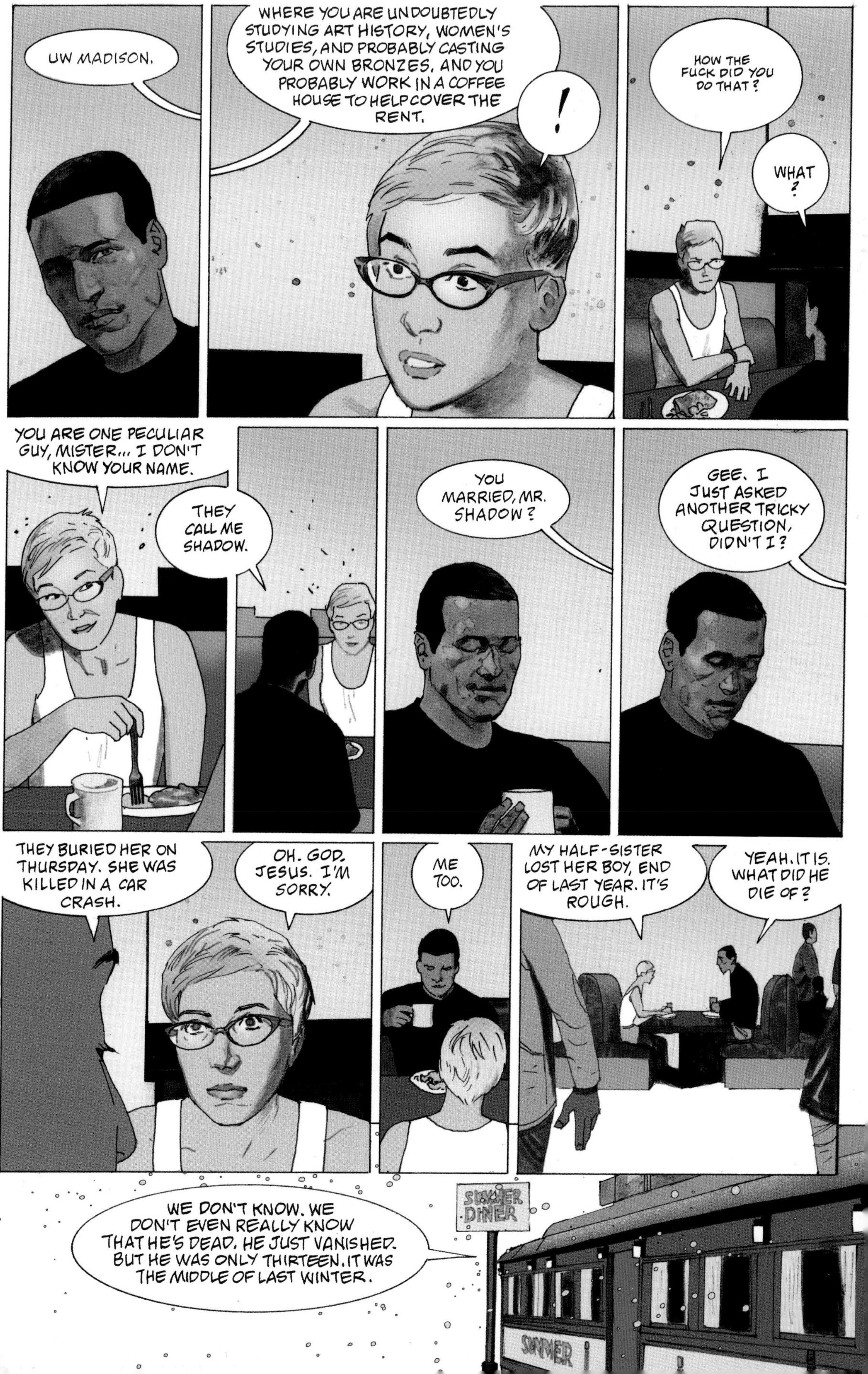
UW MADISON.
WHERE YOU ARE UNDOUBTEDLY STUDYING ART HISTORY, WOMEN'S STUDIES, AND PROBABLY CASTING YOUR OWN BRONZES. AND YOU PROBABLY WORK IN A COFFEE HOUSE TO HELP COVER THE RENT.
!
HOW THE FUCK DID YOU DO THAT?
WHAT?
YOU ARE ONE PECULIAR GUY, MISTER... I DON'T KNOW YOUR NAME.
THEY CALL ME SHADOW.
YOU MARRIED, MR. SHADOW?
GEE. I JUST ASKED ANOTHER TRICKY QUESTION, DIDN'T I?
THEY BURIED HER ON THURSDAY. SHE WAS KILLED IN A CAR CRASH.
OH. GOD. JESUS. I'M SORRY.
ME TOO.
MY HALF-SISTER LOST HER BOY, END OF LAST YEAR. IT'S ROUGH.
YEAH. IT IS. WHAT DID HE DIE OF?
WE DON'T KNOW. WE DON'T EVEN REALLY KNOW THAT HE'S DEAD. HE JUST VANISHED. BUT HE WAS ONLY THIRTEEN. IT WAS THE MIDDLE OF LAST WINTER.
SUMMER DINER
SUMMER

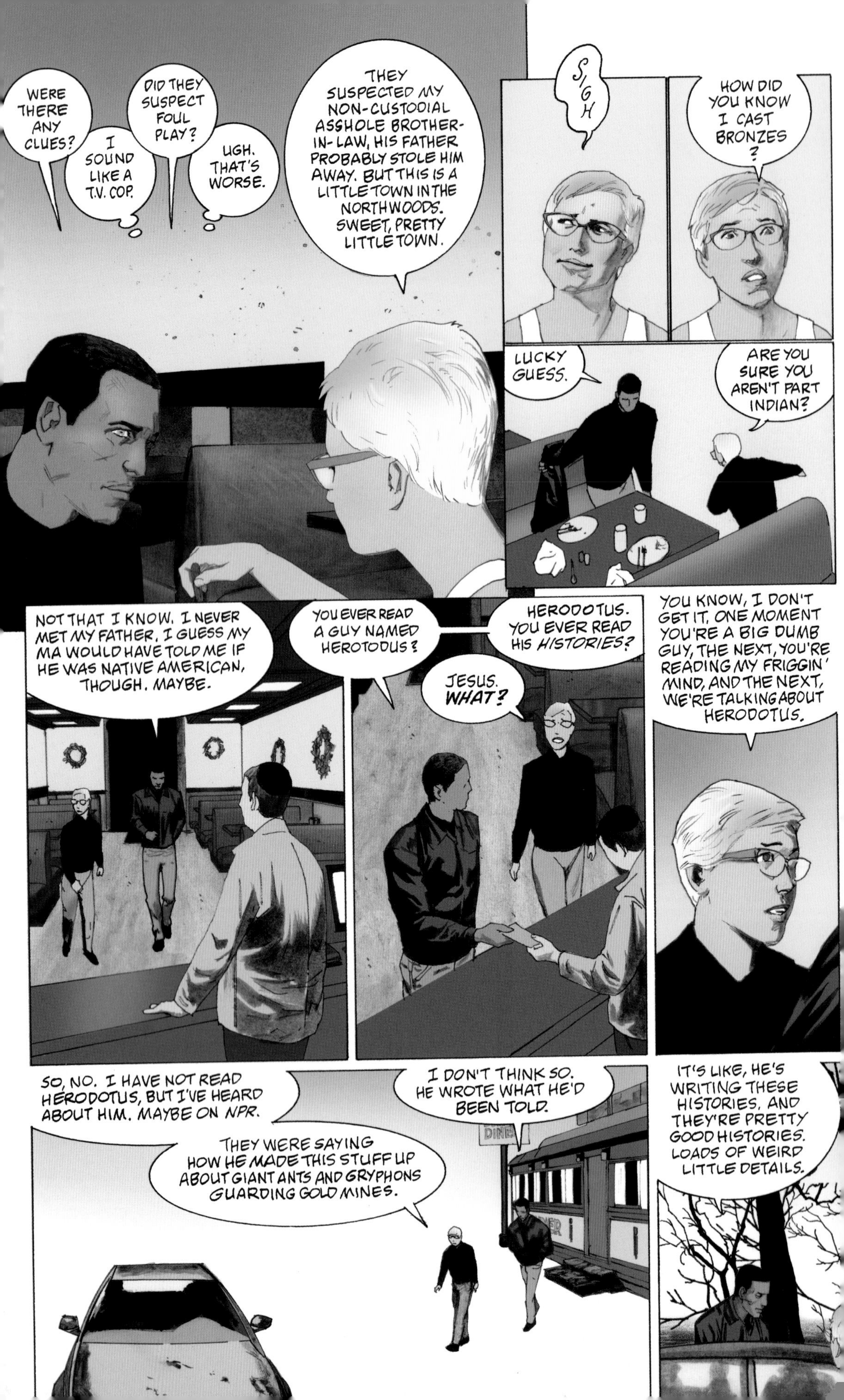
WERE THERE ANY CLUES?
I SOUND LIKE A T.V. COP.
DID THEY SUSPECT FOUL PLAY?
UGH. THAT'S WORSE.
THEY SUSPECTED MY NON-CUSTODIAL ASSHOLE BROTHER-IN-LAW, HIS FATHER PROBABLY STOLE HIM AWAY. BUT THIS IS A LITTLE TOWN IN THE NORTHWOODS. SWEET, PRETTY LITTLE TOWN.
SIGH
HOW DID YOU KNOW I CAST BRONZES?
LUCKY GUESS.
ARE YOU SURE YOU AREN'T PART INDIAN?
NOT THAT I KNOW. I NEVER MET MY FATHER. I GUESS MY MA WOULD HAVE TOLD ME IF HE WAS NATIVE AMERICAN, THOUGH. MAYBE.
YOU EVER READ A GUY NAMED HEROTODUS?
HERODOTUS. YOU EVER READ HIS *HISTORIES*?
JESUS. ***WHAT?***
YOU KNOW, I DON'T GET IT. ONE MOMENT YOU'RE A BIG DUMB GUY, THE NEXT, YOU'RE READING MY FRIGGIN' MIND, AND THE NEXT, WE'RE TALKING ABOUT HERODOTUS.
SO, NO. I HAVE NOT READ HERODOTUS, BUT I'VE HEARD ABOUT HIM. MAYBE ON *NPR*.
THEY WERE SAYING HOW HE *MADE* THIS STUFF UP ABOUT GIANT ANTS AND GRYPHONS GUARDING GOLD MINES.
I DON'T THINK SO. HE WROTE WHAT HE'D BEEN TOLD.
IT'S LIKE, HE'S WRITING THESE HISTORIES. AND THEY'RE PRETTY GOOD HISTORIES. LOADS OF WEIRD LITTLE DETAILS.

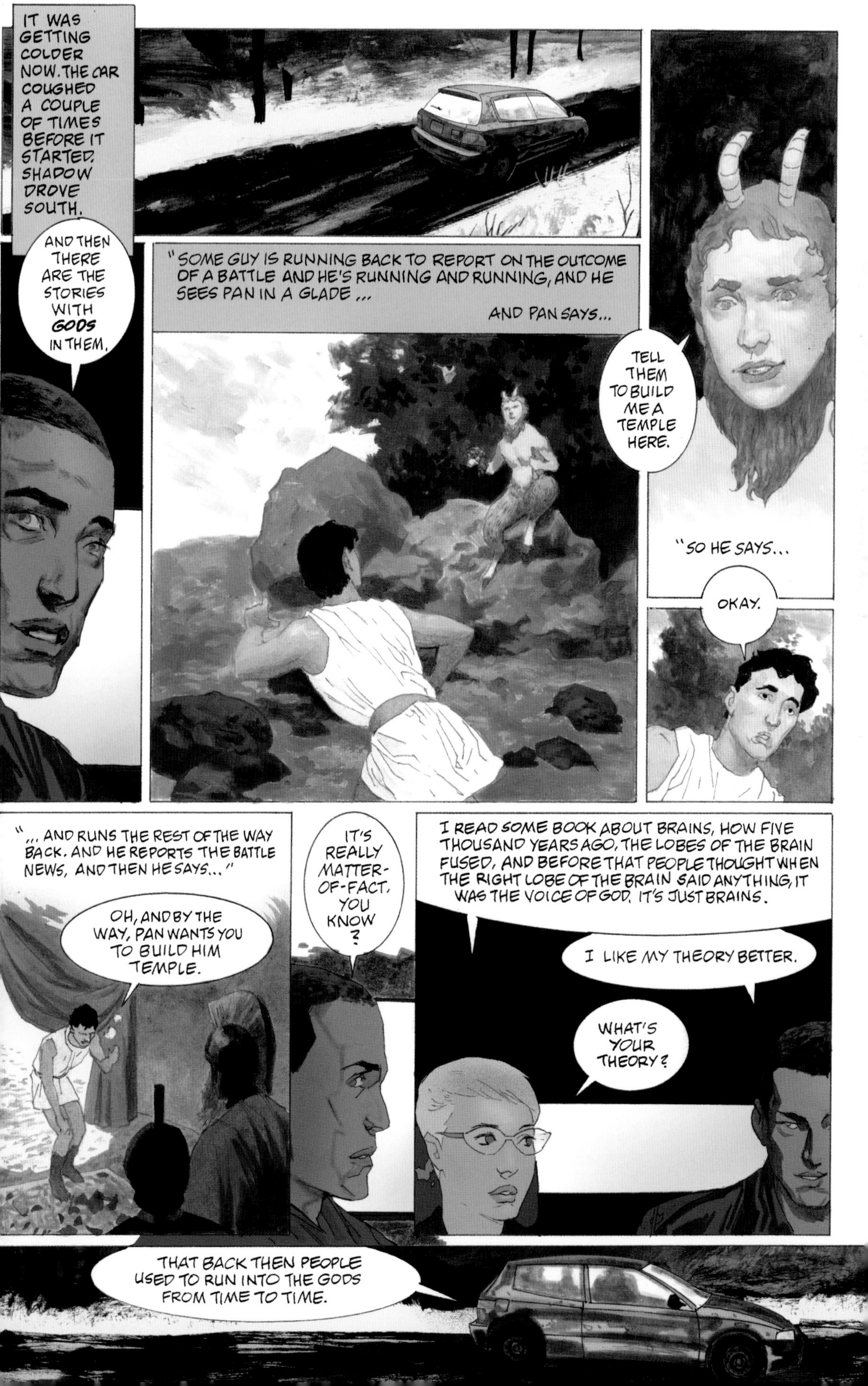
IT WAS GETTING COLDER NOW. THE CAR COUGHED A COUPLE OF TIMES BEFORE IT STARTED. SHADOW DROVE SOUTH.
AND THEN THERE ARE THE STORIES WITH **GODS** IN THEM.
"SOME GUY IS RUNNING BACK TO REPORT ON THE OUTCOME OF A BATTLE AND HE'S RUNNING AND RUNNING, AND HE SEES PAN IN A GLADE ...
AND PAN SAYS...
TELL THEM TO BUILD ME A TEMPLE HERE.
"SO HE SAYS...
OKAY.
"... AND RUNS THE REST OF THE WAY BACK. AND HE REPORTS THE BATTLE NEWS, AND THEN HE SAYS..."
OH, AND BY THE WAY, PAN WANTS YOU TO BUILD HIM TEMPLE.
IT'S REALLY MATTER-OF-FACT, YOU KNOW?
I READ SOME BOOK ABOUT BRAINS, HOW FIVE THOUSAND YEARS AGO, THE LOBES OF THE BRAIN FUSED, AND BEFORE THAT PEOPLE THOUGHT WHEN THE RIGHT LOBE OF THE BRAIN SAID ANYTHING, IT WAS THE VOICE OF GOD. IT'S JUST BRAINS.
I LIKE MY THEORY BETTER.
WHAT'S YOUR THEORY?
THAT BACK THEN PEOPLE USED TO RUN INTO THE GODS FROM TIME TO TIME.

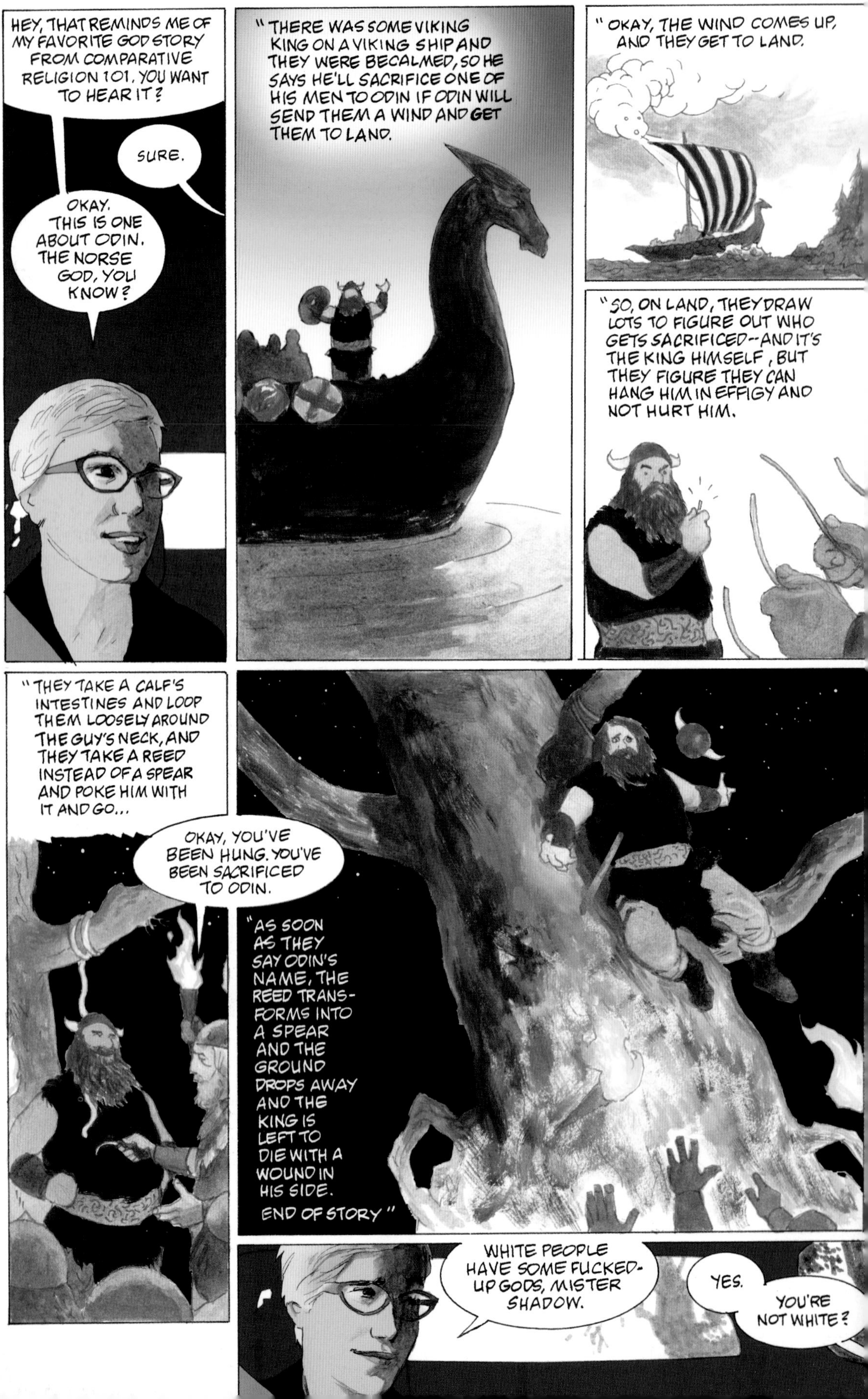
HEY, THAT REMINDS ME OF MY FAVORITE GOD STORY FROM COMPARATIVE RELIGION 101. YOU WANT TO HEAR IT?
SURE.
OKAY. THIS IS ONE ABOUT ODIN. THE NORSE GOD, YOU KNOW?
"THERE WAS SOME VIKING KING ON A VIKING SHIP AND THEY WERE BECALMED, SO HE SAYS HE'LL SACRIFICE ONE OF HIS MEN TO ODIN IF ODIN WILL SEND THEM A WIND AND GET THEM TO LAND.
"OKAY, THE WIND COMES UP, AND THEY GET TO LAND.
"SO, ON LAND, THEY DRAW LOTS TO FIGURE OUT WHO GETS SACRIFICED--AND IT'S THE KING HIMSELF, BUT THEY FIGURE THEY CAN HANG HIM IN EFFIGY AND NOT HURT HIM.
"THEY TAKE A CALF'S INTESTINES AND LOOP THEM LOOSELY AROUND THE GUY'S NECK, AND THEY TAKE A REED INSTEAD OF A SPEAR AND POKE HIM WITH IT AND GO...
OKAY, YOU'VE BEEN HUNG. YOU'VE BEEN SACRIFICED TO ODIN.
"AS SOON AS THEY SAY ODIN'S NAME, THE REED TRANS-FORMS INTO A SPEAR AND THE GROUND DROPS AWAY AND THE KING IS LEFT TO DIE WITH A WOUND IN HIS SIDE.
END OF STORY"
WHITE PEOPLE HAVE SOME FUCKED-UP GODS, MISTER SHADOW.
YES.
YOU'RE NOT WHITE?

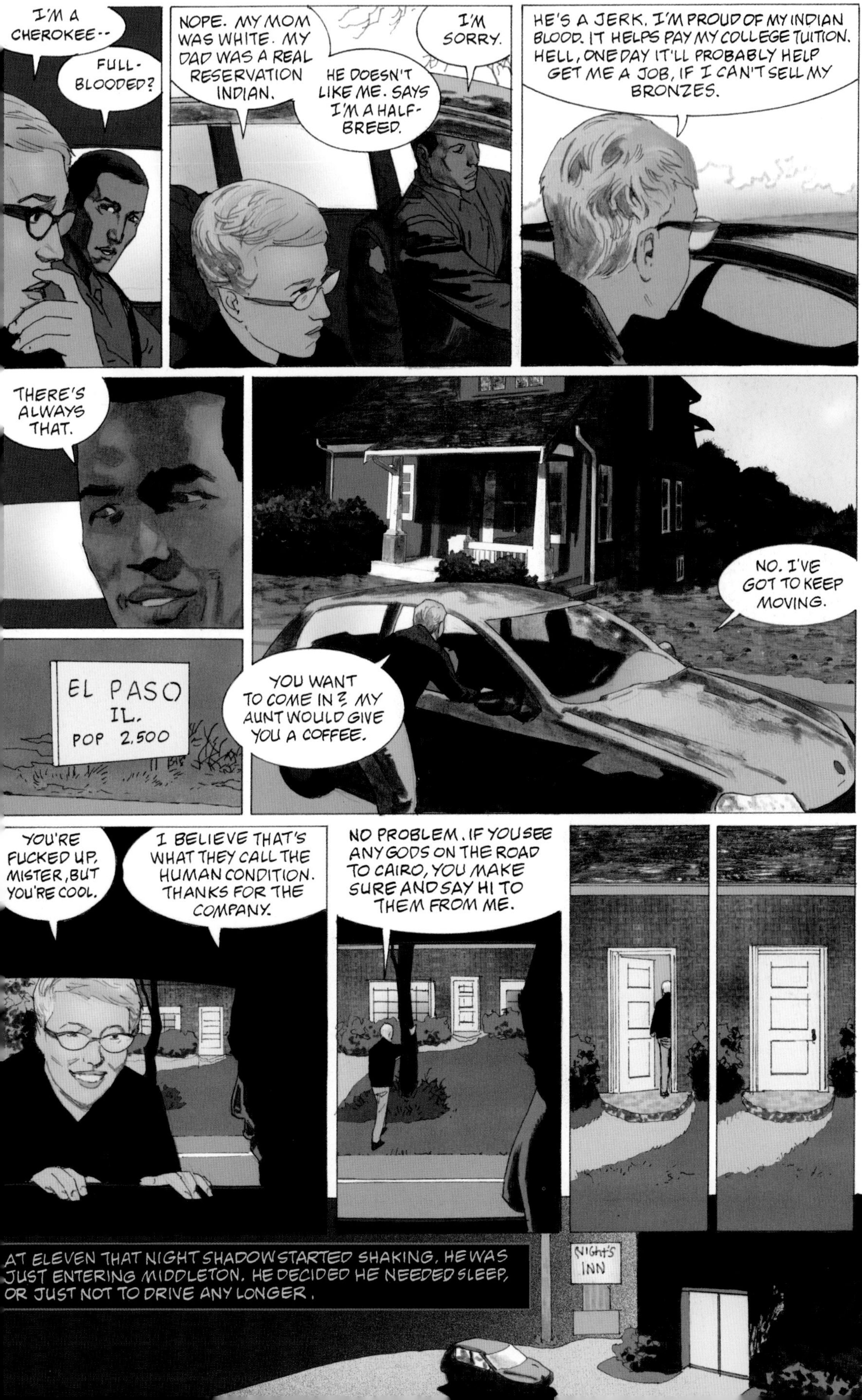
I'M A CHEROKEE--
FULL-BLOODED?
NOPE. MY MOM WAS WHITE. MY DAD WAS A REAL RESERVATION INDIAN.
HE DOESN'T LIKE ME. SAYS I'M A HALF-BREED.
I'M SORRY.
HE'S A JERK. I'M PROUD OF MY INDIAN BLOOD. IT HELPS PAY MY COLLEGE TUITION. HELL, ONE DAY IT'LL PROBABLY HELP GET ME A JOB, IF I CAN'T SELL MY BRONZES.
THERE'S ALWAYS THAT.
EL PASO IL. POP 2,500
YOU WANT TO COME IN? MY AUNT WOULD GIVE YOU A COFFEE.
NO. I'VE GOT TO KEEP MOVING.
YOU'RE FUCKED UP, MISTER, BUT YOU'RE COOL.
I BELIEVE THAT'S WHAT THEY CALL THE HUMAN CONDITION. THANKS FOR THE COMPANY.
NO PROBLEM. IF YOU SEE ANY GODS ON THE ROAD TO CAIRO, YOU MAKE SURE AND SAY HI TO THEM FROM ME.
AT ELEVEN THAT NIGHT SHADOW STARTED SHAKING, HE WAS JUST ENTERING MIDDLETON. HE DECIDED HE NEEDED SLEEP, OR JUST NOT TO DRIVE ANY LONGER.
NIGHT'S INN

SHADOW CLIMBED INTO BED AND TURNED ON THE T.V. SET FOR COMPANY. THE PICTURE WAS MOTEL-FUZZY. AN EPISODE OF **I LOVE LUCY** WAS JUST BEGINNING.

LUCY WAS TRYING TO PERSUADE RICKY TO REPLACE HER OLD ICEBOX WITH A NEW REFRIGERATOR.

WHEN HE LEFT, SHE WALKED OVER TO THE COUCH AND SAT DOWN PATIENTLY IN BLACK AND WHITE ACROSS THE YEARS.

SHADOW, WE NEED TO TALK.

?!

I'M TALKING TO YOU, SHADOW.

WELL?

THIS IS CRAZY.

LIKE THE REST OF YOUR LIFE IS SANE? GIVE ME A FUCKING BREAK.

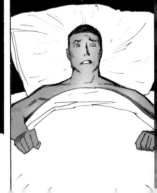
WHATEVER. LUCILLE BALL TALKING TO ME FROM THE T.V. IS WEIRDER BY SEVERAL ORDERS OF MAGNITUDE THAN ANYTHING THAT'S HAPPENED TO ME SO FAR.

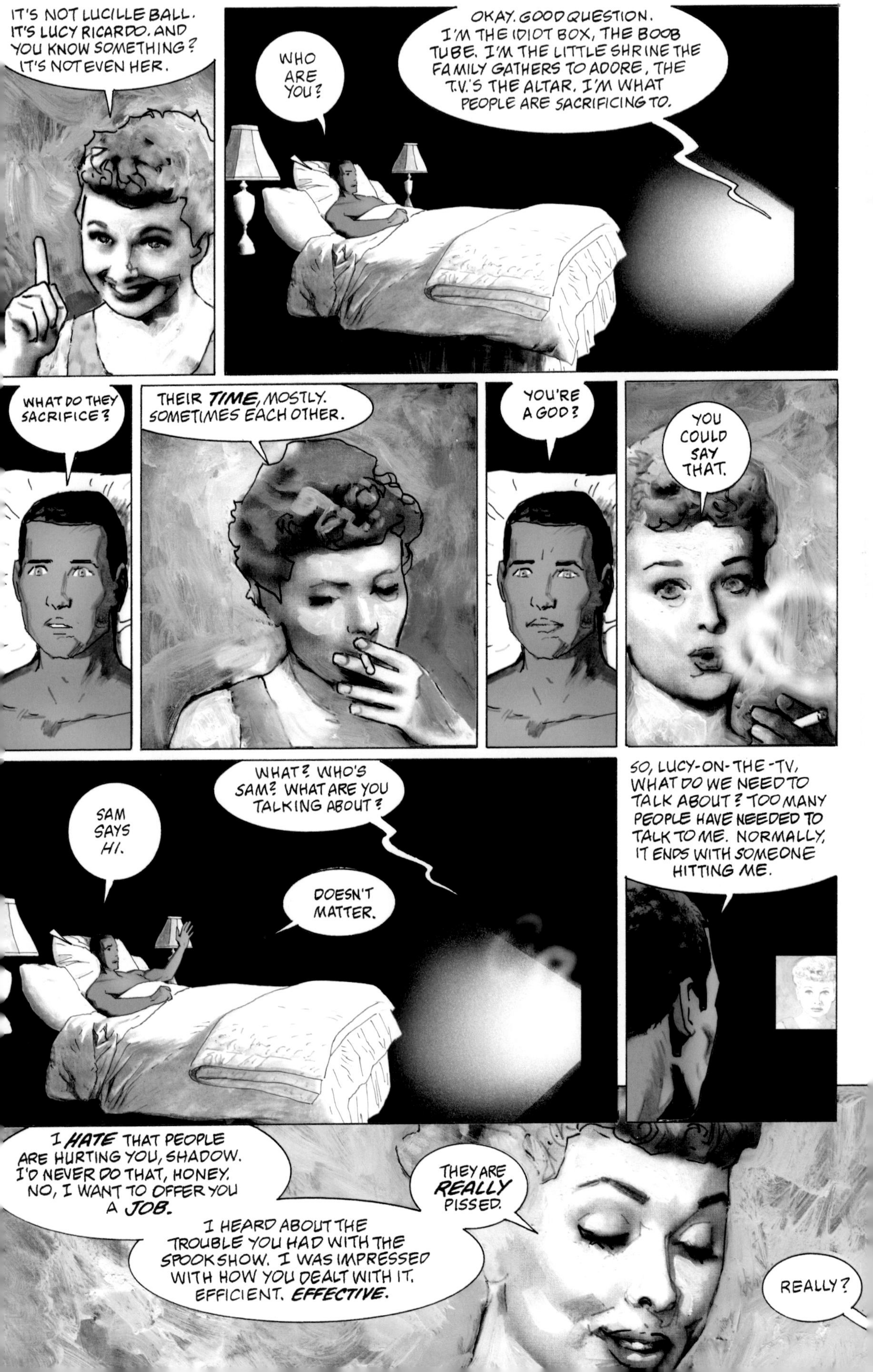

IT'S NOT LUCILLE BALL. IT'S LUCY RICARDO. AND YOU KNOW SOMETHING? IT'S NOT EVEN HER.
WHO ARE YOU?
OKAY. GOOD QUESTION. I'M THE IDIOT BOX, THE BOOB TUBE. I'M THE LITTLE SHRINE THE FAMILY GATHERS TO ADORE. THE T.V.'S THE ALTAR. I'M WHAT PEOPLE ARE SACRIFICING TO.
WHAT DO THEY SACRIFICE?
THEIR *TIME*, MOSTLY. SOMETIMES EACH OTHER.
YOU'RE A GOD?
YOU COULD SAY THAT.
SAM SAYS HI.
WHAT? WHO'S SAM? WHAT ARE YOU TALKING ABOUT?
DOESN'T MATTER.
SO, LUCY-ON-THE-TV, WHAT DO WE NEED TO TALK ABOUT? TOO MANY PEOPLE HAVE NEEDED TO TALK TO ME. NORMALLY, IT ENDS WITH SOMEONE HITTING ME.
I *HATE* THAT PEOPLE ARE HURTING YOU, SHADOW. I'D NEVER DO THAT, HONEY. NO, I WANT TO OFFER YOU A *JOB*.
THEY ARE *REALLY* PISSED.
I HEARD ABOUT THE TROUBLE YOU HAD WITH THE SPOOKSHOW. I WAS IMPRESSED WITH HOW YOU DEALT WITH IT. EFFICIENT. *EFFECTIVE*.
REALLY?

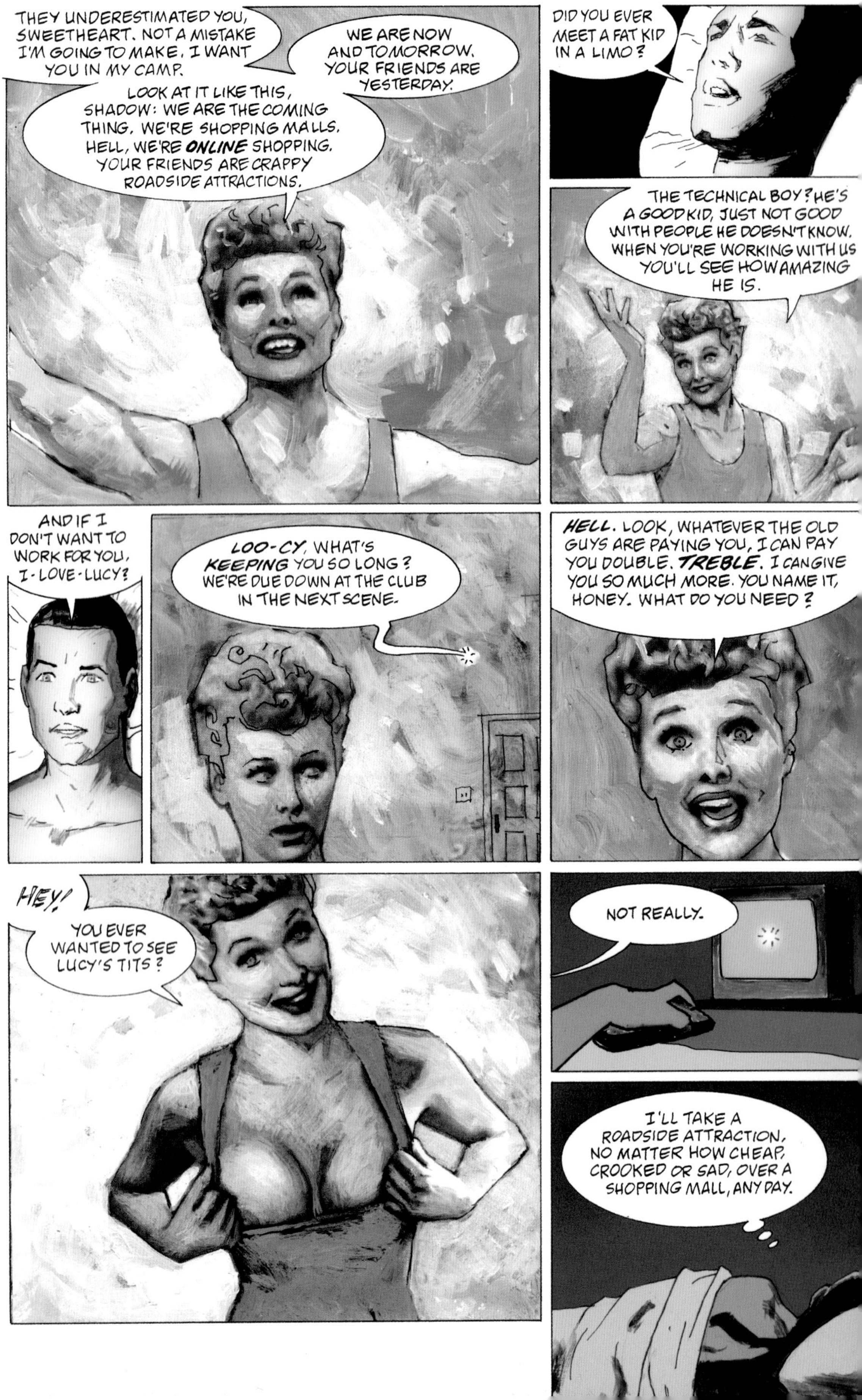

THEY UNDERESTIMATED YOU, SWEETHEART. NOT A MISTAKE I'M GOING TO MAKE. I WANT YOU IN MY CAMP.
WE ARE NOW AND TOMORROW. YOUR FRIENDS ARE YESTERDAY.
LOOK AT IT LIKE THIS, SHADOW: WE ARE THE COMING THING. WE'RE SHOPPING MALLS. HELL, WE'RE ONLINE SHOPPING. YOUR FRIENDS ARE CRAPPY ROADSIDE ATTRACTIONS.
DID YOU EVER MEET A FAT KID IN A LIMO?
THE TECHNICAL BOY? HE'S A GOOD KID, JUST NOT GOOD WITH PEOPLE HE DOESN'T KNOW. WHEN YOU'RE WORKING WITH US YOU'LL SEE HOW AMAZING HE IS.
AND IF I DON'T WANT TO WORK FOR YOU, I-LOVE-LUCY?
LOO-CY, WHAT'S KEEPING YOU SO LONG? WE'RE DUE DOWN AT THE CLUB IN THE NEXT SCENE.
HELL. LOOK, WHATEVER THE OLD GUYS ARE PAYING YOU, I CAN PAY YOU DOUBLE. TREBLE. I CAN GIVE YOU SO MUCH MORE. YOU NAME IT, HONEY. WHAT DO YOU NEED?
HEY!
YOU EVER WANTED TO SEE LUCY'S TITS?
NOT REALLY.
I'LL TAKE A ROADSIDE ATTRACTION, NO MATTER HOW CHEAP, CROOKED OR SAD, OVER A SHOPPING MALL, ANY DAY.

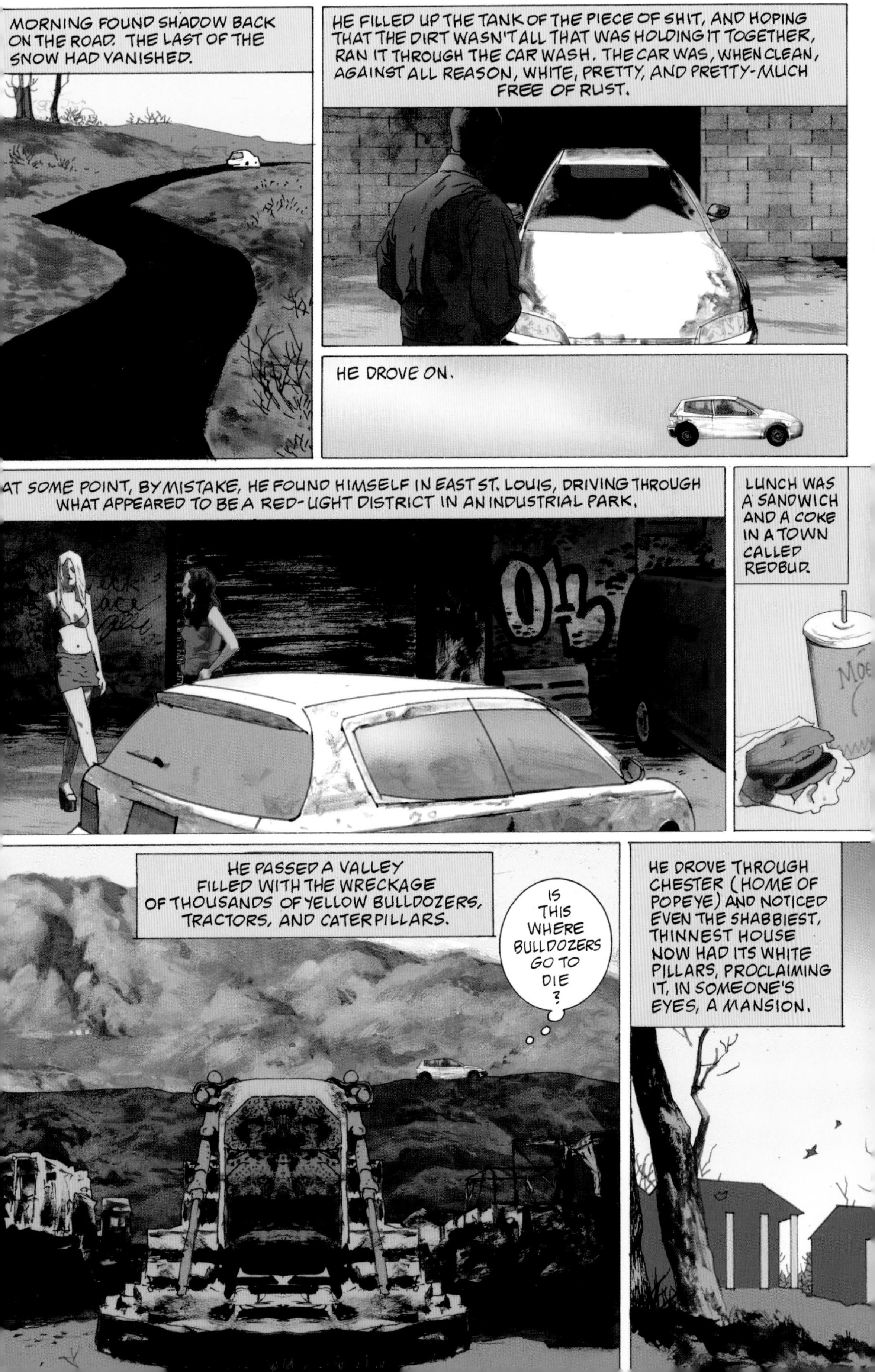
MORNING FOUND SHADOW BACK ON THE ROAD. THE LAST OF THE SNOW HAD VANISHED.
HE FILLED UP THE TANK OF THE PIECE OF SHIT, AND HOPING THAT THE DIRT WASN'T ALL THAT WAS HOLDING IT TOGETHER, RAN IT THROUGH THE CAR WASH. THE CAR WAS, WHEN CLEAN, AGAINST ALL REASON, WHITE, PRETTY, AND PRETTY-MUCH FREE OF RUST.
HE DROVE ON.
AT SOME POINT, BY MISTAKE, HE FOUND HIMSELF IN EAST ST. LOUIS, DRIVING THROUGH WHAT APPEARED TO BE A RED-LIGHT DISTRICT IN AN INDUSTRIAL PARK.
LUNCH WAS A SANDWICH AND A COKE IN A TOWN CALLED REDBUD.
HE PASSED A VALLEY FILLED WITH THE WRECKAGE OF THOUSANDS OF YELLOW BULLDOZERS, TRACTORS, AND CATERPILLARS.
IS THIS WHERE BULLDOZERS GO TO DIE?
HE DROVE THROUGH CHESTER (HOME OF POPEYE) AND NOTICED EVEN THE SHABBIEST, THINNEST HOUSE NOW HAD ITS WHITE PILLARS, PROCLAIMING IT, IN SOMEONE'S EYES, A MANSION.

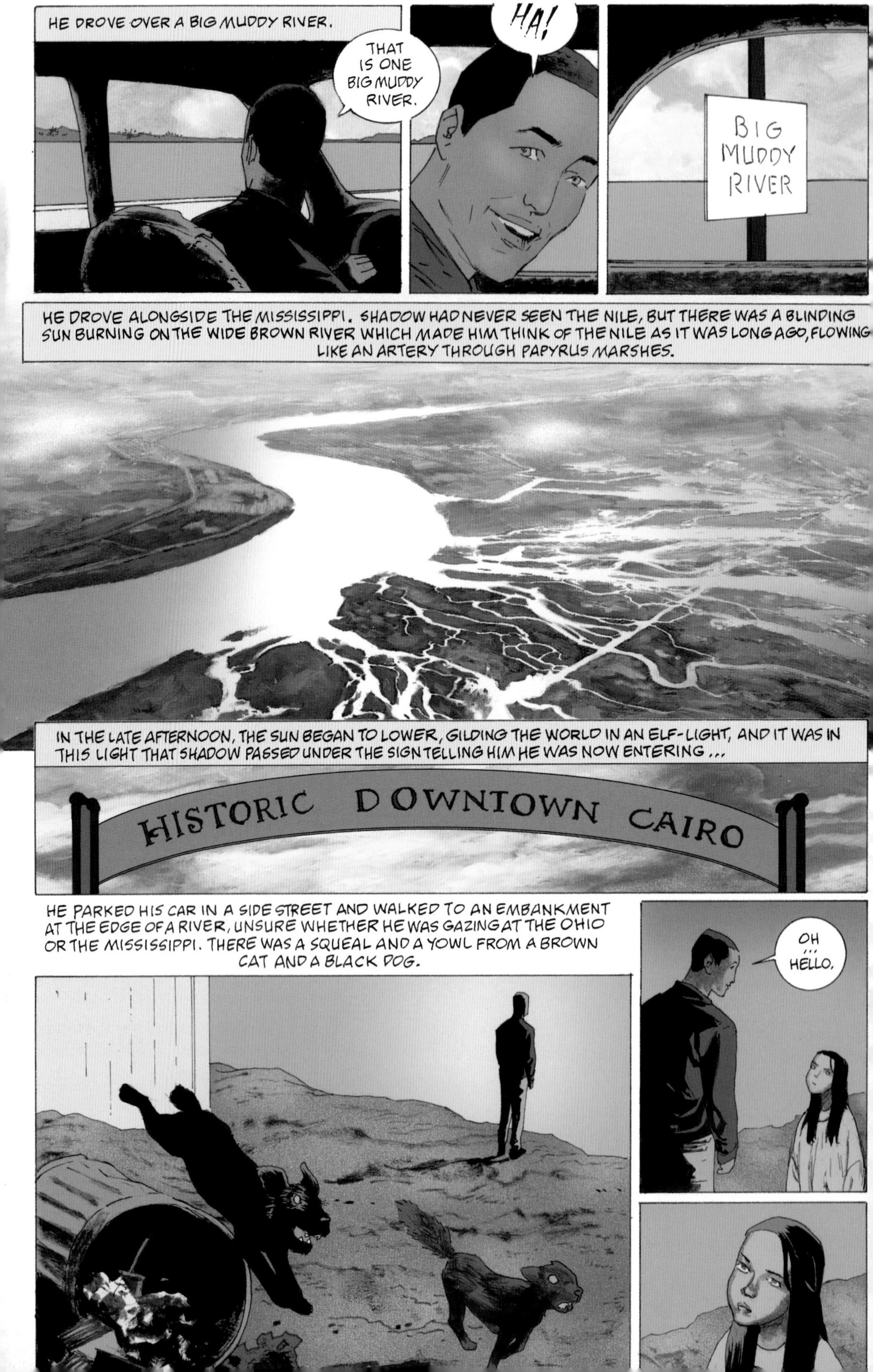
HE DROVE OVER A BIG MUDDY RIVER.
THAT IS ONE BIG MUDDY RIVER.
HA!
BIG MUDDY RIVER
HE DROVE ALONGSIDE THE MISSISSIPPI. SHADOW HAD NEVER SEEN THE NILE, BUT THERE WAS A BLINDING SUN BURNING ON THE WIDE BROWN RIVER WHICH MADE HIM THINK OF THE NILE AS IT WAS LONG AGO, FLOWING LIKE AN ARTERY THROUGH PAPYRUS MARSHES.
IN THE LATE AFTERNOON, THE SUN BEGAN TO LOWER, GILDING THE WORLD IN AN ELF-LIGHT, AND IT WAS IN THIS LIGHT THAT SHADOW PASSED UNDER THE SIGN TELLING HIM HE WAS NOW ENTERING ...
HISTORIC DOWNTOWN CAIRO
HE PARKED HIS CAR IN A SIDE STREET AND WALKED TO AN EMBANKMENT AT THE EDGE OF A RIVER, UNSURE WHETHER HE WAS GAZING AT THE OHIO OR THE MISSISSIPPI. THERE WAS A SQUEAL AND A YOWL FROM A BROWN CAT AND A BLACK DOG.
OH ... HELLO.

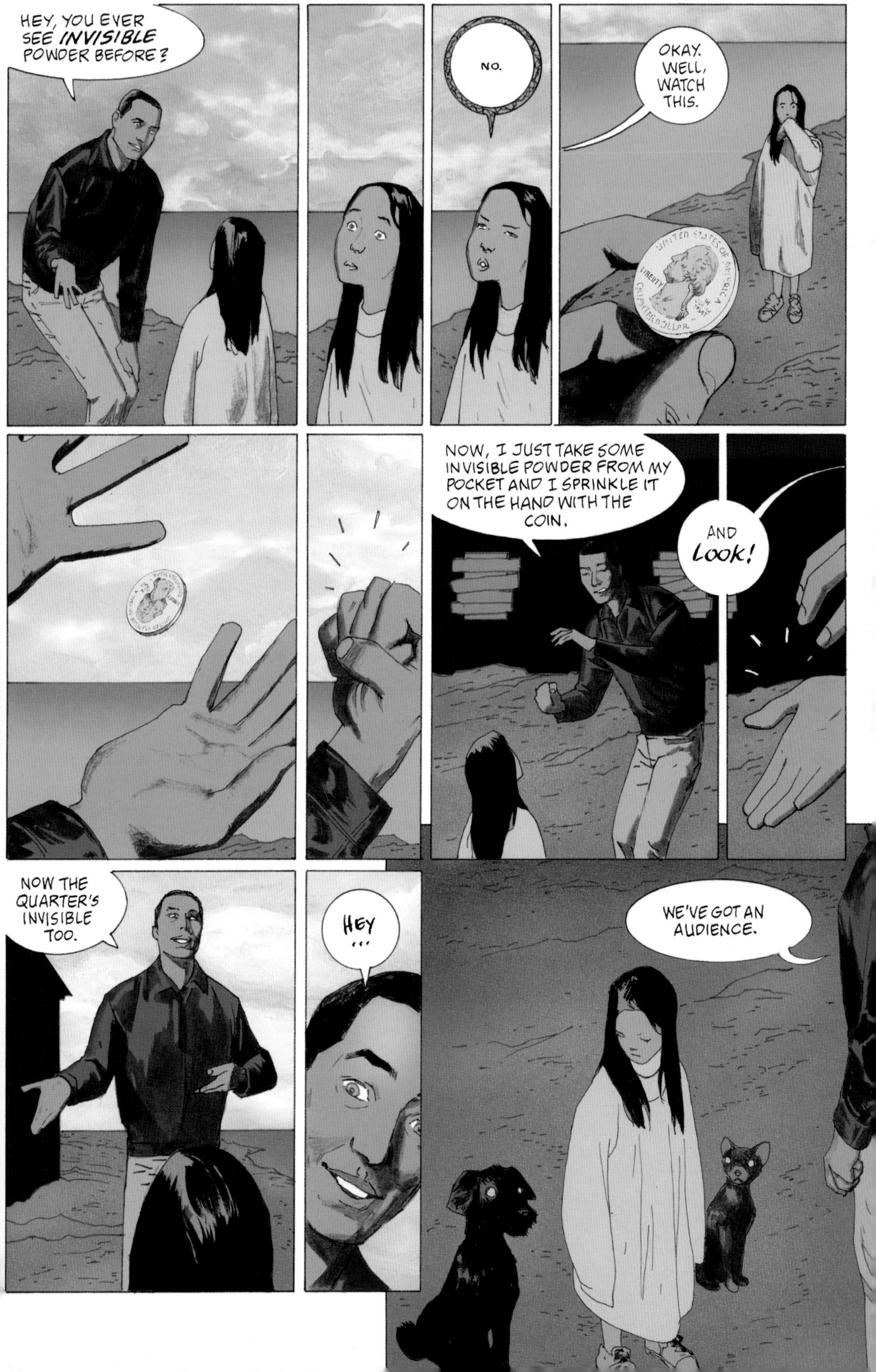
HEY, YOU EVER SEE INVISIBLE POWDER BEFORE?
NO.
OKAY. WELL, WATCH THIS.
NOW, I JUST TAKE SOME INVISIBLE POWDER FROM MY POCKET AND I SPRINKLE IT ON THE HAND WITH THE COIN.
AND LOOK!
NOW THE QUARTER'S INVISIBLE TOO.
HEY ...
WE'VE GOT AN AUDIENCE.

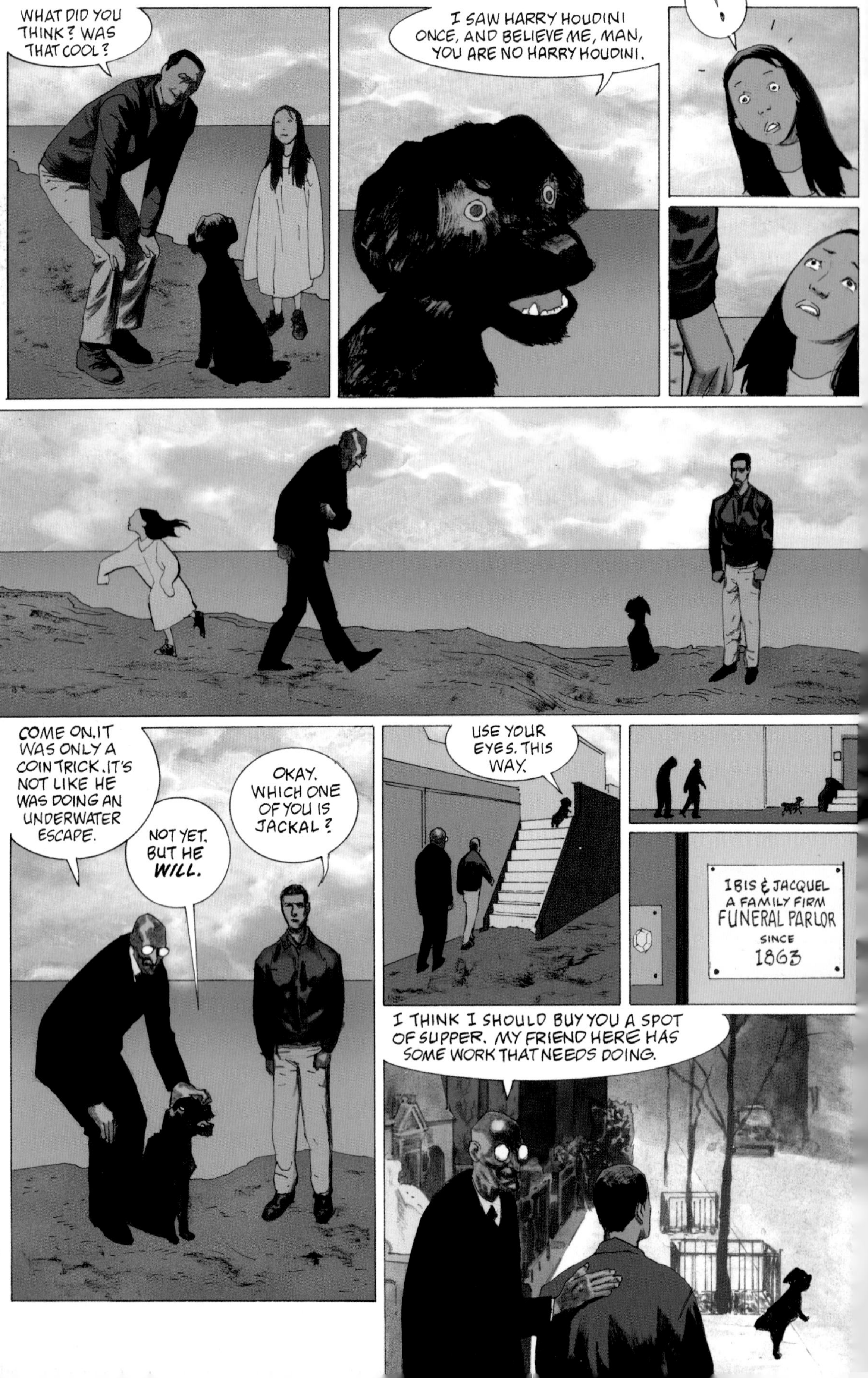
WHAT DID YOU THINK? WAS THAT COOL?
I SAW HARRY HOUDINI ONCE, AND BELIEVE ME, MAN, YOU ARE NO HARRY HOUDINI.
!
COME ON. IT WAS ONLY A COIN TRICK. IT'S NOT LIKE HE WAS DOING AN UNDERWATER ESCAPE.
NOT YET. BUT HE *WILL*.
OKAY. WHICH ONE OF YOU IS JACKAL?
USE YOUR EYES. THIS WAY.
IBIS & JACQUEL
A FAMILY FIRM
FUNERAL PARLOR
SINCE
1863
I THINK I SHOULD BUY YOU A SPOT OF SUPPER. MY FRIEND HERE HAS SOME WORK THAT NEEDS DOING.

CHAPTER EIGHT

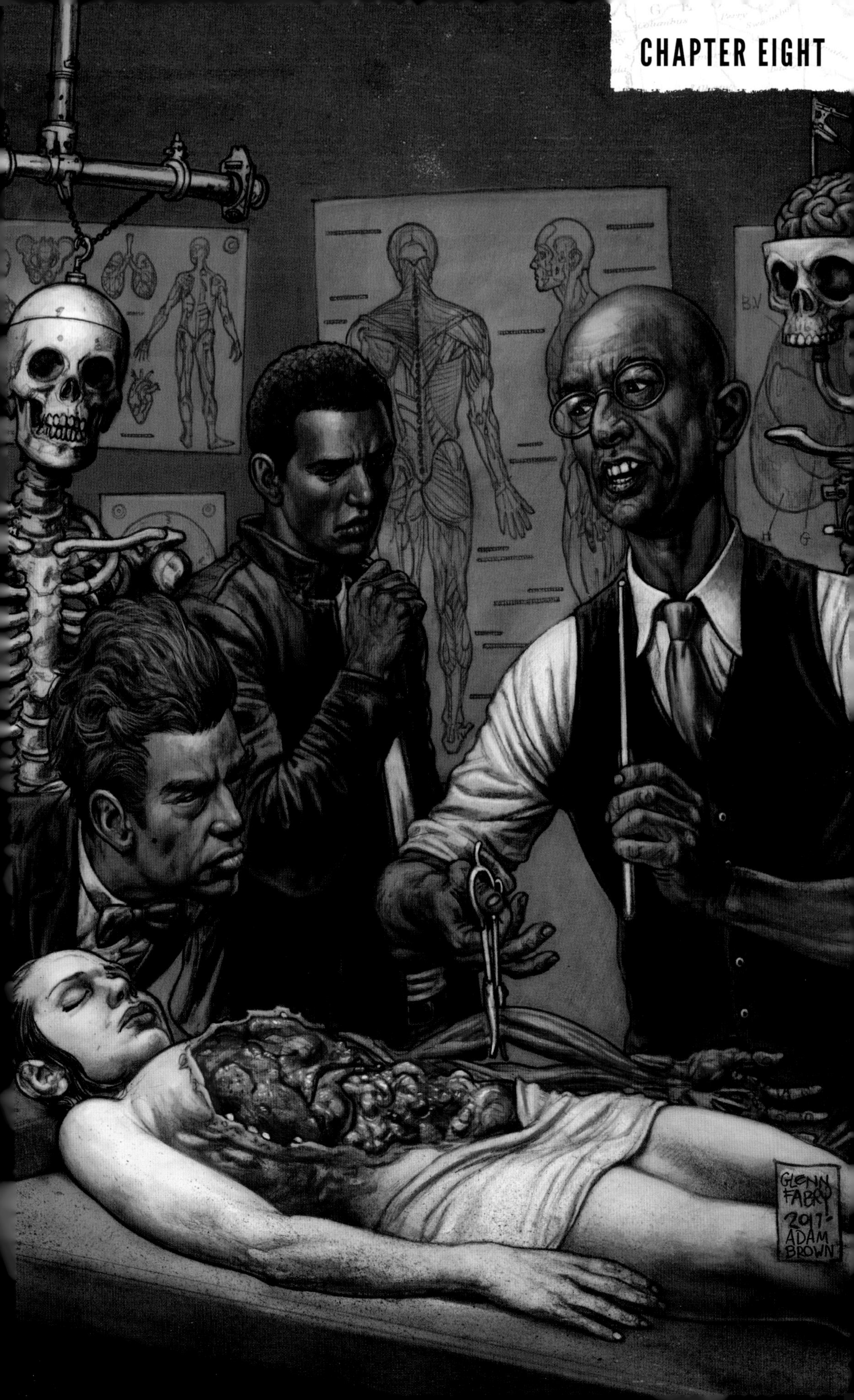
GLENN FABRY 2017 ADAM BROWN

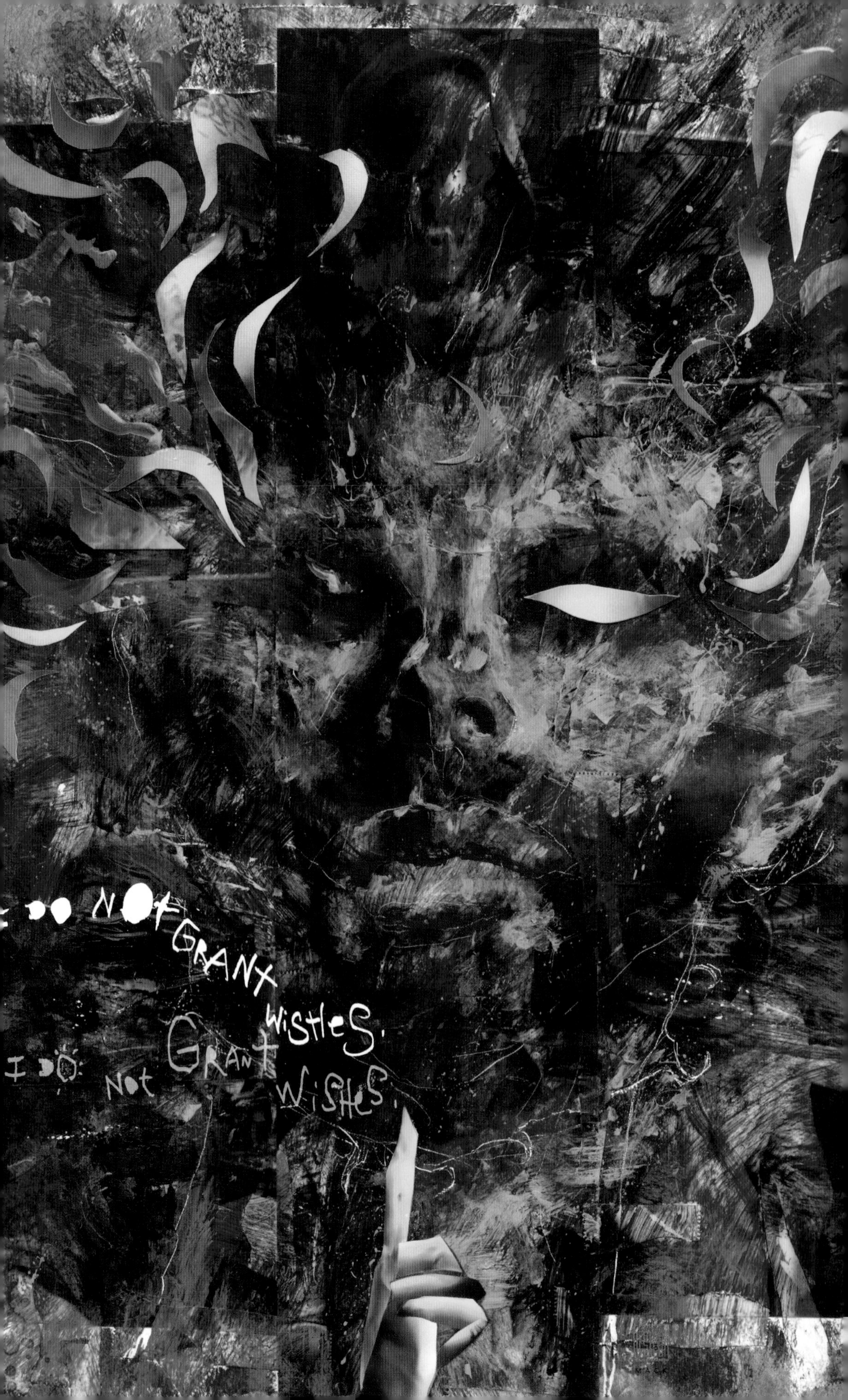
DO NOT GRANX WISTLES.
I DO NOT GRANT WISHES.

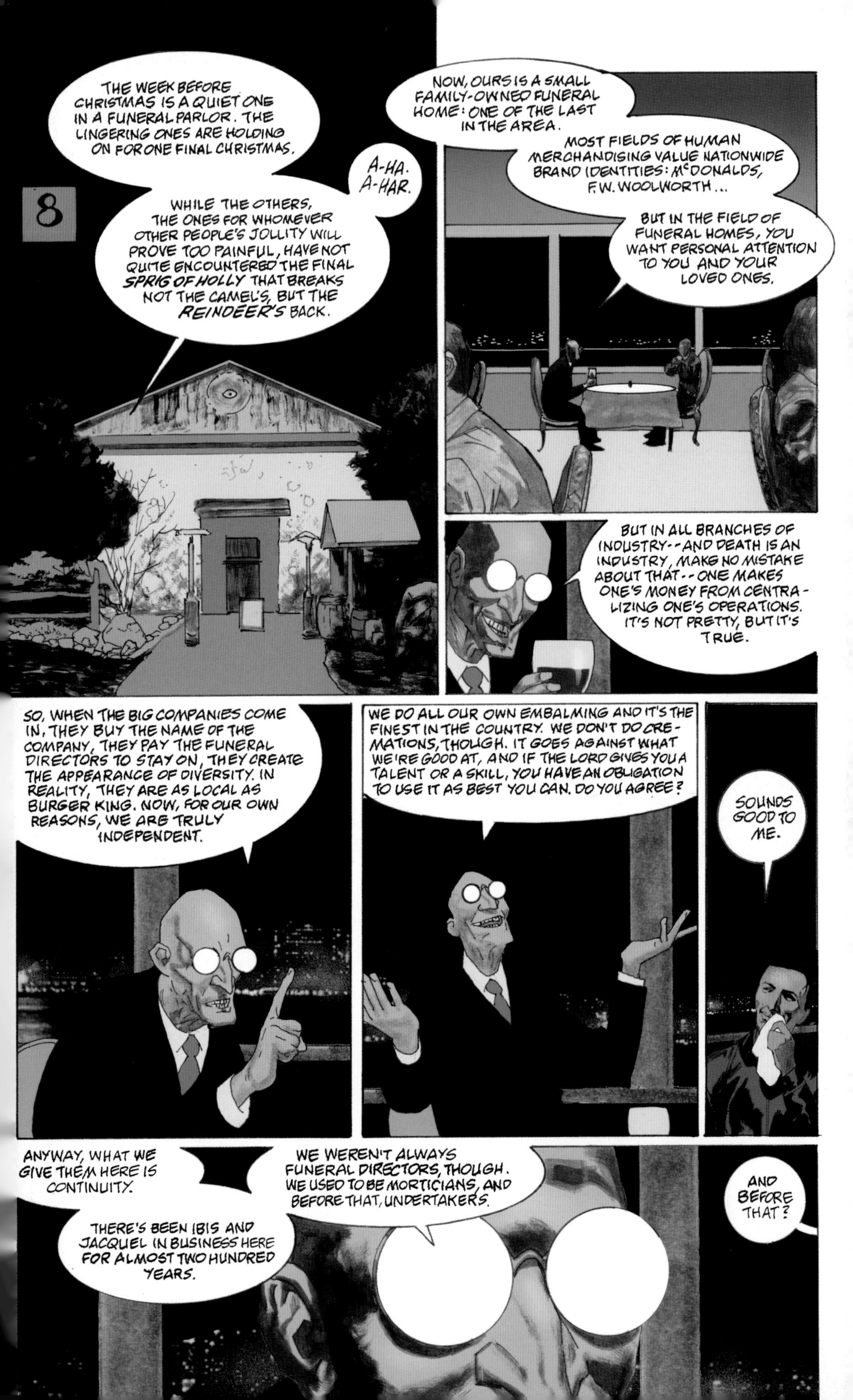
THE WEEK BEFORE CHRISTMAS IS A QUIET ONE IN A FUNERAL PARLOR. THE LINGERING ONES ARE HOLDING ON FOR ONE FINAL CHRISTMAS.
A-HA. A-HAR.
8
WHILE THE OTHERS, THE ONES FOR WHOM EVER OTHER PEOPLE'S JOLLITY WILL PROVE TOO PAINFUL, HAVE NOT QUITE ENCOUNTERED THE FINAL SPRIG OF HOLLY THAT BREAKS NOT THE CAMEL'S, BUT THE REINDEER'S BACK.
NOW, OURS IS A SMALL FAMILY-OWNED FUNERAL HOME: ONE OF THE LAST IN THE AREA.
MOST FIELDS OF HUMAN MERCHANDISING VALUE NATIONWIDE BRAND IDENTITIES: McDONALDS, F.W. WOOLWORTH...
BUT IN THE FIELD OF FUNERAL HOMES, YOU WANT PERSONAL ATTENTION TO YOU AND YOUR LOVED ONES.
BUT IN ALL BRANCHES OF INDUSTRY--AND DEATH IS AN INDUSTRY, MAKE NO MISTAKE ABOUT THAT--ONE MAKES ONE'S MONEY FROM CENTRALIZING ONE'S OPERATIONS. IT'S NOT PRETTY, BUT IT'S TRUE.
SO, WHEN THE BIG COMPANIES COME IN, THEY BUY THE NAME OF THE COMPANY, THEY PAY THE FUNERAL DIRECTORS TO STAY ON, THEY CREATE THE APPEARANCE OF DIVERSITY. IN REALITY, THEY ARE AS LOCAL AS BURGER KING. NOW, FOR OUR OWN REASONS, WE ARE TRULY INDEPENDENT.
WE DO ALL OUR OWN EMBALMING AND IT'S THE FINEST IN THE COUNTRY. WE DON'T DO CREMATIONS, THOUGH. IT GOES AGAINST WHAT WE'RE GOOD AT, AND IF THE LORD GIVES YOU A TALENT OR A SKILL, YOU HAVE AN OBLIGATION TO USE IT AS BEST YOU CAN. DO YOU AGREE?
SOUNDS GOOD TO ME.
ANYWAY, WHAT WE GIVE THEM HERE IS CONTINUITY.
THERE'S BEEN IBIS AND JACQUEL IN BUSINESS HERE FOR ALMOST TWO HUNDRED YEARS.
WE WEREN'T ALWAYS FUNERAL DIRECTORS, THOUGH. WE USED TO BE MORTICIANS, AND BEFORE THAT, UNDERTAKERS.
AND BEFORE THAT?

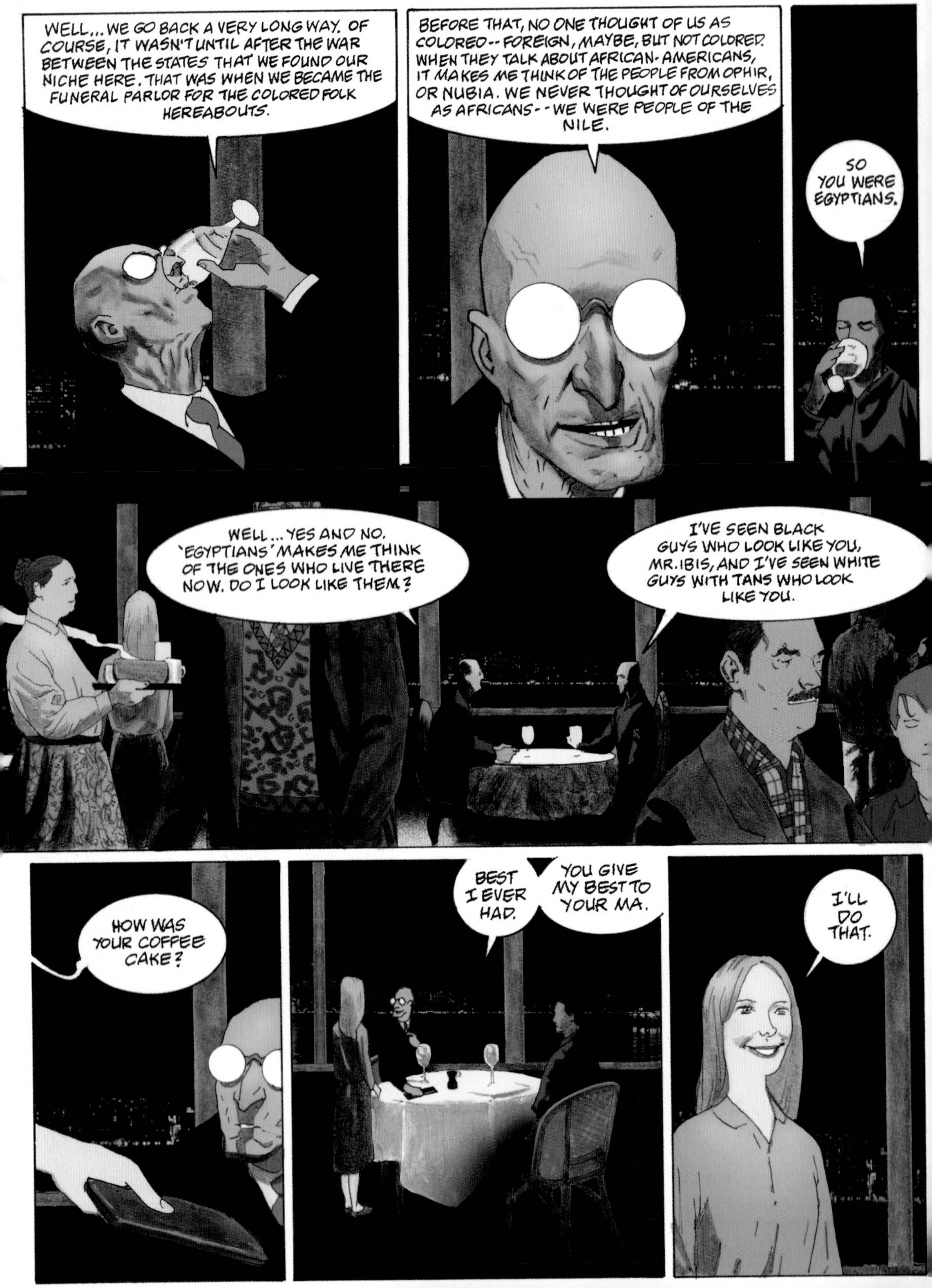
WELL... WE GO BACK A VERY LONG WAY. OF COURSE, IT WASN'T UNTIL AFTER THE WAR BETWEEN THE STATES THAT WE FOUND OUR NICHE HERE. THAT WAS WHEN WE BECAME THE FUNERAL PARLOR FOR THE COLORED FOLK HEREABOUTS.
BEFORE THAT, NO ONE THOUGHT OF US AS COLORED-- FOREIGN, MAYBE, BUT NOT COLORED. WHEN THEY TALK ABOUT AFRICAN-AMERICANS, IT MAKES ME THINK OF THE PEOPLE FROM OPHIR, OR NUBIA. WE NEVER THOUGHT OF OURSELVES AS AFRICANS-- WE WERE PEOPLE OF THE NILE.
SO YOU WERE EGYPTIANS.
WELL... YES AND NO. 'EGYPTIANS' MAKES ME THINK OF THE ONES WHO LIVE THERE NOW. DO I LOOK LIKE THEM?
I'VE SEEN BLACK GUYS WHO LOOK LIKE YOU, MR. IBIS, AND I'VE SEEN WHITE GUYS WITH TANS WHO LOOK LIKE YOU.
HOW WAS YOUR COFFEE CAKE?
BEST I EVER HAD.
YOU GIVE MY BEST TO YOUR MA.
I'LL DO THAT.

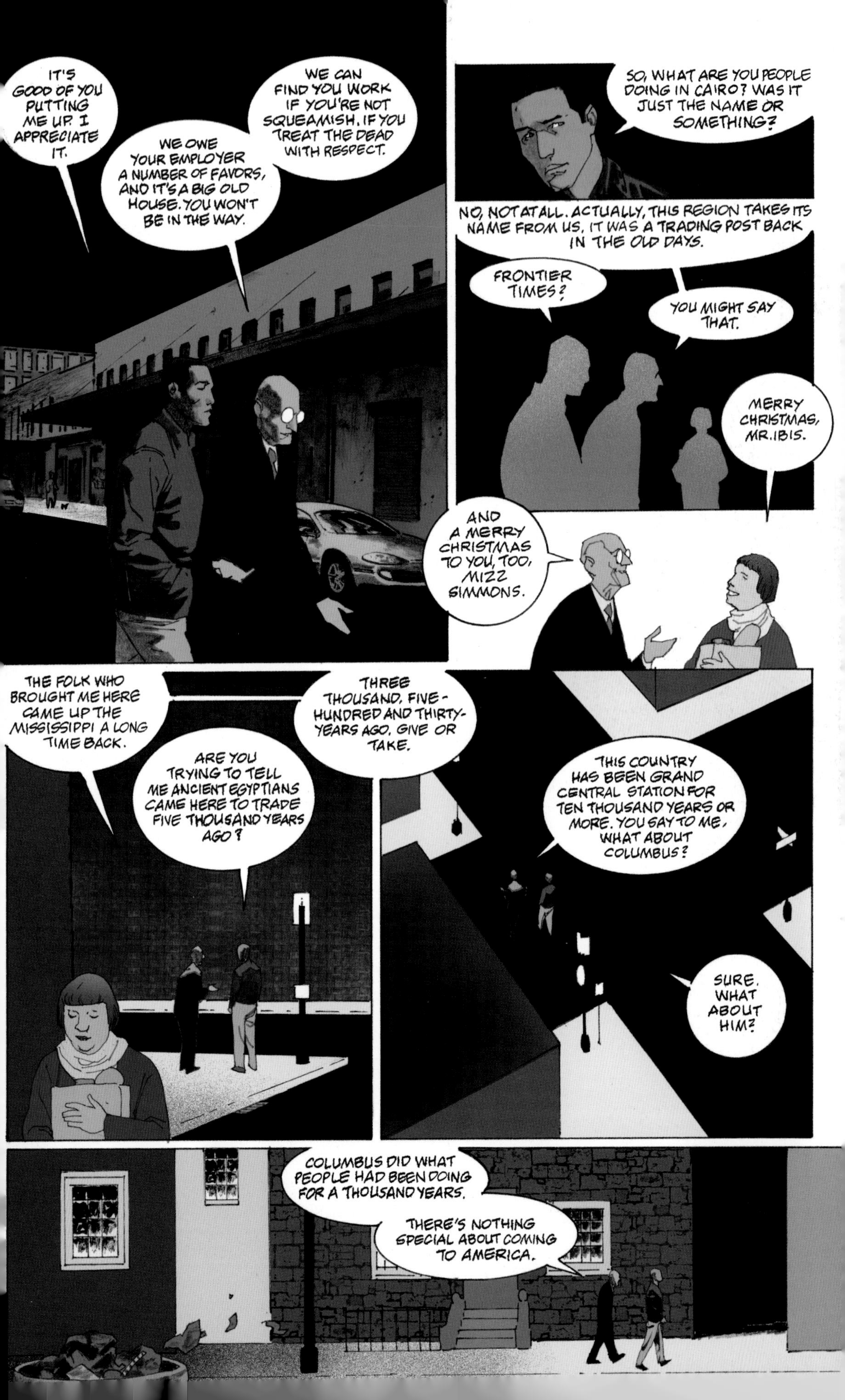
IT'S GOOD OF YOU PUTTING ME UP. I APPRECIATE IT.
WE OWE YOUR EMPLOYER A NUMBER OF FAVORS, AND IT'S A BIG OLD HOUSE. YOU WON'T BE IN THE WAY.
WE CAN FIND YOU WORK IF YOU'RE NOT SQUEAMISH. IF YOU TREAT THE DEAD WITH RESPECT.
SO, WHAT ARE YOU PEOPLE DOING IN CAIRO? WAS IT JUST THE NAME OR SOMETHING?
NO, NOT AT ALL. ACTUALLY, THIS REGION TAKES ITS NAME FROM US. IT WAS A TRADING POST BACK IN THE OLD DAYS.
FRONTIER TIMES?
YOU MIGHT SAY THAT.
MERRY CHRISTMAS, MR. IBIS.
AND A MERRY CHRISTMAS TO YOU, TOO, MIZZ SIMMONS.
THE FOLK WHO BROUGHT ME HERE CAME UP THE MISSISSIPPI A LONG TIME BACK.
ARE YOU TRYING TO TELL ME ANCIENT EGYPTIANS CAME HERE TO TRADE FIVE THOUSAND YEARS AGO?
THREE THOUSAND, FIVE-HUNDRED AND THIRTY-YEARS AGO, GIVE OR TAKE.
THIS COUNTRY HAS BEEN GRAND CENTRAL STATION FOR TEN THOUSAND YEARS OR MORE. YOU SAY TO ME, WHAT ABOUT COLUMBUS?
SURE. WHAT ABOUT HIM?
COLUMBUS DID WHAT PEOPLE HAD BEEN DOING FOR A THOUSAND YEARS.
THERE'S NOTHING SPECIAL ABOUT COMING TO AMERICA.

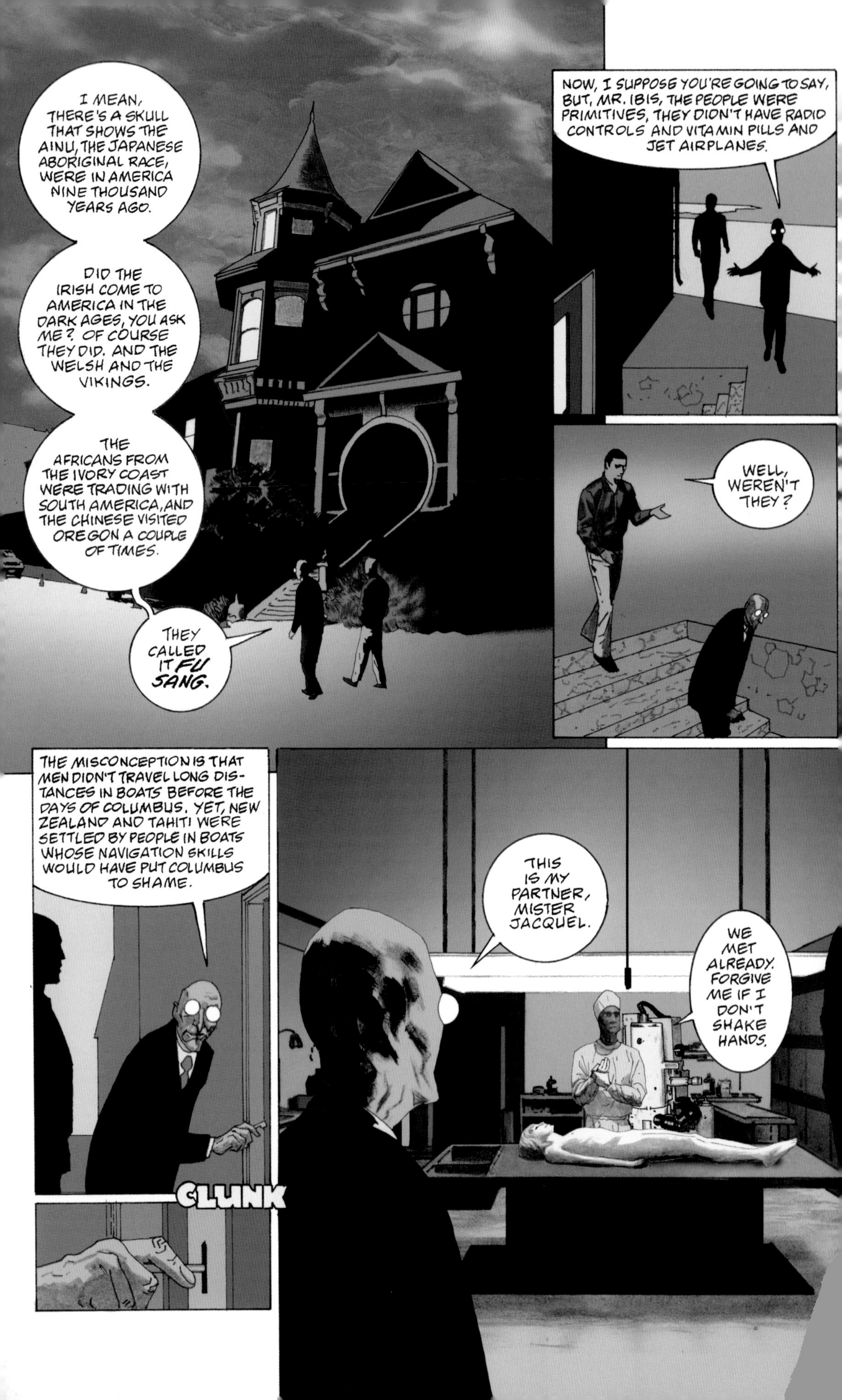
I MEAN, THERE'S A SKULL THAT SHOWS THE AINU, THE JAPANESE ABORIGINAL RACE, WERE IN AMERICA NINE THOUSAND YEARS AGO.
DID THE IRISH COME TO AMERICA IN THE DARK AGES, YOU ASK ME? OF COURSE THEY DID. AND THE WELSH AND THE VIKINGS.
THE AFRICANS FROM THE IVORY COAST WERE TRADING WITH SOUTH AMERICA, AND THE CHINESE VISITED OREGON A COUPLE OF TIMES.
THEY CALLED IT FU SANG.
NOW, I SUPPOSE YOU'RE GOING TO SAY, BUT, MR. IBIS, THE PEOPLE WERE PRIMITIVES, THEY DIDN'T HAVE RADIO CONTROLS AND VITAMIN PILLS AND JET AIRPLANES.
WELL, WEREN'T THEY?
THE MISCONCEPTION IS THAT MEN DIDN'T TRAVEL LONG DISTANCES IN BOATS BEFORE THE DAYS OF COLUMBUS. YET, NEW ZEALAND AND TAHITI WERE SETTLED BY PEOPLE IN BOATS WHOSE NAVIGATION SKILLS WOULD HAVE PUT COLUMBUS TO SHAME.
CLUNK
THIS IS MY PARTNER, MISTER JACQUEL.
WE MET ALREADY. FORGIVE ME IF I DON'T SHAKE HANDS.

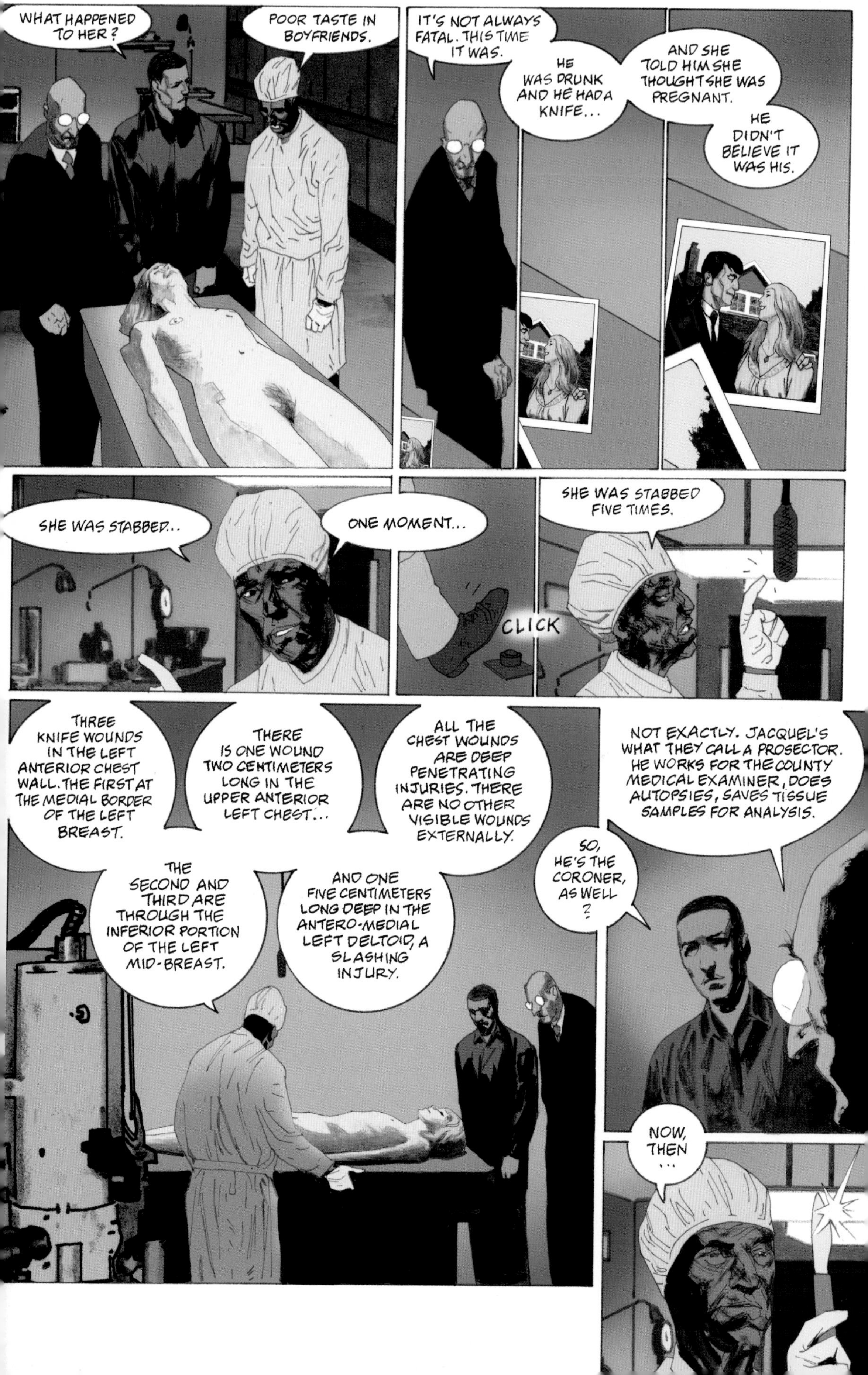
WHAT HAPPENED TO HER?
POOR TASTE IN BOYFRIENDS.
IT'S NOT ALWAYS FATAL. THIS TIME IT WAS.
HE WAS DRUNK AND HE HAD A KNIFE...
AND SHE TOLD HIM SHE THOUGHT SHE WAS PREGNANT.
HE DIDN'T BELIEVE IT WAS HIS.
SHE WAS STABBED...
ONE MOMENT...
CLICK
SHE WAS STABBED FIVE TIMES.
THREE KNIFE WOUNDS IN THE LEFT ANTERIOR CHEST WALL. THE FIRST AT THE MEDIAL BORDER OF THE LEFT BREAST.
THE SECOND AND THIRD ARE THROUGH THE INFERIOR PORTION OF THE LEFT MID-BREAST.
THERE IS ONE WOUND TWO CENTIMETERS LONG IN THE UPPER ANTERIOR LEFT CHEST...
AND ONE FIVE CENTIMETERS LONG DEEP IN THE ANTERO-MEDIAL LEFT DELTOID, A SLASHING INJURY.
ALL THE CHEST WOUNDS ARE DEEP PENETRATING INJURIES. THERE ARE NO OTHER VISIBLE WOUNDS EXTERNALLY.
SO, HE'S THE CORONER, AS WELL?
NOT EXACTLY. JACQUEL'S WHAT THEY CALL A PROSECTOR. HE WORKS FOR THE COUNTY MEDICAL EXAMINER, DOES AUTOPSIES, SAVES TISSUE SAMPLES FOR ANALYSIS.
NOW, THEN...

JACQUEL MADE A DEEP INCISION WHICH BEGAN AT BOTH SIDES OF THE COLLARBONES AND MET AT THE BOTTOM OF HER BREASTBONE...

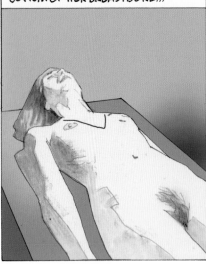

... AND ANOTHER DEEP INCISION THAT CONTINUED FROM HER BREASTBONE TO HER PUBIS.

HE PICKED UP A SMALL HEAVY CHROME DRILL --

BZZZZZZZ

-- AND CUT THROUGH THE RIBS AT BOTH SIDES OF HER BREASTBONE.

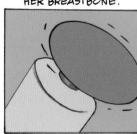

THE GIRL OPENED LIKE A PURSE.

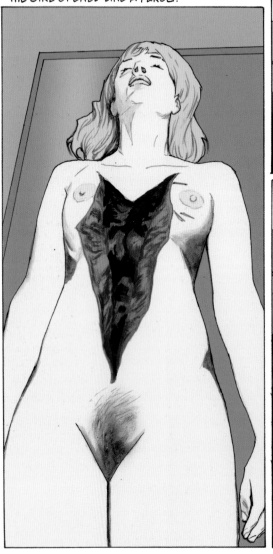

SHADOW SUDDENLY WAS AWARE OF A MILD, BUT PENETRATING, PUNGENT, MEATY SMELL.

I THOUGHT IT WOULD SMELL WORSE.

SHE'S PRETTY FRESH. AND THE INTESTINES WEREN'T PIERCED. SO IT DOESN'T SMELL OF SHIT.

SHADOW FOUND HIMSELF LOOKING AWAY...

...NOT FROM REVULSION, AS HE WOULD HAVE EXPECTED, BUT FROM A STRANGE DESIRE TO GIVE THE GIRL SOME PRIVACY.

IT WOULD BE HARD TO BE NAKEDER THAN THIS OPEN THING.

JACQUEL RAN
THE INTESTINES
THROUGH HIS
FINGERS, FOOT
AFTER FOOT OF
THEM, DESCRIBED
THEM AS...

NORMAL.

HE GRASPED HER
HEART, TURNED IT
ABOUT IN HIS HAND.

THERE
ARE TWO
LACERATIONS
OF THE MYO-
CARDIUM.

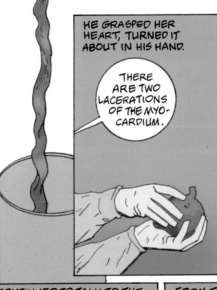

FROM EACH LUNG HE
SLICED A SMALL PIECE
OF TISSUE, WHICH HE
PLACED IN A JAR.

FORMALDEHYDE.

HE CONTINUED TO TALK TO THE
MICROPHONE AS HE REMOVED
THE GIRL'S LIVER, STOMACH,
SPLEEN, PANCREAS, BOTH
KIDNEYS, THE UTERUS, AND
THE OVARIES.

FROM EACH ORGAN HE TOOK A
SMALL SLICE AND PUT IT INTO A
JAR OF FORMALDEHYDE.

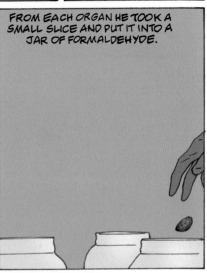

FROM THE HEART, THE
LIVER, AND FROM ONE
OF THE KIDNEYS, HE
CUT AN ADDITIONAL
SLICE.

THESE PIECES HE CHEWED,
SLOWLY, MAKING THEM LAST,
AND ATE WHILE HE WORKED.

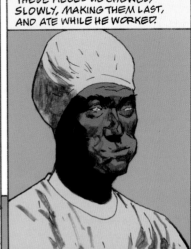

SOMEHOW IT SEEMED TO SHADOW A GOOD THING FOR
HIM TO DO: RESPECTFUL, NOT OBSCENE.

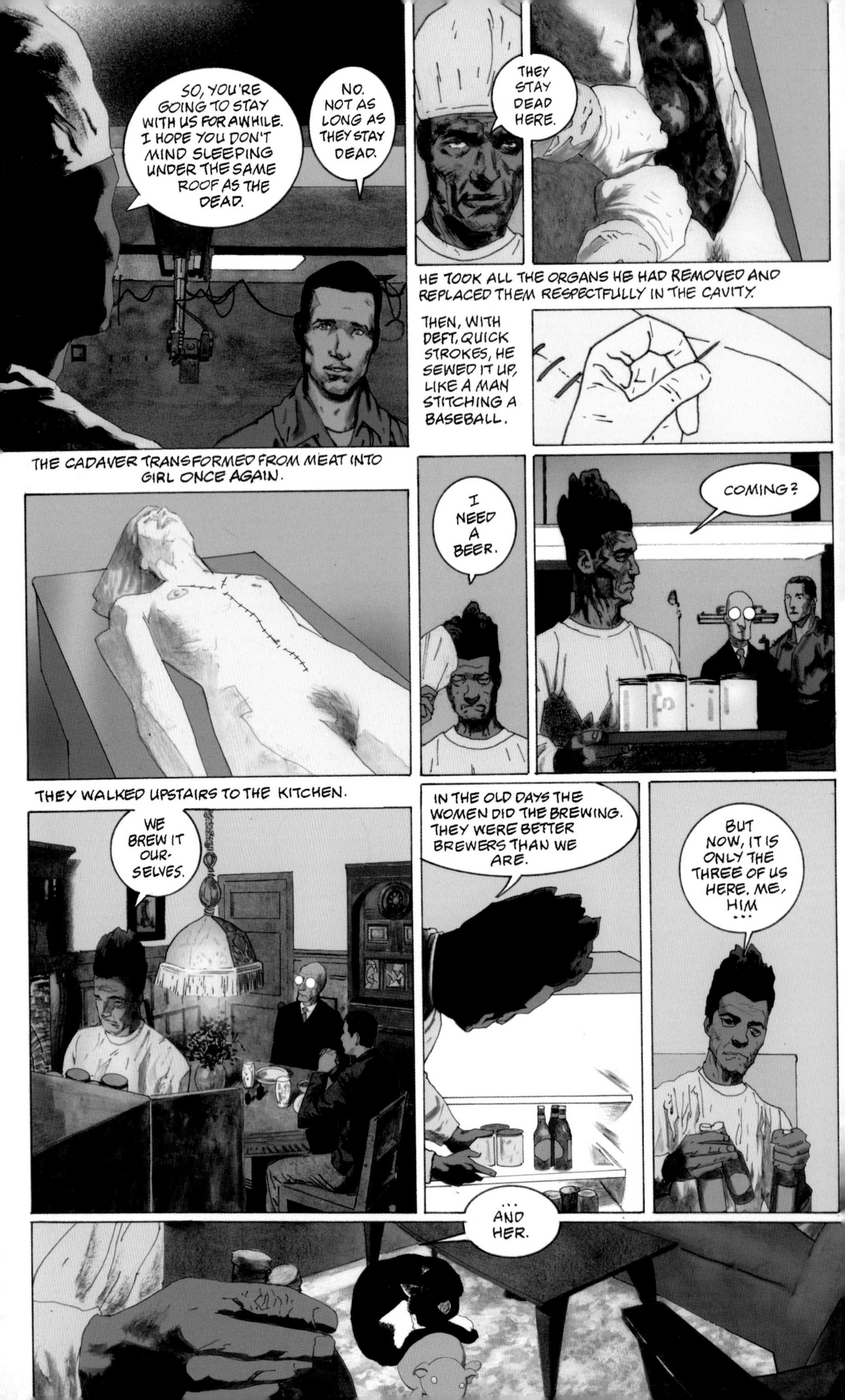
SO, YOU'RE GOING TO STAY WITH US FOR AWHILE. I HOPE YOU DON'T MIND SLEEPING UNDER THE SAME ROOF AS THE DEAD.
NO. NOT AS LONG AS THEY STAY DEAD.
THEY STAY DEAD HERE.
HE TOOK ALL THE ORGANS HE HAD REMOVED AND REPLACED THEM RESPECTFULLY IN THE CAVITY.
THEN, WITH DEFT, QUICK STROKES, HE SEWED IT UP, LIKE A MAN STITCHING A BASEBALL.
THE CADAVER TRANSFORMED FROM MEAT INTO GIRL ONCE AGAIN.
I NEED A BEER.
COMING?
THEY WALKED UPSTAIRS TO THE KITCHEN.
WE BREW IT OUR-SELVES.
IN THE OLD DAYS THE WOMEN DID THE BREWING. THEY WERE BETTER BREWERS THAN WE ARE.
BUT NOW, IT IS ONLY THE THREE OF US HERE. ME, HIM ...
... AND HER.

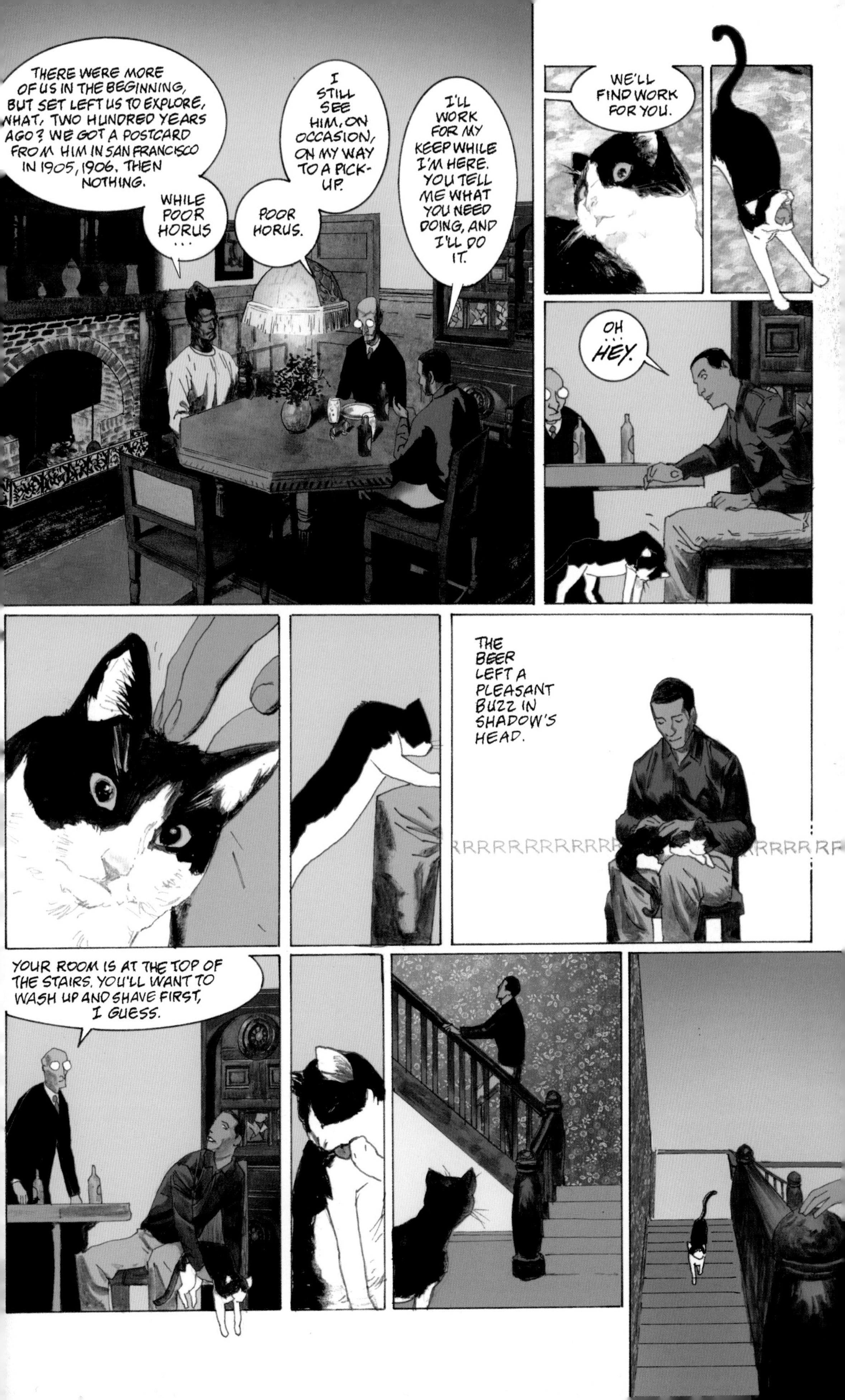
THERE WERE MORE OF US IN THE BEGINNING, BUT SET LEFT US TO EXPLORE, WHAT, TWO HUNDRED YEARS AGO? WE GOT A POSTCARD FROM HIM IN SAN FRANCISCO IN 1905, 1906. THEN NOTHING.
I STILL SEE HIM, ON OCCASION, ON MY WAY TO A PICK-UP.
WHILE POOR HORUS . . .
POOR HORUS.
I'LL WORK FOR MY KEEP WHILE I'M HERE. YOU TELL ME WHAT YOU NEED DOING, AND I'LL DO IT.
WE'LL FIND WORK FOR YOU.
OH . . . HEY.
THE BEER LEFT A PLEASANT BUZZ IN SHADOW'S HEAD.
RRRRRRRRRRRRRR RRRRRRRRRRRRR
YOUR ROOM IS AT THE TOP OF THE STAIRS. YOU'LL WANT TO WASH UP AND SHAVE FIRST, I GUESS.

SHADOW SHAVED, VERY NERVOUSLY, WITH A STRAIGHT RAZOR THAT JACQUEL LOANED HIM. IT WAS OBSCENELY SHARP.

HE WASHED OFF THE SHAVING CREAM, LOOKED AT THE BLACK BRUISES ON HIS CHEST. LOOKED AT THE MARKS ON HIS COFFEE-COLORED SKIN, LOOKED AT THE DARK GRAY EYES WHICH LOOKED BACK MISTRUST-FULLY FROM THE MIRROR AT HIM.

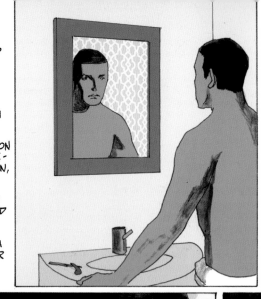

AND THEN, AS IF SOMEONE ELSE WERE HOLDING HIS HAND...

IT WOULD BE A WAY OUT. AN EASY WAY OUT. NO MORE WORRIES.

NO MORE LAURA...

NO MORE MYSTERIES AND CONSPIRACIES.

...NO MORE BAD DREAMS. JUST PEACE AND QUIET AND REST FOREVERMORE.

...ONE CLEAN SLASH FROM EAR TO EAR.

...THAT'S ALL IT'D TAKE.

SEE?

IT'S PAINLESS, TOO SHARP TO HURT. I'LL BE GONE BEFORE I KNOW IT.

CREEEEEEEK

MRR?

HEY. I THOUGHT I LOCKED THAT DOOR.

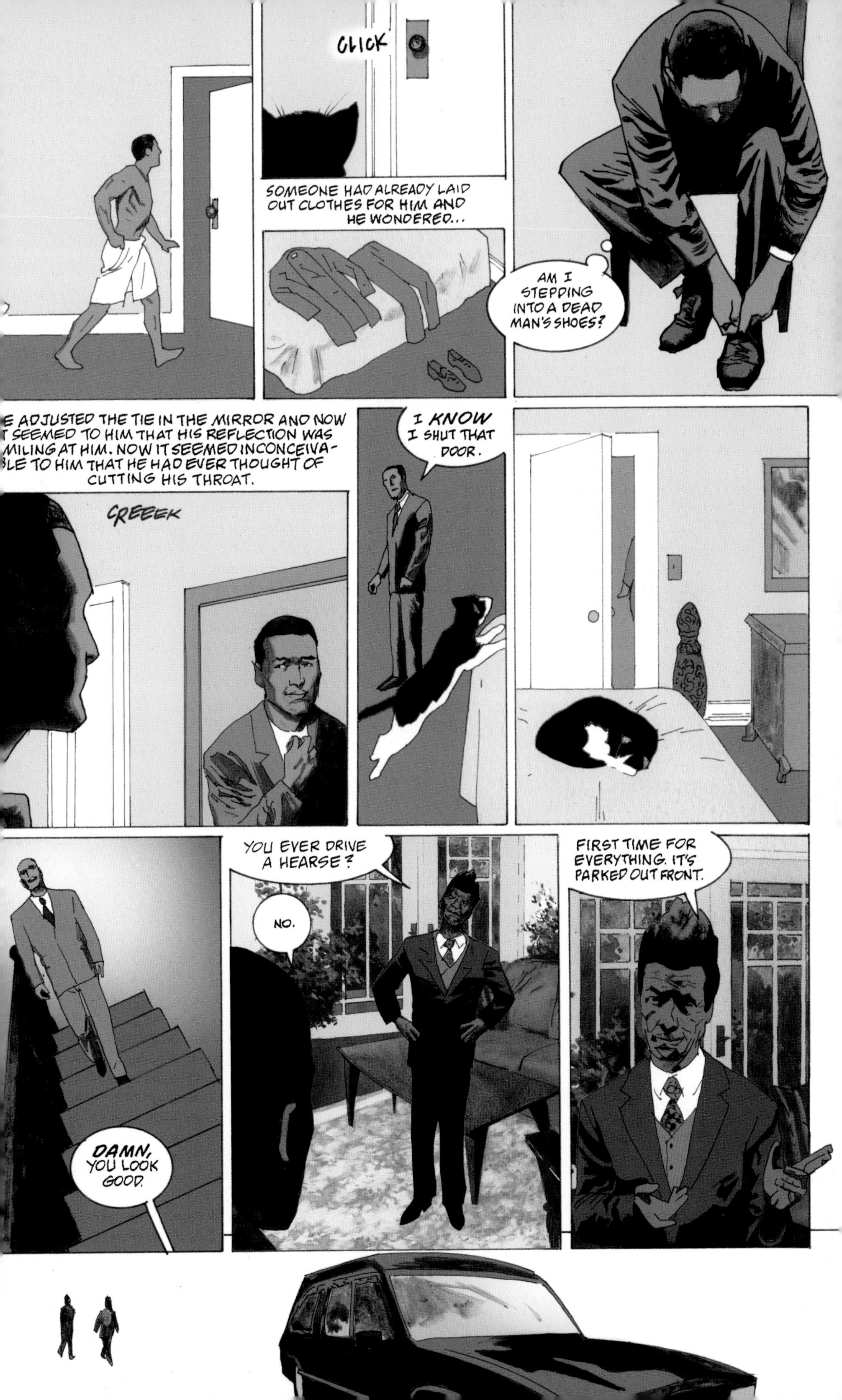
CLICK
SOMEONE HAD ALREADY LAID OUT CLOTHES FOR HIM AND HE WONDERED...
AM I STEPPING INTO A DEAD MAN'S SHOES?
E ADJUSTED THE TIE IN THE MIRROR AND NOW T SEEMED TO HIM THAT HIS REFLECTION WAS MILING AT HIM. NOW IT SEEMED INCONCEIVA-BLE TO HIM THAT HE HAD EVER THOUGHT OF CUTTING HIS THROAT.
CREEEK
I KNOW I SHUT THAT DOOR.
DAMN, YOU LOOK GOOD.
YOU EVER DRIVE A HEARSE?
NO.
FIRST TIME FOR EVERYTHING. IT'S PARKED OUT FRONT.

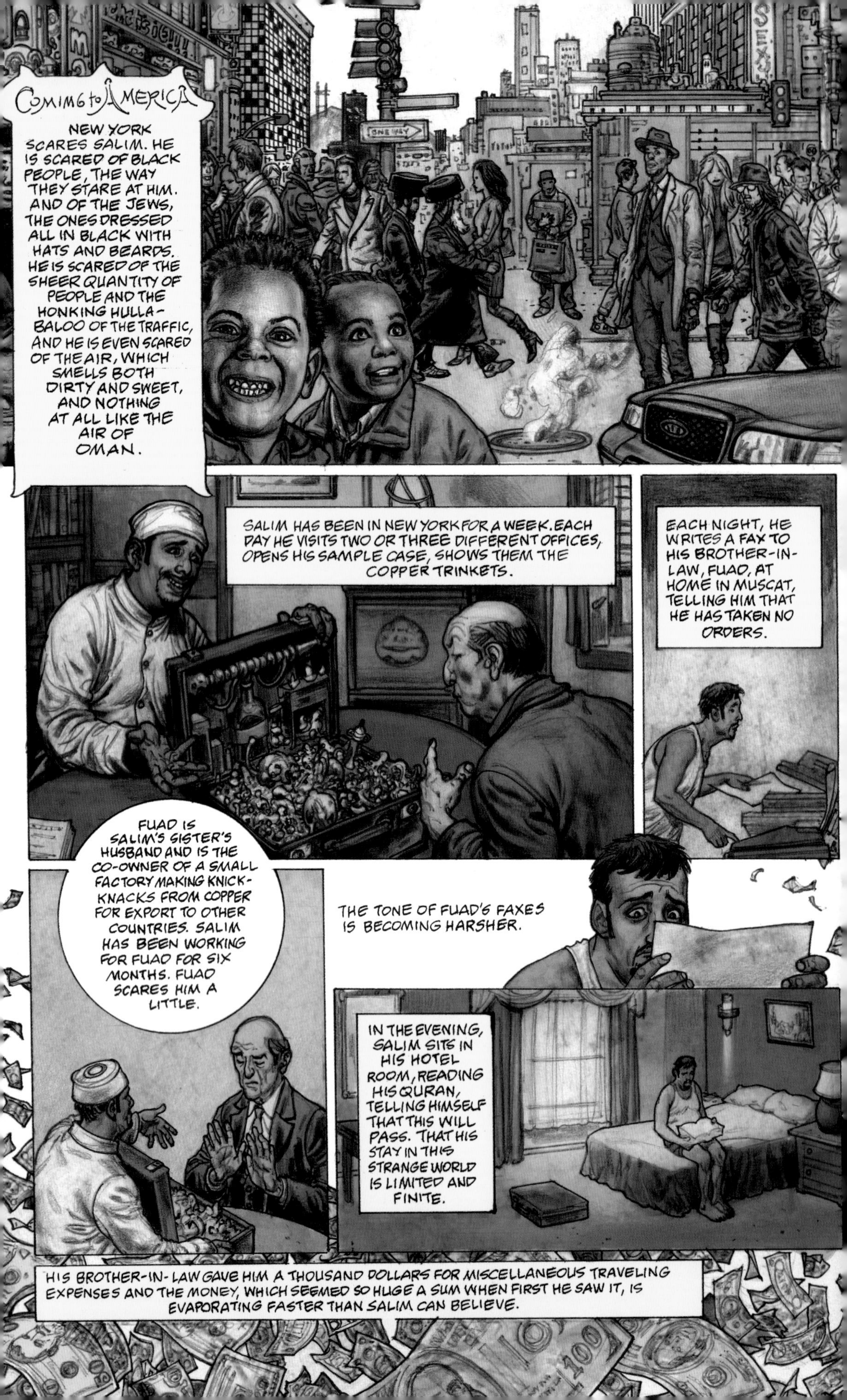
COMING TO AMERICA
NEW YORK SCARES SALIM. HE IS SCARED OF BLACK PEOPLE, THE WAY THEY STARE AT HIM. AND OF THE JEWS, THE ONES DRESSED ALL IN BLACK WITH HATS AND BEARDS. HE IS SCARED OF THE SHEER QUANTITY OF PEOPLE AND THE HONKING HULLABALOO OF THE TRAFFIC, AND HE IS EVEN SCARED OF THE AIR, WHICH SMELLS BOTH DIRTY AND SWEET, AND NOTHING AT ALL LIKE THE AIR OF OMAN.
ONE WAY
SALIM HAS BEEN IN NEW YORK FOR A WEEK. EACH DAY HE VISITS TWO OR THREE DIFFERENT OFFICES, OPENS HIS SAMPLE CASE, SHOWS THEM THE COPPER TRINKETS.
EACH NIGHT, HE WRITES A FAX TO HIS BROTHER-IN-LAW, FUAD, AT HOME IN MUSCAT, TELLING HIM THAT HE HAS TAKEN NO ORDERS.
FUAD IS SALIM'S SISTER'S HUSBAND AND IS THE CO-OWNER OF A SMALL FACTORY MAKING KNICK-KNACKS FROM COPPER FOR EXPORT TO OTHER COUNTRIES. SALIM HAS BEEN WORKING FOR FUAD FOR SIX MONTHS. FUAD SCARES HIM A LITTLE.
THE TONE OF FUAD'S FAXES IS BECOMING HARSHER.
IN THE EVENING, SALIM SITS IN HIS HOTEL ROOM, READING HIS QURAN, TELLING HIMSELF THAT THIS WILL PASS. THAT HIS STAY IN THIS STRANGE WORLD IS LIMITED AND FINITE.
HIS BROTHER-IN-LAW GAVE HIM A THOUSAND DOLLARS FOR MISCELLANEOUS TRAVELING EXPENSES AND THE MONEY, WHICH SEEMED SO HUGE A SUM WHEN FIRST HE SAW IT, IS EVAPORATING FASTER THAN SALIM CAN BELIEVE.

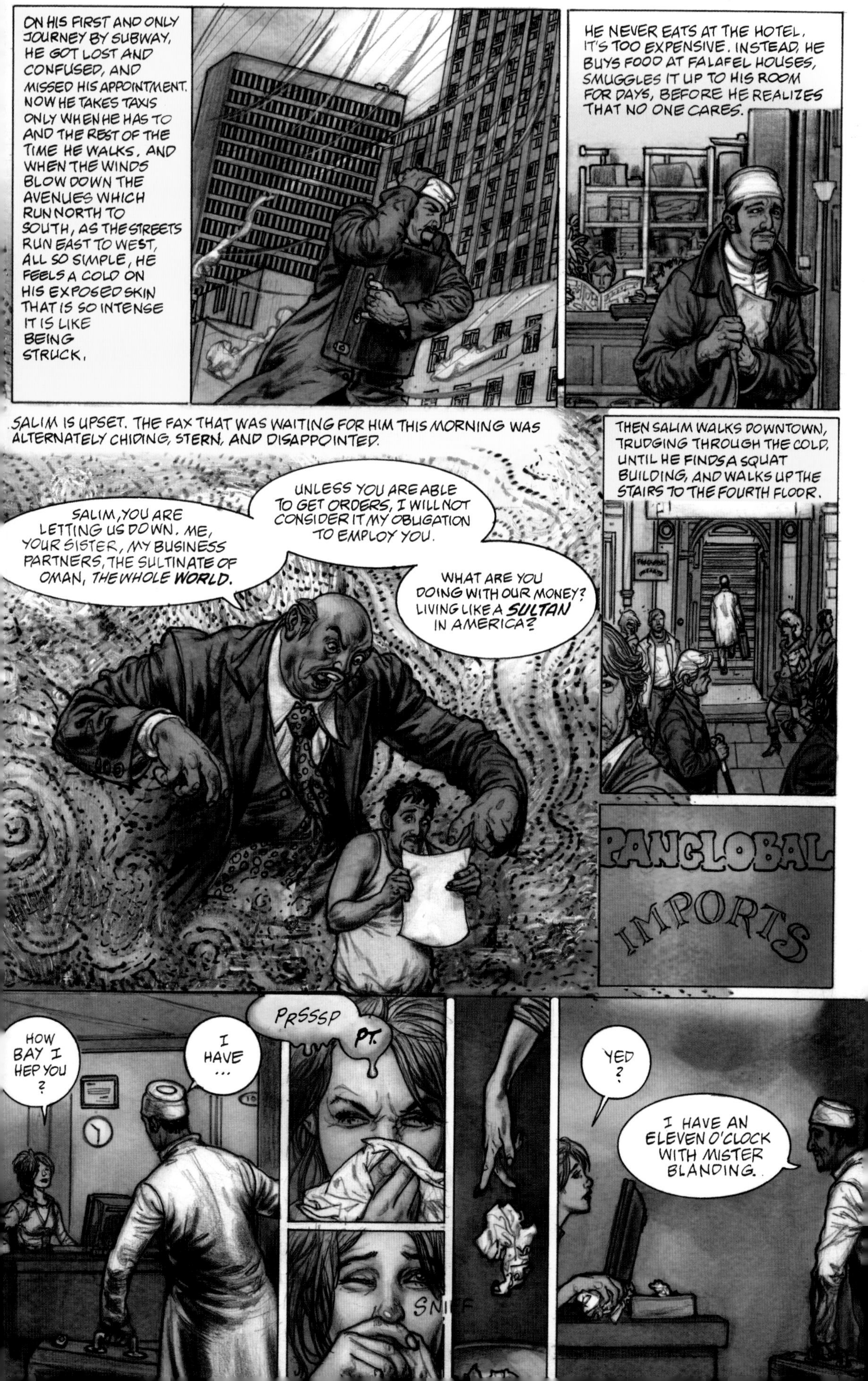
ON HIS FIRST AND ONLY JOURNEY BY SUBWAY, HE GOT LOST AND CONFUSED, AND MISSED HIS APPOINTMENT. NOW HE TAKES TAXIS ONLY WHEN HE HAS TO AND THE REST OF THE TIME HE WALKS. AND WHEN THE WINDS BLOW DOWN THE AVENUES WHICH RUN NORTH TO SOUTH, AS THE STREETS RUN EAST TO WEST, ALL SO SIMPLE, HE FEELS A COLD ON HIS EXPOSED SKIN THAT IS SO INTENSE IT IS LIKE BEING STRUCK.
HE NEVER EATS AT THE HOTEL, IT'S TOO EXPENSIVE. INSTEAD, HE BUYS FOOD AT FALAFEL HOUSES, SMUGGLES IT UP TO HIS ROOM FOR DAYS, BEFORE HE REALIZES THAT NO ONE CARES.
SALIM IS UPSET. THE FAX THAT WAS WAITING FOR HIM THIS MORNING WAS ALTERNATELY CHIDING, STERN, AND DISAPPOINTED.
SALIM, YOU ARE LETTING US DOWN. ME, YOUR SISTER, MY BUSINESS PARTNERS, THE SULTINATE OF OMAN, THE WHOLE WORLD.
UNLESS YOU ARE ABLE TO GET ORDERS, I WILL NOT CONSIDER IT MY OBLIGATION TO EMPLOY YOU.
WHAT ARE YOU DOING WITH OUR MONEY? LIVING LIKE A SULTAN IN AMERICA?
THEN SALIM WALKS DOWNTOWN, TRUDGING THROUGH THE COLD, UNTIL HE FINDS A SQUAT BUILDING, AND WALKS UP THE STAIRS TO THE FOURTH FLOOR.
PANGLOBAL
IMPORTS
HOW BAY I HEP YOU?
I HAVE ...
PRSSSP
PT.
SNIFF
YED?
I HAVE AN ELEVEN O'CLOCK WITH MISTER BLANDING.

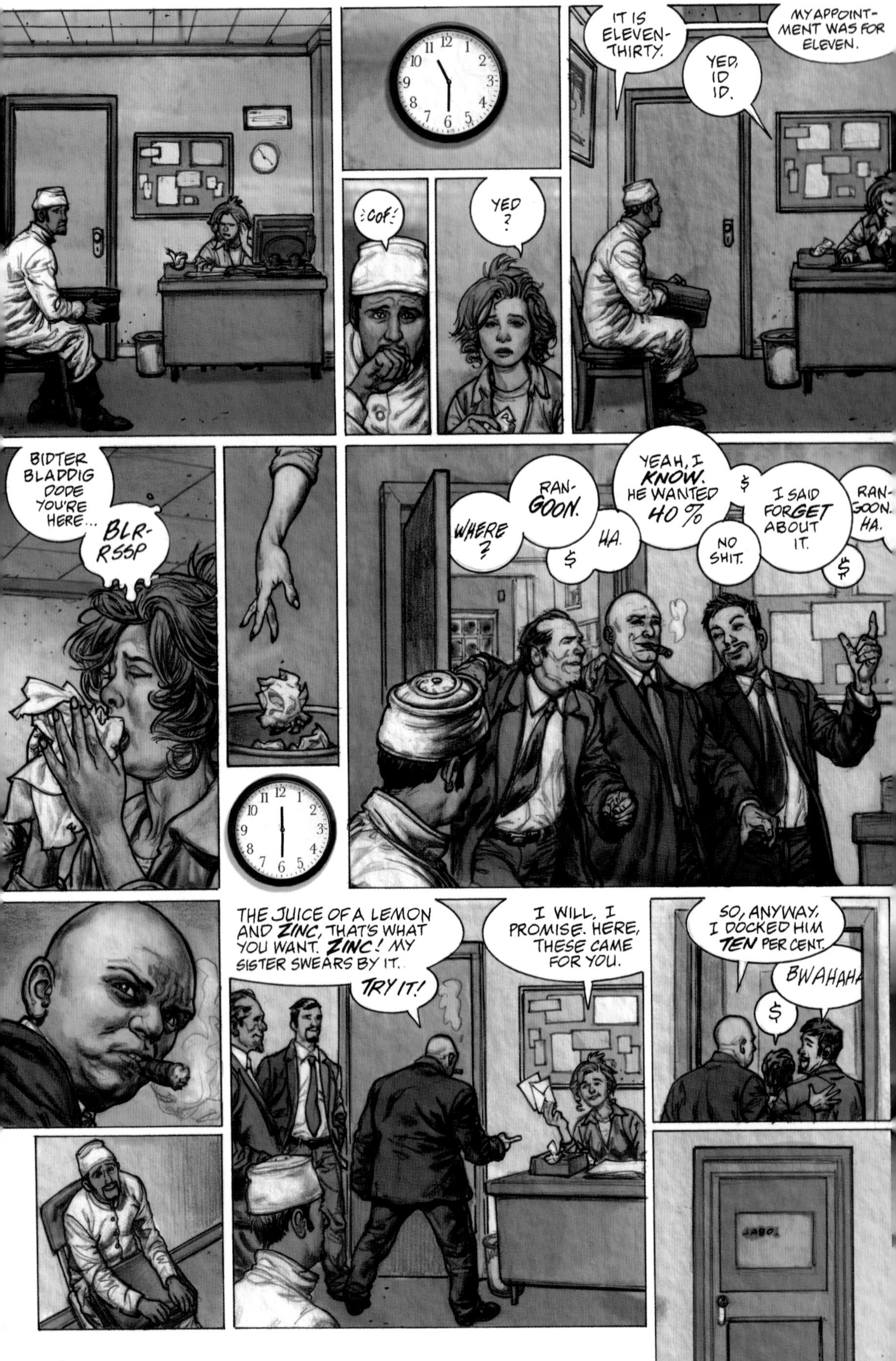

:COF:
YED ?
IT IS ELEVEN-THIRTY.
YED, ID ID.
MY APPOINTMENT WAS FOR ELEVEN.
BIDTER BLADDIG DODE YOU'RE HERE...
BLR-RSSP
WHERE ?
RAN-GOON.
$
HA.
YEAH, I KNOW. HE WANTED 40%
$
NO SHIT.
I SAID FORGET ABOUT IT.
RAN-GOON. HA.
$
THE JUICE OF A LEMON AND ZINC, THAT'S WHAT YOU WANT. ZINC! MY SISTER SWEARS BY IT.
TRY IT!
I WILL. I PROMISE. HERE, THESE CAME FOR YOU.
SO, ANYWAY, I DOCKED HIM TEN PER CENT.
BWAHAHA
$

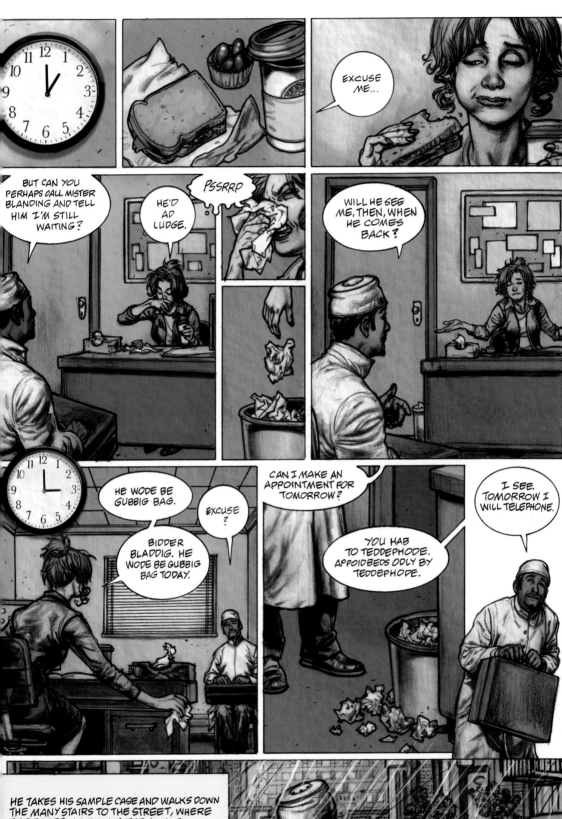

EXCUSE ME...

BUT CAN YOU PERHAPS CALL MISTER BLANDING AND TELL HIM I'M STILL WAITING?

HE'D AD LUDGE.

PSSRRP

WILL HE SEE ME, THEN, WHEN HE COMES BACK?

HE WODE BE GUBBIG BAG.

BIDDER BLADDIG. HE WODE BE GUBBIG BAG TODAY.

EXCUSE?

CAN I MAKE AN APPOINTMENT FOR TOMORROW?

YOU HAB TO TEDDEPHODE. APPOIDBEDS ODLY BY TEDDEPHODE.

I SEE. TOMORROW I WILL TELEPHONE.

HE TAKES HIS SAMPLE CASE AND WALKS DOWN THE MANY STAIRS TO THE STREET, WHERE THE FREEZING RAIN IS TURNING TO SLEET. HE CONTEMPLATES THE LONG, COLD WALK BACK TO THE HOTEL, THEN HE STEPS TO THE EDGE OF THE SIDEWALK AND WAVES AT EVERY YELLOW CAB THAT APPROACHES, AND EVERY CAB DRIVES PAST HIM.

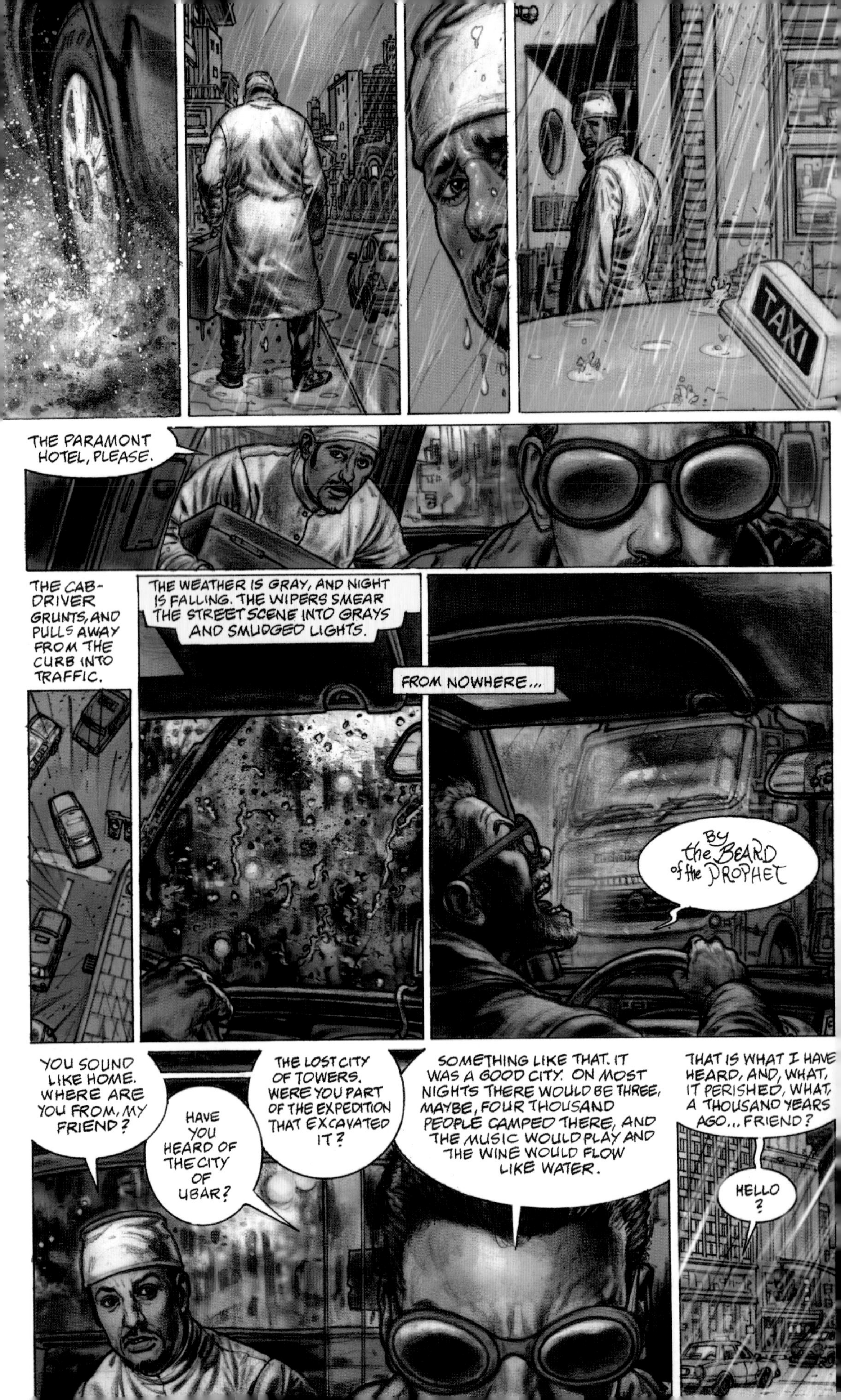

TAXI
THE PARAMONT HOTEL, PLEASE.
THE CAB-DRIVER GRUNTS, AND PULLS AWAY FROM THE CURB INTO TRAFFIC.
THE WEATHER IS GRAY, AND NIGHT IS FALLING. THE WIPERS SMEAR THE STREET SCENE INTO GRAYS AND SMUDGED LIGHTS.
FROM NOWHERE...
By the BEARD of the PROPHET
YOU SOUND LIKE HOME. WHERE ARE YOU FROM, MY FRIEND?
HAVE YOU HEARD OF THE CITY OF UBAR?
THE LOST CITY OF TOWERS. WERE YOU PART OF THE EXPEDITION THAT EXCAVATED IT?
SOMETHING LIKE THAT. IT WAS A GOOD CITY. ON MOST NIGHTS THERE WOULD BE THREE, MAYBE, FOUR THOUSAND PEOPLE CAMPED THERE, AND THE MUSIC WOULD PLAY AND THE WINE WOULD FLOW LIKE WATER.
THAT IS WHAT I HAVE HEARD, AND, WHAT, IT PERISHED, WHAT, A THOUSAND YEARS AGO... FRIEND?
HELLO?

ZZZZZ

HO HO HONK HONK HONK

FUCKSHIT FUCKSHIT

YOU MUST BE VERY TIRED, MY FRIEND.

I HAVE BEEN DRIVING THIS ALLAH-FORGOTTEN TAXI FOR THIRTY HOURS. BEFORE THAT, I SLEEP FOR FIVE HOURS, AND I DROVE FOURTEEN HOURS BEFORE THAT. WE ARE SHORT-HANDED BEFORE CHRISTMAS.

I HOPE YOU HAVE MADE A LOT OF MONEY.

HMF. NOT MUCH. THIS MORNING I DROVE A MAN FROM MIDTOWN TO NEWARK AIRPORT. WHEN WE GOT THERE, HE RAN OFF INTO THE AIRPORT. A FIFTY-DOLLAR FARE GONE. AND I HAD TO PAY THE TOLLS ON THE WAY BACK MYSELF.

I HAD TO SPEND TODAY WAITING TO SEE A MAN WHO WILL NOT SEE ME. MY BROTHER-IN-LAW HATES ME. I HAVE BEEN IN AMERICA FOR A WEEK AND IT HAS DONE NOTHING BUT EAT MY MONEY. I SELL NOTHING.

WHAT DO YOU SELL?

SHIT. WORTHLESS GEEGAWS AND BAUBLES AND TOURIST TRINKETS, HORRIBLE, CHEAP, FOOLISH, UGLY SHIT.

AND THEY WILL NOT BUY IT?

NO.

STRANGE. YOU LOOK AT THE STORES AND THAT IS ALL THEY SELL.

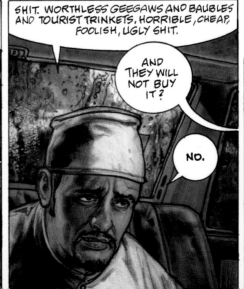

THEY TURN ONTO A STREET WHERE THE TRAFFIC HAS STOPPED COMPLETELY. THERE IS A CACOPHONY OF HORNS, BUT THE CARS DO NOT MOVE. THE DRIVER SWAYS IN HIS SEAT, HIS HEAD DIPS, THEN HE BEGINS, GENTLY, TO SNORE.

FRIEND? ARE YOU . . .

TAP TAP

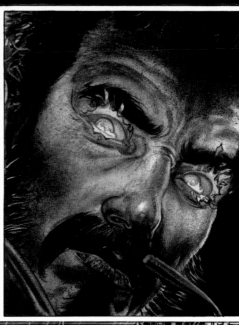

THE CAR CRAWLS FORWARD IN THE RAIN, THE NUMBERS ON THE METER INCREASE.

ARE YOU GOING TO KILL ME?

NO.

MY GRANDMOTHER SWORE THAT SHE HAD SEEN AN IFRIT LATE ONE EVENING ON THE EDGE OF THE DESERT. SHE SAW ITS FACE, AND ITS EYES, LIKE YOURS, WERE BURNING FLAMES.

THE GRAND-MOTHERS CAME HERE, TOO.

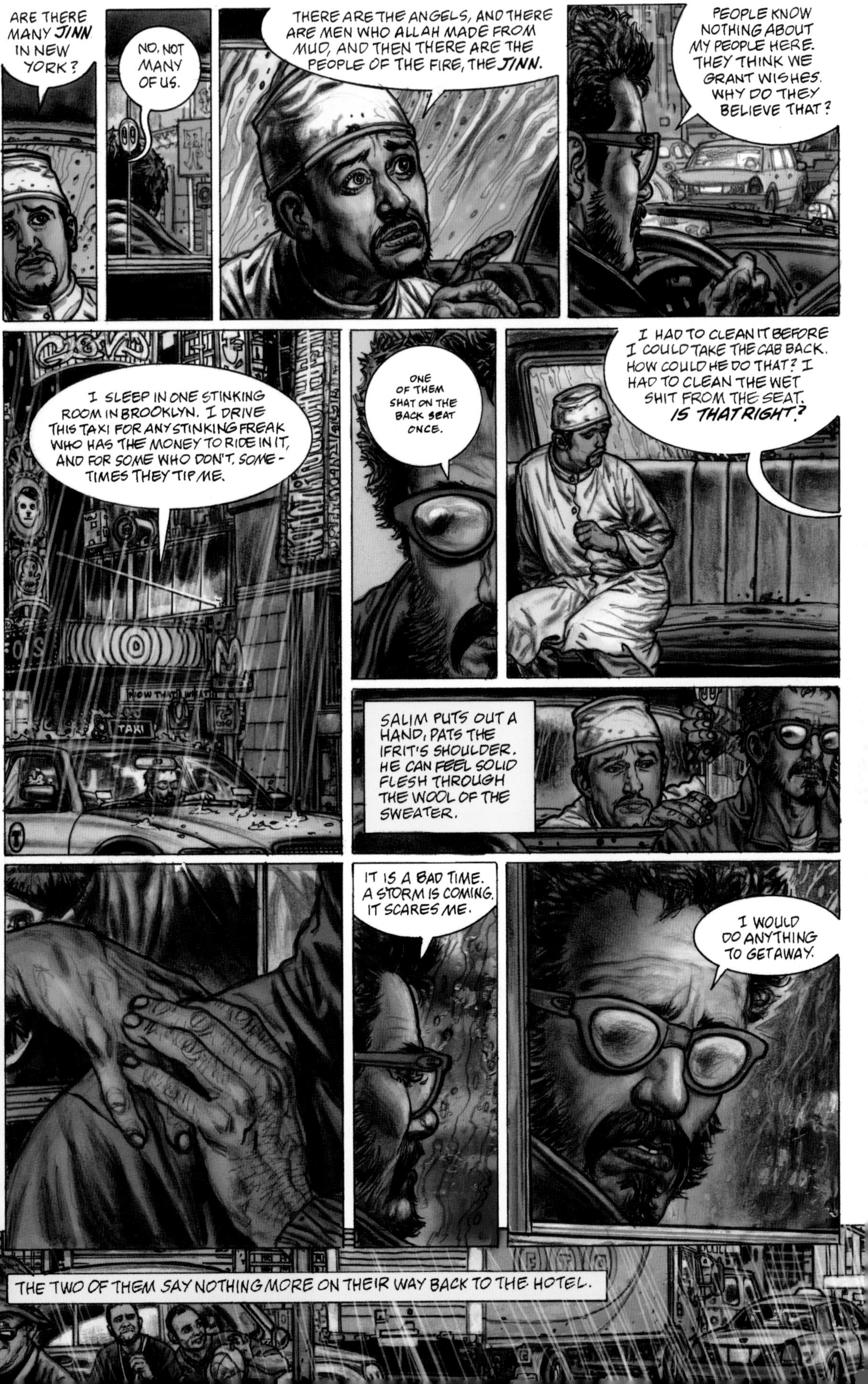
ARE THERE MANY JINN IN NEW YORK?
NO, NOT MANY OF US.
THERE ARE THE ANGELS, AND THERE ARE MEN WHO ALLAH MADE FROM MUD, AND THEN THERE ARE THE PEOPLE OF THE FIRE, THE JINN.
PEOPLE KNOW NOTHING ABOUT MY PEOPLE HERE. THEY THINK WE GRANT WISHES. WHY DO THEY BELIEVE THAT?
I SLEEP IN ONE STINKING ROOM IN BROOKLYN. I DRIVE THIS TAXI FOR ANY STINKING FREAK WHO HAS THE MONEY TO RIDE IN IT, AND FOR SOME WHO DON'T. SOMETIMES THEY TIP ME.
ONE OF THEM SHAT ON THE BACK SEAT ONCE.
I HAD TO CLEAN IT BEFORE I COULD TAKE THE CAB BACK. HOW COULD HE DO THAT? I HAD TO CLEAN THE WET SHIT FROM THE SEAT. IS THAT RIGHT?
TAXI
SALIM PUTS OUT A HAND, PATS THE IFRIT'S SHOULDER. HE CAN FEEL SOLID FLESH THROUGH THE WOOL OF THE SWEATER.
IT IS A BAD TIME. A STORM IS COMING. IT SCARES ME.
I WOULD DO ANYTHING TO GET AWAY.
THE TWO OF THEM SAY NOTHING MORE ON THEIR WAY BACK TO THE HOTEL.

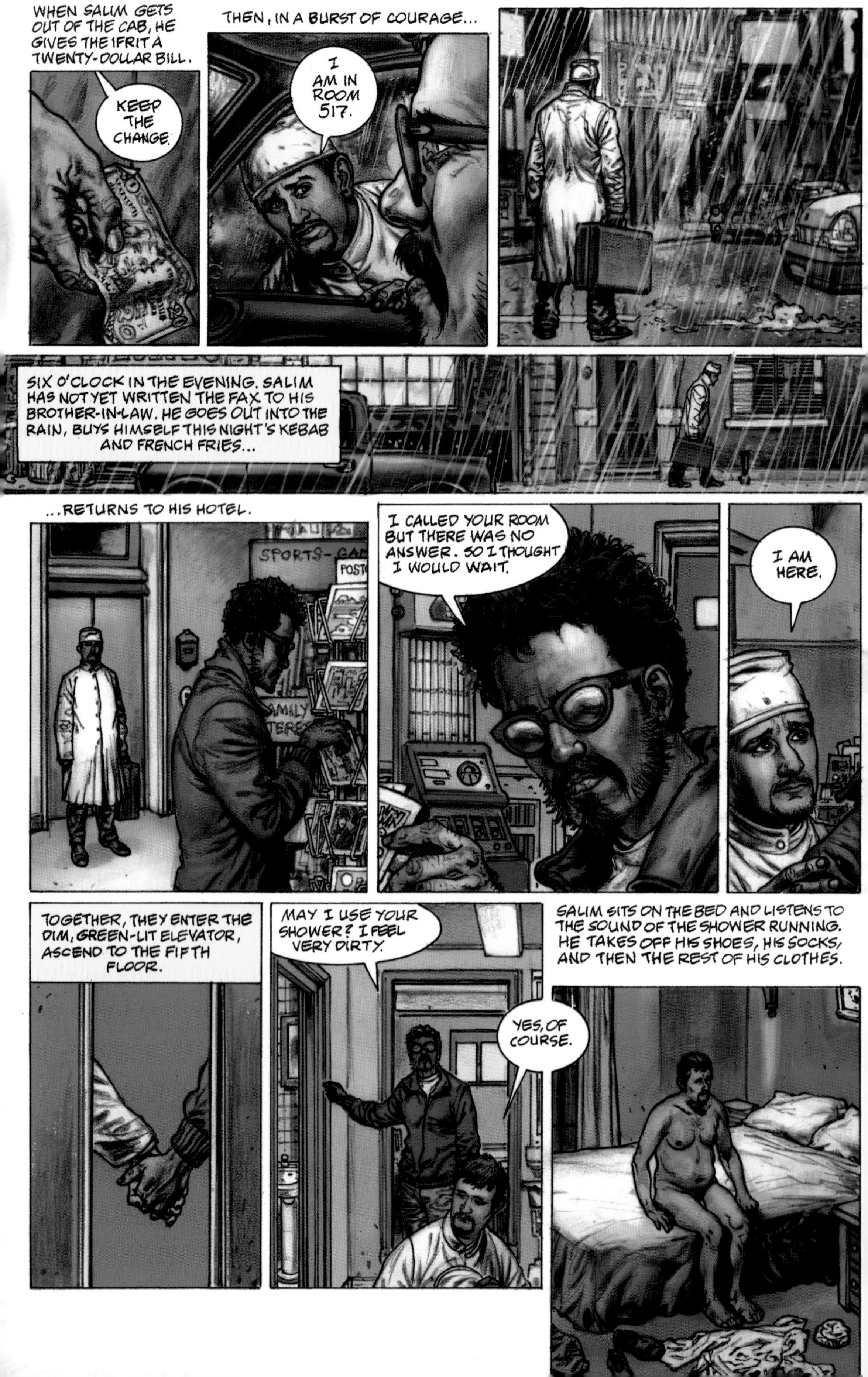
WHEN SALIM GETS OUT OF THE CAB, HE GIVES THE IFRIT A TWENTY-DOLLAR BILL.
KEEP THE CHANGE.
THEN, IN A BURST OF COURAGE...
I AM IN ROOM 517.
SIX O'CLOCK IN THE EVENING. SALIM HAS NOT YET WRITTEN THE FAX TO HIS BROTHER-IN-LAW. HE GOES OUT INTO THE RAIN, BUYS HIMSELF THIS NIGHT'S KEBAB AND FRENCH FRIES...
...RETURNS TO HIS HOTEL.
I CALLED YOUR ROOM BUT THERE WAS NO ANSWER. SO I THOUGHT I WOULD WAIT.
I AM HERE.
TOGETHER, THEY ENTER THE DIM, GREEN-LIT ELEVATOR, ASCEND TO THE FIFTH FLOOR.
MAY I USE YOUR SHOWER? I FEEL VERY DIRTY.
YES, OF COURSE.
SALIM SITS ON THE BED AND LISTENS TO THE SOUND OF THE SHOWER RUNNING. HE TAKES OFF HIS SHOES, HIS SOCKS, AND THEN THE REST OF HIS CLOTHES.

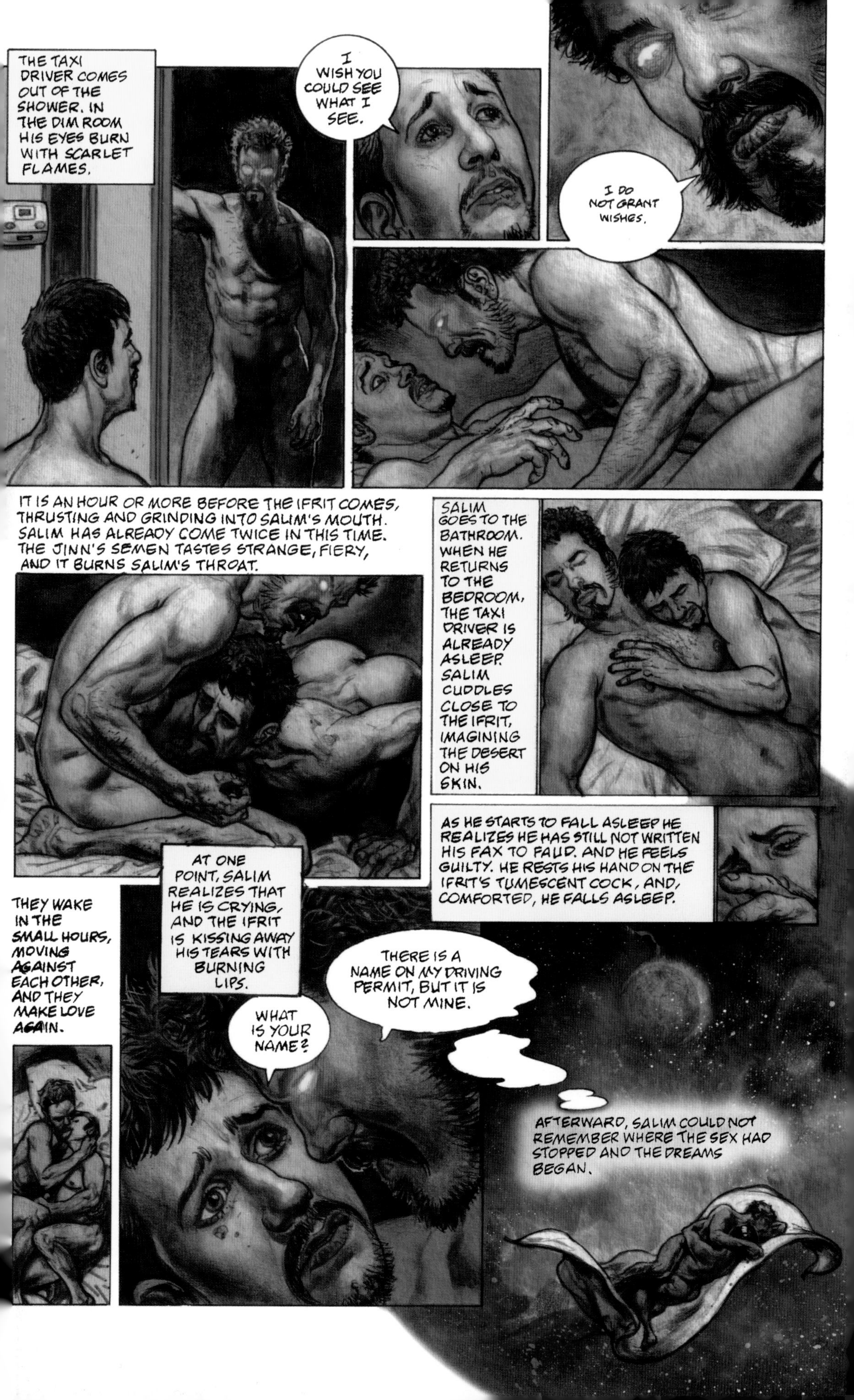
THE TAXI DRIVER COMES OUT OF THE SHOWER. IN THE DIM ROOM HIS EYES BURN WITH SCARLET FLAMES.
I WISH YOU COULD SEE WHAT I SEE.
I DO NOT GRANT WISHES.
IT IS AN HOUR OR MORE BEFORE THE IFRIT COMES, THRUSTING AND GRINDING INTO SALIM'S MOUTH. SALIM HAS ALREADY COME TWICE IN THIS TIME. THE JINN'S SEMEN TASTES STRANGE, FIERY, AND IT BURNS SALIM'S THROAT.
SALIM GOES TO THE BATHROOM. WHEN HE RETURNS TO THE BEDROOM, THE TAXI DRIVER IS ALREADY ASLEEP. SALIM CUDDLES CLOSE TO THE IFRIT, IMAGINING THE DESERT ON HIS SKIN.
AS HE STARTS TO FALL ASLEEP HE REALIZES HE HAS STILL NOT WRITTEN HIS FAX TO FAUD. AND HE FEELS GUILTY. HE RESTS HIS HAND ON THE IFRIT'S TUMESCENT COCK, AND, COMFORTED, HE FALLS ASLEEP.
AT ONE POINT, SALIM REALIZES THAT HE IS CRYING, AND THE IFRIT IS KISSING AWAY HIS TEARS WITH BURNING LIPS.
THEY WAKE IN THE SMALL HOURS, MOVING AGAINST EACH OTHER, AND THEY MAKE LOVE AGAIN.
WHAT IS YOUR NAME?
THERE IS A NAME ON MY DRIVING PERMIT, BUT IT IS NOT MINE.
AFTERWARD, SALIM COULD NOT REMEMBER WHERE THE SEX HAD STOPPED AND THE DREAMS BEGAN.

WHEN SALIM AWAKES, HE IS ALONE. ALSO, HE DISCOVERS HIS SAMPLE CASE IS GONE, THE SOUVENIR COPPER TRINKETS, ALL GONE, ALONG WITH HIS WALLET, HIS PASSPORT, AND HIS AIR TICKETS BACK TO OMAN.

ONLY THE IFRIT'S CLOTHES ARE LEFT BEHIND. BENEATH THEM, HE FINDS A DRIVER'S LICENSE IN THE NAME OF...

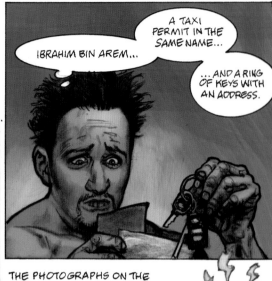

IBRAHIM BIN AREM...

A TAXI PERMIT IN THE SAME NAME...

...AND A RING OF KEYS WITH AN ADDRESS.

THE PHOTOGRAPHS ON THE LICENSE AND THE PERMIT DO NOT LOOK MUCH LIKE SALIM, BUT THEN, THEY DID NOT LOOK MUCH LIKE THE IFRIT.

THE FRONT DESK CALLS TO POINT OUT THAT SALIM HAD ALREADY CHECKED OUT, AND HIS GUEST NEEDS TO LEAVE SOON, SO THAT THEY CAN SERVICE THE ROOM.

I DO NOT GRANT WISHES.

HE FEELS STRANGELY LIGHT-HEADED AS HE DRESSES.

NEW YORK IS VERY SIMPLE.

THE AVENUES RUN NORTH TO SOUTH...

...THE STREETS RUN WEST TO EAST--

--HOW HARD CAN IT BE?

HA.

HE PUTS ON THE BLACK PLASTIC SUNGLASSES HE FOUND IN THE POCKETS...

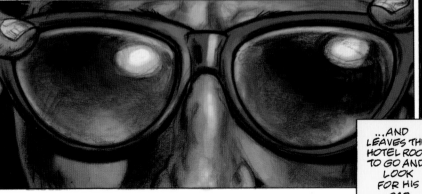

...AND LEAVES THE HOTEL ROOM TO GO AND LOOK FOR HIS CAB.

CHAPTER NINE

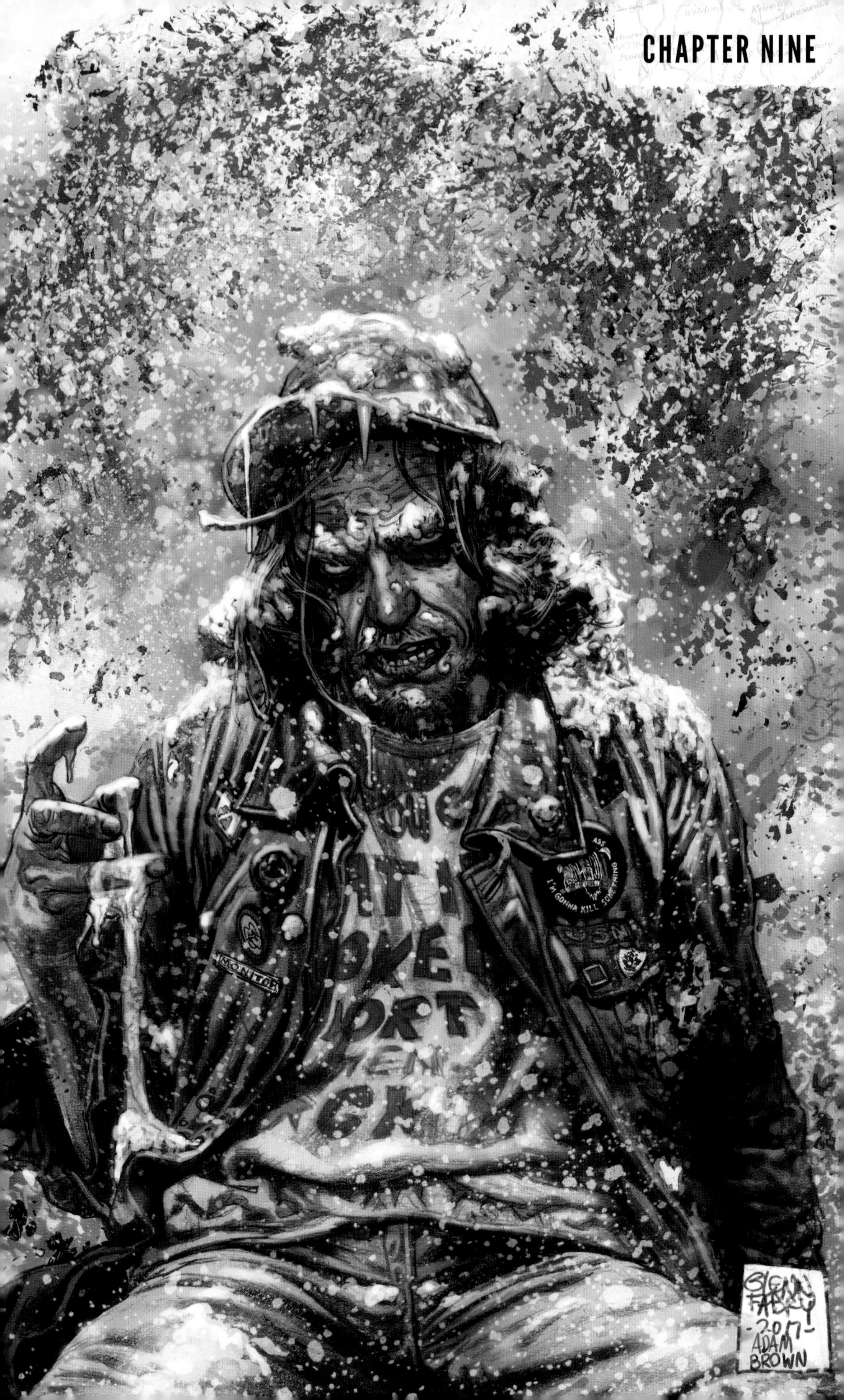
I'M GONNA KILL SOMETHING
MONITOR
USN
GLENN FABRY -2017- ADAM BROWN

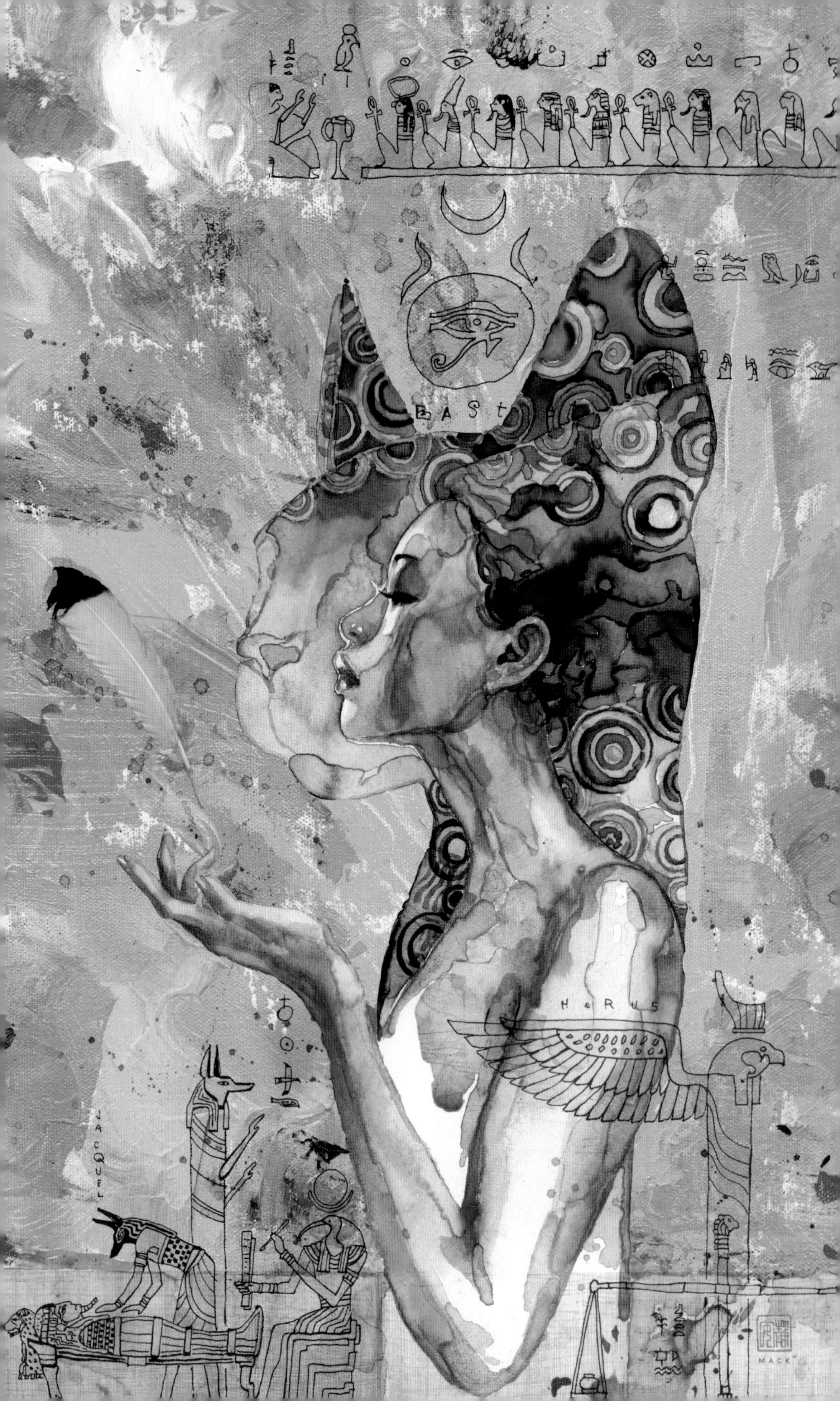
BAST
HORUS
JACQUEL
MACK

AN OLD WOMAN HAD DIED. HER NAME HAD BEEN LILA GOODCHILD.

AT MR. JACQUEL'S DIRECTION, SHADOW CARRIED THE FOLDED ALUMINUM GURNEY UP THE NARROW STAIRS TO HER BEDROOM, AND UNFOLDED IT NEXT TO HER BED. HE TOOK OUT A BLUE PLASTIC BODY BAG, LAID IT NEXT TO THE DEAD WOMAN, AND UNZIPPED IT OPEN. SHADOW LIFTED HER, FRAGILE AND ALMOST WEIGHTLESS, PLACED HER IN THE BAG, AND ZIPPED THE BAG SHUT.

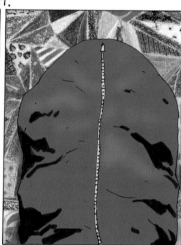

SHADOW CLOSED THE HEARSE WHILE JACQUEL TALKED TO A VERY OLD MAN WHO HAD, WHEN SHE WAS ALIVE, BEEN MARRIED TO LILA GOODCHILD. THE OLD MAN WAS EXPLAINING HOW UNGRATEFUL HIS CHILDREN HAD BEEN, AND GRANDCHILDREN, TOO, ALTHOUGH THAT WASN'T THEIR FAULT. AFTER ALL...

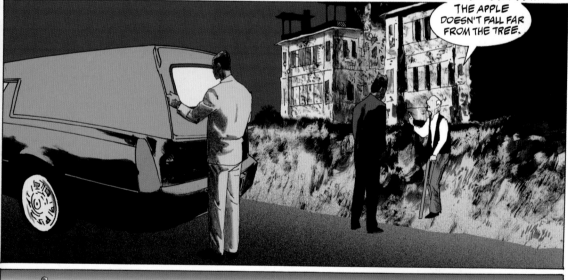

THE APPLE DOESN'T FALL FAR FROM THE TREE.

THEY'VE GOT NO MONEY. HE'LL CHOOSE THE CHEAPEST FUNERAL. HER FRIENDS WILL PERSUADE HIM TO GIVE HER A PROPER SENDOFF IN THE FRONT ROOM. BUT HE'LL GRUMBLE: GOT NO MONEY.

...ANYWAY, HE'LL BE DEAD IN SIX MONTHS. A YEAR AT THE OUTSIDE.

IS HE SICK?

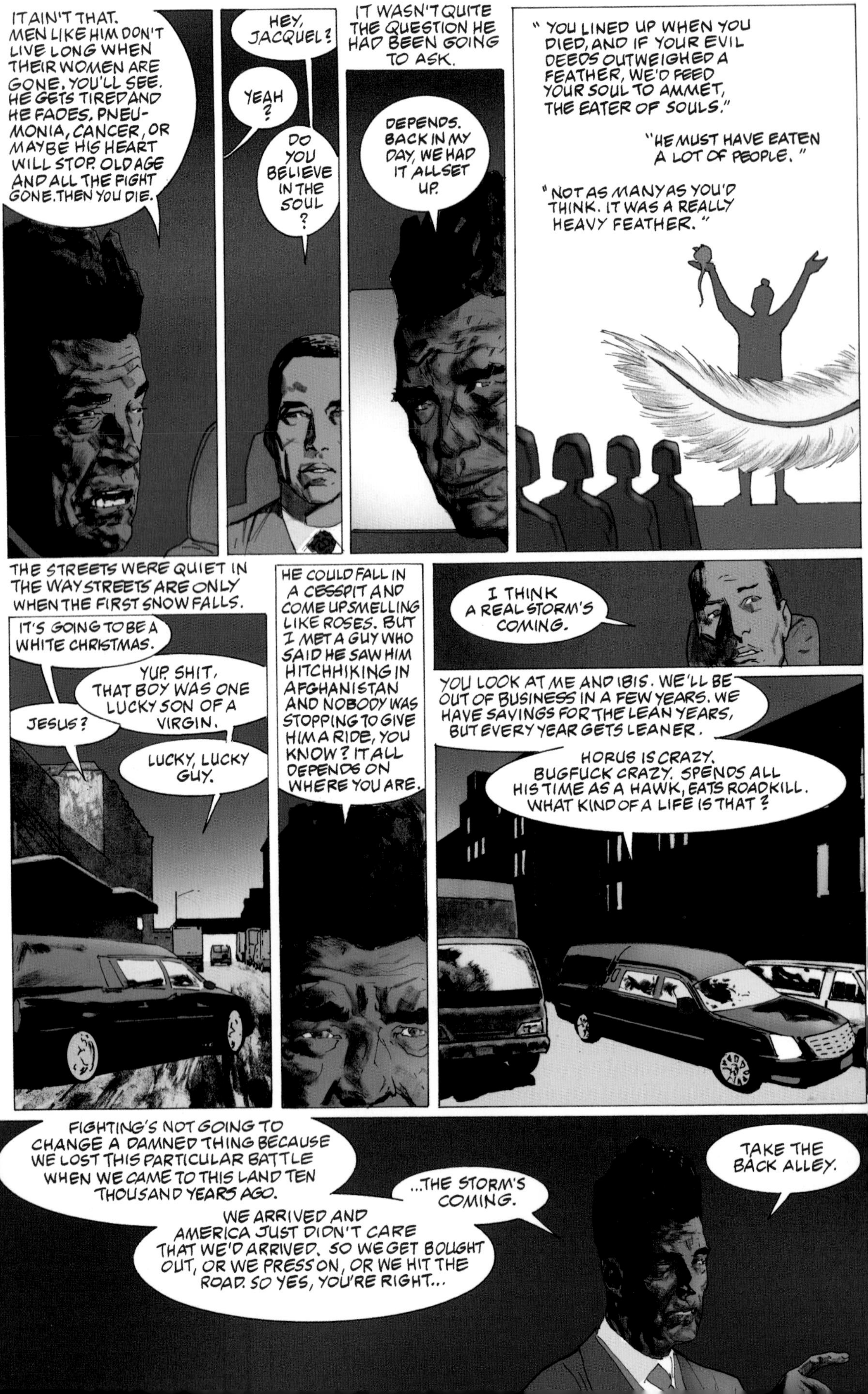
IT AIN'T THAT. MEN LIKE HIM DON'T LIVE LONG WHEN THEIR WOMEN ARE GONE. YOU'LL SEE. HE GETS TIRED AND HE FADES. PNEUMONIA, CANCER, OR MAYBE HIS HEART WILL STOP. OLD AGE AND ALL THE FIGHT GONE. THEN YOU DIE.
HEY, JACQUEL?
YEAH?
DO YOU BELIEVE IN THE SOUL?
IT WASN'T QUITE THE QUESTION HE HAD BEEN GOING TO ASK.
DEPENDS. BACK IN MY DAY, WE HAD IT ALL SET UP.
"YOU LINED UP WHEN YOU DIED, AND IF YOUR EVIL DEEDS OUTWEIGHED A FEATHER, WE'D FEED YOUR SOUL TO AMMET, THE EATER OF SOULS."
"HE MUST HAVE EATEN A LOT OF PEOPLE."
"NOT AS MANY AS YOU'D THINK. IT WAS A REALLY HEAVY FEATHER."
THE STREETS WERE QUIET IN THE WAY STREETS ARE ONLY WHEN THE FIRST SNOW FALLS.
IT'S GOING TO BE A WHITE CHRISTMAS.
JESUS?
YUP. SHIT, THAT BOY WAS ONE LUCKY SON OF A VIRGIN.
LUCKY, LUCKY GUY.
HE COULD FALL IN A CESSPIT AND COME UP SMELLING LIKE ROSES. BUT I MET A GUY WHO SAID HE SAW HIM HITCHHIKING IN AFGHANISTAN AND NOBODY WAS STOPPING TO GIVE HIM A RIDE, YOU KNOW? IT ALL DEPENDS ON WHERE YOU ARE.
I THINK A REAL STORM'S COMING.
YOU LOOK AT ME AND IBIS. WE'LL BE OUT OF BUSINESS IN A FEW YEARS. WE HAVE SAVINGS FOR THE LEAN YEARS, BUT EVERY YEAR GETS LEANER.
HORUS IS CRAZY. BUGFUCK CRAZY. SPENDS ALL HIS TIME AS A HAWK, EATS ROADKILL. WHAT KIND OF A LIFE IS THAT?
FIGHTING'S NOT GOING TO CHANGE A DAMNED THING BECAUSE WE LOST THIS PARTICULAR BATTLE WHEN WE CAME TO THIS LAND TEN THOUSAND YEARS AGO.
WE ARRIVED AND AMERICA JUST DIDN'T CARE THAT WE'D ARRIVED. SO WE GET BOUGHT OUT, OR WE PRESS ON, OR WE HIT THE ROAD. SO YES, YOU'RE RIGHT...
...THE STORM'S COMING.
TAKE THE BACK ALLEY.

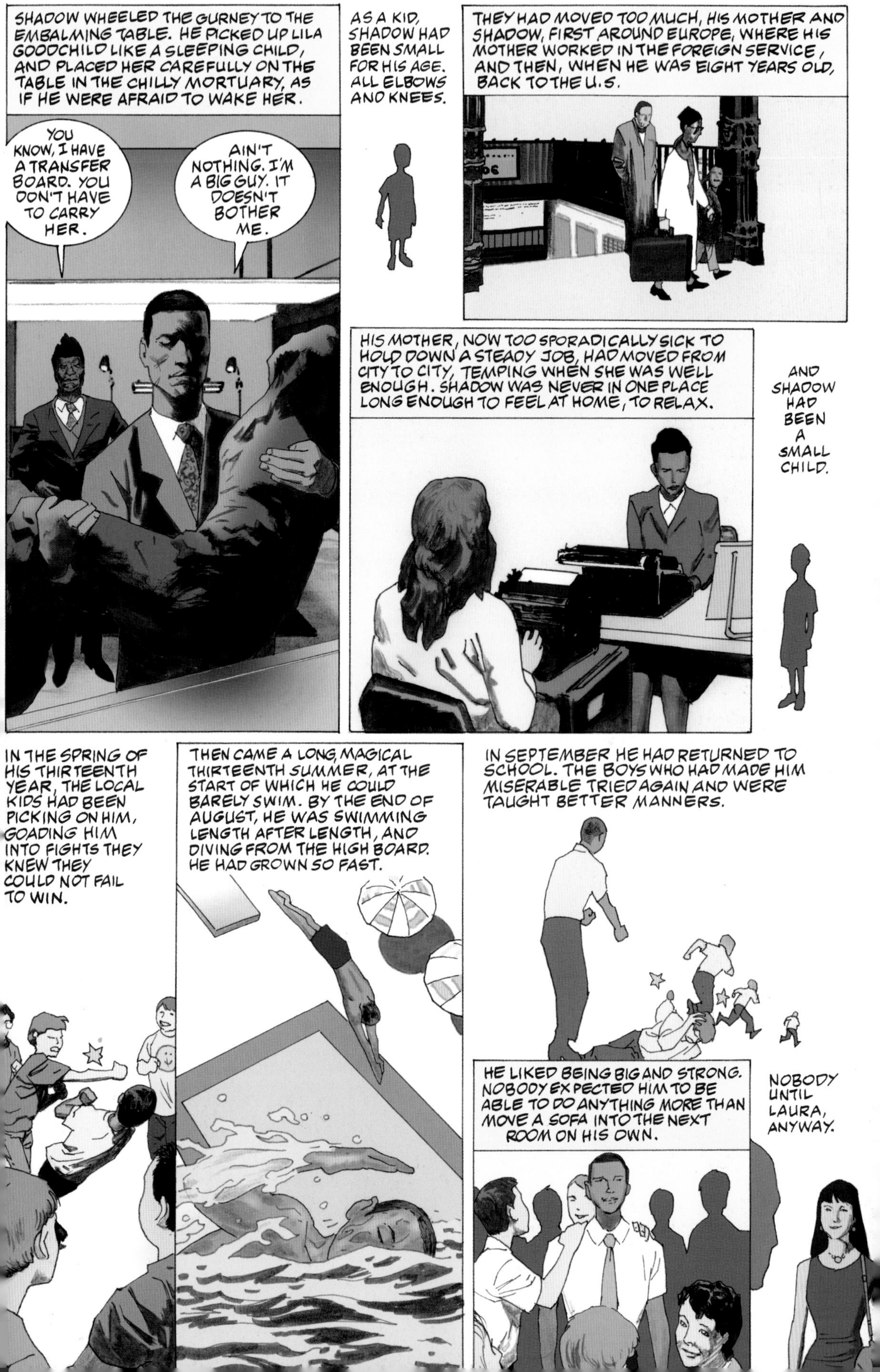
SHADOW WHEELED THE GURNEY TO THE EMBALMING TABLE. HE PICKED UP LILA GOODCHILD LIKE A SLEEPING CHILD, AND PLACED HER CAREFULLY ON THE TABLE IN THE CHILLY MORTUARY, AS IF HE WERE AFRAID TO WAKE HER.
YOU KNOW, I HAVE A TRANSFER BOARD. YOU DON'T HAVE TO CARRY HER.
AIN'T NOTHING. I'M A BIG GUY. IT DOESN'T BOTHER ME.
AS A KID, SHADOW HAD BEEN SMALL FOR HIS AGE. ALL ELBOWS AND KNEES.
THEY HAD MOVED TOO MUCH, HIS MOTHER AND SHADOW, FIRST AROUND EUROPE, WHERE HIS MOTHER WORKED IN THE FOREIGN SERVICE, AND THEN, WHEN HE WAS EIGHT YEARS OLD, BACK TO THE U.S.
HIS MOTHER, NOW TOO SPORADICALLY SICK TO HOLD DOWN A STEADY JOB, HAD MOVED FROM CITY TO CITY, TEMPING WHEN SHE WAS WELL ENOUGH. SHADOW WAS NEVER IN ONE PLACE LONG ENOUGH TO FEEL AT HOME, TO RELAX.
AND SHADOW HAD BEEN A SMALL CHILD.
IN THE SPRING OF HIS THIRTEENTH YEAR, THE LOCAL KIDS HAD BEEN PICKING ON HIM, GOADING HIM INTO FIGHTS THEY KNEW THEY COULD NOT FAIL TO WIN.
THEN CAME A LONG, MAGICAL THIRTEENTH *SUMMER*, AT THE START OF WHICH HE COULD BARELY SWIM. BY THE END OF AUGUST, HE WAS SWIMMING LENGTH AFTER LENGTH, AND DIVING FROM THE HIGH BOARD. HE HAD GROWN SO FAST.
IN SEPTEMBER HE HAD RETURNED TO SCHOOL. THE BOYS WHO HAD MADE HIM MISERABLE TRIED AGAIN AND WERE TAUGHT BETTER MANNERS.
HE LIKED BEING BIG AND STRONG. NOBODY EXPECTED HIM TO BE ABLE TO DO ANYTHING MORE THAN MOVE A SOFA INTO THE NEXT ROOM ON HIS OWN.
NOBODY UNTIL LAURA, ANYWAY.

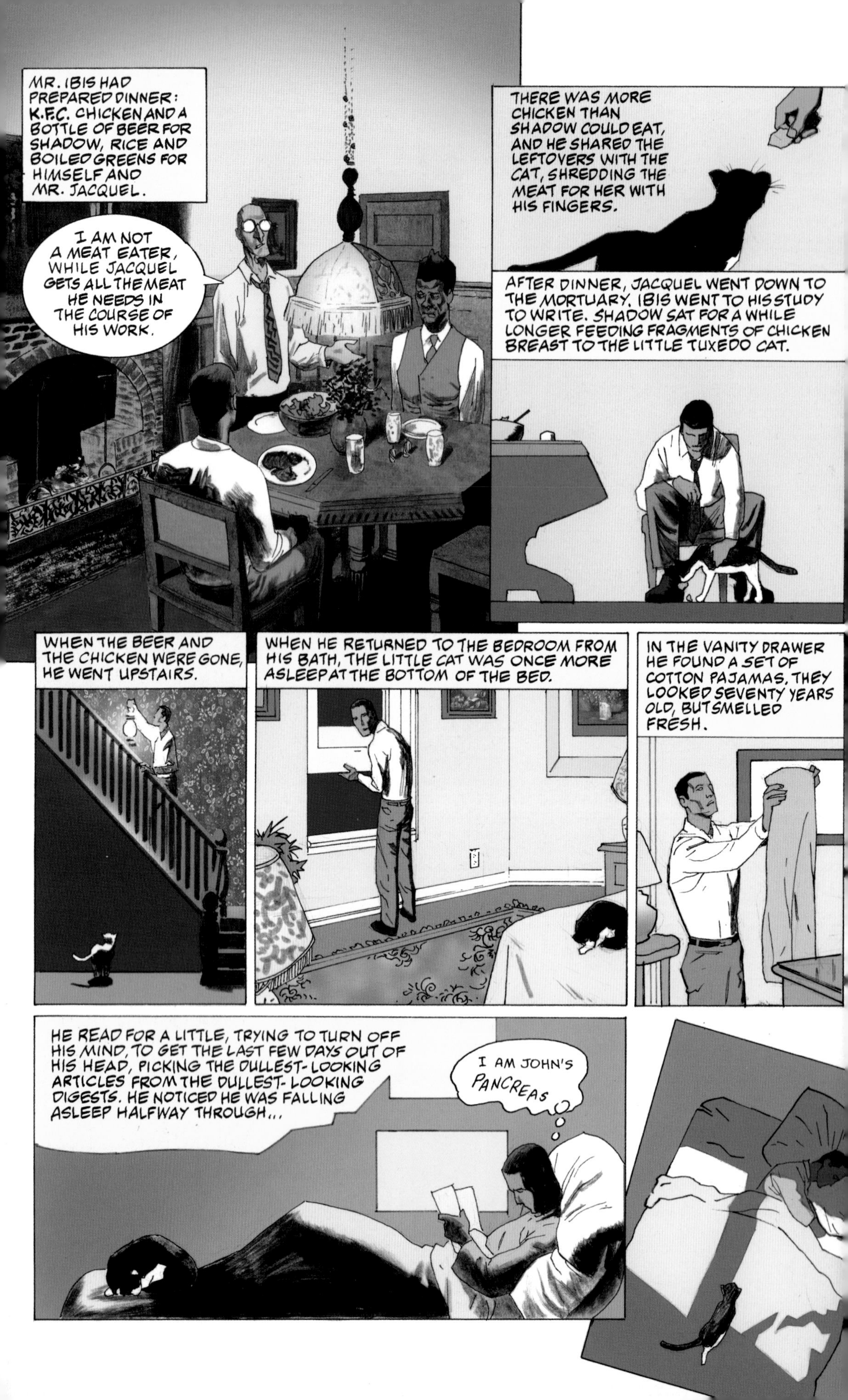
MR. IBIS HAD PREPARED DINNER: K.F.C. CHICKEN AND A BOTTLE OF BEER FOR SHADOW, RICE AND BOILED GREENS FOR HIMSELF AND MR. JACQUEL.
I AM NOT A MEAT EATER, WHILE JACQUEL GETS ALL THE MEAT HE NEEDS IN THE COURSE OF HIS WORK.
THERE WAS MORE CHICKEN THAN SHADOW COULD EAT, AND HE SHARED THE LEFTOVERS WITH THE CAT, SHREDDING THE MEAT FOR HER WITH HIS FINGERS.
AFTER DINNER, JACQUEL WENT DOWN TO THE MORTUARY. IBIS WENT TO HIS STUDY TO WRITE. SHADOW SAT FOR A WHILE LONGER FEEDING FRAGMENTS OF CHICKEN BREAST TO THE LITTLE TUXEDO CAT.
WHEN THE BEER AND THE CHICKEN WERE GONE, HE WENT UPSTAIRS.
WHEN HE RETURNED TO THE BEDROOM FROM HIS BATH, THE LITTLE CAT WAS ONCE MORE ASLEEP AT THE BOTTOM OF THE BED.
IN THE VANITY DRAWER HE FOUND A SET OF COTTON PAJAMAS. THEY LOOKED SEVENTY YEARS OLD, BUT SMELLED FRESH.
HE READ FOR A LITTLE, TRYING TO TURN OFF HIS MIND, TO GET THE LAST FEW DAYS OUT OF HIS HEAD, PICKING THE DULLEST-LOOKING ARTICLES FROM THE DULLEST-LOOKING DIGESTS. HE NOTICED HE WAS FALLING ASLEEP HALFWAY THROUGH...
I AM JOHN'S PANCREAS

LATER, HE WAS NEVER ABLE TO
RECOLLECT THE SEQUENCES
AND DETAILS OF THAT DREAM.

THERE WAS A GIRL.

AND A BRIDGE.

DOWN
THERE.

SHADOW
WENT
TO HIS
KNEES.

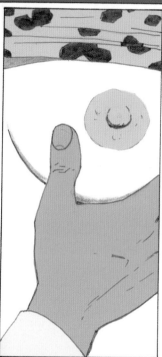

THE WOMAN
PURRED AGAINST
HIM ECSTATICALLY.
HER HAND
MOVING DOWN TO
THE HARDNESS
OF HIM. HE
PUSHED THE BED
SHEETS AWAY, AND
ROLLED ON TOP OF
HER, WHERE
ONE THRUST, ONE
MAGICAL PUSH...

NOW HE WAS BACK IN HIS OLD PRISON CELL,
AND HE WAS KISSING HER DEEPLY, HER
LIPS WERE SO SOFT. HER TONGUE, THOUGH,
WAS SANDPAPER-ROUGH.

SHE MADE NO ANSWER, JUST PUSHED HIM
ONTO HIS BACK AND BEGAN TO RIDE HIM.
HER NAILS WERE NEEDLE-SHARP, BUT HE
FELT NO PAIN, ONLY UTTER PLEASURE.

WHO
ARE
YOU?

WHO
ARE
YOU?

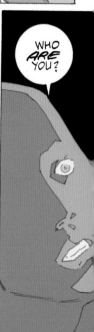

WHO
ARE
YOU?

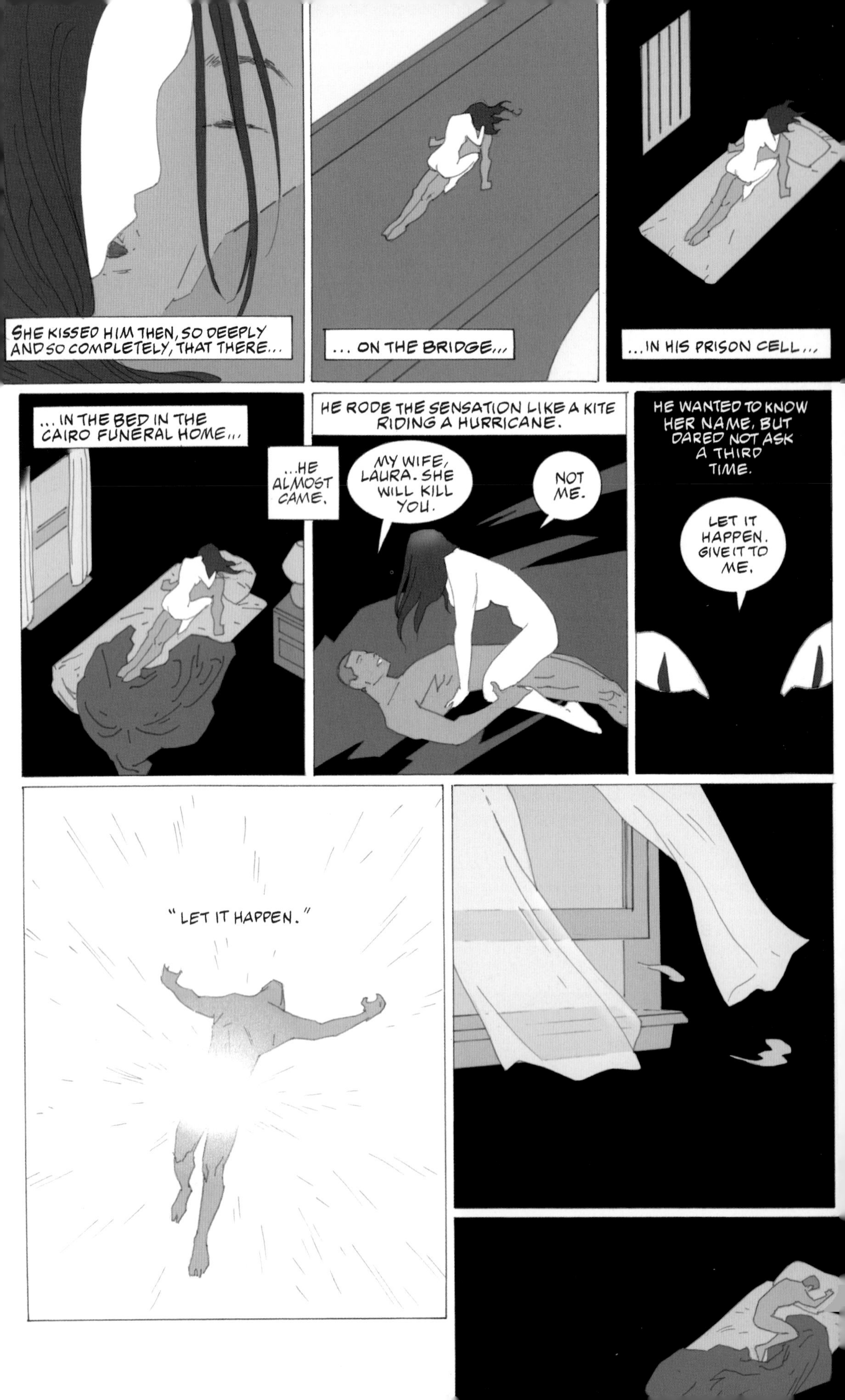
SHE KISSED HIM THEN, SO DEEPLY AND SO COMPLETELY, THAT THERE...
... ON THE BRIDGE...
...IN HIS PRISON CELL...
... IN THE BED IN THE CAIRO FUNERAL HOME...
...HE ALMOST CAME.
HE RODE THE SENSATION LIKE A KITE RIDING A HURRICANE.
MY WIFE, LAURA. SHE WILL KILL YOU.
NOT ME.
HE WANTED TO KNOW HER NAME, BUT DARED NOT ASK A THIRD TIME.
LET IT HAPPEN. GIVE IT TO ME.
"LET IT HAPPEN."

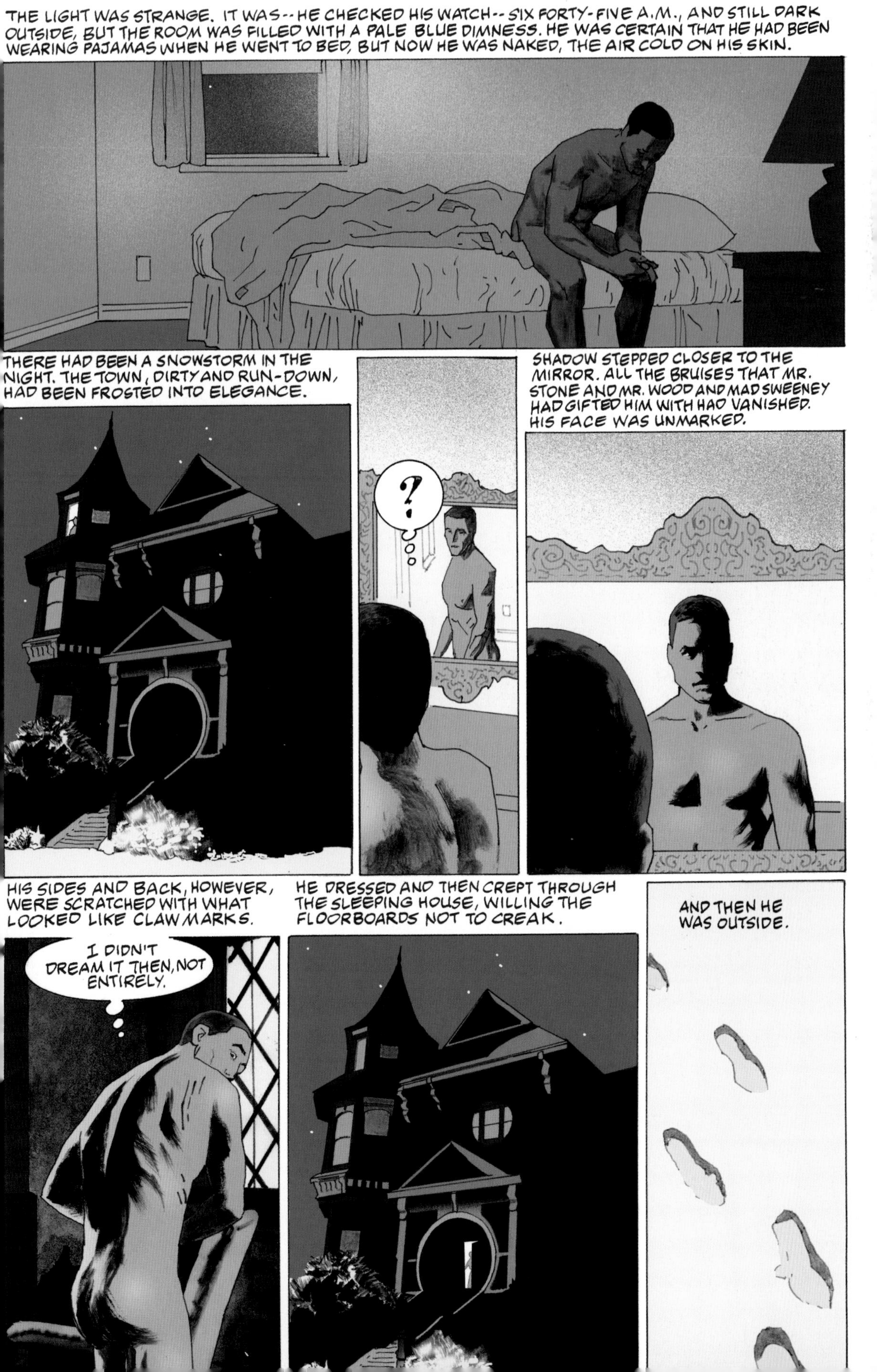
THE LIGHT WAS STRANGE. IT WAS -- HE CHECKED HIS WATCH -- SIX FORTY-FIVE A.M., AND STILL DARK OUTSIDE, BUT THE ROOM WAS FILLED WITH A PALE BLUE DIMNESS. HE WAS CERTAIN THAT HE HAD BEEN WEARING PAJAMAS WHEN HE WENT TO BED, BUT NOW HE WAS NAKED, THE AIR COLD ON HIS SKIN.
THERE HAD BEEN A SNOWSTORM IN THE NIGHT. THE TOWN, DIRTY AND RUN-DOWN, HAD BEEN FROSTED INTO ELEGANCE.
?
SHADOW STEPPED CLOSER TO THE MIRROR. ALL THE BRUISES THAT MR. STONE AND MR. WOOD AND MAD SWEENEY HAD GIFTED HIM WITH HAD VANISHED. HIS FACE WAS UNMARKED.
HIS SIDES AND BACK, HOWEVER, WERE SCRATCHED WITH WHAT LOOKED LIKE CLAW MARKS.
I DIDN'T DREAM IT THEN, NOT ENTIRELY.
HE DRESSED AND THEN CREPT THROUGH THE SLEEPING HOUSE, WILLING THE FLOORBOARDS NOT TO CREAK.
AND THEN HE WAS OUTSIDE.

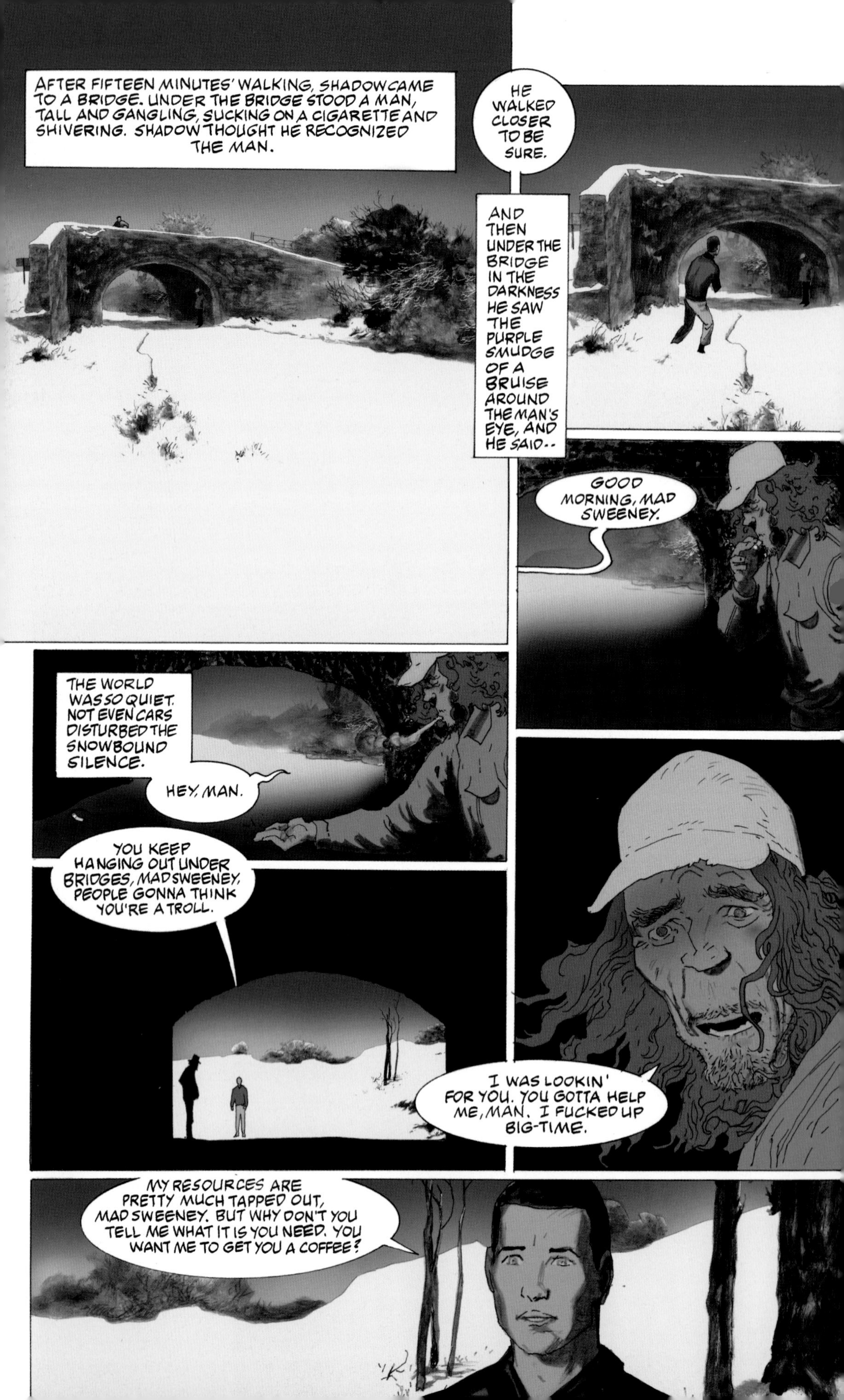
AFTER FIFTEEN MINUTES' WALKING, SHADOW CAME TO A BRIDGE. UNDER THE BRIDGE STOOD A MAN, TALL AND GANGLING, SUCKING ON A CIGARETTE AND SHIVERING. SHADOW THOUGHT HE RECOGNIZED THE MAN.
HE WALKED CLOSER TO BE SURE.
AND THEN UNDER THE BRIDGE IN THE DARKNESS HE SAW THE PURPLE SMUDGE OF A BRUISE AROUND THE MAN'S EYE, AND HE SAID..
GOOD MORNING, MAD SWEENEY.
THE WORLD WAS SO QUIET. NOT EVEN CARS DISTURBED THE SNOWBOUND SILENCE.
HEY, MAN.
YOU KEEP HANGING OUT UNDER BRIDGES, MAD SWEENEY. PEOPLE GONNA THINK YOU'RE A TROLL.
I WAS LOOKIN' FOR YOU. YOU GOTTA HELP ME, MAN. I FUCKED UP BIG-TIME.
MY RESOURCES ARE PRETTY MUCH TAPPED OUT, MAD SWEENEY. BUT WHY DON'T YOU TELL ME WHAT IT IS YOU NEED. YOU WANT ME TO GET YOU A COFFEE?

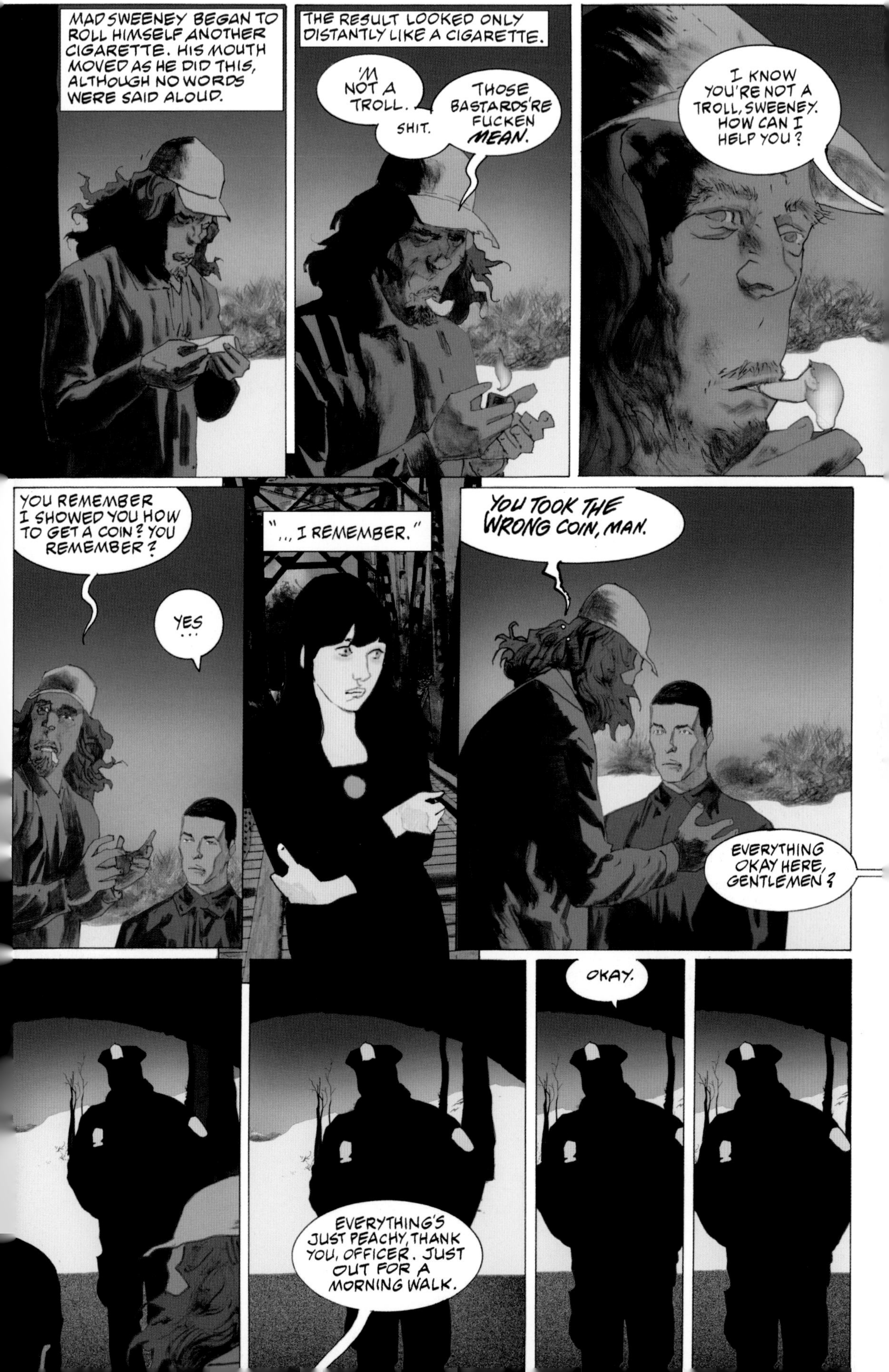
MAD SWEENEY BEGAN TO ROLL HIMSELF ANOTHER CIGARETTE. HIS MOUTH MOVED AS HE DID THIS, ALTHOUGH NO WORDS WERE SAID ALOUD.
THE RESULT LOOKED ONLY DISTANTLY LIKE A CIGARETTE.
'M NOT A TROLL.
SHIT.
THOSE BASTARDS'RE FUCKEN MEAN.
I KNOW YOU'RE NOT A TROLL, SWEENEY. HOW CAN I HELP YOU?
YOU REMEMBER I SHOWED YOU HOW TO GET A COIN? YOU REMEMBER?
YES...
"... I REMEMBER."
YOU TOOK THE WRONG COIN, MAN.
EVERYTHING OKAY HERE, GENTLEMEN?
EVERYTHING'S JUST PEACHY, THANK YOU, OFFICER. JUST OUT FOR A MORNING WALK.
OKAY.

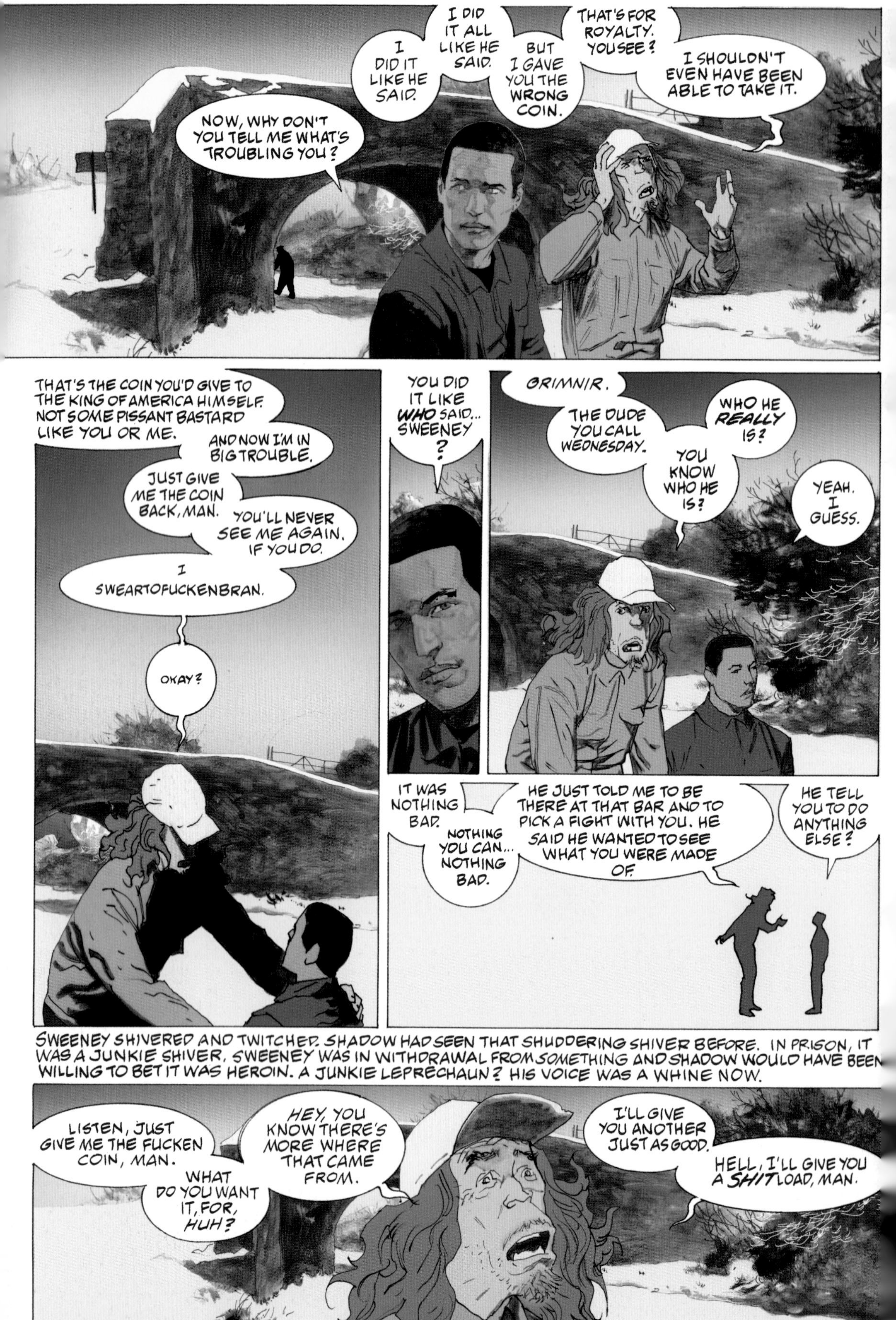
NOW, WHY DON'T YOU TELL ME WHAT'S TROUBLING YOU?
I DID IT LIKE HE SAID.
I DID IT ALL LIKE HE SAID.
BUT I GAVE YOU THE WRONG COIN.
THAT'S FOR ROYALTY. YOU SEE?
I SHOULDN'T EVEN HAVE BEEN ABLE TO TAKE IT.
THAT'S THE COIN YOU'D GIVE TO THE KING OF AMERICA HIMSELF. NOT SOME PISSANT BASTARD LIKE YOU OR ME.
AND NOW I'M IN BIG TROUBLE.
JUST GIVE ME THE COIN BACK, MAN.
YOU'LL NEVER SEE ME AGAIN, IF YOU DO.
I SWEARTOFUCKENBRAN.
OKAY?
YOU DID IT LIKE *WHO* SAID... SWEENEY?
GRIMNIR.
THE DUDE YOU CALL WEDNESDAY.
WHO HE *REALLY* IS?
YOU KNOW WHO HE IS?
YEAH. I GUESS.
IT WAS NOTHING BAD.
NOTHING YOU CAN... NOTHING BAD.
HE JUST TOLD ME TO BE THERE AT THAT BAR AND TO PICK A FIGHT WITH YOU. HE SAID HE WANTED TO SEE WHAT YOU WERE MADE OF.
HE TELL YOU TO DO ANYTHING ELSE?
SWEENEY SHIVERED AND TWITCHED. SHADOW HAD SEEN THAT SHUDDERING SHIVER BEFORE. IN PRISON, IT WAS A JUNKIE SHIVER. SWEENEY WAS IN WITHDRAWAL FROM *SOMETHING* AND SHADOW WOULD HAVE BEEN WILLING TO BET IT WAS HEROIN. A JUNKIE LEPRECHAUN? HIS VOICE WAS A WHINE NOW.
LISTEN, JUST GIVE ME THE FUCKEN COIN, MAN.
WHAT DO YOU WANT IT, FOR, *HUH*?
HEY, YOU KNOW THERE'S MORE WHERE THAT CAME FROM.
I'LL GIVE YOU ANOTHER JUST AS GOOD.
HELL, I'LL GIVE YOU A *SHIT* LOAD, MAN.

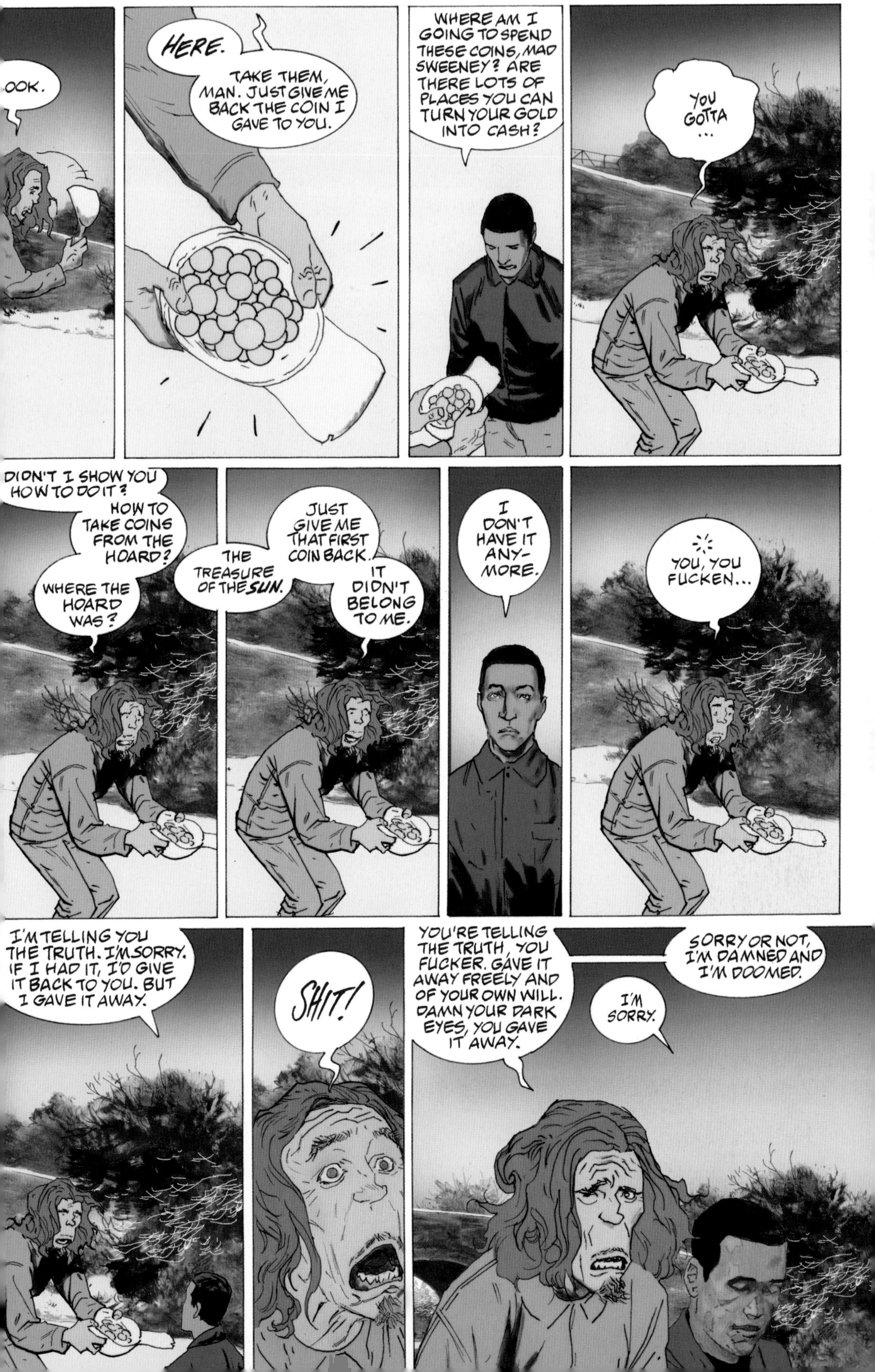
OOK.
HERE.
TAKE THEM, MAN. JUST GIVE ME BACK THE COIN I GAVE TO YOU.
WHERE AM I GOING TO SPEND THESE COINS, MAD SWEENEY? ARE THERE LOTS OF PLACES YOU CAN TURN YOUR GOLD INTO CASH?
YOU GOTTA ...
DIDN'T I SHOW YOU HOW TO DO IT?
HOW TO TAKE COINS FROM THE HOARD?
WHERE THE HOARD WAS?
THE TREASURE OF THE SUN.
JUST GIVE ME THAT FIRST COIN BACK.
IT DIDN'T BELONG TO ME.
I DON'T HAVE IT ANY-MORE.
YOU, YOU FUCKEN...
I'M TELLING YOU THE TRUTH. I'M SORRY. IF I HAD IT, I'D GIVE IT BACK TO YOU. BUT I GAVE IT AWAY.
SHIT!
YOU'RE TELLING THE TRUTH, YOU FUCKER. GAVE IT AWAY FREELY AND OF YOUR OWN WILL. DAMN YOUR DARK EYES, YOU GAVE IT AWAY.
SORRY OR NOT, I'M DAMNED AND I'M DOOMED.
I'M SORRY.

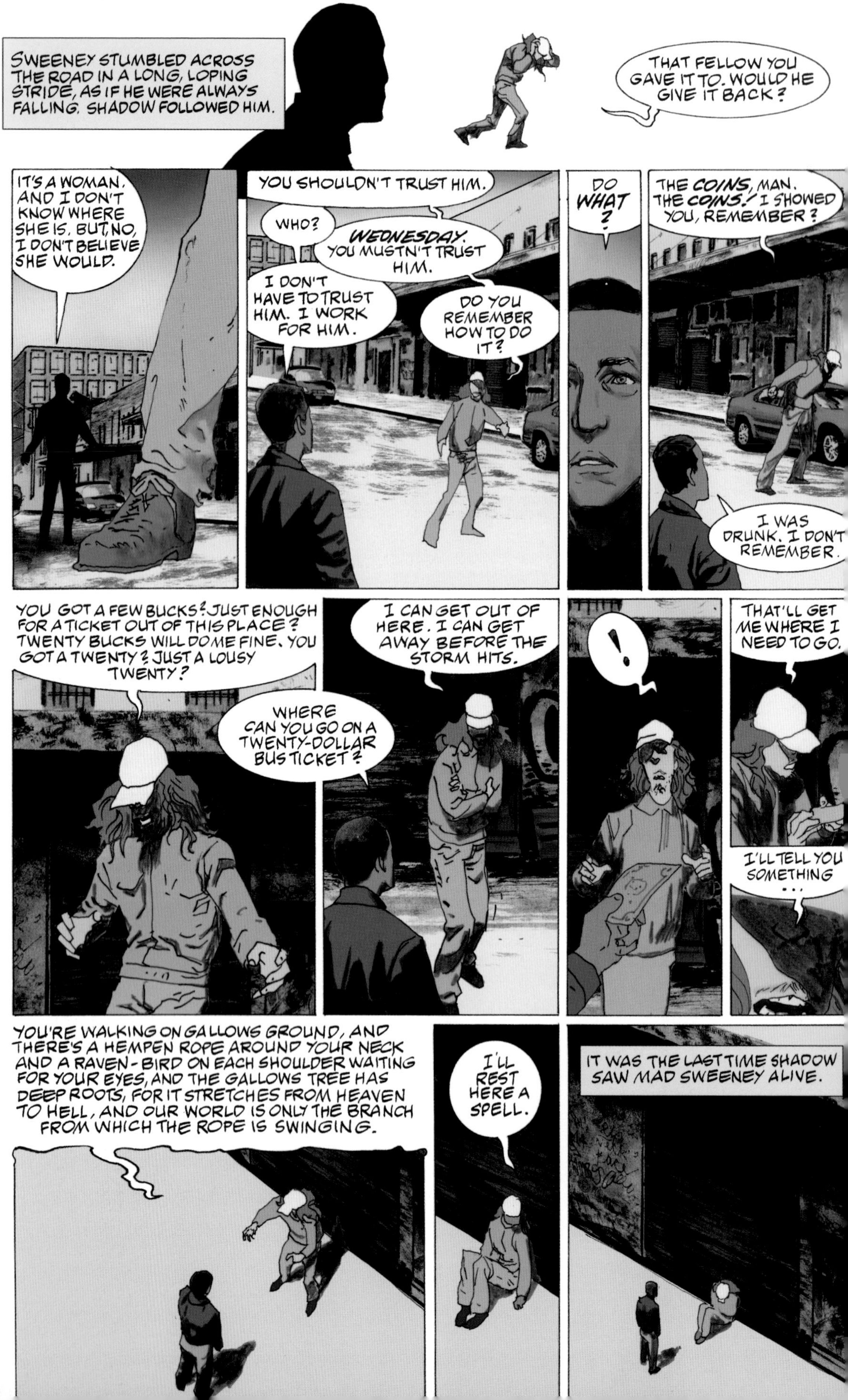

SWEENEY STUMBLED ACROSS THE ROAD IN A LONG, LOPING STRIDE, AS IF HE WERE ALWAYS FALLING. SHADOW FOLLOWED HIM.
THAT FELLOW YOU GAVE IT TO. WOULD HE GIVE IT BACK?
IT'S A WOMAN. AND I DON'T KNOW WHERE SHE IS. BUT, NO, I DON'T BELIEVE SHE WOULD.
YOU SHOULDN'T TRUST HIM.
WHO?
WEDNESDAY. YOU MUSTN'T TRUST HIM.
I DON'T HAVE TO TRUST HIM. I WORK FOR HIM.
DO YOU REMEMBER HOW TO DO IT?
DO WHAT?
THE COINS, MAN. THE COINS! I SHOWED YOU, REMEMBER?
I WAS DRUNK. I DON'T REMEMBER.
YOU GOT A FEW BUCKS? JUST ENOUGH FOR A TICKET OUT OF THIS PLACE? TWENTY BUCKS WILL DO ME FINE. YOU GOT A TWENTY? JUST A LOUSY TWENTY?
WHERE CAN YOU GO ON A TWENTY-DOLLAR BUS TICKET?
I CAN GET OUT OF HERE. I CAN GET AWAY BEFORE THE STORM HITS.
!
THAT'LL GET ME WHERE I NEED TO GO.
I'LL TELL YOU SOMETHING...
YOU'RE WALKING ON GALLOWS GROUND, AND THERE'S A HEMPEN ROPE AROUND YOUR NECK AND A RAVEN-BIRD ON EACH SHOULDER WAITING FOR YOUR EYES, AND THE GALLOWS TREE HAS DEEP ROOTS, FOR IT STRETCHES FROM HEAVEN TO HELL, AND OUR WORLD IS ONLY THE BRANCH FROM WHICH THE ROPE IS SWINGING.
I'LL REST HERE A SPELL.
IT WAS THE LAST TIME SHADOW SAW MAD SWEENEY ALIVE.

THE BRIEF WINTER DAYS LEADING UP TO CHRISTMAS FLED FAST IN THE HOUSE OF THE DEAD.

IT WAS THE TWENTY-THIRD OF DECEMBER, AND JACQUEL AND IBIS'S PLAYED HOST TO A WAKE FOR LILA GOODCHILD.

BUSTLING WOMEN FILLED THE TABLE ON THE OTHER SIDE OF THE ROOM WITH COLESLAW AND CORNMEAL, HUSH PUPPIES AND CHICKEN AND RIBS AND BLACK-EYED PEAS.

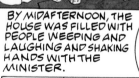

BY MIDAFTERNOON, THE HOUSE WAS FILLED WITH PEOPLE WEEPING AND LAUGHING AND SHAKING HANDS WITH THE MINISTER.

THAT WAS THE POLICE. CAN YOU MAKE A PICKUP?

SURE.

BE DISCREET. DRIVE SLOWLY. HERE'S THE ADDRESS. THERE WILL BE A POLICE CAR WAITING.

SHADOW DROVE CAREFULLY DOWN THE STREET. IT SEEMED RIGHT TO GO SLOW IN A HEARSE, ALTHOUGH HE COULD BARELY REMEMBER THE LAST TIME HE HAD SEEN A HEARSE ON THE STREET. DEATH HAD VANISHED FROM THE STREETS OF AMERICA, THOUGHT SHADOW. NOW IT HAPPENED IN HOSPITAL ROOMS AND IN AMBULANCES.

WE MUST NOT STARTLE THE LIVING.

SHADOW PARKED THE HEARSE BEHIND THE POLICE CRUISER.

YEAH?

I'M FROM THE FUNERAL HOME.

WE'RE WAITING FOR THE MEDICAL EXAMINER.

BACK THIS WAY.

DEAD WINO.

LOOKS LIKE IT.

DON'T TOUCH ANYTHING YET. MEDICAL EXAMINER SHOULD BE HERE ANYTIME NOW.

YOU ASK ME, THE GUY DRANK HIMSELF INTO A STUPOR AND FROZE HIS ASS.

YES. THAT'S CERTAINLY WHAT IT *LOOKS* LIKE.

A TWENTY-DOLLAR TICKET OUT OF THIS PLACE.

HE'S BACK HERE.

THE MEDICAL EXAMINER TOUCHED THE CORPSE'S NECK.

HE'S DEAD. ANY *I.D.*?

HE'S A JOHN DOE.

YOU WORKING FOR JACQUEL AND IBIS?

YES...

TELL JACQUEL TO GET DENTALS AND PRINTS FOR I.D. AND IDENTITY PHOTOS. HE SHOULD JUST DRAW BLOOD FOR TOXICOLOGY. GOT THAT? DO YOU WANT ME TO WRITE IT DOWN FOR YOU?

NO, IT'S FINE. I CAN REMEMBER.

THE MAN SCOWLED FLEETINGLY. THEN SCRIBBLED ON A BUSINESS CARD.

GIVE THIS TO JACQUEL.

MERRY CHRIST-MAS.

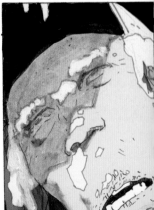

SHADOW SIGNED FOR THE JOHN DOE. THE BODY WAS PRETTY STIFF, SO HE STRAPPED IT, SITTING, TO THE GURNEY, AND PUT HIM IN THE BACK OF THE HEARSE, FACING FORWARD.

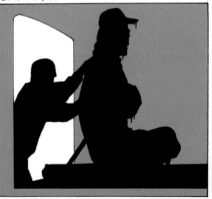

MIGHT AS WELL GIVE HIM A GOOD RIDE.

AND IT'S A FINE WAKE I'LL BE WANTING, WITH THE BEST OF EVERYTHING, AND BEAUTIFUL WOMEN SHEDDING TEARS AND THEIR CLOTHES IN THEIR DISTRESS, AND BRAVE MEN LAMENTING AND TELLING FINE TALES OF ME IN MY GREAT DAYS.

YOU'RE DEAD, MAD SWEENEY. YOU TAKE WHAT YOU'RE GIVEN WHEN YOU'RE DEAD.

AYE, THAT I SHALL.

THE JUNKIE WHINE HAD VANISHED FROM HIS VOICE NOW, REPLACED WITH A RESIGNED FLATNESS, DEAD WORDS BEING SENT OUT ON A DEAD FREQUENCY.

BUT GIVE ME A STINKING DRUNK WAKE TONIGHT, NONETHELESS. YOU KILLED ME, SHADOW. YOU OWE ME THAT MUCH.

I NEVER KILLED YOU, MAD SWEENEY. IT WAS THE DRINK AND THE COLD KILLED YOU, NOT ME.

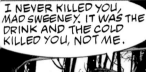

THERE WAS NO REPLY AND THERE WAS SILENCE IN THE CAR FOR THE REST OF THE JOURNEY.

AFTER HE PARKED AT THE BACK, SHADOW WHEELED THE GURNEY INTO THE MORTUARY. HE MANHANDLED MAD SWEENEY ONTO THE EMBALMING TABLE AS IF HE WERE HANDLING A SIDE OF BEEF.

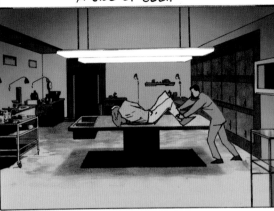

HE COVERED HIM WITH A SHEET AND LEFT HIM THERE, WITH THE PAPERWORK BESIDE HIM.

AND WHAT WOULD DRINK OR COLD BE DOING KILLING ME, A LEPRECHAUN OF THE BLOOD?

NO. IT WAS *YOU* LOSING THE LITTLE GOLDEN SUN KILLED ME, SHADOW, KILLED ME DEAD, AS SURE AS WATER'S WET AND DAYS ARE LONG AND A FRIEND WILL ALWAYS DISAPPOINT YOU IN THE END.

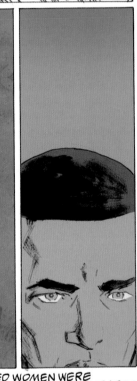

HE WENT UPSTAIRS TO THE MAIN HOUSE, WHERE A NUMBER OF MIDDLE-AGED WOMEN WERE PUTTING SARAN WRAP ON CASSEROLE DISHES AND MR. GOODCHILD, THE HUSBAND OF THE DECEASED, WAS TELLING MR. IBIS HOW HE KNEW NONE OF HIS CHILDREN WOULD COME OUT TO PAY THEIR RESPECTS TO THEIR MOTHER. HE WAS TELLING ANYONE WHO WOULD LISTEN...

THE APPLE DON'T FALL FAR FROM THE TREE.

THAT EVENING SHADOW LAID AN EXTRA PLACE AT THE TABLE. HE PUT A GLASS AT EACH PLACE, AND A NEW BOTTLE OF JAMESON GOLD IN THE MIDDLE OF THE TABLE.

AFTER THEY ATE (A LARGE PLATTER OF LEFTOVERS LEFT FOR THEM BY THE MIDDLE-AGED WOMEN), SHADOW POURED A GENEROUS TOT INTO EACH GLASS--

HIS, IBIS'S, JACQUEL'S...

...AND MAD SWEENEY'S.

SO WHAT IF HE'S SITTING ON A GURNEY IN THE CELLAR ON HIS WAY TO A PAUPER'S GRAVE? TONIGHT WE'LL TOAST HIM AND GIVE HIM THE WAKE HE WANTED.

I ONLY MET MAD SWEENEY TWICE, ALIVE. THE FIRST TIME, I THOUGHT HE WAS A WORLD-CLASS JERK, THE SECOND TIME, A MAJOR FUCKUP, AND I GAVE HIM THE MONEY TO KILL HIMSELF. HE SHOWED ME A COIN TRICK I DON'T REMEMBER HOW TO DO, GAVE ME SOME BRUISES, AND CLAIMED HE WAS A LEPRECHAUN. REST IN PEACE, MAD SWEENEY.

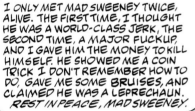

"MAD SWEENEY!"

MR. IBIS PULLED OUT A NOTEBOOK AND READ OUT A SUMMARIZED VERSION OF MAD SWEENEY'S LIFE.

MAD SWEENEY STARTED HIS LIFE AS THE GUARDIAN OF A SACRED ROCK IN A SMALL IRISH GLADE OVER THREE THOUSAND YEARS AGO.

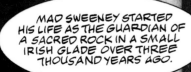

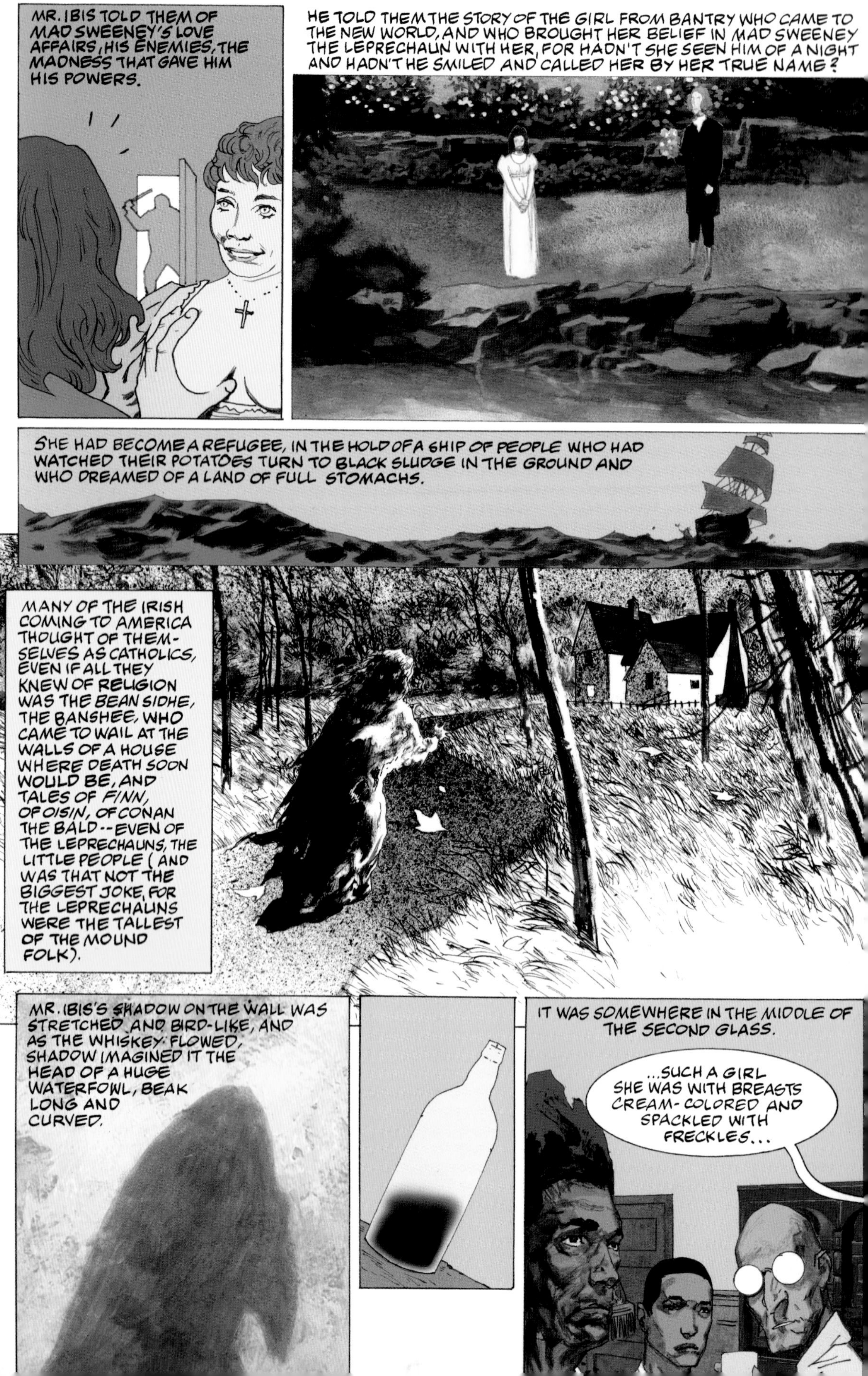
MR. IBIS TOLD THEM OF MAD SWEENEY'S LOVE AFFAIRS, HIS ENEMIES, THE MADNESS THAT GAVE HIM HIS POWERS.
HE TOLD THEM THE STORY OF THE GIRL FROM BANTRY WHO CAME TO THE NEW WORLD, AND WHO BROUGHT HER BELIEF IN MAD SWEENEY THE LEPRECHAUN WITH HER, FOR HADN'T SHE SEEN HIM OF A NIGHT AND HADN'T HE SMILED AND CALLED HER BY HER TRUE NAME?
SHE HAD BECOME A REFUGEE, IN THE HOLD OF A SHIP OF PEOPLE WHO HAD WATCHED THEIR POTATOES TURN TO BLACK SLUDGE IN THE GROUND AND WHO DREAMED OF A LAND OF FULL STOMACHS.
MANY OF THE IRISH COMING TO AMERICA THOUGHT OF THEMSELVES AS CATHOLICS, EVEN IF ALL THEY KNEW OF RELIGION WAS THE BEAN SIDHE, THE BANSHEE, WHO CAME TO WAIL AT THE WALLS OF A HOUSE WHERE DEATH SOON WOULD BE, AND TALES OF FINN, OF OISIN, OF CONAN THE BALD--EVEN OF THE LEPRECHAUNS, THE LITTLE PEOPLE (AND WAS THAT NOT THE BIGGEST JOKE, FOR THE LEPRECHAUNS WERE THE TALLEST OF THE MOUND FOLK).
MR. IBIS'S SHADOW ON THE WALL WAS STRETCHED AND BIRD-LIKE, AND AS THE WHISKEY FLOWED, SHADOW IMAGINED IT THE HEAD OF A HUGE WATERFOWL, BEAK LONG AND CURVED.
IT WAS SOMEWHERE IN THE MIDDLE OF THE SECOND GLASS.
...SUCH A GIRL SHE WAS WITH BREASTS CREAM-COLORED AND SPACKLED WITH FRECKLES...

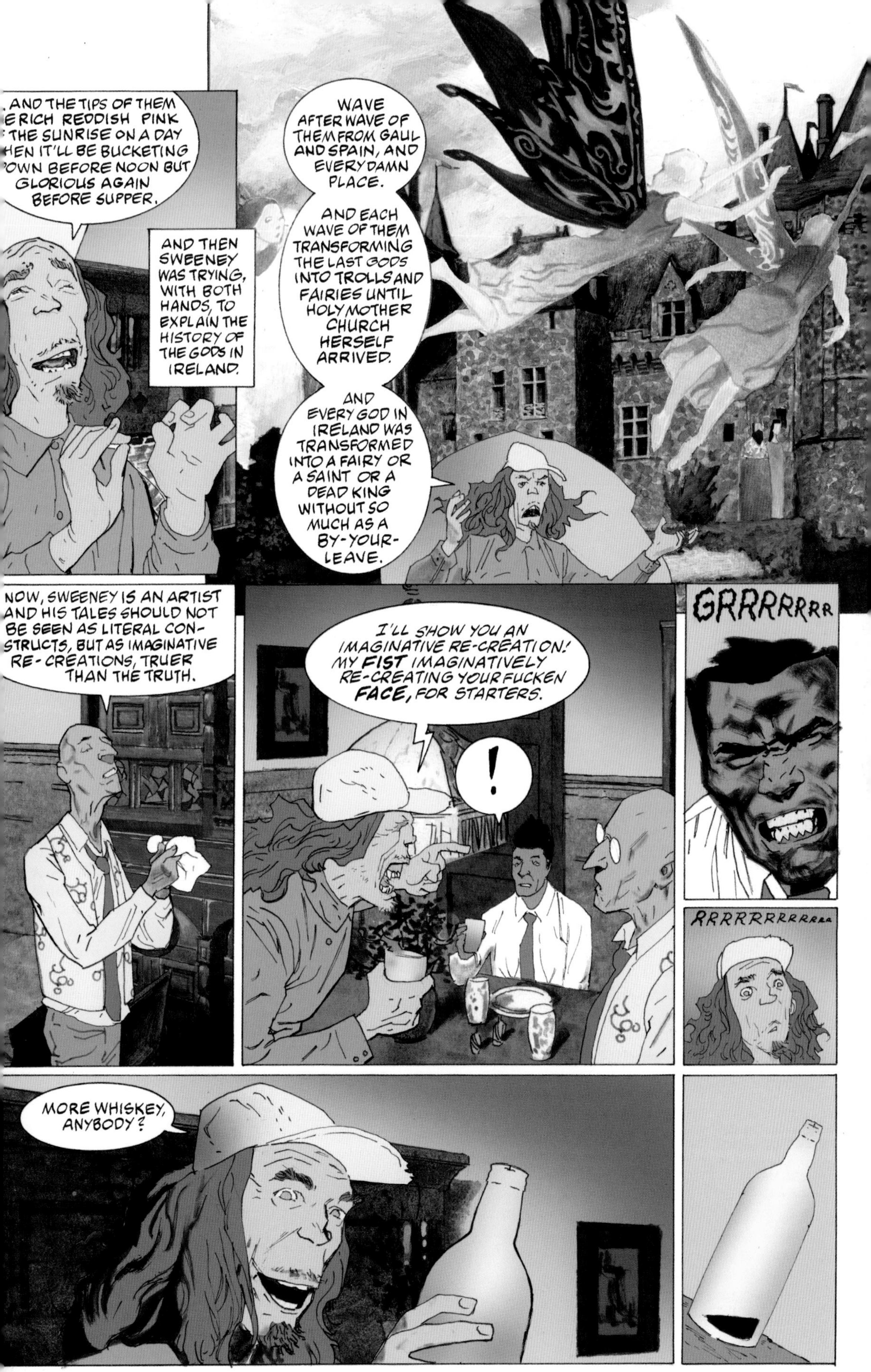

. AND THE TIPS OF THEM E RICH REDDISH PINK F THE SUNRISE ON A DAY HEN IT'LL BE BUCKETING OWN BEFORE NOON BUT GLORIOUS AGAIN BEFORE SUPPER.
AND THEN SWEENEY WAS TRYING, WITH BOTH HANDS, TO EXPLAIN THE HISTORY OF THE GODS IN IRELAND.
WAVE AFTER WAVE OF THEM FROM GAUL AND SPAIN, AND EVERY DAMN PLACE.
AND EACH WAVE OF THEM TRANSFORMING THE LAST GODS INTO TROLLS AND FAIRIES UNTIL HOLY MOTHER CHURCH HERSELF ARRIVED.
AND EVERY GOD IN IRELAND WAS TRANSFORMED INTO A FAIRY OR A SAINT OR A DEAD KING WITHOUT SO MUCH AS A BY-YOUR-LEAVE.
NOW, SWEENEY IS AN ARTIST AND HIS TALES SHOULD NOT BE SEEN AS LITERAL CONSTRUCTS, BUT AS IMAGINATIVE RE-CREATIONS, TRUER THAN THE TRUTH.
I'LL SHOW YOU AN IMAGINATIVE RE-CREATION! MY FIST IMAGINATIVELY RE-CREATING YOUR FUCKEN FACE, FOR STARTERS.
!
GRRRRRRR
RRRRRRRRRRRR
MORE WHISKEY, ANYBODY?

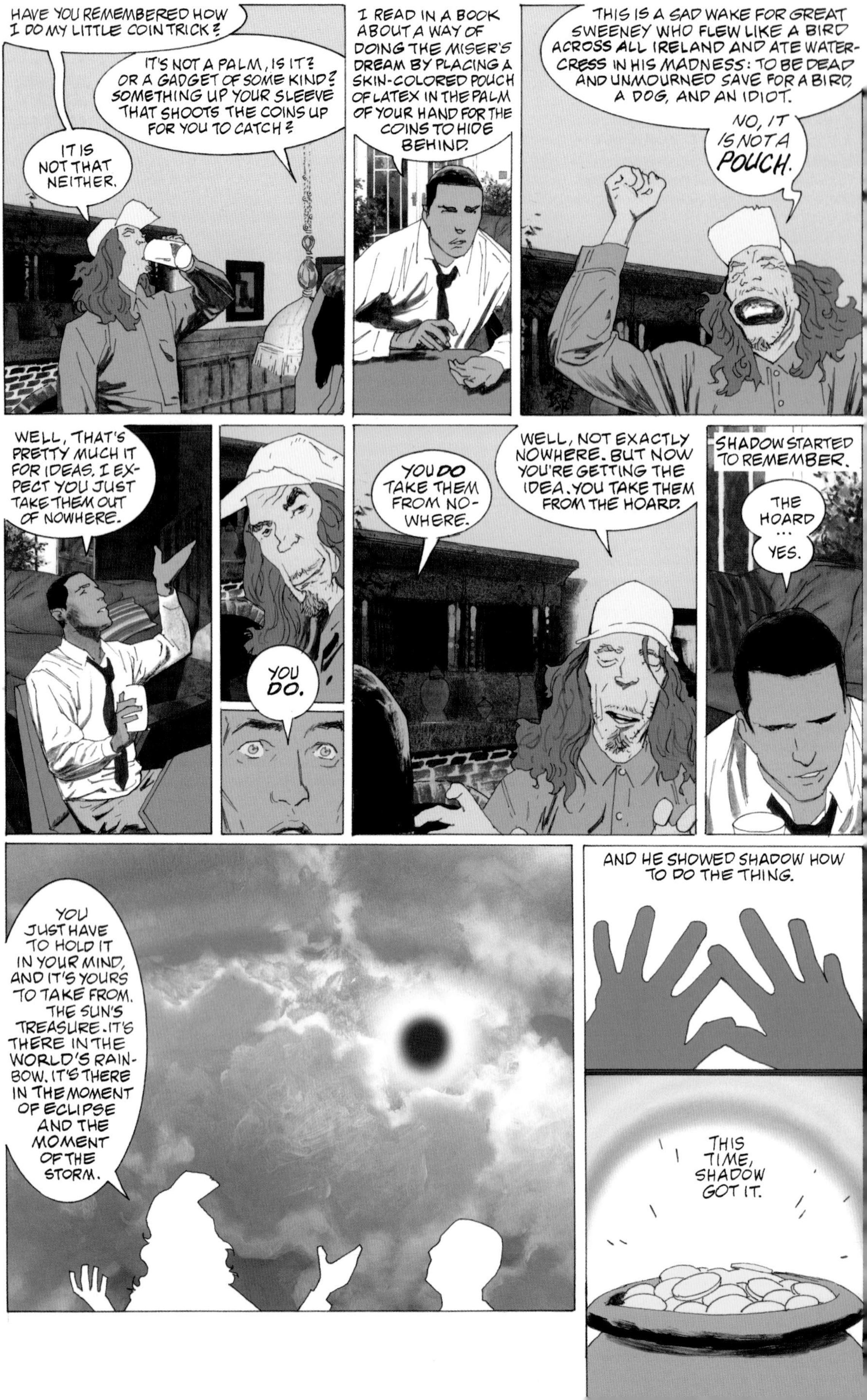
HAVE YOU REMEMBERED HOW I DO MY LITTLE COIN TRICK?
IT'S NOT A PALM, IS IT? OR A GADGET OF SOME KIND? SOMETHING UP YOUR SLEEVE THAT SHOOTS THE COINS UP FOR YOU TO CATCH?
IT IS NOT THAT NEITHER.
I READ IN A BOOK ABOUT A WAY OF DOING THE MISER'S DREAM BY PLACING A SKIN-COLORED POUCH OF LATEX IN THE PALM OF YOUR HAND FOR THE COINS TO HIDE BEHIND.
THIS IS A SAD WAKE FOR GREAT SWEENEY WHO FLEW LIKE A BIRD ACROSS ALL IRELAND AND ATE WATER-CRESS IN HIS MADNESS: TO BE DEAD AND UNMOURNED SAVE FOR A BIRD, A DOG, AND AN IDIOT.
NO, IT IS NOT A POUCH.
WELL, THAT'S PRETTY MUCH IT FOR IDEAS. I EXPECT YOU JUST TAKE THEM OUT OF NOWHERE.
YOU DO.
YOU DO TAKE THEM FROM NO-WHERE.
WELL, NOT EXACTLY NOWHERE. BUT NOW YOU'RE GETTING THE IDEA. YOU TAKE THEM FROM THE HOARD.
SHADOW STARTED TO REMEMBER.
THE HOARD...
YES.
YOU JUST HAVE TO HOLD IT IN YOUR MIND, AND IT'S YOURS TO TAKE FROM. THE SUN'S TREASURE. IT'S THERE IN THE WORLD'S RAIN-BOW. IT'S THERE IN THE MOMENT OF ECLIPSE AND THE MOMENT OF THE STORM.
AND HE SHOWED SHADOW HOW TO DO THE THING.
THIS TIME, SHADOW GOT IT.

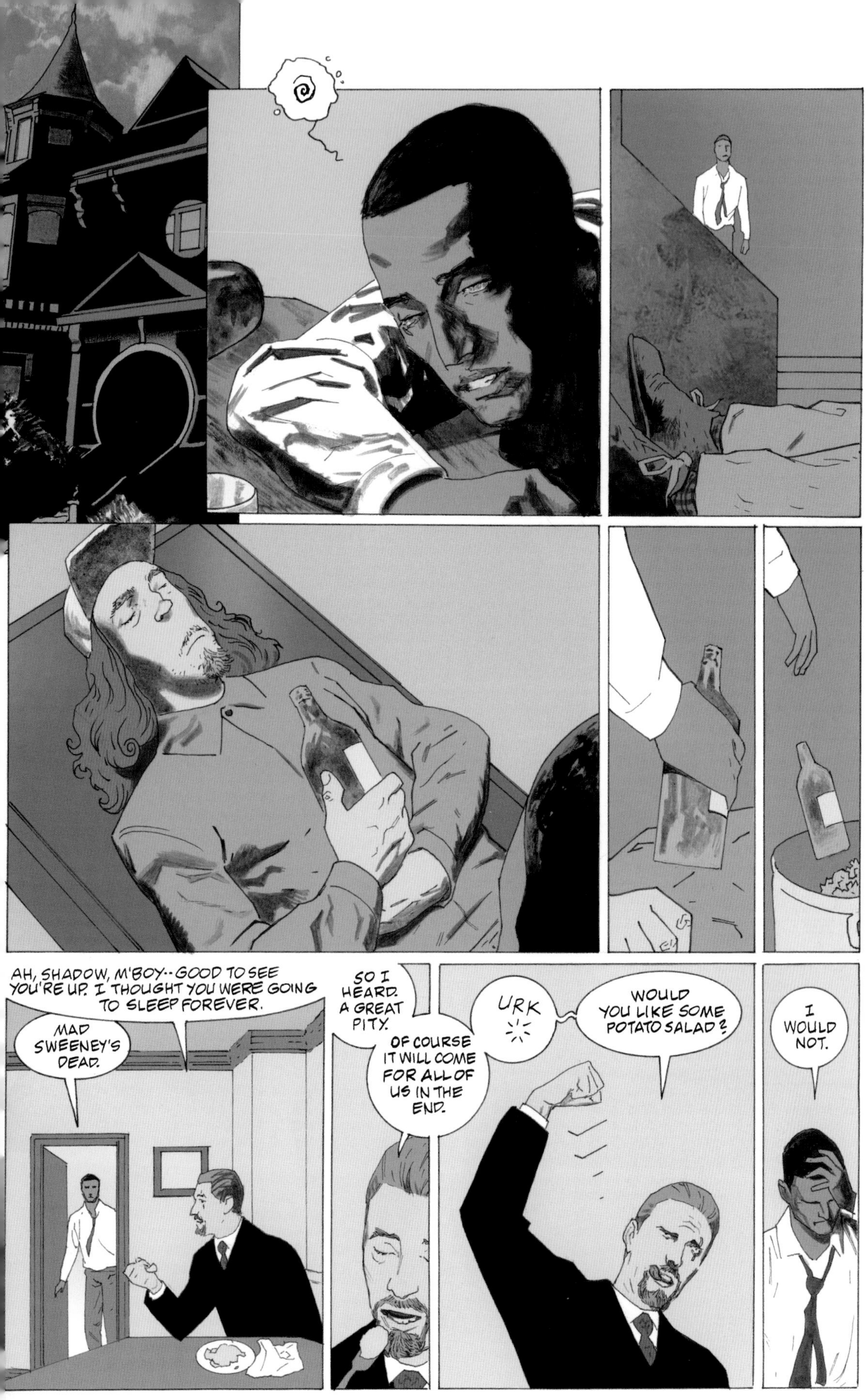
MAD SWEENEY'S DEAD.
AH, SHADOW, M'BOY.. GOOD TO SEE YOU'RE UP. I THOUGHT YOU WERE GOING TO SLEEP FOREVER.
SO I HEARD. A GREAT PITY.
OF COURSE IT WILL COME FOR ALL OF US IN THE END.
URK
WOULD YOU LIKE SOME POTATO SALAD?
I WOULD NOT.

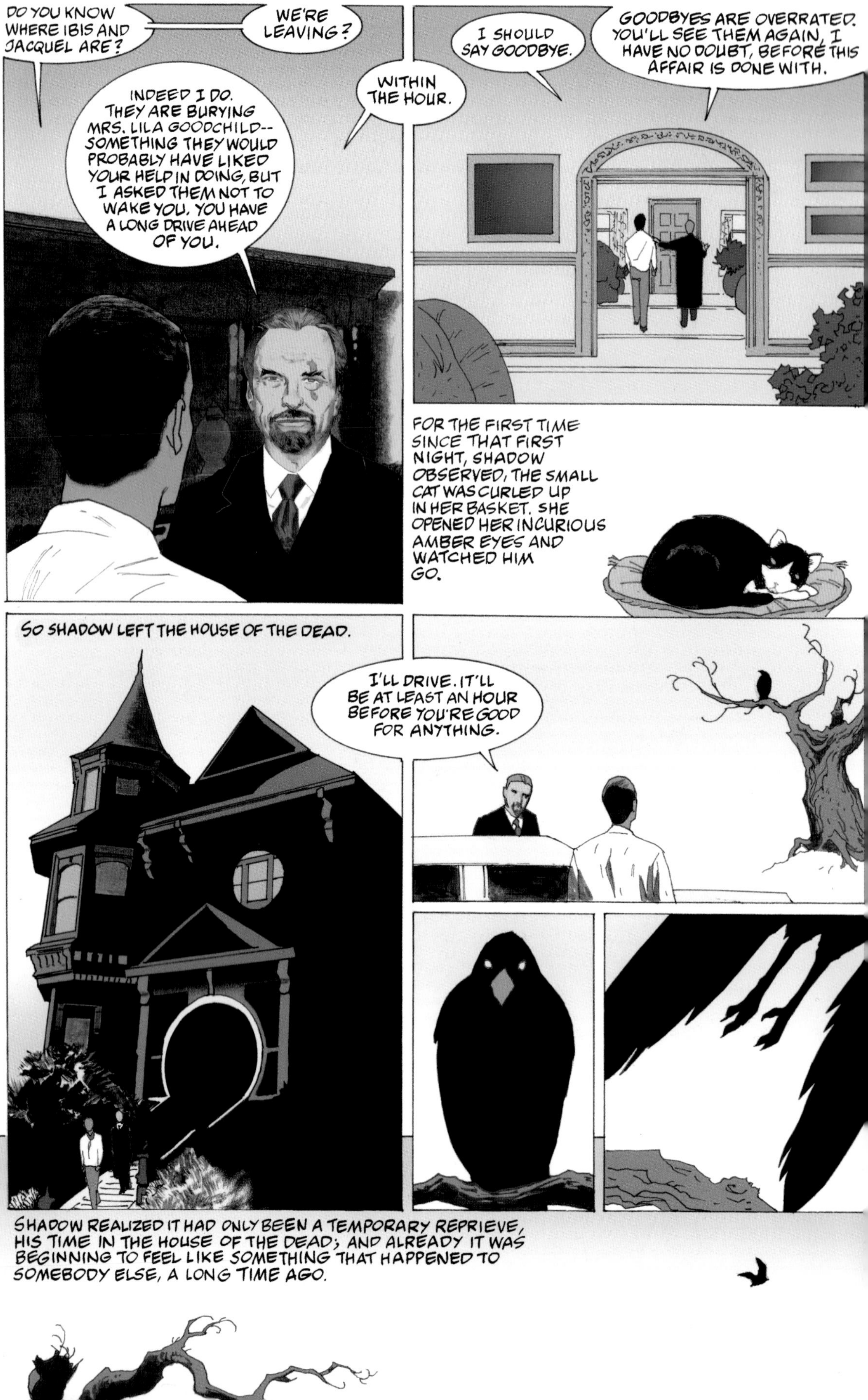
DO YOU KNOW WHERE IBIS AND JACQUEL ARE?
WE'RE LEAVING?
INDEED I DO. THEY ARE BURYING MRS. LILA GOODCHILD-- SOMETHING THEY WOULD PROBABLY HAVE LIKED YOUR HELP IN DOING, BUT I ASKED THEM NOT TO WAKE YOU. YOU HAVE A LONG DRIVE AHEAD OF YOU.
WITHIN THE HOUR.
I SHOULD SAY GOODBYE.
GOODBYES ARE OVERRATED. YOU'LL SEE THEM AGAIN, I HAVE NO DOUBT, BEFORE THIS AFFAIR IS DONE WITH.
FOR THE FIRST TIME SINCE THAT FIRST NIGHT, SHADOW OBSERVED, THE SMALL CAT WAS CURLED UP IN HER BASKET. SHE OPENED HER INCURIOUS AMBER EYES AND WATCHED HIM GO.
SO SHADOW LEFT THE HOUSE OF THE DEAD.
I'LL DRIVE. IT'LL BE AT LEAST AN HOUR BEFORE YOU'RE GOOD FOR ANYTHING.
SHADOW REALIZED IT HAD ONLY BEEN A TEMPORARY REPRIEVE, HIS TIME IN THE HOUSE OF THE DEAD; AND ALREADY IT WAS BEGINNING TO FEEL LIKE SOMETHING THAT HAPPENED TO SOMEBODY ELSE, A LONG TIME AGO.

AMERICAN GODS
SKETCHBOOK
NOTES BY **DANIEL CHABON**

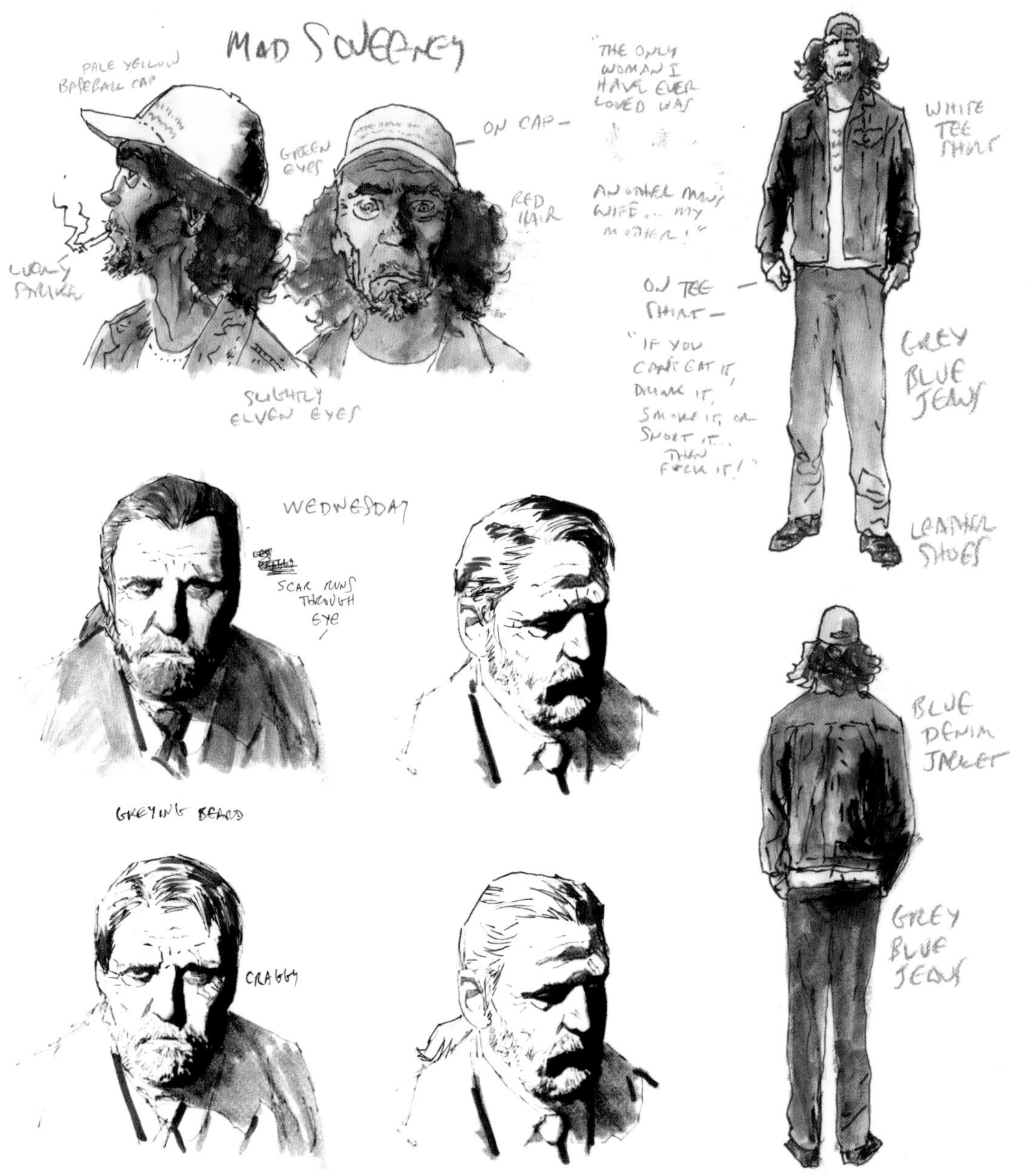
MAD SWEENEY
PALE YELLOW BASEBALL CAP
LUCKY STRIKE
GREEN EYES
ON CAP—
RED HAIR
SLIGHTLY ELVEN EYES
"THE ONLY WOMAN I HAVE EVER LOVED WAS
ANOTHER MAN'S WIFE... MY MOTHER!"
ON TEE SHIRT—
"IF YOU CAN'T EAT IT, DRINK IT, SMOKE IT, OR SNORT IT... THEN FUCK IT!"
WHITE TEE SHIRT
GREY BLUE JEANS
LEATHER SHOES
WEDNESDAY
SCAR RUNS THROUGH EYE
GREYING BEARD
CRAGGY
BLUE DENIM JACKET
GREY BLUE JEANS

Designs by artist Scott Hampton for the characters Mr. Wednesday and Mad Sweeney. We tried to keep the characters on model as much as possible to how Neil described them in the original novel.

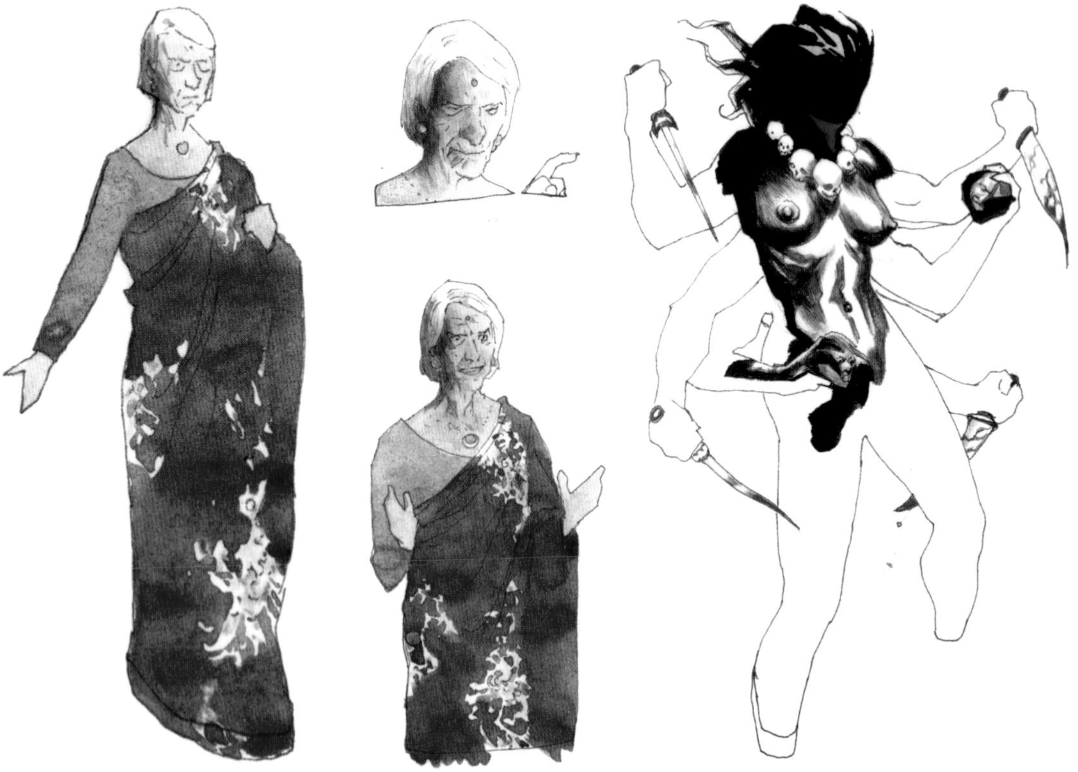

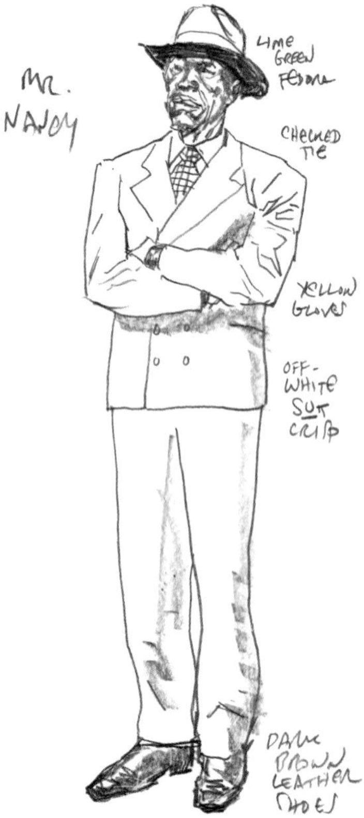
MR.
NANCY
LIME
GREEN
FEDORA
CHECKED
TIE
YELLOW
GLOVES
OFF-
WHITE
SUIT
CRISP
DARK
BROWN
LEATHER
SHOES

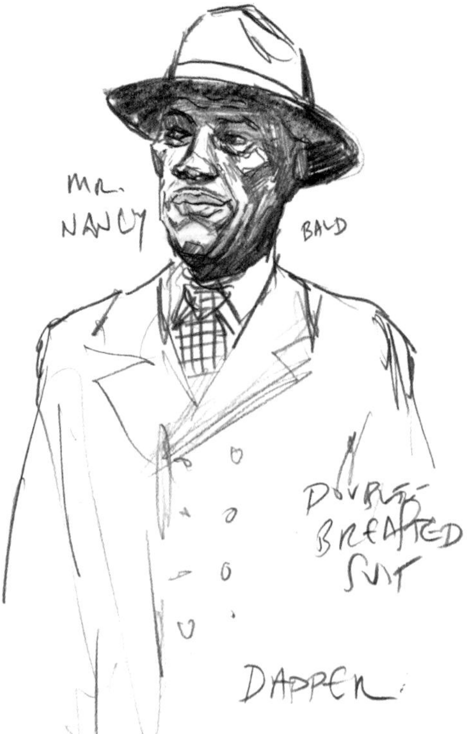
MR.
NANCY
BALD
DOUBLE-
BREASTED
SUIT
DAPPER.

Here are character designs for Mr. Nancy and Kali by Scott. On the right page are his designs for Ibis and Jacquel.

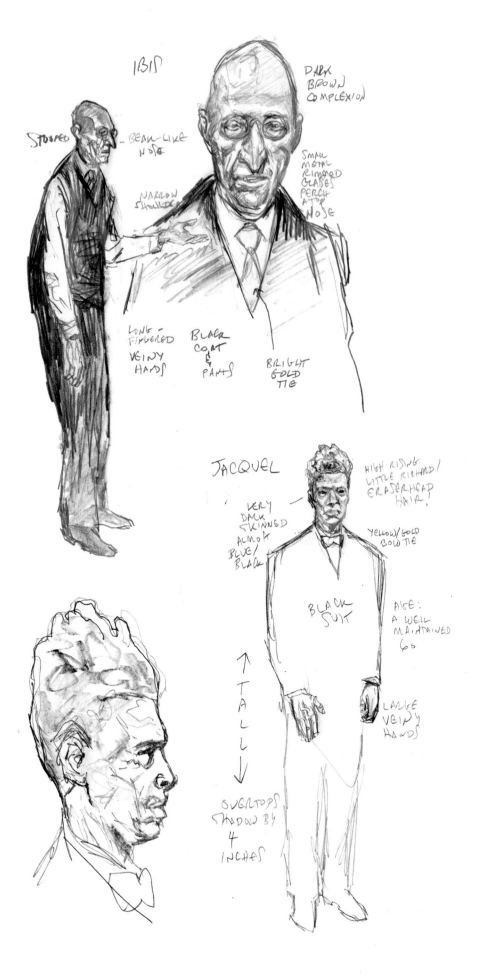

IBIS

DARK BROWN COMPLEXION

STOOPED

BEAK-LIKE NOSE

NARROW SHOULDER

SMALL METAL RIMMED GLASSES PERCH ATOP NOSE

LONG-FINGERED VEINY HANDS

BLACK COAT & PANTS

BRIGHT GOLD TIE

JACQUEL

VERY DARK SKINNED ALMOST BLUE/BLACK

HIGH RIDING LITTLE RICHARD/ ERASERHEAD HAIR.

YELLOW/GOLD BOLO TIE

BLACK SUIT

AGE: A WELL MAINTAINED 60

LARGE VEINY HANDS

TALL

OVERTOPS SHADOW BY 4 INCHES

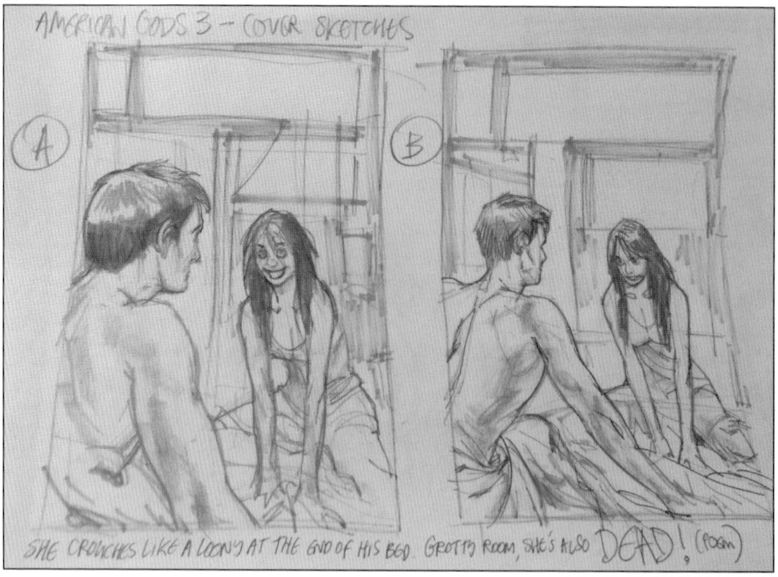
AMERICAN GODS 3 – COVER SKETCHES
A
B
SHE CROUCHES LIKE A LOONY AT THE END OF HIS BED. GROTTY ROOM, SHE'S ALSO DEAD!

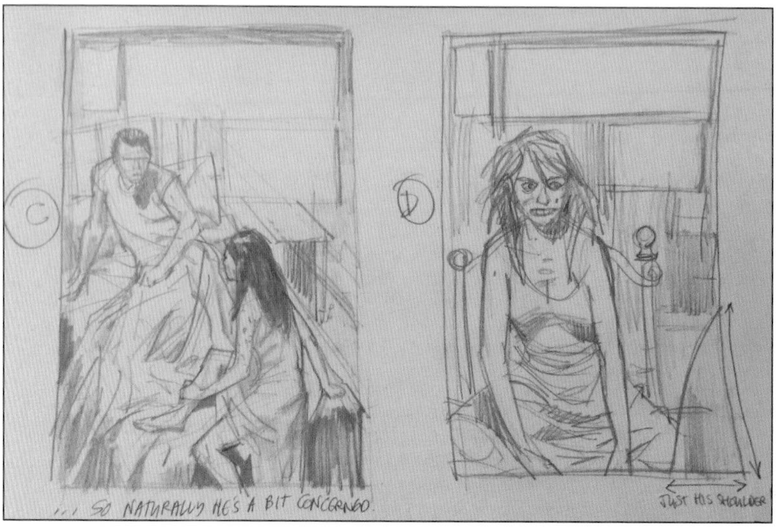
C
D
... SO NATURALLY HE'S A BIT CONCERNED.
JUST HIS SHOULDER

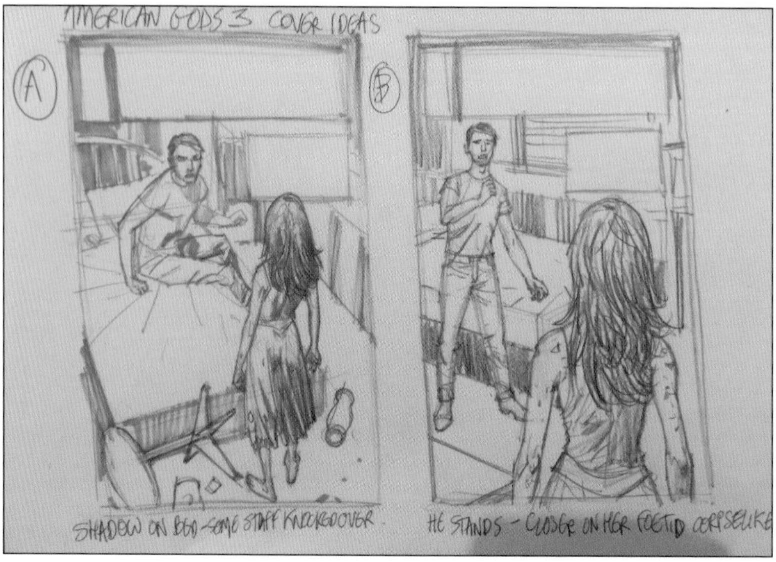
AMERICAN GODS 3 COVER IDEAS
A
B
SHADOW ON BED – SOME STUFF KNOCKED OVER
HE STANDS – CLOSER ON HER FOETID CORPSELIKE

Cover sketches by Glenn Fabry for his chapter three cover. I love all the weird notes Glenn writes on the sides of his art.

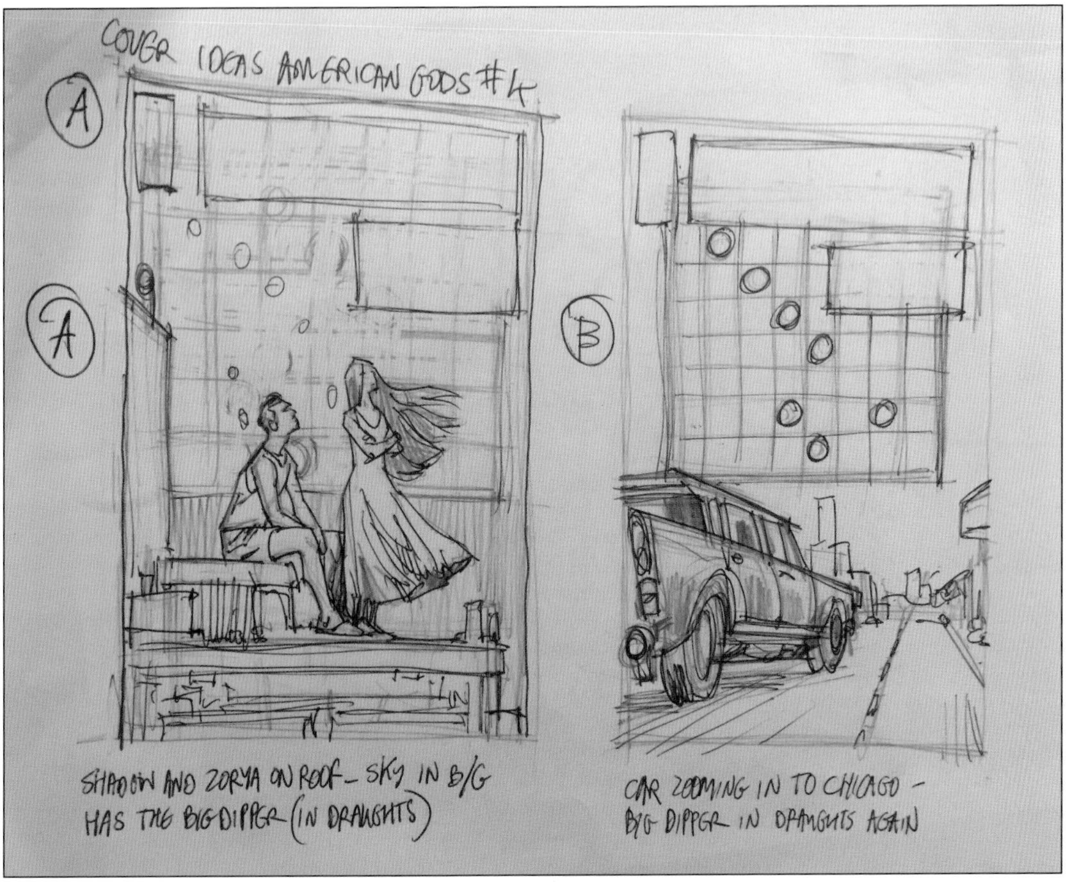

COVER IDEAS AMERICAN GODS #4
A
A
B
SHADOW AND ZORYA ON ROOF - SKY IN B/G
HAS THE BIG DIPPER (IN DRAUGHTS)
CAR ZOOMING IN TO CHICAGO -
B/G DIPPER IN DRAUGHTS AGAIN

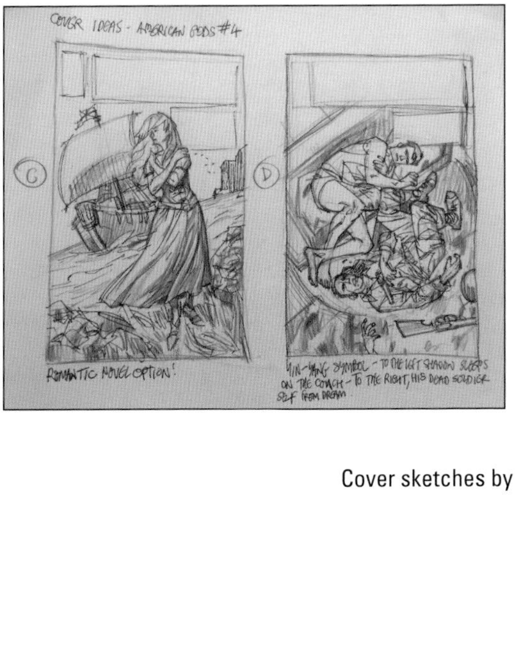

COVER IDEAS - AMERICAN GODS #4
C
D
ROMANTIC NOVEL OPTION!
YIN-YANG SYMBOL - TO THE LEFT SHADOW SLEEPS ON THE COUCH - TO THE RIGHT, HIS DEAD SOLDIER SELF FROM DREAM

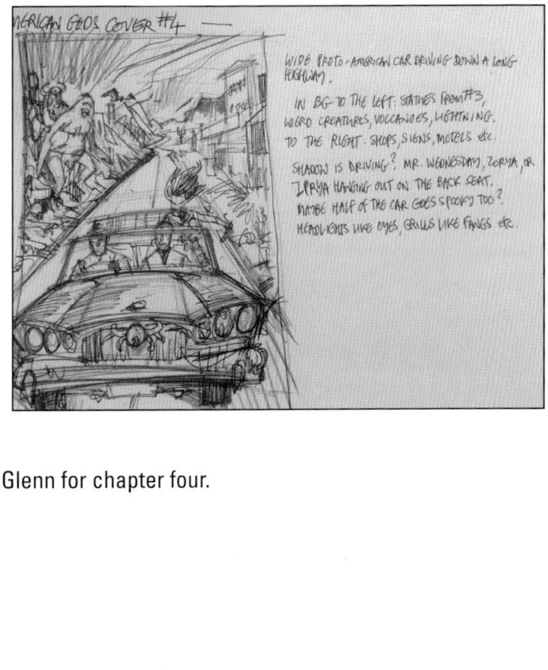

AMERICAN GODS COVER #4
WIDE PROTO-AMERICAN CAR DRIVING DOWN A LONG HIGHWAY.
IN BG TO THE LEFT: STATUES FROM #3, WEIRD CREATURES, VOLCANOES, LIGHTNING.
TO THE RIGHT: SHOPS, SIGNS, MOTELS etc.
SHADOW IS DRIVING? MR. WEDNESDAY, ZORYA, OR ZORYA HANGING OUT ON THE BACK SEAT.
MAYBE HALF OF THE CAR GOES SPOOKY TOO?
HEADLIGHTS LIKE EYES, GRILLS LIKE FANGS etc.

Cover sketches by Glenn for chapter four.

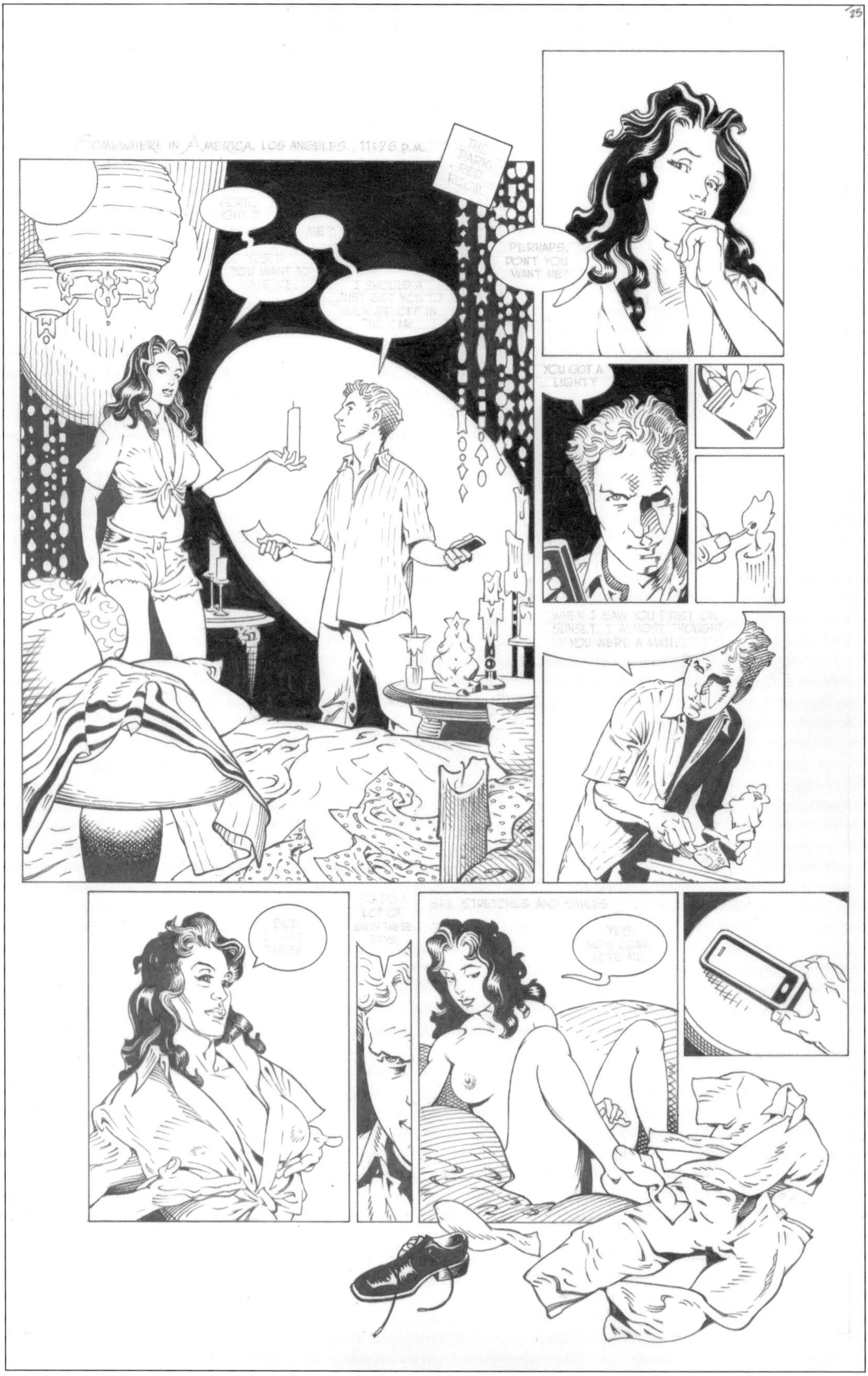
25
SOMEWHERE IN AMERICA. LOS ANGELES 11:26 P.M.
THE DARK RED ROOM
ME?
PERHAPS. DON'T YOU WANT ME?
YOU GOT A LIGHT?
WHEN I SAW YOU FIRST ON SUNSET, I ALMOST THOUGHT YOU WERE A MAN...
SHE STRETCHES AND SMILES.
YES. NOW COME LOVE ME.

This double-page spread features high resolution scans of P. Craig Russell's original art for the infamous Bilquis sex scene from chapter one.

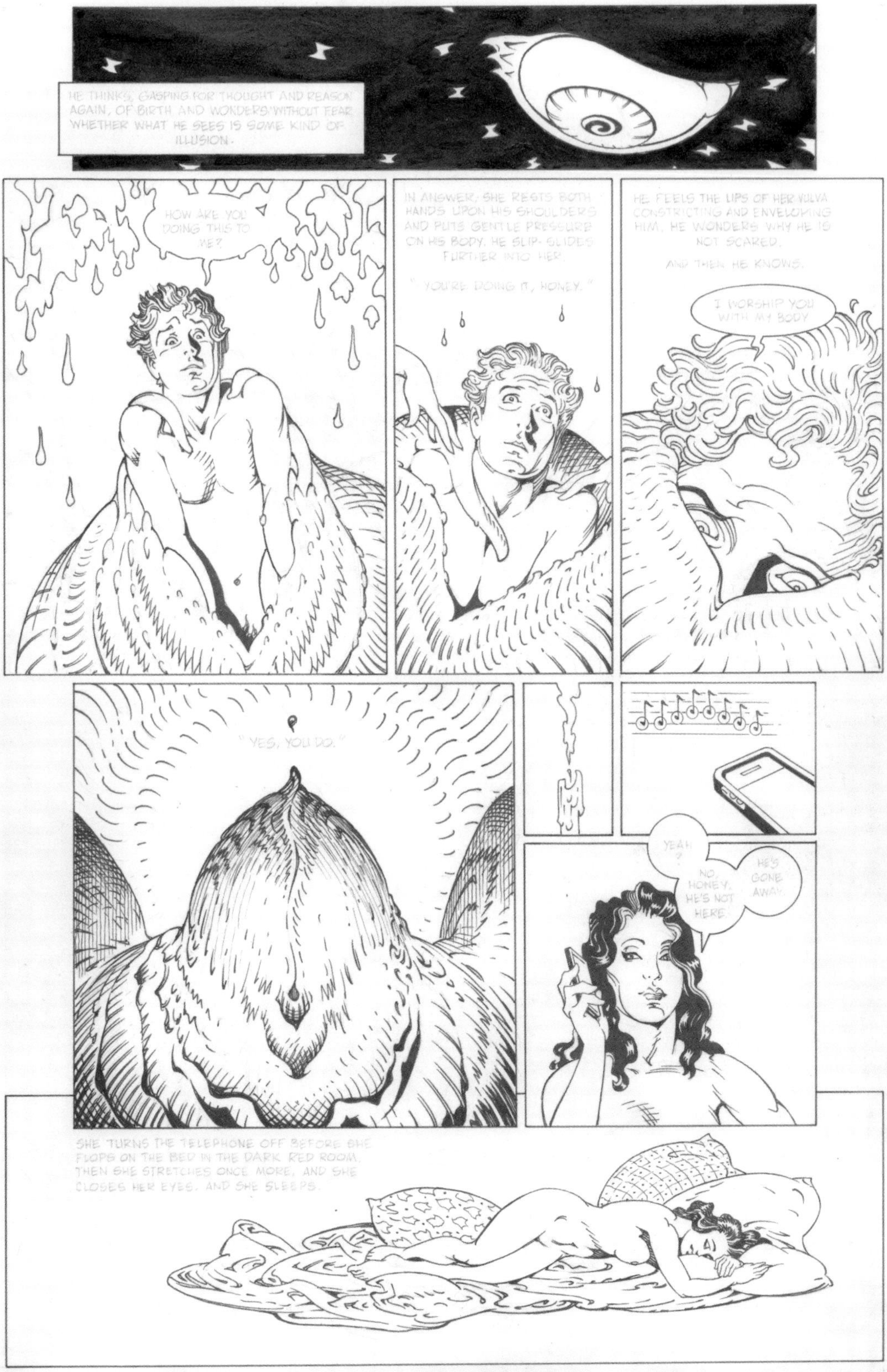

HE THINKS, GASPING FOR THOUGHT AND REASON AGAIN, OF BIRTH AND WONDERS WITHOUT FEAR WHETHER WHAT HE SEES IS SOME KIND OF ILLUSION.
HOW ARE YOU DOING THIS TO ME?
IN ANSWER, SHE RESTS BOTH HANDS UPON HIS SHOULDERS AND PUTS GENTLE PRESSURE ON HIS BODY. HE SLIP-SLIDES FURTHER INTO HER.
"YOU'RE DOING IT, HONEY."
HE FEELS THE LIPS OF HER VULVA CONSTRICTING AND ENVELOPING HIM. HE WONDERS WHY HE IS NOT SCARED.
AND THEN HE KNOWS.
I WORSHIP YOU WITH MY BODY
"YES, YOU DO."
YEAH?
NO, HONEY, HE'S NOT HERE.
HE'S GONE AWAY.
SHE TURNS THE TELEPHONE OFF BEFORE SHE FLOPS ON THE BED IN THE DARK RED ROOM. THEN SHE STRETCHES ONCE MORE, AND SHE CLOSES HER EYES. AND SHE SLEEPS.

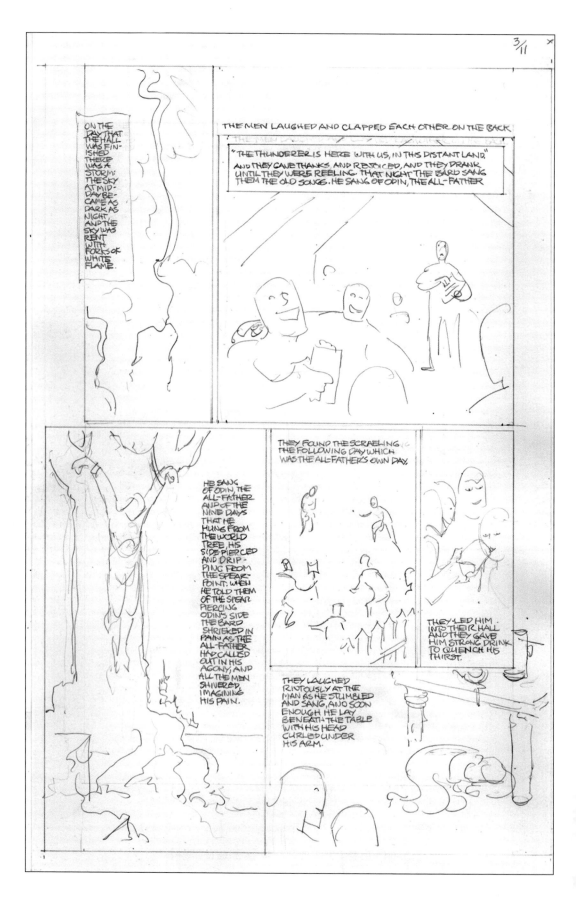

These next six pages feature scans of the original layouts, pencils, and inks for the "Coming to America" sequence from chapter three—the layouts are by P. Craig Russell and the pencils and inks are by Walter Simonson.

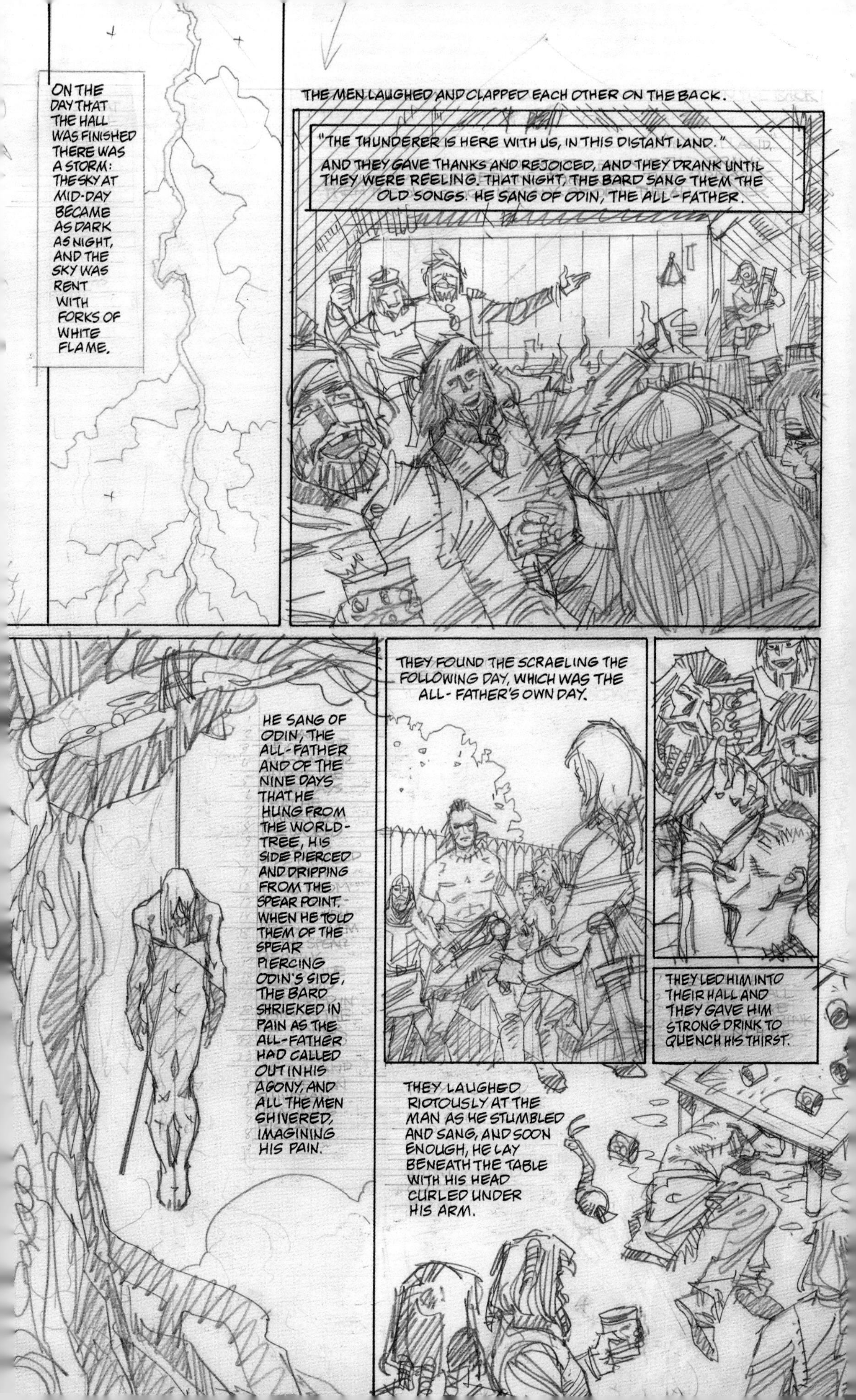

ON THE DAY THAT THE HALL WAS FINISHED THERE WAS A STORM: THE SKY AT MID-DAY BECAME AS DARK AS NIGHT, AND THE SKY WAS RENT WITH FORKS OF WHITE FLAME.
THE MEN LAUGHED AND CLAPPED EACH OTHER ON THE BACK.
"THE THUNDERER IS HERE WITH US, IN THIS DISTANT LAND."
AND THEY GAVE THANKS AND REJOICED, AND THEY DRANK UNTIL THEY WERE REELING. THAT NIGHT, THE BARD SANG THEM THE OLD SONGS. HE SANG OF ODIN, THE ALL-FATHER.
HE SANG OF ODIN, THE ALL-FATHER AND OF THE NINE DAYS THAT HE HUNG FROM THE WORLD-TREE, HIS SIDE PIERCED AND DRIPPING FROM THE SPEAR POINT. WHEN HE TOLD THEM OF THE SPEAR PIERCING ODIN'S SIDE, THE BARD SHRIEKED IN PAIN AS THE ALL-FATHER HAD CALLED OUT IN HIS AGONY, AND ALL THE MEN SHIVERED, IMAGINING HIS PAIN.
THEY FOUND THE SCRAELING THE FOLLOWING DAY, WHICH WAS THE ALL-FATHER'S OWN DAY.
THEY LED HIM INTO THEIR HALL AND THEY GAVE HIM STRONG DRINK TO QUENCH HIS THIRST.
THEY LAUGHED RIOTOUSLY AT THE MAN AS HE STUMBLED AND SANG, AND SOON ENOUGH, HE LAY BENEATH THE TABLE WITH HIS HEAD CURLED UNDER HIS ARM.

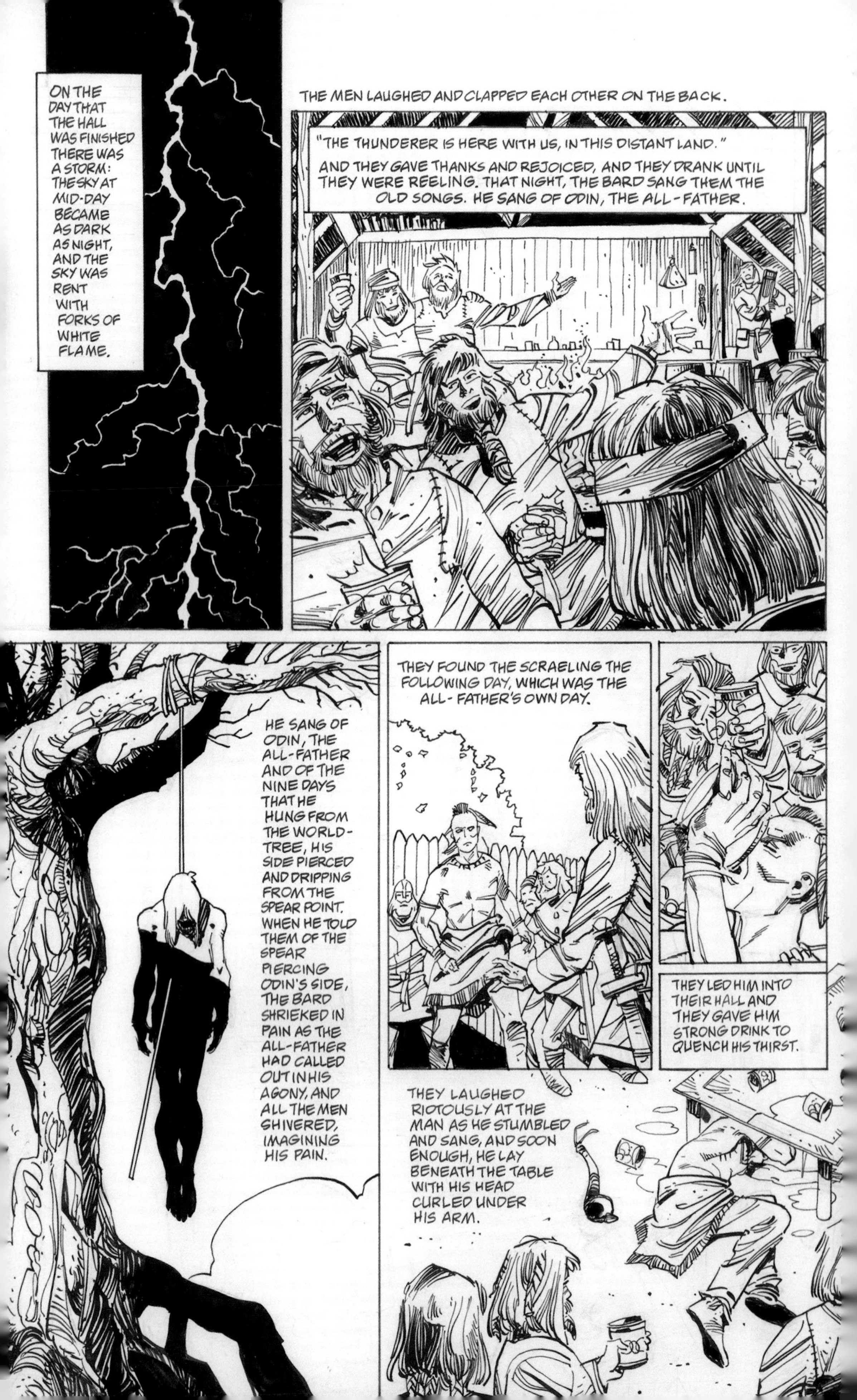

ON THE DAY THAT THE HALL WAS FINISHED THERE WAS A STORM: THE SKY AT MID-DAY BECAME AS DARK AS NIGHT, AND THE SKY WAS RENT WITH FORKS OF WHITE FLAME.
THE MEN LAUGHED AND CLAPPED EACH OTHER ON THE BACK.
"THE THUNDERER IS HERE WITH US, IN THIS DISTANT LAND."
AND THEY GAVE THANKS AND REJOICED, AND THEY DRANK UNTIL THEY WERE REELING. THAT NIGHT, THE BARD SANG THEM THE OLD SONGS. HE SANG OF ODIN, THE ALL-FATHER.
HE SANG OF ODIN, THE ALL-FATHER AND OF THE NINE DAYS THAT HE HUNG FROM THE WORLD-TREE, HIS SIDE PIERCED AND DRIPPING FROM THE SPEAR POINT. WHEN HE TOLD THEM OF THE SPEAR PIERCING ODIN'S SIDE, THE BARD SHRIEKED IN PAIN AS THE ALL-FATHER HAD CALLED OUT IN HIS AGONY, AND ALL THE MEN SHIVERED, IMAGINING HIS PAIN.
THEY FOUND THE SCRAELING THE FOLLOWING DAY, WHICH WAS THE ALL-FATHER'S OWN DAY.
THEY LED HIM INTO THEIR HALL AND THEY GAVE HIM STRONG DRINK TO QUENCH HIS THIRST.
THEY LAUGHED RIOTOUSLY AT THE MAN AS HE STUMBLED AND SANG, AND SOON ENOUGH, HE LAY BENEATH THE TABLE WITH HIS HEAD CURLED UNDER HIS ARM.

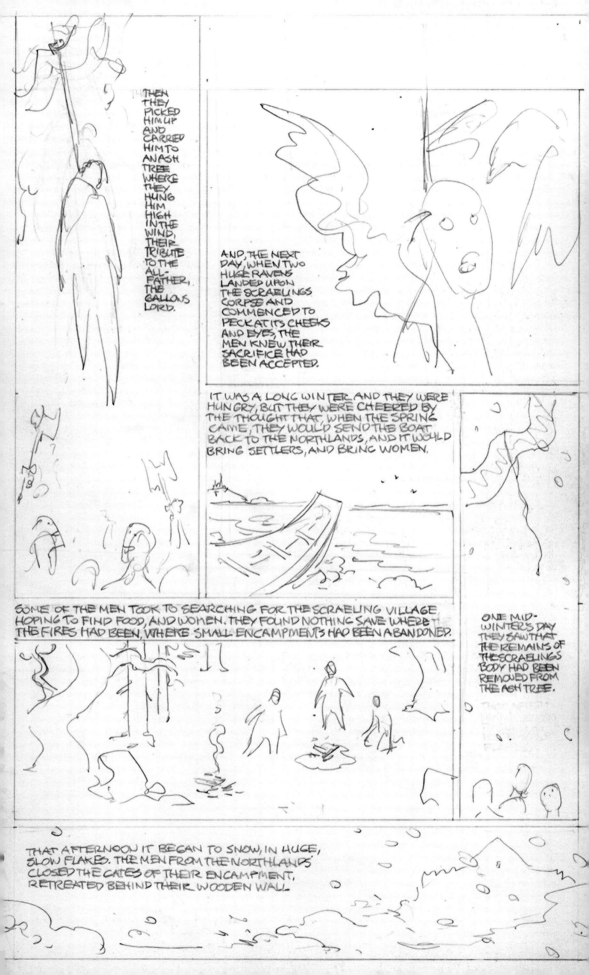

THEN THEY PICKED HIM UP AND CARRIED HIM TO AN ASH TREE WHERE THEY HUNG HIM HIGH IN THE WIND, THEIR TRIBUTE TO THE ALL-FATHER, THE GALLOWS LORD.

AND, THE NEXT DAY, WHEN TWO HUGE RAVENS LANDED UPON THE SCRAELING'S CORPSE AND COMMENCED TO PECK AT ITS CHEEKS AND EYES, THE MEN KNEW THEIR SACRIFICE HAD BEEN ACCEPTED.

IT WAS A LONG WINTER, AND THEY WERE HUNGRY, BUT THEY WERE CHEERED BY THE THOUGHT THAT, WHEN THE SPRING CAME, THEY WOULD SEND THE BOAT BACK TO THE NORTHLANDS, AND IT WOULD BRING SETTLERS, AND BRING WOMEN.

SOME OF THE MEN TOOK TO SEARCHING FOR THE SCRAELING VILLAGE, HOPING TO FIND FOOD, AND WOMEN. THEY FOUND NOTHING SAVE WHERE THE FIRES HAD BEEN, WHERE SMALL ENCAMPMENTS HAD BEEN ABANDONED.

ONE MID-WINTER'S DAY THEY SAW THAT THE REMAINS OF THE SCRAELING'S BODY HAD BEEN REMOVED FROM THE ASH TREE.

THAT AFTERNOON IT BEGAN TO SNOW, IN HUGE, SLOW FLAKES. THE MEN FROM THE NORTHLANDS CLOSED THE GATES OF THEIR ENCAMPMENT, RETREATED BEHIND THEIR WOODEN WALL.

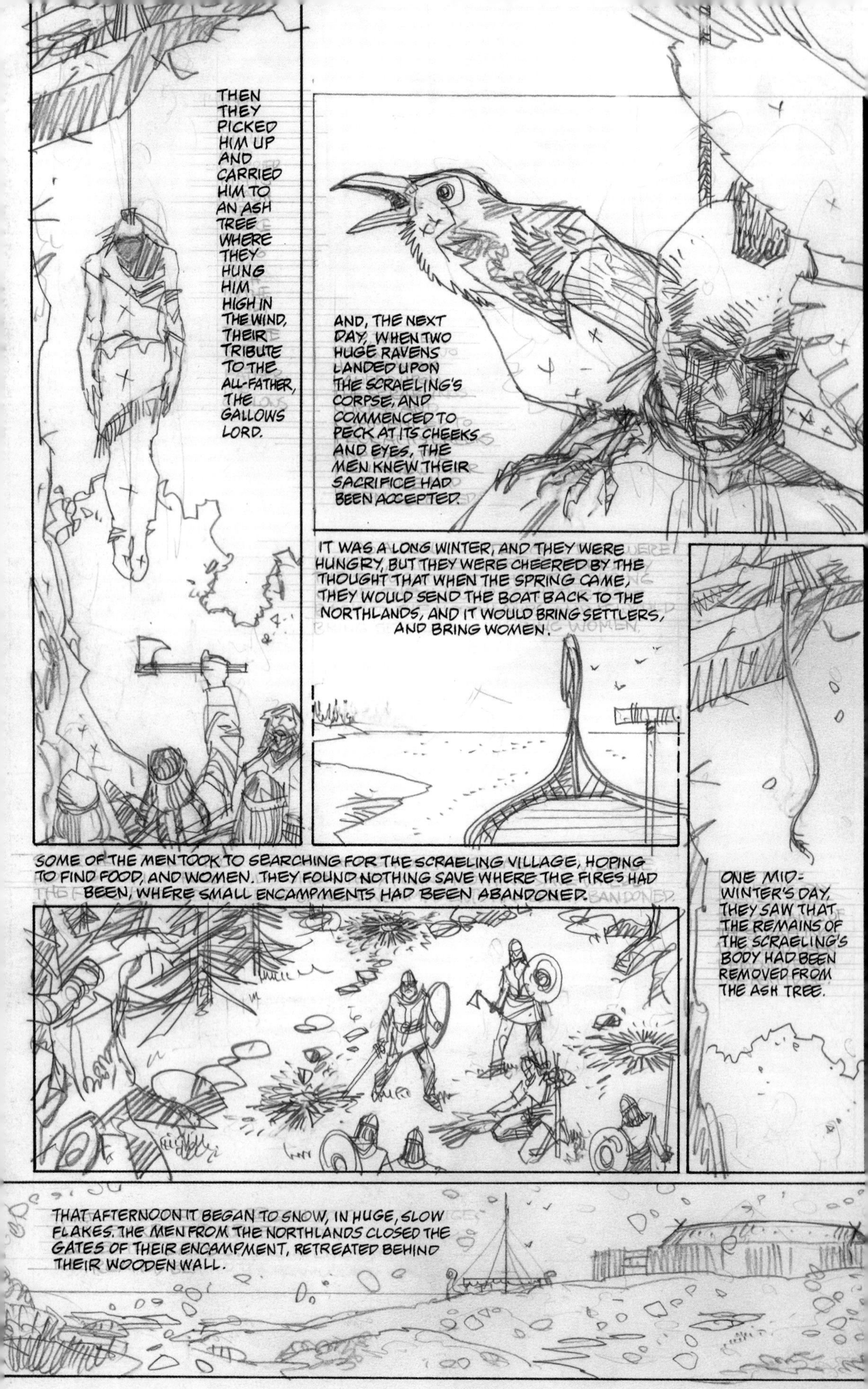
THEN THEY PICKED HIM UP AND CARRIED HIM TO AN ASH TREE WHERE THEY HUNG HIM HIGH IN THE WIND, THEIR TRIBUTE TO THE ALL-FATHER, THE GALLOWS LORD.
AND, THE NEXT DAY, WHEN TWO HUGE RAVENS LANDED UPON THE SCRAELING'S CORPSE, AND COMMENCED TO PECK AT ITS CHEEKS AND EYES, THE MEN KNEW THEIR SACRIFICE HAD BEEN ACCEPTED.
IT WAS A LONG WINTER, AND THEY WERE HUNGRY, BUT THEY WERE CHEERED BY THE THOUGHT THAT WHEN THE SPRING CAME, THEY WOULD SEND THE BOAT BACK TO THE NORTHLANDS, AND IT WOULD BRING SETTLERS, AND BRING WOMEN.
SOME OF THE MEN TOOK TO SEARCHING FOR THE SCRAELING VILLAGE, HOPING TO FIND FOOD, AND WOMEN. THEY FOUND NOTHING SAVE WHERE THE FIRES HAD BEEN, WHERE SMALL ENCAMPMENTS HAD BEEN ABANDONED.
ONE MID-WINTER'S DAY, THEY SAW THAT THE REMAINS OF THE SCRAELING'S BODY HAD BEEN REMOVED FROM THE ASH TREE.
THAT AFTERNOON IT BEGAN TO SNOW, IN HUGE, SLOW FLAKES. THE MEN FROM THE NORTHLANDS CLOSED THE GATES OF THEIR ENCAMPMENT, RETREATED BEHIND THEIR WOODEN WALL.

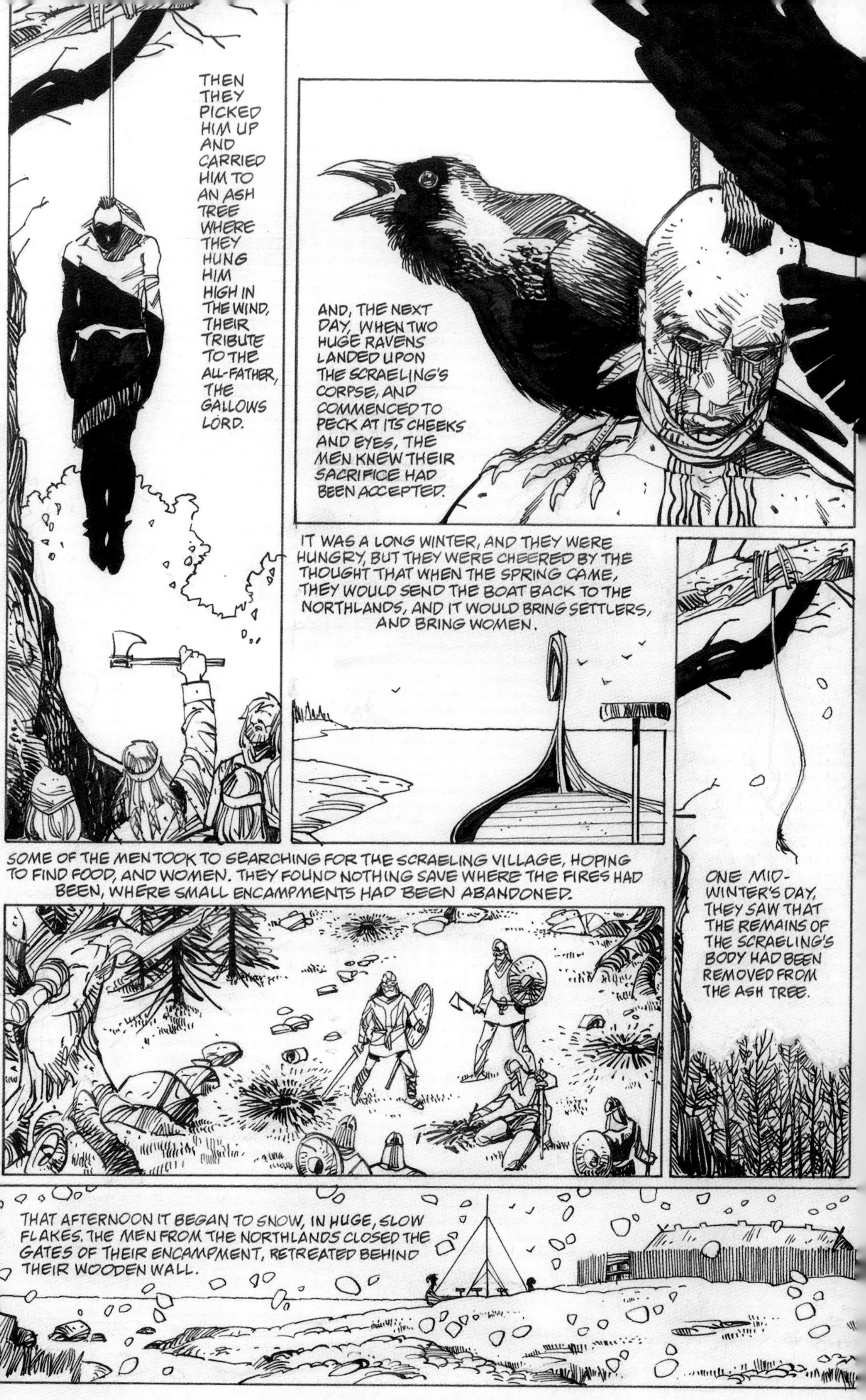
THEN THEY PICKED HIM UP AND CARRIED HIM TO AN ASH TREE WHERE THEY HUNG HIM HIGH IN THE WIND, THEIR TRIBUTE TO THE ALL-FATHER, THE GALLOWS LORD.
AND, THE NEXT DAY, WHEN TWO HUGE RAVENS LANDED UPON THE SCRAELING'S CORPSE, AND COMMENCED TO PECK AT ITS CHEEKS AND EYES, THE MEN KNEW THEIR SACRIFICE HAD BEEN ACCEPTED.
IT WAS A LONG WINTER, AND THEY WERE HUNGRY, BUT THEY WERE CHEERED BY THE THOUGHT THAT WHEN THE SPRING CAME, THEY WOULD SEND THE BOAT BACK TO THE NORTHLANDS, AND IT WOULD BRING SETTLERS, AND BRING WOMEN.
SOME OF THE MEN TOOK TO SEARCHING FOR THE SCRAELING VILLAGE, HOPING TO FIND FOOD, AND WOMEN. THEY FOUND NOTHING SAVE WHERE THE FIRES HAD BEEN, WHERE SMALL ENCAMPMENTS HAD BEEN ABANDONED.
ONE MID-WINTER'S DAY, THEY SAW THAT THE REMAINS OF THE SCRAELING'S BODY HAD BEEN REMOVED FROM THE ASH TREE.
THAT AFTERNOON IT BEGAN TO SNOW, IN HUGE, SLOW FLAKES. THE MEN FROM THE NORTHLANDS CLOSED THE GATES OF THEIR ENCAMPMENT, RETREATED BEHIND THEIR WOODEN WALL.

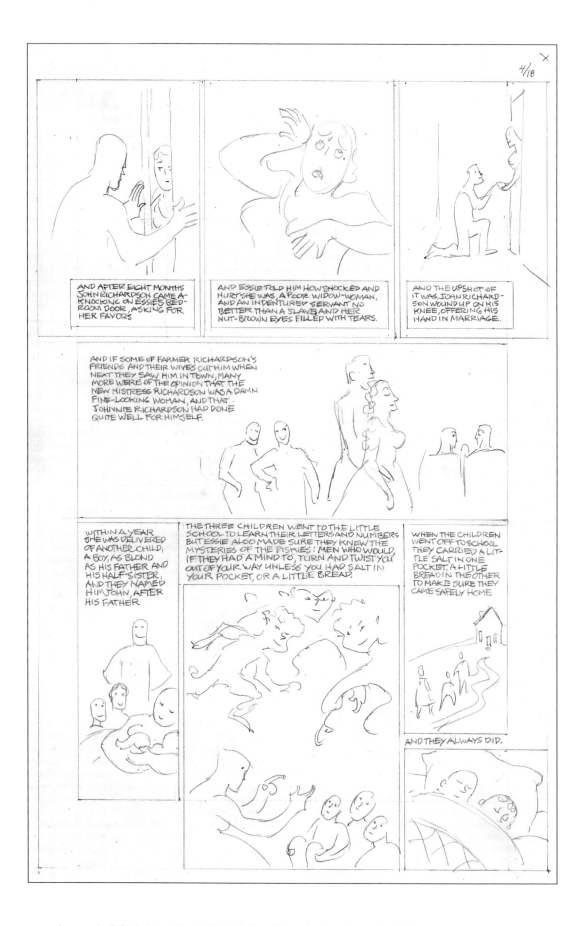

AND AFTER EIGHT MONTHS JOHN RICHARDSON CAME A-KNOCKING ON ESSIE'S BEDROOM DOOR, ASKING FOR HER FAVORS

AND ESSIE TOLD HIM HOW SHOCKED AND HURT SHE WAS, A POOR WIDOW-WOMAN, AND AN INDENTURED SERVANT NO BETTER THAN A SLAVE AND HER NUT-BROWN EYES FILLED WITH TEARS.

AND THE UPSHOT OF IT WAS, JOHN RICHARDSON WOUND UP ON HIS KNEE, OFFERING HIS HAND IN MARRIAGE.

AND IF SOME OF FARMER RICHARDSON'S FRIENDS AND THEIR WIVES CUT HIM WHEN NEXT THEY SAW HIM IN TOWN, MANY MORE WERE OF THE OPINION THAT THE NEW MISTRESS RICHARDSON WAS A DAMN FINE-LOOKING WOMAN, AND THAT JOHNNIE RICHARDSON HAD DONE QUITE WELL FOR HIMSELF.

WITHIN A YEAR SHE WAS DELIVERED OF ANOTHER CHILD, A BOY, AS BLOND AS HIS FATHER AND HIS HALF-SISTER, AND THEY NAMED HIM JOHN, AFTER HIS FATHER

THE THREE CHILDREN WENT TO THE LITTLE SCHOOL TO LEARN THEIR LETTERS AND NUMBERS BUT ESSIE ALSO MADE SURE THEY KNEW THE MYSTERIES OF THE PISKIES: MEN WHO WOULD, IF THEY HAD A MIND TO, TURN AND TWIST YOU OUT OF YOUR WAY UNLESS YOU HAD SALT IN YOUR POCKET, OR A LITTLE BREAD.

WHEN THE CHILDREN WENT OFF TO SCHOOL THEY CARRIED A LITTLE SALT IN ONE POCKET, A LITTLE BREAD IN THE OTHER TO MAKE SURE THEY CAME SAFELY HOME

AND THEY ALWAYS DID.

Layouts by P. Craig Russell and inks by Colleen Doran for the chapter four "Coming to America" story.

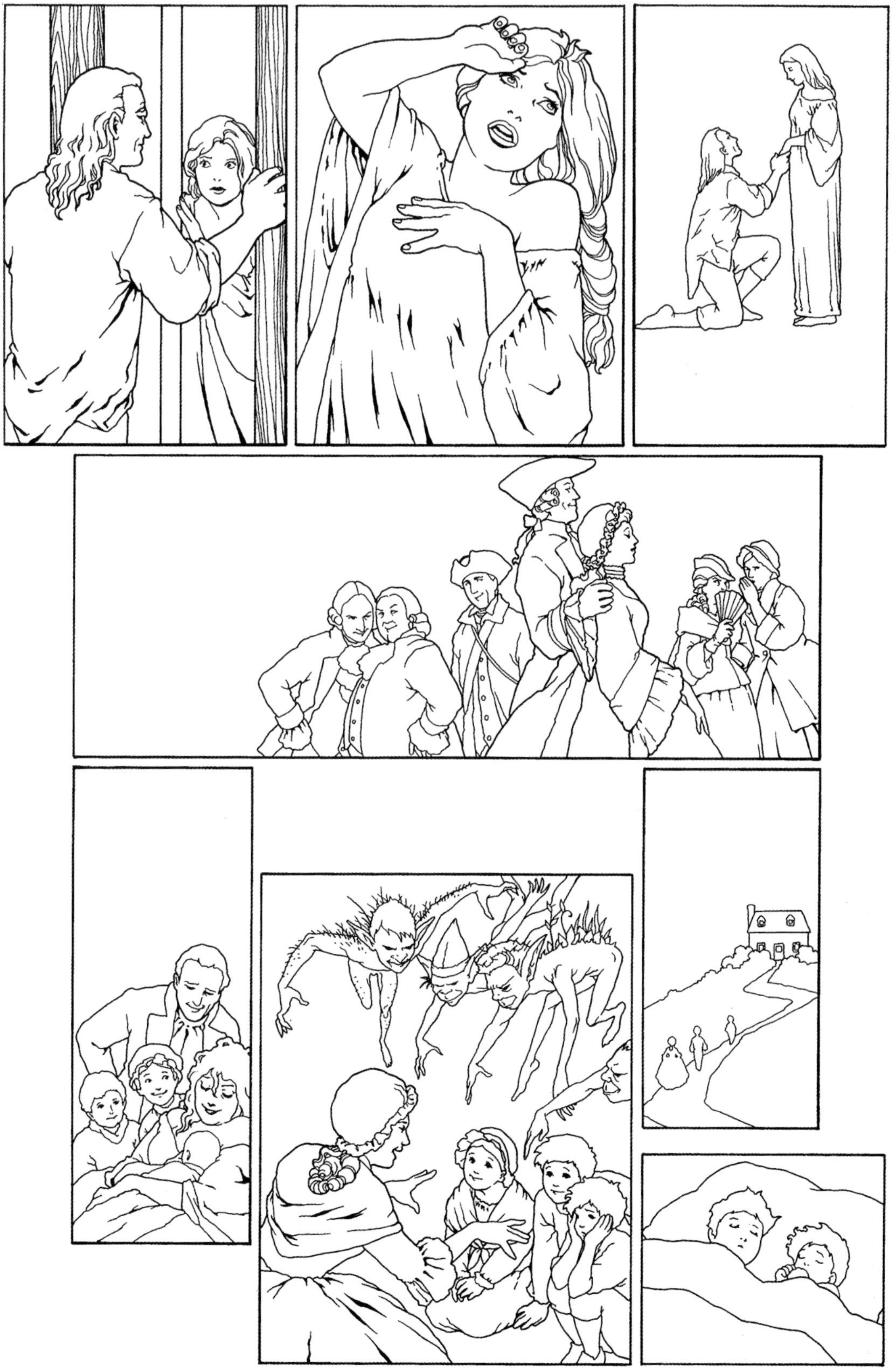

Layouts by P. Craig Russell and mid-stage pencils/colors for chapter six, page one by Scott Hampton.

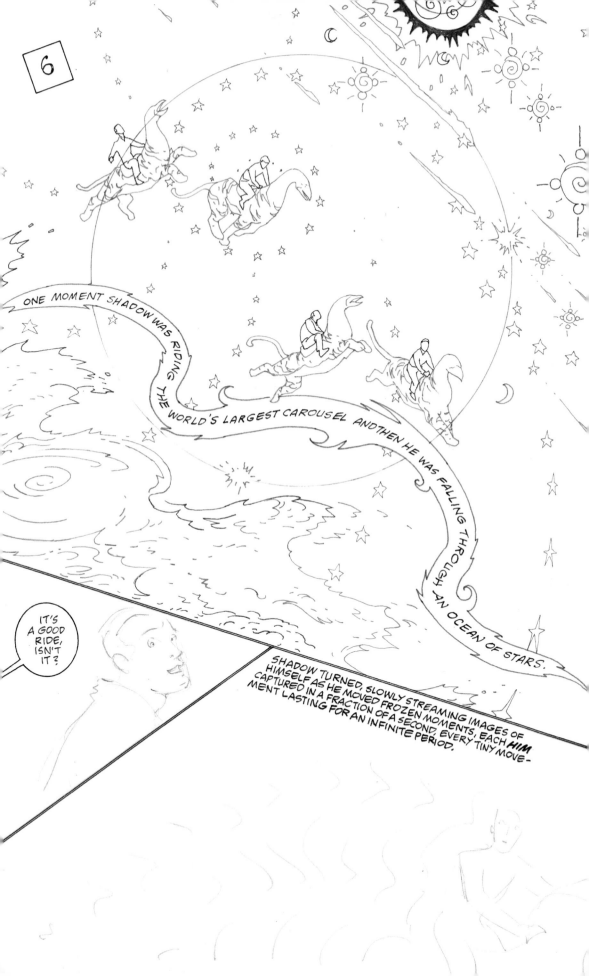

The next few pages feature layouts by P. Craig Russell and pencils by Glenn Fabry for the chapter eight "Coming to America" story. There's a special Glenn Fabry Easter egg appearance by him, walking in the background of page one, panel one—he's wearing the sunglasses and walking to the left.

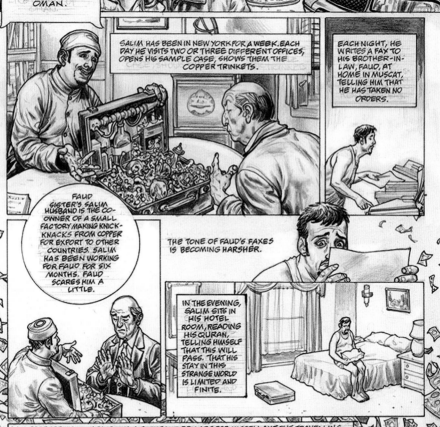

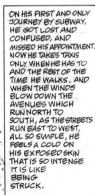

ON HIS FIRST AND ONLY JOURNEY BY SUBWAY, HE GOT LOST AND CONFUSED, AND MISSED HIS APPOINTMENT. NOW HE TAKES TAXIS ONLY WHEN HE HAS TO AND THE REST OF THE TIME HE WALKS, AND WHEN THE WINDS BLOW DOWN THE AVENUES WHICH RUN NORTH TO SOUTH, AS THE STREETS RUN EAST TO WEST, ALL SO SIMPLE, HE FEELS A COLD ON HIS EXPOSED SKIN THAT IS SO INTENSE IT IS LIKE BEING STRUCK.

HE NEVER EATS AT THE HOTEL. IT'S TOO EXPENSIVE. INSTEAD, HE BUYS FOOD AT FALAFEL HOUSES, SMUGGLES IT UP TO HIS ROOM FOR DAYS, BEFORE HE REALIZES THAT NO ONE CARES.

SALIM IS UPSET. THE FAX THAT WAS WAITING FOR HIM THIS MORNING WAS ALTERNATELY CHIDING, STERN AND DISAPPOINTED.

THEN SALIM WALKS DOWNTOWN, TRUDGING THROUGH THE COLD, UNTIL HE FINDS A SQUAT BUILDING, AND WALKS UP THE STAIRS TO THE FOURTH FLOOR.

SALIM, YOU ARE LETTING US DOWN. ME, YOUR SISTER, MY BUSINESS PARTNERS, THE SULTINATE OF OMAN, *THE WHOLE WORLD.*

UNLESS YOU ARE ABLE TO GET ORDERS, I WILL NOT CONSIDER IT MY OBLIGATION TO EMPLOY YOU.

WHAT ARE YOU DOING WITH OUR MONEY? LIVING LIKE A *SULTAN* IN AMERICA?

PANGLOBAL IMPORTS

MAKE THIS AS MUCH VAN GOGH AS YOU CAN GOGH

HOW BAY I HEP YOU?

I HAVE—

PRSSSP PT.

SNIFF

YED?

I HAVE AN ELEVEN O'CLOCK WITH MISTER BLANDING.

SECRETARY PULLING KLEENEX FROM BOX

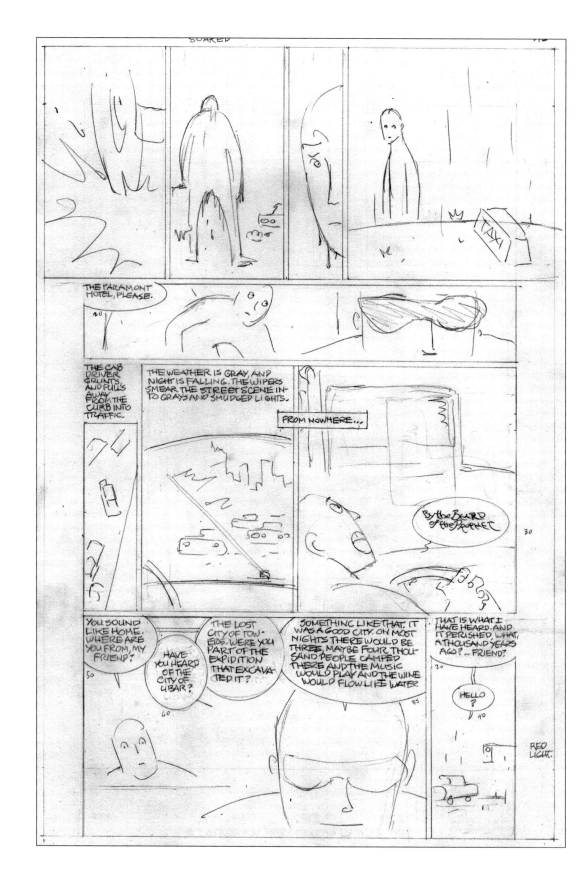

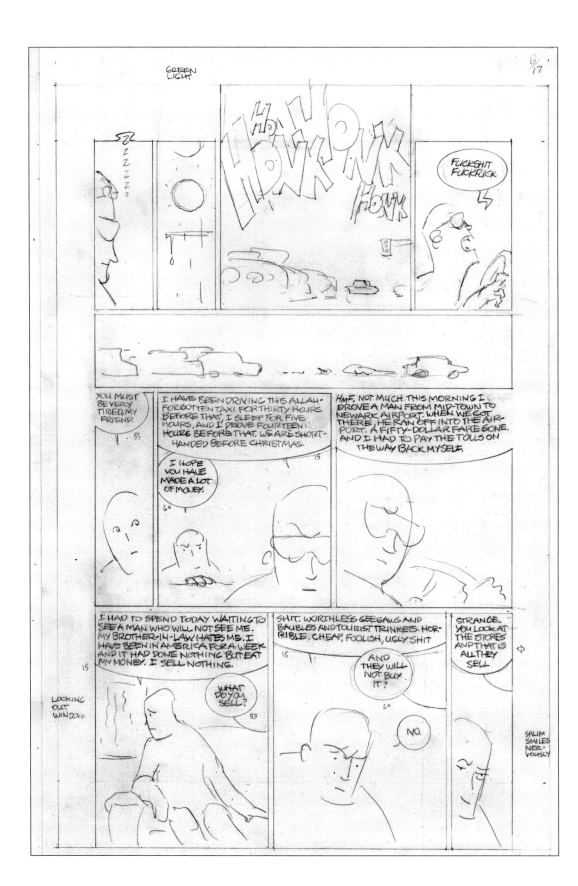

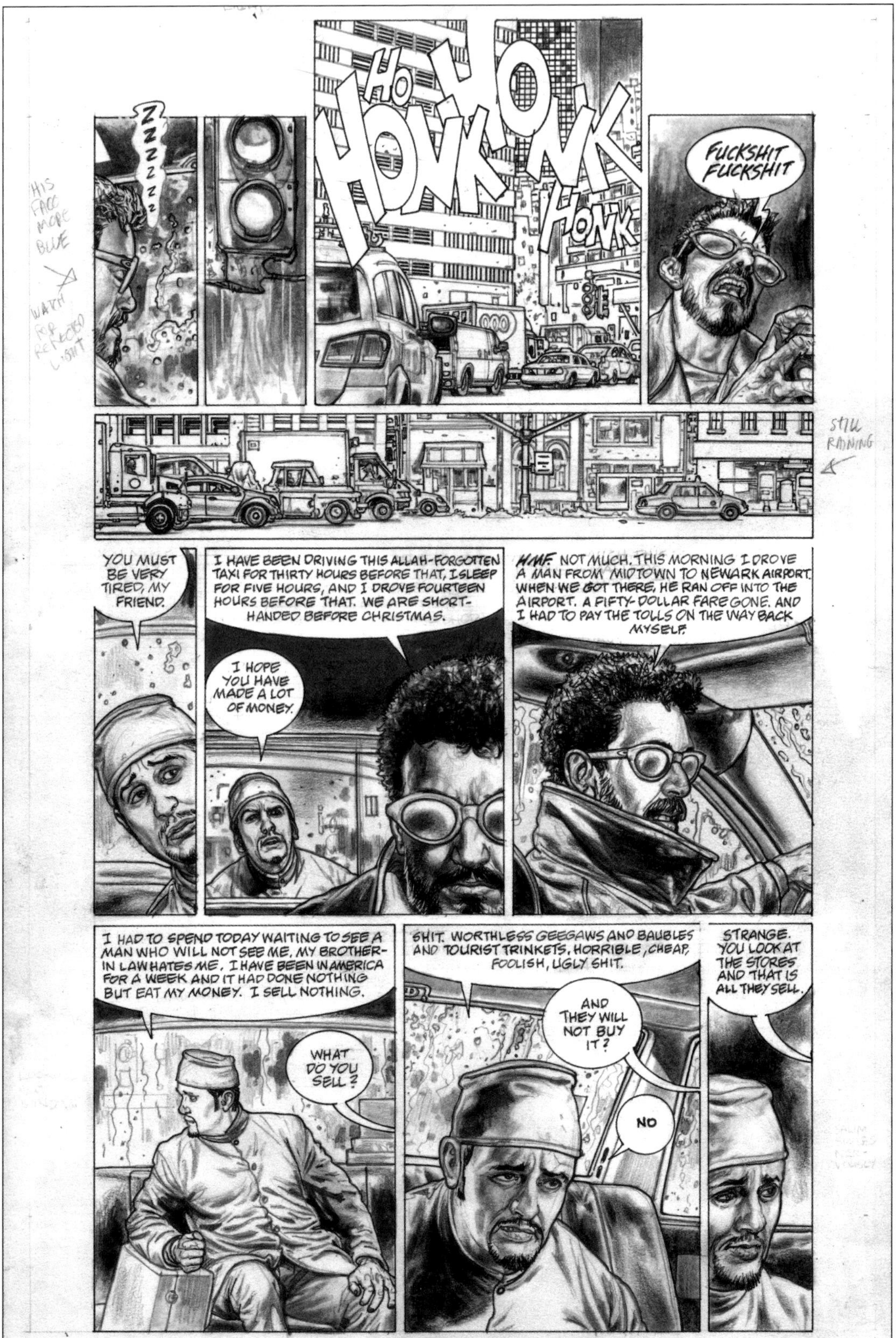
HIS FACE MORE BLUE
WATCH FOR REFLECTED LIGHT
ZZZZZZZ
HO
HONK
HONK
HONK
FUCKSHIT FUCKSHIT
STILL RAINING
YOU MUST BE VERY TIRED, MY FRIEND.
I HAVE BEEN DRIVING THIS ALLAH-FORGOTTEN TAXI FOR THIRTY HOURS BEFORE THAT, I SLEEP FOR FIVE HOURS, AND I DROVE FOURTEEN HOURS BEFORE THAT. WE ARE SHORT-HANDED BEFORE CHRISTMAS.
I HOPE YOU HAVE MADE A LOT OF MONEY.
HMF. NOT MUCH. THIS MORNING I DROVE A MAN FROM MIDTOWN TO NEWARK AIRPORT. WHEN WE GOT THERE, HE RAN OFF INTO THE AIRPORT. A FIFTY-DOLLAR FARE GONE. AND I HAD TO PAY THE TOLLS ON THE WAY BACK MYSELF.
I HAD TO SPEND TODAY WAITING TO SEE A MAN WHO WILL NOT SEE ME, MY BROTHER-IN LAW HATES ME. I HAVE BEEN IN AMERICA FOR A WEEK AND IT HAD DONE NOTHING BUT EAT MY MONEY. I SELL NOTHING.
WHAT DO YOU SELL?
SHIT. WORTHLESS GEEGAWS AND BAUBLES AND TOURIST TRINKETS. HORRIBLE, CHEAP, FOOLISH, UGLY SHIT.
AND THEY WILL NOT BUY IT?
NO
STRANGE. YOU LOOK AT THE STORES AND THAT IS ALL THEY SELL.

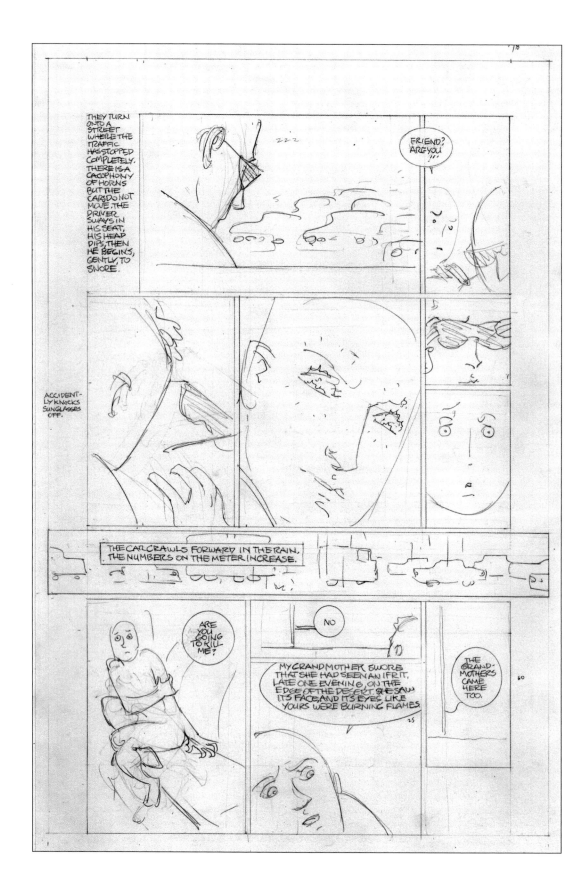

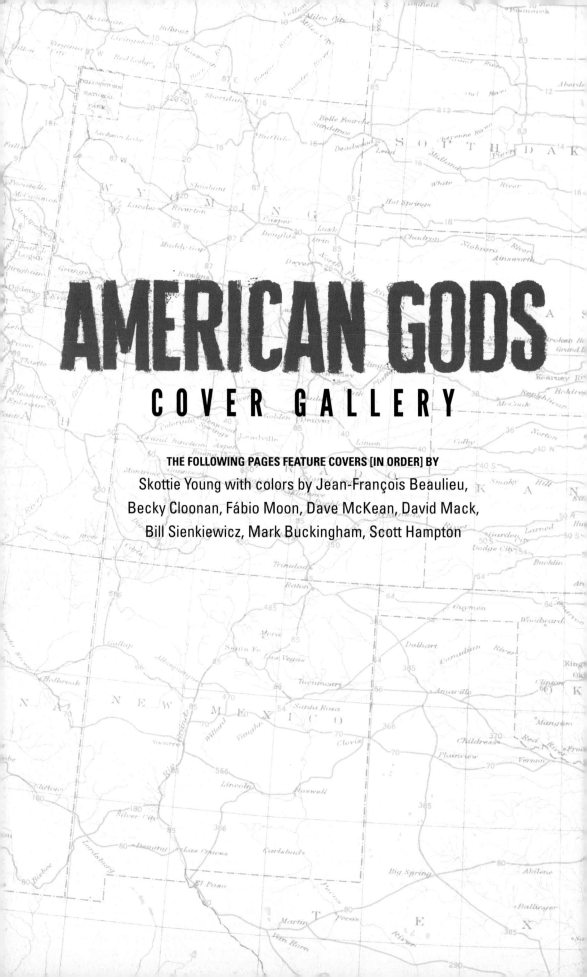

AMERICAN GODS

COVER GALLERY

THE FOLLOWING PAGES FEATURE COVERS [IN ORDER] BY

Skottie Young with colors by Jean-François Beaulieu,

Becky Cloonan, Fábio Moon, Dave McKean, David Mack,

Bill Sienkiewicz, Mark Buckingham, Scott Hampton

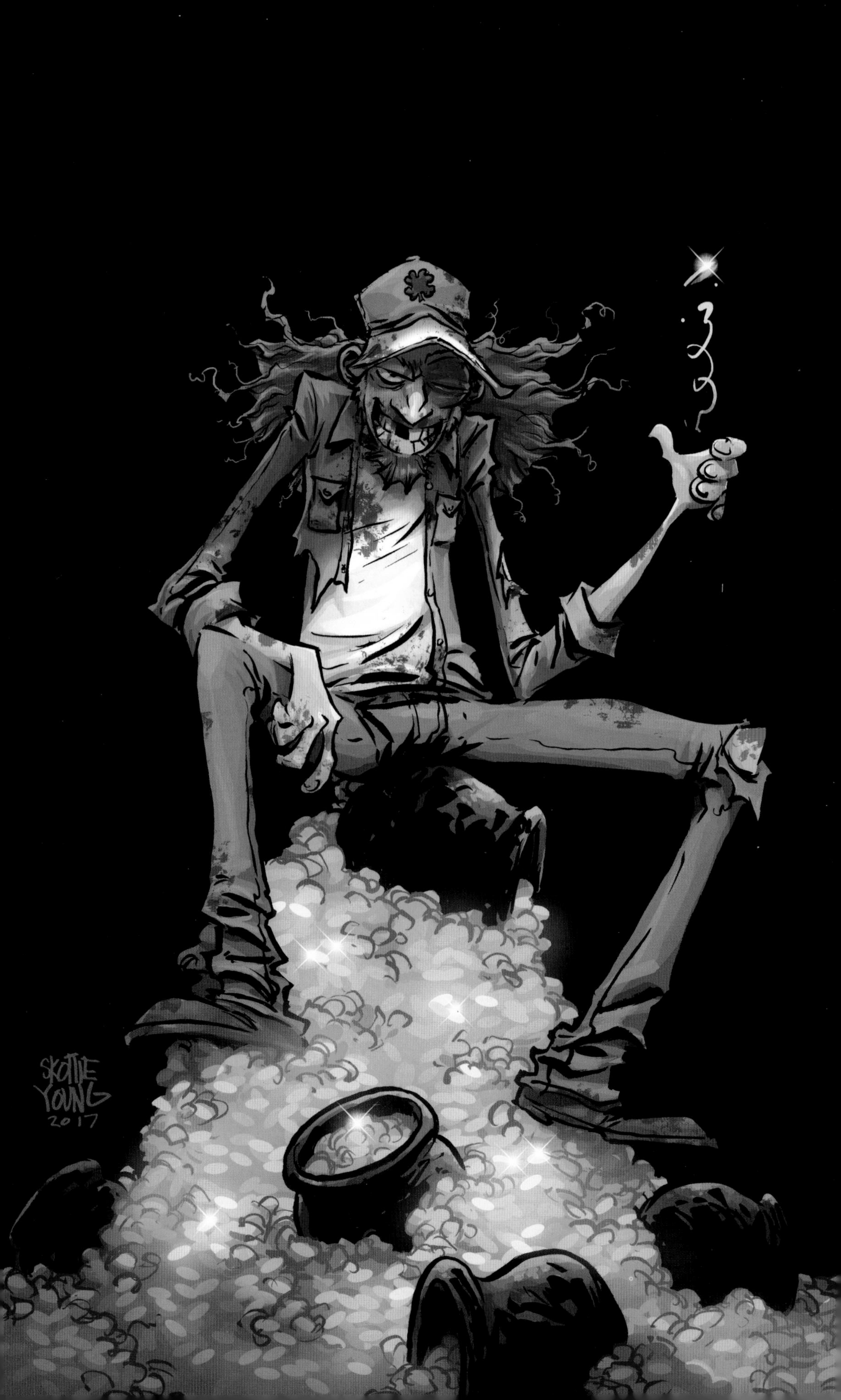
SKOTTIE
YOUNG
2017

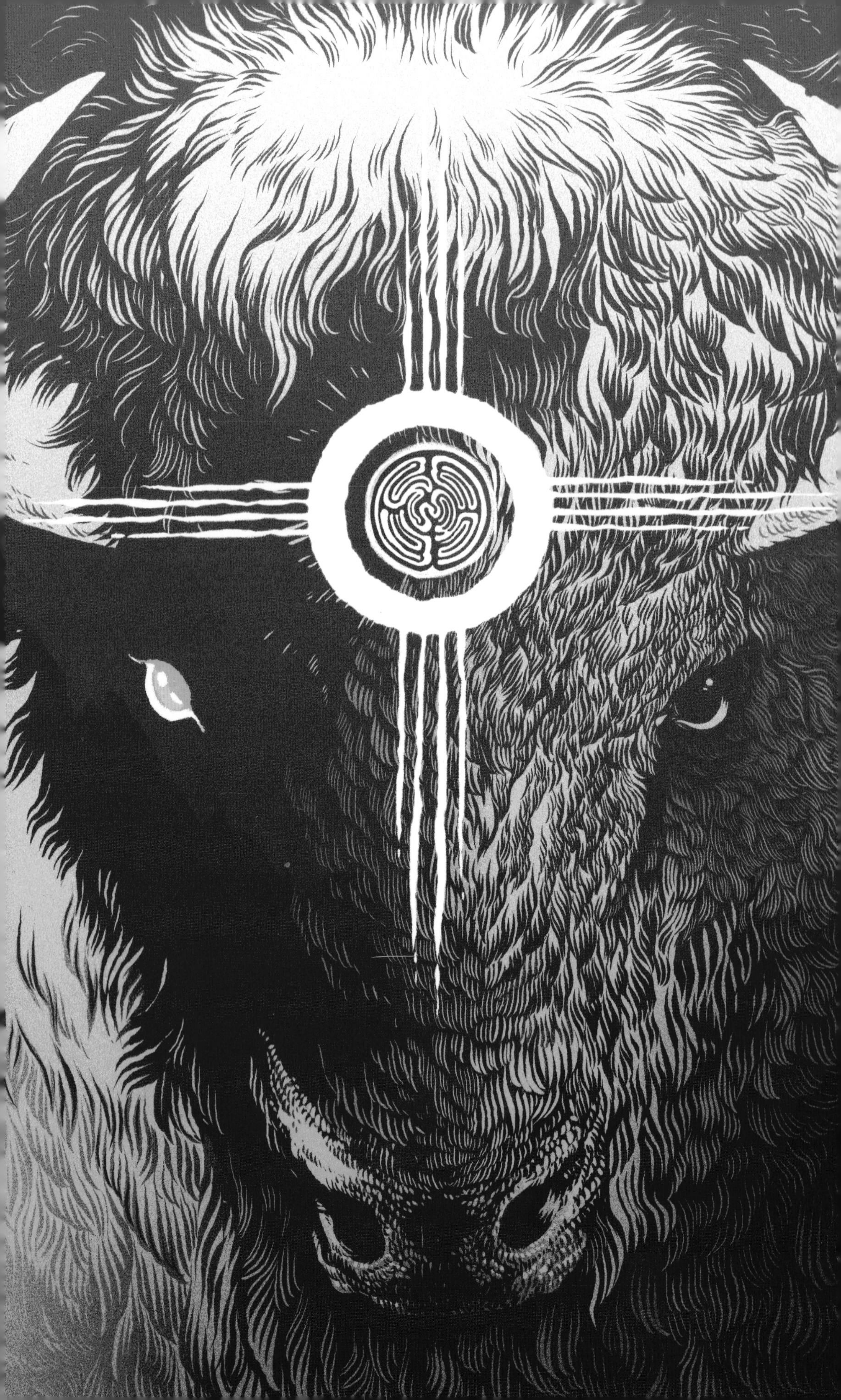

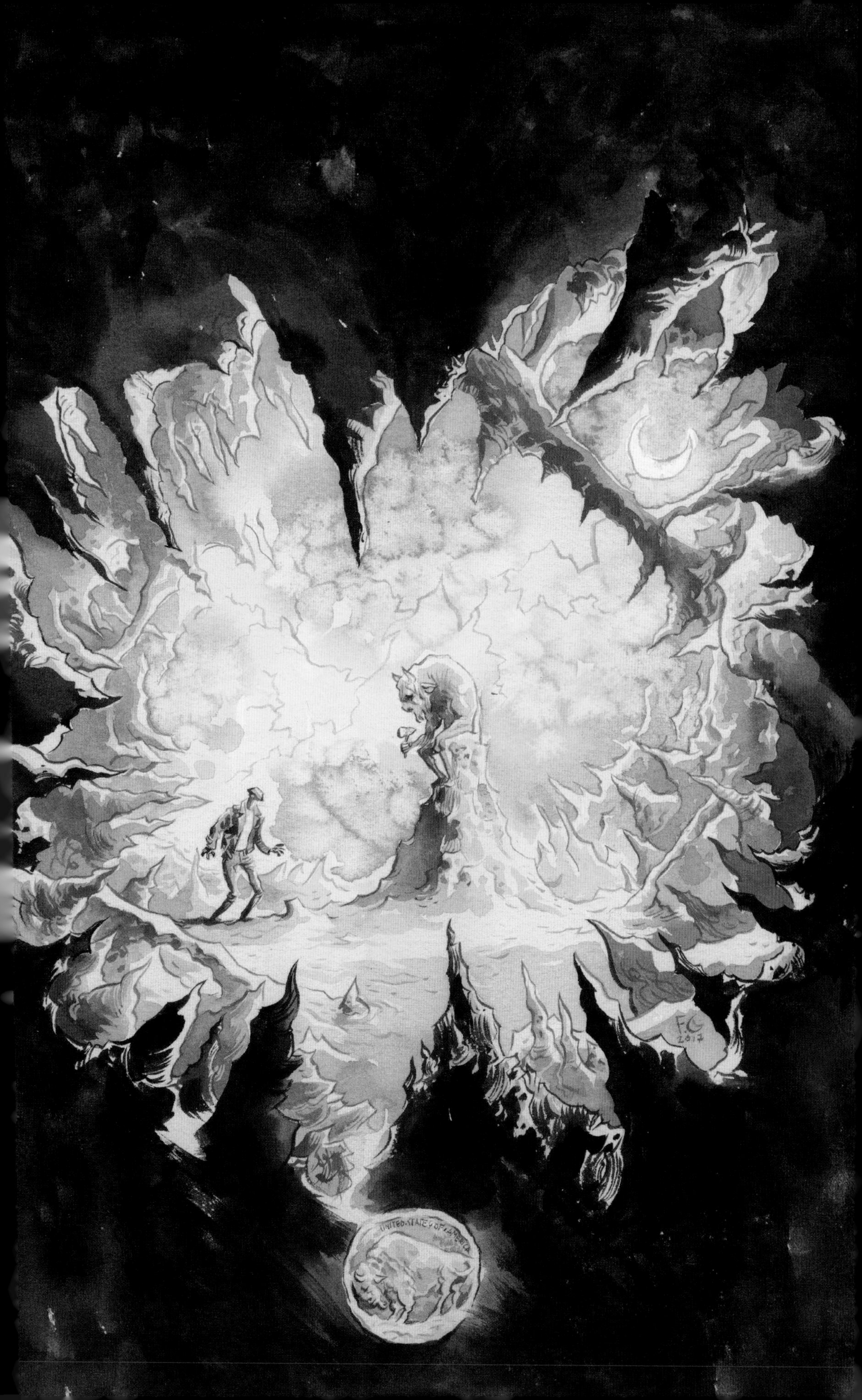
F.C
2017
UNITED STATES OF AMERICA

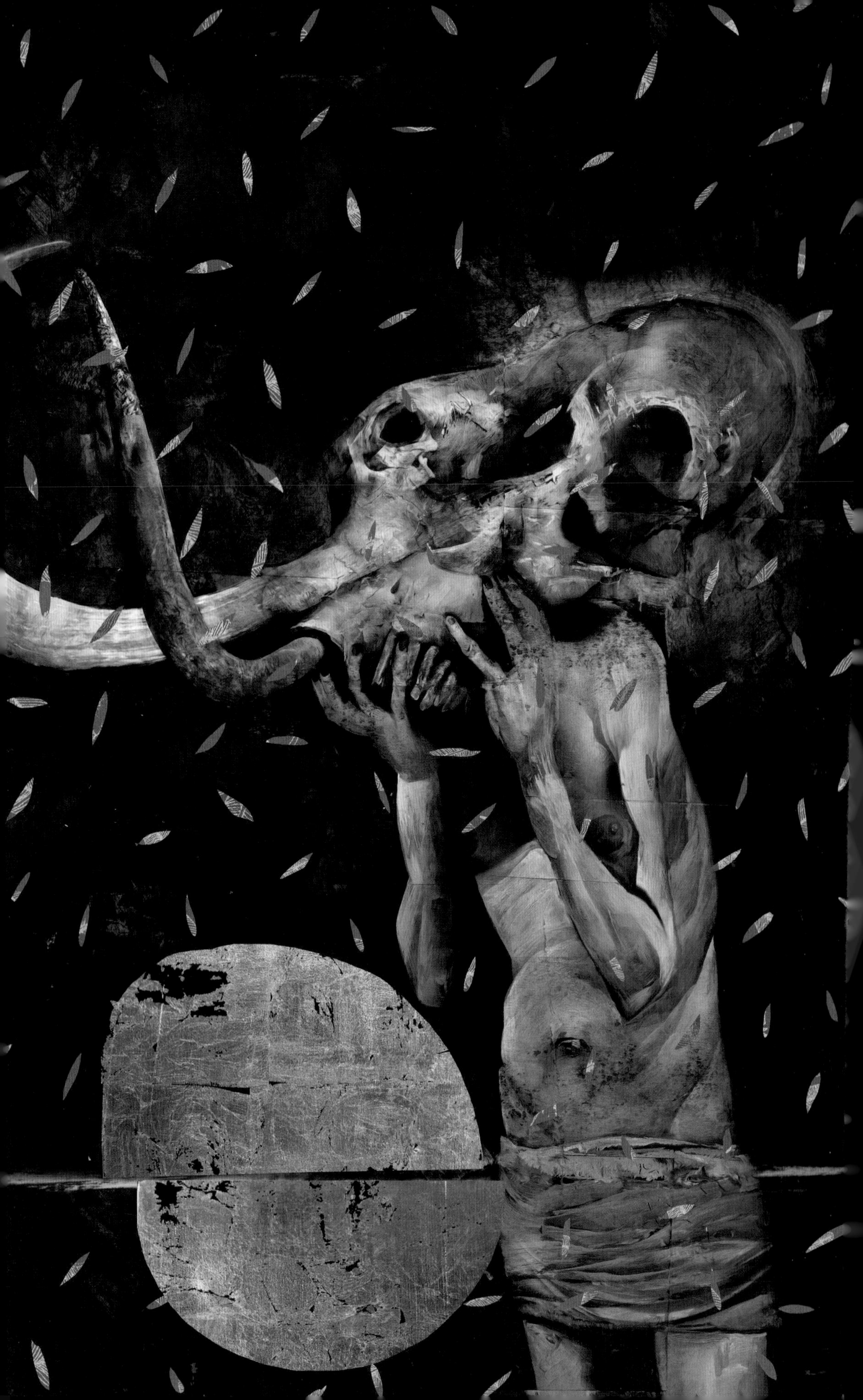

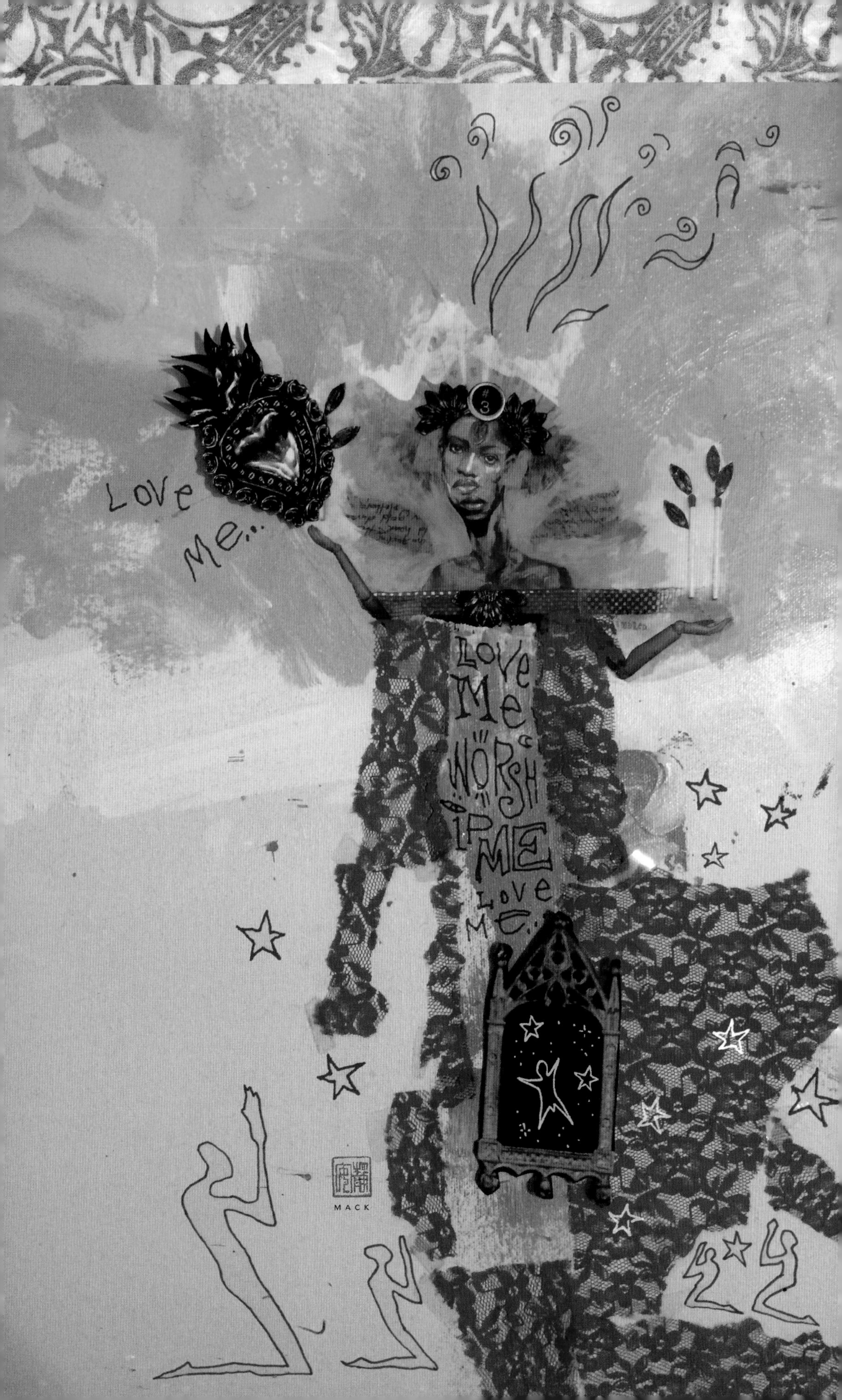
Love Me...
Love Me
WORSHIP ME
Love Me
MACK

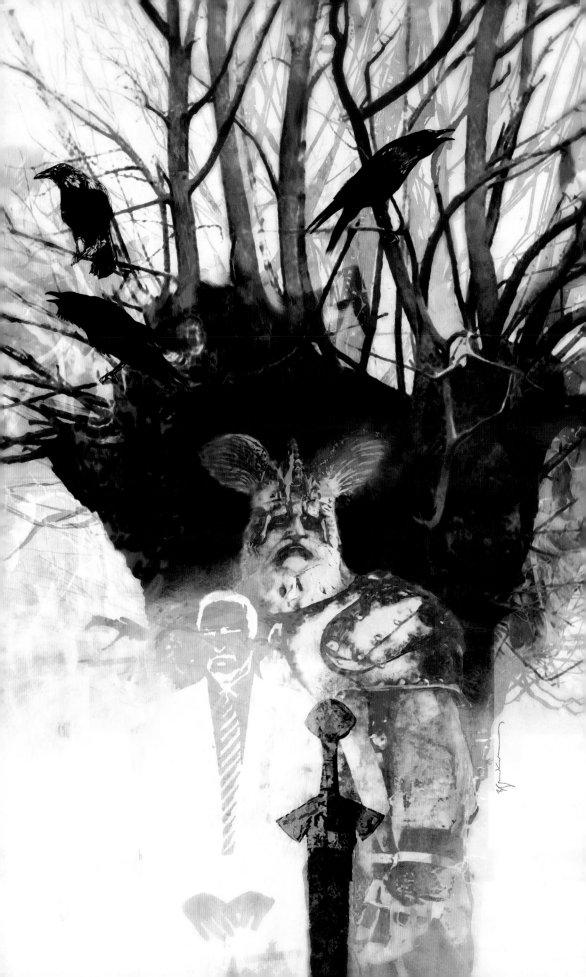

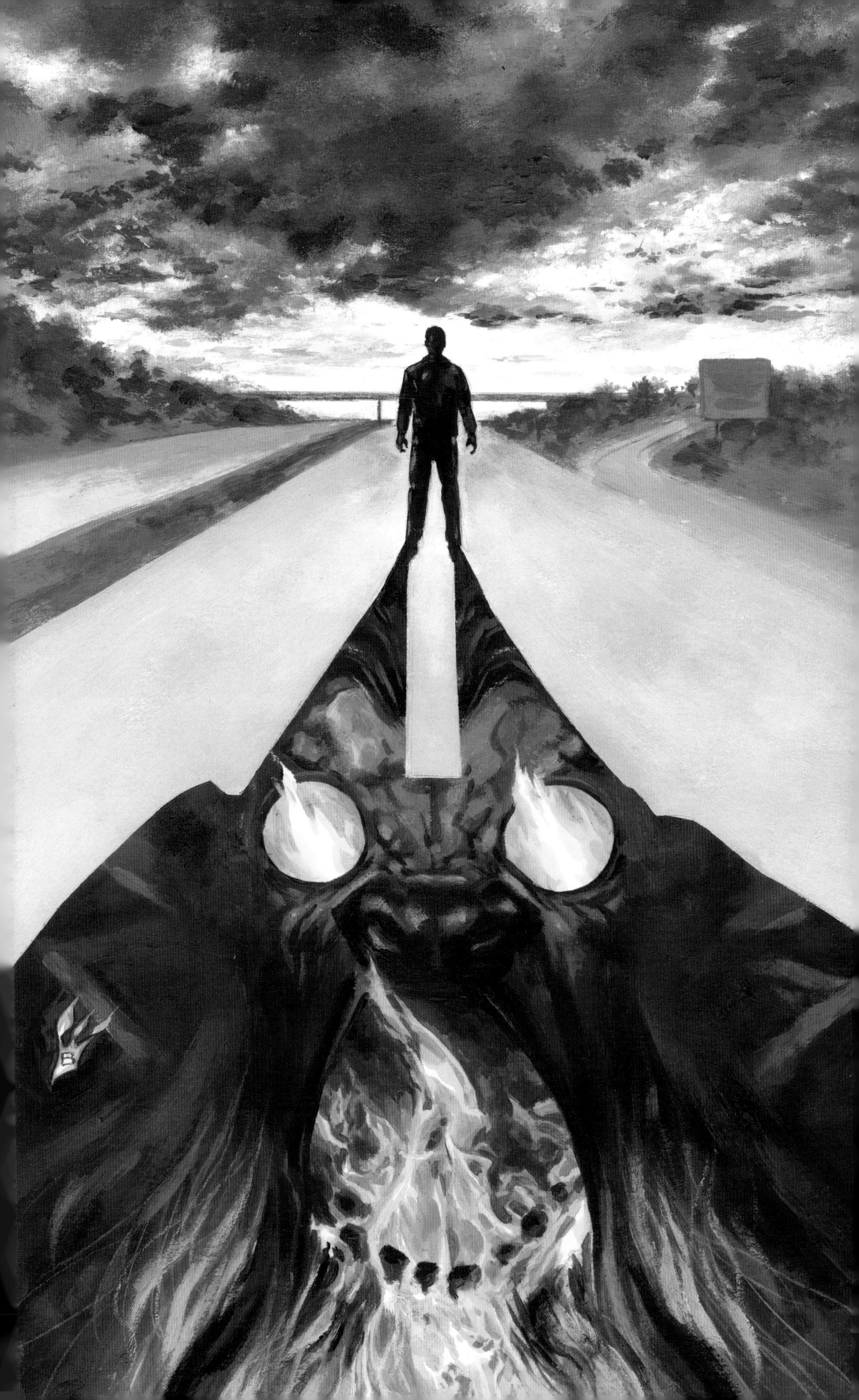

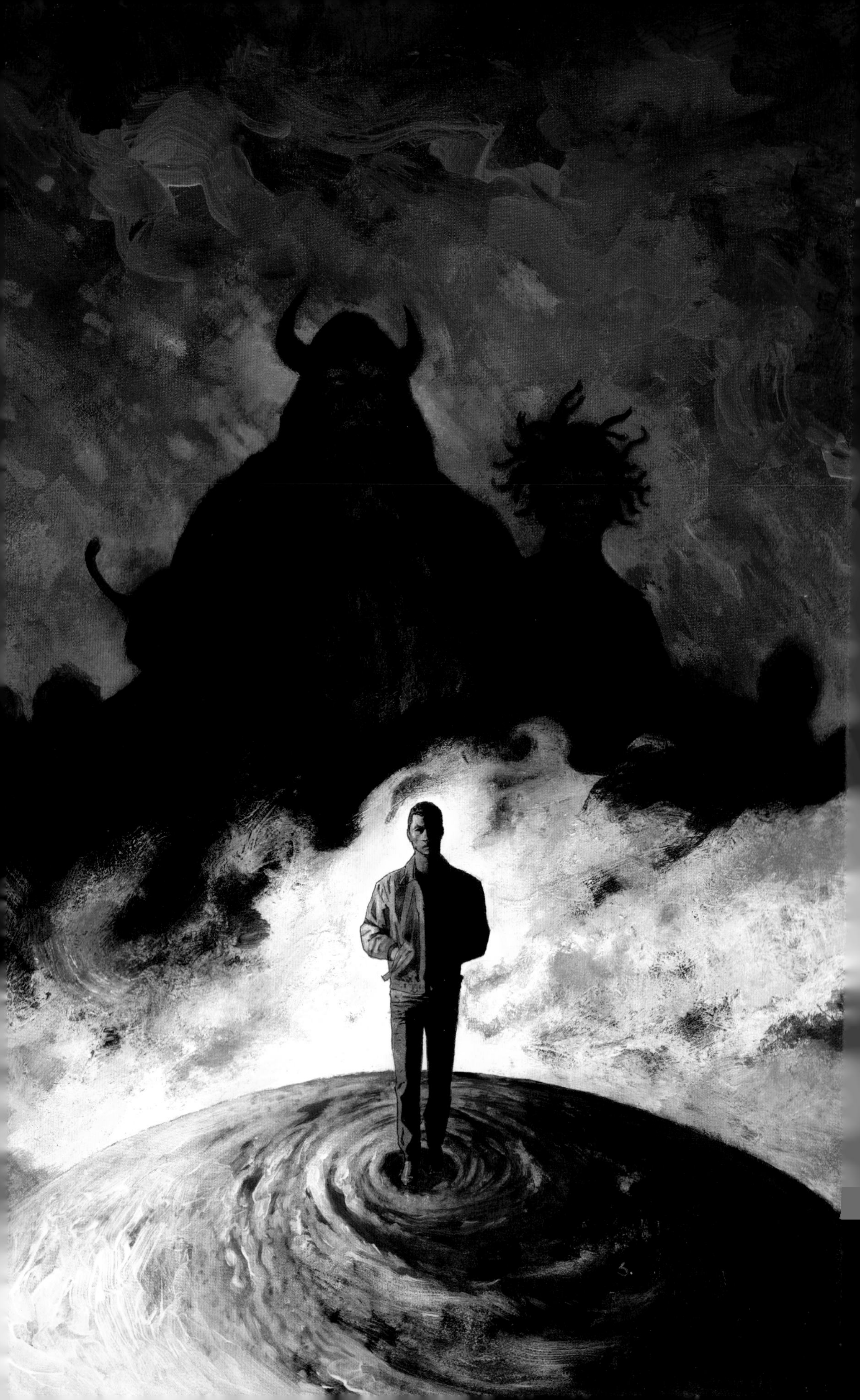

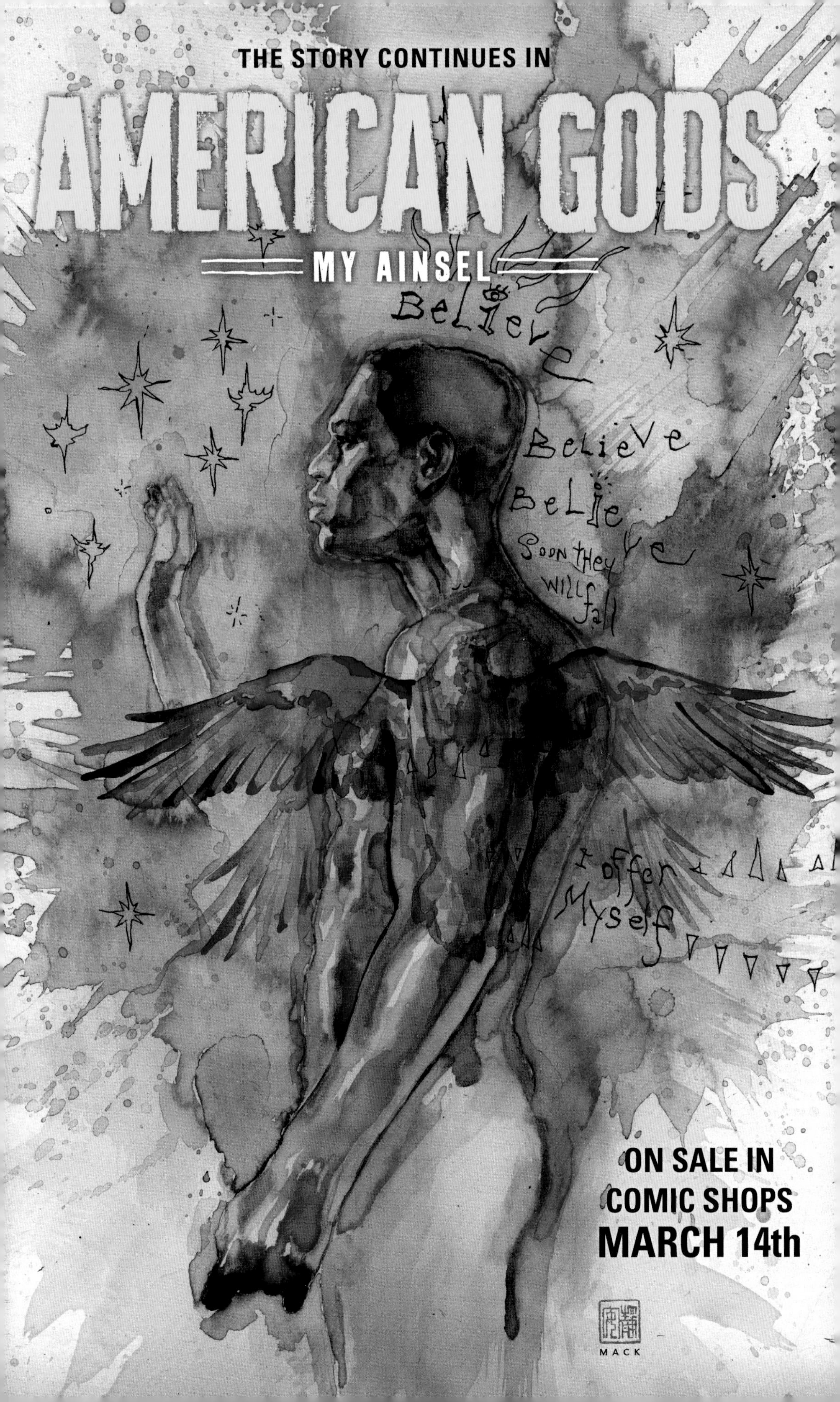
THE STORY CONTINUES IN
AMERICAN GODS
MY AINSEL
Believe
Believe
Believe
Soon they will fall
I offer Myself
ON SALE IN
COMIC SHOPS
MARCH 14th
MACK

MORE TITLES FROM THE NEIL GAIMAN LIBRARY

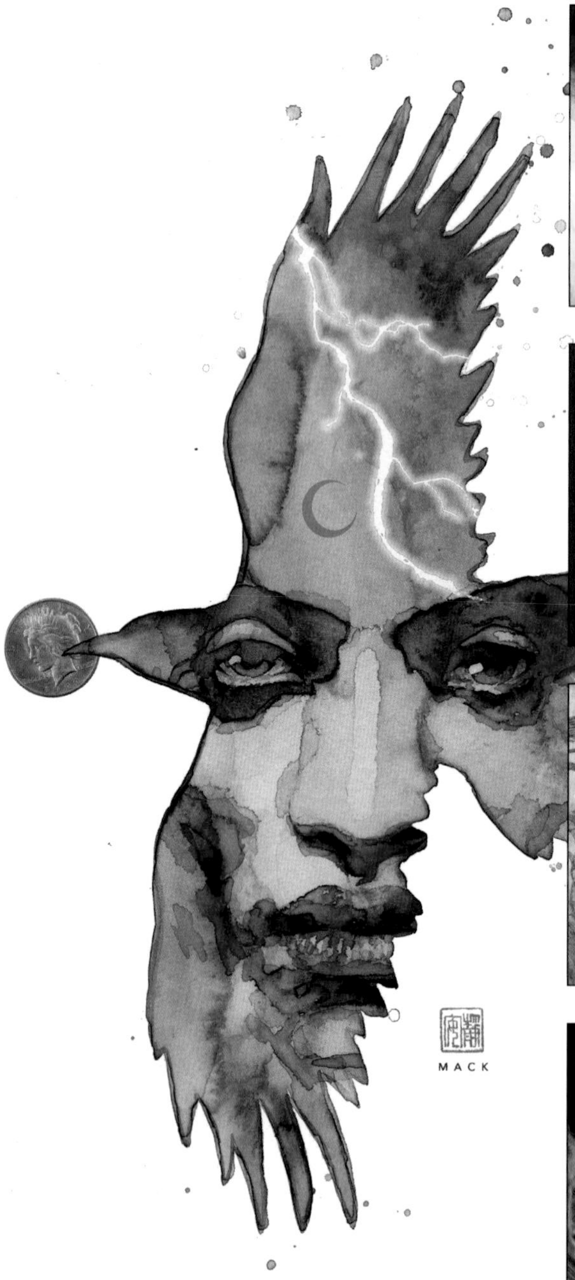

MACK

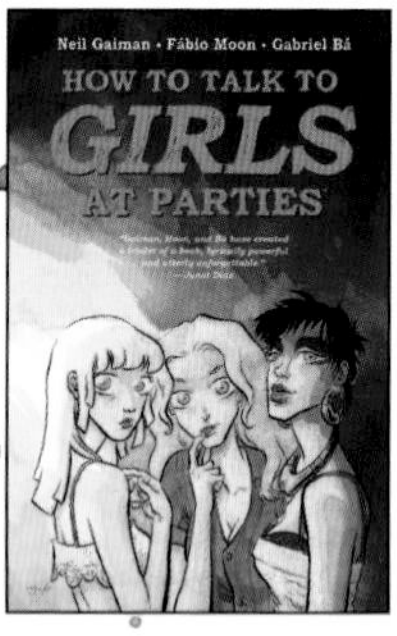

Neil Gaiman • Fábio Moon • Gabriel Bá
HOW TO TALK TO
GIRLS
AT PARTIES

THE FACTS IN THE CASE OF THE DEPARTURE OF MISS FINCH
2nd Edition
Neil Gaiman and Michael Zulli
$13.99 | 978-1-61655-949-6

NEIL GAIMAN'S HOW TO TALK TO GIRLS AT PARTIES
Neil Gaiman, Fábio Moon, and Gabriel Bá
$17.99 | ISBN 978-1-61655-955-7

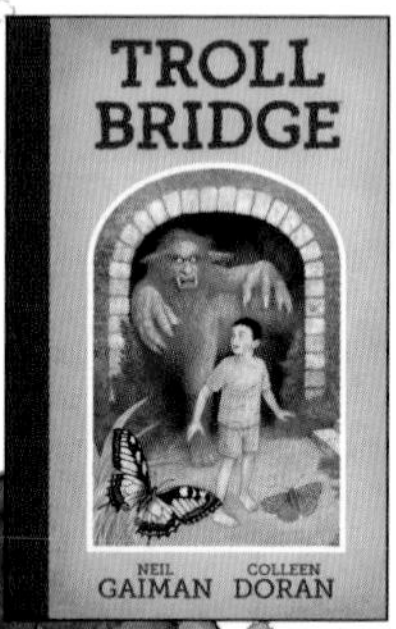

TROLL
BRIDGE
NEIL
GAIMAN
COLLEEN
DORAN

NEIL GAIMAN'S TROLL BRIDGE
Neil Gaiman and Colleen Doran
$14.99 | ISBN 978-1-50670-008-3

FORBIDDEN BRIDES OF THE FACELESS SLAVES IN THE SECRET HOUSE OF THE NIGHT OF DREAD DESIRE
Neil Gaiman and Shane Oakley
$17.99 | ISBN 978-1-50670-140-0

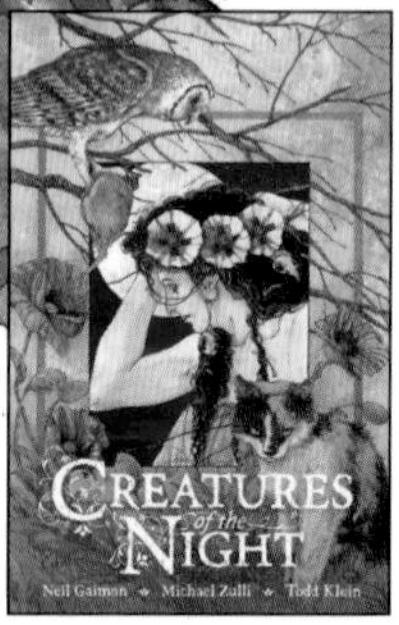

CREATURES
of the
NIGHT
Neil Gaiman • Michael Zulli • Todd Klein

CREATURES OF THE NIGHT
2nd Edition
Neil Gaiman and Michael Zulli
$12.99 | ISBN 978-1-50670-025-0

SIGNAL TO NOISE
Neil Gaiman and Dave McKean
$24.99 | ISBN 978-1-59307-752-5

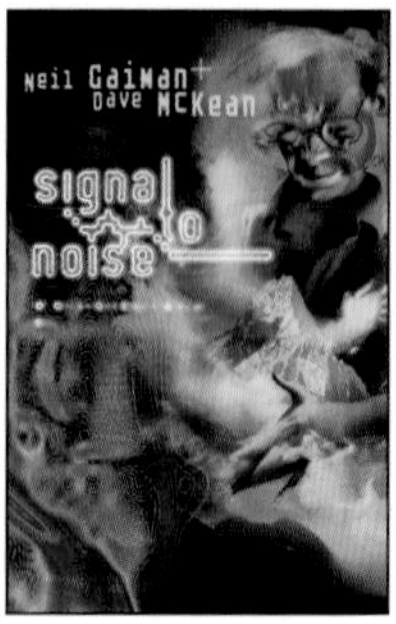

Neil Gaiman+
Dave McKean
signal
to
noise

HARLEQUIN VALENTINE
2nd Edition
Neil Gaiman and John Bolton
$12.99 | ISBN 978-1-50670-087-8

AMERICAN GODS: SHADOWS
Neil Gaiman, P. Craig Russell, Scott Hampton, and others
$29.99 | ISBN 978-1-50670-386-2